MEREOLOGY

MEREOLOGY

A. J. COTNOIR AND ACHILLE C. VARZI

OXFORD
UNIVERSITY PRESS

OXFORD
UNIVERSITY PRESS

Great Clarendon Street, Oxford, OX2 6DP,
United Kingdom

Oxford University Press is a department of the University of Oxford.
It furthers the University's objective of excellence in research, scholarship,
and education by publishing worldwide. Oxford is a registered trade mark of
Oxford University Press in the UK and in certain other countries

First published 2021

First published in paperback 2024

Published in the United States of America by Oxford University Press
198 Madison Avenue, New York, NY 10016, United States of America

British Library Cataloguing in Publication Data
Data available

Library of Congress Cataloging in Publication Data
Data available

ISBN 978–0–19–874900–4 (Hbk.)
ISBN 978–0–19–890893–7 (Pbk.)

DOI: 10.1093/oso/9780198749004.001.0001

Printed and bound by
CPI Group (UK) Ltd, Croydon, CR0 4YY

In memory of Josh Parsons (1973–2017)

CONTENTS

PREFACE

This book has one purpose and some related, more specific aims. The purpose is to meet a growing demand for a systematic and up-to-date treatment of mereology. Since the publication of Peter Simons's acclaimed book, *Parts: A Study in Ontology* (1987), interest in this discipline has grown tremendously. Mereology is now a central field of philosophical research, not only in ontology, but in metaphysics more broadly, witness the publication of two recent volumes of essays devoted to mereological issues in the metaphysics of identity (Cotnoir and Baxter, 2014) and in the theory of location (Kleinschmidt, 2014). Mereological questions and techniques have also become central in other areas of philosophy, including logic, the philosophy of language, and the foundations of mathematics (especially thanks to Lewis, 1991) as well as in neighboring disciplines such as linguistics and formal semantics (from Moltmann, 1997 to Champollion, 2017) and the information sciences (Guarino *et al.*, 1996; Lambrix, 2000). Even in the natural sciences mereology has become an established framework within which to address long-standing foundational questions, for instance, in physics, in chemistry, or in certain branches of biology; the recent publication of a collection entitled *Mereology and the Sciences* (Calosi and Graziani, 2014) is but one notable sign of this broader interest. Most importantly, however, this growth in interest and applications has been accompanied by unprecedented developments in the study of mereology itself, understood as a field of theoretical inquiry in its own right, and keeping track of all the findings is an ever-increasing challenge. In his review of Simons's book, Timothy Williamson wrote that "*Parts* could easily be the standard book on mereology for the next twenty or thirty years" (Williamson, 1990, p. 210). And Williamson was no doubt correct. As we passed the third decade mark, Simons's book has served admirably in this role. Nonetheless the field has grown; and while five other monographs have appeared in the meantime—Massimo Libardi's *Teorie delle parti e dell'intero* (1990), Andrzej Pietruszczak's *Metamereologia*

(2000b) and *Podstawy teorii części* (2013), Lothar Ridder's *Mereologie* (2002), and Giorgio Lando's *Mereology: A Philosophical Introduction* (2017)—only one of them is in English* and none covers the latest technical and philosophical developments in a systematic fashion. The purpose of this book is to fill that gap.

Our more specific aims are threefold. First, we aim to clarify the varieties of formal systems that have been put forward and discussed over the years, including different axiomatizations of the theory known as 'classical mereology' along with the motivations and main criticisms of each approach. Second, we aim to contribute to the development and systematization of new, non-classical mereological theories, with an eye on their potential impact on debates in relevant areas of metaphysics, philosophical logic, the philosophy of language, and the philosophy of mathematics. Third, we aim to do all this in a way that might prove useful to experts in the field and newcomers alike. This is probably the hardest aim to achieve, but we have tried to do so by making the text concise and self-contained while at the same time sacrificing very little in terms of detail and accuracy. We have also tried to be as neutral as possible in our presentation of philosophically controversial material—not because we do not have views, or because our personal views may not coincide, but because we thought a non-opinionated treatment would better serve our present purpose and aims. We know in advance that each of these aims can only be attained partially. We hope this is also true of our failures.

Although the book as a whole has been written from scratch, some parts have ancestors in material that has previously appeared in print. In chapter 1, sections 1.2.1 and 1.3 draw slightly on Gruszczyński and Varzi (2015, §§2–3) and on Varzi (2016, §1), respectively. In chapter 2, section 2.1 is based on the axiom system presented in Cotnoir and Varzi (2019). In chapter 3, sections 3.1 and 3.2 include some material from Cotnoir (2013b) and Cotnoir and Bacon (2012) and section 3.3.1 draws on material from Varzi (2006a). In chapter 4, section 4.1.3 draws slightly on Varzi (2016, §3.3), sections 4.3.2 and 4.4 use results from Varzi (2009) and Cotnoir (2016a), and sections 4.5 and 4.6 expand on Varzi (2007a, §1.3.4, 2016, §3.4). In chapter 5, sections 5.2.1 and 5.2.3 draw slightly on Varzi (2016, §4.5) and on Cotnoir (2014b), sections 5.3.3 and 5.3.4 on Cotnoir (2015), and section 5.5 on Cotnoir (2014a). Finally, in chapter 6, sections 6.3.1 and 6.3.3 draw on Varzi (2016, §5) and section 6.3.4 on Weber and Cotnoir (2015). We are thankful to our co-authors and to the editors and publishers of the original sources for their kind permission to reuse this material in the present form.

* As we go to press, an English edition of Pietruszczak (2000b) has appeared. We have made an effort to update our references accordingly. Professor Pietruszczak informs us that an English translation of his 2013 book is also scheduled.

Our further debts of gratitude are extensive and deep. For written comments on the entire manuscript at different stages of its development, our greatest thanks go to Rafał Gruszczyński, Kris McDaniel, David Nicolas, Andrzej Pietruszczak, Marcus Rossberg, and two anonymous referees for Oxford University Press. Moreover, a number of other friends and colleagues have helped us think through this project in a variety of ways, directly or indirectly, and our thanks extend to them all: Simona Aimar, Andrew Arlig, Andrew Bacon, Ralf Bader, Don Baxter, J. C. Beall, Franz Berto, Arianna Betti, Einar Bøhn, Andrea Borghini, Martina Botti, Claudio Calosi, Colin Caret, Roberto Casati, Damiano Costa, Vincenzo De Risi, Maureen Donnelly, Tim Elder, Haim Gaifman, Cody Gilmore, Marion Haemmerli, Joel Hamkins, Katherine Hawley, Paul Hovda, Hud Hudson, Ingvar Johansson, Shieva Kleinschmidt, Kathrin Koslicki, Tamar Lando, Matthew Lansdell, Paolo Maffezioli, Ofra Magidor, Wolfgang Mann, Massimo Mugnai, Kevin Mulligan, Hans-Georg Niebergall, Daniel Nolan, the late Josh Parsons, Laurie Paul, Greyson Potter, Graham Priest, Fred Rickey, Jeff Russell, Thomas Sattig, Kevin Scharp, Oliver Seidl, Stewart Shapiro, Anthony Shiver, Ted Sider, Peter Simons, Alex Skiles, Matthew Slater, Jereon Smid, Barry Smith, Reed Solomon, Hsing-chien Tsai, Gabriel Uzquiano, Peter van Inwagen, Zach Weber, and Jan Westerhoff.

We would also like to express a special note of thanks to our students at the University of St Andrews and at Columbia University, particularly the participants in the Arché Metaphysics Research Group, who provided detailed feedback on the very first draft of the manuscript (Spring 2016), and the participants in a graduate Mereology seminar held at Columbia, who did the same on a later draft (Fall 2017). And many special thanks to Peter Momtchiloff at the Press, both for his help and warm encouragement and for his patience through all the phases of the project.

Finally, we are deeply grateful to our families. Without their loving and unceasing support, the project would never have been completed, or even started.

The preparation of the book has benefited from financial support from the Arché Research Centre at the University of St Andrews, from a 2017–2018 Leverhulme Research Fellowship from the Leverhulme Trust, and from a 2019–2020 sabbatical leave from Columbia University and a Fellowship at the Wissenschaftskolleg zu Berlin, which we acknowledge most gratefully.

NOTE For convenient reference, all labeled formulas corresponding to definitions, axioms, and theorems of mereological theories discussed in the text are reproduced in a list at the end of the volume. In the electronic edition, the labels of such formulas, when cited in the text, appear as active hyperlinks to the locations where the formulas themselves are first introduced.

NOTE ON THE PAPERBACK EDITION

This paperback edition reproduces the text of the original 2021 edition in its entirety, with only a few small corrections. The primary correction involves axiom L.3 on pages 20 and 397, where a negation sign was inadvertently omitted in the consequent. Other typos and minor errors were rectified on pages 74, 96, 98, 108, 141, 148, 222, 263, and 280, as well as in the Bibliography. We are grateful to Paolo Crivelli, Alejandro G. Di Rienzo, Binghe Gong, Giorgio Lando, and Daniel Nolan for bringing some of these oversights to our attention.

All titles listed in the Bibliography as "in press" have now appeared in print, with the only exception of Gilmore (in press). In addition, the scheduled English translation of Pietruszczak (2013) announced in the Preface has now been published by Springer, in revised and extended form, with the title *Foundations of the Theory of Parthood. A Study of Mereology*.

LIST OF FIGURES

1

WHAT IS MEREOLOGY?

Whole and part—partly concrete parts and partly abstract parts—are at the bottom of everything. They are most fundamental in our conceptual system.

— Kurt Gödel (reported in Wang, 1996, p. 295)

Mereology (from the Greek μέρος, meaning 'share', or 'part') is concerned with the study of parthood relationships: relationships of part to whole and of part to part within a common whole. The term itself was originally coined in the twentieth century by the Polish logician Stanisław Leśniewski to designate a specific theory of such relationships, corresponding to the third component of the formal system with which he aimed to provide a comprehensive foundation for logic and mathematics[1] (the other components being a generalized theory of propositions and their functions, or Protothetic, and a calculus of names and functors, or Ontology).[2] Today, however, it is common practice to speak of mereology with reference to any theory of parthood, and more generally to the broad field of inquiry within which such theories originate, and in this book we shall follow suit. In fact, Leśniewski's own theory turned out to be enormously influential and will occupy us a great deal, at least insofar as it can be isolated from the rest of his system, but it is by no means the only one. More importantly, it certainly does not epitomize the only way of doing mereology. To see why, and to better appreciate the meaning and scope of mereology as we shall understand it here, it will be instructive to begin with a brief look at the history of the subject.

1 See Leśniewski (1927–1931), p. 166 of Part I; the Polish word is *mereologia*. As Simons (1997a, fn. 4) notes, the term was probably chosen by Leśniewski as a variant of 'merology' (*merologia*), which was already in use to indicate the field of anatomy dealing with elemental tissues and body fluids (see Robin, 1851, p. 16 for the original French coinage, *mérologie*, and Dunglison, 1857, p. 586 for the English conversion). Following Hutchinson (1978, pp. 214ff), today 'merology' is also used for the school of ecological thought that seeks to explain higher levels of organization in terms of individual organisms (in contrast to the 'holological' school, which focuses instead on the flow of energy and materials at the level of ecosystems).

2 Logically, Protothetic comes first, followed by Ontology and then Mereology, though Leśniewski worked out the three components in reverse order. For overviews of the overall system, see Kearns (1967), Rickey (1977), Clay (1980), and Simons (2009a, 2015); for extensive studies, see Luschei (1962), Miéville (1984), Urbaniak (2014a), and the essays in Srzednicki and Stachniak (1984) (on Protothetic) and Srzednicki and Rickey (1984) (on Ontology).

Mereology. A. J. Cotnoir and Achille C. Varzi, Oxford University Press. © A. J. Cotnoir and Achille C. Varzi 2021. DOI: 10.1093/oso/9780198749004.003.0001

1.1 A BIT OF HISTORY

As a general field of inquiry, mereology is actually as old as philosophy. Already among the Presocratics, metaphysical and cosmological controversies focused to a great extent on the part-whole structure of the world, and some of the main schools of thought may be seen as disagreeing precisely on a mereological question, namely, whether everything, something, or nothing has parts. Thus, the Eleatics held that Being is a uniform, 'undivided whole' (Parmenides) and that the very thought that there may be further parts, spatial or temporal, would lead to paradox (Zeno); the Atomists maintained that some things have parts, though all division must come to an end: at bottom there must be a layer of partless things, or atoms (literally: 'indivisibles'), out of which everything else is composed (Democritus); and some Pluralists went as far as claiming that all things, no matter what size, divide forever into smaller and smaller parts (Anaxagoras). Similar concerns were central also to other ancient traditions. The pluralist view, for instance, prevailed among the Míngjiā, the Chinese school of logicians led by Huì Shī and Gōngsūn Lóng, whereas the atomistic stance was prominent in Indian philosophy, with the Vaiśeṣika cosmology of Kaṇāda relying on atoms of different elemental kinds and the Jain school championing a conception of the world as consisting wholly of atoms, or Paramāṇus, of just one sort, except for souls.

In the Western tradition, metaphysical analyses in terms of parts and wholes continue to figure prominently both in the writings of Plato (especially *Parmenides*, *Theaetetus*, and *Timaeus*) and in those of Aristotle (most notably in the *Metaphysics*, where the hylomorphic theory of substances is presented, but also throughout his logical and natural philosophical treatises, such as the *Topics*, the *Physics*, and *De partibus animalium*, and even his ethical treatises). In Hellenistic times, too, the Epicurean and Stoic schools relied on claims about the kinds of parts and wholes that exist in order to frame some of their central theses, or to challenge the views of their opponents. Chrysippus, for example, devoted one of his books to what came to be known as the 'growing paradox', which he took from Epicharmus: how can something gain or lose parts over time without ceasing to be the thing it is? Similarly, we know from Plutarch's *Lives* that the question of mereological change was amply discussed in connection with the puzzle of the ship of Theseus—the ship of the mythical king of Athens that was preserved down to the time of Demetrius Phalereus by constantly replacing the old, decaying parts with new and stronger timber. (And, again, this was not a question exclusive to Western philosophy. According to the *Nihon Shoki*, for instance, the Grand Shrine of Ise was established by the daughter of the Japanese emperor Suinin precisely pursuant to the Shinto beliefs concerning the impermanence of all things, with the two main temples being taken apart and rebuilt on adjacent sites every twenty years.)

The interest in mereology continues throughout antiquity, as evidenced e.g. by Neoplatonist thinkers such as Plotinus, Proclus, and Philoponus, and especially Boethius, who played a crucial role in transmitting ancient views on these matters to the Middle Ages through his treatises *De divisione* and *In Ciceronis Topica*. Among medieval philosophers, mereological questions were taken up extensively, for instance, by Garland the Computist and by Peter Abelard, and eventually by all the major Scholastics: William of Sherwood, Peter of Spain, Thomas Aquinas, Ramon Llull, John Duns Scotus, Walter Burley, William of Ockham, Adam de Wodeham, Jean Buridan, Albert of Saxony, and Paul of Venice, whose monumental logical treatise, the *Logica magna* (1397–1398), contained ample sections devoted expressly to various forms of part-whole reasoning.

Mereological questions occupy a prominent place also in modern philosophy, from Jungius's *Logica Hamburgensis* (1638) and Cavendish's *Opinions* (1655) through Leibniz's *De arte combinatoria* (1666) and *Monadology* (1714) (and many shorter essays in between) to Wolff's *Ontologia* (1730). Among the Empiricists, they are central e.g. to the debate on infinite divisibility, witness Hume's arguments in the *Treatise* (1739) and in the *Enquiry* (1748). And, of course, we find mereological concerns in Kant, from the early writings (e.g. the *Monadologia physica* of 1756) to the famous Second Antinomy in the *Critique of Pure Reason* (1781–1787). Thesis: Every composite substance is made up of simple parts, and nothing anywhere exists save the simple or what is composed of the simple. Anti-thesis: No composite thing is made up of simple parts, and there nowhere exists in the world anything simple.

With all this, it is not an exaggeration to say that mereological theorizing forms a central chapter of philosophy throughout its history.[3] Nonetheless, it bears emphasis that such extensive theorizing focused by and large on substantive treatments of metaphysical questions concerning the actual part-whole structure of the world. Few philosophers engaged in the systematic study of part-whole relations *as such*, as if the properties of such relations were in some sense obvious, or easily recoverable. For example, it is natural to consider whether parthood behaves transitively, so that the parts of a

3 For a fuller picture, see Kaulbach *et al.* (1974), Burkhardt and Dufour (1991), and the historical entries in Burkhardt *et al.* (2017). On ancient theories, especially Plato's and Aristotle's, see also Bogaard (1979), Barnes (1988), Harte (2002), Koslicki (2006, 2008), and Arci (2012). On medieval mereology, see Henry (1989, 1991a), Arlig (2011a,b, 2019), Normore and Brown (2014), and the essays in Klima and Hall (2018) and Amerini *et al.* (2019). On modern views, see Costa (in press) along with Peterman (2019) on Cavendish; Schmidt (1971), Burkhardt and Degen (1990), Cook (2000), Hartz (2006), and Mugnai (2019) on Leibniz; Favaretti Camposampiero (2019a,b) on Wolff; and Baxter (1988c), Jacquette (1996), and Holden (2002) on Hume. On Kant, see Bell (2001) together with Van Cleve (1981), Engelhard (2005), Marschall (2019), and Watt (2019).

whole always include the parts of its parts. Yet it is hard to find anywhere an explicit discussion of this general principle, or of the conditions under which it holds. Aristotle, for one, seems to endorse it when he says that some parts, "while entire in themselves, have within themselves other parts" (*History of Animals*, I, 1, 486a11; Aristotle, 1984, p. 774), and some ancient commentators reinforce this view—for instance, Simplicius:

> He says that ... something can be in something as a part in a whole, like a finger in a hand or in the whole body, in the hand as a part and in the whole body as a part of a part. (*On Aristotle's Physics*, 551.19–20; Simplicius, 1992, p. 45)[4]

On the other hand, Aristotle recognizes several senses of 'part', including a sense in which "the genus is called a part of the species" and another in which "the species is part of the genus" (*Metaphysics*, V, 25, 1023b18–25; Aristotle, 1984, p. 1616), and it is not clear whether the corresponding parthood relation obeys the same laws in each case, or across cases. If an individual substance includes its form among its parts, and the form in turn includes the genus, does it follow that Socrates, who is part of the species human being, which is part of the genus animal, which is part of Coriscus's form, is himself in some sense part of Coriscus?[5] And what of transitivity itself—may it be said to hold in one sense but not in another, even within the same domain of application, as in the following passage from Boethius?

> The letters, syllables, names and verses are in some sense parts of the whole book. Nevertheless, when taken in another manner, they are not parts of the whole, rather they are parts of parts. (*De divisione*, 888b; Boethius, 1998, p. 40)

This is just an illustration, but it is indicative of a pattern that is typical of mereological discussions throughout history. We are given some examples, and inferences are drawn therefrom, but exactly what part-whole principles those inferences are supposed to instantiate is generally left in the dark.

One exception to this lack of systematic treatments was Leibniz, who explicitly formulated a set of general laws in his essays on so-called 'real addition'. A good example is a short untitled text from around 1690, which begins with a formulation of Leibniz's famous Identity Law ("Same or coincident are those terms that can be substituted for each other anywhere *salva veritate*") and continues by introducing a binary operation of composition, $\oplus$, which Leibniz axiomatizes as being both commutative ($B \oplus N = N \oplus B$) and idempotent ($A \oplus A = A$). From this, Leibniz infers—correctly[6]—that the

4 This is still a limited thesis. Some scholars (e.g. Barnes, 1988, §2) actually doubt anyone in antiquity ever held the transitivity of parthood in its general form.

5 The puzzle is raised in Koslicki (2007, pp. 138f; 2008, p. 158). Whether forms are themselves parts, however, is controversial; see e.g. Galluzzo (2018), Rotkale (2018), and Shields (2019).

6 Using also associativity, i.e. $A \oplus (B \oplus N) = (A \oplus B) \oplus N$, which Leibniz takes for granted.

corresponding relation of mereological containment is not only transitive, but also reflexive and antisymmetric, which is to say a partial order:

> 'B ⊕ N = L' means that B is in L, or, that L contains B, and that B and N together constitute or compose L ...
> *Proposition 7*. A is in A ...
> *Proposition 15*. If A is in B and B is in C, then A is in C ...
> *Proposition 17*. If A is in B and B is in A, then A = B. (Leibniz, 1966, pp. 132–136)

Another important principle listed by Leibniz is the following, which he adds to the basic axioms on ⊕. It suggests that Leibniz regarded mereological composition as a structural operation that obtains automatically as soon as several things are posited, regardless of what they are:[7]

> *Postulate 2*. Any plurality of things, such as A and B, can be taken together to compose one thing, A ⊕ B. (*ibid.*, p. 132)[8]

Whether or not these principles should hold unrestrictedly may, of course, be a matter of controversy. But it is precisely on principles of this sort that a robust mereological theory needs to rest. Indeed we shall see that Leibniz's intuitions here are pretty much in line with those of most contemporary theorists. Unfortunately, however, they were an isolated episode. Leibniz's forays into a general theory of parthood had no impact whatsoever on what came after, if anything because the essays in question were not published until 1890, and even then as minor writings with no apparent connection with the most important parts of his extensive philosophical production.[9]

1.2 CONTEMPORARY PERSPECTIVES

This lack of a systematic study of the part-whole relation *per se* was overcome only at the beginning of the twentieth century. There were two major impulses toward this change of perspective. One came from the school of

7 Cf. the following passage, from an earlier fragment dating mid-1685:

> If when several things are posited, by that very fact some unity is immediately understood to be posited, then the former are called *parts*, the latter a *whole*. Nor is it even necessary that they exist at the same time, or at the same place ... Thus from all the Roman emperors together, we construct one aggregate. (Leibniz, 2002, p. 271)

8 Here the 1966 English translation (by G. H. R. Parkinson) has 'term' instead of 'thing'. However, in the Latin original it seems clear that Leibniz is using the neuter, singular or plural, to speak of generic things ("Plura quæcunque ut A, B ..."), so we follow Mugnai (2019, p. 55).

9 The untitled essay cited above appeared for the first time in Gerhardt's edition of the *Philosophischen Schriften* (Leibniz, 1890, pp. 236–247), along with another short essay on the same subject entitled *Non inelegans specimen demonstrandi in abstractis* (pp. 228–235). Other relevant essays were published only in Couturat's later collection (Leibniz, 1903). For detailed studies of Leibniz's calculus, see Swoyer (1994), Lenzen (2000, 2004), and, again, Mugnai (2019).

Franz Brentano (who emphatically maintained that the problems of Aristotle's theory of categories had their origins in the underlying mereology)[10] through Edmund Husserl; the other came from Leśniewski.[11] Their specific motivations were different: in Husserl's case, the theory of parts and wholes was pivotal to the development of a general framework for *formal ontology*; Leśniewski's mereology, by contrast, issued primarily from his *austere nominalism*, and specifically from the need of a nominalistically acceptable alternative to set theory. Neither of these motivations is by itself intrinsic to mereology as such. Nonetheless it is precisely these two sorts of motivations that, together, have fixed the coordinates of most later developments.

1.2.1 *Mereology as Formal Ontology*

Husserl's conception of mereology as a piece of formal ontology receives its fullest formulation in the third of his *Logical Investigations* (1900–1901). Broadly speaking, the goal of this Investigation was the development of

> the *pure (a priori) theory of objects as such*, in which we deal with ideas pertinent to the *category of object* ... as well as the *a priori* truths which relate to these. (Husserl, 1900–1901, p. 435)

Husserl mentioned several other "ideas" besides Part and Whole, including Genus and Species, Subject and Quality, Relation and Collection, Unity, Number, Magnitude, etc. Yet the bulk of the Investigation is devoted to the first of these ideas and the title itself, "On the theory of wholes and parts", spotlights the centrality of the part-whole relation in Husserl's project.

The very notion of an "object as such" is, of course, heavily laden with philosophical meaning, as is Husserl's notion of an *a priori* truth. For our purposes, however, the central idea can be put rather simply as follows. Don't think of ontology in Quinean terms, i.e. as a theory aimed at drawing up an inventory of the world, a catalogue of those entities that must exist in order for our best theories about the world to be true (Quine, 1948). Rather, think of ontology in the old sense, as a theory of being *qua* being (Aristotle), or perhaps of the possible *qua* possible (Wolff). In this sense, the task of ontology is not to find out what there is; it is to lay bare the formal structure of what there is *no matter what it is*. Regardless of whether our inventory of the world includes objects along with events, concrete entities along with abstract ones, and so on, it must exhibit some general features and obey some general laws, and the task of ontology—understood formally—is to

10 See Brentano (1933, pt. 2, §1). On Brentano's views on mereology, see Baumgartner and Simons (1993), Baumgartner (2013), Salice (2017), and Kriegel (2018a, §1.6; 2018b, §3).

11 Leśniewski did his doctoral studies under Kazimierz Twardowski, himself a pupil of Brentano and an early mereologist (see Twardowski, 1894, §§9–11). For connections, see Rosiak (1998a).

figure out such features and laws. For instance, it would pertain to the task of formal ontology to assert that every entity, no matter what it is, is governed by certain laws concerning identity, such as transitivity:

If x is identical to y and y is identical to z, then x is identical to z.

Ideally, the truth of this law does not depend on what (kinds of) entities are assigned to the individual variables 'x', 'y', and 'z', exactly as the truth of the following law concerning entailment does not depend on what propositions are assigned to the sentential variables 'p', 'q', and 'r':

If p entails q and q entails r, then p entails r.

Both laws are meant to possess the same sort of generality and topic neutrality. Both are meant to hold as a matter of necessity and should be discovered, in some sense, *a priori*. And just as the latter law may be said to pertain to formal logic insofar as the relevant variables range over propositions, i.e. *claims about* the world (no matter what they say), the former would pertain to formal ontology insofar as their variables range over *things in* the world (no matter what they are).[12]

Now, Husserl's view was that the general principles of mereology should constitute a formal ontological theory precisely in this sense, like the formal principles governing identity. Transitivity, for example, would hold in the same way: no matter what x, y, and z happen to be, if x is part of y and y is part of z, then x must be part of z. And what goes for transitivity goes for any other mereological principle that a theory of this sort should contain. Husserl himself did not go as far as providing a full account, describing the laws put forward in his Investigation as "mere indications of a future treatment" (p. 484). Moreover, such indications are presented in a way that makes it difficult to disentangle the analysis of the part-whole relation from that of other ontologically relevant relations (such as foundation).[13] Husserl's concluding remarks, however, leave no doubts as to the nature and scope of the task. It is worth quoting them in full, for they represent the first explicit statement of a full-fledged project in mereology:

> A proper working out of the pure theory we here have in mind, would have to define all concepts with mathematical exactness and to deduce all theorems by

12 In the Prolegomena to the *Investigations*, Husserl speaks of these laws as governing the "interconnections of truths" and the "interconnections of things", respectively (§ 62). The parallel will return repeatedly in Husserl's writings, from *Ideas I* (1913, §10) to *Formal and Transcendental Logic* (1929, §54) to *Experience and Judgment* (1939, §1). For a general analysis, see Smith (1989); for discussion, see Crosson (1962), Scanlon (1975), Poli (1993), Rosiak (1998b), and Smith (2003).

13 The list of attempts in this direction, some of which are quite thorough, is long; see Ginsberg (1929), Sokolowski (1968), Simons (1982a), Null (1983), Blecksmith and Null (1990), Fine (1995), Rosiak (1995, 1996), Casari (2000, 2007), Ridder (2002, § VI.2), and Correia (2004).

> *argumenta in forma*, i.e. mathematically. Thus would arise a complete law-determined survey of the *a priori* possibilities of complexity in the form of wholes and parts, and an exact knowledge of the relations possible in this sphere. That this end can be achieved, has been shown by the small beginnings of purely formal treatment in our present chapter. (Husserl, 1900–1901, p. 484)

As we shall see, much current work in mereology has been influenced by this way of thinking. The last claim is especially important if we want to understand the philosophical motivation behind some of the most recent technical developments. For clearly Husserl's project raises a difficult challenge—the challenge of determining which, among the many things one can say about parthood, should be taken as formal laws in the relevant sense. After all, not every general thesis concerning identity qualifies as formal, either; the principle of Identity of Indiscernibles, for instance, is a substantive thesis that can hardly be claimed to hold *a priori*, if at all. Likewise for parthood. The vexed question of whether there are mereological *atoms*, or whether everything is ultimately *composed of* atoms, is obviously a substantive question about the actual make-up of the world; any answer would amount to a substantive metaphysical (or physical) thesis that goes beyond a "pure theory of objects as such". The same could be said of other mereological theses that come to mind, such as Leibniz's postulate to the effect that any plurality of things whatsoever can be added together to compose a further thing. Where, then, should the line be drawn? What else should be included in the "pure theory" of parthood besides transitivity? Indeed, is transitivity a good candidate to begin with, given the puzzles mentioned earlier in connection with Aristotle and Boethius?[14] These questions admit of no simple answer. But precisely for this reason, the challenges they raise may be said to have set the agenda for the development of formal mereological theories well beyond the narrow scope of Husserlian scholarship.

1.2.2 *Mereology as an Alternative to Set Theory*

Leśniewski's motivations for the development of mereology were, as we said, significantly different, originating entirely within the philosophy of mathematics. Here the incentive was the nominalistic persuasion that set

---

14 As a matter of fact, transitivity has sometimes been questioned also in the case of identity, beginning with Carneades. As Galen writes:

> He did not even believe this principle, which is the most evident of all: that quantities which are equal to the same quantity are also equal to one another. (*De optima doctrina*, §2; Galen, 1821, p. 45)

For contemporary examples, see Prior (1966), Garrett (1985), and Priest (2003). The same is true of the transitivity of logical entailment, at least since Geach (1958). For logics in which transitivity fails, see e.g. Zardini (2008), Ripley (2012), Cobreros *et al.* (2012), and Weir (2015).

theory had been conceived in sin—the sin of founding all of mathematics on such *abstracta* as Cantorian sets—and that a theory of the part-whole relation could provide a more solid foundation. In Leśniewski's own words:

> Scenting in the 'classes' of Whitehead and Russell and in the 'extensions of concepts' of Frege the aroma of mythical specimen from a rich gallery of 'invented' objects, I am unable to rid myself of an inclination to sympathize 'on credit' with the authors' doubts as to whether such 'classes' do exist in the world. (Leśniewski, 1927–1931, p. 224)

Leśniewski produced several versions of his theory. The first version appeared in an essay entitled *Foundations of the general theory of sets* (1916);[15] the others are presented in a series of articles called "On the foundations of mathematics" (1927–1931), where the theory was officially named "Mereology". The various versions differ in their choice of primitives, resulting in different sets of axioms and definitions: in the first version, the basic notion is *proper part*, which Leśniewski takes to apply to those parts of an object that are not identical with the object itself; later versions use as primitive the notion of *part* in its broader, proper or improper sense, or other notions such as *disjoint* (lacking a common part).[16] Since these notions are all interdefinable, however, such differences prove to be immaterial and we can speak of Leśniewski's Mereology as a single theory. And in this case, unlike Husserl's, it is a theory that was meant to be complete. Here are its axioms stated in terms of parthood (adapted from Leśniewski, 1927–1931, pt. VII):[17]

(a) If x is part of y and y is part of x, then x is y.
(b) If x is part of y and y is part of z, then x is part of z.
(c) If every φ is part of both x and y, and if every z that is part of either x or y has some part that is part of some φ, then x is y.
(d) If something is φ, then there is some x such that every φ is part of x and every part of x has some part that is part of some φ.

Whether this theory could in fact serve as an adequate foundation for mathematics is a question that goes beyond our present concerns.[18] Leśniewski

15 Published as Part I; the continuation never appeared in print (cf. Leśniewski, 1927–1931, p. 227).
16 This is our terminology, following current usage. Leśniewski used 'part' (*część*) for the notion of proper part and 'ingredient' (*ingredyens*) for the broader notion. His term for 'disjoint' was 'exterior' (*zewnętrzny*). Later developments by Sobociński (1954), Lejewski (1954a), and Clay (1961) display an even wider range of possible primitives; for a full picture, see Welsh (1978).
17 Strictly speaking, these axioms should be read against the background of Leśniewski's peculiar understanding of the meaning and logic of the copula 'is' and of the quantifiers 'every' and 'some'. This is where the other components of his overall system, especially Ontology, become relevant. For our purposes we can ignore such aspects, but see note 2 for some literature and Simons (1982c) for helpful guidance. For compact expositions, see also Simons (1987, §2.6; 2018), Ridder (2002, §1.1.2), and Urbaniak (2014a, ch. 5); for an extensive study, Gessler (2005).
18 For a first assessment, see Simons (1993) and Urbaniak (2014a, §5.3; 2015).

did show that his Mereology does not lead to Russell's (1902) antinomy (see Leśniewski, 1916, propositions XVI–XVII)[19] and he did go as far as proving mereological counterparts for a large number of set-theoretic facts, including an analogue of Zermelo's (1908) version of Cantor's theorem to the effect that every set is strictly smaller than the set of its subsets (thm. CXCVIII in Leśniewski, 1927–1931), but obviously much more than that is needed to pass muster.[20] More important, for our purposes, is whether the axioms of the theory were intended to capture some peculiar parthood relation needed to implement that program or rather the laws pertaining to part-whole relationships in general (whence the program would follow from the nominalist's conception of sets as mereological wholes). And in this regard, Leśniewski could not be more explicit:

> I tried to write my work so that it would not concern exclusively some kind of 'free creations' of various more or less Dedekindian creative souls; ... my theorems, while possessing as exact [a] form as possible, should harmonise with the 'common sense' of the representatives of 'esprit laique' who are engaged in investigating a reality not 'created by them'. (Leśniewski, 1927–1931, p. 228)

Of course, some of Leśniewski's axioms are admittedly not straightforward, so it remains to be seen whether they enjoy the "esprit laique" he attached to them. Yet precisely for this reason, precisely because they were meant to hold unrestrictedly and somewhat intuitively, Leśniewski's Mereology may be considered the first fully worked out example of a mereological theory in the sense we are interested in. In fact, roughly at the same time as he was working on it, other authors were producing semi-formal theories of the part-whole relation, but no such theory aimed at the same sort of generality as Leśniewski's. The mereological analyses contained in Alfred Whitehead's writings are perhaps the best case in point. Whitehead proposed several such analyses, first in his lecture on "The relational theory of space" (1916), then again in *An Enquiry Concerning the Principles of Natural Knowledge* (1919), in *The Concept of Nature* (1920), and in *Process and Reality* (1929).[21] These analyses are not without interest, and bear witness to the fact that contemporary philosophers had finally began to feel the need to be more specific in matters of mereology than their predecessors. But in each

19 Leśniewski addressed Russell's antinomy as early as Leśniewski (1914) and returned to it in Part II of Leśniewski (1927–1931). We shall look at these treatments in chapter 5, section 5.4.1.

20 There have been attempts to go further. For instance, Słupecki (1958) developed a "generalized mereology" that was meant to allow a full mereological reconstruction of type theory. The resulting system, however, is defective; see Urbaniak (2014b).

21 On Whitehead's mereological theories, see Simons (1987, §2.9.1; 1991b; 2017b), Ridder (2001; 2002, §IV.3), and Richard (2011). Leśniewski himself was familiar with the version presented in Whitehead (1919, ch. 8) and discussed it at some length in Part IV of Leśniewski (1927–1931); see Sinisi (1966) and Srzednicki and Stachniak (1988, ch. 6) for details.

case it is clear that Whitehead's work was crucially driven by his philosophical agenda. He was interested in the part-whole organization of specific domains of entities—initially three-dimensional physical objects, then the four-dimensional manifold of events—and the mereological principles he laid out were in each case meant to capture that organization. The very fact that they are not uniform across his writings shows that such principles were functional to this agenda and developed accordingly. Not so with Leśniewski. His motivations stemmed from his nominalistic stance toward logic and mathematics. But the mereological framework on which he erected his overall system was meant to stand by itself, and remained the same throughout his writings.

One final remark is due here. A few years after the appearance of Leśniewski's essays, Henry Leonard and Nelson Goodman published their article on the Calculus of Individuals (1940), which they presented as a powerful and expedient instrument for "the constructional analysis of the world" based on the mereological structure of individuals rather than on the set-theoretic structure of classes.[22] Their motivations for developing such a calculus were not dissimilar from Leśniewski's, as was their understanding of the basic difference between 'wholes' and 'classes':

> The difference in the concepts lies in this: that to conceive a segment as a whole or individual offers no suggestion as to what [its] subdivisions, if any, must be, whereas to conceive a segment as a class imposes a definite scheme of subdivision—into subclasses and members. (Leonard and Goodman, 1940, p. 45)

A consequence of this view is that in the Calculus of Individuals there is no way to reproduce the set-theoretic distinction between an object, x, and something consisting of just that object, i.e. its singleton $\{x\}$. This is a key feature of Leśniewski's Mereology, too, and one that Leśniewski advertised as a virtue of his theory *vis-à-vis* "the contemporary 'non-naive' theory of sets", which is in "startling conflict with intuitions of the 'commonalty'" (Leśniewski, 1916, p. 130). There is, therefore, a close connection between the two systems, and between the motives that inspired them. And since Leśniewski's writings, in Polish, have been inaccessible to larger readerships for a long time,[23] Leonard and Goodman's Calculus has for some time been credited as the first systematic treatment of mereology motivated on

22 The Calculus has its roots in Chapter 4 of Leonard's (1930) doctoral thesis (written under Whitehead's supervision) and a joint version was presented by Leonard and Goodman at the 1936 meeting of the Association for Symbolic Logic (Leonard and Goodman, 1937). For a detailed history, see Cohnitz and Rossberg (2006, ch. 4) and Rossberg (2009).

23 The *Collected Works*, in two volumes, have been published in English translation as Leśniewski (1992). An earlier translation of Leśniewski (1927–1931) appeared in Sinisi (1983) and two more essays (Leśniewski, 1931, 1938, both in German) were translated in McCall (1967). An edition of Leśniewski's lecture notes in logic was published as Srzednicki and Stachniak (1988).

nominalistic grounds.[24] It was not, as is now well known. In a way, however, the appellation is not inappropriate. For as Leonard and Goodman themselves pointed out, their Calculus turns out to be essentially *equivalent* to Leśniewski's Mereology.[25] It is not surprising, therefore, that this common theory is nowadays known as *classical mereology*. And it is from this theory that we shall begin the technical exposition of our subject in chapter 2. The rest of the book will then be devoted to a critical analysis of its postulates and to a detailed study of the many 'non-classical' theories that can be obtained by changing, dropping, or strengthening them in various ways.

1.3 'PART' AND PARTHOOD

Before we can proceed, there is still an important question that needs to be addressed. We said that part-whole considerations have occupied a prominent place throughout the history of philosophy. But we also said that already Aristotle distinguished different notions of parthood, different senses in which something can be said to be part of something else, as with genus and species (in one sense) and species and genus (in another). Indeed, Aristotle distinguished at least five senses. Here is the relevant passage in full:

> We call a part (1) that into which a quantity can in any way be divided; for that which is taken from a quantity *qua* quantity is always called a part of it, e.g. two is called in a sense a part of three.—(2) It means, of the parts in the first sense, only those which measure the whole; this is why two, though in one sense it is, in another is not, a part of three.—(3) The elements into which the kind might be divided apart from the quantity, are also called parts of it; for which reason we say the species are parts of the genus.—(4) Those into which the whole is divided, or of which it consists—'the whole' meaning either the form or that which has the form; e.g. of the bronze sphere or of the bronze cube both the bronze—i.e. the matter in which the form is—and the characteristic angle are parts.—(5) Those in the formula which explains a thing are parts of the whole; this is why the genus is called a part of the species, though in another sense the species is part of the genus. (*Metaphysics*, v, 25, 1023b12–25; Aristotle, 1984, p. 1616)

24 The original Calculus of Individuals, based on disjointness as a primitive, involved quantification over classes, as did the version included in Goodman's (1941) dissertation, written under C. I. Lewis. A class-free version, based on overlap, was later given in Goodman (1951) (where Leśniewski's Mereology is actually cited as an earlier "calculus of individuals"; see p. 42n). For detailed comparisons and discussion, see Cohnitz and Rossberg (2019) and section 2.4.2.

25 That is, they are essentially equivalent *modulo* the peculiarities of Leśniewski's logic mentioned in note 17; see Simons (1987, §2.8). It is not clear whether Leonard and Goodman were aware of such peculiarities when they wrote that the two systems are "virtually the same" (p. 46). Footnote 8 of their article actually suggests they were not, as the axiomatization of Mereology they mention seems to be taken from Tarski (1937), which is based on standard logic. (Apparently, Leonard and Goodman first heard of Leśniewski's Mereology from Quine in 1935; see Quine, 1985, p. 122. Cf. also Leonard, 1967, p. 127.)

The question that needs to be addressed is—which of these notions are to be regarded as forming the proper subject matter of mereology? Should mereology concern the basic organizing relationships between parts and wholes in all of these senses, and possibly others, or only in some senses, possibly just one?

This is not a question that admits of a simple, uncontroversial answer. One response, for instance, might go as follows. One might say that in spite of the relevant differences, all these notions share a common core, and the business of mereology is precisely to investigate that core. After all, if 'part' is the right word in each case, then there must be something to the meaning of that word that justifies its use, a "unity of analogy", as van Inwagen (1990, p. 19) calls it; let *that* something fix the scope of mereology. This seems plausible also in view of how the word 'part' is used in ordinary language, regardless of the subtle distinctions drawn by metaphysicians. Consider:

(1) The handle is part of the knife.
(2) The remote-control unit is part of the stereo system.
(3) This half is your part of the cake.
(4) The cutlery is part of the tableware.
(5) This pile is part of the trash.
(6) The circle is part of the area.
(7) The vertices are part of the boundary.
(8) The bombing was part of the attack.

Each of these uses of 'part' is perfectly appropriate, despite the obvious differences among them.[26] A part may be attached to the remainder, as in (1), or detached, as in (2); it may be cognitively or functionally salient, as in (1) and (2), or arbitrarily demarcated, as in (3); self-connected, as in (1)–(3), or disconnected, as in (4); homogeneous or otherwise well-matched, as in (1)–(4), or gerrymandered, as in (5); material, as in (1)–(5), or immaterial, as in (6); extended, as in (1)–(6), or unextended, as in (7); spatial, as in (1)–(7), or temporal, as in (8); and so on.[27] These differences are not immaterial, and each use may justify the development of specific part-whole theories incorporating principles that may not apply across the board. A Whiteheadian mereology of events, for instance, might be a good candidate for an account of cases such as (8), though it might prove too strong, or too weak, for the

26 Sometimes 'part' is used more narrowly to designate only the cognitively or functionally salient cases illustrated in (1) and (2). Such narrow use trades on the subtle difference between 'part of' and '*a* part of', to which we shall return. See Sharvy (1980, 1983), Krecz (1986), Tversky (1986, 1989), Moltmann (1998), Sanford (2017), and the brief discussion in Simons (1987, pp. 234f).

27 For more variety and tentative taxonomies, see Winston *et al.* (1987), Iris *et al.* (1988), Odell (1994), Gerstl and Pribbenow (1995), Pribbenow (1999, 2002), Westerhoff (2004), Simons (2013a), and Schalley (2017).

other cases. Yet all such theories would presumably have something in common. They would, presumably, all agree on some general features of 'part' in the broadest sense of the term, and it is such general features that mereology should investigate. In short, one may distinguish here between *local* and *global* mereologies, as Simons (1987, p. 363) puts it. And according to this first line of response it is the latter that truly matters; the truths of the former do not lie in the part-whole relation itself but in the nature of the entities to which they apply. (This is perhaps best understood in the spirit of a broadly Husserlian conception of mereology as a piece of formal ontology, though we have seen that Leśniewski, too, was aiming at a global mereology of sorts, a theory of parts and wholes consistent with 'common sense'.)

On the other hand, there is a legitimate worry that such an approach may not result in anything of value. Indeed, in section 1.1 we saw that combining different senses of 'part' may lead to trouble already with respect to transitivity, and it may lead to trouble precisely *insofar as* transitivity applies to each sense taken individually. The union of two transitive relations need not be transitive. This suggests that even principles that belong to the 'common core', even principles that appear to be valid in *every* sense of 'part', such as transitivity, may no longer hold when taken globally. And if this is true of some principles, then it may well be true of all candidate principles, jeopardizing the whole project. Accordingly, one might favor a different sort of response to our question. One might take the many senses of 'part' at face value and investigate the corresponding parthood relations in the spirit of a genuinely pluralist mereology. In its plainest form, this strategy would simply yield a family of mereologies, one for each relevant sense and each with its own set of laws. (Determining exactly *which* senses of 'part' should be distinguished, or how many, is of course part of the challenge, though Aristotle is always a good start.) Alternatively, one might understand the relevant pluralism to involve the further task of explaining how the several parthood relations interact with one another, so as to determine, for instance, whether and in what sense Socrates is part of Coriscus, whether the handle, which is part of the knife in sense (1), is in some sense part of the tableware insofar as the knife itself is part of the tableware in sense (4), and so on. One may even construe mereological pluralism as involving substantive metaphysical work in the spirit of a thorough 'constructional analysis of the world'. And here, again, there is room for weaker and stronger forms of pluralism, depending on whether, following McDaniel (2010a), the different part-whole relations are taken to be fundamental insofar as they are irreducible to one another (weak pluralism) or insofar as they cannot be analyzed in terms of any other property or relation (strong pluralism).

A careful assessment of these options is obviously vital for a proper understanding of the tasks of mereology, and the recent literature on the topic bears witness to its importance.[28] In this work, however, we shall refrain from taking a definite stand. Generally speaking, we take it that an abductive approach would be methodologically appropriate. One first identifies the role mereological considerations are meant to play in theoretical inquiry (and, hence, in relation to larger metaphysical projects) and then proceeds to characterize the parthood relations that best fit the bill. Each characterization would then be assessed on the usual criteria for theory choice. Yet this sort of assessment goes beyond our present concerns. For the most part, our treatment will focus on theories that are defined entirely by the axioms they take to govern a specific parthood relation, P, as represented in a simplified language whose vocabulary contains no other predicate except for the identity relation, =. The interaction between these two relations will be within the purview of those theories, which may differ significantly in the accounts they offer. (For instance: should parthood and identity conform to the doctrine of 'extensionality', to the effect that no two composite things can have the same proper parts?) But the lack of further linguistic resources will block from the start the possibility of studying P from a broader perspective, including its interaction with other sorts of (irreducible) parthood relations. While this is admittedly a limit, it need not be construed as a tacit endorsement of the monist position corresponding to the first stance mentioned above, as if all possible parthood relations were subsumed under a single, overarching relation represented by P. More simply, it is a fact that most theories available in the literature are of this kind, and there is much to learn from their careful study before any further development can even get off the ground. For a mereological monist, that may well be all that mereology is about; for a pluralist, those further developments will be of chief importance, and it may well be that the interesting work, philosophically and technically, lies there. Yet both can gain a lot, we trust, by locally joining forces.

1.4 PARTS AND WHOLES

One final clarification is in order. It is common, and somewhat intuitive, to speak of mereology as dealing with the *part-whole* relation (or relations), and in this book we follow this common usage. Strictly speaking, however, the

---

28 For the record, classical mereology is normally aligned with mereological monism (see Lewis, 1991, for a classic endorsement and Lando, 2017, for a sustained defense), whereas the authors mentioned in note 27 tend to favor a pluralist stance of the first sort (a plurality of mereologies). The same stance is urged, among others, by McDaniel (2004), Mellor (2006), Johansson (2015), and Wallace (in press) and hinted at in van Inwagen (1990, pp. 19f). Stronger forms of pluralism have also been advocated, from Nagel (1952) and Grossmann (1973) to Armstrong (1986) or Fine (1994, 1999, 2010). See also Hawley (2006) and McDaniel (2009a). On the other hand, there are authors who recognize *no* parthood relations, so that the world would lack any part-whole structure altogether; for a defense of this sort of mereological antirealism, see Cowling (2014).

relation P that our mereological theories seek to characterize is just *parthood*, i.e. a relation expressed by the binary predicate 'x is part of y', with no presumption that it holds exclusively when y qualifies as a 'whole' in any substantive sense (e.g. as an integral, cohesive, unitary entity). Mereologically speaking, there is no difference between the sense in which a finger is part of a hand and the sense in which it is part of a whole human body. Indeed, mereologically the distinction between parts and wholes is entirely context-dependent. As Jonathan Barnes puts it:

> As parts are relative, so too—and trivially—are wholes. That is to say, corresponding to the relation of *being a part of* there is its converse—which we may as well call the relation of *being a whole for* ... One thing is a part of a second if and only if the second is a whole for the first. (Barnes, 1988, p. 244)

The very fact that parthood may be construed as a transitive relation bears witness to this point. For whenever transitivity obtains, the middle term y will count as a whole with respect to the first, x, and as a part with respect to the third, z.[29]

This is not to deny that a mereological theory can be developed in such a way that the relation expressed by 'x is part of y' will obtain only when the second argument, y, satisfies certain special conditions. Consider, for instance, the following thesis:

If x is part of y, then y is not part of z unless $x = y$ or $y = z$.

Surely this thesis trivializes the transitivity of parthood (without contradicting it), and may be read as asserting that parthood can only relate parts and *wholes*, i.e. things that are mereologically maximal. Yet this is what the *thesis* says. It may be taken as an axiom or it may be derived as a theorem. But no such claim can be read directly into the predicate itself, 'x is part of y'.

More generally, there is no question that mereology can prove useful for the purpose of drawing important ontological distinctions among wholes of various kinds. Aristotle and many medieval mereologists may be read as engaging precisely in that sort of task, and the same can be said of Husserl, whose third Investigation used mereological concepts to characterize "the pregnant concept of a whole" (Husserl, 1900–1901, p. 475). The growing interest in mereology among contemporary analytic metaphysicians is also indicative of its promise in connection with projects of this kind.[30] Typically,

29 Some authors would speak of y as a 'holon', following Koestler (1967). The term comes from the Greek ὅλος (meaning 'whole') but with the suffix 'on' (suggesting a particle) to designate precisely those 'Janus-faced' nodes on a hierarchic tree that look both inward and outward and behave "partly as wholes or wholly as parts" (p. 48). See also Koestler (1969, 1978), where such 'holarchies' are investigated in the spirit of Bertalanffy's (1968) system theory.

30 As in Part III of Simons (1987). Other examples include Lowe (1989), van Inwagen (1990), Moltmann (1997), Meirav (2003), Koslicki (2008), and Priest (2014b).

however, such projects draw on conceptual and linguistic resources that go well beyond the expressive power of a purely mereological theory in our sense, with just a parthood predicate and an identity predicate.[31] Aristotle, for example, relied on the notions of naturalness and unity:

> We call a whole (1) that from which is absent none of the parts of which it is said to be naturally a whole, and (2) that which so contains the things it contains that they form a unity; and this in two senses—either as each and all one, or as making up the unity between them. (*Metaphysics*, v, 26, 1023b26–29; Aristotle, 1984, p. 1616)

Likewise, Husserl relied explicitly on the interplay between 'x is part of y' and 'x is founded on y':

> By a Whole we understand a range of contents which are all covered *by a single foundation* without the help of further contents. The contents of such a range we call its parts. (Husserl, 1900–1901, p. 475)

This is all fine, and it is our hope that this book will provide useful material for metaphysical applications of this sort. But to engage in such projects is to go beyond mereology. It is to engage in something which, for lack of better terminology, might be called 'hology', the theory of wholeness.[32] Mereology may well be part of it. It has, however, no claim to being the whole.

1.5 THE FORMAL SETTING

We now introduce the formal apparatus with which we shall be working through the rest of the book. This apparatus will help avoid ambiguities stemming from ordinary language and will facilitate systematic comparisons across the different mereological theories that we shall consider.

As already noted, for the most part we shall focus on theories formulated in a first-order language whose basic vocabulary consists of the identity predicate, $=$, and just one more binary predicate constant, P, for the parthood relation.[33] Thus we shall write, for instance, $x = y$ for 'x is identical

31 Typically, but not necessarily. See e.g. Mormann (2013) for a purely mereological characterization of 'whole' in the topological sense of 'self-connected'. We take this opportunity to rectify the stronger claim made in Varzi (1996, §3) and Casati and Varzi (1999, §2.1).

32 The term is actually present in some relevant literature. It was coined, in Italian, in Dappiano (1993) and introduced into English by Libardi (1994), though it does not seem to have caught on.

33 In the literature, the parthood relation is often represented by non-alphabetic symbols supporting infix notation, such as $\leq$, $\sqsubseteq$, or $\trianglelefteq$. Similarly for other mereological relations, whether defined or treated as primitive: proper parthood is often symbolized as $<$ (but also, again, as $\ll$, $\sqsubset$, $\triangleleft$, etc.), overlap as $\circ$ or $\between$, disjointness as $|$, $)($, $\wr$, $\rceil$, $\Vert$, etc. This plethora of symbols is both overwhelming and confusing. Here we stick to the safer practice of sacrificing all infix notation in favor of mnemonic upper-case letters (single or compound), with the only exception of identity. Note that we will not observe use/mention distinctions unless required by the context.

to y' (or, more simply, 'x is y') and Pxy for 'x is part of y', using x, y, z, etc. as individual variables. Other mereologically salient predicates, corresponding to such relations as proper parthood, disjointness, overlap, etc., will be introduced by definition as we proceed (or treated as primitive in a similar fashion). In addition, the language of these theories will include symbols for the usual logical operators: the sentential connectives $\neg$, $\wedge$, $\vee$, $\rightarrow$, and $\leftrightarrow$, respectively for negation ('it is not the case that'), conjunction ('and'), disjunction ('or'), conditional ('only if', or 'if ... then'), and biconditional ('if and only if'); the universal and existential quantifiers $\forall$ ('for all') and $\exists$ ('for some'); and parentheses. Thus, we shall write $\neg Pxy$ for 'x is not part of y', $Pxy \wedge Pyz$ for 'x is part of y and y is part of z', $\forall x(Pxy \rightarrow Pxz)$ for 'For all x, if x is part of y, then x is part of z' (i.e. 'Every x that is part of y is part of z'), and so on. To indicate arbitrary well-formed formulas we will generally use lower-case letters from the middle of the Greek alphabet: φ, ψ, ξ, etc.

All other syntactic conventions and terminology concerning this language will be either obvious from the context or used in accordance with standard practice. Only two conventions need to be defined explicitly, since they will be central to the understanding of several axioms and theorems to be discussed.

The first convention concerns the distinction between bound and free occurrences of a variable. Given any formula φ, we shall speak of an occurrence of a variable x in φ as *bound* if it is either next to a quantifier or within the scope of a quantifier associated with x; otherwise we shall speak of that occurrence of x as *free* in φ. Thus, for instance, in the formula

$$\forall x(Pxy \rightarrow Pxz) \rightarrow Pyx$$

(where the parentheses mark the quantifier's scope), the first three occurrences of x are bound while the fourth one is free, as are all occurrences of y and z. When dealing with an arbitrary formula φ, we may want to indicate that a certain variable x occurs free in φ. We shall do so by writing φx, thus signaling that the formula behaves effectively like a predicate. Moreover, we shall generally write φ^x_y for the formula obtained by replacing every free occurrence of x in φ by y, whereas $\varphi(^x_y)$ will indicate any formula that can be obtained from φ by substituting y for any number of such occurrences (not necessarily all). If no free occurrence of x in φ lies within the scope of a quantifier binding the variable y, as in the example displayed above, then y is said to be *free for* x in φ.

The second convention concerns the iota operator, ι. This will be used to represent expressions that in English can be formulated with the help of the definite article 'the', i.e. definite descriptions, and our usage will conform to the standard account due to Russell (1905). Thus, given any formula φ, we shall write $\iota x \varphi x$ for 'the x such that φx', or simply 'the φ', and this, in turn, is to be understood in accordance with the following contextual definition: to say 'the φ is ψ' is to say 'there is at least one and at most one x such that φx, and this unique x is such that ψx'. In symbols:

$$\exists x((\varphi x \wedge \forall w(\varphi^x_w \to w = x)) \wedge \psi x)$$

(where w is any variable foreign to φ). As a simple example, consider the definite description 'the (unique) part of y'. Using the iota operator, this can be written in formal notation as $\iota x Pxy$, and a statement such as 'the (unique) part of y is z' will correspond to the formula $\exists x((Pxy \wedge \forall w(Pwy \to w = x)) \wedge x = z)$, which can be abbreviated as $\iota x Pxy = z$.

On the semantic side, our language will be just as standard. An interpretation of the language will simply consist of a non-empty domain of objects, D, along with a binary relation on that domain, $\leqslant$, corresponding to the parthood predicate P. We shall say that an interpretation is a *model* of a certain mereological theory if and only if it satisfies every axiom of the theory. And we shall understand the latter notion thus: an interpretation $\langle D, \leqslant \rangle$ *satisfies* a formula φ, with free variables among $x_1, \ldots, x_n$, if and only if φ is satisfied by some n-tuple of objects $a_1, \ldots, a_n$ in D (each a_i providing a value for the corresponding x_i) in accordance with the following recursive clauses. (i) If φ is an atomic formula, of the form Px_jx_k or $x_j = x_k$, then φ is satisfied by $a_1, \ldots, a_n$ if and only if $a_j \leqslant a_k$ or $a_j = a_k$, respectively. (ii) If φ is a truth-functional compound, then φ is satisfied by $a_1, \ldots, a_n$ if and only if the immediate components of φ are satisfied or not satisfied by $a_1, \ldots, a_n$ in conformity with the standard truth table for the main connective of φ: if φ is of the form $\neg\psi$, it is satisfied by $a_1, \ldots, a_n$ if and only if ψ is not satisfied by $a_1, \ldots, a_n$; if φ is of the form $\psi \wedge \xi$, it is satisfied by $a_1, \ldots, a_n$ if and only if both ψ and ξ are satisfied by $a_1, \ldots, a_n$; and so on. (iii) If φ is a quantified formula of the form $\forall x\psi$ or $\exists x\psi$, then φ is satisfied by $a_1, \ldots, a_n$ if and only if ψ is satisfied by every or, respectively, by some x-variant of $a_1, \ldots, a_n$, where an x-variant of $a_1, \ldots, a_n$ is any tuple of objects in D that deviates from $a_1, \ldots, a_n$ at most in containing a different or an additional element assigned to x depending on whether x is or is not among $x_1, \ldots, x_n$. Thus, for example, the universally quantified formula $\forall x_1 Px_1x_2$ (with just x_2 free and $x_1 \neq x_2$) is satisfied by $a_1, \ldots, a_n$ if and only if Px_1x_2 is satisfied by $a, a_2, \ldots, a_n$ for every a in D, hence if and only if $a \leqslant a_2$ for every such a; the existentially quantified formula $\exists x_{n+1}(Px_1x_{n+1} \wedge Px_{n+1}x_2)$ (with x_1 and x_2 free and $x_{n+1} \neq x_1, x_{n+1} \neq x_2$) is satisfied by $a_1, \ldots, a_n$ if and only if $Px_1x_{n+1} \wedge Px_{n+1}x_2$ is satisfied by $a_1, \ldots, a_n, a$ for some a in D, hence if and only if $a_1 \leqslant a$ and $a \leqslant a_2$ for some such a; and so on.

So much for the linguistic framework. As for the deductive apparatus, for the most part our mereological theories will be based on classical predicate logic with identity. We need not be too precise about this. When it comes to showing that certain formulas are among the theorems of a certain theory, or that they stand in certain logical relations, object-language derivations tend to be tedious and unperspicuous; we shall rely instead on semi-formal proofs, with just enough rigor to give the feeling that a full formalization is possible. However, occasionally it will be necessary to be more precise and refer to a specific version of classical logic. For definiteness, we shall assume it to be the first-order predicate calculus defined by the following axiom schemas, with *modus ponens* (from φ and $\varphi \to \psi$ infer ψ) and *generalization* (from φ infer $\forall x\varphi$) as the only rules of inference:

(L.1) $\varphi \to (\psi \to \varphi)$

(L.2) $(\varphi \to (\psi \to \xi)) \to ((\varphi \to \psi) \to (\varphi \to \xi))$

(L.3) $(\neg\varphi \to \neg\psi) \to ((\neg\varphi \to \psi) \to \varphi)$

(L.4) $\forall x\varphi \to \varphi^x_y$ provided y is free for x in φ

(L.5) $\forall x(\varphi \to \psi) \to (\varphi \to \forall x\psi)$ provided x is not free in φ

(L.6) $x = x$

(L.7) $x = y \to (\varphi \to \varphi(^x_y))$ provided y is free for x in φ

Such an axiomatization of the classical predicate calculus may be found, for instance, in Mendelson (1964). The last axiom is a version of so-called Leibniz's law, and we shall occasionally refer to it that way.

This logico-linguistic machinery will suffice for chapters 2 through 5, where we shall examine classical mereology along with a good number of other theories.[34] The use of classical predicate logic, however, is not without consequences, as is the decision to treat parthood as a simple binary relation. In chapter 6 we shall therefore consider various ways in which these assumptions may be relaxed or modified so as to address certain questions, and account for certain phenomena, that run afoul of the theories examined up to that point. Among other things, this will include forays into mereologies formulated in second-order logic, in first-order logic with plural reference and quantification, in tense and modal logic, and in various systems tolerating failures of the two fundamental laws that govern classical logic: the law of excluded middle and the law of non-contradiction. The relevant technical details, however, will be introduced in due time.

34 We shall confine ourselves to Hilbert-style axiomatic systems, which is the preferred format of most mereological theories discussed in the literature. For Gentzen-style sequent calculi, see Tennant (2013, 2019) and Maffezioli (2016a,b).

CLASSICAL MEREOLOGY 2

Everything is surely related to everything as follows:
either it is the same or different; or, if it is not the same or different,
it would be related as part to whole or as whole to part.

— Plato, *Parmenides*, 146b2–5 (1997, p. 379)

The primary aim of this chapter is to provide a comprehensive account of *classical mereology*, the theory stemming from the work of Leśniewski (1916, 1927–1931) and of Leonard and Goodman (1940) mentioned in section 1.2.2. This theory is by now well known and has been studied *axiomatically*, *algebraically*, and *set-theoretically*. We will examine classical mereology in each of these three settings, sketching proofs of their equivalence.

It can be somewhat difficult for newcomers to get a sense for the structures that classical mereology is meant to capture. Rather than working directly with Leśniewski's axioms, or with Leonard and Goodman's, our approach is to begin with a slightly non-standard axiom system that displays the spirit of the theory more clearly. This is done in section 2.1, where we also introduce several auxiliary notions as they are usually defined in classical mereology: proper parthood, overlap, disjointness, etc. In section 2.2 we use this axiomatic formulation to prove the important result, originally due to Alfred Tarski (1935),[1] that models of classical mereology have a familiar algebraic structure: they are complete Boolean algebras without a bottom element. A straightforward example of these algebras is the *powerset* structure, where a powerset is the set of all subsets of a given set. We discuss the precise relationship between powersets and classical mereology in section 2.3. Finally, in section 2.4 we present a number of alternative axiom systems that can be used to characterize classical mereology, some of which rely on different primitive mereological concepts. We begin with two closely related versions of Leśniewski's (1916) system due to Tarski (1929, 1935),[2]

1 Tarski did his doctoral studies at the University of Warsaw and completed his dissertation (partly published as Tarski, 1923) under Leśniewski's supervision. On Tarski's Leśniewskian background, see Feferman and Feferman (2004, ch. 2) and Betti (2004, 2008).

2 Strictly speaking, the axiom system of Tarski (1929) only appears in the English translation included in Tarski (1956). The French original gives no axioms and simply refers to Leśniewski (1916) and to the first two essays of Leśniewski (1927–1931). For a detailed reconstruction of the reasons that may have led Tarski to proceed this way, see Betti and Loeb (2012) and Betti (2014).

Mereology. A. J. Cotnoir and Achille C. Varzi, Oxford University Press. © A. J. Cotnoir and Achille C. Varzi 2021. DOI: 10.1093/oso/9780198749004.003.0002

both of which use *proper parthood* as a primitive. Next we consider a version of Leonard and Goodman's (1940) system, which uses *disjointness* and is akin to the system of Goodman (1951), based on *overlap*. Lastly, we present two *parthood*-based systems, due to Tarski (1937) and Eberle (1970), which differ from ours in significant ways, followed by a few more variants. As we shall see, while all these systems are equivalent (and the list is by no means exhaustive of the options), they use a variety of 'decomposition' and 'composition' axioms of varying strengths. Introducing these axioms here, and the definitions on which they rely, will prepare the way for their philosophical evaluation, to which we shall attend in chapters 4 and 5, respectively.

2.1 A PERSPICUOUS AXIOM SYSTEM

When dealing with formal theories, starting from a purely syntactic axiom system is not usually the most enlightening way to proceed. (Imagine trying to learn and understand classical logic via the predicate calculus, with nothing but some rules of inference and a few schematic formulas treated as axioms.) Still, classical mereology is often presented axiomatically, so understanding the axioms and how they relate to the underlying mereological structure is essential. Toward this end, we begin here with an axiom system that is virtually new to the literature,[3] but has the advantage of wearing its intended interpretation 'on its sleeve', as it were. Each of the axioms is simple and easy to grasp intuitively, and together they will allow for a smooth comparison to well-known mathematical structures.

2.1.1 *A Partial Order*

As with every axiomatic theory, before we present and begin to explore our axioms, we need to fix a formal logical apparatus in which to operate. Classical mereology is nearly always formulated within *classical logic*,[4] so we reserve a preliminary axiom set for this purpose.

(A.0) Any axiom set adequate for classical first-order logic with identity.

One such axiom set is given at the end of chapter 1, with *modus ponens* and generalization as rules of inference.

3 Our axiomatization is inspired by the system N2 discussed in Hovda (2009); it was first presented in Cotnoir and Varzi (2019). As we go to press, we learn from Świętorzecka and Łyczak (in press) that a notable precedent may be found in an unpublished 1920s manuscript by Jan Drewnowski, who studied mereology with Leśniewski. We shall provide details on this historical precedent in due course (sections 4.1.1 and 5.1.1).

4 Though see again chapter 1, notes 17 and 24, for the original formulations of Leśniewski's and Leonard and Goodman's systems. Other logical variants will be discussed in chapter 6.

Next, like all axiom systems for mereology, we must choose a primitive mereological concept to axiomatize, and then define other concepts in terms of it. For our system, we will simply choose the parthood relation, P. Here is our first cluster of axioms:

(A.1) $\forall x Pxx$ *Reflexivity*
(A.2) $\forall x \forall y ((Pxy \wedge Pyx) \rightarrow x = y)$ *Antisymmetry*
(A.3) $\forall x \forall y \forall z ((Pxy \wedge Pyz) \rightarrow Pxz)$ *Transitivity*

These axioms are sometimes called *ordering* axioms, since they impose a kind of 'order' on the elements that stand in the parthood relation. A.1 says that everything is part of itself; by this, we just mean that the identity relation counts as a limit case of parthood. In other words, this first axiom forces parthood to be a *reflexive* relation. A.2 says that things that are parts of each other are identical; it rules out any cases of symmetric parthood while still being compatible with the symmetry of identity. This condition on parthood forces it to be an *antisymmetric* relation. Lastly, A.3 says that if something is part of some part of a thing, it is itself part of that thing. This means that parthood must be a *transitive* relation. Mathematically, any relation that is both reflexive and transitive is called a *pre-order*, and any pre-order that is also antisymmetric is called a *partial order*. Partial orders are fairly common relations; consider, for example, the relation *less than or equal to* on the integers, or the relation *later than or simultaneous with* on events, or the relation *included in* in the spatial sense. That parthood, too, is a partial order may not be so obvious, and in chapter 3 we shall examine the philosophical case for thinking that it is (or that it isn't). For now, the purpose of A.1–A.3 is simply to register that this is a fundamental assumption of classical mereology. (It may be recalled that it was already Leibniz's view; see section 1.1.)

Given the minimal characterization of parthood afforded by these three axioms, we are now in a position to define some of the other mereological relations we wish to make use of.

(D.1) $PPxy :\equiv Pxy \wedge \neg x = y$ *Proper Parthood*
(D.2) $Oxy :\equiv \exists z(Pzx \wedge Pzy)$ *Overlap*
(D.3) $Uxy :\equiv \exists z(Pxz \wedge Pyz)$ *Underlap*
(D.4) $Dxy :\equiv \neg \exists z(Pzx \wedge Pzy)$ *Disjointness*

According to D.1, something is a proper part of a thing just in case it is a part distinct from the thing itself (as a finger is part of a hand). Because we have already stipulated that the parthood relation is a partial order, it will follow that proper parthood is also a kind of order. It is called a *strict partial order*, for it is irreflexive and—given A.2—asymmetric: no two things can be proper parts of each other. D.2 says that a thing overlaps another whenever there is something they both have as a part—a part they share in common (as two streets may share a part where they intersect). This relation, too, has some interesting properties. For instance, it follows from A.1 that it is reflexive (everything has a part in common with itself, namely itself), and since the conjunction connective used in the definition is commutative by A.0, overlap is also symmetric. However, it is not a transitive relation, for something can have a part in common with one thing and also a part in common with another thing without those two things having any part in common between themselves. (A case in point would be a street that intersects two parallel streets.) A relation that is reflexive and symmetric, but not necessarily transitive, is sometimes called a *tolerance relation*. D.3 tells us that a thing underlaps another when there is something of which both are parts (as with two fingers that are part of the same hand). This is also a tolerance relation. Finally, D.4 says that two things are disjoint when they have no common parts. Thus, disjointness is simply the negation of overlap (symmetric but irreflexive).

As a simple model for these relations, consider figure 2.1. Here we interpret parthood as spatial inclusion. On the understanding that the only things in this model are the five circular regions $x_1, \ldots, x_5$ (with $x_4 = y$) along with their subregions, our mereological relations obtain as follows: Px_iy obtains for $i = 2$ and $i = 4$; PPx_iy only for $i = 2$; Ox_iy for $i = 1, 2, 4, 5$; Ux_iy for $i = 1, 2, 3, 4, 5$; and Dx_iy for $i = 3$ (the one case when Ox_iy does not obtain).

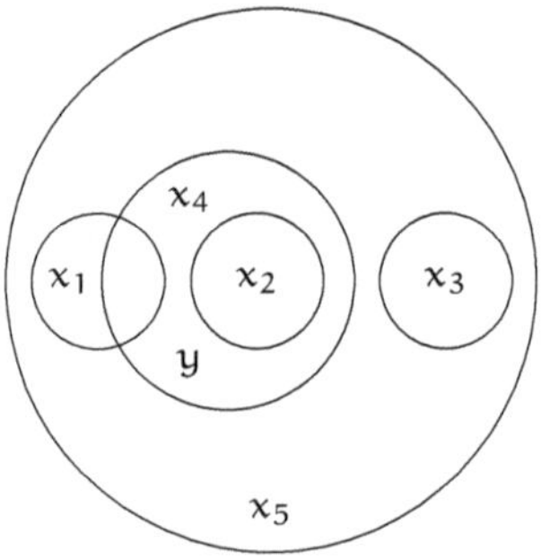

Figure 2.1: A spatial model for the main mereological relations

Other intuitive mereological concepts could be defined in a similar fashion. For instance, one may define *proper overlap* as the relation that obtains between overlapping things when neither is part of the other, and similarly for *proper underlap*. Or one might say that a thing *(properly) extends over* a second when the latter is (a proper) part of the former. However, such notions are merely variants or simple combinations of the four notions defined in D.1–D.4 and play no significant role in axiomatic treatments of mereology,[5] so we shall not bother here to introduce them formally. For the time being, D.1–D.4 will suffice.

2.1.2 *Decomposition*

After we have our ordering axioms, mereological questions regarding the *decomposition* of objects arise naturally. When does an object have parts at all—that is, proper parts? Can an object have exactly one proper part? If an object has a proper part, must it have a 'remainder'—a proper part made up of the rest of the object?

In the literature, these are controversial questions. There is class of principles—called *supplementation* principles[6]—that are used to enforce certain answers. Supplementation principles, however, are among the most difficult aspects of mereology to master; we shall devote a good part of chapter 4 to formulating them and exploring their connections to various philosophical views about decomposition. Here we start with the following principle, which encapsulates the distinctive view of classical mereology. Given A.1–A.3, this fourth axiom will imply an affirmative answer to the third question raised above and, derivatively, a negative answer to the second, though classical mereology leaves the first question open.

(A.4) $\forall x \forall y(\neg Pxy \to \exists z \forall w(Pwz \leftrightarrow (Pwx \wedge Dwy)))$ *Remainder*

To understand this principle in full generality, we first notice that it is in conditional form: it stipulates the existence of a certain sort of thing under the conditions outlined in the antecedent. The antecedent says that $\neg Pxy$; when is it true? Because of the Reflexivity axiom A.1, we know that $x \neq y$. We thus have three sorts of case: (i) the case where y is a proper part of x; (ii) the case where y is not a proper part of x but where x and y overlap; and (iii) the case in which x and y are completely disjoint. So A.4 asserts that in each of these cases, the consequent holds. What does the consequent say? It asserts the existence of something, z, that has as parts all and only those parts of x that are disjoint from y. Intuitively, one can think of this z as what remains of x when y is 'removed' (whence the name of this axiom). In case (i) and case (ii), z will include every part of x that is disjoint from y and exclude those parts of x that overlap y. In case (iii), there are no parts

5 One notable exception are the mereological theories of Whitehead (1919, 1920), which use *extends over* as a primitive.

6 The notion of supplementation comes from Husserl (1900–1901). In the sense used here, it has entered the literature with Simons (1987).

of x that overlap y, and so our original object x can serve as a witness for z. These three cases are depicted in figure 2.2, where the remainder of y in x is represented by the shaded areas.

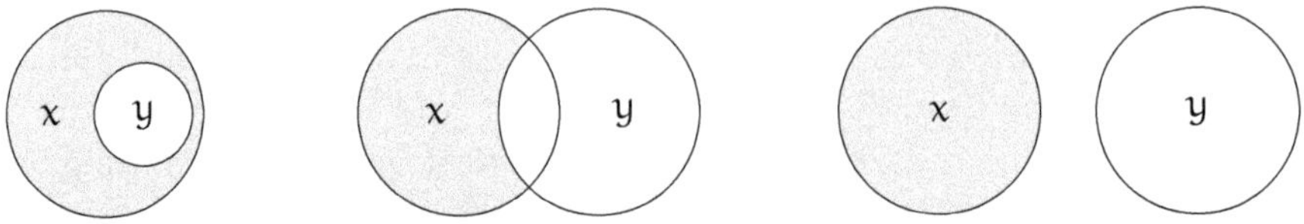

Figure 2.2: Cases where $\neg Pxy$

Those familiar with Euler diagrams (or even Venn diagrams) from the set-theoretic context will be reminded here of the notion of *set difference*, $X \setminus Y$, namely the set of all members of X that are not members of Y. In mathematics, these sorts of remainders are called *relative complements*, and the same notion is also familiar from logic: where p and q are propositions, the relative complement of q in p is just the proposition $p \wedge \neg q$. Borrowing from this terminology, we can by analogy speak of remainders, too, as relative complements: z is a relative complement of y in x.[7] In fact, the analogy is stronger. For just as set differences or relative complements are unique, so the ordering axioms guarantee that mereological remainders are also unique. This can be seen by noting that if z_1 and z_2 are remainders of y in x (assuming $\neg Pxy$), then z_1 and z_2 must have the same parts, since in each case these parts must be exactly those parts of x that are disjoint from y. But if z_1 and z_2 have the same parts, then A.1 (Reflexivity) implies that z_1 and z_2 are part of each other, whence we can infer that $z_1 = z_2$ by A.2 (Antisymmetry). Because of this, we are justified in speaking of *the* (unique) relative complement of y in x, and we can rely on a definite description to introduce a notation paralleling the common notation for set difference.[8]

(D.5) $x - y := \iota z \forall w(Pwz \leftrightarrow (Pwx \wedge Dwy))$ *Difference*

Now, we said that A.4 implies answers to the second and third questions with which we started, and it is not difficult to see why. Case (i) above, with y a proper part of x, is in fact the case envisaged by the third question, yielding an affirmative answer: whenever an object x has a proper part y, the difference $x - y$ is a further proper part of x entirely disjoint from y. *A fortiori*, it follows that the second question is answered in the negative: nothing can have a single proper part. The first question, however, concerning

7 In some literature, A.4 is actually called 'Complementation'; see Varzi (2016, §3.3).
8 On the use of the iota operator ι, see section 1.5.

whether an object must have proper parts at all, is left open by A.4 and, more generally, by the axioms of classical mereology. Among other things, this means that this theory is neutral with regard to Kant's famous Antinomy mentioned in section 1.1: it is compatible with an *atomistic* stance, according to which everything is ultimately composed of parts that have no further parts (Democritus's 'indivisibles', or atoms), and it is also compatible with an *anti-atomistic* stance, which says instead that everything can be divided forever into smaller and smaller proper parts (as Anaxagoras claimed). We shall come back to these issues in section 4.6. For now, two more consequences of A.4 are worth registering, both of which betoken the non-neutrality of classical mereology in other respects.

The first consequence is that decomposition is unique; whenever a thing has proper parts, it is the *only* thing with just those proper parts. Formally:

(T.1) $\forall x(\exists w PPwx \rightarrow \forall y(\forall z(PPzx \leftrightarrow PPzy) \rightarrow x = y))$ PP–*Extensionality*

We can also read this thesis as asserting that no composite thing can have exactly the same proper parts as another. That is why the thesis is called Extensionality, by analogy with the extensionality principle of set theory, which says that two sets cannot have the same members (or, for that matter, the same proper subsets). To see why the thesis follows from A.4, given also the ordering axioms, assume according to the antecedent of T.1 that x has at least one proper part, w, and suppose that $x \neq y$. By A.2 (Antisymmetry), it must be that either $\neg Pxy$ or $\neg Pyx$. The two cases are symmetric, so suppose $\neg Pxy$. This is the antecedent of A.4, so we can infer the consequent: there must be a remainder, z, whose parts are those parts of x that are disjoint from y. By A.1 (Reflexivity), we have Pzz, so it follows that Pzx and Dzy. If $z = x$, this means that x and y are disjoint, and hence that w, which is a proper part of x, is not a proper part of y. If $z \neq x$, then we must have $PPzx$, so in this case z itself counts as a proper part of x but not of y (for if z were a proper part of y, it would overlap y, again by A.1). Thus, either way the assumption that $x \neq y$ implies that x and y do not have exactly the same proper parts. From this, the consequent of T.1 follows by contraposition.

The Extensionality thesis T.1 expresses a substantive mereological claim,[9] and in chapters 3 and 4 we shall examine several philosophical reasons why it may be deemed problematic. The second consequence of A.4 worth noting is of different import. As we shall see in section 2.2, in a setting where we have a 'universe'—an all-encompassing entity extending over everything—we can define a non-relative notion of complement: the complement of any

9 The label itself comes from Goodman (1956, §2), for whom the extensional character of the Calculus of Individuals embodies the fundamental 'principle of nominalism': no distinction of entities without distinction of content. See also Goodman (1951, p. 26) and Lewis (1991, p. 78).

object y is the relative complement of y in the whole universe.[10] In other words, it is just what we get when y is 'removed' from the universe. What about the complement of the universe itself? Intuitively, the universe is the largest thing, a mereological 'top' of which everything is part, so its complement (were it to exist) would have to be the smallest thing, a mereological 'bottom' that is part of everything, a 'null' object, a 'zero'. Now, A.4 does not require a complement of the universe, since the universe can never satisfy its antecedent: where y is the universe, there is no x such that $\neg Pxy$. But something stronger is true: A.4 actually *rules out* the null object. That is, A.4 (together with A.1 and A.2) entails the following thesis:

(T.2) $\exists x \exists y \neg x = y \rightarrow \neg \exists x \forall y \, Pxy$ *No Zero*

This theorem says that as long as there is more than one thing, there is nothing which is part of everything—no mereological zero.[11] To see why T.2 follows, assume according to the antecedent that there are at least two things, say, a and b. By A.2 (Antisymmetry), a and b cannot be part of each other, so without loss of generality let $\neg Pab$. By A.4, we have for some z that $\forall w(Pwz \leftrightarrow (Pwa \wedge Dwb))$. Now suppose there were an object—call it 0—such that $\forall w P0w$. Then we would have that $P0z$, and hence $P0a \wedge D0b$. But by A.1 (Reflexivity) the latter conjunct conflicts with $P0b$, which holds by supposition. Hence, there can be no such 0.

In chapter 4 we shall have more to say about the reasons for discarding the null object in mereology. Leśniewski himself was adamant about its non-existence, speaking of its set-theoretic analogue—the empty set—as a "mythological conception" (Leśniewski, 1927–1931, p. 202).[12] But apart from any philosophical considerations, the fact that classical mereology rejects its existence is important mathematically. For as we shall see in section 2.2, precisely here lies the main difference between this theory and the more familiar structures known as Boolean algebras. As Tarski put it:[13]

> The formal difference between mereology and the extended system of Boolean algebra reduces to one point: the axioms of mereology imply (under the assumption of the existence of at least two different individuals) that there is no individual corresponding to the Boolean-algebraic zero, i.e. an individual which is a part of every other individual. (Tarski, 1935, p. 333, fn. 4)

10 We shall come back to this in section 4.1.2, where we discuss stronger (non-relative) remainder principles called 'Absolute' or 'Strong' Complementation.

11 In some versions of classical mereology, T.2 is listed as an axiom; see e.g. Hovda (2009, §4) (but cf. *infra*, chapter 4, note 27 for qualifications).

12 It is precisely from the rejection of this "myth" that Leśniewski (1914) explained his way out of Russell's paradox; see Urbaniak (2014a, §2.8.4).

13 Leonard and Goodman (1940, p. 46) stress the same point: "The calculus ... differs from the Boolean analogue in ways consequent upon the refusal to postulate a null element".

2.1.3 *Composition*

After settling questions regarding decomposition, we move on to questions regarding mereological organization in the opposite direction—composition. What is it for some objects to compose another? Under what conditions does mereological composition occur?

To begin, we need a formal definition of mereological composition, sometimes called 'fusion'.[14] There are a number of options that we explore in detail in chapter 5. For our purposes, we begin with the following.

(D.6) $F_\varphi z :\equiv \forall x(\varphi x \to Pxz) \land \forall y(\forall x(\varphi x \to Pxy) \to Pzy)$ *Fusion*

Here φ is any formula in which x occurs free, and '$F_\varphi z$' may be read: 'z is a fusion of every x such that φx', or simply 'z is a fusion of the φs'. The definiens has two conjuncts, giving necessary and jointly sufficient conditions for when z is such a fusion. The first conjunct says that everything satisfying φ must be part of z. This is a stipulation that z must be an *upper bound* of the φs in the parthood ordering. To illustrate with a concrete example, imagine that φx stands for 'x is a cat'; then a fusion of the cats must, at the very least, have each cat as a part. The second conjunct says that z itself must be part of any (other) object that has all the φs as parts. This is a stipulation that a fusion must be *minimal* among the upper bounds of the φs. That's because a fusion of the cats should be a smallest thing made up of the cats; we shouldn't get any extra dogs in the fusion, for example.

In mathematics, these sorts of entity are also known as *least upper bounds* of the φs, or *suprema*. As we will see in detail in section 2.2, suprema satisfy a number of important properties. In particular, the Antisymmetry axiom A.2 guarantees that they are always *unique*. That is, if $F_\varphi z$ and $F_\varphi w$, then by the first conjunct of D.6 we have that z and w are both upper bounds of the φs, hence Pzw and Pwz by the second conjunct, and so $z = w$ by A.2.

(T.3) $\forall z \forall w((F_\varphi z \land F_\varphi w) \to z = w)$ *Fusion Uniqueness*

In this setting it therefore makes sense to speak of *the* fusion of the φs, and similarly *the* least upper bound, where 'least' has the sense of uniqueness.

(D.7) $\sigma x \varphi x := \iota z F_\varphi z$ *Unique Fusion*

---

14 The term is from Leonard and Goodman (1940), though their definition is different (see D.18 in section 2.4). Leśniewski's term, which corresponds to yet another definition (see D.13), was 'sum' (*suma*). This term, too, is widely used today, often interchangeably, sometimes to mark the difference (as in Gruszczyński and Pietruszczak, 2010, though see e.g. Russell, 2016 for the opposite usage). Here we shall always speak of fusions, reserving 'sum' for the special binary case defined below, D.9.

Now that we have a definition of fusions, we need to specify under what conditions fusion occurs. And the answer provided by classical mereology is perfectly simple: under *any* conditions! That is, classical mereology endorses what is known as the doctrine of mereological *universalism* (after van Inwagen, 1987), which says that for any formula φ, so long as there is something satisfying that formula, there is a fusion of all the things that satisfy it.[15] We take this as our fifth axiom.

(A.5) $\exists x \varphi x \rightarrow \exists z F_{\varphi} z$ *Unrestricted Fusion*

(What if nothing satisfies φ? Then the corresponding fusion would have to be part of everything—a null object—by the second conjunct of D.6, and we already know from T.2 that no such thing exists except in trivial cases.)

Technically, A.5 is not a single axiom but an axiom *schema*. The occurrence of 'φ' is a placeholder for any formula we like.[16] The idea is that for *any* first-order formula with x free, there is an individual axiom with that formula substituted in for 'φ' in the universal closure of A.5. To give a feel for how this works, let's examine a few of the more useful instances of the schema.

First, let φ be the formula '$\exists y\, x = y$'. Then A.5 tells us there is some z that is the fusion of everything satisfying this formula; and since the formula simply says that x is something, this means z is the fusion of absolutely everything whatsoever. Note that this universal fusion is bound to exist, since within the logical framework set by A.0 the existential closure of $\exists y\, x = y$ is a theorem, verifying the antecedent of A.5. As the fusion is also unique, we can give it a name, 'u' (for 'universe'), and define it explicitly.

(D.8) $u := \sigma x \exists y\, x = y$ *Universe*

We could have done the same using any other formula φ that is satisfied by absolutely everything, such as any theorem of classical logic (with x free) or the relevant instance of the Reflexivity axiom for parthood, Pxx. Indeed, the universe could already have been defined without going through the machinery of fusions: $u := \imath z \forall y P y z$. What the above example shows is that the universe is actually required to exist by A.5.

For a second example, we let φ be the disjunction '$x = a \vee x = b$', where 'a' and 'b' are singular terms (variables or definite descriptions). Then we can define the *sum* of a and b as follows.

(D.9) $a + b := \sigma x (x = a \vee x = b)$ *Sum*

15 Universalism is also known as "conjunctivism" (Hestevold, 1981; Van Cleve, 1986; Chisholm, 1987), "collectivism" (Hoffman and Rosenkrantz, 1994), or "maximalism" (Simons, 2006).

16 So A.5 is really an infinity of axioms. Strictly speaking, a few well chosen instances would suffice, yielding a finite axiomatization. We'll come back to this possibility in chapter 6.

The sum is really just a binary version of the general form of fusion. It defines the smallest thing composed of a and b. The sum of Munkustrap and Jellylorum, for instance, is just that—the two cats taken together.[17]

A third example uses an instance of A.5 where φ is '$Pxa \wedge Pxb$'. Notice that this formula is only satisfiable in the case where 'Oab' is true. In that case, then, we can define the *product* of a and b:

(D.10) $a \times b := \sigma x(Pxa \wedge Pxb)$ *Product*

This defines the maximal common part of a and b, which exists whenever they have a common part at all. Thus, Munkustrap and Jellylorum have no product, but Munkustrap + Quaxo and Jellylorum + Quaxo have an obvious one: Quaxo.

Our final example takes φ to be the formula 'Dxa'; this instance of A.5 yields the fusion of everything disjoint from any object a other than u.

(D.11) $-a := \sigma x\, Dxa$ *Complement*

In fact, these complements are precisely the relative complements that are guaranteed to exist by A.4 in the special case when the variable x in the antecedent is the universe. That is, we always have $-a = u - a$. We shall come back to this in section 4.1.2; for now we leave the proof as an exercise.

D.8–D.11 are defined via instances of the A.5 schema. There will be infinitely many other instances, since we have infinitely many suitable formulas φ in the language of first-order logic. In each case, A.5 will guarantee the existence of something that is composed exactly of those things that satisfy φ. The axiom schema is, therefore, a fairly straightforward formal implementation of the philosophical doctrine of universalism. There are others, however. We could formulate universalism using a number of other definitions of fusion, or using resources that go beyond first-order logic. We'll come back to the first of these options in section 2.4 and then again, more extensively, in chapter 5; in chapter 6 we shall consider the second option.

And that's all we need for classical mereology. Our five axioms, together with a handful of definitions, complete the picture. To recap: we have our partial order axioms A.1 (Reflexivity), A.2 (Antisymmetry), A.3 (Transitivity); a decomposition axiom A.4 (Remainder); and a composition axiom A.5 (Unrestricted Fusion). The consistency of this axiom system is easily verified: each of A.1–A.5 is satisfied in any trivial, one-element model. What do the other models of classical mereology look like? As it turns out, there

17 It is probably this notion of sum that Leibniz meant to capture with his composition operator $\oplus$ (see chapter 1, section 1.1). His Postulate to the effect that any plurality of things, such as A and B, can be taken together to compose $A \oplus B$ would then be a binary version of our fusion axiom A.5.

is a well-studied class of mathematical structures that our axioms uniquely specify. It is to those structures we now turn.

2.2 ALGEBRAIC MODELS

In a nutshell, the models of classical mereology turn out to be complete Boolean algebras with the zero element removed. This fundamental result is due to Tarski (1935), who put it as follows:[18]

> If a set B of elements (together with the relation of inclusion) constitutes a model of the extended system of Boolean algebra, then, by removing the zero element from B, we obtain a model for mereology; if, conversely, a set C is a model for mereology, then, by adding a new element to C and by postulating that this element is in the relation of inclusion to every element of C, we obtain a model for the extended system of Boolean algebra. (Tarski, 1935, p. 333, fn. 4)

In this section we provide an explanation of what this amounts to along with a detailed proof of the result insofar as it applies to our axiomatization. We proceed by first defining complete Boolean algebras. Then we prove Tarski's result in the two steps outlined in the passage just cited: we show that complete Boolean algebras without a zero element satisfy the axioms of classical mereology, and then we show that models of classical mereology, when adjoined to a zero element, satisfy the definition of a Boolean algebra.[19]

2.2.1 *Boolean Algebras*

Boolean algebras (after Boole, 1847) are familiar structures to many philosophers; we encounter them when learning about classical propositional logic. The truth values 1 and 0 (true and false), together with the operations of disjunction $\vee$, conjunction $\wedge$, and negation $\neg$, form a Boolean algebra. Likewise, the class of all propositions (treating logically equivalent sentences as expressing the same proposition), including the logically true proposition $\top$ and the logical falsehood $\bot$, is a Boolean algebra under the same operations.

More generally, a Boolean algebra is defined as a structure $\langle B, \sqcup, \sqcap, -, 0, 1\rangle$ where B is any non-empty set, $\sqcup$ is a binary operation called *join*, $\sqcap$ is

18 The passage follows immediately the text cited in section 2.1.2. It should be noted that while Tarski was referring explicitly to Leśniewski's Mereology, his result was meant to apply to that theory insofar as it can be understood against the background of classical logic (as is our version of classical mereology), not on the grounds of Leśniewski's Ontology and Protothetic. Understood strictly in Leśniewskian terms, the link between Mereology and Boolean algebras is not as straightforward. See Clay (1974a) (*pace* Grzegorczyk, 1955, §4).

19 For other presentations of Tarski's result (based on different axiomatizations of classical mereology), see Pietruszczak (2000b, chs. 3 and 6), Ridder (2002, ch. 3), Pontow and Schubert (2006, §§4–5), and Hovda (2009, §4). For a detailed historical reconstruction, see Loeb (2014).

another binary operation called *meet*, $-$ is a unary operation called *complement*, and 0 and 1 are two distinguished elements in B called *bottom* and *top*, respectively, and where the following six conditions are satisfied by all elements a, b, c in B.[20]

(2.1) $a \sqcup (b \sqcup c) = (a \sqcup b) \sqcup c$ *Associativity*
$a \sqcap (b \sqcap c) = (a \sqcap b) \sqcap c$

(2.2) $a \sqcup b = b \sqcup a$ *Commutativity*
$a \sqcap b = b \sqcap a$

(2.3) $a \sqcup (b \sqcap c) = (a \sqcup b) \sqcap (a \sqcup c)$ *Distributivity*
$a \sqcap (b \sqcup c) = (a \sqcap b) \sqcup (a \sqcap c)$

(2.4) $a \sqcup a = a$ *Idempotence*
$a \sqcap a = a$

(2.5) $a \sqcup (a \sqcap b) = a$ *Absorption*
$a \sqcap (a \sqcup b) = a$

(2.6) $a \sqcup -a = 1$ *Complementation*
$a \sqcap -a = 0$

The key idea behind each of these conditions is that it forces the algebraic operations $\sqcup$, $\sqcap$, and $-$ to interact with each other and with 1 and 0 in the way suggested by their logical interpretation. It is good exercise to go through 2.1–2.6 to verify that these conditions are in fact satisfied by the logical operators of classical logic, $\vee$, $\wedge$, and $\neg$. Generally speaking, however, there is no constraint on the sort of entities that make up the base set B.

A simple example of a Boolean algebra is given by the subsets of a given set, say, $A = \{a, b, c\}$. A set X is called a *subset* of Y, written '$X \subseteq Y$', whenever every member of X is a member of Y, and the set of all subsets of Y is called the *powerset* of Y, written '$\mathcal{P}(Y)$'. Note that $\subseteq$ is a transitive relation although set membership, $\in$, is not. Taking $B = \mathcal{P}(A)$ and treating $\sqcup$ as $\cup$ (set union), $\sqcap$ as $\cap$ (set intersection), $-$ as $\overline{\cdot}$ (set complement), 0 as $\emptyset$ (the empty set, also written '$\{\}$'), and 1 as A itself, we obtain a Boolean algebra. This algebra is shown in figure 2.3, where an arrow connecting two sets indicates that the first set is a subset of the second. Note, for example, that we have $\{a\} \cup (\{a\} \cap \{a, b\}) = \{a\} \cup \{a\} = \{a\}$, as required by Absorption, or that $\{a\} \cap \overline{\{a\}} = \{a\} \cap \{b, c\} = \emptyset$, as required by Complementation.

The notational similarity between $\vee$, $\cup$, $\sqcup$, and between $\wedge$, $\cap$, $\sqcap$, is of course not a coincidence. Indeed, just as in set theory we can characterize

20 This list of conditions is overkill, but having the redundant ones around will prove useful. For a general overview of Boolean algebras, see Givant and Halmos (2009). For a history of their axiomatization (in terms of conditions on $\sqcup$, $\sqcap$, $-$, 1, and 0), see Padmanabhan and Rudeanu (2008, ch. 4).

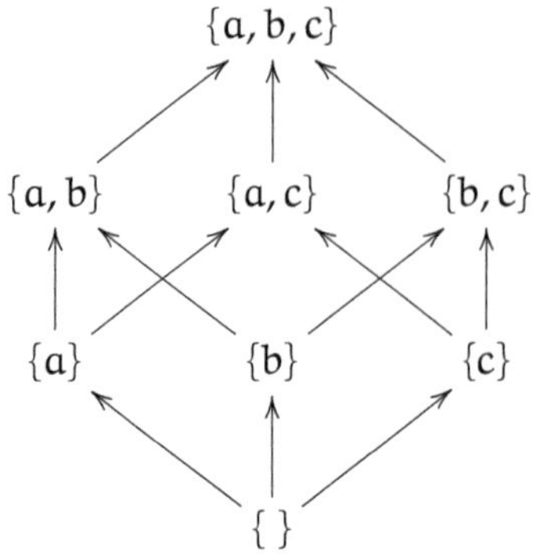

Figure 2.3: A Boolean algebra

the subset relation in terms of the operations of set union and intersection, noting e.g. that $X \subseteq Y$ if and only if $X \cup Y = Y$, so in a Boolean algebra we can define a corresponding relation $\sqsubseteq$ on B:

(2.7) $a \sqsubseteq b :\equiv a \sqcup b = b$ *Order*

(Equivalently, $a \sqsubseteq b :\equiv a \sqcap b = a$.) It is easy to see that this relation, like $\subseteq$, is a partial order:

- $\sqsubseteq$ is reflexive; since we always have that $a \sqcup a = a$ (by 2.4), hence $a \sqsubseteq a$.
- $\sqsubseteq$ is antisymmetric; for if $a \sqsubseteq b$ and $b \sqsubseteq a$, then $a \sqcup b = b$ and $b \sqcup a = a$ (by definition), and since $a \sqcup b = b \sqcup a$ (by 2.2), it follows that $a = b$.
- $\sqsubseteq$ is transitive; for if $a \sqsubseteq b$ and $b \sqsubseteq c$, then $a \sqcup b = b$ and $b \sqcup c = c$ (by definition), hence $(a \sqcup b) \sqcup c = c$ (by substitution), hence $a \sqcup (b \sqcup c) = c$ (by 2.1), which implies that $a \sqcup c = c$ (again by substitution), i.e. $a \sqsubseteq c$.

Now, it follows from 2.7 that the join and the meet of any pair of elements in B are just their least upper bound and their greatest lower bound (respectively) relative to the ordering determined by $\sqsubseteq$: $a \sqcup b$ is always an upper bound of $\{a, b\}$ because $a \sqsubseteq a \sqcup b$ and $b \sqsubseteq a \sqcup b$ (by 2.1 and 2.4), and it is the least because $a \sqcup b \sqsubseteq c$ for all upper bounds c of $\{a, b\}$ (by 2.1); similarly, $a \sqcap b$ is always a lower bound of $\{a, b\}$ because $a \sqcap b \sqsubseteq a$ and $a \sqcap b \sqsubseteq b$, and it is the greatest because $c \sqsubseteq a \sqcap b$ for all lower bounds c. Generalizing, given the ordering set by $\sqsubseteq$ we can speak of the least upper bound, $\bigsqcup X$, and of the greatest lower bound, $\bigsqcap X$, for any subset X of B. These need not always exist. When they do, i.e. when B contains both $\bigsqcup X$ and $\bigsqcap X$ for *every* subset X of B, we have a *complete* Boolean algebra. The powerset algebra of figure 2.3, where $\sqsubseteq$ is just $\subseteq$, is a case in point.

2.2.2 *Complete Boolean Algebras Are Models*

We are now in a position to prove Tarski's fundamental result: the models of classical mereology are essentially those structures that can be obtained from a complete Boolean algebra by removing the bottom element 0. Every model of mereology consists of a certain non-empty domain, D, along with a binary relation on that domain, $\leqslant$, interpreting the parthood predicate P.[21] Thus, to prove Tarski's result we have to show two things: (1) that removing the zero element from a complete Boolean algebra yields a model of the form $\langle D, \leqslant \rangle$ that satisfies the axioms of classical mereology, A.1–A.5; and (2) that all models of classical mereology, when supplemented with a zero element, determine a structure of the form $\langle B, \sqcup, \sqcap, -, 0, 1 \rangle$ that satisfies the conditions on Boolean algebras, 2.1–2.6.[22] We begin with (1).

Let $\langle B, \sqcup, \sqcap, -, 0, 1 \rangle$ be a complete Boolean algebra, with B partially ordered by $\sqsubseteq$. To 'remove' the bottom element, let $B^- = B \setminus \{0\}$. Now let $\sqsubseteq^-$ be the restriction of $\sqsubseteq$ to B^-:

(2.8) $a \sqsubseteq^- b :\equiv a \sqsubseteq b$ and $a \neq 0$ *Order–*

We want to show that $\langle B^-, \sqsubseteq^- \rangle$ is a model of classical mereology, i.e. that $\sqsubseteq^-$ can serve as an interpretation of the parthood predicate P relative to the domain B^-.[23] We do so by showing that the relation $\sqsubseteq^-$ satisfies each of the five axioms A.1–A.5.

- *Re* A.1, A.2, A.3 (Reflexivity, Antisymmetry, Transitivity): These axioms are satisfied by virtue of the fact that $\sqsubseteq$ is a partial order, which means that $\sqsubseteq^-$ is also a partial order.
- *Re* A.4 (Remainder): We begin by noting that with parthood interpreted as $\sqsubseteq^-$, disjointness in B^- amounts to having a meet in B that equals 0. For to say that a and b are disjoint in B^- is to say that there is no c in B^- such that $c \sqsubseteq^- a$ and $c \sqsubseteq^- b$, and since any a and b in B always have a greatest lower bound relative to $\sqsubseteq$, namely $a \sqcap b$, the condition in question obtains only when $a \sqcap b = 0$. Now assume for some arbitrary a and b in B^- that $a \not\sqsubseteq^- b$. We need to show that there is some z in B^- such that, for all w in B^-, $w \sqsubseteq^- z$ if and only if $w \sqsubseteq^- a$ and $w \sqcap b = 0$.

21 On these basic semantic notions (model, satisfaction of a formula, etc.) see section 1.5.

22 What about the requirement that the algebra be complete? As we shall see, this further requirement is only partly satisfied, owing to the specific format of our Unrestricted Fusion axiom A.5.

23 Note that $B^- \neq \varnothing$, since we have defined Boolean algebras by requiring 0 and 1 to be *two* distinguished elements of the base set B. Some authors allow for degenerate Boolean algebras with just one element (in which case $0 = 1$). As already pointed out, such structures are models of classical mereology as they stand; for recall that the No Zero theorem T.2 is in conditional form, ruling out the existence of a null object only in the presence of at least two objects.

We let $z = a \sqcap -b$. Note that z is in B^-, since $a \sqcap -b = 0$ only if $a \sqsubseteq b$,[24] which is not the case (since $a \not\sqsubseteq^- b$). To see that z satisfies the left-to-right direction of the biconditional, assume that $w \sqsubseteq^- z$. That just means that $w \sqsubseteq a \sqcap -b$; and since $(a \sqcap -b) \sqcup a = a \sqcup (a \sqcap -b) = a$ (by 2.2 and 2.5), i.e. $a \sqcap -b \sqsubseteq a$, we immediately have that $w \sqsubseteq a$ (by transitivity), and hence $w \sqsubseteq^- a$. By parallel reasoning, we also have that $w \sqsubseteq -b$, i.e. $w \sqcap -b = w$. To show that $w \sqcap b = 0$, suppose not. Then $w \sqcap b \neq 0$, and hence $(w \sqcap -b) \sqcap b \neq 0$ (by substitution). So $w \sqcap (b \sqcap -b) \neq 0$ (by 2.1). Hence, $w \sqcap 0 \neq 0$ (by 2.6). But that is impossible, as $w \neq 0$ by supposition. So we also have that $w \sqcap b = 0$, as desired. For the right-to-left direction, assume for arbitrary w in B^- that $w \sqsubseteq^- a$ and $w \sqcap b = 0$. As above, notice that $w \sqcap b = 0$ entails that $w \sqsubseteq -b$. And since $w \sqsubseteq a$ and $w \sqsubseteq -b$, we have that $w \sqsubseteq a \sqcap -b$, and hence $w \sqsubseteq^- a$.

- *Re* A.5 (Unrestricted Fusion): The fusion of some things is just the least upper bound of those things relative to parthood. Thus, with P interpreted as $\sqsubseteq^-$, the fusion of a subset X of B^- will be the least upper bound relative to $\sqsubseteq^-$. In a complete Boolean algebra, *every* subset X in B has a least upper bound in B relative to the order $\sqsubseteq$, namely $\bigsqcup X$. Since B^- is a subset of B, every *non-empty* subset of B^- has a $\sqsubseteq$-least upper bound in B. *A fortiori*, every non-empty *first-order definable* subset of B^- has a $\sqsubseteq$-least upper bound in B. That is, every subset X of B which is the interpretation of some satisfiable first-order formula φ with a free variable is such that $\bigsqcup X$ is in B. Is $\bigsqcup X$ also in B^-? Well, $\bigsqcup X = 0$ if and only if $X = \varnothing$ or $X = \{0\}$. The second case can be dismissed, since we are only interested in subsets of B^-. As to the first case, any formula φ whose interpretation is $\varnothing$ is unsatisfiable and hence it is not required to exist in B^- by A.5 (in fact, it is ruled out). Hence, complete Boolean algebras satisfy A.5.[25]

Our structure $\langle B^-, \sqsubseteq^- \rangle$ is a complete Boolean algebra without 0, and we have just seen that structures of this kind are models of classical mereology. It should be noted that while classical mereology posits the existence of a fusion for every (specifiable) non-empty set of things, i.e. a least upper bound of those things with respect to parthood, it does not also posit the existence of a corresponding nucleus, or product, i.e. a greatest lower bound. Mereologically, a set of things has a lower bound only when all members of the set share a common part. Thus, while in a complete Boolean algebra

24 Suppose $a \sqcap -b = 0$. So $b \sqcup (a \sqcap -b) = b \sqcup 0$. But $b \sqcup (a \sqcap -b) = (b \sqcup a) \sqcap (b \sqcup -b) = (b \sqcup a) \sqcap 1 = (b \sqcup a) \sqcap ((b \sqcup a) \sqcup -(b \sqcup a)) = b \sqcup a = a \sqcup b$ (by 2.1, 2.6, 2.6, 2.5, 2.2). Moreover $b \sqcup 0 = b \sqcup (b \sqcap -b) = b$ (by 2.6 and 2.5). Thus $a \sqcup b = b$, hence $a \sqsubseteq b$ (by 2.7).

25 Because A.5 is a first-order axiom schema, we are only requiring the first-order definable subsets to have fusions. This puts some limits to the strict claim that models of classical mereology are *complete* Boolean algebras without 0. This issue will be relevant below (section 2.2.3), and will be taken up in full detail in chapter 6 (section 6.1).

$\bigsqcap X$ is guaranteed to exist for all $X \subseteq B$, this is not so in models of classical mereology. Why? The answer has to do with the removal of 0 from B. Since 0 is the least element of B on the $\sqsubseteq$ ordering, we have it that $0 \sqsubseteq b$ for all b in B. This means that in a complete Boolean algebra everything overlaps everything else; for any set X whatsoever, all members of X will perforce share at least one common part, namely 0. Not so if we model parthood with $\sqsubseteq^{-}$. Structures like $\langle B^{-}, \sqsubseteq^{-}\rangle$ are sometimes called *complete join semilattices* to reflect the fact that $\bigsqcup X$, but not $\bigsqcap X$, always exists.[26] Similarly, models of classical mereology are not strictly closed under complementation; the complement to 1 (i.e. to the universe u) would have to be 0, which does not belong to the domain.

2.2.3 *Models Are Complete Boolean Algebras*

Stage (2) in the proof of Tarski's result is to show that all models of classical mereology are complete Boolean algebras without a zero element. We begin by proving that the models, when supplemented with a zero element, do in fact determine a Boolean algebra. Then we shall turn to the further requirement of completeness, which requires some qualification.

Recall that models of classical mereology have the form $\langle D, \leqslant\rangle$, where D is a non-empty domain and $\leqslant$ an interpretation for the parthood predicate P (satisfying A.1–A.5). To supplement these models with a zero element, we use a process called 'lifting' (Davey and Priestly, 2002, pp. 15f). Fix some element $0 \notin D$. Let $D^{+} = D \cup \{0\}$ and define a new order relation on D^{+}:

(2.9) $x \leqslant^{+} y :\equiv x \leqslant y \text{ or } x = 0$ *Order+*

Each of these 'lifted' models $\langle D^{+}, \leqslant^{+}\rangle$ can be associated with a corresponding Boolean structure $\langle D^{+}, \sqcup, \sqcap, -, 0, 1\rangle$ defined as follows:[27]

- For all a, b in D^{+}: $a \sqcup b$ is the mereological sum $a + b$ (see D.9) if a and b are in D; otherwise $a \sqcup b = a$ if $b = 0$ and $a \sqcup b = b$ if $a = 0$.
- For all a, b in D^{+}: $a \sqcap b$ is the mereological product $a \times b$ (see D.10) if a and b overlap in D; otherwise $a \sqcap b = 0$.
- For all a in D^{+}: $-a$ is the mereological complement of a (see D.11) for $a \neq 1$ in D; otherwise $-0 = 1$ and $-1 = 0$.

26 Lattice theory is an outgrowth of the study of Boolean algebras; it comes from Birkhoff (1940).

27 For ease of exposition, aside from P we play fast and loose regarding the distinction between our syntactic vocabulary and its interpretation in a model, using the same notation and terminology in both cases. Thus, we write e.g. '$\sigma x \varphi x$' for the value of this very expression, the fusion of the φs in the model (effectively: the $\leqslant$-least upper bound of the elements of D that satisfy φ); similarly, we write '$a + b$', '$a \times b$', etc. for the sum, the product, etc. of any given objects a and b in D (effectively: their $\leqslant$-least upper bound, their $\leqslant$-greatest lower bound, etc.).

- 0 is just the object added during 'lifting', the $\leqslant^+$-minimal element of D^+.
- 1 is the 'universe' u (see D.8), which is the $\leqslant^+$-maximal element of D^+.

We want to show that these structures are Boolean algebras, i.e. satisfy the conditions in 2.1–2.6. (For each condition, we only prove the first half; the proofs of the second half are perfectly dual and are left for the reader.)

- *Re* 2.1 (Associativity): Where a, b, c are all in D, we need to show that $a + (b + c) = (a + b) + c$. The definition of sum gives us $a + (b + c) = \sigma x(x = a \vee x = \sigma y(y = b \vee y = c)) = \sigma x(x = a \vee (x = b \vee x = c))$.[28] Similarly, $(a+b)+c = \sigma x(x = \sigma y(y = a \vee y = b) \vee x = c) = \sigma x((x = a \vee x = b) \vee x = c)$. So the desired equality follows from the associativity property of the disjunction connective. If any or all of a, b, c are 0, then they just drop out of the calculation (e.g. $0 \sqcup (b \sqcup c) = b \sqcup c = (0 \sqcup b) \sqcup c$).
- *Re* 2.2 (Commutativity): Where both a and b are in D, we need to show that $a + b = b + a$. This follows immediately from the commutativity of the disjunction connective: $a + b = \sigma x(x = a \vee x = b) = \sigma x(x = b \vee x = a) = b + a$. If $a = 0$, then $a \sqcup 0 = a = 0 \sqcup a$, and similarly for b.
- *Re* 2.3 (Distributivity): We need to show that $a \sqcup (b \sqcap c) = (a \sqcup b) \sqcap (a \sqcup c)$. If $a = 0$ then $0 \sqcup (b \sqcap c) = b \sqcap c = (0 \sqcup b) \sqcap (0 \sqcup c)$. Similarly, if either b or c is 0, or b and c do not overlap, then $b \sqcap c = 0$. So $a \sqcup (b \sqcap c) = a \sqcap 0 = a$. But because b and c have no common non-zero parts, $a \sqcup b$ and $a \sqcup c$ can only have a (and its parts) in common. Thus, $(a \sqcup b) \sqcap (a \sqcup c) = a$ as well. In the cases where b and c overlap, for a in D we have it that $a \leqslant a + b$ and $a \leqslant a + c$, and also $b \times c \leqslant b \leqslant a + b$ and $b \times c \leqslant c \leqslant a + c$. As a result, we have it that $a + (b \times c) \leqslant (a + b) \times (a + c)$. Now if we can prove the converse, namely $(a + b) \times (a + c) \leqslant a + (b \times c)$, we can infer the identity by A.2 (Antisymmetry). To prove this converse claim, we note that in classical mereology Pxy is provably equivalent to $\forall w(Owx \to Owy)$.[29] Hence we assume that some arbitrary w in D overlaps $(a + b) \times (a + c)$ and show that w must also overlap $a + (b \times c)$. So pick some $d \neq 0$ such that $d \leqslant w$ and $d \leqslant (a + b) \times (a + c)$. Then $d \leqslant (a + b)$ and $d \leqslant (a + c)$. We have two cases: either (i) d overlaps a, or (ii) d is disjoint from a. In case (i) there must be some $e \neq 0$ such that $e \leqslant d$ (hence $e \leqslant w$) and $e \leqslant a$ (hence $e \leqslant a + (b \times c)$). So w overlaps $a + (b \times c)$. In case (ii), because $d \leqslant (a + b)$ with d disjoint from a, $d \leqslant b$; similarly, $d \leqslant c$. So $d \leqslant b \times c$ and hence $d \leqslant a + (b \times c)$. Since $d \leqslant w$, w overlaps $a + (b \times c)$.

---

28 The second equality requires careful unpacking of D.9. We leave the details as an exercise.

29 If Pxy, then for any w such that Owx there will be some v such that Pvw and Pvx. By A.3, Pvy, and therefore Owy. Conversely, suppose $\neg Pxy$. By A.4, there must be some z such that, for all w, Pwz if and only if Pwx and Dwy. Since Pzz (by A.1), this means that Pzx and Dzy, i.e. $\neg Ozy$. But clearly Ozx (again by A.1).

- *Re* 2.4 (Idempotence): For a in D, we need to show that $a + a = a$. This follows from the idempotence of the disjunction connective: $a + a = \sigma x(x = a \vee x = a) = \sigma x(x = a) = a$. Where $a = 0$, we just have $0 \sqcup 0 = 0$.
- *Re* 2.5 (Absorption): For a, b in D, we need to show that $a + (a \times b) = a$. This follows from the distributivity of $\times$ over $+$ proved above (*re* 2.3) together with the fact that the product of a thing with the universe coincides with the thing itself. Thus, $a + (a \times b) = (a \times 1) + (a \times b) = a \times (1 + b) = a \times 1 = a$. For $a = 0$, we have that $0 + (0 \times b) = 0 + 0 = 0$. For $b = 0$, $a + (a \times 0) = a + 0 = a$.
- *Re* 2.6 (Complementation): We need to show that $a \sqcup -a = 1$. If $a = 1$, then $-a = 0$ and $1 \sqcup 0 = 1$. Similarly for $a = 0$. Where $a \neq 1$ in D, note that since everything is part of the universe, we have it that $a + -a \leqslant 1$. If we can show that $1 \leqslant a + -a$, by A.2 we can infer the identity. Let y be an arbitrary member of the domain; note that y overlaps 1. Either y overlaps a or y is disjoint from a. In the latter case, $y \leqslant -a$ (by D.11), and hence y overlaps $-a$. In either case, y overlaps $a + -a$. So $1 \leqslant a + -a$.[30]

So, the structures $\langle D^+, \sqcup, \sqcap, -, 0, 1\rangle$ determined by our lifted models satisfy 2.1–2.6 and, hence, are Boolean algebras by definition. Are they *complete* Boolean algebras?

It follows from our axiom schema A.5 that any non-empty *first-order definable* subset of the domain—i.e. any subset whose members are all and only those things that satisfy a satisfiable formula φ in the language—has a $\leqslant^+$-least upper bound in D. Moreover, the empty set has a $\leqslant^+$-least upper bound in D^+, namely 0. Thus, when D^+ is finite, the algebra is indeed complete, for in that case every subset is first-order definable.

However, when D^+ is infinite, this is not necessarily the case. The reason is that the vocabulary of our language (including all variables) is denumerable, hence the set of distinct formulas of the language is also denumerable, and thus at most denumerably many sets in a given domain can be specified by means of a formula φ with a free variable. When the domain is infinite, though, the number of all subsets may be greater than that. Indeed, it is a consequence of Cantor's (1891) theorem that even the set of all subsets of a countably infinite set is *not* denumerable. It follows, therefore, that some of those subsets—in fact, an uncountable infinity—will run afoul of the expressive resources of our language, and hence that our axiom schema A.5 is not strong enough to guarantee that our lifted models are always complete. Moving to a stronger logic, such as second-order or plural logic, would avoid this problem, and indeed it should be noted that Tarski himself stated his result in relation to an axiomatization of classical mereology that

30 Again, this uses the equivalence between Pxy and $\forall w(Owx \rightarrow Owy)$ proved in note 29.

involved explicit quantification over sets. We shall come back to this issue in chapter 6. For now we simply register the limits of A.5 in a purely first-order axiomatization. Alongside complete Boolean algebras, classical mereology will have other, non-standard models.[31]

2.3 SET-THEORETIC MODELS

Boolean algebras are familiar structures, but they are rather abstract in nature. To get a better sense of the models of classical mereology, in this section we consider some set-theoretic ways of interpreting the parthood predicate. Since we have just shown that *all* models of classical mereology are Boolean algebras, these set-theoretic interpretations will be no more than a special case. However, they are particularly intuitive and easy to grasp, and it will be instructive to check independently that they satisfy the mereological axioms A.1–A.5. Moreover, there is an important result, due to Stone (1936), which relates all Boolean algebras to set-theoretic structures of this sort, so it will pay to look at them closely. We begin with the simple case of models with a finite domain; then we consider models with infinite domains, where things become slightly less straightforward.

2.3.1 *Finite Models*

Consider any finite, non-empty set A. This set will have a certain number of subsets—in fact a total of 2^n, where n is the number of elements of A—and we may think of the relation of set inclusion, $\subseteq$, as representing the relation of parthood among those subsets. That is, whenever every element of a subset X is also an element of subset Y, we may think of X as a part of Y. We do not, of course, want to consider the empty subset $\varnothing$; for that would be part of every other subset, hence it would count as a null individual, which classical mereology rules out. But all the other subsets of A may be taken as entities that are related by parthood in the relevant sense. This conforms to common usage. We say, for instance, that the set of all cats is part of the set of all felines, or that the set of knives is part of the set of silverware. (Indeed, as Lewis, 1991, p. 5 reminds us, in German the word for 'subset' is 'Teilmenge', literally 'part-set'; see Cantor, 1878.) Whether this means that the subset relation really *is* a case of parthood, as e.g. Armstrong (1978, p. 37) says, or whether this use of the word 'part' is merely metaphorical (Oliver, 1994), need not concern us here. It's just that when it comes to sets, the subset relation $\subseteq$ provides a natural interpretation of the parthood predicate P.

31 For rigorous proofs, see Pietruszczak (2000b, § III.2 and 2015). Of course, a philosopher who is only ready to accept *specifiable entities* might think this is not a limit at all; cf. Eberle (1970, §2.7).

The basic idea, then, is simply to consider set-theoretic models of the form $\langle D, \subseteq \rangle$, where $D = \mathcal{P}(A) \setminus \{\varnothing\}$ for some finite non-empty set A. A formula 'Pxy' will be satisfied in such a model if and only if $x \subseteq y$ (i.e., more precisely, if and only if the assignment of x is a subset of the assignment of y).[32] From here, our defined mereological predicates will directly correspond to a number of standard set-theoretic relations.

- '$PPxy$' is satisfied whenever $x \subset y$ (x is a proper subset of y).
- 'Oxy' is satisfied whenever $x \cap y \neq \varnothing$ (the intersection of x and y is non-empty).
- 'Uxy' is satisfied whenever $x \cup y \neq \varnothing$ (the union of x and y is non-empty).
- 'Dxy' is satisfied whenever $x \cap y = \varnothing$ (the intersection of x and y is empty).
- '$F_\varphi z$' is satisfied whenever $z = \bigcup\{x \in D : \varphi x\}$ (the union of the set of those sets x in D that satisfy φx).

One way to convince ourselves of these interpretations is to use Euler or Venn diagrams to represent the subset relation itself in terms of spatial inclusion, as we did earlier in figures 2.1 and 2.2.[33] This is helpful at least with regard to the first four relations. Regarding the fusion predicate, we can reason as follows. In set theory, the union $\bigcup X$ of a set X is the set whose members are the members of some member of X. Thus, when X is a set of sets, each member of X will be a subset of $\bigcup X$. Now, the definition of 'fusion' in D.6 has two main conjuncts. The first says that everything satisfying the relevant formula φ is part of the fusion of the φs. In the present context, this means that every non-empty subset of A satisfying φ—i.e. every $x \in D$ such that φx—must be a subset of $\bigcup\{x \in D : \varphi x\}$, which is true for the set-theoretic reason just explained. The second conjunct of D.6 says that the fusion of the φs is part of every (other) thing whose parts include all the φs. So, consider any $y \in D$ such that every $x \in D$ satisfying φ is a subset of y. Let w be an arbitrary element of $\bigcup\{x \in D : \varphi x\}$. By definition, w must be a member of some $x \in D$ such that φx; and because $x \subseteq y$, it follows that w itself is a member of y. Thus, by generalization, $\bigcup\{x \in D : \varphi x\} \subseteq y$, which is precisely what the second conjunct of D.6 amounts to in the present context.

Do these models actually satisfy the axioms of classical mereology? Yes. We have already mentioned that finite powerset structures are Boolean algebras, and they are complete, so the answer follows from Tarski's general result. But we can also verify the answer directly by going through each of the five axioms A.1–A.5.

32 For ease of notation, in the following we shall again play fast and loose regarding use/mention, often writing 'x' when we really mean the value of x under an assignment.

33 The usefulness of Euler diagrams in this connection was already stressed by Frege (1895).

- *Re* A.1–A.3: These order axioms are all satisfied owing to the fact that $\subseteq$ itself is a partial order on $\mathcal{P}(A)$, with or without $\varnothing$.
- *Re* A.4: Assume that x is not a subset of y, i.e. $x \not\subseteq y$. Let $z = x \setminus y$ be the set of all members of x that are not members of y. Then $z \subseteq A$ and $z \cap y = \varnothing$. And since $x \neq y$, z is non-empty, hence in the domain D.
- *Re* A.5: For this axiom schema, we need to check that every satisfiable predicate φ has a fusion in D. In the model, the satisfiable predicates stand for the *definable* non-empty subsets of D. But for finite models, *every* subset of the domain is definable. So, we just need to show that every non-empty $X \subseteq D$ has a fusion in D. As we have seen, in models of this sort the fusion in question is just $\bigcup X$. And since every member of X is a subset of A, it follows from the definition of $\bigcup$ that $\bigcup X$ is a subset of A, too. Moreover, $\bigcup X$ must be non-empty if X is non-empty. Thus, $\bigcup X$ is in D.

So we have an independent proof that these simple finite structures are models of classical mereology. Now, one good thing about this fact is that it allows us to understand the parthood relation in terms of the familiar subset relation. But there is more to it. For there is an important sense in which these models are *all* the finite models we need to consider. Here is why:

> FINITE REPRESENTATION Every finite complete Boolean algebra is isomorphic to a finite powerset Boolean algebra.

Finite representation is a standard textbook fact about finite Boolean algebras.[34] And since we know that all models of classical mereology are complete Boolean algebras, what this means is that the set-theoretic models given above are representative of the whole class. Any other finite model of classical mereology has the same structure as one of them.

There is another important fact about these set-theoretic models: they are always built up from an initial set of *atoms*, elements that have no proper subsets in the domain. For example, if we start with $A = \{a, b, c\}$, the corresponding powerset model is shown in figure 2.4, where it is clear that the domain 'bottoms out' in the singletons of a, b, and c. (The only proper subset of these singletons would be $\varnothing$, which is not in the model.) More generally, we can see that all these structures satisfy a further axiom besides A.1–A.5. They satisfy an axiom that says that everything has 'atomic' parts.

(A.6) $\forall x \exists y (Pyx \wedge \neg \exists z PPzy)$ *Atomism*

This is not surprising. In a finite model, the process of mereological decomposition cannot go on forever. So every finite model is, as we may say,

34 For proofs, see e.g. Davey and Priestly (2002, ch. 5) and Givant and Halmos (2009, ch. 15).

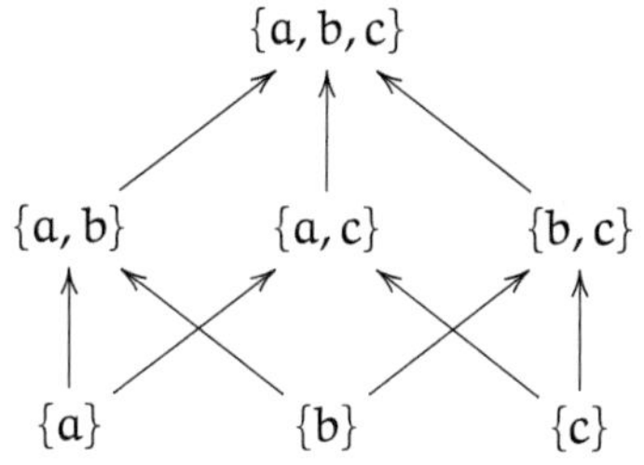

Figure 2.4: Three-atom powerset Boolean algebra without ∅

atomistic. On the other hand, not every model of mereology is finite; and while it is possible for an infinite model to satisfy A.6, there are also infinite models that are not atomistic. It is for this reason that we said classical mereology is actually neutral with regard to the question of atomism. So let us turn to infinite models and see why.

2.3.2 *Infinite Models*

What do infinite set-theoretic models of mereology look like? In section 2.3.1, we started with a finite set A and looked at the model $\langle \mathcal{P}(A) \setminus \{\varnothing\}, \subseteq \rangle$. What happens if we begin instead with an infinite set A, and look at the resulting powerset?

The answer is that as soon as we remove the empty set ∅, we get again a model of classical mereology; after all, our proof that the finite models satisfy A.1–A.5 did not rely on the assumption that A was finite. And as before, these models are *atomistic*. In fact, these infinite models together with their finite companions are *all* the atomistic models of classical mereology (up to isomorphism). This is again a basic fact about Boolean algebras, extending the finite representation theorem mentioned above.[35]

ATOMISTIC REPRESENTATION Every complete atomic Boolean algebra is isomorphic to a powerset Boolean algebra.

So, again, powersets provide an important intuitive way of thinking about the structures we are concerned with.

Yet not all of the models of classical mereology are atomistic. It is perfectly compatible with A.1–A.5 that A.6 might fail. We might have a structure in which some, but not all, objects are built of atoms; or we might have a structure in which everything has proper parts. Such models are perhaps a little harder to imagine, and in chapter 4 we shall see that there is a rich

35 For a proof, see e.g. Givant and Halmos (2009, ch. 14).

philosophical debate as to whether they represent genuine possibilities at all. But there is no question that such models exist. And among them, there are some that can again be defined in set-theoretic terms.

To see this, we need to look at a certain sort of substructures of powersets. A *field of sets* over a set A is a subset X of $\mathcal{P}(A)$ that is closed under set unions, intersections, and complements; that is, if x and y are in X, then so are $x \cup y$, $x \cap y$, and $-y$. (If we think of $\mathcal{P}(A)$ as a Boolean algebra, these structures are also called *subalgebras*.) We can now appeal to another important representation theorem, due to Stone (1936).

STONE REPRESENTATION Every Boolean algebra is isomorphic to a field of sets.

Given Tarski's result, this immediately implies that every model of classical mereology—including non-atomic ones—is isomorphic to a field of sets of some sort of other.

Can we be more precise about the sort of field that does the job? One might hope that we can simply look at *complete* fields of sets, i.e. those subalgebras of $\mathcal{P}(A)$ such that, for every subset $X \subseteq \mathcal{P}(A)$, both $\bigcup X$ and $\bigcap X$ exist. Unfortunately, this will not work: every field of sets which is closed under the operators of arbitrary unions $\bigcup$ and arbitrary intersections $\bigcap$ is again atomic.[36] This is not by itself incompatible with the claim that mereology admits of non-atomistic models. But it means that to obtain such models we need to look to different operations to get the set-theoretic analogues of mereological fusions; identifying fusions with ordinary set unions won't do.

As it turns out, specifying those set-theoretic operations is not easy. It requires a detour through a generalization of Stone's representation theorem known as *Stone Duality*, which concerns certain basic dualities between Boolean algebras and topological spaces. Such a detour would take us deep into topological territory, something which is beyond the scope of this book, so we shall omit the details. For the interested reader, however, here's the bottom line in brief: every complete Boolean algebra turns out to be isomorphic to the Boolean algebra of regular open sets of its induced Boolean topological space, with the closure of $\bigcup X$ representing the supremum of X.[37]

2.4 OTHER AXIOM SYSTEMS

So much for our presentation of classical mereology. We have given a set of axioms, A.1–A.5, and have shown that all complete Boolean algebras without a bottom element satisfy them, i.e. the axioms are *sound* with respect to

36 For a proof, see Pontow and Schubert (2006, p. 131).

37 For a thorough explanation of this general result, see again Pontow and Schubert (2006, §5).

those algebraic structures. We have also shown that all structures satisfying the axioms are complete Boolean algebras without a bottom element, i.e. the axioms are *complete* with respect to these structures (modulo certain limitations regarding non-standard models, to which we'll return in chapter 6). Finally, we have given a purely set-theoretic characterization of these algebras, showing that the finite structures correspond straightforwardly to powerset models and noting that infinite structures, too, admit a set-theoretic representation. All in all, this gives a full picture of classical mereology.

We conclude this chapter by returning to our starting point and reviewing briefly a number of alternative ways in which the theory can be characterized axiomatically. The axiom system we introduced in section 2.1 is new (and unfamiliar), so presenting a few more will offer a better picture and facilitate comparisons with the systems most frequently found in the literature. In particular, we shall consider systems that differ in their choice of a primitive mereological concept. Since in classical mereology all such concepts are interdefinable, formally a different choice does not call for different axioms. However, philosophically one may see the choice as reflecting a different starting point, and the corresponding axiomatization as an attempt to elucidate a particular intuitive notion, so in each case the outcome may well be an axiom system that is more appropriate, or more 'natural', for that primitive. Reviewing such alternative axiomatizations may therefore be illuminating, and will shed further light on the properties of our defined predicates, which we mentioned only briefly in sections 2.1.1 and 2.1.3. In each case, we shall assume the underlying logic to be governed by A.0.

2.4.1 *Proper Parthood as Primitive*

Instead of beginning with parthood, we could have taken the relation of proper parthood defined in D.1 as our primitive mereological concept and axiomatized that concept directly, defining P and the other relational predicates from PP. This was Leśniewski's (1916) original choice (modulo notation and terminology) and it is the strategy followed by Simons (1987), so it is especially worth consideration.

To begin with, in this case the partial ordering axioms define a *strict* partial order, as against the *weak* partial order given by A.1–A.3.

(A.7) $\forall x \neg PPxx$ *Irreflexivity*

(A.8) $\forall x \forall y (PPxy \rightarrow \neg PPyx)$ *Asymmetry*

(A.9) $\forall x \forall y \forall z ((PPxy \wedge PPyz) \rightarrow PPxz)$ *Transitivity*

This is actually a redundant characterization, since A.7 is an immediate consequence of A.8 and A.8 itself follows logically from A.7 and A.9, but listing all three principles will facilitate comparisons (and will be helpful in connection with some issues discussed in chapter 3). At any rate, it is easy to check that a system with A.1–A.3 will have each of A.7–A.9 as a theorem.[38] This confirms the well-known fact that every weak partial order has a corresponding strict order. Likewise, it is a fact that every strict partial order has a corresponding weak partial order; thus, parthood can be defined in terms of proper parthood and A.1–A.3 derived from A.7–A.9.[39]

(D.12) $Pxy :\equiv PPxy \vee x = y$ *Parthood*

Once we have defined P, the auxiliary predicates O, U, and D can be defined as before (definitions D.2–D.4).

To complete the picture, we need a decomposition axiom and a composition axiom. For the former, we could of course use our A.4, but this is not the common way to go. The common way, following Simons (1987), is to use the following axiom instead, which places constraints directly on PP.[40]

(A.10) $\forall x \forall y (PPyx \rightarrow \exists z (PPzx \wedge Dzy))$ *Weak Supplementation*

This axiom says that if something has a proper part, then it has a second, supplemental proper part entirely disjoint from the first. It is easy to see that in our original axiom system A.10 is derivable as a theorem,[41] and indeed it may be thought that Weak Supplementation is an unassailably intuitive principle governing decomposition; we will explore this thought in chapter 4. For now, we just note that A.10 together with A.9 entails Asymmetry, making A.8 (and hence A.7) redundant.[42]

Regarding composition, we can make up for the difference introduced by A.10 using a somewhat different definition of fusion than D.6.

(D.13) $F'_{\varphi}z :\equiv \forall x(\varphi x \rightarrow Pxz) \wedge \forall y(Pyz \rightarrow \exists x(\varphi x \wedge Oyx))$ *Fusion'*

38 Given D.1, A.7 follows immediately by the reflexivity of identity (L.6). For A.8, suppose that $PPxy$; then $\neg x = y$, and hence $\neg Pxy \vee \neg Pyx$ by A.2, from which it follows that $\neg PPyx$. For A.9, suppose $PPxy$ and $PPyz$. Then Pxz by A.3 and D.1, and $\neg x = z$ by A.8. So $PPxz$.

39 Given D.12, A.1 follows by the reflexivity of identity; A.2 follows from A.8 by the symmetry of identity; and A.3 follows from A.9 by the transitivity of identity.

40 Simons calls this axiom *weak* supplementation to distinguish it from a similar but stronger decomposition principle, corresponding to A.18 below. In the literature, A.10 is sometimes called "Witness" (Landman, 1991), "Separation" (Pietruszczak, 2000a), "Leftover" (Yablo, 2014), or even "Remainder" (Smith, 1997; Hudson, 2002a), though it really differs from our A.4. The exact relationships between these decomposition principles will be fully examined in chapter 4.

41 Suppose $PPyx$. By D.1 and A.2, this implies $\neg Pxy$. By A.4, this means there is a z such that, for all w, Pwz if and only if $Pwx \wedge Dwy$. Since Pzz by A.1, it follows that $Pzx \wedge Dzy$; and since $PPyx$ implies $\neg Dxy$, we must have $\neg z = x$. Thus, by D.12, $PPzx \wedge Dzy$.

42 Suppose $PPxy$ and $PPyx$. By A.10, we have $PPzx$ and Dzy for some z. By A.9 we have $PPzy$, hence Pzy by D.12. But D.12 also gives us Pzz. Thus $\neg Dzy$ by D.4. Contradiction.

This is actually akin to the original definition used by Leśniewski (1916) and endorsed by his pupil Tarski (1929, 1935), and it is also popular in contemporary literature.[43] It states that a fusion of the φs is such that every φ is part of it, and every part of it overlaps some φ. Correspondingly, A.5 will be replaced by the following axiom schema.

(A.11) $\exists x \varphi x \rightarrow \exists z F'_{\varphi} z$ *Unrestricted Fusion'*

With A.7 and A.8 shown to be redundant, it can be verified that the three axioms A.9, A.10, and A.11 amount to a complete axiomatization of classical mereology.[44] Indeed, we can reduce this list even further. Following Tarski (1929, 1935), we can drop the decomposition axiom A.10 altogether if we strengthen the composition axiom a bit.

(A.12) $\exists x \varphi x \rightarrow \exists z \forall y (F'_{\varphi} y \leftrightarrow y = z)$ *Unique Unrestricted Fusion'*

This axiom schema states for every non-empty condition φ that the φs have exactly one fusion, and together with A.9 it is enough to axiomatize classical mereology.[45] This is also the gist of Leśniewski's (1916) original axiomatization, though Leśniewski included the redundant axiom A.8 and split A.12 into the corresponding uniqueness and existence claims.[46] A few years later, Leśniewski (1927–1931, pt. VII) gave a similar axiomatization using P as a primitive, with just the Transitivity axiom A.9 replaced by A.3. It is precisely that axiomatization, modulo logical idiosyncrasies, that we met informally in chapter 1.[47]

2.4.2 *Overlap or Disjointness as Primitive*

The Calculus of Individuals of Leonard and Goodman (1940), which represents the main alternative to Leśniewski's and Tarski's axiomatizations,

43 Simons (1987) uses yet another notion of fusion, corresponding to D.16 below, along with the matching axiom schema A.15. The resulting system, given A.9 and A.10 (along with the redundant A.8), is offered as an axiomatization of classical mereology (p. 37) and has been treated as such in much of the literature that followed (including Casati and Varzi, 1999). In fact, it is not; only the fusions defined in D.13 will do. See Pietruszczak (2000a, §7.3; 2000b, §IV.8) and Pontow (2004, §5.2). For a thorough diagnosis of the error, see Hovda (2009). We shall return to the subtle relationships between these various notions of fusion in chapter 5, section 5.1.

44 For a proof, cf. Pietruszczak (2000b, §IV.1).

45 Cf. Pietruszczak (2000a, §7.1; 2000b, §IV.1) or Ridder (2002, §I.2.1.1). See also Tennant (2019).

46 On the redundancy of A.8 in Leśniewski's original setting (based on Ontology) there has been some controversy. See e.g. Rickey (1977, p. 412) and the response in Lejewski (1983).

47 The clean version of this axiomatization, using A.12, is given in Carnap (1954, §52). It is also offered by Hovda (2009) as the "fourth way" to classical mereology. Lewis (1991) follows the same approach, though in a language with plural quantification (cf. chapter 6). That the axiomatization requires fusions to be defined as in D.13, rather than D.6, was shown in Clay (1966).

used as a primitive the disjointness predicate D (in their terminology: discreteness).[48] Goodman (1951, § II.4) gave virtually the same axiom system, but using O instead. We present Goodman's system first, and briefly outline Leonard and Goodman's afterward.[49]

With O as a primitive, we need definitions of other mereological notions in terms of it. D can be defined simply as the negation of O. For the other basic notions, Goodman gives the following.

(D.14) $Pxy :\equiv \forall z(Ozx \rightarrow Ozy)$ *Parthood*

(D.15) $PPxy :\equiv Pxy \wedge \neg Pyx$ *Proper Parthood*

(D.16) $F''_{\varphi}z :\equiv \forall y(Oyz \leftrightarrow \exists x(\varphi x \wedge Oyx))$ *Fusion''*

Since P in D.14 is quantificational, logic alone gives us A.1 (Reflexivity) and A.3 (Transitivity) as theorems.[50] D.15 is an alternative definition of proper parthood; in classical mereology it is equivalent to D.1.[51] Similarly, the definition of fusion in terms of overlap, D.16, is different from both D.6 and D.13 (and we shall examine the differences in section 5.1), but the axiomatic treatment of O will force the equivalence. Intuitively, it says that a fusion of the φs is something that overlaps exactly those things that overlap at least one of the φs. In the recent literature, this notion is perhaps even more common than the others.[52]

Using D.14 and D.16, Goodman's axiomatization of classical mereology has only two axioms, plus a schema.

(A.13) $\forall x \forall y(Oxy \leftrightarrow \exists z(Pzx \wedge Pzy))$ *Overlapping Parts*

(A.14) $\forall x \forall y(\forall z(Ozx \leftrightarrow Ozy) \rightarrow x = y)$ *O–Extensionality*

(A.15) $\exists x \varphi x \rightarrow \exists z F''_{\varphi}z$ *Unrestricted Fusion''*

A.13 is of course just our definition D.2 treated as an axiom; and given D.14, A.14 turns out to be equivalent to A.2, the Antisymmetry axiom for P (since $\forall z(Ozx \leftrightarrow Ozy)$ is tantamount to $Pxy \wedge Pyx$).[53] Thus, since we also have A.1 and A.3 from D.14, another way of looking at this axiomatization is that

48 The idea of using D as a primitive may also be found in Leśniewski, who gave an axiomatization of Mereology based on this predicate already in 1921; see Leśniewski (1927–1931, pt. x).

49 Both systems are extensively studied in Eberle (1970), and Goodman's in Breitkopf (1978). The version of the Calculus presented in Leonard's dissertation (1930) used yet another primitive, the sum operator +, though the resulting system is weaker; see section 2.4.4.

50 This is already noted in Quine and Goodman (1940).

51 If Pxy, then $\neg Pyx$ implies $x \neq y$ by Leibniz's law (L.7) and $x \neq y$ implies $\neg Pyx$ by A.2. The latter implication may however break down in weaker systems; see section 3.2.

52 See e.g. Simons (1987, p. 37), Casati and Varzi (1999, p. 46), Niebergall (2011, p. 277).

53 Actually, Goodman uses both directions of the conditional in A.14 to *define* the identity predicate. Since here we are treating identity as a primitive, and the right-to-left direction would be an instance of Leibniz's law (our logical axiom L.7), we list the other direction as an axiom.

classical mereology can be obtained by adding A.13 and A.15 to the initial partial order axioms for P, and then dropping the redundancies.[54]

The Leonard and Goodman (1940) system differs in only minor ways from the above.[55] In nearly every case, the definitions and axioms given using D are just the *duals* of the ones given for O, and are logically equivalent.

(D.17) $Pxy :\equiv \forall z(Dzy \rightarrow Dzx)$ *Parthood (D–Variant)*

(D.18) $F''_{\varphi}z :\equiv \forall y(Dyz \leftrightarrow \forall x(\varphi x \rightarrow Dyx))$ *Fusion″ (D–Variant)*

With O defined standardly as in D.2 (but using D.17), Leonard and Goodman's system consists of the Antisymmetry axiom A.2 and the Unrestricted Fusion″ axiom schema A.15 (using D.18) together with the following.

(A.16) $\forall x \forall y(Oxy \leftrightarrow \neg Dxy)$ *Exclusion*

So we are just trading an axiom (A.13) for a definition (D.2) and a definition (D.4) for an axiom (A.16). As for A.2, we have already noted that it is equivalent to A.14 under D.14, and the equivalence is inherited by D.17.

2.4.3 *More Parthood Axiomatizations*

Both ways into classical mereology—Leśniewski's and Leonard and Goodman's—have also been formulated using P as a primitive, with axioms that differ from ours in significant ways.

Concerning the former, we already mentioned Leśniewski's own axiomatization, but there is an interesting variant due to Tarski (1937). It uses the same notion of fusion defined in D.13 and is based on the corresponding Unrestricted Fusion axiom schema (A.11)[56] and the Transitivity axiom for P (A.3). In addition, it has the following special axiom.

(A.17) $\forall z \forall y(F'_{x=y}z \rightarrow z = y)$ *Singular Fusion′*

Intuitively, this says that everything qualifies as a fusion′ of its own singleton. Since identity is symmetric and transitive, such a fusion′ is bound to be unique, and this in turn implies uniqueness of φ-fusions′ for any condition φ (Tarski, 1937, thm. 1·25). Thus, the conjunction of A.11 and A.17

54 It must be stressed that the adequacy of these axioms depends crucially on the notion of fusion involved in A.15. Using the regular fusion axiom A.5 would result in a weaker system while the fusion′ axiom A.11 would be unnecessarily strong. A proof of these claims will be given in section 5.1. It is also worth reiterating that replacing A.13 with the Weak Supplementation axiom A.10, as in some recent treatments, won't do. See note 43.

55 We ignore here the fact that Leonard and Goodman's original axiomatization involves quantification over classes (see chapter 1, note 24). We shall come back to the issue in chapter 6.

56 Again, we set aside the fact that Tarski's actual formulation involves quantification over classes.

ultimately amounts to the Unique Unrestricted Fusion' schema A.12, justifying Tarski's claim that this is another 'simplification' of Leśniewski's original system. It is, however, one that carries special historical interest, as it amounts to the first axiomatic presentation of classical mereology to appear in English (in strict *Principia Mathematica* notation).

Regarding the Calculus of Individuals, the main variant based on P comes from Eberle (1970, §2.9).[57] The definitions for O and for D are standard (D.2 and D.4), but Eberle follows Goodman in using D.15 for proper parts and D.16 for fusions. His axioms are: the ordering axioms A.1–A.3,[58] the composition axiom schema A.15, and a decomposition axiom we have not yet seen.

(A.18) $\forall x \forall y(\neg Pxy \rightarrow \exists z(Pzx \wedge Dzy))$ *Strong Supplementation*

This axiom is similar to the Weak Supplementation axiom A.10 except for having $\neg Pxy$ in the antecedent instead of $PPyx$ (and Pzx in the consequent instead of $PPzx$). As our nomenclature suggests, following Simons (1987, p. 29), this is not a negligible difference. We shall explore the difference in detail in chapter 4, where we shall also take a closer look at some philosophical issues that these two Supplementation principles—both of which are of course provable in our axiom system—may raise.

2.4.4 *Further Options*

Lastly, it is worth mentioning the possibility of axiomatizing classical mereology using as primitives some of the 'algebraic' functors defined in section 2.1.3, such as sum and product.

The first option is especially interesting. Recall that Leibniz's pioneering attempts to develop a systematic theory of the part-whole relation were indeed based on an operation of binary composition, $\oplus$, with parthood (containment) defined so that Pxy if and only if $x \oplus z = y$ for some z (see section 1.1). Leśniewski himself considered this idea, noting that his theory had the following theorem (Leśniewski, 1927–1931, thm. CCLXIV).[59]

(T.4) $\forall x \forall y(Pxy \leftrightarrow \exists z\, x + z = y)$ *Addition*

A similar idea was in fact used by Leonard in the initial formulation of the Calculus of Individuals included in his dissertation, which takes the binary

57 Eberle's system is based on a non-classical (free) logic. Here we assume A.0 instead, as in Pontow and Schubert (2006, §2.1) and Hovda (2009, §3.3) (both with completeness proofs).

58 Actually A.1 turns out to be redundant, as shown in Pietruszczak (2000b, § IV.5), though this is often neglected in the literature.

59 More precisely, Leśniewski proved the analogue of T.4 for $+$ defined in terms of F' (D.13).

sum operator $+$ as primitive and defines the parthood relation as follows (Leonard, 1930, p. 190):

(D.19) $\mathsf{P}xy :\equiv x + y = y$ *Parthood*

Now, as it turns out, the axiom system proposed by Leonard is weaker than classical mereology (see Rossberg, 2009, §3).[60] Nonetheless, our discussion of Boolean algebras in section 2.2.1 suggests a natural way of obtaining a full axiomatization along precisely these lines.

There are, strictly speaking, two possibilities. The most direct would be to follow Leonard literally and allow our language to include $+$ as a primitive function symbol, extending A.0 (the underlying logic) accordingly.[61] Alternatively, one may work with a primitive three-place predicate, S (reading $\mathsf{S}zxy$ as 'z is a sum of x and y'), and require that it behaves functionally.

(A.19) $\forall x \forall y \forall z \forall w((\mathsf{S}zxy \wedge \mathsf{S}wxy) \rightarrow z = w)$ *Sum Uniqueness*

The operator $+$ could then be introduced by definition, by analogy to the definition of the general fusion operator σ in terms of F (D.7).

(D.20) $a + b := \imath z \mathsf{S}zab$ *Sum*

Either way, one may then proceed as follows. Start with Leibniz's axioms for $+$, which correspond to the algebraic properties of the join operator $\sqcup$ in 2.1–2.3 (and are therefore provable in our original axiom system).[62]

(A.20) $\forall x\ x + x = x$ *Idempotence*

(A.21) $\forall x \forall y\ x + y = y + x$ *Commutativity*

(A.22) $\forall x \forall y \forall z\ x + (y + z) = (x + y) + z$ *Associativity*

Next, adopt Leonard's definition for P, which matches the algebraic definition of $\sqsubseteq$ in 2.7. We know that A.20, A.21, and A.22 imply the three ordering axioms A.1, A.2, and A.3, respectively.[63] Moreover, the reader can check that $+$ and the fusion predicate F (defined again as in D.6) will interact as they should, in the sense that $x + y$ will always equal the fusion of x and y. Thus, adding now A.4 and A.5 (or A.15 and A.18, as in Eberle's system)

60 D.19 has been used by other authors, independently of Leonard (1930); see e.g. Link (1983, p. 307) and Krifka (1998, p. 199). Their systems, however, while intended to generate classical mereology, are also provably weaker; see Hovda (2009, p. 68).

61 See e.g. Mendelson (1964, §2.7).

62 Recall that Leibniz did not officially state that composition is associative, though he took it for granted; see chapter 1, note 6.

63 See the proofs after definition 2.7 in section 2.2.1. Note that those proofs require $x \sqcup y$ to exist for every x and y. In the present context, the relevant existential assumption is guaranteed by A.21, which logically implies $\forall x \forall y \exists z\ x + y = z$.

will immediately result in an axiomatization of classical mereology.[64] Indeed, since A.22 suffices to show that the parthood predicate defined in D.19 is transitive, one may even consider an axiomatization based on just this axiom, A.22, together with Tarski's Unique Unrestricted Fusion′ axiom A.12. This elegant 'fusion only' axiomatization may be found, for instance, in Ketland and Schindler (2016, §4); they call it "Fusion Theory".[65]

The picture is somewhat different when it comes to other mereological functors, such as the product operator $\times$. Algebraically, we know that $a \sqsubseteq b$ holds if and only if $a \sqcap b = a$. One could therefore consider a matching definition to introduce the parthood relation, P, in terms of $\times$.

(D.21) $Pxy :\equiv x \times y = x$ *Parthood*

This would be perfectly dual to Leonard's definition D.19, and indeed it's easy to verify that the biconditional corresponding to D.21 is a theorem of classical mereology when $\times$ is defined as in D.10.[66] However, in this case the option of treating $\times$ as a primitive functor is not quite available. The reason is that we want to allow for $x \times y$ not to exist (x and y need not overlap) and that is impossible if the underlying logic is classical. In classical logic, a term-forming functor must be defined for all arguments. Thus, short of weakening A.0, with the major structural revisions that this would involve,[67] in this case the only possibility is to treat $\times$ as an operator defined via a more basic relational predicate, by analogy to the second option mentioned in connection with $+$. (The details are similar, using the relevant counterparts of A.19 and D.20.) Moreover, in this case one cannot just require $\times$ to match the properties of the meet operator $\sqcap$ in 2.1–2.3. Idempotence is fine, but Commutativity and Associativity would need to be in conditional form.

(A.23) $\forall x\, x \times x = x$ *Idempotence*

(A.24) $\forall x \forall y \forall w\, (w = x \times y \rightarrow w = y \times x)$ *Commutativity*

(A.25) $\forall x \forall y \forall z \forall w\, (w = x \times (y \times z) \rightarrow w = (x \times y) \times z)$ *Associativity*

---

64 With some redundancy. For instance, the existence of binary sums is guaranteed twice, by A.5 and by A.21 (see note 63).

65 The adequacy of this Tarski-style axiomatization depends crucially on the provability of $\forall x \forall y \forall z (x + y = z \leftrightarrow F'_{w=x \vee w=y} z)$. See Lemmas 10 and 11 in Ketland and Schindler (2016).

66 When Pxy, A.3 gives us $\forall z(Pzx \rightarrow Pzy)$, which entails $\forall z((Pzx \wedge Pzy) \leftrightarrow Pzx)$, whence $\sigma z(Pzx \wedge Pzy) = \sigma z\, Pzx$ by D.6 and D.7 and so $x \times y = x$ by D.10 and A.1. Conversely, if $x \times y = x$, D.10 and D.6 give us $\forall z((Pzx \wedge Pzy) \rightarrow Pzy) \rightarrow Pxy$, which entails Pxy.

67 One could, for instance, shift to a so-called free logic, where *bona fide* empty terms are allowed (see Simons, 1987, §2.5 and 1991a). The original version of Eberle's (1970) system actually uses such a logic, though we set that feature aside in our brief outline in section 2.4.3 (see note 57). Leśniewski's Mereology, too, was originally set in a logical framework that is 'free' in this sense, and in fact it admits an axiomatization based on the product operator (see Welsh, 1978, §2). On the affinities of Leśniewski's system with free logic, see Simons (1981, 1985b, 1995).

Even so, these axioms would suffice to secure the ordering properties for P.[68] It is also easy to check that, together with D.21, they guarantee that (i) $a \times b$ exists whenever a and b have a common part, and (ii) if $a \times b$ exists, it is itself a common part and, indeed, qualifies as a product of a and b in the sense of D.10.[69] One can thus proceed as above and add the necessary decomposition and composition axioms to get classical mereology.

Indeed, one can do better. Supplementing A.23–A.25 with a composition axiom such as A.5 would be legitimate, yet somewhat at odds with taking the concept of mereological product as a fundamental primitive. However, a 'product only' axiomatization is also possible. To see this, note that in classical mereology there is a notion that generalizes $\times$ in a way that parallels the generalization of $+$ afforded by the fusion predicate F. Just as a fusion of the φs is a minimal upper bound of the φs, so we can define their general product, or *nucleus*,[70] as the corresponding maximal lower bound:

(D.22) $N_\varphi z :\equiv \forall y(\varphi y \to Pzy) \land \forall x(\forall y(\varphi y \to Pxy) \to Pxz)$ *Nucleus*

And just as a maximal lower bound of a set of things is always a minimal upper bound of the lower bounds of that set,[71]

(T.5) $\forall z(N_\varphi z \leftrightarrow F_{\forall y(\varphi y \to Pxy)} z)$ *Upward Duality*

68 A.1 is just A.23 under D.21. For A.2, suppose Pab and Pba. By D.21, this means $a = a \times b$ and $b = b \times a$. Since $a = a \times b \to a = b \times a$ by A.24, we obtain $a = b \times a$ by modus ponens and hence, substituting, $a = b$. The proof of A.3 from A.25 is similar.

69 For (i), suppose there is some c such that Pca and Pcb. By D.21, $c = c \times a$ and $c = c \times b$, whence $c = (c \times a) \times b$ and thus, by A.25, $c = c \times (a \times b)$, i.e. $Pc(a \times b)$. Since '$a \times b$' is a definite description, this can only be true if $a \times b$ exists. For (ii), suppose $a \times b$ exists. Then we have $a \times b = (a \times a) \times b = a \times (a \times b) = (a \times b) \times a$ (using A.23, A.25, and A.24), and so $P(a \times b)a$ by D.21, as desired. Similarly, $P(a \times b)b$. Now, it follows from this that $a \times b$ meets the second conjunct of D.6 with regard to being a fusion of the common parts of a and b, hence a product of a and b in the sense of D.10. For insofar as $a \times b$ is itself among those common parts, it is part of anything whose parts includes them all. And $a \times b$ meets the first condition as well, since the proof of (i) shows that $Pc(a \times b)$ for *any* common part c.

70 The term is from Leonard and Goodman (1940, p. 47). Their definition is different, paralleling the definition of fusion″ in D.18:

$$N''_\varphi z :\equiv \forall y(Pyz \leftrightarrow \forall x(\varphi x \to Pyx)).$$

However, given A.1 and A.3, this reduces to D.22. In recent literature the term 'general product' is more common, following Simons (1987, p. 35) (if not Goodman himself, 1951, p. 37).

71 Let's check for arbitrary a that $N_\varphi a \leftrightarrow F_{\forall y(\varphi y \to Pxy)} a$. From left to right, assume $N_\varphi a$. By D.22, this means that (i) $\forall y(\varphi y \to Pay)$ and (ii) $\forall x(\forall y(\varphi y \to Pxy) \to Pxa)$. Suppose for arbitrary b that $\forall x(\forall y(\varphi y \to Pxy) \to Pxb)$. Then $\forall y(\varphi y \to Pay) \to Pab$, and so Pab by (i). Thus, since b was arbitrary, by conditionalization and generalization we get (iii) $\forall w(\forall x(\forall y(\varphi y \to Pxy) \to Pxw) \to Paw)$. Conjoining (ii) and (iii), we obtain by D.6 that $F_{\forall y(\varphi y \to Pxy)} a$. Conversely, assume $F_{\forall y(\varphi y \to Pxy)} a$. This gives us (ii) and (iii). Let c be any φ. We have that $\forall x(\forall y(\varphi y \to Pxy) \to Pxc)$ and hence, by (iii), Pac. Since c was arbitrary, by generalization we get (iv) $\forall y(\varphi y \to Pay)$. (Note that if there are no φs, this is vacuously true

it's easy to see that, dually, a minimal upper bound is a maximal lower bound of the upper bounds:[72]

(T.6) $\forall z(F_\varphi z \leftrightarrow N_{\forall y(\varphi y \to Pyx)} z)$ *Downward Duality*

It follows, therefore, that we can trade the Unrestricted Fusion axiom A.5 for the following schema:

(A.26) $\exists x \varphi x \to \exists z N_{\forall y(\varphi y \to Pyx)} z$ *Unrestricted Upper Nucleus*

Together with A.23–A.25 (plus the Remainder axiom A.4), this will yield the full strength of classical mereology directly in terms of products (nuclei).

2.4.5 *Primitivity in Mereology*

One final remark is in order. In view of the variety of alternative options outlined in the foregoing sections, one may wonder whether *any* functor or predicate of classical mereology can be used as a primitive instead of P. The answer to this question is in the negative, and it is important to convince ourselves that it is so. Adapting from Simons (1987, p. 73), this can be done with the classic method of Padoa (1901). Let $\mathcal{A}$ and $\mathcal{B}$ be any two functors or predicates, and suppose we know $\mathcal{A}$ can serve as sole primitive. Then $\mathcal{B}$ can serve in this capacity only if it permits an adequate definition of $\mathcal{A}$, hence only if there are no distinct models in which $\mathcal{A}$ receives the same interpretation while the interpretation of $\mathcal{B}$ changes. And surely this is not always the case. For example, the two models in figure 2.5, where the arrows represent proper parthood, show that the third functor introduced in section 2.1.3, the complement operator (D.11), is not a good candidate: its interpretation is

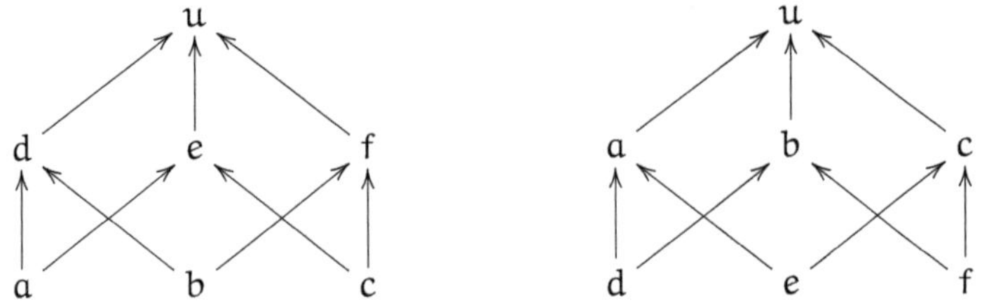

Figure 2.5: Two models of classical mereology

and $a = u$, the universe.) Conjoining (iv) and (ii), we obtain that $N_\varphi a$ by D.22. This completes the proof. Note that, as a result, the biconditional in T.5 could be used as a definition instead of D.22. This is also a common way of defining N when 'fusion' is understood via the alternative definitions in D.13 and D.16; see e.g. Tarski (1937, def. 1·31) and Simons (1987, p. 37).

72 The proof is similar to that of T.5. For a purely algebraic treatment of both equivalences, with $\bigsqcup$ and $\bigsqcap$ in place of F and N, see e.g. Davey and Priestly (2002, ch. 2).

the same in both models whereas that of P (as well as the interpretation of PP, O, D, +, and ×) is not. For the same reason, the zero-place functor u (D.8) cannot serve as sole primitive, either.

This leaves us with the general question of *which* functors and predicates can do the job, besides the ones we already considered. Furthermore, there is the question of which operators or predicates, while unfit to serve as sole primitives, can nonetheless serve as primitives in conjunction with others. A simple case in point would be the following pair.

(D.23) $\mathsf{PO}xy :\equiv \mathsf{O}xy \wedge \neg \mathsf{P}xy \wedge \neg \mathsf{P}yx$ *Proper Overlap*

(D.24) $\mathsf{IO}xy :\equiv \mathsf{P}xy \vee \mathsf{P}yx$ *Improper Overlap*

Neither of these predicates can serve as sole primitive, as can be seen by the method above.[73] Yet clearly their disjunction amounts to the overlap predicate O, and so the two predicates together can provide an adequate basis for classical mereology.

These last questions open an interesting area of research, and their treatment has generated a considerable amount of literature especially among early Leśniewskian scholars (see Welsh, 1978 and references therein).[74] Unfortunately, it is not easy to extrapolate their results from the idiosyncrasies of Leśniewski's original logical apparatus, and doing so would take us too far afield. For our purposes these brief remarks will suffice. In the following we shall for the most part hold to our official axiom system anyway, as defined by A.1–A.5. Nevertheless, it bears emphasis that the full character of classical mereology, as of any formal theory, lies precisely here, in the exact range of alternative options that are available to capture its intended truths. As we shall see, this becomes especially important when we turn to theories that *depart* from classical mereology in some respect or other. Such theories, and their philosophical motivations, will be our main concern in the remaining chapters.

---

73 The two models in figure 2.5 are enough to show the inadequacy of IO. For PO, just take the model on the left along with a model obtained by switching two adjacent atoms, say a and b.

74 This literature goes hand in hand with research devoted to identifying short, single-axiom foundations for Leśniewski's Mereology. The shortest axiom is due to Le Blanc (1983) and is based on overlap. See also Le Blanc (1985a,b). Earlier examples include Sobociński (1954), a series of papers by Lejewski (1955, 1963, 1967, 1973, 1978, 1980), and Clay (1961, 1975). For a brief overview, see Simons (1987, §2.7.3).

ORDERING 3

Nature being a wise and provident lady,
governs her parts very wisely, methodically, and orderly.

— Margaret Cavendish, *Observations upon Experimental Philosophy* (2001, p. 105)

Classical mereology is by far the best-known mereological theory, and we have seen that it is *sound* and *complete* with respect to a well-defined class of mathematical models. This makes it a 'classical' theory not only in view of its history and pedigree, but also because it constitutes a robust starting point for anyone interested in rigorous treatments of formal part-whole relationships. Moreover, while we shall not prove it here, classical mereology turns out to be *decidable*, i.e. there exist effective methods for determining whether any given formula in the language is or is not among its theorems (Tsai, 2013a). This adds extra value, making the theory attractive also from a practical (e.g. computational) standpoint. Philosophically, however, classical mereology is just a theory, and there is room for alternatives. Indeed, since the pioneering work of Leśniewski, Leonard, and Goodman, several 'non-classical' mereologies have been proposed, mainly stemming from philosophical concerns regarding some aspect or other in the classic treatment of the parthood relation. To appreciate the import and motivations of such developments, and to get a better picture of the range of views that define the field, it is therefore important that we take a closer look at our five axioms. We begin in this chapter by re-examining the very idea that parthood is a partial order, as determined by A.1–A.3. Here are those axioms again:

(A.1) $\forall x Pxx$ *Reflexivity*

(A.2) $\forall x \forall y((Pxy \wedge Pyx) \rightarrow x = y)$ *Antisymmetry*

(A.3) $\forall x \forall y \forall z((Pxy \wedge Pyz) \rightarrow Pxz)$ *Transitivity*

One kind of confusion about these axioms should be dealt with immediately: there is something odd about saying that a whole is part of itself. Most ordinary uses of 'part' seem to fly in the face of A.1 and A.2 for the sheer reason that we do not usually consider identity to be a case of parthood.

Mereology. A. J. Cotnoir and Achille C. Varzi, Oxford University Press. © A. J. Cotnoir and Achille C. Varzi 2021. DOI: 10.1093/oso/9780198749004.003.0003

Rescher (1955, pp. 9f) famously objected to Leonard and Goodman's Calculus of Individuals precisely on these grounds, citing the biologists' use of 'part' for the functional subunits of an organism as a case in point: no organism is a subunit of itself. As Lejewski (1957) noted, however, this worry appears to be merely terminological; taking parthood to include identity as a limit (or 'improper') case is simply a stipulation "to get rid of ambiguities", and it is in this sense that we decided to take P to represent a partial order.[1] As we saw, a different relational predicate PP of proper parthood, to the effect that nothing counts as part of itself, can easily be defined in terms of P via D.1. If so, then PP satisfies the conditions on strict orderings, conforming to the uses in question.

(A.7) $\forall x \neg PPxx$ *Irreflexivity*

(A.8) $\forall x \forall y (PPxy \rightarrow \neg PPyx)$ *Asymmetry*

(A.9) $\forall x \forall y \forall z ((PPxy \wedge PPyz) \rightarrow PPxz)$ *Transitivity*

Moreover, we saw that we could have started with PP as a primitive and use A.7–A.9 as axioms. Our P could then be defined accordingly, as in D.12, and A.1–A.3 derived as theorems. The wide and the strict relations are therefore inter-definable, and hence picking one over the other means no loss of generality. There may well be philosophical reasons for thinking that one or the other is ontologically more 'basic', or more 'natural' in the sense of Lewis (1983a).[2] But either way, nothing is lost from a purely formal perspective.

With this understanding, the thought behind A.1–A.3 and A.7–A.9 is that there should be nothing controversial about these principles. Indeed, there is something of a consensus that it is a conceptual truth that parthood and proper parthood satisfy the respective ordering axioms. Peter Simons writes:

> These principles are partly constitutive of the meaning of 'part', which means that anyone who seriously disagrees with them has failed to understand the word. (Simons, 1987, p. 11)

Such a view is reminiscent of Husserl's conception of mereology as belonging to the realm of a purely formal ontology, and has been very influential

1 Already Whitehead was candid about this:

> It is purely a matter of words and of technical convenience that we allow as an extreme case that a spatial object must always be considered as part of itself, or that we consider that 'part' signifies 'part properly speaking' in such a way that no spatial object can be part of itself. (Whitehead, 1916, p. 725)

2 For example, since A.2 could be used to define identity (see D.27), one could argue with Sharvy (1983, p. 234) that the relation expressed by P is conceptually prior to the identity relation; and since no such definition can be given in terms of PP except in the presence of stronger axioms, the argument would provide evidence in favor of P being a more basic, natural primitive. See Smid (2017b, fn. 9) for a clear statement of this view.

also among contemporary mereologists. However, there have been dissenters, and each principle calls for close scrutiny.

3.1 REFLEXIVITY AND IRREFLEXIVITY

The reflexivity of P (A.1) is the least controversial of the partial ordering principles. As long as we are conceiving of parthood as including identity as a limit case, the only possible counterexamples to A.1 would have to be counterexamples to the reflexivity of identity (hence to A.0, the classical logical apparatus that we have assumed in the background of classical mereology). For example, a dialetheist may countenance the possibility of contradictory, self-different individuals, as with Priest's (1997) Sylvan's box. Or one might think with Schrödinger (1952), or more recently French and Krause (2006), that subatomic particles are not self-identical, because they differ from ordinary individuals due to quantum phenomena. Clearly, entities of this sort would fail to be (improper) parts of themselves and thus constitute genuine counterexamples to A.1. But, equally clearly, such counterexamples require widespread revisions of other standard metaphysical doctrines, too. So, it is only insofar as one is willing to go that far that the generality and metaphysical neutrality of A.1 may be questioned.

The irreflexivity of PP as expressed in A.7 may seem only mildly more controversial. We tend to think of parthood as a kind of inclusion relation, and it seems counterintuitive to think that something might be 'properly included within itself'. Indeed, there is no way one could even represent the mereological structure of such an object using a Euler or Venn diagram, for such diagrams have the irreflexivity of PP built in, as it were. We can only rely on abstract models, such as the one in figure 3.1, where the proper parthood relation is represented by an arrow.

Figure 3.1: A self-part

What would a have to be like in such a case? Aren't models of this sort, which violate A.7, simply a sign that we are failing to understand the meaning of 'part'?

Following Kearns (2011), here is one way to argue that the question is not as straightforward as it might seem. Suppose we take 'x loves y' to mean that either x loves y in the ordinary sense of the English word 'loves' or x is identical with y. Correspondingly, let 'x properly loves y' mean that x loves y but is not identical with y. It follows from these definitions that 'loves' is reflexive and 'properly loves' is irreflexive; these two properties are, we may say, constitutive of the intended meaning of our predicates. Yet this just goes to show that neither predicate is really about love, since genuine love is neither reflexive nor irreflexive. Now consider the mereological understanding of 'part' and 'proper part'; what reasons do we have to resist a similar diagnosis? What we said about the inter-definability of P and PP leaves the question open. Either these predicates are really meant to express genuine parthood, or at least one of the genuine parthood relations expressed by the ordinary and philosophical senses of the English word 'part'; or else P and PP are not genuinely about parthood but about some other relations conveniently defined *in terms of* parthood, as 'love' and 'properly love' are about relations defined in terms of love.[3] In the latter case, A.1 and A.7 would indeed be unobjectionable, but at the price of changing the subject: mereology would cease to be the theory it is meant to be. So it is the former option that we must have in mind when doing mereology. And in that case, the status of A.1 and A.7 is no longer trivial. For then it would seem that these axioms do not simply register something about the meaning of 'part'; they say something substantive about parthood. In particular, with PP treated as primitive, the truth of A.1 will still depend on how we feel about self-identity, but A.7 may be disputed in its own right. *Can* there be genuine self-parts—things that are parts of themselves not by virtue of being self-identical, but by being properly included within themselves in some sense?

3.1.1 *Concrete Self-parts*

While few philosophers have offered explicit examples towards a positive answer, several possibilities come to mind. Consider, for instance, the Christian doctrine of the Trinity. The orthodox view is that the trinitarian God is a simple, partless substance, and hence each person of the Trinity is strictly identical with God. In Peter Lombard's words:

> Nor is any of the three persons a part of God or of the divine essence, because each of them is truly and fully God and is the whole and full divine essence. (*Sententiarum*, I, XIX, 5; Lombard, 2007, p. 108)

Sometimes, however, this view is contrasted with a different conception, according to which each person of the Trinity *is* a part of God, in the sense of being properly included within the godhead, and yet also identical with God, by virtue of having the same divine essence. (See. e.g. Abelard, *Theologica Christiana*, bk. IV.) If the latter conception is accepted, then we would have a counterexample to the Irreflexivity axiom A.7.

3 See e.g. van Inwagen (1994, p. 207), where 'part' and 'proper part' are defined exactly this way.

For a second example, consider the metaphysical puzzle of Dion and Theon raised by the Stoic Chrysippus in his book on the 'growing argument'. Philo of Alexandria puts it thus:

> Having first established that it is impossible for two peculiarly qualified individuals to occupy the same space jointly, he says: "For the sake of argument, let one individual be thought of as whole-limbed, the other as minus one foot. Let the whole-limbed one be called Dion, the defective one Theon. Then let one of Dion's feet be amputated." The question arises which one of them has perished. (*De aeternitate mundi*, 48; in Long and Sedley, 1987, p. 171)

The literature is filled with responses to this puzzle (and to the structurally similar puzzles of Tibbles and Tib, from Wiggins, 1968, of Charlie and Sam, from Cartwright, 1975, and of Descartes and Descartes-minus, from van Inwagen, 1981).[4] Chrysippus himself maintained that it is Theon who perished, since only Dion can be grieving over his severed foot. For his part, Philo held the opposite view, since Dion's body was mutilated whereas nothing happened to Theon.[5] Today it is also popular to claim survival for both Dion and Theon as *coincident* entities, rejecting the assumption that two individuals cannot "occupy the same space jointly".[6] But another possible response would be to hold that Theon is a proper part of Dion that is identical to Dion also before the amputation, by virtue of being identical to Dion afterwards. Indeed, Abelard appears to have held such a view.[7]

> [W]hen a hand has been cut off, that which then stays a human was also staying a human before the amputation, although it was hidden as a part in the human who was the whole ... Therefore, although before all amputations there were many parts in one human each of which was human, still there were not for this reason many humans ... For the humans here have the same essence. (*Theologia Christiana*, IV, 25–26, in Bosley and Tweedale, 2006, p. 302)

There are drawbacks to such a view, including the apparent discernibility of Dion and Theon before the amputation. But one may attempt to explain

4 For comparisons and further cases, see Rea (1995) and Wasserman (2018a). The puzzle is also present in medieval philosophy; see e.g. the case of Socrates and Socrates-minus-his-foot in William of Sherwood's *Syncategoremata*, x, 6, and the analogous case (with a finger instead of the foot) discussed in William Heytesbury's *Sophismata*, XXVII (*Totus Socrates est Minor Socrate*) and in Albert of Saxony's *Sophismata*, XLVI (*Totus Socrates est pars Socratis*) *inter alia*. The latter case is reviewed extensively in Kretzmann (1982, pp. 234–240) and Fitzgerald (2009).

5 For detailed accounts of these views, see Sedley (1982), Bowin (2003), Sorabji (2005, pp. 184f; 2006, pp. 83ff). In recent literature, Chrysippus's stance has been revived by Burke (1994, 1996) (with replies by Denkel, 1995; Olson, 1997; Carter, 1997; Noonan, 1999; Stone, 2002; Ujvári, 2004; *et al.*) and Moran (2018), while Philo's finds support in Chisholm (1973). The latter is normally associated with the thesis of 'mereological essentialism', which we examine in chapter 6.

6 This view has become popular with Wiggins (1968). On a natural construal, it involves a rejection of A.2 and/or the extensionality thesis T.1, on which see section 3.2.3.

7 For more on Abelard's view, which is rather complex, see Henry (1991b) and Arlig (2012b).

away their distinguishing characteristics.[8] And if such a project could be successfully carried out, then one might be motivated to reject A.7.

For a third putative example of concrete self-parthood, we look to the growing literature on the topic of mereology and time travel.[9] Nikk Effingham offers the following scenario.

> Imagine a cube, with each side measuring 10m, made of a homogeneous substance ... Not only do we take it back to a time that it previously existed at, but we use a shrinking machine and miniaturize by a factor of 100. We then remove a cube-shaped portion, with edges measuring 10cm, from the earlier, larger version of the cube and replace that portion with the miniaturized future version (which now fits perfectly). The cube is now a proper part of itself at that time. (Effingham, 2010a, p. 335)

If such time-travel stories are accepted as legitimate metaphysical possibilities, then again one might have reason to doubt A.7, confirming that it is a substantive and controversial metaphysical principle.

3.1.2 *Abstract Self-parts*

There are also a range of cases regarding parthood relations among abstract entities. A case in point would be the theory of structured propositions originated with Russell (1903). As Kearns (2011) argues, if the relevant structure is construed mereologically, then there is good reason to accept self-parthood. Consider a sentence such as

(p) Proposition p is abstract.

On the assumption that (p) succeeds in expressing any proposition at all, it must express proposition p. And since p says something about itself, it appears to have itself as a constituent, i.e. to be a proper part of itself. (The existence of such 'cyclical' propositions is of course contentious; but it is, for instance, a central component of the solution to the semantic paradoxes defended by Barwise and Etchemendy, 1987.)

For a different case, also due to Kearns (2011), suppose that shapes are construed as abstract universals. Then qualitative identity may be viewed as sufficient for numerical identity. If so, self-similar shapes such as fractals might be said to contain themselves as parts in a sense other shapes do not.[10]

---

8 See Eagle (2010a, §3) for resources.

9 Initially aimed against endurantism (Effingham and Robson, 2007, with a response by Smith, 2009 and reply in Effingham, 2010a) or against perdurantism (Gilmore, 2007, with further discussion in Eagle, 2010a,b and Gilmore, 2010a). Cf. also Daniels (2014), Eagle (2016), Wasserman (2018b, ch. 6). On the use of time-travel stories in mereology, see Proietti and Smid (in press).

10 On fractal geometry, see Mandelbrot (1983). The idea has also been exploited in the arts. A classic example is Johannes Misset's 1904 design for the advertisement of Droste cacao, where

Indeed, the same could be said of abstract structures more generally. Gödel once claimed:

> Nor is it self-contradictory that a proper part should be identical (not merely equal) to the whole, as is seen in the case of structures in the abstract sense. The structure of the series of integers, e.g. contains itself as a proper part and it is easily seen that there exist also structures containing infinitely many different parts, each containing the whole structure as a part. (Gödel, 1944, p. 139).

Similarly, suppose one accepts a conception of immanent universals as being 'wholly present' wherever they are instantiated. Then it seems perfectly possible that, say, a universal such as *whiteness* is wholly present in some extended region, r, and also wholly present in smaller portions of r. This is how Thomas Aquinas put it:

> If wholeness of nature is meant, whiteness is wholly present everywhere on a surface, its full specific nature being realized in every part. (*Summa Theologiae*, I, q. 8, a. 2; Aquinas, 2006, vol. 2, p. 117)

On the assumption that the mereological structure of an entity always 'mirrors' or is in perfect 'harmony' with that of its spatial receptacle,[11] and that this is also true of multi-located entities such as universals, it follows therefore that *whiteness* can be a proper part of itself: it can have more than one receptacle, with some receptacles related to others by proper parthood.

One last example may be drawn from the metaphysics of sets. Suppose we count a set's members as among its parts;[12] then non-wellfounded sets, i.e. sets that allow for membership loops (Aczel, 1988),[13] could easily bring about failures of the Irreflexivity axiom A.7. For instance, in Quine's alternative set theory, *New Foundations* (1937), there exist certain self-membered singletons $\{a\} = a$. Such sets, called 'Quine atoms', could be considered part of themselves in a non-trivial way.

---

the front-face of the package repeats itself in the drawing, potentially *ad infinitum*. For more examples (and a mathematical analysis) see Leys (2007).

11 The terminology is from Varzi (2007a, §3.3) and Uzquiano (2011b), respectively. For more on the relationship between mereology and spatial or spatio-temporal location, see Saucedo (2011), Leonard (2016), Gilmore (2018), and the essays in Kleinschmidt (2014).

12 This is by itself controversial. As we saw in section 2.3, the natural set-theoretic counterpart of parthood is the relation of set inclusion, and today most philosophers would follow Lewis (1991, 1993b) in taking that to be the correct metaphysics of sets (*pace* Oliver, 1994). On the other hand, see Fine (1999, 2010) for the contrary view that the 'hierarchical' conception of sets and their members provides a better model for parthood than the 'linear' conception of set and subset. For the view that a set's members are among its parts (*pace* Oliver, 1993), see also Forrest (2002) and Hovda (2016); for a sustained defense of this view in the case of singletons, see Caplan *et al.* (2010). For an early discussion, see Weingartner (1981).

13 The origins of non-wellfounded set theory date back to Scott (1960), Boffa (1968), and Forti and Honsell (1983). For a thorough introduction, see Barwise and Moss (1996).

Let us stress again that these are only *potential* counterexamples to A.7. Whether any such scenarios correspond to genuine metaphysical possibilities is by itself a controversial issue, as it depends on a number of controversial background questions concerning persistence through time, location in space, and the nature of such entities as sets, universals, abstract structures, or propositions. Yet this just goes to show that the acceptance of A.7 is not merely a matter of understanding the meaning of 'part', or 'proper part'; it reflects substantive metaphysical views. Indeed, as Donnelly (2011, p. 242) notes, in many cases those scenarios provide reasons to question the generality of many other claims that underlie the way we ordinarily talk, such as the claim that nothing can be *larger* than itself, or *next* to itself, or *older than* itself.[14] Such claims might be even more entrenched in common sense than the claim that nothing can be a *proper part* of itself. Yet this is hardly a reason to regard those scenarios as inconceivable. It simply shows that our ordinary talk does not take into account situations which, if possible, would be out of the ordinary.

So let us say that there *may* be uses of 'proper part' that violate the Irreflexivity axiom A.7. Such uses are in direct conflict with the definition of PP given in D.1, for that definition explicitly requires every proper part to be distinct from the whole. It is also in contrast with the alternative definition given in D.15 (Goodman's definition), since $\mathsf{PP}xx \wedge \neg \mathsf{PP}xx$ is a contradiction. But if PP is taken as a primitive—and we have seen that this is always an option—then there are no formal constraints, and one may consider departing from classical mereology already here, at the very start. That this can result in a coherent theory is shown by Cotnoir and Bacon (2012), whose "non-wellfounded mereology" dispenses with A.7 altogether thereby allowing for self-parts. More precisely, the theory in question dispenses with A.7 along with A.8, the Asymmetry axiom, keeping only the Transitivity axiom A.9. For the rest, the decomposition and composition axioms are exactly as in our axiomatization of classical mereology, i.e. A.4 (Remainder) and A.5 (Unrestricted Fusion).[15] The resulting axiom system is obviously consistent; and as it turns out, it is sound and complete with respect to a well-defined class of 'non-wellfounded algebras' that generalize in a natural way the complete Boolean algebras (minus zero) of classical mereology.[16]

---

14 Think e.g. of a time traveler meeting her younger self when she was a small child.

15 Equivalently, the theory can be axiomatized by taking A.9 along with A.18 and A.15. See Cotnoir and Bacon (2012, §3). See also Maffezioli (2016b) for a sequent-calculus axiomatization.

16 Specifically, the relevant non-wellfounded algebras can be defined as quintuples of the form $\langle A, \sqsubset, D, \leqslant, ' \rangle$, where $\langle D, \leqslant \rangle$ is a model of classical mereology (to be thought of as the well-founded portion of the algebra), A is any non-empty set including D, $'$ is a map from A into D such that $d' = d$ for every $d \in D$, and $\sqsubset$ is the irreflexive kernel of the relation $\{\langle x, y \rangle \in A \times A : x' \leqslant y'\}$. Note that when $A = D$, $'$ is just the identity map and the algebra reduces to a well-founded model of classical mereology.

It should not be surprising that allowing for self-parts requires dispensing, not only with A.7, but also with A.8. As already noted, the latter axiom implies the former by sheer logic, so one cannot give up Irreflexivity and still require PP to be asymmetric. But there may be other, independent reasons for questioning A.8, and such reasons would also lead to a non-wellfounded mereology. So let us turn to those, and to the parallel question of whether the antisymmetry of P, corresponding to A.2, may also be challenged.

3.2 ANTISYMMETRY AND ASYMMETRY

Though logically related, the Asymmetry axiom A.8 is in fact more controversial than A.7. And even though Rescher (1955, p. 10) thought the Antisymmetry axiom A.2 is "surely unobjectionable", it turns out to be more controversial than A.1. We shall start by considering a number of cases that appear to involve proper-parthood 'loops', as in figure 3.2.

Figure 3.2: A mereological loop

Models of this sort, where a and b are distinct objects, violate A.8 as well as A.2. Indeed, in the presence of Transitivity, a and b would count as self-parts, violating A.7 as well. Later we shall consider the possibility of mutual (symmetric) parthood relations even when A.7 and A.8 are both satisfied.

3.2.1 *Loops*

To begin with some of exotic cases, Sanford (1993) brings attention to the structure of Borges's Aleph:

> [I] saw the Aleph from everywhere at once, saw the earth in the Aleph, and the Aleph once more in the earth, and the earth in the Aleph... (Borges, 1945, pp. 283f)

As Sanford notes, Borges uses the 'in' of containment, but it seems fair to assume that whatever the Aleph contains is part of it. If so, then we seem to have a structure violating the asymmetry of proper parthood. The Aleph, a, contains everything as a part, including the earth; and the earth, b, contains the Aleph, since this sits on the cellar stairs in Beatriz Viterbo's house.

One immediate response, following van Inwagen (1993a), is that fictional examples of this sort do not constitute counterevidence to conceptual truths. This is contentious (see Parsons, 2013c). But even if Borges had been knowingly and intentionally writing fiction, other authors have offered similar examples in works that were clearly *not* intended as fiction. For instance, strikingly similar to Borges's example is a passage in the *Upanishads* that outlines the structural relations between Brahman and persons:

> In the center of the castle of Brahman, our own body, there is a small shrine in the form of a lotus-flower, and within can be found a small space ... This little space within the heart is as great as this vast universe. The heavens and earth are there, and the sun, and the moon, and the stars; fire and lightning and winds are there; and all that now is and all that is not; for the whole universe is in Him and He dwells within our heart. (*Chandogya Upanishad*, §8.1, in Mascaró, 1965, p. 120)

Jones (2009, 2010) and Priest (2014b, ch. 11; 2015) suggest the same could be said of the 'Net of Indra' of the Huayan school of Chinese Buddhism, based on the *Avataṃsaka Sūtra*—a net of jewels that stretches infinitely in every direction, but in which each jewel is contained in every other, symbolizing the interconnectedness of the universe. And in Christian theology, too, there are models that follow the same pattern, mainly inspired by the Gospel of John: "I am in the Father, and the Father in Me" (14:10). For example, according to the doctrine of perichoresis,

> [T]hese Beings can reciprocally contain One Another, so that One should permanently envelope, and also be permanently enveloped by, the Other, whom yet He envelopes. (Hilary of Poitiers, *De Trinitate*, III, 1, in Schaff and Wace, 1899, p. 62).

Such structures "seem to contradict the laws of the universe", as Hilary himself admits; yet they can hardly be dismissed as mere Borgesian fiction. Philosophically, their conceivability and metaphysical possibility appear to be a substantive question that raises genuine challenges to the antisymmetry of parthood (Cotnoir, 2017; Molto, 2018).

In recent philosophical literature, a structurally similar example has been put forward by Chris Tillman and Gregory Fowler.

> Suppose that the universe exists ... a thing such that absolutely everything is a part of it ... Assuming there is a unique such thing, let's name it U. According to a popular view of semantic content, 'U exists' semantically encodes a singular, structured proposition that has U itself as a constituent as well as the property of existing. By hypothesis, this proposition is a proper part of U. But U is in turn a proper part of the relevant proposition. (Tillman and Fowler, 2012, p. 525)

Tillman and Fowler take this as evidence that proper parthood cannot be asymmetric (and hence that parthood cannot be antisymmetric), a point made also by Yablo (2016, p. 143). Of course, such evidence relies on crucial assumptions, not least of which is the assumption that the constituents of propositions are parts of those propositions. Yet again this appears to be a thesis that cannot be rejected merely by appealing to the ordinary meaning of 'part'. Gilmore (2014), for instance, defends it at length.

It is worth highlighting that this sort of case need not involve the existence of a universal fusion. For example, suppose that each of the following sentences expresses a proposition.[17]

(1) The proposition expressed by (2) is true.
(2) The proposition expressed by (1) is contingent.

Then it would seem that the proposition expressed by (1) is a constituent of—and hence a part of—the proposition expressed by (2), and vice versa. And since the two propositions are distinct, it would follow that they are mutual parts.[18]

For a last example, we look again to the literature on time travel. Consider a case from Kleinschmidt (2011). Clifford is a dog statue which was made partly of other, smaller statues, including Kibble. But Kibble, too, has statue parts, including a time-traveling future version of Clifford itself, suitably reduced in size. As a result, it would seem as though Kibble is a proper part of Clifford that has Clifford as a proper part.

3.2.2 *Irregular Parts*

All of the above are purported examples of proper-parthood loops that would provide straightforward reasons for rejecting the Asymmetry axiom A.8 in theories where PP is taken as primitive, paving the way to a non-wellfounded mereology. If we are in a system where the primitive mereological concept is P, and if we wish to dispense with the Antisymmetry axiom A.2, the picture is somewhat more complex. In particular, the tight connection between parthood and proper parthood may break down.

To see this, recall our two definitions of 'proper part' from chapter 2, namely D.1 and D.15.

(D.1) $PP_1xy := Pxy \wedge \neg x = y$ *Proper Parthood 1*
(D.15) $PP_2xy := Pxy \wedge \neg Pyx$ *Proper Parthood 2*

(The subscripts are added here for convenient reference.) While most authors use D.1, others have relied on the identity-free version in D.15, following Goodman (1951) and Eberle (1970).[19] In classical mereology the choice is

17 As with (p) above, the existence of such propositions is central to the solution of the liar paradox offered by Barwise and Etchemendy (1987).

18 A similar case is discussed in Merricks (2015, pp. 166f), though as a *reductio*, given A.2, of the view that the entities a proposition is directly about should be counted among its parts.

19 Examples include Simons (1991a, p. 286; 2017a, p. 268), Casati and Varzi (1999, p. 36), Niebergall (2009a, p. 338; 2011, p. 274), Calosi (2011, p. 32), Valore (2016, p. 37). Some authors refer to PP_2 as "strict parthood" (Parsons, 2013b, §3.1; Vakarelov, 2015, p. 271; Varzi, 2016, §2.2), "non-mutual parthood" (Parsons, 2014, p. 7), or "asymmetric parthood" (Kleinschmidt, 2017, §1).

immaterial, as the two definitions amount to the same. However, they are not *logically* equivalent, and their equivalence in classical mereology depends crucially on the assumption that P is antisymmetric. More precisely, PP_2 logically entails PP_1, at least as long as identity behaves classically:

(T.7) $\forall x \forall y(PP_2xy \rightarrow PP_1xy)$ PP–*Strength*

This is because Pxy and $\neg Pyx$ jointly imply $\neg x = y$ by Leibniz's law. However, the converse entailment requires A.2. The model given in figure 3.2 shows why: if a and b are mutual parts, then we have it that PP_1ab but not PP_2ab (and PP_1ba but not PP_2ba). Thus, failures of A.2 generate PP_1 loops, but *not* PP_2 loops.

To put it differently, D.15 rules out proper-parthood loops by definition, whereas D.1 does not. Those who find such loops conceivable may therefore wish to stick to the D.1 definition. However, D.1 itself is less than ideal; in the presence of mutual parts, such as a and b, we have PP_1ab and PP_1ba but not PP_1aa (unless $a \neq a$). Hence, absent A.2, in classical logic PP_1 fails to be transitive even when P is transitive. By contrast, PP_2 is sure to be transitive as long as P is, since A.3 will always yield Pxz from Pxy and Pyz, and $\neg Pzx$ from Pxy and $\neg Pzy$.

These remarks bring out what will be a recurring theme: definitions that are equivalent in classical mereology may fail to be so in other, weaker theories. When considering non-classical axiom systems, one should therefore pay careful attention to definitional matters. There may be formal or philosophical reasons to think that one definition better expresses an intuitive mereological concept than others, but those reasons may depend crucially on what axioms are in play. If one wants to allow for mutual parts, but thinks that proper parthood is transitive, as per A.9, then the way forward is to use D.15 (Cotnoir, 2010). On the other hand, suppose one wants to model proper-parthood loops; then one must either accept D.1 and the corresponding failures of Transitivity (as do Tillman and Fowler, 2012) or else treat PP as primitive (as do Cotnoir and Bacon, 2012). The last strategy is the only option also in case one wishes to develop a non-wellfounded mereology that allows for mutual parts *and* self-parts, for we have seen that both D.1 and D.15 entail Irreflexivity by definition.

In fact the picture is even more delicate. We have it that failures of A.8 by two or more objects (proper-parthood loops) result in failures of A.2 (mutual parts), whereas the converse holds just in case proper parthood is defined as PP_1 or treated as primitive. However, with PP as primitive, the latter claim is true only insomuch as P is defined classically as in D.12, so that Pxy if and only if $PPxy \vee x = y$. That is not the only possibility. And, again, a different definition would deliver a different result.

The main suggestion comes from Simons (1987, p. 112). Consider the binary relation introduced by the following definition.

(D.25) $Ixy :\equiv \forall z(PPzx \rightarrow PPzy)$ *Inclosure*

Clearly, this relation would not by itself be a good candidate for parthood, since Ixy holds vacuously whenever x has no proper parts. Yet one may plausibly rely on inclosure in the case of composite objects, and Simons invites us to compare the standard definition in D.12 with the alternative in D.26.

(D.12) $P_1xy := PPxy \vee x = y$ *Parthood 1*

(D.26) $P_2xy :\equiv (\exists zPPzx \rightarrow Ixy) \wedge (\neg\exists zPPzx \rightarrow (PPxy \vee x = y))$ *Parthood 2*

(Again, we add subscripts for convenient reference.) In classical mereology, the two definitions coincide, confirming the adequacy of D.26. In weaker contexts, however, P_1 and P_2 may come apart. In particular, while the inference from P_1 to P_2 requires only the Transitivity of PP,[20] the converse may fail even when PP obeys all the ordering axioms. The model in figure 3.3 is a case in point. It satisfies each of A.7–A.9 along with P_2ab, yet P_1ab is false.

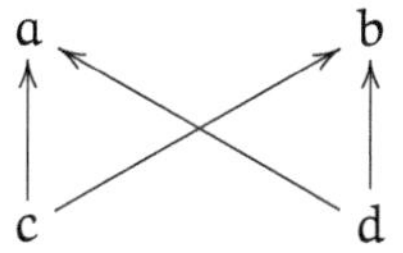

Figure 3.3: Parthood 2 without parthood 1

Now, precisely this model shows also the fact we alluded to, namely, that one can take PP as primitive and define the parthood relation so as to allow for mutual parts even without proper-parthood loops. For along with P_2ab we have P_2ba even though $a \neq b$. To put it differently, the model shows that the following classical principle may fail when P is understood as P_2.

(T.8) $\forall x\forall y(Pxy \rightarrow (PPxy \vee x = y))$ *Regularity*

An object may have parts other than itself that are not proper parts. This is exactly parallel to what may happen if we take P as primitive and define proper parthood as PP_2. Following Null (1995, 1997), let us call such parts *irregular*. Then the point is that, either way, irregular parts may result in failures of A.2 (Antisymmetry) even in the presence of A.8 (Asymmetry).[21]

20 Given A.9, the definiens of D.26 is equivalent to the disjunction $PP_1xy \vee (\exists zPPzx \wedge Ixy)$.
21 Rea (2010) makes the same point. See also Molto (2018, pp. 410ff). Null himself offers a full analysis of irregular parthood in the context of a mereology based on PP with Transitivity and Weak Supplementation (hence Asymmetry) as axioms, though without composition principles.

3.2.3 *Mutual Parts and Extensionality*

As in the case of self-parts, mereological loops and irregular parts may strike us as pure exotica, as the result of odd thought experiments or conceptual wizardry that any mature metaphysics should discard. Ordinary objects, one might think, are surely not structured like that. As it turns out, however, controversy surrounding the antisymmetry of parthood is not restricted to exotica but concerns everyday objects as well.

Returning, for instance, to Chrysippus's case of Dion and his footless proper part Theon, recall that one of the popular solutions among contemporary philosophers is to assert that both survive the amputation of Dion's foot. We said that this requires rejecting the original assumption that two entities cannot occupy "the same space jointly", following Wiggins (1968). But if both Dion and Theon survive, then after the amputation they coincide in every respect, not only spatially but also mereologically. Each will have exactly the same proper parts as the other. And just as Theon will continue to be a part of Dion, one might say that after the amputation Dion becomes a part of Theon as well. Short of saying that two things can become one, which few philosophers would be willing to concede,[22] this would mean that Dion and Theon survive as mutual parts.

A similar scenario arises in connection with the problem of material constitution. Consider a statue and the amount of matter (clay, marble, etc.) out of which it is shaped; one thing or two? Several philosophers would count at least two things, on account of the fact that the statue and the amount of matter appear to have different properties. For instance, already Mnesarchus of Athens (another Stoic philosopher) argued that such things have different persistence conditions.

> That what concerns the peculiarly qualified [thing] is not the same as what concerns [its constituent] substance, Mnesarchus says is clear. For things which are the same should have the same properties. For if, for the sake of argument, someone were to mould a horse, squash it, then make a dog, it would be reasonable for us on seeing this to say that this previously did not exist but now does exist. So what is said when it comes to the qualified thing is different. (Stobaeus, *Anthology* I, 179, 6–12; in Long and Sedley, 1987, p. 168)

The idea, here, is that the amount of matter (constituent substance) remains the same even though different statues (qualified things) can be shaped out of it.[23] Those who share this view may in turn consider whether a statue and

22 Notable exceptions include Myro (1986), Gallois (1998), and Allen (2000). Cf. also Moyer (2006).

23 Variants of this line of reasoning involve claiming that the amount of matter, but not a statue, *can* survive squashing; that a statue is in a certain *style* (e.g. Romanesque) whereas the corresponding amount of matter is not; that a statue has certain *legal* properties (e.g. is insured) that

the corresponding amount of matter are mereologically related. Some think they only share the same constituents at some level of decomposition, say, material atoms (Burke, 1992; Doepke, 1996; Baker, 2000); others, following Aristotle,[24] hold that the whole amount of matter is part of the statue, though not vice versa (Fine, 1982; Haslanger, 1994; Rea, 1998b; Koslicki, 2008; Lowe, 2013); and, finally, some hold that parthood goes both ways, so that the statue and its matter, though distinct and asymmetrically related in terms of constitution, are part of each other (Thomson, 1983, 1998).[25] If the latter position is accepted, then we have a perfectly ordinary, non-exotic case of mutual parthood of the sort depicted in figure 3.2.

It is not our concern here to assess the validity of these purported counterexamples to A.2 (and of others that could be constructed along similar lines).[26] As with the other cases considered so far, these too rest on contentious philosophical assumptions, beginning with the idea that two things can be in the same place at the same time, so their tenability is an open question.[27] Yet precisely this is the point one might want to push: even without resorting to exotic scenarios of dubious legitimacy, the thought that the Antisymmetry axiom A.2 expresses a simple conceptual truth appears to be unwarranted; the axiom calls for explicit philosophical defense.

These last examples also help to bring out an important aspect of Antisymmetry that might easily be overlooked. For if Dion and Theon turn out to be mutual parts, or if this is true of a statue and the corresponding amount of matter, then the entities in question are not just part of each other; as long as parthood is transitive, they have *all* their parts in common. All additional parts of a (Dion, the statue) will be parts of b (Theon, the amount of matter) and *vice versa*. More generally, and schematically, this means that whenever a and b are composite objects with further proper parts, in the presence of the Transitivity axiom A.3 the model of figure 3.2

the matter lacks; etc. See e.g. Yablo (1987), Johnston (1992), and Fine (2003). For an overview of such arguments, and relevant references, see Paul (2010), Magidor (2011), Blatti (2012), and Wasserman (2018a).

24 See the fourth sense of 'part' in the taxonomy of the *Metaphysics* cited in section 1.3.

25 See also Sider (2001, p. 155) for an argument to the effect that *if* the statue and its matter share the same ultimate constituents, as most constitution theorists think, then they must be mutual parts. The argument uses the Strong Supplementation principle A.18, which we shall discuss at some length in chapter 4. We shall come back to the relation between Antisymmetry and Supplementation principles in sections 4.2 and 4.3.

26 Consider, for instance, the classic problem of the relationship between actions and bodily movements, such as raising one's arm and one's arm's rising. Here, too, it is common to argue that there are two coinciding events, distinguished by virtue of their having different properties, and again the relevant mereology may lead to violations of A.2. For some discussion, see Goldman (1970), Thomson (1977), Pfeifer (1980), Bennett (1988, ch. 10), Ruben (1999), and Allen (2005) (who actually holds that an event may be identical with one of its proper parts).

27 For the record, one of us is more sympathetic to the counterexamples in question than the other; see Cotnoir (2010, 2016a) vs. Varzi (2000a, 2008), respectively.

expands to models of the sort illustrated in figure 3.4 (where, for simplicity, we suppose the additional proper parts to be just two atoms, c and d).

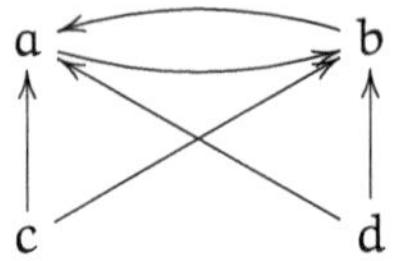

Figure 3.4: Mereological loop for composite objects

This is also the picture we get from figure 3.3 if we read the arrows as expressing parthood in the sense of P_2. And pretty clearly, models like this are not just symmetric; they also show that non-identical mutual parts would be, in an important sense, mereologically indiscernible.

Now, the idea that non-identity calls for some degree of mereological differentiation—that two things cannot have exactly the same compositional makeup—is a major tenet of classical mereology. Specifically, we saw in section 2.1.2 that the following Extensionality thesis is a consequence of the Remainder axiom A.4.

(T.1) $\forall x(\exists w PPwx \rightarrow \forall y(\forall z(PPzx \leftrightarrow PPzy) \rightarrow x = y))$ PP–*Extensionality*

This is the standard way of expressing the tenet in question, and indeed we shall have more to say about this consequence of A.4 in section 4.2. But what emerges from the above considerations is that the extensional character of classical mereology is already present—and crucially—in the Antisymmetry axiom A.2. Not only did the proof of T.1 from A.4 depend on A.2. More importantly, T.1 itself is *not* in conflict with the model of figure 3.4. For T.1 says that composite objects with the same *proper* parts must be identical; but with P taken as a primitive, and PP defined as in D.1 (i.e. as PP_1), the two objects a and b in the model do not have the same proper parts, since we have PPab but not PPaa, and PPba but not PPbb.[28] It is only through an explicit appeal to A.2 that the model in question can be ruled out. (With PP treated as a primitive, the picture is only slightly different. In that case PP can be transitive, and this would suffice to render the structure in figure 3.4 incompatible with T.1. Yet again T.1 itself would not follow from A.4 unless PP is also assumed to be asymmetric or P defined standardly as in D.12. Two cases in point are the system of non-wellfounded mereology of Cotnoir and Bacon, 2012, whose theorems do not include T.1 even though A.4 is one of the axioms, and the theory of irregular parts of Null, 1995, 1997.[29])

28 Remember that, absent A.2, PP_1 is not transitive even if P is.

29 Null's theory does not include A.4, but it is easy to verify that the entailment does not hold if P is defined as in D.26, i.e. as P_2. The model in figure 3.3 is already a counterexample.

This connection between Antisymmetry and extensionality can be made more precise. Consider the following three theses, each of which is also a theorem of classical mereology.

(T.9) $\forall x \forall y(\forall z(Pzx \leftrightarrow Pzy) \rightarrow x = y)$ P–*Extensionality*

(T.10) $\forall x \forall y(\forall z(Ozx \leftrightarrow Ozy) \rightarrow x = y)$ O–*Extensionality*

(T.11) $\forall x \forall y(\forall z(Dzx \leftrightarrow Dzy) \rightarrow x = y)$ D–*Extensionality*

The first of these theses is the natural counterpart of T.1 for the parthood relation (proper or improper),[30] and we know that it fails in the model of figure 3.4. It is, therefore, closely related to the Antisymmetry axiom A.2. But there is more; for in the presence of the other ordering axioms, T.9 turns out to be *equivalent* to A.2. This is because Transitivity ensures the implication from $Pxy \wedge Pyx$ to $\forall z(Pzx \leftrightarrow Pzy)$ (as we have seen) while Reflexivity ensures the converse implication. Thus, there is an important sense in which the Antisymmetry axiom A.2 *just is* the P–Extensionality thesis T.9.[31] And this is true regardless of whether P itself is treated as primitive or defined in terms of PP. The other two theses, T.10 and T.11, are generally stronger, as can be seen from the fact that they also rule out the earlier model in figure 3.3. (T.9 has that effect only when P is defined as P_2.) Yet, again, we know that T.10 is logically equivalent to A.2 if P is defined in terms of O (D.14), as in the axiom system of Goodman (1951) presented in section 2.4.2. Similarly, T.11 is equivalent to A.2 if P is defined in terms of D (D.17), as in the system of Leonard and Goodman (1940). So there is a clear sense in which these extensionality theses, too, express the same fundamental intuition as Antisymmetry. From the perspective of classical mereology, exchanging A.2 for any one of T.9, T.10, or T.11 would make no difference whatsoever.[32]

The extensional import of Antisymmetry can also be appreciated by direct comparison with the extensionality axiom of set theory. Consider Zermelo's classic formulation:[33]

> If every element of a set M is also an element of N and vice versa, if, therefore, both $M \subseteq N$ and $N \subseteq M$, then always $M = N$; or, more briefly: Every set is determined by its elements. (Zermelo, 1908, §1.4)

30 Never mind the extra condition in the antecedent of T.1; that is just to allow the possibility that there is more than one mereological atom, for obviously all atoms have the same proper parts, viz. none.

31 Simons (2017a, p. 268) actually refers to A.2 as "Extensionality".

32 It is telling that while Leonard and Goodman (1940) adopted A.2 as an axiom rather than T.11, Goodman (1951) decided to trade A.2 for T.10, i.e. A.14.

33 Zermelo's nomenclature was "Axiom of Determinateness" (*Axiom der Bestimmtheit*); the familiar terminology, Axiom of Extensionality, only entered common usage in the 1930s, mostly through Carnap (1934, p. 98) and Quine (1936, p. 45).

Assuming the domain is restricted to sets, this is usually put in terms of a general condition on the membership relation $\in$.[34]

$$\forall x \forall y (\forall z (z \in x \leftrightarrow z \in y) \rightarrow x = y) \tag{3.1}$$ *$\in$–Extensionality*

Yet Zermelo's formulation makes it clear that the axiom could equally be taken to assert the antisymmetry of the subset relation $\subseteq$.

$$\forall x \forall y ((x \subseteq y \wedge y \subseteq x) \rightarrow x = y) \tag{3.2}$$ *$\subseteq$–Antisymmetry*

So, here the intimate tie between extensionality and antisymmetry is literally 'built into' the relevant notions of set membership and inclusion. Having the same constituents (members) just is being mutual parts (subsets).

Now, that sets are extensional entities in this sense is hardly controversial. Although non-classical set theories that do away with extensionality have occasionally been considered,[35] most authors agree in regarding 3.1 and 3.2 as encoding a defining characteristic of sets, indeed as constitutive of the very meaning of 'set'. Here, for instance, is a clear statement by George Boolos:

> One might be tempted to call the axiom of extensionality 'analytic', true by virtue of the meanings of the words contained in it ... A theory that did not affirm that the objects with which it dealt were identical if they had the same members would only by charity be called a theory of *sets* alone. (Boolos, 1971, pp. 229–230)

The same view is echoed repeatedly in the philosophical literature on axiomatic set theory, from Wang (1974, p. 184) to Maddy (1988, pp. 483f) to John Burgess:

> While extensionality may not be an utter triviality, it is still in a sense less a substantive assumption than a partial explication of the concept of set. It would be inappropriate to use the word 'set', rather than 'whole' or 'property' or whatever, for a concept of which extensionality was not a feature. (Burgess, 2004, p. 199)

However, this is because sets are meant to be entities of a certain kind, entities which, as Quine (1973, p. 103) once put it, have expressly been introduced as the "extensional distillates" of intensional entities such as properties or concepts. Mereology is not like that; it is not about entities of a certain kind. Whether or not one agrees with Husserl's formal ontological conception, mereology is meant to be a general theory of parthood relations. And

34 If the domain is not restricted to sets, allowing for so-called *urelements* (as in Zermelo's theory), then the axiom must be explicitly restricted in a way similar to T.1:

$$\forall x (\exists w\, w \in x \rightarrow \forall y (\forall z (z \in x \leftrightarrow z \in y) \rightarrow x = y))$$

35 For instance, in the context of constructive mathematics (Friedman, 1973; Beeson, 1979, 1985, §VIII.2), partial set theory (Gilmore, 1974), or fuzzy logic (Hájek and Haniková, 2003).

as a general theory, its commitment to extensionality pertains to entities of *any* kind. Do x and y have the same parts? Identical. Do they overlap the same things? Identical. Are they disjoint from the same things? Identical. The claims that come with T.9–T.11 are obviously more ambitious and contentious than the extensionality principle of set theory. After all, given that identicals are indiscernible, each claim implies that things that are mereologically indiscernible in one way or other are indiscernible *tout court*. For many a philosopher, this is simply beyond the pale. And at least in the case of T.9 (P–Extensionality), such misgivings translate directly into misgivings about the Antisymmetry axiom A.2.

As mentioned, we shall have more to say about mereological extensionality in chapter 4. For now, the bottom line is that much of the philosophical debate surrounding such matters is importantly tied up with A.2, whose status is therefore open to questioning independently of the exotic properparthood loops with which we began. On the other hand, it is also worth noting that the friends of mereological extensionality may turn the above considerations to their advantage. For it follows that A.2 could be turned into a *definition* of the identity predicate, which could therefore be dispensed with as a separate primitive.[36]

(D.27) $x = y :\equiv Pxy \wedge Pyx$ *Identity*

To ensure standard identity behavior, one would just need to add the following axiom schema for Leibniz's law.

(A.27) $\forall x \forall y((Pxy \wedge Pyx) \rightarrow (\varphi \rightarrow \varphi(^{x}_{y})))$ *Indiscernibility*

Several authors (from Goodman, 1951, ch. 5 to Smid, 2017b) take this to afford significant ideological parsimony, if not to show that the parthood relation is "logically more primary" than identity (Sharvy, 1983, p. 234).[37] Others (from Johnston, 1992, §2 to Sider, 2013, fn. 14) disagree. What is clear is that this route embraces the full consequences of extensionality. It should, therefore, be affirmed or denied on the basis of serious philosophical reflection. Moreover, given D.27, the reflexivity of identity would depend on the reflexivity of P itself, i.e. A.1, which would therefore require independent philosophical defense.

36 See Leonard and Goodman (1940), fn. 6. This is actually how Goodman (1951) proceeds, though based on T.10 rather than A.2; see, chapter 2, note 53. The same option is available in set theory when it comes to identity restricted to sets; see Fraenkel (1927) and the discussion in Fraenkel and Bar-Hillel (1958, §II.2) and Quine (1963, ch. II).

37 See also Armstrong (1997, §2.32), who holds that identity may be regarded as a limit case of the more general notion of "partial identity" afforded by parthood and overlap, and that mereology may therefore be thought of as "an extended logic of identity" (an idea to be found already in Armstrong, 1978, §15.2).

3.3 TRANSITIVITY

The third and last ordering axiom is Transitivity, A.3, whose counterpart for proper parthood is A.9. In classical mereology these two principles are equivalent, the equivalence itself reflecting the relationship between any partial order and the corresponding strict order. Generally speaking, however, we have seen that the relationship between P and PP may vary depending on whether these predicates behave antisymmetrically and asymmetrically, respectively, so we need to be more specific. The exact picture is as follows.

- If P is taken as primitive and PP defined as in D.1 (= PP_1), then: (i) A.9 implies A.3, but (ii) A.3 implies A.9 if and only if P is antisymmetric.[38]
- If P is taken as primitive and PP defined as in D.15 (= PP_2), then: (i) A.3 implies A.9, but (ii) A.9 implies A.3 if and only if P is antisymmetric.[39]
- If PP is taken as primitive and P defined as in D.12 (= P_1), then: (i) A.9 implies A.3, but (ii) A.3 implies A.9 if and only if PP is asymmetric.[40]
- If PP is taken as primitive and P defined as in D.26 (= P_2), then: (i) A.9 implies A.3, but (ii) A.3 does not imply A.9 even if PP is asymmetric.[41]

---

38 For (i), pick arbitrary a, b, c and suppose that Pab and Pbc. If either $a = b$ or $b = c$, then we immediately get Pac by substitution. On the other hand, if neither $a = b$ nor $b = c$, then we have PP_1ab and PP_1bc by D.1, hence PP_1ac by A.9, and hence Pac (again by D.1). For (ii), suppose first that P is antisymmetric. Pick arbitrary a, b, c such that PP_1ab and PP_1bc. Then we also have Pab and Pbc by D.1, and hence Pac by A.3. Moreover, we must have $a \neq c$, for otherwise Pab would amount to Pcb, which together with Pbc would imply $b = c$ by A.2, contradicting PP_1bc. Thus PP_1ac by D.1. Conversely, suppose P is not antisymmetric. Then we know that the P-reflexive closure of the model in figure 3.2 satisfies A.3 but not A.9, since it verifies both PP_1ab and PP_1ba but not PP_1aa (by D.1).

39 For (i), we have already hinted at the proof in section 3.2.1. Pick arbitrary a, b, c and suppose that PP_2ab and PP_2bc. Then we also have Pab and Pbc by D.15, and hence Pac by A.3. Moreover, we must have $\neg Pca$, otherwise A.3 would imply Pcb (from Pab), which together with Pbc would contradict PP_2bc. Thus PP_2ac. For (ii), suppose first that P is antisymmetric. Pick a, b, c so that Pab and Pbc. If neither Pba nor Pcb, then we have PP_2ab and PP_2bc by D.15, hence PP_2ac by A.9, and thus Pac (again by D.15). On the other hand, if either Pba or Pcb, then we have either $a = b$ or $b = c$ by A.2, and in each case it follows immediately that Pac by substitution. Conversely, suppose P is not antisymmetric. Then the model in figure 3.2, with Pab and Pba but neither Paa nor Pbb, satisfies A.9 (vacuously) but not A.3.

40 The proof of (i) parallels the corresponding case for PP_1 in note 38, with D.12 in place of D.1. For (ii), suppose first that PP is asymmetric. Pick arbitrary a, b, c such that $PPab$ and $PPbc$. Then we also have P_1ab and P_1bc by D.12, hence P_1ac by A.3, and hence $PPac \vee a = c$ (again by D.12). But $a = c$ is impossible, otherwise $PPab$ would amount to $PPcb$, which together with $PPbc$ would contradict A.8. Thus, $PPac$. Conversely, suppose PP is not asymmetric. Then the model in figure 3.2, with $PPab$ and $PPba$ but neither $PPaa$ nor $PPbb$, satisfies A.3 (since the reflexivity of identity implies P_1aa and P_1bb by D.12) but not A.9.

41 For a proof of (i), see Null (1997, thm. 22). Concerning (ii), note that whenever $PPab$ and $PPbc$ with $\neg PPac$, D.26 gives us $\neg P_2bc$, so A.9 fails but the relevant instance of A.3 is vacuously satisfied. On the other hand, if we had P_2bc, then $PPac$ would follow automatically from D.26, regardless of A.3.

The subtle connection between the Transitivity axioms and the axioms of Antisymmetry for P and Asymmetry for PP goes also in the opposite direction. For if either A.3 or A.9 fails to hold, then A.2 and A.8 may not suffice to do all the work they are intended to do. Intuitively, the latter axioms are not only meant to rule out cases of immediate mutual parthood and proper self-parthood of the sort illustrated in figures 3.2 and 3.1; they are meant to rule out mereological loops or 'cycles' of any length, including patterns such as that in figure 3.5.

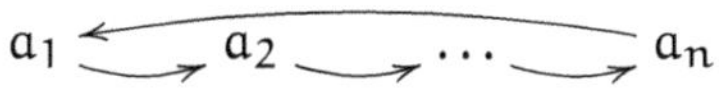

Figure 3.5: A cyclic model

(A simple case in point, generalizing from one of the examples of section 3.2.1, would be a sequence of structured propositions, each of which says something about its predecessor, starting with a proposition that says something about the proposition that happens to come at the end.) Absent A.3 and A.9, models such as this would be perfectly acceptable even in the presence of A.2 and A.8. To rule them out, these axioms would therefore have to be strengthened. For instance, one could replace A.2 and A.8 with the following axiom schemas, where n is any natural number and P^n is defined recursively by setting $P^0xy :\equiv Pxy$ and $P^{k+1}xy :\equiv \exists z(P^kxz \wedge Pzy)$. Similarly for PP^n.

(A.28) $\forall x \forall y((P^nxy \wedge Pyx) \to x = y)$ *Anticyclicity*

(A.29) $\forall x \forall y(PP^nxy \to \neg PPyx)$ *Acyclicity*

This amounts to requiring that the *transitive closures* of P and PP be antisymmetric and asymmetric, respectively. The notion of transitive closure is not first-order definable, so one cannot express these requirements by means of individual axioms. As axiom schemas, however, A.28 and A.29 would do.

Now, are there any reasons to suppose that A.3 or A.9 may actually fail, over and above those already seen in connection with putative failures of Antisymmetry and Asymmetry? In a way, both forms of transitivity are among the oldest and most fundamental principles considered in the context of part-whole theorizing, as we saw in the brief historical survey of chapter 1. Yet we also saw that transitivity is potentially problematic, witness the complications raised by Aristotle's metaphysics of genus and differentia. It is also among the most widely criticized aspects of mereology in contemporary literature, often based on intuitions that do not depend on any sophisticated metaphysics. So let us finally turn to these intuitions, and to the further issues that failures of transitivity would raise.

3.3.1 *Distinguished Parts*

One general sort of worry has been voiced repeatedly by authors concerned with the ordinary use of 'part' in natural language. Already Rescher (1955), for instance, complained that the word is often used non-transitively.

> In military usage, persons can be parts of small units, and small units parts of larger ones; but persons are never parts of large units. Other examples are given by the various hierarchical uses of 'part'. A part (i.e. biological subunit) of a cell is not said to be a part of the organ of which that cell is a part. (Rescher, 1955, p. 10)

Examples would also include: (i) a handle can be part of a door and the door of a house, but we do not say that the parts of a house include handles (Lyons, 1977, p. 312); (ii) the eye is usually regarded as part of the face and the retina as part of the eye, yet the retina is not part of the face (Fiorini *et al.*, 2014, p. 137); (iii) Sonia's fingers are part of Sonia and Sonia is part of the team, yet the fingers themselves are not part of the team (Winston *et al.*, 1987, p. 431); (iv) Mark's father was part of the Normandy Invasion, and his liver and earlobes were parts of him, but none of these parts was part of the Normandy Invasion (Johnston, 2002, p. 143; 2005, p. 646).

Authors who find such examples convincing have offered various accounts of the underlying phenomena. For example, it has been suggested that 'part' is context-sensitive (Cruse, 1979), or that transitivity only holds relative to certain conditions (Moltmann, 1997), or that there really are several meronymic relations, only some of which are transitive (Iris *et al.*, 1988) if not all (van Inwagen, 2007), or again that each such relation can be meaningfully (and transitively) predicated only relative to entities of a restricted sort, such as masses and quantities but not, say, living organisms or hierarchical group structures (Odell, 1994).[42] Alternatively, some authors have argued that precisely because parthood is transitive, the examples in question—or some of them—are indicative of the fact that the relevant relation is not strictly mereological. For instance, Schmitt (2003a, p. 5), Uzquiano (2004, pp. 136f), and Effingham (2010b, p. 255) all read the failure of transitivity in case (iii) as a *reductio* of the very idea that the group-membership relation is a genuine case of parthood.[43] One way or other, all these views

42 The last point goes back to Bolzano (1837, §83.2). For further examples and proposals, see Sanford (1993), Gerstl and Pribbenow (1995), Hossack (2000), Johansson (2004), Ghiselin (2007), Keet and Artale (2008), Guizzardi (2009), Herre (2010), and Seibt (2015, 2017), among others.

43 This is a particularly vexed case. The view that teams and other groups are mereological wholes has a long pedigree, from Oppenheim and Putnam (1958) to Quinton (1976), Mellor (1982), Copp (1984), or Martin (1988). See Hawley (2017) and Strohmaier (2018) for recent defenses. On the other hand, a growing number of authors prefer to see group membership as a *sui generis* relation; besides the titles cited in the text, see e.g. Simons (1980), Ruben (1983, 1985), Gilbert (1989), Meixner (1997), Sheehy (2006a,b), Ritchie (2013), Epstein (2015), and Uzquiano (2018b).

have important ramifications, formally and philosophically. Among other things, they would once again be detrimental to the claim that the parthood relation modeled by classical mereology is governed by purely formal and domain-independent ontological laws, as opposed to principles that reflect substantive views about the multiplex make-up of the world.

There is, however, a standard way of resisting such conclusions on behalf of classical mereology. Peter Simons puts it thus:

> In each of these cases, non-transitivity arises by narrowing or specifying some basic broad part-relation, the specifications introducing concepts themselves extrinsic to part–whole theory, such as function, causal contribution, and lines of command. The existence of such examples does not in any way entail that there are not more basic senses of 'part' which are transitive. (Simons, 1987, p. 108)

In other words, just as in ordinary discourse we do not distinguish between 'part' and 'proper part', so we generally do not distinguish between 'part' and several other, more specific senses in which something can be a mereological constituent of something else—and this can interfere with our judgements. With reference to Rescher's example, if a cell's nucleus is not said to be a part of the organ of which that cell is part, it is because the nucleus does not count as a *biological* part of the organ. Yet this is not to say that the nucleus is not part of the organ at all. On the contrary, it has all those features a genuine part is supposed to have: it contributes to the mass of the organ, it occupies part of the space occupied by the organ, it gets annihilated if the organ is annihilated, and if something happens to it, then the organ itself is affected by the change (albeit insignificantly). Similarly, if there is a sense of 'part' in which a door handle is not part of the house to which it belongs, or the retina not part of the face, it is a restricted sense: the handle is not a *functional* part of the house, though it is a functional part of the door and the door a functional part of the house; the retina is not a *salient* part of the face, though it is a salient part of the eye and the eye a salient part of the face; and so on. It is obvious that if the interpretation of 'part' is narrowed by some additional condition φ, requiring that the parts make a functional, salient, or otherwise special contribution to the whole, then transitivity may fail. In general, if x is a φ-part of y and y is a φ-part of z, x need not be a φ-part of z: the condition expressed by 'φ' may not distribute over parthood. But that would only show the non-transitivity of 'φ-part', not of 'part', regardless of whether 'φ' is explicitly mentioned in our statements. (It may also be that different narrowing conditions are operating within the same context. The liver is an anatomic part of the soldier, who is a military part of the Army. The anatomic and military languages do not recognize any relationship between liver and Army; yet this is no denial that "ontologically", as Ghiselin, 1997, p. 41 puts it, the one is part of the other.)

This line of response has its dissenters. For instance, Ingvar Johansson protests that it would give rise to an "odd subsumption relation":[44]

> What is true of 'red' is necessarily also true of the 'light red' which it subsumes, what is true of 'running' is necessarily also true of 'running quickly', and what is true of 'x is part of y' ought necessarily [to] be true of 'x is a φ-part of y'. Since 'x is part of y' is transitive, 'x is a φ-part of y' ought to be so as well. (Johansson, 2004, p. 165, notation adapted)

As it stands, however, this rebuttal trades on an ambiguity. We can fairly speak of subsumption if 'φ-part' is understood as involving a qualification acting solely on the subject term, so that a φ-part is just a part that is φ.[45]

(D.28) $P_{\varphi}xy :\equiv Pxy \wedge \varphi x$ *φ–Parthood 1*

This is certainly a legitimate notion, and in some cases it corresponds precisely to the way in which we qualify the parts we are interested in. When we talk about the red parts of a thing, for instance, we are talking about parts that are red. There is no question that this way of 'narrowing' the relevant parthood relation would leave the transitivity issue intact, since the monadic condition φ would go through holus-bolus. In other words, the following thesis would be tautologically equivalent to A.3.

(T.12) $\forall x \forall y \forall z((P_{\varphi}xy \wedge P_{\varphi}yz) \rightarrow P_{\varphi}xz)$ *φ–Transitivity*

Any failure of T.12 would therefore result in a counterexample to the original axiom. But D.28 is not the only way to understand 'φ-part'. A *proper* part, for example, is not a part that is proper (whatever that might mean); it is a part that is properly *related to* the relevant whole—viz. by virtue of not being identical to the whole (if we go for D.1), or by virtue of not containing the whole as a mutual part (if we go for D.15). This is why we do not speak of classical mereology as involving an "odd subsumption relation" just because its treats P as, say, reflexive and PP as irreflexive. The two predicates are related, and we may even say that one subsumes the other, but the subsumption principle does not apply. The case of such modifiers as 'functional', 'biological', 'military', etc. is arguably similar. The qualification they

44 The reference is to the subsumption principle familiar from description logics: "When a concept is more specific than some other concept, it inherits the properties of the more general one" (Nardi and Brachman, 2003, p. 5).

45 We say 'if', but really other conditions appear to be relevant as well; not everything that is true of a general concept need be true of the more specific one. Thus, if it is true that 'red' stands for a color, then 'light red' must stand for a color, too. But although 'red' can properly be predicated of the wine in this glass, the same is not true of 'light red'. Predicate modification is in fact a complex affair, and here we can barely scratch the surface. For a thorough survey of the issues, see Morzycki (2016) and references therein.

add is relational. It does not just apply to the part; it qualifies the relevant part-whole relationship, as per the following definitional schema.[46]

(D.29) $P_{\varphi}xy :\equiv Pxy \wedge \varphi xy$ *φ–Parthood 2*

And with 'P_{φ}' construed this way, the conditional in T.12 is logically independent of A.3. One can insist on the transitivity of P while acknowledging the non-transitivity of the relevant cases of φ-parthood.

Of course, if this line of reasoning is accepted, there remains work to be done to explain in each case how the relational condition φ should be characterized, and to determine how exactly φ-parts interact with parts *simpliciter*. This is by itself an interesting area of research. It is, however, extrinsic to the theory of parthood as such, at least insofar as the condition φ is beyond the pure language of mereology, so here we shall not pursue it further.[47]

3.3.2 *Immediate Parts*

As Simons (1987, p. 108) notes, there is nonetheless one restricted sense of 'part' that is intrinsic to mereology, as is 'proper part', and yet fails to be transitive. This is the notion of an 'immediate part', definable as follows.

(D.30) $IPxy :\equiv PPxy \wedge \neg\exists z(PPxz \wedge PPzy)$ *Immediate Parthood*

In other words, something is an immediate part of another thing whenever it is a 'maximal' proper part of that thing. For example, in the three-atom Boolean algebra reproduced in figure 3.6, the as are immediate parts of the bs, which are immediate parts of c, but the as themselves are only mediate (i.e. non-immediate) parts of c.

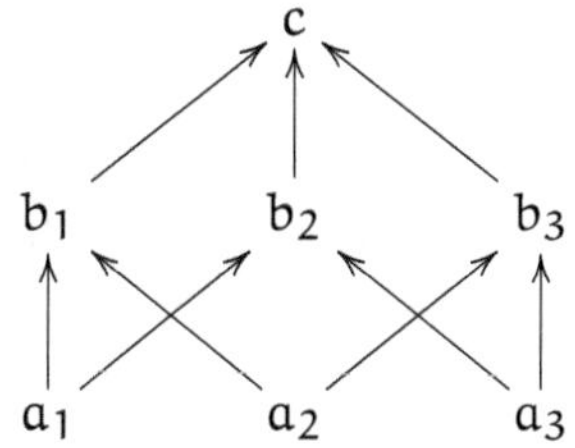

Figure 3.6: Immediate and mediate parts

46 Here we follow Varzi (2006a). For further discussion, see Johansson (2006a) and Seibt (2017).

47 Some developments in this direction may be found in the treatment of "significant part" by Tzouvaras (1993, 1995) and in the theories of functional parthood of Simons and Dement (1996), Vieu (2006), Vieu and Aurnague (2007), Garbacz (2007), and Vermaas and Garbacz (2009). See also Haber (2015, §15.3.2) for indications on relevant research concerning biological parthood.

Given the standard ordering axioms, it is clear that this relation inherits from PP the properties of irreflexivity and asymmetry, but not transitivity. Indeed, it follows directly from D.30 that IP is antitransitive:

(T.13) $\forall x \forall y \forall z((\mathrm{IP}xy \wedge \mathrm{IP}yz) \rightarrow \neg \mathrm{IP}xz)$ *Antitransitivity*

This is not to say that we now have a counterexample to the Transitivity axioms A.3 and A.9. In the terminology of section 3.3.1, we are simply narrowing the relation of proper part by a condition φ—expressed by the negative existential $\neg\exists z(\mathrm{PP}xz \wedge \mathrm{PP}zy)$—that does not distribute over the broader notion. Precisely because this condition is entirely mereological, IP is, however, especially interesting from the present perspective, for its antitransitive behavior captures an important sense in which decomposition into parts may be structured more orderly than P and PP might suggest. For instance, Kit Fine has argued that IP is in some sense metaphysically (if not conceptually) fundamental, at least in the domain of material objects.

> The majority of material objects ... will submit to a hierarchical division into parts. Just as a car will have an engine, a chassis, and a body as immediate parts (these being the components of the rigid embodiment that is the current manifestation of the car), these immediate parts will themselves have further immediate parts, and so on all the way down until we reach the most basic forms of matter. Thus a material object will be like a set, with its hierarchical division into members, members of members, and so on. (Fine, 1999, p. 72)

In fact, the distinction between immediate and mediate parts plays a central role already in Husserl (1900–1901), though Husserl's view is almost opposite to Fine's. Husserl defines immediate parts exactly as in D.30, as parts "such as may enter into *no* [proper] part of the same whole" (p. 469).[48] However, Husserl brings attention to the fact that in many cases the distinction arises only subjectively, i.e. relative to "some psychologically compulsive preference for a certain order of division" that makes us hit on some parts before others, but that corresponds to "no fixed, factually determined gradation in the relation of parts to wholes" (p. 470). In particular, with material objects there is no way of privileging some parts as absolutely immediate.[49]

> In an extended whole there is no division which is intrinsically primary, and no definitely delimited group of divisions forming the first grade in division; from a given division there is also no progress determined by the thing's nature to a new division or grade in division. We could *begin* with each division without violating an intrinsic prerogative. (Husserl, 1900–1901, pp. 470f)

48 We follow Simons (1987, p. 108, fn. 18) in repairing J. N. Findlay's translation, which wrongly has 'any' instead of 'no'. Husserl's definition can already be found in Husserl (1894, I, §2).

49 Here Husserl is following Twardowski (1894, §9), who in turn draws on Bolzano (1837, §58).

Yet Husserl, too, insists on the absolute character of the distinction in other cases. In a melody, for instance, we find individual tones as parts, and each individual tone has further parts of its own, such as a quality, an intensity, etc. These further parts, Husserl says, are also part of the melody, for parthood is transitive. Nonetheless,

> it is clear in this case that the mediacy with which the qualitative 'moment' of the individual tone enters the whole cannot be attributed to our subjective series of divisions ... The tone in itself is a prior part in the whole melody, and its quality a later, mediate part. (Husserl, 1900–1901, p. 471)[50]

Returning to the formal details, there are two important aspects of the relation IP that need mentioning. The first concerns the conditions for the very existence of immediate parts, and hence of non-vacuous instances of Antitransitivity. These conditions will depend on how exactly PP is assumed to behave. In case PP satisfies the classical ordering axioms A.7–A.9, it is obvious that finite models will generally involve relations of immediate parthood. Indeed, all finite models satisfy the following thesis, to the effect that every proper part is either an immediate part or a proper part of an immediate part.[51]

(T.14) $\forall x \forall y(PPxy \leftrightarrow (IPxy \vee \exists z(PPxz \wedge IPzy)))$ *Finite Parts*

Infinite models, however, may well contain mereologically *dense* elements that fail to have maximal proper parts. Classical mereology is actually compatible with an axiom (to be found already in Whitehead, 1919, ch. VIII) asserting that *every* composite element is dense:[52]

(A.30) $\forall x \forall y(PPxy \rightarrow \exists z(PPxz \wedge PPzy))$ *Denseness*

Clearly this axiom would render IP null and void. Similarly, just as classical mereology is, as we know, consistent with the Atomism axiom A.6, so there

50 This idea will continue to be central in Husserl's later work, notably *Experience and Judgment* (1939). For a thorough formal study, see Null (2007).

51 Pick arbitrary a and b. From right to left, the biconditional in T.14 follows directly from D.30 and A.9. From left to right, assume $PPab$. If there is no c such that $PPac$ and $PPcb$, then $IPab$ by D.30. Otherwise we can find a witness for $\exists z(PPaz \wedge IPzb)$ as follows. Pick c_1 so that $PPac_1$ and PPc_1b. By A.7, c_1 must be distinct from both a and b, and either IPc_1b or there is some c_2 such that PPc_1c_2 and PPc_2b. In the first case, c_1 will do. Otherwise, again, c_2 must be distinct from both c_1 and b (by A.7) and also from a (since $PPac_2$ by A.9). If the domain is finite, this pattern will eventually lead to some c_{n+1} distinct from $a, b, c_1, \ldots, c_n$ such that (i) PPc_nc_{n+1} and $PPc_{n+1}b$, and (ii) there is no further c such that $PPc_{n+1}c$ and $PPcb$. Since $PPac_{n+1}$ by A.9, this means c_{n+1} is a witness for $\exists z(PPaz \wedge IPzb)$.

52 The consistency of A.30 with classical mereology is guaranteed by the trivial one-element model. The existence of non-trivial, infinite models will follow from the relationship with the Atomlessness axiom A.31 introduced below.

are consistent extensions of classical mereology that embody the opposite view, to the effect that there are no atoms at all. As we shall see in section 4.6, where the question of atomism will be addressed in detail, that view is usually expressed by the following axiom (also from Whitehead, 1919).

(A.31) $\forall x \exists y \mathrm{PP} y x$ *Atomlessness*

Unlike Denseness, this axiom does not quite *say* that nothing can ever be an immediate part of anything. Still, in classical mereology A.31 entails A.30,[53] so again any model of such theories would force IP to be empty.[54] Generally speaking, in classical mereology the existence of immediate parts goes hand in hand with the existence of atomic remainders: $\mathrm{IP}ab$ will hold if, and only if, there is an atom c such that $\mathrm{PP}cb$ and $a = b - c$ (and $c = b - a$).[55]

If PP violates the standard ordering axioms, the picture is different. In particular, it's easy to see that failures of Irreflexivity or Asymmetry may impact on the existence of immediate parthood relationships even in finite models. A simple case in point is the model of figure 3.1, where the only element in the domain, a, counts as a proper but not immediate part of itself (since $\mathrm{PP}aa$ gives us $\mathrm{PP}aa \wedge \mathrm{PP}aa$, and therefore $\exists z(\mathrm{PP}az \wedge \mathrm{PP}za)$). Likewise, the transitive and hence reflexive closure of the two-element mereological loop of figure 3.2 would be a finite model in which everything is a proper part of everything, but nothing an immediate part of anything (since we would again have $\neg\mathrm{IP}aa$ as well as $\mathrm{PP}ab \wedge \mathrm{PP}bb$, hence $\neg\mathrm{IP}ab$ —and similarly for $\neg\mathrm{IP}bb$ and $\neg\mathrm{IP}ba$). Of course, insofar as models of this

53 For a proof, pick arbitrary a, b so that $\mathrm{PP}ab$. By A.4, the difference $b - a$ exists, and by A.31 it has a proper part, c. Now, $a + c$ exists by A.5, and clearly $\mathrm{P}a(a + c)$. Moreover $a \neq a + c$, since c is part of $b - a$. Thus $\mathrm{PP}a(a + c)$. The desired result will now follow if we show that $\mathrm{PP}(a + c)b$. To this end, note that $\mathrm{P}(b - a)b$ (via A.1). Since $\mathrm{PP}c(b - a)$, A.3 implies that $\mathrm{PP}cb$, and since we also have $\mathrm{PP}ab$, it follows that $\mathrm{P}(a + c)b$. Suppose $a + c = b$. Then $(a + c) - a = b - a$, and hence $\mathrm{PP}c((a + c) - a)$ (from $\mathrm{PP}c(b - a)$). But the remainder of a in $a + c$ is part of c, i.e. $\mathrm{P}((a + c) - a)c$, so we obtain $\mathrm{PP}cc$ by A.9. As this contradicts A.7, we must therefore reject the assumption that $a + c = b$ and conclude that $\mathrm{PP}(a + c)b$.

54 The existence of such models will be documented in section 4.6.

55 To see this, pick arbitrary a, b and suppose that $\mathrm{IP}ab$. Then $\mathrm{PP}ab$ and hence, by A.4 (along with A.1 and A.2), there must be a remainder $c = b - a$, whence $a = b - c$. We need to show that c is an atom. To this end, suppose for *reductio* that $\mathrm{PP}dc$ for some d. Then, again, we have a remainder $e = c - d$. Consider $a + e$, whose existence follows by A.5. Since $\mathrm{D}ac$, and hence $\mathrm{D}ae$, we must have that $\mathrm{PP}a(a + e)$. Moreover, since $\mathrm{P}ab$ and (by A.3) $\mathrm{P}eb$, we have that $\mathrm{P}(a + e)b$, and since $\mathrm{P}db$ but $\neg\mathrm{P}d(a + e)$, it follows that $a + e \neq b$ and therefore $\mathrm{PP}(a + e)b$, contradicting the hypothesis that $\mathrm{IP}ab$ (by the second conjunct of D.30). So c must be atomic, as desired. Conversely, suppose b has an atomic proper part, c, such that $a = b - c$. Clearly $\mathrm{PP}ab$ and $\mathrm{D}ac$, and moreover $b = a + c$. Suppose for *reductio* that there is some d such that $\mathrm{PP}ad$ and $\mathrm{PP}db$. By A.4 (with A.1 and A.2) there must be a remainder $e = d - a$, and by A.3 we have $\mathrm{P}eb$, which is to say $\mathrm{P}e(a + c)$. Since $\mathrm{D}ea$, it follows that $\mathrm{P}ec$ and, hence, $e = c$ (because c is atomic). Thus, $d = a + e = a + c = b$, contradicting the hypothesis that $\mathrm{PP}db$. So there exists no such d after all, which means that $\mathrm{IP}ab$ (by D.30).

sort defy the standard meaning of 'PP', it comes as no surprise that the meaning of 'IP' is equally affected. One may therefore consider adjusting D.30 accordingly, e.g. by replacing PP with PP_2, or with the corresponding definiens if PP is treated as primitive.[56]

The second remark is related. In his treatment of the mediate/immediate distinction, Husserl pointed out that while it may be difficult to identify cases of "absolute" immediate parthood, or even cases of "subjective" immediate parthood in infinite domains, things are easier if we restrict our attention to "parts of one and the same sort" (Husserl, 1900–1901, p. 469). For instance, every geometrical part of a dense extension is in the absolute sense a mediate part of that extension, for there are always "other geometric parts that include it"; but the same is not true if we focus on those geometric parts that are "congruent in all except position" (*ibid.*). Similarly, while a leg (say) is in the absolute sense only a mediate part of a cat, for it is contained in larger cat parts, it is an immediate part relative to certain sortal distinctions: no leg is part of another part of the same kind—another *leg*, another *limb*, another *organ*.[57] Generally speaking, where ξ is any unary predicate, let a proper ξ–part be defined in analogy with D.28.

(D.31) $PP_\xi xy :\equiv PPxy \wedge \xi x$ *Proper ξ–Parthood*

Then Husserl's point is that the basic notion of immediate part defined in D.30 can be expanded to the following sort-relative notion.

(D.32) $IP_\xi xy :\equiv PP_\xi xy \wedge \neg\exists z(PPxz \wedge PP_\xi zy)$ *Immediate ξ–Parthood*

And pretty clearly, the existence of immediate ξ–parts is a possibility even in infinite models that satisfy Denseness. That is, it is a genuine possibility as long as the ξs are not themselves densely ordered.

This generalization has several benefits to offer. Among other things, D.32 provides a perspicuous way to model the interplay between conceptual and mereological criteria—between "taxonomies" and "partonomies", in the influential terminology of Brown *et al.* (1976)—that governs the hierarchical structural representation of composite entities in ordinary and scientific

56 Another option is to treat IP itself as primitive. See e.g. Batchelor (2013), whose "Stoichiology" is based on a binary relation of "immediate constituency" that is irreflexive, asymmetric, and non-transitive (though not antitransitive). Cf. also Jacinto and Cotnoir (2019), who give a model theory for Fine's (1999) "theory of embodiments" (discussed in section 5.3.1) with immediate parthood as the only primitive.

57 At least, this would be true on the common understanding of 'leg'. It is a controversial question—an instance of the so-called 'problem of the many' of Unger (1980a) and Geach (1980, §110)—whether a slightly smaller leg-shaped proper part of a leg should itself qualify as a leg, and hence as a limb or an organ. If so, then the point is meant to apply to *maximal* legs (a notion that may itself be problematic owing to issues of vagueness; see section 6.3.)

discourse.[58] On the other hand, the sortal relativization introduced by ξ is obviously a step beyond the theory of parthood as such. Indeed, formally the notion defined in D.32 is just a special case of the general notion of a distinguished part discussed in section 3.3.1. Whenever x is an immediate ξ–part of y, it is a φ–part of y in the sense of D.29, where φ is the relational condition expressed by the definiens of D.32. The non-transitivity of IP_ξ can therefore be handled the same way.[59]

3.3.3 *Parts of Parts*

Finally we come to some challenges to the Transitivity axioms that have nothing or very little to do with the restricted use of 'part' in ordinary language but rather stem from the contemplation of metaphysical possibilities that are genuinely at odds with the orthodox behavior of parthood.

The time-travel and multi-location scenarios invoked in relation to A.1 and A.2 are perhaps the most immediate source of potential counterexamples. Consider, for instance, the case of Clifford mentioned in section 3.2.1, the dog statue made partly of a time-traveling future version of Clifford itself suitably reduced in size. Kleinschmidt (2011) offered it as a counterexample to the asymmetry of proper parthood. As she notes, however, the case may also be construed as a counterexample to transitivity, since the reduced Clifford would be a proper part of a proper part of Clifford itself.

> But nothing can be a proper part of itself—proper parts are parts that are distinct from their wholes. So, the Clifford ... case involves an outright violation of the Transitivity of Proper Parthood. (Kleinschmidt, 2011, p. 258)

As the quotation makes clear, one could resist the conclusion by renouncing instead the Irreflexivity axiom. But precisely because one may not wish to do so, the Transitivity axiom is in jeopardy.

The same could be said of other cases of parthood loops discussed earlier, beginning with Borges's Aleph. The Aleph is part of the earth, which in turn is part of the Aleph. Either we accept that the Aleph is a proper part

58 This has been a central topic of research in the cognitive sciences, where the taxonomy/partonomy distinction (on which see also Brown, 1976) has a parallel in the hyponymy/partonymy duality introduced by Miller and Johnson-Laird (1976, §4.2). See e.g. Palmer (1977), Kosslyn *et al.* (1980), Markman (1981), Hoffman and Richards (1984), Engehausen *et al.* (1997), Górska (1999, 2002a,b), and especially Tversky and Hemenway (1984) and Tversky (1989, 1990, 2005). For a general perspective, see Johansson and Lynøe (2008, ch. 11). Most of this work is informal, though more recently the interplay between taxonomic and mereological modes of decomposition has received formal treatment in some information-science theories; see e.g. Lambrix (2000, ch. 3), Keet and Artale (2008), and Dapoigny and Barlatier (2013).

59 So can other features of IP_ξ, such as its failure to be closed under fusion. Cf. Monaghan (2016), whose 'refutation' of classical mereology via IP trades entirely on tacit sortal restrictions.

of itself, or the symmetry of the situation turns immediately into a counterexample to the transitivity of proper parthood. In fact, this sort of case would be even stronger, for it does not depend on controversial metaphysical views concerning the nature of persisting entities. In the Clifford case, we have a puzzle insofar as the large dog statue (Clifford before time travel) and the reduced dog statue (Clifford after time travel) are taken to be one and the same thing.[60] In the language of Lewis (1986c, §4.2), this betrays a conception of material objects as *enduring* entities, entities that are wholly present at every time at which they exist; as a result of time travel, Clifford is wholly *bi*located. With Clifford construed as a *perduring* entity that persists by having different temporal parts, the puzzle dissolves, for small Clifford and large Clifford would be numerically distinct spatial parts of a proper temporal part of the whole perduring Clifford. Not so with the Aleph case.

Note that these cases would only violate the transitivity of *proper* parthood, as expressed by A.9. The transitivity of parthood, corresponding to A.3, would not be affected, at least insofar as this relation behaves reflexively. Here, by contrast, is a scenario where both forms of transitivity would fail.

> Imagine a car has a wheel as a part at t. At t* the wheel is removed from the car, and then lined with exotic matter to facilitate its travelling through time. The wheel (but not the car) travels through time and returns to t. The car has the wheel as a proper part at t, and the future version of the wheel has a lump of exotic matter as a proper part at t, but it is false (contra *Transitivity*) that the car has a lump of exotic matter as a proper part at t. (Effingham, 2010a, p. 335)

Effingham puts it in terms of 'proper part', for obviously the car, the (bilocated) wheel, and the lump of exotic matter are all distinct. However, each occurrence of 'proper part' could be replaced by 'part' *salva veritate*, so the scenario in question, if accepted, would constitute a counterexample to both A.9 and A.3 (and would do so regardless of Asymmetry).

So much for exotica. For a less extravagant case, consider again the Russellian view that the constituents of a structured proposition are literally part of it. As Keller (2013, §3.2) and Gilmore (2014) point out, already Frege found it hard to reconcile this view with the transitivity of parthood.

> For each individual piece of frozen, solidified lava which is part of Mount Etna would then also be part of the thought that Etna is higher than Vesuvius. But it seems to me absurd that pieces of lava, even pieces of which I had no knowledge, should be parts of my thought. (Draft to Jourdain, Jan. 1914, in Frege, 1976, p. 79)

60 Actually, one may also view the case in question as indicative of a more general problem affecting the standard conception of parthood as an absolute, binary relation, as opposed to a three- or four-place relation that holds only relative to places and/or times. We shall address this general question in section 6.2.2. In the special case at issue, this line of response is mentioned by Kleinschmidt herself and fully articulated by Gilmore (2009).

As a *reductio ad absurdum*, this may leave some philosophers unconvinced.[61] Yet the problem is serious if one thinks that grasping a proposition requires some way of grasping each of its constituent parts.[62] It is also serious, Gilmore notes, if one thinks that propositions have their parts essentially; for while the proposition that Etna is higher than Vesuvius would in that case depend crucially on its having the two volcanos as proper parts, its existence and identity conditions would seem to be independent of which pieces of hardened lava happen to be part of Etna, of Vesuvius, or of the mereological sum of the two. Too bad for Russell's theory of structured propositions, concluded Frege. Too bad, one could reply, for the transitivity of parthood.

Gilmore also brings attention to following passage, where Frege makes a similar point concerning the structure of atomic facts:

> The part of a part is part of the whole ... I want to have an example for the claim that Vesuvius is a constituent of an atomic fact. Then it appears that constituents of Vesuvius must also be constituents of this fact; the fact will therefore also consist of hardened lava. That does not seem right to me. (Letter to Wittgenstein, 28 June 1919, in Frege, 1989, p. 53)

Here the target is the metaphysics of the *Tractatus*.[63] Wittgenstein himself seems to have thought that Frege's remark was "silly" (McGuinness, 1988, p. 164), betraying a deep misunderstanding of his views,[64] but the problem arises more generally for any theory of facts as structured entities. Provided the relevant structure is mereological, it would seem that a fact has many more constituents than one may be willing to admit. And yet, again, one could respond by *modus tollens*. Frege argues from the transitivity of parthood to something that "does not seem right"; one could turn the argument around and reject instead the transitivity assumption.

Presumably, few philosophers would be willing to make this move. A defender of facts or of structured propositions is more likely to think that Frege is just mistaken in construing the relevant notion of constituency in

---

61 See e.g. King (2007), who finds "nothing objectionable" about the claim that, in his example, "Wendy's nose is a part of the proposition that Wendy loves Carl" (p. 120, fn. 42).

62 To be sure, one might think that it is enough to grasp the *immediate* parts of the proposition, which in this case would only include Etna and Vesuvius but not the little rocks inside them. Gilmore rules out this option as "somewhat *ad hoc* and artificial" (2014, p. 166).

63 The *Tractatus* was published in 1921, but Wittgenstein had sent Frege a copy of the manuscript already in late 1918 or early 1919; see Schmitt (2003b, p. 16) and Floyd (2011, p. 12).

64 Upon receiving Frege's letter, Wittgenstein actually wrote to Russell: "I also sent my MS. to Frege. He wrote me a week ago and I gather that he doesn't understand a word of it all" (19 Aug. 1919, in Wittgenstein, 1974, p. 74). Unfortunately there is no written record of Wittgenstein's response to Frege himself, as his letters were lost in the fire that in 1945 destroyed the Frege-Archiv in Münster (see Frege, 1969, pp. x–xi). Years later, however, when Wittgenstein became disillusioned with all talk of facts and their constituents, he acknowledged Frege's point. See the remarks on "Complex and fact" in Wittgenstein (1964), esp. p. 302.

mereological terms. David Armstrong, for instance, is adamant that facts, and states of affairs more generally, "hold their constituents together in a non-mereological form of composition" (Armstrong, 1997, p. 118), and it is debatable whether such a relation is transitive (McDaniel, 2009a, §4.1).[65] Similarly, with regard to structured propositions, proponents such as Salmon (1986), Soames (1987), and others construe them set-theoretically, typically as ordered sets of some sort. On such views Frege's worry does not get off the ground. However, precisely for this reason one might say that the transitivity of parthood ceases to be the general, metaphysically neutral law it is supposed to be. A.3 and A.9 would be safe, but at the cost of restricting the domain of application of mereology—and this is something that can hardly be justified or explained by appealing to the meaning of the word 'part'.

To be sure, one could still say that mereology does apply to facts and structured propositions thus construed; it's just that such things would be mereologically atomic, entities with no *proper* parts. Then A.3 would hold trivially and A.9 vacuously. From the perspective of classical mereology, however, this move would be less agreeable than it might seem.[66] For recall that classical mereology has an axiom of Unrestricted Fusion. Provided there is more than one thing, this axiom guarantees the existence of more things than there are atoms: n atoms generate at least $2^n - 1$ fusions.[67] Thus, if facts or propositions were mereologically atomic, Unrestricted Fusion would imply that their number is less than the overall number of things. But as Tillman and Fowler (2012, p. 529) point out, we also have the following. For any object, x, there is the fact/proposition that x exists; and for any two objects x and y, the facts/propositions that x exists and that y exists are distinct, at least insofar as facts and propositions are construed as structured entities.[68] So really there are as many facts/propositions as there are things—contradiction. It would seem, therefore that something has to give: either facts/propositions are not mereologically atomic, or mereological composition is not unrestricted.[69] We shall come back to the second option in chapter 5. For now we simply note that the first option generates Frege's problem, with the consequence that one might want to reject the

65 Specifically with reference to Wittgenstein's notion of fact, see Lando (2007), where the worry is addressed at length. For a mereological reading of the *Tractatus*, see Simons (1985a, 1986).

66 One may also object that this way of saving the generality of mereology is too easy, as it piggybacks on the generality of identity; see e.g. McDaniel (2010b, p. 413).

67 Strictly speaking, in the present context this is only true for finite n, since our A.5 is a first-order axiom schema. However, this limitation is not intrinsic to classical mereology; see section 6.1.

68 As Tillman and Fowler note, this second claim would not be true if, say, propositions were construed as sets of possible worlds, as in the popular theory of Lewis (1986c) and Stalnaker (1984). For then the proposition that Vesuvius exists and the proposition that the singleton of Vesuvius exists may turn out to be the same even though Vesuvius $\neq$ {Vesuvius}.

69 This argument has an ancestor in Rosen (1995), who objects to Armstrong's (1991) theory of classes as states of affairs on similar grounds.

transitivity axioms after all (on pain of biting the bullet and accepting what Frege finds absurd, if not denying that facts and propositions exist at all).

Finally, it is worth mentioning that the *modus tollens* strategy consisting in rejecting A.3 and A.9 in the face of problematic inferences has in fact been considered by some authors in other contexts. Most notably, Johanna Seibt (2009, 2015) argues that cases that are usually viewed as involving violations of mereological extensionality (in any of the forms discussed in section 3.2.3) could be treated as involving failures of Transitivity instead. Consider, for instance, the dualist view according to which a person and their body are distinct entities. The traditional Aristotelian-Thomistic account would of course explain the difference by treating the body as a proper part of the person, i.e. as the matter of a hylomorphic composite whose form is the soul. Some contemporary dualists, however, do not hesitate to treat persons and bodies as mereologically indiscernible, grounding their numerical difference in the possession of different non-mereological properties, e.g. persistence conditions. For example, Simons puts it thus:

> My body and I share all our parts at any time at which both exist, yet we are distinct, because my body may outlast me. (Simons, 1986, pp. 171f)

Obviously, this kind of dualism violates extensionality, at least on an endurantist construal of persons and bodies. We know that at bottom this could be seen as a challenge to Antisymmetry (a case of mutual parthood, as with the statue and the clay, or Dion and Theon after the amputation). But as Seibt points out, such dualists have an alternative. For where does the idea that a person and her body share *all* of their parts? There may be good reasons to think that they share the same head, trunk, and limbs; yet this is not to say that they also share the parts of these parts unless one assumes that (proper) parthood is transitive.[70] Absent this assumption,

> the example would cease to be counterexample to [extensionality], since a person has as spatial parts all those parts of her body she can have concerns about (feel pain in or feel shame or pride about) but not the millions of cells that are part of her body. (Seibt, 2015, p. 173)[71]

The claim that a person's body cells are not among her parts (as opposed to parts-she-can-have-concerns-about, which would be another restricted notion of the sort discussed in section 3.3.1) is of course as debatable as the

70 This was in fact the assumption we made in establishing the link between extensionality and antisymmetry in section 3.2.3; see again the discussion preceding figure 3.4.

71 We put 'extensionality' where Seibt has 'PPP'. This label refers to a principle we shall examine in section 4.2.2, the Proper Parts principle T.24, which says that whenever all proper parts of x are proper parts of y (non-vacuously), x itself is part of y. Together with Antisymmetry, which Seibt accepts, that principle is equivalent to the PP–Extensionality thesis T.1.

claim that they are.[72] But this is no bar to Seibt's point. Person/body dualists are inclined to think their view is incompatible with classical mereology because it violates extensionality; they could, instead, keep extensionality and forgo transitivity.

3.3.4 *Local Transitivity and Beyond*

With all this, it should be stressed that the transitivity of parthood and proper parthood are still the most robust among the ordering axioms of classical mereology, together with P-Reflexivity. Virtually every formal theory in the literature subscribes to these axioms unrestrictedly, and those that refrain from doing so have only been worked out in sketchy detail. The notable exception is the work of Pietruszczak (2014), which is driven by the specific desire to investigate an account of transitivity that "may be satisfactory for both its advocates and its opponents" (p. 359).[73] We conclude with a few general remarks on precisely this task.

One important point has already been mentioned at the beginning. Absent Transitivity, the Antisymmetry and Asymmetry axioms A.2 and A.8 may not suffice to do all the work they are intended to do; to rule out non-well-founded mereological cycles one would need something stronger, such as the Anticyclicity and the Acyclicity axiom schemas A.28 and A.29 (respectively). This is the course followed by Pietruszczak, whose theory is formulated with PP as a primitive and begins with replacing A.8 with A.29 (unlike Seibt, 2015, who sticks to Asymmetry while allowing for the possibility that something "may well be part of ... part of itself"). With P as a primitive, the obvious analogue is to replace A.2 with A.28.

A second point concerns the possibility of limited forms of transitivity. Following again Pietruszczak (2014), it seems plausible to require that (proper) parthood be, if not transitive, at least *locally transitive*. If Sonia's finger is part of her hand, which is part of her arm, which in turn is part of her body, then to say that the finger itself is part of the body should entail that it is also part of the arm, and that the hand is part of the body. In other words, there should be no parthood 'jumps' (see figure 3.7).

Figure 3.7: A non-transitive model with jump

72 The question of what counts as a part of a person has no straightforward answer even among biologists and medical scientists. See e.g. the exchange between Fried (2013) and Khushf (2013). Notice that if Seibt's view is accepted, PPP would imply that a person is a proper part of her body—exactly the opposite of the traditional Aristotelian-Thomistic doctrine.

73 Earlier treatments may be found in Pietruszczak (2012; 2013, ch. 4).

Formally, this requirement can be put in terms of an axiom to the effect that whenever something is part of some (other) thing, any 'path' of parthood relationships connecting these things must be closed under transitivity. In our language this amounts again to an axiom schema, or rather the conjunction of two axiom schemas. They can be formulated as follows, where m and n range over natural numbers.[74]

(A.32) $\forall x \forall y \forall z((P^m xy \wedge P^n yz \wedge Pxz) \rightarrow Pxy)$ *Left Transitivity*

(A.33) $\forall x \forall y \forall z((P^m xy \wedge P^n yz \wedge Pxz) \rightarrow Pyz)$ *Right Transitivity*

It is easy to see that the first of these schemas is indeed equivalent to the statement that, for every z, P behaves transitively relative to the set $\{y : Pyz\}$, i.e. the set of those things that lie on the 'left' of z with respect to parthood. For let a, b, c be any elements of this set and suppose that Pab and Pbc. This means that P^1ac. But we have Pcz. Thus we have $P^m ac \wedge P^n cz$ for $m = 1$ and $n = 0$. Since we also have Paz, A.32 implies that Pac. Similarly, A.33 is equivalent to the statement that, for all x, P behaves transitively in $\{y : Pxy\}$, the set of things on the 'right' of x.

The kit consisting of A.1, A.28 (Anticyclicity), and A.32–A.33 suggests itself as a good alternative to the standard ordering axioms A.1, A.2, and A.3 for those who wish to forgo Transitivity without losing too much structure. Similarly, with PP as primitive, the natural suggestion is to replace A.8 and A.9 with A.29 (Acyclicity) and the analogues of A.32–A.33 for PP. One could also consider the analogues of A.32–A.33 for the restricted notion of φ-parthood defined in D.29.[75] This would capture the intuition that, in actual cases, local transitivity is sortally constrained. In the intuitive example of Sonia's finger, hand, arm, and body, all the relevant items are *anatomic* parts.

If these changes are accepted, the third and final point concerns their impact on the rest of our mereological theory. What further adjustments would be required in order to have a non-transitive parthood relation that is otherwise classically well-behaved? Specifically, suppose one agrees with the basic intuitions behind the other axioms of classical mereology, viz. the Remainder axiom A.4 and the axiom schema of Unrestricted Fusion A.5. The first of these axioms reflects the idea that, when a whole has a proper part, it has a remainder, i.e. another proper part that is made up of all the rest; the second reflects the idea that any number of things has a mereological fusion, something composed of exactly those things. If P and PP are only locally transitive, are these intuitions still captured by A.4 and A.5 or should these axioms, too, be modified to make up for the loss of structure?

74 Again, in classical mereology both schemas hold trivially, since $P^m xy$ and $P^n yz$ always imply Pxy and Pyz (respectively) by repeated applications of A.3.

75 Or for other ways of identifying suitable restrictions on P. See e.g. Nolan (2018, §5).

For a concrete example, consider again the three-atom structure of figure 3.6, reproduced below. On the assumption that parthood behaves transitively, this is a Boolean model of classical mereology. But suppose the assumption is dropped altogether, to the point that parthood coincides with immediate parthood. Then both A.4 and A.5 end up being false. For example, an intermediate element such as b_1 will have no remainder in c. Classically this would be a_3, the atom disjoint from b_1; but if a_3 is no longer part of c, it no longer meets the condition set by the axiom. Similarly, the three atoms a_1, a_2, a_3 will have no fusion. Classically this would be c; but if c's parts do not extend to include the bottom atoms, c no longer counts as being composed of those atoms. Nothing does. So, both axioms end up being false in the model. All the same, it might be thought that this simply shows their inadequacy to capture the relevant intuitions in the absence of Transitivity. After all, if b_1 were annihilated, a_1 and a_2 would be gone and we'd be left with just a_3, so there seems to be a clear sense in which a_3 should still count as the remainder of b_1 in c even if it isn't *part* of c. Similarly, there seems to be a clear sense in which c should still count as a fusion of the three atoms a_1, a_2, a_3: after all, c is *ultimately* composed of them; it is entirely composed of things that are entirely composed of those atoms. The foes of transitivity must therefore choose: either A.4 and A.5 are fine as they stand, and hence the model is ruled out; or the model is fine after all and A.4 and A.5 must be adjusted accordingly.

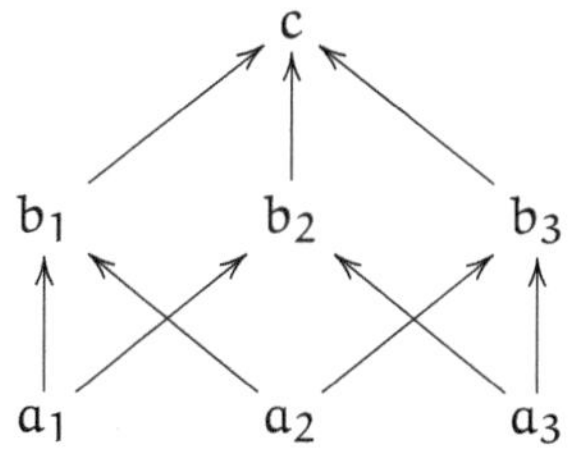

Figure 3.6: Immediate and mediate parts

Needless to say, this is hardly a decision that can be left to intuition. It requires serious reconsideration of some of the most basic mereological notions, which in classical mereology rely crucially on the assumption that P and PP are fully transitive. The notion of a fusion, for instance, was defined in D.6 by explicit appeal to the order-theoretic properties of these relations: something qualifies as a fusion of a given class of things if and only if it is a *minimal upper bound* of that class with respect to parthood. Absent Transitivity, this definition will obviously work differently, and the same can be said of the alternative definitions mentioned towards the end of chapter 2

(D.13 and D.16). So the challenge, here, is not just to decide whether A.5 should be modified; it is to explain how the very notion of fusion should be understood if P is not transitive. And what goes for 'fusion' in relation to A.5 goes for 'remainder' in relation to A.4—and indeed for many other notions as well (think of 'overlap' and 'disjoint').

The work of Pietruszczak (2014) goes precisely in this direction. The details are too complex to be summarized here, but it should be clear that the range of options is in principle quite wide. For all the help that may come from Anticyclicity, Acyclicity, and Local Transitivity, there is no obvious, unique way of redefining our conceptual apparatus once A.3 or A.9 are relinquished.

4

DECOMPOSITION

Take a pole one foot long, cut away half of it every day,
and at the end of ten thousand generations,
there will still be some left.

— Huì Shī (according to Zhuangzi, 2013, p. 298)

In chapter 3, we saw that the ordering axioms that govern the parthood relation of classical mereology are not as straightforward and metaphysically neutral as one might initially think. Perhaps in the end none of the putative counterexamples will be accepted. But this verdict would seem to require philosophical argumentation, or at least a decision of some sort, contrary to the thought that the axioms in question are constitutive of the meaning of 'part'. If that is so, then departing from classical mereology in this regard need not amount to a failure to "understand the word" (to quote again from Simons, 1987, p. 11),[1] just as departing from the basic principles of classical logic need not amount to a "change of subject" (Quine, 1970, p. 80). More generally, the very fact that the ordering axioms may be challenged on metaphysical grounds would seem to undermine any Husserlian understanding of classical mereology as a chapter of formal ontology, in the sense of section 1.2.1, and indeed there are philosophers who would draw this conclusion for *any* mereological theory, whether classical or weaker. Maureen Donnelly, for instance, sees "no reason to assume that any useful core mereology ... functions as a common basis for *all* plausible metaphysical theories" (Donnelly, 2011, p. 246). Similarly, Mark Johnston has been upfront in arguing that "there is no metaphysically neutral, *logical* conception of a part" (Johnston, 1992, p. 97), going so far as saying that in grounding a metaphysics, as opposed to implementing one, "mereology is about as useful as Mariology" (*ibid.* and 2002, p. 130, 2005, p. 637).

Any such conclusion should, of course, be assessed on its own merits. We already commented on this in chapter 1, where we expressed our sympathy for a broadly abductive methodology (section 1.3), and we shall have

1 In earlier work, one of us put things similarly in speaking of the ordering axioms as "lexical" principles (Varzi, 1996, p. 260; Casati and Varzi, 1999, p. 33; Varzi, 2007a, p. 950). While this was mainly meant to signal the intended function of such axioms *vis-à-vis* the other, more substantive principles of classical mereology, we now reckon this terminology is infelicitous.

Mereology. A. J. Cotnoir and Achille C. Varzi, Oxford University Press. © A. J. Cotnoir and Achille C. Varzi 2021. DOI: 10.1093/oso/9780198749004.003.0004

more to say below. Here let us simply note that there is in fact some leeway concerning the exact scope of the worry. For while it is natural to construe it as a worry about the status of mereology *vis-à-vis* the general tasks of formal ontology, one might as well contend that it is the very possibility of a formal ontology that is at stake. After all, we have seen that similar concerns may be raised with regard to the putative formal properties of the identity relation, some of which have been questioned since the Academic skeptics (Carneades). And what goes for parthood and identity goes for every relation that may be taken to admit of a formal ontological characterization, such as Husserl's relation of foundation, or existential dependence, or grounding.[2] From this perspective, one might therefore think that the question is not whether there is any useful core *mereology* that functions as a common basis for all metaphysical theories; the question, deep down, is whether there is any useful ontological core *tout court*.[3]

With this picture in the background, let us now proceed to an examination of the other axioms of classical mereology. Recall that a mereological theory typically involves, besides axioms governing the ordering properties of the parthood relation (if any), two sorts of principles. On the one hand, we need some sort of *decomposition principles* concerning the admissible ways a whole is decomposed into its parts. On the other hand, we also need *composition principles* that go in the opposite direction—principles that tell us the permissible ways a whole is composed from its parts. In the case of classical mereology, these two tasks are accomplished respectively by the Remainder axiom A.4 and by the Unrestricted Fusion axiom schema A.5 (in our axiomatization), or by principles that serve the same purpose such as the Weak Supplementation axiom A.10 and the Fusion′ axiom schema A.11, or the Strong Supplementation axiom A.18 and the Fusion″ axiom schema A.15 (in other axiomatizations). As it turns out, these decomposition and composition principles, too, have been the subject of extensive debates in the philosophical literature, indeed to a much greater degree than the ordering axioms, so we need to say more. In this chapter we shall deal with

2 For example, orthodox theories of grounding treat this relation as irreflexive, asymmetric, and transitive (Correia and Schnieder, 2012a; Raven, 2013), but each of these features has been challenged; see e.g. Jenkins (2011), Barnes (2018), and Schaffer (2012a), respectively. Some authors actually think there are multiple grounding relations, and rather than looking for a common core we should "understand the generic relation as some kind of 'disjunction' of the special relations" (Fine, 2012, p. 4), if not give up "big-G Grounding" altogether (Wilson, 2014).

3 Thus, e.g., McDaniel (2017, §4.1). Indeed, there is a parallel question regarding formal logic. The existence of widespread disagreement concerning which laws should count as purely 'logical' may lead one to conclude that there is no core set—that in the end the only principle to be found in the intersection of all candidate logics may well be the identity inference $\varphi \vdash \varphi$ (Beall and Restall 2006, p. 92), and perhaps not even that much (Williamson, 2013, pp. 146f; Russell, 2018; Cotnoir, 2019a). For more on this aspect of the logic/ontology parallel, see Varzi (2010). On the prospects of an abductive methodology in relation to logic, see Williamson (2017).

the former sort of principle, leaving composition principles for chapter 5. It is worth bearing in mind, however, that mereological decomposition and composition can be seen as 'two sides of the same coin'. Considerations regarding decomposition principles may have impact on questions regarding composition, and vice versa. Along the way, we will therefore foreshadow ways in which composition principles can already be brought to bear here.

Our plan is to proceed in steps. We shall begin by taking a closer look at the Remainder axiom A.4, which is based on the familiar notion of Boolean *complementation*. Then we shall extend our understanding of the underlying issues by gradually discussing weaker and weaker variants of this notion, each of which corresponds to a different notion of *supplementation* as reflected in A.18, in A.10, and in a few other supplementation principles discussed in the literature. Doing this will allow us to appreciate the relevant differences, which may be sometimes difficult to grasp intuitively, as well as the relationship between decomposition principles and other mereological theses with which we are already familiar, such as the Extensionality thesis T.1 and its cognates. Finally, we shall consider the extent to which decomposition may take place: can we continually decompose objects into smaller and smaller parts, or must there ultimately be a bottom level of mereological simples? This is the question of *atomism*, which we have already met in passing and which now calls for a fuller treatment. Relatedly, we shall also discuss some issues concerning the No Zero thesis T.2. This thesis rules out the existence of a mereological correlate of the empty set—a *null thing* that is part of everything—and is the main source of difference between classical mereology and the theory of complete Boolean algebras. We have seen that it follows from the Remainder axiom A.4 (given A.1 and A.2); how does it relate to the other, weaker decomposition principles?

4.1 COMPLEMENTATION

Let us begin with Remainder, which is the official decomposition principle of our axiomatization of classical mereology from chapter 2.

(A.4) $\forall x \forall y(\neg Pxy \rightarrow \exists z \forall w(Pwz \leftrightarrow (Pwx \wedge Dwy)))$ *Remainder*

As we explained in that chapter, this is a conditional existence claim. It says that as long as x is not itself part of y, it has a part that is composed of all and only those parts of x that are disjoint from y. In other words, there is always something that qualifies as a *relative complement* of y in x, corresponding to what would 'remain' of x if y were somehow deleted, or annihilated.[4] (This

4 To our knowledge, A.4 appears for the first time as an axiom in Bostock (1979, p. 119), though Bostock's system is weaker than classical mereology and the label 'Remainder' comes from

is why the claim is in conditional form; if x were part of y, there would be *nothing* left of x upon deleting y.) We have seen that as long as P is reflexive and antisymmetric, this relative complement is always unique: it is the mereological *difference* $x - y$ (see D.5). Thus, given A.1 and A.2, the Remainder axiom is equivalent to the following simpler thesis.[5]

(T.15) $\forall x \forall y(\neg Pxy \rightarrow \exists z\, z = x - y)$ *Unique Remainder*

For the rest of this section we shall in fact work under the assumption that P satisfies all the standard ordering axioms, so it will prove convenient to identify A.4 with T.15. The reader should, however, keep in mind that A.4 is in principle available also for theories where P behaves non-standardly.[6]

4.1.1 *Remainders*

The first thing we want to be clear about is the full import of Remainder. Sometimes the underlying idea is expressed in the literature by means of principles that do not quite coincide with our formulation, and the differences are not immaterial. There are two sorts of variant worth considering.

On the one hand, there are formulations that differ from ours in the antecedent. For example, sometimes the Remainder principle is identified with the following thesis (as in Parsons, 2004b, p. 87).[7]

(T.16) $\forall x \forall y(PPyx \rightarrow \exists z\, z = x - y)$ *Weak Remainder*

Leśniewski himself asserts an analogue of this thesis to illustrate the meaning of part-whole complementation in his Mereology (see Leśniewski, 1916, thm. XLVIII). It is clear, however, that T.16 is generally weaker than T.15, for

Simons (1987, p. 88). The closest precursor of A.4 is due to Grzegorczyk (1955, p. 91), whose postulate M4 has the following form:

$$\forall x \forall y(\neg Pxy \rightarrow \exists z(Pzx \wedge Dzy \wedge \forall w((Pwx \wedge Dwy) \rightarrow Pwz)))$$

This postulate entails A.4 so long as P is transitive, and is entailed by A.4 so long as P is reflexive. A version of Grzegorczyk's postulate, formulated in the language of Leśniewski's Mereology, may also be found in the unpublished axiomatization due to Jan Drewnowski mentioned in chapter 2, note 3, and is stated informally in Part II of Drewnowski (1934), where it is called "Existence of Subtractions" (§126). For details, see Świętorzecka and Łyczak (in press). In recent literature, the postulate is known as "Super-Strong Supplementation" (Pietruszczak, 2000b, §II.11) or "Strong Super-Supplementation" (Pietruszczak, 2013, §III.6.1). (This last reference also contains a thorough analysis and discussion of Grzegorczyk's system; see §III.7.)

5 Recall that D.5 uses the definite descriptor ι, which we understand as an abbreviatory device *à la* Russell (see section 1.5). Failing uniqueness, *the* difference $x - y$ does not exist and T.15 may therefore be false even in the presence of A.4.

6 A case in point is the non-wellfounded mereology of Cotnoir and Bacon (2012) (where A.4 is called "Complementation"). See also Cotnoir (2016a).

7 This thesis is also known as "Exact Remainder"; see e.g. Smith (1997, p. 542).

it ensures the existence of a relative complement in only one of the three possible cases in which $\neg Pxy$, namely when y is a proper part of x (see chapter 2, figure 2.2). To be sure, the case in which x and y are disjoint is also covered, for then $x - y$ is just x.[8] But in the third case, when x and y properly overlap, T.16 is only partially informative as to whether $x - y$ exists. In special circumstances, repeated applications of T.16 may suffice. For instance, if all the parts x and y have in common are composed out of finitely many atoms, $z_1 \ldots, z_n$, we have $(\ldots((x - z_1) - z_2) - \ldots) - z_n = x - y$. In general, however, a model of T.16 will violate T.15 unless all overlappers have a unique product, so in this sense T.16 is weaker than T.15. Similarly for the corresponding variant of A.4.[9]

Another principle that is sometimes offered to secure the existence of relative complements is the following (e.g. Niebergall, 2011, p. 276).[10]

(T.17) $\forall x \forall y(\exists z(Pzx \wedge Dzy) \rightarrow \exists z\, z = x - y)$ *Maximal Remainder*

What this says is that if y leaves *some* residual part in x, it leaves a *maximal* residual part, which is what the relative complement amounts to. This is very close to the intuition T.15 is meant to express, and it obviously covers cases in which y is not a proper part of x. Yet, again, given only the ordering axioms, T.17 turns out to be weaker than T.15. Whenever the antecedent of T.17 is true, A.1 and A.3 guarantee the truth of $\neg Pxy$,[11] and hence the entailment from T.15 to T.17. The converse entailment, however, may fail. A simple countermodel is the two-element structure in figure 4.1, left, which satisfies T.17 (vacuously) but not T.15. Actually this structure does not even satisfy T.16, showing that T.17 is *not* a way of strengthening that thesis. Another example is provided by the four-element structure on the right, which

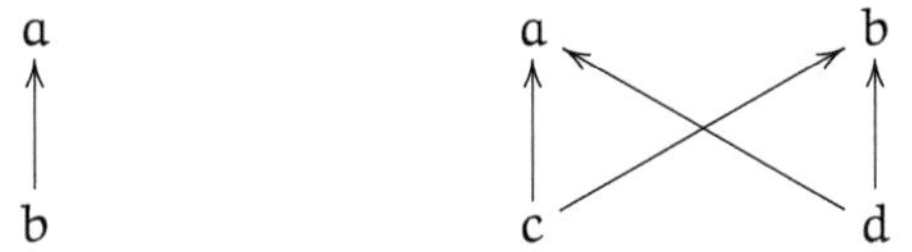

Figure 4.1: Two failures of (Unique) Remainder

8 If Dxy, then we have $\forall w(Pwx \leftrightarrow (Pwx \wedge Dwy))$ by logic, hence $x = x - y$ by D.5.

9 Strictly speaking, there are two possible variants, one of which differs also in the consequent:

$$\forall x \forall y(PPyx \rightarrow \exists z \forall w(Pwz \leftrightarrow (Pwx \wedge Dwy)))$$
$$\forall x \forall y(PPyx \rightarrow \exists z \forall w(Pwz \leftrightarrow (PPwx \wedge Dwy)))$$

In the presence of A.1, these two variants are equivalent; see Pietruszczak (2013, pp. 94f).

10 It should be noted that Niebergall understands P in terms of O, as in Goodman's D.14.

11 Assume $\exists z(Pzx \wedge Dzy)$ and let c be a witness for z, so that $Pcx \wedge Dcy$. If we had Pxy, the first conjunct would imply Pcy (by A.3), and since Pcc (by A.1), it would follow that $\exists z(Pzc \wedge Pzy)$. As this contradicts the second conjunct (by D.4), we must have $\neg Pxy$.

we already met in chapter 3. Here one can check that both T.16 and T.17 hold, and yet T.15 is clearly false (b has no complement in a). This second example is especially interesting, because it illustrates one important sense in which both T.16 and T.17 are weaker than T.15: they admit of partially ordered *non-extensional* models, whereas we know from chapter 2 that the Remainder axiom A.4, and hence T.15, imply the PP–Extensionality thesis T.1 (given Reflexivity and Antisymmetry). That is an important implication, to which we shall return in the next sections.

There are, on the other hand, formulations of Remainder that differ from ours (also) in the consequent. The intuition behind these formulations reflects an important property of the algebraic notion of relative complement: when one thing is a proper part of a second, the remainder must be "a third thing which, when added to the former, would yield the latter" (Smith, 1990, p. 170). In our language, this can be put formally as follows.[12]

(T.18) $\forall x \forall y (PPyx \rightarrow \exists z(Dzy \wedge y + z = x))$ *Additive Remainder*

One can see why this thesis may be taken to reflect the same intuition expressed by our Remainder axiom, or at least by the Weak Remainder principle T.16, and indeed in classical mereology T.18 and T.16 are provably equivalent.[13] Generally speaking, however, the two theses come apart. For example, the non-extensional model of figure 4.1, which satisfies T.16, does not satisfy T.18, since the bottom elements have no least upper bound; thus we have, say, $d = a - c$ but not $c + d = a$. Conversely, the four-element structure in figure 4.2 satisfies T.18 but not T.16. We have e.g. that $a - b_1$ does not exist even though $b_1 + b_2 = a$ (and also $b_1 + b_3 = a$).

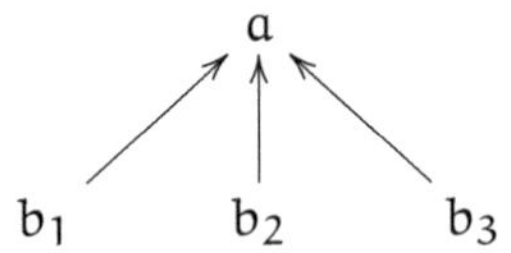

Figure 4.2: A model of Additive Remainder without remainders

More importantly, appealing to the sum operator in the consequent of T.18 involves a step into the logic of composition, and this is a significant deviation. Indeed, we saw in chapter 2 that there are several ways of characterizing

12 This is just one possibility. A weaker formulation would simply require y and z to compose x, without presuming uniqueness; see e.g. McDaniel (2009a, §4.2). Alternatively, in Krifka (1998, p. 199), the thesis is strengthened by requiring z itself to be unique. Krifka calls it the "Remainder Principle"; in Champollion and Krifka (2016, p. 74) it is called "Unique Separation". See also Ojeda (2009, p. 25), where the same principle is called "Subtraction".

13 This follows immediately from the algebraic characterization of section 2.2.

composition in terms of mereological fusion, corresponding to our original definition in terms of least upper bounds (D.6) or to the alternative definitions due to Leśniewski (D.13) or to Leonard and Goodman (D.16, D.18). Each definition will deliver a corresponding sum operator, and each operator may behave differently depending on what other axioms one assumes. We shall provide a full account of these differences in chapter 5. For now, the point is simply that the exact import of T.18 may vary accordingly.[14] For example, with + understood in terms of one of the alternative notions of fusion defined in D.13 and D.16 (or D.18), T.18 would result in a principle that rules out, not only the non-extensional model of figure 4.1, but also the model in figure 4.2.[15] Additive Remainder is not a pure decomposition principle; it is a principle that depends also, and crucially, on the mechanisms of mereological composition.

4.1.2 *Boolean Complements*

Returning to the official formulation of the Remainder axiom A.4, a second point that bears emphasis concerns the strength of this axiom in those settings where we have a universal element of which everything is part (as we always do in classical mereology). Given Antisymmetry, if such an element exists, it is bound to be unique, so D.8 applies and we can simply speak of *the* universe, u. And the point is this: when it comes to a proper part of u, which is to say anything whatsoever except for u itself, its relative complement in u is just its absolute, Boolean complement, as defined in D.11.

(T.19) $\exists z\, z = u \to \forall x(\neg x = u \to u - x = -x)$ *Boolean Complementation*

We already commented on this fact in connection with D.11, but it is important to stress that T.19 does not require the full strength of classical mereology.[16] It is an immediate consequence of Unique Remainder—hence of Remainder—given only the ordering axioms A.1 and A.2.[17]

---

14 Similar considerations apply to the variants of T.18 mentioned in note 12, whose original formulations are actually based on a reading of + in terms of D.13 (McDaniel, Ojeda), if not as a primitive operator (Krifka). See also Gilmore (in press, §1.4), whose "Moderate Supplementation" is essentially a version of T.18 itself based on D.13.

15 The former model would be ruled out because, while the bottom atoms would then have a sum of the appropriate sort, they would not have a *unique* sum. The latter model would be ruled out because no pair of atoms would sum up to a in either sense of 'sum'.

16 In the context of classical mereology, Boolean complements are sometimes *defined* this way, setting $-a := u - a$. See e.g. Simons (1987, p. 37).

17 Assume u exists and pick $a \neq u$. Given A.2 and D.8, we must have $\neg Pua$, hence T.15 applies and there must be a unique remainder $c = u - a$. To see that $c = -a$, recall that c must satisfy $\forall x(Pxc \leftrightarrow (Pxu \wedge Dxa))$ (by D.5), and since $\forall x Pxu$ (again by D.8), we have that $\forall x(Pxc \leftrightarrow Dxa)$. It follows that $\forall x(Dxa \to Pxc)$, which means c is an upper bound of the

This result captures a fundamental intuition. Set-theoretically, Boolean complementation is perhaps the most familiar notion from logic. If we think of a proposition p as a set of possible worlds—namely, those worlds in which it is true—then the *negation* of that proposition is just the set of all and only those worlds not in p. That is, where W is our space of possible worlds, the proposition $\neg p$ is just the Boolean complement of p, which is to say $W \setminus p$. Of course, in set theory we also have the empty set, so the limit case in which p is the set of *all* possible worlds (e.g. when p is a truth-functional tautology) is no exception: $W \setminus W = \varnothing$. Since here we are not assuming the existence of a mereological counterpart of $\varnothing$,[18] the mereological analogue of this general fact about negation—which is what the consequent of T.19 amounts to—is in conditional form. The underlying intuition, however, is exactly the same.

Now, what about those cases where the universe, too, fails to exist (and so the antecedent of T.19 fails to apply)? Does it follow from Remainder that every non-universal object has a Boolean complement *regardless* of the existence of u, and hence of the identity $-x = u - x$? After all, in D.11 the complement operator was defined independently, setting $-a := \sigma x Dxa$, so the thesis in question is readily available:

(T.20) $\forall x(\neg\forall y Pyx \to \exists z\, z = -x)$ *Absolute Complementation*

This is a theorem of classical mereology.[19] Is it already a consequence of A.4 (given only the ordering axioms)?

The answer is in the negative. A simple counterexample is given in figure 4.3, where b_2 is now an isolated atom and a is composed only of b_1 and b_3. This structure is a model of A.4 and, vacuously, of T.19 (there is no

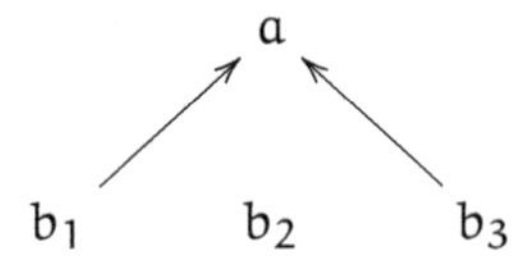

Figure 4.3: A model of Remainder with missing complements

things disjoint from a. Moreover we obtain that $\forall x(Pxc \to Dxa)$, hence $Pcc \to Dca$, and therefore Dca by A.1, whence it follows by logic alone that $\forall y(\forall x(Dxa \to Pxy) \to Pcy)$. This means that c is a *least* upper bound of the things disjoint from a, hence that $F_{Dxa}c$ (by D.6). Since least upper bounds are always unique (by T.3, which only requires A.2), we conclude that $c = \iota z F_{Dxa} z$, i.e. $c = \sigma x Dxa$ (by D.7), hence $c = -a$ (by D.11).

18 Indeed, we are excluding its existence in almost every case, since A.4 together with A.1 and A.2 imply T.2 (No Zero). We shall come back to this below.

19 Suppose, for arbitrary a, that there is some b such that $\neg Pba$. In classical mereology Pba is equivalent to $\forall w(Owb \to Owa)$, as shown in chapter 2, note 29. Thus there must be some c such that Ocb and $\neg Oca$, and hence such that Dca (by D.2 and D.4). Given A.5 and A.2, this immediately implies the existence of a unique z such that $F_{Dxa}z$, hence of $-a$ (by D.11).

universe). Yet there is no fusion of b_2 and b_3, or of b_2 and b_1, which means that neither $-b_1$ nor $-b_3$ exists. Thus, while each atomic part of a counts as a relative complement of the other *in* a, both lack an absolute, Boolean complement, contrary to T.20.

In fact, it's easy to see that the converse implication does not hold either. The model we saw in figure 4.2 is a case in point. There we have a total of three non-universal elements, the b_is, and each of them has a unique Boolean complement, namely a (since in each case a counts as the least upper bound of the things disjoint from b_i). So T.20 is true in that model. Yet we already know that A.4 is false, as none of the b_is has a relative complement in a.

What this latter example shows, however, is simply that the definition of complement in D.11 is not as straightforward as we made it sound. For notice that the model of figure 4.2 allows for a thing to *overlap* its complement, indeed to be part of it (we have $PPb_i(-b_i)$ for each i), and this is obviously at odds with the Boolean concept D.11 was meant to capture. There are, to be sure, cases where the Boolean notion itself might seem too strict. The puzzles raised by the mereology of spatial and temporal boundaries are a good example. As Peirce once put it:

> There is a line of demarcation between the black [drop of ink] and the white [paper]. Now I ask about the points of this line, are they black or white? Why one more than the other? (Peirce, 1893, p. 98)

Mereologically, this amounts to asking whether the boundary that separates a thing from its complement, treated as an entity in its own right, belongs to one or to the other, and it is very hard indeed to come up with a principled answer.[20] Since nothing can be left as a third thing between two entities that are *in contact*, one may therefore be inclined to conclude that the boundary belongs to both, and hence that a thing and its complement need not be disjoint: the boundary points are black *and* white. It is clear, however, that this would go beyond a mere departure from the Boolean notion of mereological complementation. This sort of answer violates no less than the principle of non-contradiction, so it would require a thorough rethinking of the underlying *logic*, e.g. a step from classical to paraconsistent logic (Weber and Cotnoir, 2015). We shall therefore postpone its treatment to chapter 6, which is devoted entirely to the alternative logical frameworks one may consider in developing a mereological theory. For now, let us simply register that D.11 does not, by itself, deliver the Boolean notion of complement unless models such as that of figure 4.2 are independently ruled out.[21]

20 For some discussion, see Varzi (1997, 2015) and references therein.

21 D.11 is patterned after the standard definition of Tarski (1937, def. 1·35), but using F rather than F'. Leonard and Goodman (1940, p. 48) give the same definition using F'' (their word

To properly assess the relationship between Remainder and complementation—and, more generally, to study the properties of specific mereological principles given only the ordering axioms A.1–A.3—we need to work with a stronger definition.

In the literature we find two main options, both of which can be formulated without resorting to fusions.

(D.33) $a' := \iota z \forall x (Pxz \leftrightarrow Dxa)$ *Complement′*

(D.34) $a^* := \iota z (Dza \wedge \forall x ((Dxa \rightarrow Pxz) \wedge (Dxz \rightarrow Pxa)))$ *Complement**

The first of these definitions comes from Goodman (1951, p. 36). Given the ordering axioms, it is easy to verify that it coincides with D.11 if we also assume Remainder;[22] otherwise D.33 is strictly stronger, as it requires explicitly that the complement be a separate, disjoint entity. The second definition, which comes from Hovda (2009, §4), is even stronger. For not only does it say that the complement (and hence its proper parts) must be fully disjoint from a, and that everything disjoint from a must be part of the complement; D.34 is also explicit in requiring that everything disjoint from a's complement be part of a, as it should be, and this is not something that can be inferred from D.11 or from D.33 unless we assume the general equivalence between Pxa and $\forall y(Oyx \rightarrow Oya)$.[23] In the model of figure 4.4, for instance, we have that $-a = a' = b_2$ and yet c, which is disjoint from b_2, is not part of a.

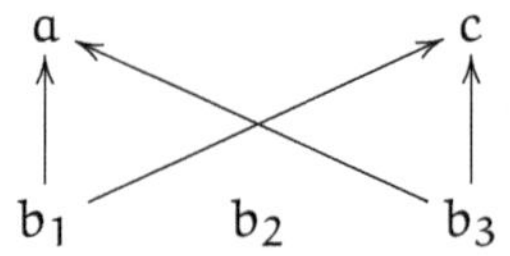

Figure 4.4: A case where neither $-a$ nor a' amounts to a^* (which doesn't exist)

for 'complement' is 'negate'). In classical mereology these differences are immaterial, but the model of figure 4.2 shows they may matter in weaker settings: in that model a counts as the complement of each b_i under our definition, not under its F' and F'' counterparts.

22 Let φx be the open formula 'Dxa'. D.33 immediately implies that $\forall x(\varphi x \rightarrow Pxa')$, so a' must be an upper bound of the φs. Moreover, it implies that $Da'a$ (since $Pa'a'$ by A.1), and hence that $\forall x(\varphi x \rightarrow Pxw) \rightarrow Pa'w$, so a' is sure to be a *least* upper bound of the φs, which is to say that $F_\varphi a'$. Since fusions are unique by A.2 (see T.3), this means that D.33 implies the identity $a' = -a$. Conversely, we know from T.19 that $-a = u - a$, which implies that $D(-a)a$ by D.5, and hence $\forall x(Px(-a) \rightarrow \varphi x)$ by A.3. Since D.11 requires $-a$ to be an upper bound of the φs, we also have that $\forall x(\varphi x \rightarrow Px(-a))$, and so we may conclude that $\forall x(Px(-a) \leftrightarrow Dxa)$. Moreover, any z satisfying $\forall x(Pxz \leftrightarrow Dxa)$ must also satisfy $\forall x(Pxz \leftrightarrow Px(-a))$, so must be identical to $-a$ by A.2. Thus D.11 implies that $-a = a'$. Note that Remainder (via T.19), was used in the second derivation, but not in the first.

23 As Goodman actually does; see again D.14 in section 2.4.2. We leave the proof that under this condition D.33 coincides with D.34 as an exercise.

So we have two ways of revisiting the Absolute Complementation principle T.20, corresponding to the following axioms.[24]

(A.34) $\forall x(\neg\forall y Pyx \to \exists z\, z = x')$ *Strong Complementation′*

(A.35) $\forall x(\neg\forall y Pyx \to \exists z\, z = x^*)$ *Strong Complementation**

Let us focus on the latter, which rests exclusively on the ordering properties of P. Since it is stronger than T.20, we already know that A.35 doesn't follow from A.4 (the model of figure 4.3 is still a counterexample).[25] Does the converse hold now? The answer is, again, in the negative, though for reasons that now are in full compliance with the Boolean meaning of these axioms. A counterexample is shown in figure 4.5. Here each of the a_is counts as the complement of the corresponding b_i, and vice versa, so the model satisfies A.35. Yet none of the bottom atoms leaves a remainder in the top elements that contain it. For instance, b_1 is a proper part of a_4, but there is nothing whose parts are just the other two atoms of which a_4 is composed, b_2 and b_3. So A.4 is false.[26]

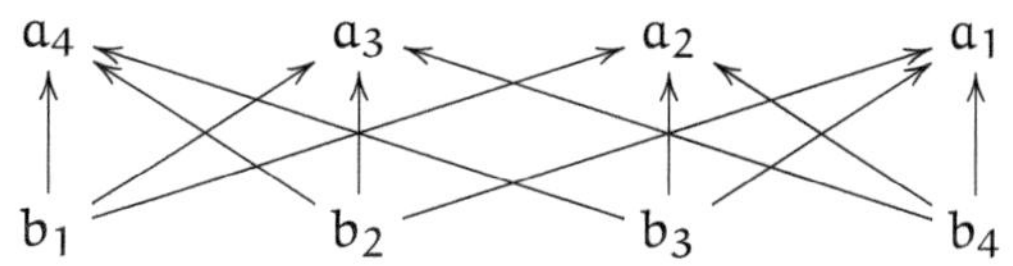

Figure 4.5: A model of Strong Complementation* with missing remainders

The bottom line, then, is that relative complementation and Boolean complementation are really distinct, independent notions. Given only the ordering axioms, neither A.4 nor A.35 implies the other. On the other hand, it should be clear that the difference dissolves as soon as the composition axiom A.5 is added back to the picture. For then the universe is bound to exist, and so A.35 follows from A.4 via T.19 (the model of figure 4.3 is ruled out); and conversely, we always get the relative complement $x - y$ (when $\neg Pxy$) by taking the Boolean complement of y if $x = u$, and otherwise the Boolean complement of $x^* + y$, whose existence is guaranteed by A.5, and so we get A.4 from A.35 (the model of figure 4.5 is ruled out).

Putting all of this together, we can appreciate the relative independence of Remainder and Strong Complementation, but also their intimate connection.

24 Hovda (2009) actually adopts A.35 in one of his axiomatizations of classical mereology. For axiomatizations using A.34, see e.g. Niebergall (2009a, 2011), where the axiom is labeled 'NEG' (for 'Negate'), and Tsai (2009, 2013a,b), where it is simply called "Complementation".

25 We leave it to the reader to check that the x^*-counterpart of the Boolean Complementation principle T.19 is still derivable from A.4.

26 Exercise: Why does the counterexample require no less than *four* atoms?

Starting from our axiom set A.1–A.5, we can replace A.4 with A.35 and the outcome will be the same. Indeed, as Hovda (2009, p. 75) notes, A.35 is strong enough to entail the Reflexivity axiom A.1. For if $\forall y Pyx$, we immediately have that Pxx; and if $\neg\forall y Pyx$, then A.35 implies the existence of x^*, whence Pxx follows from the definitional requirements that Dxx^* and $\forall y(Dyx^* \rightarrow Pyx)$. Thus, as an alternative way to get classical mereology, the four axioms A.2 + A.3 + A.35 + A.5 would suffice.[27]

4.1.3 *Complementation and Composition*

Philosophically, the difference between our Remainder axiom A.4 and the Strong Complementation axiom A.35 is not without import. For it should be noted that A.35 is not truly a 'decomposition' principle. It is not just about how an entity may be decomposed; it effectively stipulates the existence of something *outside* the entity in question. Since there are things that are not part of, say, Dion, according to A.35 there is a single, humongous entity composed of absolutely everything disjoint from Dion. Since there is more to this world than the State of Maine, there is something that consists of everything except for Maine. Entities of this sort—Dion's complement, Maine's complement—will not be objectionable to those philosophers who accept unrestricted mereological fusions, but everyone else may well think that A.35 oversteps its bounds. By contrast, A.4 is truly a decomposition principle in that it tells us one critical way in which any entity x may be decomposed. Provided it is not part of y, x may be decomposed entirely into the following two parts: the product $x \times y$ (where it exists) and the difference $x - y$. That is, A.4 only stipulates the existence of *parts* of x.

Some philosophers may think this is already too much. For instance, van Inwagen (1981) famously argued against what he calls the "doctrine of arbitrary undetached parts", according to which any subregion whatever of the region of space occupied by a material object is occupied by something, i.e. a part of that object. This is really a general doctrine concerning the existence of parts, and as such it goes beyond the provisions of Remainder. It is clear, however, that its rejection may result in a rejection of Remainder as well. For whatever reason one may have to endorse the existence of only *some* things located within the space occupied by a given object may lead one to reject the existence of the corresponding remainders, or of some of them. If the only existing things were things that φ (e.g. fundamental particles and functional units), it may well be that a certain subregion of the space occupied

27 This is Hovda's "fifth way" (2009, p. 82). To be sure, Hovda's system includes a further axiom, corresponding to our No Zero (T.2). However, No Zero follows from A.35 as it follows from A.4. No object that is part of everything, were it to exist, could have a complement *disjoint* from it. So the inclusion of No Zero in Hovda's axiom set is redundant. See Varzi (2019, §3).

by an existing φ is occupied by something—a proper part—that is also a φ, even though there is no φ corresponding to the mereological remainder. Dion is a functional unit, and so is, say, Dion's foot, but there is no functional unit corresponding to Dion minus his foot; those particles add up to nothing. (This is actually another possible response to Chrysippus's puzzle of section 3.1.1: before the amputation, there simply would be no such thing as Theon, so the question of Theon's survival would not even arise.[28])

As always, there is room for serious metaphysical disagreements on these matters,[29] so in this sense Remainder is hardly less controversial than Strong Complementation. But such disagreements are truly about the status of parts; they concern the scope and import of mereological decomposition.

There is nonetheless a sense in which the Remainder axiom, too, bleeds into the territory of composition principles. For the remainder of y in x is not just a part of x. It is, by definition, a part *composed* of parts, viz. those parts of x that are disjoint from y. And while sometimes this amounts to an ordinary undetached portion, as with Dion minus his foot, in other cases the entity composed of those parts can be quite extraordinary—as extraordinary and problematic as the entities postulated by Strong Complementation. Indeed, if x is the universe, and Dion is y, then the remainder of y in x—the universe minus Dion—just *is* Dion's humongous complement.

Nor is it necessary to assume the existence of the universe to see why remainders may be found objectionable in this sense. Consider a simple wine glass. The glass, x, is composed of three main parts: the base, the stem, and the bowl. It is plausible to think that the base and the stem jointly compose a larger part of the glass itself; and similarly, the stem and the bowl jointly compose a larger part of the glass. But is it obvious that there is something composed just of the base and the bowl? The base and the bowl are two pieces that stand apart; they are spatially separated. Yet together they make up the difference between the glass and the stem—their scattered sum is the remainder of y, the stem, within x, the glass.

More generally, it appears that A.4 would force us to accept the existence of a wealth of bizarre entities, such as the aggregate consisting of Dion's body minus his torso (just his head and limbs), or the aggregate of all the land mass of the State of Maine except for the bottom half of Mt. Katahdin, or perhaps the Earth without the 'slice' between the Tropic of Cancer and the Tropic of Capricorn. Entities such as these are spatially 'irregular', even discontinuous, lacking the sort of unity that is so characteristic of ordinary objects. As Lowe (1953, p. 121) complained, they go "far beyond what one

28 See Carmichael (in press). Van Inwagen himself comes to this conclusion, though for him Dion's foot does not exist either; the φs must be living organisms. See van Inwagen (1990).

29 For more discussion of the doctrine of arbitrary undetached parts, see Carter (1983), Zimmerman (1996a, §4), Parsons (2004b), and Varzi (2013) (in defense) and Olson (1995) (against).

ordinarily means by individuals", and many philosophers would agree. Yet this ontological discomfort is not by itself a sign of one's standards concerning mereological decomposition. Even those who accept the strictest laws of extensionality may feel uneasy about the existence of scattered entities (Chisholm, 1987, is a notable case in point). The discomfort, here, comes from one's misgivings about the compositional implications of A.4.

4.2 STRONG SUPPLEMENTATION

For those who have such misgivings, there are other decomposition principles on offer besides A.4. The first of these, in terms of strength, is the supplementation axiom we met in section 2.4.3.[30]

(A.18) $\forall x \forall y(\neg Pxy \rightarrow \exists z(Pzx \wedge Dzy))$ *Strong Supplementation*

This axiom states that whenever x is not part of y, x must have *some* part that is disjoint from y. The similarity with the Remainder axiom A.4 is apparent, but the two are clearly not equivalent, for the consequent of A.18 does not require the additional part of x to be *maximal*. (In fact, the consequent coincides with the antecedent of the Maximal Remainder principle, T.17.) Thus, as long as P is reflexive, A.4 implies A.18, since the remainder of y in x *is* a part of x disjoint from y. However, the model in figure 4.6 shows that A.18 does not imply A.4 even in contexts where P is a full partial order, so the latter axiom is strictly stronger.[31] This model satisfies A.18. In particular, b has two 'supplements' in a, namely c_1 and c_2. Yet the model contains no element whose parts are exactly those two supplements (no maximal remainder of b), and thus A.4 fails.

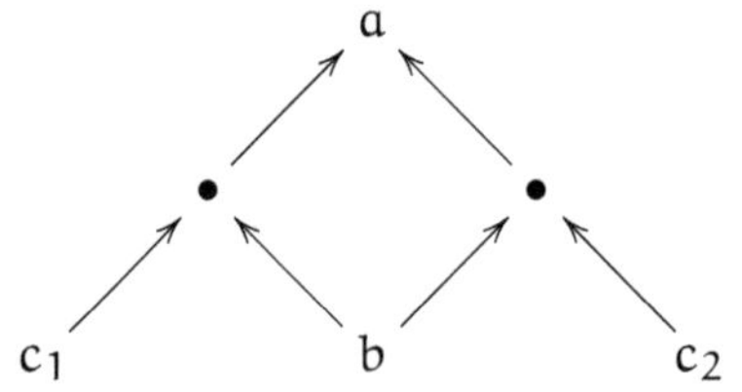

Figure 4.6: A model of Strong Supplementation with missing remainders

30 Again, terminology may vary. Here we are following Simons (1987, p. 29). Other authors (e.g. Donnelly and Smith, 2003, p. 53) refer to A.18 as the "Remainder Principle", though we shall see momentarily that A.18 is weaker than A.4. Further terms for A.18 are "Freedom" (van Benthem, 1983, p. 62) and "Separation" (Link, 1998; Pietruszczak, 2000a). The latter term is also standard in the set-theoretic literature dealing with partial orders; see e.g. Jech (1978, p. 152).

31 In some literature, the Remainder axiom A.4 is actually called "Super-Strong Supplementation"; see Cotnoir (2016a, §2) (though cf. above, note 4, for a slightly different use of this terminology).

Returning to our example of the wine glass, we may think of the model in figure 4.6 as depicting precisely the situation we described, with a representing the glass, b the stem, c_1 the base, and c_2 the bowl. Since the stem is a proper part of the glass, the glass in not part of it, so A.18 requires the existence of some other part of the glass disjoint from the stem. There are two such parts, the bowl and the base, and so A.18 is satisfied. But A.18 is silent as to the existence of a further thing composed of the bowl and the base, as would be required by A.4. So Strong Supplementation manages to avoid the potential misgivings about the Remainder axiom while still ensuring that objects have an intuitive decompositional structure.

Two further features of A.18 are worth noting. First, while Reflexivity ensures that A.4 is stronger than A.18, A.18 itself is stronger than A.4 in the following sense: as long as P is transitive, A.18 entails the Reflexivity axiom A.1.[32] To see this, suppose for some a that $\neg Paa$. By A.18, this implies the existence of some z such that Pza and Dza. From the second conjunct, it follows that no part of z can be part of a (by D.4) and hence, from the first conjunct, that z has no parts at all (by A.3). On the other hand, this means that $\neg Pzz$, and so there must be some w such that Pwz and Dwz (by A.18), which means that z does have parts. Contradiction.

Second, adding the Unrestricted Fusion axiom A.5 to the theory defined by A.18 and the ordering axioms (minus Reflexivity) does not result in classical mereology, as can be seen by considering again the model in figure 4.2.[33] This confirms that Strong Supplementation is a genuine alternative to Remainder. (To get back Remainder, and hence classical mereology, one would also need the Maximal Remainder principle T.17; see Bostock, 1979, p. 119.) However, adding the F''-variant of Unrestricted Fusion, i.e. the axiom A.15 of Goodman (1951), does result in full classical mereology. That is precisely the system of Eberle (1970) given in section 2.4.3. The same is true if we add instead the F'–variant due to Leśniewski (1916) and Tarski (1929, 1935), i.e. A.11.[34] Thus, generally speaking, the exact strength of A.18 *vis-à-vis* A.4 depends crucially on which notion of fusion one works with.

4.2.1 *Supervenience*

Following Parsons (2014, §2), one may actually think of Strong Supplementation as giving (non-modal) expression to a kind of supervenience principle:

32 To our knowledge, this entailment was first noted in Pietruszczak (2000b, § IV.5), though it is generally neglected. This is the source of the redundancy mentioned in chapter 2, note 58.

33 This is sometimes overlooked. See e.g. Russell (2016, p. 252).

34 Indeed, given A.11, one already gets classical mereology if Remainder is replaced with the Weak Supplementation axiom A.10 (discussed below) and taking only Transitivity instead of the whole set A.1–A.3. See the "second way" of Hovda (2009) and below, note 60.

no two things can differ regarding what parts they have (or what they are parts of) without differing regarding what they overlap. To see why, consider the contrapositive of A.18:

(4.1) $\forall x \forall y(\neg\exists z(Pzx \wedge Dzy) \to Pxy)$

Given D.2 and D.4, this is equivalent to:

(4.2) $\forall x \forall y(\forall z(Pzx \to Ozy) \to Pxy)$

Since Pzx entails Ozx by Reflexivity, 4.2 immediately implies:

(T.21) $\forall x \forall y(\forall z(Ozx \to Ozy) \to Pxy)$ O–*Supervenience*

And given Transitivity, the converse implication holds as well. For suppose we have $\forall z(Pza \to Ozb)$ and assume for arbitrary c that Oca. By D.2, this means there's some d with Pdc and Pda. Applying our initial hypothesis to d we can infer that Odb and so, again, there's some e with Peb and Ped. Since Pdc, Transitivity gives us Pec, whence Ocb by D.2. This shows that $Oca \to Ocb$, and since c was arbitrary, we obtain that $\forall z(Oza \to Ozb)$ and, hence, Pab by T.21. Thus $\forall z(Pza \to Ozb) \to Pab$, which generalizes to 4.2.

Now, in one direction the inter-derivability of Strong Supplementation and O–Supervenience is mainly of conceptual value. Much like the definition of overlap in terms of parthood (D.2), O–Supervenience connects parthood to overlap. Indeed, Transitivity also secures the converse of T.21.

(T.22) $\forall x \forall y(Pxy \to \forall z(Ozx \to Ozy))$ O–*Inclusion*

Thus, provided we are willing to accept this thesis in its own right, T.21 would allow us to *define* parthood in terms of overlap. As we saw in chapter 2, Goodman (1951) followed precisely this strategy, trading D.2 for D.14.

But Parsons's point is instructive also in the opposite direction. For it follows that Strong Supplementation *must* hold in any mereology axiomatized using O as a primitive, at least insofar as O continues to obey the standard meaning fixed by D.2 (as in Goodman's Overlapping Parts axiom A.13). Ditto of any mereology based on D, as in the original version of the Calculus of Individuals of Leonard and Goodman (1940); for clearly the same line of argument will show the inter-derivability of A.18 and

(T.23) $\forall x \forall y(\forall z(Dzy \to Dzx) \to Pxy)$ D–*Supervenience*

(See e.g. Bostock, 1979, p. 113.) Thus, here we see that the choice of a mereological primitive is not as free as one might initially think. In some cases it carries substantive weight. We can use either P or PP and decide in complete freedom how to axiomatize these relations, including whether they should obey Strong Supplementation or something weaker (as we shall see below). But taking O or D as primitives would quickly commit us to A.18 and its consequences.

4.2.2 *Strong Supplementation and Extensionality*

Despite its plausibility and its avoidance of the problems with the Remainder axiom A.4, Strong Supplementation has in fact one consequence that is generally thought to be problematic: it entails extensionality for overlap in any antisymmetric mereology. This is why the theory obtained by positing A.18 along with the ordering axioms (or just A.2–A.3) is known in the literature as Extensional Mereology (Casati and Varzi, 1999, p. 40).[35]

To see this, consider that by substituting variables in T.21 we have:

(4.3) $\forall x \forall y(\forall z(Ozy \to Ozx) \to Pyx)$

When conjoined with T.21, this yields the following:

(4.4) $\forall x \forall y(\forall z(Ozx \leftrightarrow Ozy) \to (Pxy \wedge Pyx))$

And in the presence of Antisymmetry A.2, this is just the extensionality principle for O we met in section 3.2.3, and adopted by Goodman (1951) as an axiom of his Calculus of Individuals (A.14).

(T.10) $\forall x \forall y(\forall z(Ozx \leftrightarrow Ozy) \to x = y)$ O–*Extensionality*

Not only does A.18 entail the extensionality of overlap (and of disjointness, T.11); like A.4, it also entails the extensionality of proper parthood:

(T.1) $\forall x(\exists w PPwx \to \forall y(\forall z(PPzx \leftrightarrow PPzy) \to x = y))$ PP–*Extensionality*

To see why this already follows from A.18, consider the following principle identified by Simons (1987, p. 28).[36]

(T.24) $\forall x(\exists w PPwx \to \forall y(\forall z(PPzx \to PPzy) \to Pxy))$ *Proper Parts*

35 Simons (1987, p. 31) reserves the label "Minimal Extensional Mereology" for the theory obtained from the ordering axioms by adding instead the Weak Supplementation axiom A.10 along with an axiom to the effect that every pair of overlapping things has a unique product, corresponding to A.37 below. In that theory Strong Supplementation and hence extensionality are derivable as theorems, hence the label. Both Extensional Mereology and Minimal Extensional Mereology are now known to be undecidable, as proved in Tsai (2009, thm. 1) and Tsai (2011, thm. 5). The same applies to the several other theories discussed below, for which see also Tsai (2013b).

36 This principle may already be found in Whitehead's mereology of events, where it is treated as a postulate; see Whitehead (1919, p. 101).

As above, if we conjoin two instances of T.24 we can use Antisymmetry to obtain T.1. But T.24 follows from A.18. This is shown by the following proof (due to Simons himself). Assume A.18 and suppose the antecedent of T.24 holds, so that x has at least one proper part. We need to derive the consequent. Actually, it is easier to derive the contrapositive, viz. $\forall y(\neg Pxy \rightarrow \exists z(PPzx \wedge \neg PPzy))$. So assume for arbitrary y that $\neg Pxy$. We have two cases: (i) Oxy, and (ii) $\neg Oxy$, i.e. Dxy. For case (i), since $\neg Pxy$, we know by A.18 that there's a z such that Pzx and Dzy. Plainly, whenever Oxy and Dzy it cannot be that $x = z$ on pain of contradiction. Hence, by D.1, we must have it that $PPzx$. (With PP defined via D.15 we have the same, at least as long as P is transitive; for then, given Oxy, Pxz would imply Ozy, and we know that Dzy.) Moreover, z cannot be a proper part of y, otherwise it would be a common part of y and z (by A.1), contradicting Dzy. So $\neg PPzy$, and hence $\exists z(PPzx \wedge \neg PPzy)$ as required. In case (ii), since Dxy, x and y have no proper parts in common, and so $\forall z(PPzx \rightarrow \neg PPzy)$. But we know by assumption that x has at least one proper part, and thus, again, $\exists z(PPzx \wedge \neg PPzy)$.

So, given Antisymmetry (and Reflexivity), Strong Supplementation yields the extensionality of PP along with that of O and D. And these theses, as we saw in chapter 3, are highly controversial. Indeed, putative counterexamples abound. Besides the classic cases already mentioned (Dion and Theon, the statue and the clay, persons and their bodies), here are a few more cases featured prominently in contemporary literature: (i) two words can be made up of the same letters (Hempel, 1953, p. 110; Rescher, 1955, p. 10), as different tunes can consist of the same notes (Rosen and Dorr, 2002, p. 154); (ii) the arrangement of the parts matters, so a bouquet of roses is not the same as their 'mere' fusion (Eberle, 1970, p. 210) as a ham sandwich is not 'just' a ham+bread sum (Fine, 1999, p. 65), a watch a pile of springs and gears (Maudlin, 1998, p. 47), or a molecule a bunch of atoms (Harré and Llored, 2013); (iii) the fusion of a roof, walls, and floor made of Tinkertoys is not identical to the fusion of the Tinkertoys (as neither is identical to the Tinkertoy house), for the former is destroyed when its parts are destroyed, and destroying the roof, walls, and floors doesn't require destroying any Tinkertoy (Sanford, 2003); (iv) a cat and the corresponding amount of feline tissue have the same proper parts, yet the cat can survive the loss of certain parts whereas *that* amount of tissue cannot by definition (Wiggins, 1968, 1979).[37]

37 For more examples along these lines, see e.g. Doepke (1982), Lowe (1989), Johnston (1992), Baker (1997), Fine (2003), Meirav (2000), and Crane (2012). See also Simons (1987, chs. 3, 6) for distinctions and connections between the various cases. With regard to (iv), which builds on Locke (*Essay*, II, xxvii, 3), some variants trade on the further distinction between the matter an object is made of and the specific amount that constitutes the object (about which see Steen, 2016, and references therein). We won't go into this here, but the literature is extensive; see esp. Grandy (1975), Burge (1977), Cartwright (1984), Zimmerman (1995), Koslicki (1999), Barnett (2004), Kleinschmidt (2007), Donnelly and Bittner (2009), Tanksley (2010), and Laycock (2011).

Now, as always, each of these cases appeals to intuitions or hidden assumptions that may be disputed. With reference to case (i), for instance, consider two words made up of the same letters, say, 'TIM' and 'MIT'. Following Lewis (1991, pp. 78f), one could say a number of things on behalf of extensionality. As word *tokens*, a 'TIM'-inscription and a 'MIT'-inscription are certainly not identical; but then the letter tokens that compose them are also not identical, and so the counterexample misfires. Perhaps the three letter tokens are suitably arranged so as to form both words at once, as in a street sign that reads 'TIM' from one side and 'MIT' from the opposite side; but then we really have *one* object, a single array of letters that reads differently depending on one's vantage point. What if the three letters are movable items, first formed into a 'TIM'-inscription and later rearranged into a 'MIT'-inscription? Then one could insist that we are facing a case of diachronic identity, with all that it entails. An endurantist, for instance, might still speak of a single whole that persists through (spatial) change; a perdurantist might say that the inscriptions consist of different (temporal) parts; et cetera. So really one should construe the counterexample in terms of word and letter *types*. And don't think of a type as a fusion of its inscriptions, otherwise our two words would be composed of parts of the same three letter types, but not the *same* parts. To yield a counterexample to PP–Extensionality, the two word types must be construed literally as structural universals made up of the same three letter types. But then, again, we would have a counterexample only if the structure in question is truly mereological, and one may just deny that (Lewis, 1986a; Armstrong, 1986).

The other cases can be more challenging; yet even there the friends of extensionality will have things to say in response (Varzi, 2008; 2016, §3.2). Some may even be satisfied with rejecting all cases holus-bolus simply because of the "crazy arithmetic" that they entail—a phrase that Plutarch used to scorn the views of the Stoics (*On common conceptions*, 1084A) and that nominalistically-inclined mereologists would happily endorse. No distinction of entities without distinction of content, says Goodman (1951, p. 26). No difference without a difference-maker, echoes Lewis (1991, p. 78).

All this notwithstanding, it is a fact that any such response on behalf of mereological extensionality is bound to be as contentious as the cases it is meant to address. There is no neutral way of settling the matter, no response that would satisfy all plausible metaphysical views. Moreover, we have seen in chapter 3 that there are other issues at stake as well. For our present purposes, then, the moral to be drawn is quite simple: if any of the counterexamples is accepted, then the extensionality theses T.1, T.10, and T.11 are in jeopardy. And since these theses follow from the Strong Supplementation axiom A.18 together with the Antisymmetry axiom A.2, it might be concluded that one of these two axioms is too strong. In chapter 3 we saw that there are reasons to think the culprit is A.2, and someone willing to drop this axiom is indeed free to endorse A.18 along with the Proper Parts principle T.24. (A case in point is the non-wellfounded mereology of Cotnoir and Bacon, 2012, which has exactly the same decomposition and composition axioms of classical mereology; but see also Obojska, 2012, 2013a and Parsons, 2013b. Another case in point would be the theory of irregular parts of Null, 1995, 1997.) Not everyone will agree, though, and indeed the popular verdict is to blame A.18 instead. If so, then this decomposition axiom, like the Remainder axiom A.4, is unsuitable and one needs to look for further alternatives.

4.3 WEAK SUPPLEMENTATION

The next decomposition principle on offer is Weak Supplementation. We introduced this principle in section 2.4.1 as axiom A.10 for a version of classical mereology based on PP, but in the literature it is often considered independently, not least because of its intuitive appeal. Here it is again.

(A.10) $\forall x \forall y (PPyx \rightarrow \exists z (PPzx \wedge Dzy))$ *Weak Supplementation*

As the name suggests,[38] A.10 is not altogether too dissimilar from the Strong Supplementation axiom A.18. It says that whenever a whole has a proper part, it has another one disjoint from the first. Some standard treatments actually state A.10 using P in the consequent rather than PP:[39]

(T.25) $\forall x \forall y (PPyx \rightarrow \exists z (Pzx \wedge Dzy))$ *Weak P–Supplementation*

Given the standard interaction between the two predicates, this formulation is entailed by A.10, and entails A.10 so long as P is reflexive, showing that the difference with A.18 is really just in the antecedent.[40] Where Strong Supplementation requires the existence of a supplementary part whenever $\neg Pxy$, Weak Supplementation only requires it when $PPyx$ (much like Remainder versus Weak Remainder).

38 From Simons (1987, p. 28); but see chapter 2, note 40 for further nomenclature. Sometimes A.10 is simply called 'Supplementation' (e.g. Simons, 2013b), as is T.25 below (e.g. Varzi, 2016).

39 See e.g. Casati and Varzi (1999, p. 39), Sider (2007a, p. 60), Hovda (2009, p. 63), Koons and Pickavance (2017, p. 516), and Lando (2017, p. 140).

40 With P as a primitive, the entailment from A.10 to T.25 follows immediately by D.1. Conversely, assume $PPyx$. Given T.25, there must be a z such that Pzx and Dzy. But we cannot have $z = x$, for this would imply Dxy, contradicting $PPyx$ (by A.1). Thus $z \neq y$, and hence $PPzy$ by D.1. The same argument applies if PP is taken as a primitive and P defined by D.12. With PP defined via D.15 (i.e. as PP_2), or P defined via D.26 (as P_2), things are slightly different. We will consider these alternatives in section 4.3.3. For the rest of this section and the next, we shall confine ourselves to the basic framework determined by D.1 and D.12.

Now, in the presence of Antisymmetry we know that $PPyx$ implies $\neg Pxy$, so A.18 entails T.25 and hence, given Reflexivity, A.10. However, the converse is not true, which means that Weak Supplementation is (in reflexive antisymmetric mereologies anyway) strictly weaker than Strong Supplementation. The easiest way to check this is to consider again the four-element 'butterfly' model, reproduced in figure 4.7. In this model A.10 is true (as is T.25), since each proper part of a counts as a supplement of the other, and similarly for b. Yet A.18 is false. For while, say, a is not part of b, satisfying the antecedent of A.18, a has no parts disjoint from b, and so the consequent fails. Note that this model also violates PP–Extensionality, since a and b have the same proper parts. Ditto for O– and D–Extensionality. So this also shows that adding A.10 to the partial order axioms has no extensional implications. It is precisely for this reason that A.10 may be preferred to A.18.

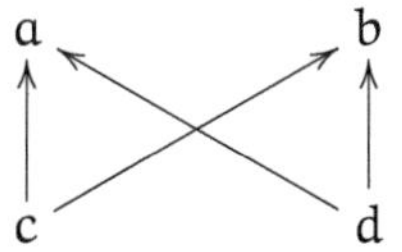

Figure 4.7: A model of Weak Supplementation without strong supplements

We shall come back below to the effects of dropping Antisymmetry. For now let us continue to assume A.2. The difference between Weak and Strong Supplementation becomes sharper if we consider the following principle (from Pietruszczak, 2013, p. 44):

(T.26) $\forall x \forall y (POxy \rightarrow \exists z(PPzx \wedge Dzy))$ *Over-Supplementation*

Here PO is the relation of proper overlap defined in D.23, which obtains whenever two things overlap without either being part of the other. Since $POxy$ implies $\neg Pxy$, it's clear that T.26 is entailed by Strong Supplementation. And since T.26 admits models that Strong Supplementation rules out, for instance, models in which something has a single proper part (as in the two-element pattern of figure 4.1), the converse entailment does not hold. Thus, generally speaking, in reflexive antisymmetric mereologies we have it that Strong Supplementation entails both Weak and Over-Supplementation and is entailed by neither. However, it is entailed by (and therefore equivalent to) their conjunction. For, given $\neg Pxy$, we know there are only three possible cases: either $PPyx$ or $POxy$ or Dxy. The third case is trivial, since Reflexivity immediately yields Pxx, and hence $\exists z(Pzx \wedge Dzy)$ as required. And the other two cases are exactly the ones covered by Weak and Over-Supplementation, each of which delivers $\exists z(PPzx \wedge Dzy)$ and thus, again, $\exists z(Pzx \wedge Dzy)$. So it's not just that these two principles are weaker; they are weaker in the precise sense that each of them captures one 'half' of Strong Supplementation. Indeed, it's easy to see that as long as P is reflexive (and PP defined via D.1), T.26 suffices for PP–Extensionality.[41] So really we can put it this way: in ordinary circumstances the extensional import of A.18 rests entirely on that half, T.26; Weak Supplementation is, so to speak, the 'innocuous' leftover.

4.3.1 *Solitary Parts*

Historically, Weak Supplementation is relatively recent. It is stated by Whitehead (1919, p. 102) as a general principle of his semi-formal mereology of events, but neither Leśniewski (or Tarski) nor Leonard and Goodman include it among the axioms of their systems, or list it explicitly as a theorem.[42] The first clear formulation is due to Simons (1987, p. 28). Nonetheless, Weak Supplementation captures a constraint on mereological decomposition that is so natural and deeply entrenched in common sense as to have served, in some form or other, as an example of a self-evident truth throughout history. Consider Plato's problem of the one and the many:

> Then the one would be composed of parts ... So the one would thus be many rather than one. (*Parmenides*, 137c–d; Plato, 1997, p. 372)

In his commentary, and then again in his own metaphysical compendium, Proclus comes close to stating the principle explicitly:

> We use a general meaning of part [read: proper part] to describe everything that is in any way linked with other things for the completion of some one entity. (*In Parmenides*, VI, 1113; Proclus, 1987, p. 456)

> If it is a part, it is a part of some whole; and ... since the parts of any whole are at least two, this whole will include a further element. (*Elements of Theology*, 68; Proclus, 1933, p. 65)

41 Pick any a with proper parts and suppose, for arbitrary b, that $\forall z(\mathsf{PP}za \leftrightarrow \mathsf{PP}zb)$. Given D.1 and D.2 we immediately have $\mathsf{O}ab$. Assume for *reductio* that $a \neq b$. Then we must have $\neg\mathsf{P}ab$; for otherwise we'd have $\mathsf{PP}ab$ (by D.1) and hence, given our initial supposition, $\mathsf{PP}aa$, which is impossible (again by D.1). By parallel reasoning we obtain that $\neg\mathsf{P}ba$. So $\mathsf{O}ab \wedge \neg\mathsf{P}ab \wedge \neg\mathsf{P}ba$, which is to say $\mathsf{PO}ab$. But then T.26 applies, requiring some part of a to be disjoint from b. This is impossible, since a itself overlaps b and all of its proper parts are also proper parts of b by hypothesis, and hence overlap b (by D.1 and A.1). So, given T.26, we conclude by *reductio* that $a = b$, as required.

42 As we mentioned, Leśniewski does, however, list Weak Remainder (T.16), from which A.10 follows easily. Concerning Whitehead, it should be noted that he does not state A.10 as a postulate but, rather, as a general truth that his postulates should warrant (along with the O–Supervenience principle T.21). In fact it doesn't follow, as conjectured by Tarski and shown by Leśniewski himself (1927–1931, pp. 260ff). For details about Leśniewski's independence proof, see also Sinisi (1966).

Or consider Aristotle:

> If it is a compound, clearly it will be a compound not of one but of many (or else it will itself be that one). (*Metaphysics*, VII, 17, 1041b22–24; Aristotle, 1984, p. 1644)

Aquinas's gloss:

> If this something when found is not an element but is composed of elements, it is evident that it is not composed of one element only but of many; because if it were not composed of many but of only one, it would follow that that element would be the same as the whole. (*On Aristotle's Metaphysics*, VII, 17, 1677; Aquinas, 1961, vol. 2, p. 617)

Abelard:

> No composite consists of one part; nor is there any part that the quantity of the whole fails to exceed; and if there were one, surely that part would be identical with the whole. (*Dialectica*, V, i, 4; Abelard, 1956, p. 554)

Of course Weak Supplementation is more specific than these statements. It asks for a supplementary part that is, not simply distinct, but disjoint from the first (on the proviso that nothing is disjoint from itself, as implied by Reflexivity). Yet the underlying thought is much the same and so intuitive that contemporary philosophers have gone as far as taking A.10 to express an *analytic* truth. In Simons's own words:[43]

> How could an individual have a *single* proper part? This goes against what we mean by 'part' ... [Weak Supplementation] is indeed analytic—constitutive of the meaning of 'proper part'. (Simons, 1987, pp. 26, 116)

It appears, then, that we are dealing with a decomposition principle that is significantly different from the ones considered thus far. Whereas Remainder and Strong Supplementation express constraints on decomposition that embody substantive metaphysical views, Weak Supplementation would simply encapsulate a minimal requirement that any binary relation must satisfy in order to qualify as parthood at all. The status of this axiom would be on a par with the special status traditionally accorded to the partial order axioms, to the point that Simons uses the exact same words: "constitutive of the meaning". Indeed, not every partial order (if any) qualifies as a parthood relation, and it is plausible to think of Weak Supplementation as providing the missing crucial ingredient in the formal characterization of 'part' as a truly mereological predicate. It is precisely for this reason that the theory

43 Similar statements may be found in Parsons (2004b, p. 88), Pineda (2006, p. 255), Effingham and Robson (2007, p. 635), Koslicki (2008, pp. 167f), Bøhn (2009a, fn. 3), and Evnine (2016, p. 58), among others. One of us, too, stated this view sympathetically in earlier works (Varzi, 2008, p. 110; 2009, p. 601). For a critical examination of the analyticity claim, see Cotnoir (in press).

defined by A.1–A.3 and A.10 has come to be known as Minimal Mereology (Casati and Varzi, 1999, p. 39).[44]

As we know, however, when it comes to claims of this sort there is room for skepticism. We have already commented extensively on the putative status of A.1–A.3 in this regard, seeing that their reputation as purely formal ontological laws is more dubious than traditionally supposed. And there is, we said, a deep connection between Husserl's conception of a formal law that applies to everything there is, no matter what it is, and a law that is in some sense true in virtue of the meaning of the words we use to express it. Of course this is not the same as saying that a formal-ontological law is analytic. After all, we saw that for Husserl these laws must express *a priori* truths, and a law such as the transitivity of P, were it to pass muster, might well be an instance of a *synthetic a priori*.[45] Still, these are details that do not affect the skeptic stance, which is really about the metaphysical neutrality of the axioms in question, the thought that their rejection would somehow amount to a failure to understand the word 'part'. And this applies just as well to the case in point. Is the Weak Supplementation axiom A.10 as self-evident and universally valid as is usually supposed? Does it capture a purely formal truth which, if not genuinely analytic, must nonetheless hold *a priori*, no matter what, just by virtue of the meaning of 'part'?

A growing number of philosophers think it doesn't. One important reason is that A.10 is not an isolated principle. It may be 'innocuous' insofar as adding it to the ordering axioms has no extensional implications, but that doesn't mean the addition is purely cumulative. Indeed, we saw in section 2.4.1 that Weak Supplementation *entails* the Irreflexivity and Asymmetry axioms for PP, A.7 and A.8, in any system where PP satisfies Transitivity, A.9. This yields an elegant simplification in the formal system. But clearly whoever thinks the former axioms are problematic—and in sections 3.1 and 3.2 we saw several reasons why one might think so—will have problems with A.10 as well. Similarly, one can see that if P satisfies Transitivity, A.3, Weak Supplementation entails the Antisymmetry axiom A.2, at least insofar as PP is understood as in D.1.[46] For if x and y are part of each other, then every z that is part of one is also part of the other; and since this falsifies the consequent of A.10, it follows that x and y must be *improper* parts of each other, which is to say identical. Again, formally this is a notable result.

44 Simons himself would add one more minimal principle, called "Falsehood", to the effect that (proper) parthood relations are existence-entailing (see Simons, 1987, p. 362; 1991a, p. 293). We shall come back to this in chapter 6, section 6.2, where the existential assumptions of classical logic, as imported via A.0, will play a role. For now notice that all our axioms are universally quantified and hence apply only to entities in the domain of quantification.

45 Not one of Kant's examples, to be sure, but see e.g. BonJour (1998, p. 29) on the transitivity of 'taller than'. Specifically in regard to the transitivity of 'part of', see Smith (1996b, p. 181).

46 We shall come back to this, and consider other options, in section 4.3.3.

Among other things, it means that Minimal Mereology, as defined above, is, strictly speaking, redundant; the three axioms A.1, A.3, and A.10 would suffice. Philosophically, however, the moral is the same: any independent misgivings concerning Antisymmetry turn immediately into reasons for questioning the truth of Weak Supplementation. Indeed, whoever thinks that, say, a statue and the corresponding lump of clay are part of each other will have reasons to find A.10 unreasonable. After all, such parts are perfectly coextensive; why should we expect anything to be left over when, say, the clay is 'subtracted' from the statue (Donnelly, 2011, p. 230)?[47]

This sort of worry can be generalized. On closer look, *any* case of material coincidence resulting from mereological diminution, as in certain solutions of the puzzle of Dion and Theon and its modern variants (see section 3.1.1), is at odds with A.10. Suppose that, contrary to Chrysippus's and Philo's competing judgments, one thinks that both Theon and Dion survive the amputation of Dion's right foot—a view which, as we mentioned, is not unpopular among contemporary philosophers, from Wiggins (1968) to Lowe (2013) and many others in between. Before the surgery, Theon is a proper part of Dion, hence distinct. If both survive, then they survive as perfectly *coincident* entities. Short of holding that two things have become one, or that Theon did not really exist as a proper undetached part, this violates A.10; for after the surgery there *is* nothing that makes up for the difference between a proper part (Theon) and the whole with which it comes to coincide (Dion).[48]

Similarly, consider the neo-Thomist doctrine known as 'survivalism', according to which the human person continues to exist, bodiless, in the interim period between physical death and resurrection (Stump, 1995).[49] On the assumption that living persons are mereological body-soul composites, this doctrine implies that upon losing our body we will for a while coincide with our soul; the soul will be, literally, "our only proper part" (Hershenov and Koch-Hershenov, 2006, p. 440). It is controversial whether this was in fact Aquinas's view. Pretty clearly, however, the view is incompatible with Weak Supplementation.[50]

47 Bigelow (2010, p. 474) makes the same point.

48 At least, this would be a plausible diagnosis on an endurantist conception of persistence (see Guillon, in press). On a perdurantist conception, one could argue that both Theon and Dion survive as one without *becoming* one, viz. by merging into the same post-surgery person stage. See e.g. Heller (2000), Hawley (2001), and Sider (2001); but see also Wasserman (2002), McGrath (2007a), Sattig (2008), and Moyer (2009) for reservations and Hawley (2008), Eddon (2009), and Rychter (2011) for refinements. We'll return to these issues in section 6.2.

49 See also Stump (2006, 2012). Other defenders of this view include Oderberg (2005), Brown (2005, 2007), Hershenov (2008), Eberl (2009), and Brower (2014).

50 This raises the scholarly question of whether the passage by Aquinas quoted above should really be read as an endorsement of Weak Supplementation; see Oderberg (2012), who also gives a thorough analysis of the impact of survivalism on A.10. The question is less pressing on a more traditional reading of Aquinas, according to which the human person as a whole ceases

Nor is mereological diminution the only source of trouble. Time-travel scenarios such as those already mentioned in chapter 3 can also be seen to cause problems with A.10. If a brick wall may be composed entirely of a single, time-traveling brick, then there won't be any parts of the wall disjoint from that brick, at least so long as parthood is reflexive, even though the brick itself is a proper part of the wall (see Effingham and Robson, 2007).[51] Actually, the source of problem here is independent of time travel. As argued by Donnelly (2010) and Kleinschmidt (2011), A.10 seems to be in trouble as soon as one accepts the possibility of objects being located in multiple places at once (though not everyone would agree; see e.g. Eagle, 2016).

There are, in addition, distinguished metaphysical views that rest on an outright rejection of Weak Supplementation. Perhaps the best-known example is Brentano's theory of accidents. On this theory, a substance (Socrates) is a proper part of an accident (sitting Socrates) even though nothing needs to be added to the former to get the latter.[52]

> Among the things that have parts, there are certain wholes which are not composed of a plurality of parts. Such a whole would seem to be a thing which is such that one of its parts has been enriched but not as a result of the whole acquiring a second part. (Brentano, 1933, p. 47)

Similarly, on Fine's (1999) theory of embodiments, an individual such as Socrates involves a principle of variable embodiment that picks out a concrete manifestation (a bundle of fleshy parts arranged in a suitable way) at each time at which Socrates exists. Insofar as this principle is literally part of Socrates,[53] it must be a proper part; yet there would seem to be no supplement. Indeed Fine is plain-spoken in rejecting A.10. As he writes elsewhere:

> Socrates is a part of singleton Socrates even though there is no proper part of singleton Socrates that is not a part of Socrates. (Fine, 2007, p. 162)[54]

Another example, from the domain of intensive magnitudes, is offered by Geach (1991), who tells us that if a lesser light persists as part of a greater

to exist at death and begins to exist again at resurrection; see Toner (2009, 2010) and references therein. On Aquinas's mereology, see also Henry (1991a, ch. 3), Svoboda (2012), Galluzzo (2015).

51 Gilmore (2007) presents a similar case. To be sure, as mentioned in chapter 3, note 9, things may once again differ according to whether one takes the bricks to be enduring entities or perduring entities composed of distinct temporal parts. For relevant discussion, see Smith (2009), Gilmore (2010a), Eagle (2010a), Effingham (2010a), Toner (2013, §2), and Daniels (2014).

52 For useful discussion, see Chisholm (1978), Smith (1987), Baumgartner and Simons (1993, §6), and Kriegel (2015, §4; 2018a, §1.6). Brentano's view has a parallel in Kotarbiński's (1929) theory of qualitative extensions; see Smith (1990, §§12f).

53 Fine (1999) is not explicit in this regard, but see Fine (2007) in response to Koslicki (2007) for a clear statement. Evnine (2016, p. 55, fn. 36) reports that Fine has since changed his mind.

54 Caplan *et al.* (2010, p. 512) also express sympathy toward the rejection in the context of mereological construals of set theory, though their overall view is different.

light, "there is no identifiable individual which *is* the increment of light" (p. 254).[55] And even simpler is the geopolitical case of Smith (1999, p. 270): the City of Hamburg is part of the German Federal State of Hamburg, and since they are distinct, it must be a proper part; yet mereologically there appears to be nothing to make up for the difference.

Finally, it is worth noting that Weak Supplementation is incompatible with certain views concerning the fundamental structure of space (or time). Suppose, for instance, that space is Whiteheadian: each spatial region has smaller regions as proper parts, but all regions are of the same dimension (Whitehead, 1929, pt. IV, ch 2). If space is three-dimensional, this means there are no boundary elements such as points, lines, or surfaces. Nonetheless, for Whitehead we should still acknowledge a difference between regions that overlap and regions that barely touch 'externally', hence a difference between 'interior parts' and 'tangential parts'. In the presence of suitably strong fusion principles, this suffices to reconstruct the classical topological opposition between open regions and closed ones (as detailed in Clarke, 1981). And that's enough to cause trouble for A.10.[56] For every closed region, x, will include its open interior, y, as a proper part (the interior of a region being the fusion of its interior parts); and yet every part of x will overlap y, since it will overlap some interior part of x. The only difference between tangential and interior parts lies at the boundary, and in Whiteheadian space there *are* no boundaries.[57]

Perhaps one doesn't even need Whiteheadian space to cause trouble. Yablo (2016, p. 144) gives a simple measure-theoretic argument that would apply whenever the standard open/closed distinction is accepted. For a closed region and its open interior have the same volume: were there to be a supplementary part, it would not take up any space, by additivity of measure. But then how can there *be* a supplementary part?

4.3.2 *Weak Supplementation and Extensionality*

There is, then, a long list of facts, scenarios, and philosophical theories that clash with Weak Supplementation. As with the ordering axioms, we have

55 As Geach notes, this peculiarity of intensive magnitudes is already emphasized by McTaggart (1927, §568) and plays a crucial role for a proper understanding of his C series of time.

56 We noted that Whitehead himself endorsed A.10 in the context of his earlier, purely mereological theory (Whitehead, 1919). However, the postulates of Whitehead (1929) only guarantee that A.10 holds for those regions that would qualify as open (cf. Clarke, 1981, thm. T0.31). It doesn't follow that it continues to hold for such regions in relation to their closures.

57 The failure of A.10 in this setting is discussed more extensively in Varzi (1997, pp. 33f; in press), Cohn and Varzi (2003, pp. 373f), and Hudson (2002a, pp. 437ff; 2005, pp. 53ff). Hudson further argues that admitting only closed regions, or only open ones, would be independently problematic if regions are to serve as the receptacles of material bodies. See also Forrest (2010).

a mereological principle that seems very intuitive and self-evident, to the point of being sometimes classified as 'analytic', and yet does not fit all possible cases. One may attempt to discard all putative counterexamples as *im*possible, and indeed whoever thinks Weak Supplementation is non-negotiable will stick to Antisymmetry and reject all other putative counterexamples precisely on such grounds.[58] Anyone else, however, might reach the opposite conclusion and reject A.10 instead.

The fact that A.10 entails Antisymmetry is especially disturbing here. In section 3.2.3 we saw that Antisymmetry is closely connected with extensionality, and actually coincides with P–Extensionality (T.9) whenever P is transitive and reflexive. One may therefore complain that Weak Supplementation is not as 'innocuous' with respect to extensionality as its comparison with Over-Supplementation (T.26) suggested. Of course, it remains true that Weak Supplementation does not suffice for the stronger forms of extensionality that follow from Antisymmetry in conjunction with Strong Supplementation, such as O–Extensionality (T.10) or PP–Extensionality (T.1), and it is these stronger forms that most philosophers find problematic. One need not accept the possibility of parthood loops to believe that a statue and the corresponding lump of clay are distinct, or that a bouquet of roses is not the 'mere' fusion of the individual flowers. For such philosophers, P–Extensionality is unproblematic and A.10 would be innocuous enough. Yet there is more. For decomposition is only part of the picture, and adding some assumptions about composition may suffice for A.10 to entail the stronger forms of extensionality as well. In particular, it bears emphasis that accepting A.10 makes it virtually impossible for an anti-extensionalist to endorse a liberal view concerning composition.

Consider, for instance, the most liberal view—universalism. That is the view according to which any specifiable plurality of objects composes something, as expressed by the axiom schema of Unrestricted Fusion, A.5. Given just Reflexivity, the conjunction of A.10 and A.5 turns out to be sufficient for every composite object to count as the unique fusion of its own proper parts.[59] That immediately implies PP–Extensionality. A similar result applies if we express universalism in terms of the alternative notion of fusion defined in D.13 (following Leśniewski, 1916). In that case, given just Transitivity, the conjunction of A.10 and the corresponding Unrestricted Fusion′

58 Such is, for instance, Simons's attitude. See his comments about Brentano and about the Whitehead-Clarke theory of space in Simons (1987, pp. 26 and 98).

59 Suppose a is a composite object. Let the φs be the proper parts of a and, given A.5, let b be a fusion of the φs. By D.1, every φ is part of a, which implies that $\mathrm{P}ba$ (by the second conjunct of D.6). Suppose $a \neq b$. Then $\mathrm{PP}ba$ (again by D.1) and, given A.10, a should have a proper part disjoint from b. But that is impossible, since such a part would be a φ, and every φ overlaps b (by the first conjunct of D.6 and A.1). So $a = b$ by *reductio*. Since b was an arbitrary fusion of the φs, the argument generalizes, showing that a is *the* fusion of the φs.

axiom schema A.11 yields classical mereology, and so again PP–Extensionality and the like will follow as theorems.[60] The picture would be different if we expressed universalism in terms of the third notion of fusion mentioned in chapter 2, corresponding to D.16 (from Goodman, 1951) or, equivalently, D.18 (from Leonard and Goodman, 1940). However, we shall see in chapter 5 that this option is independently problematic in the absence of Strong Supplementation. In the present context, the only viable options are the first two—and the non-extensionalist can accept neither (short of relinquishing Reflexivity or Transitivity).

These results may come as a surprise. One might have thought that one's views about extensionality are independent of questions concerning composition. Just as there are philosophers who endorse extensionalism while rejecting universalism (e.g. Chisholm, 1976, 1987), others might be inclined to endorse the latter while rejecting extensionalism. Indeed, since the anti-extensionalist thinks that objects with the same parts can be distinct, anti-extensionalism should be *prima facie* compatible with more fusions, not fewer. Well, that is just not so.[61]

Of course, universalism is only one possible view about composition, and a radical one at that. But one may get PP–Extensionality from Weak Supplementation also in conjunction with more modest views. For example, in the presence of Transitivity it is enough to assume that every *pair* of objects has a fusion, or rather a fusion′ in the sense of D.13. That is, endorsing the following composition principle will suffice:

(A.36) $\forall x \forall y \exists z S'zxy$ *Unrestricted Sum′*

where S' is the relation of binary sum ('z is a sum of x and y') determined by D.13. It can also be defined directly as follows:

(D.35) $S'zxy :\equiv Pxz \wedge Pyz \wedge \forall w(Pwz \rightarrow (Owx \vee Owy))$ *Binary Sum′*

Here is the proof. Imagine we had a counterexample to PP–Extensionality: two composite objects, a and b, with the same proper parts. Notice we must have both $\neg Pab$ and $\neg Pba$. For if we had Pab, D.1 would imply that $PPab$ (because $a \neq b$) and also that $\neg PPaa$ (because $a = a$), contradicting

60 In section 2.4.1 we saw that classical mereology can be axiomatized taking A.10 and A.11 along with A.9, the Transitivity axiom for PP (Asymmetry follows by D.12). However, we also saw that A.9 follows from D.1, A.3, and A.2, and we know A.2 follows from A.10 and A.3. Thus trading A.9 for A.3 will not affect the strength of the system. (This is similar to the "second way" to classical mereology of Hovda, 2009, though Hovda additionally trades A.10 for T.25.)

61 There are other consequences worth noting. For example, in the debate over the metaphysics of persistence, the above results undermine the viability of any form of plenitudinous coincidentalism—an endurantist view (held e.g. by Bennett, 2004 and Hawthorne, 2006, ch. 5) that allows for as many objects as a perdurantist would countenance. See Gilmore (in press).

the assumption that a and b have the same proper parts. *Mutatis mutandis* for the supposition that Pba. Now, given A.36, we know there is something, c, which is a sum′ of a and b. Moreover, c must be distinct from both a and b, for we have just seen that neither of these is part of the other, while D.35 requires that both be part of c. It follows that $PPac \wedge PPbc$. Take one of these conjuncts, say, $PPac$. This is a typical situation when A.10 applies. So there must exist some d such that $PPdc$ and Dda. Using again D.35, we know that Odb, which means d and b have a common part, e. By our definition of PP (D.1), there are only two ways e could be part of b: either $PPeb$ or $e = b$.[62] The first case, however, is impossible. For it implies that $PPea$ (by hypothesis) and hence that Oda, contradicting Dda. And the second case is impossible, too. For let f be any proper part of b (a composite object by assumption). Then we have that $PPfe$. Since Ped, Transitivity gives us Pfd, and since we also have $PPfa$ (by hypothesis), we obtain again that Oda, contradicting Dda. As both cases are impossible, we conclude that no such thing as d can exist, i.e. c has no proper parts disjoint from a even though $PPac$. This violates A.10. So if A.10 is true, the counterexample we hypothesized cannot obtain: Transitivity and Unrestricted Sum′ will force PP–Extensionality.

For another illustration, we get PP–Extensionality out of Weak Supplementation (together with Reflexivity and Transitivity) as soon as we make the assumption that every pair of overlapping objects has, not a sum′, but a product:

(A.37) $\forall x \forall y(Oxy \rightarrow \exists z\, z = x \times y)$ *Unrestricted Product*

Note that this is really a composition principle, since $a \times b$ is just the fusion of the common parts of a and b (see D.10). And many will find it plausible enough; after all, if two objects have a part in common, why should they not have a *maximal* common part? Yet this principle is enough to turn Weak Supplementation into Strong Supplementation. To see why (following Simons, 1987, p. 30), suppose $\neg Pab$. This is an instance of the antecedent of Strong Supplementation, so we need to derive the consequent. We have two cases: either Dab or Oab. In the first case, Reflexivity guarantees that Paa, and so there is some z—namely a itself—with $Pza \wedge Dzb$ as required. In the second case, A.37 guarantees the existence of $a \times b$, which is part of both a and b. Since $\neg Pab$, we know that $a \times b \neq a$, and hence $PP(a \times b)a$. By A.10, we

62 Rea (2010) objects to this step in response to Varzi (2009), where the present proof was originally put forward. In fact the step follows from D.1 by sheer logic, and we have used it before. There is, however, something to be said about the crucial role of D.1 in this context (or, if PP were taken as primitive, about the crucial role of D.12 in defining P, which would warrant the same step). We shall come back to this in section 4.3.3. For a detailed diagnosis, see also Calosi (2014; in press-a, §3).

have it that there's a z such that Pza and $Dz(a \times b)$. But every part of a that is disjoint from $a \times b$ is itself disjoint from b. Hence, $Pza \wedge Dzb$ as required. So Strong Supplementation follows. And since we know that this axiom and Reflexivity entail the Proper Parts principle T.24, PP–Extensionality follows immediately by Antisymmetry (which follows from Weak Supplementation and Transitivity).

We shall have much more to say about how decomposition and composition principles interact, sometimes in surprising ways, in chapter 5, where compositional theses of varying strengths will also be examined more closely. Here the point of these facts and examples is simply to illustrate their bearing on the status of Weak Supplementation. Particularly with regard to extensionality, the *prima facie* innocuousness of this axiom is, on closer look, much more fragile than one might expect.

4.3.3 *Strictly Weak Supplementation*

There is, however, a sense in which the extensionalist consequences of Weak Supplementation could be avoided. For both the arguments of section 4.3.2 and the proof that Antisymmetry follows from Weak Supplementation rest on understanding PP via the standard definition in D.1, i.e. as PP_1: a proper part is a part distinct from the whole. We know there is an alternative definition, D.15, whereby PP is characterized as asymmetric parthood, PP_2. If this definition is used instead, or if PP is treated as primitive, the picture changes.

Consider first the alternative reading of PP as PP_2.[63] That is, suppose we read Weak Supplementation, as follows:

(A.38) $\forall x \forall y (PP_2 yx \rightarrow \exists z (PP_2 zx \wedge Dzy))$ *Strict Supplementation*

and similarly for Weak P–Supplementation:[64]

(T.27) $\forall x \forall y (PP_2 yx \rightarrow \exists z (Pzx \wedge Dzy))$ *Strict* P–*Supplementation*

In an antisymmetric setting, the two notions of proper parthood coincide and so these principles reduce to A.10 and T.25, respectively. Generally speaking, however, we know that PP_2 is stronger than PP_1, which means that A.38 and T.27 may be weaker than A.10 and T.25.[65] And one sense in which

63 This is the course suggested in Cotnoir (2010). See also Obojska (2013b) and Cotnoir (2016a, in press) for related remarks and Walters (2019) for discussion.

64 In Varzi (2016, §3.1), 'Strict Supplementation' is used for this latter thesis.

65 The different strength of A.38 and T.27 also shows in their mutual relationships. For while we saw that T.25 entails A.10 as long as P is reflexive, the entailment from T.27 to A.38 requires in addition that P be transitive. We leave the proof as an exercise.

they are weaker is precisely that they do *not* imply Antisymmetry even when P is transitive. This is shown by the model in figure 4.8, which we briefly discussed in connection with the possibility of parthood loops (section 3.2.3). Since this model is non-antisymmetric, A.10 and T.25 are both false: we have that PP_1ba even though every part of a overlaps b, and similarly for PP_1ab. Yet the strict variants in A.38 and T.27 are both true in this model, as we have it that neither PP_2ba nor PP_2ab (and all cases where PP_2 obtains are properly supplemented).

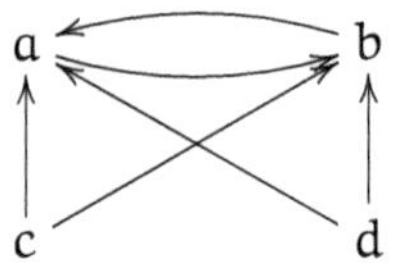

Figure 4.8: A model of Strict Supplementation without weak supplements

So, two consequences follow immediately. First, since A.38 (or T.27) does not imply Antisymmetry, hence P–Extensionality, one basic worry about Weak Supplementation can be handled accordingly: the anti-extensionalist can insist on reading the axiom in these strict terms. While the strict reading may not reflect the language used in some of the classic texts cited earlier, the basic intuition is certainly retained. (Indeed, when Peter Abelard says that there is no [proper] part that the quantity of the whole fails to "exceed", the asymmetric reading of 'proper part' seems just right.) Second, with Weak Supplementation understood as Strict Supplementation, the anti-extensionalist is now free to endorse this principle along with any liberal views about composition without fear of PP–Extensionality, i.e., effectively, PP_2–Extensionality. For the impossibility arguments of section 4.3.2 cease to be valid if PP is treated as PP_2 (and A.10 as A.38). This can be checked, again, by looking at the model in figure 4.8. The model satisfies universalism in the two relevant senses expressed by the axiom schemas A.5 and A.11, and it also satisfies Reflexivity and Transitivity; yet PP_2–Extensionality fails. The same is true, of course, if Strict Supplementation is combined with weaker compositional principles, such as the Unrestricted Sum′ principle A.36. The only case that would remain problematic for the anti-extensionalist is the conjunction of Strict Supplementation with the Unrestricted Product principle expressed by A.37 (which fails in the model of figure 4.8). However, this is not so surprising. After all, A.37 is not altogether neutral with regard to extensionality: it asserts that every pair of overlapping things has a *unique* product.[66]

66 Simons (1987, p. 31) actually lists A.37 as an axiom for the theory he calls "Minimal Extensional Mereology"; see note 35.

Reading PP via D.15 is thus an option the anti-extensionalist should seriously consider. So long as Antisymmetry is not assumed on independent grounds, Strict Supplementation is more 'innocuous' than Weak Supplementation *cum* D.1. We leave it as an exercise to check whether this is true also of the mixed variants of these principles that employ both notions of proper part, one in the antecedent and the other in the consequent.

The other option is to treat PP as a primitive (which is how the Weak Supplementation axiom A.10 was originally introduced). We know that in transitive contexts A.10 entails the Asymmetry axiom A.8, and we know A.8 immediately entails the Antisymmetry axiom A.2 if P is defined standardly as in D.12. Hence, short of rejecting Transitivity, this doesn't seem a viable route. However, an anti-extensionalist may wish to adopt the non-standard definition in D.26, reading P as P_2 (see section 3.2.2).[67] As with the shift from PP_1 to PP_2, trading P_1 for P_2 will allow for an object to have improper parts other than itself, and that will suffice to block the inference from A.10 to A.2. This is shown once more by the weakly supplemented model in figure 4.7, where P_2ab and P_2ba. Thus, again, the anti-extensionalist will be on safe ground and the foregoing remarks will apply *mutatis mutandis*.[68] Weak Supplementation *cum* D.26 is as innocuous as Strict Supplementation.

So, both alternative ways of dealing with proper parts can take care of the anti-extensionalist's worries. At least, they can take care of those worries insofar as PP–Extensionality itself is understood in terms of the relevant readings of PP, as PP_2 or as a primitive in conjunction with P_2. On the original reading, as PP_1–Extensionality, the worries will persist. For instance, the argument concerning the Unrestricted Sum′ principle A.36 would still go through with Strict Supplementation in place of Weak Supplementation.[69] (Notice that PP_1–Extensionality will in fact continue to be available as a general principle in spite of the linguistic revisions, since D.1 is still at hand.)

67 This is the course advocated in Null (1995, 1997) and independently suggested by Rea (2010). A slightly different proposal comes from Molto (2018), who prefers the following definition.

$$P_3xy := PPxy \vee (\exists zPPzx \wedge \forall z(PPzx \leftrightarrow PPzy))$$

As with P_2, this relation need not be antisymmetric even if PP is asymmetric. However, in that case P_3 may also fail to be reflexive, since no mereological atom would have any parts. It can be made reflexive by adding $x = y$ as a third disjunct in the definiens. But then, given Transitivity, P_3 comes very close to the disjunctive version of P_2 mentioned in chapter 3, note 20, except for having a biconditional in place of a conditional—a difference that dissolves in all relevant cases (mutual parthood).

68 With one qualification: working with P_2, the relationship between A.10 and T.25 will be even less straightforward than with PP_2. In particular, each direction of the equivalence will require the PP–Transitivity axiom A.9. Again, we leave the proof as an exercise.

69 This is pointed out in Gilmore (in press, §1.6.1). But the reader can check things directly. For notice that early in the argument we can easily replace $PPac \wedge PPbc$ with $PP_2ac \wedge PP_2bc$ (using Transitivity). Then it suffices to apply PP–Strength (T.7) and continue reading PP as PP_1 where D.1 is invoked.

That being said, it remains that not everyone is willing to forgo the antisymmetry of parthood in order to redeem Weak Supplementation. Indeed, it bears emphasis that this move will automatically redeem the Strong Supplementation axiom as well, for the reasons we saw at the end of section 4.2: Strong Supplementation entails the Proper Parts principle T.24, but the further step from T.24 to PP–Extensionality requires Antisymmetry (as does the original entailment from Strong to Weak Supplementation[70]). Insofar as a major motivation for considering A.10 was precisely to avoid the extensionalist implications of Strong Supplementation without questioning the standard ordering axioms for P, this payoff is hardly satisfactory. Moreover, we know that the extensionalist implications of Weak Supplementation do not exhaust all concerns about this axiom. The putative counterexamples involving solitary parts, or the worries about the impossibility to allow for proper-parthood loops, arise regardless. Thus, whoever deems Antisymmetry non-negotiable, or finds any such worries and counterexamples problematic, will still feel uneasy. As a general decomposition principle, Weak or even Strict Supplementation will not be weak enough.

4.4 EVEN WEAKER SUPPLEMENTATION

There are further options. We have looked at ways of weakening A.10 mainly by strengthening the antecedent, using a stronger notion of 'proper part'; but one may also weaken the axiom by adjusting the consequent. We shall conclude our analysis by considering two main ways of doing so.

A first, immediate way is illustrated by the following principles (from Simons, 1987, p. 27):[71]

(A.39) $\forall x \forall y(PPyx \rightarrow \exists z(PPzx \wedge \neg z = y))$ *Weak Company*

(A.40) $\forall x \forall y(PPyx \rightarrow \exists z(PPzx \wedge \neg Pzy))$ *Strong Company*

These principles are obtained directly from A.10 by replacing the second conjunct in the consequent with conditions that are normally weaker than disjointness: in the presence of Reflexivity, Dzy implies $\neg Pzy$, which in turn implies $\neg z = y$, though obviously we don't have the converse implications. So both principles are correspondingly weaker.

Weak Company is actually a natural option here. It says that every proper part must be accompanied by another, and this is a literal rendering of the

70 By contrast, the entailment from Strong to Strict Supplementation only requires the Transitivity axiom A.3; see Obojska (2013b, thm. 3.2).

71 Simons mentions these principles only to reject them as overly weak. Our nomenclature is from Varzi (2007a, p. 955). Other authors speak of "Non-identity Supplementation" and "Non-parthood Supplementation", respectively (e.g. Bynoe, 2011, pp. 93f).

principal idea behind every supplementation principle: a whole cannot have a single proper part. Accordingly, the main effect of A.39 is to exclude the model in figure 4.9 and the like.

Figure 4.9: A failure of Weak Company

This may already be too much for some of the views mentioned in section 4.3.1. A neo-Thomist survivalist, for instance, would insist that the condition of a person between death and resurrection is precisely as in the model above, with the indivisible soul as the person's only proper part, and would therefore reject A.39 along with A.10. However, as soon as the solitary part is allowed to have proper parts of its own, as in most other cases, A.39 is clearly more tolerant than A.10, witness the model in figure 4.10.

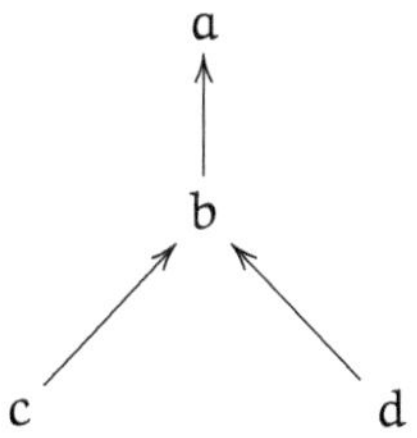

Figure 4.10: A model of Weak Company

Brentano's theory of accidents is a case in point. Socrates (b) is the only immediate part of sitting Socrates (a). Since both are composed of the same ultimate constituents, say, c and d, there is nothing to make up for the distinction and Weak Supplementation fails. Strict Supplementation fails, too. But Weak Company holds, since b, c, and d are all distinct. The same could be said of other problematic cases mentioned in section 4.3.1, such as those deriving from mereological diminution (Dion and surviving Theon) or time travel (the brick wall). Moreover, Weak Company is compatible with certain cases of mutual parthood, such as the model of figure 4.8, and so it will also be suitable in the context of mereological theories that forgo Antisymmetry. Finally, the principle is weak enough to avoid the incompatibility between anti-extensionalism and compositional universalism even when P and PP obey all the ordering axioms. This is shown by the model in figure 4.11. Here PP–Extensionality is false, since b_1 and b_2 have the same proper parts, and universalism holds, at least in the version based on A.11: every collection of elements has a fusion′. Obviously Weak Supplementation fails, since a has no parts disjoint from b_1 (or from b_2). But A.39 is true.

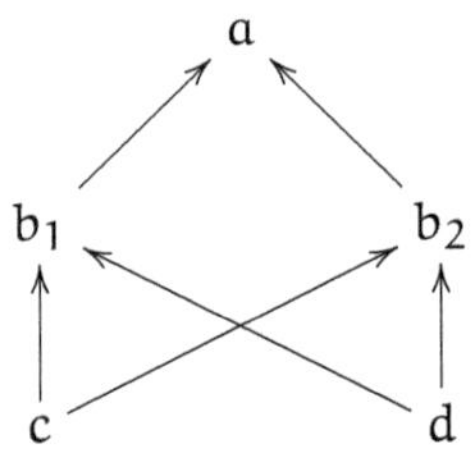

Figure 4.11: A non-extensional model of Weak Company satisfying universalism

Unfortunately, all of this comes at a price. Not only is A.39 weak enough to permit such scenarios; there is a sense in which A.39 is *too* weak. For while it rules out models where a whole is decomposed into a single proper part, as in figure 4.9, it is compatible with other models that seem to suffer from the same 'defect'. A simple example (from Simons, *ibid.*) is given in the left diagram of figure 4.12, where proper-part decomposition results in an (infinitely) descending linear chain. In this model, each proper part is indeed accompanied by another one; but the latter does not supplement the former, it just piles up. Similarly for the non-extensional diagram on the right, where *two* wholes decompose into the same chain of proper parts. It is hard to find satisfaction in this picture. Weak Company is a literal rendering of the idea that a whole cannot have a single proper part; but for all its virtues, it would seem it only captures the letter of the idea, not the spirit.

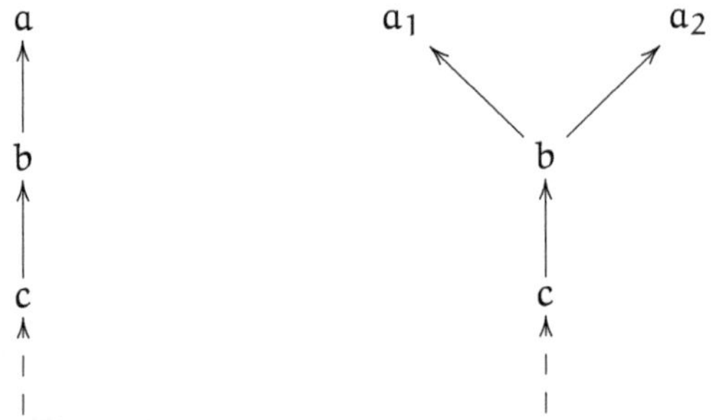

Figure 4.12: Two more models of Weak Company

The Strong Company principle, A.40, avoids this problem. This principle says that every proper part must be accompanied by a second proper part that is not already included in the first. Since a linear proper-parthood chain violates this stronger requirement, the models of figure 4.12 are thereby excluded. However, notice that this result is achieved at the cost of excluding also the model in figure 4.10, whose admission spoke in favor of A.39. Moreover, Strong Company rules out the mutual-part model of figure 4.8, and will therefore be unsuitable in the context of non-antisymmetric mereologies. So this principle is not just a stronger variant of A.39; as a general decomposition principle, some will find it *too* strong.

On the other hand, one might think Strong Company is still too weak. It does rule out the descending chains of figure 4.12, but it still allows for models with *dense* descending chains, i.e. chains with no immediate parts. To exclude such models, A.40 would have to be strengthened accordingly:[72]

(A.41) $\forall x \forall y(PPyx \rightarrow \exists z(PPzx \wedge \neg Pzy \wedge \neg Pyz))$ *Super-Strong Company*

Moreover, even this stronger formulation admits models that seem equally implausible, such as the bottomless 'pyramid' in the left diagram of figure 4.13 (also from Simons) or the non-extensional 'ladder' in the right diagram. In these models, the top elements decompose into an infinity of parts *all* of which overlap one another. So these are not just cases where Weak Supplementation fails; here Weak Supplementation fails at every level of decomposition, which means that the removal of *any* proper part, at any level, will result in the annihilation of the whole. Formally there is nothing wrong, and indeed both models are in perfect compliance with the standard ordering axioms. But it's hard to imagine a philosophical view that would treat such partial orders as representing genuine part-whole configurations.[73]

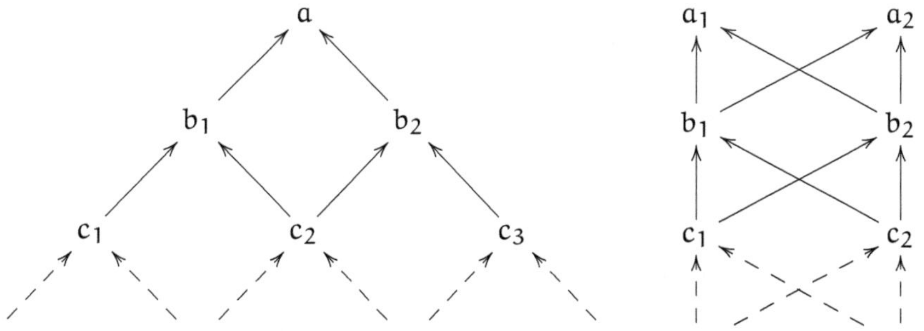

Figure 4.13: Two models of (Super-)Strong Company

72 This principle may be found in Koons (2014, §5.1), who calls it "Very Strong Companionship".

73 Commenting on Simons's quick dismissal of the left model, Donnelly (2011, p. 244) says a neo-Aristotelian metaphysics might plausibly hold that all objects share a common formal part, e.g. a part representing a general condition such as self-identity; or it might even be that all objects share a common material part, e.g. a frenzied time-traveling particle that manages to squeeze into everything. These would indeed be cases of universal overlap. Yet the relevant mereology

So each of these Company principles has something to offer, and each reflects a natural way of weakening A.10 by relaxing the provision on the requisite supplementary part; yet all involve a complex trade-off of strengths and weaknesses that makes them less straightforward than their simple format might suggest. Ditto for the obvious variants one could consider, obtained by tinkering with the various occurrences of P and PP in the consequent or in the antecedent of A.39 and A.40 (or A.41).[74] Such variants may be weaker in some respects and stronger in others, but all will agree, for instance, in admitting the models of figure 4.13.

The second way of weakening A.10 by weakening the consequent comes from Gilmore (2009, p. 119n).[75] Consider the following principle.

(T.28) $\forall x \forall y(PPyx \rightarrow \exists w \exists z(Pwx \wedge Pzx \wedge Dwz))$ *Quasi-P–Supplementation*

Reading PP as PP_1, this principle says that anything that has a *distinct* part has *disjoint* parts. Given Reflexivity, it is equivalent to the following.[76]

(A.42) $\forall x \forall y(PPyx \rightarrow \exists w \exists z(PPwx \wedge PPzx \wedge Dwz))$ *Quasi-Supplementation*

And since disjointness implies non-identity, the latter principle literally says that if something has a proper part, it has at least *two* disjoint proper parts. This is how the supplementation intuition is often stated informally. Simons himself (1987, p. 27) uses these words to motivate and introduce the Weak Supplementation axiom A.10, and some authors even *identify* Weak Supplementation with A.42 (as in Bennett, 2011, p. 286). So A.42 is certainly a good candidate to capture the 'self-evident' truth A.10 was meant to express—and so is T.28. Yet again these principles are strictly weaker than A.10.

Let us assume Reflexivity, so we can just focus on A.42. That this principle follows from A.10 should be obvious, since whenever b is a proper part of a and c is a further proper part of a disjoint from b, as required by A.10, we have it that a has two disjoint proper parts, namely b and c, meeting

would not quite correspond to the model in question, for in the pyramid everything overlaps everything without there being any *one* part that everything shares. Donnelly also suggests the possibility that all pairs of objects have *some* time-traveling particle in common, though not the same in all cases. That would fit the bill. However, it is unclear how the relevant time traveling would work, short of assuming such particles to be atomic (which the model rules out).

74 For example, Evnine (2011, p. 214) considers a principle called "Complementarity", a variant of A.39 in which PP is replaced by P in a non-reflexive setting, while Lowe (2001, p. 140) has a variant of A.40, which he simply calls "Weak Supplementation", in which P is replaced by PP. Other variants along these lines are easily constructed. And of course there are variants based on treating PP as a primitive, some of which are considered in Cotnoir and Bacon (2012, §3.1).

75 See also Gilmore (2014, §5, and in press). Gilmore actually reserves 'Quasi-Supplementation' for T.28. Our nomenclature differs for uniformity with the principles of the previous sections.

76 A.1 ensures that nothing is disjoint from its parts, and this suffices for the consequent of T.28 to entail the consequent of A.42. The converse entailment is obvious, since P includes PP.

the requirement of A.42. But, equally obviously, the converse entailment does not hold. For one thing, A.42 admits the non-antisymmetric model in figure 4.8, which is not weakly supplemented. In this regard, A.42 behaves like Weak Company and Strict Supplementation, as opposed to Strong Company. Second, even in contexts where PP is a strict partial order, A.42 admits models that are not strictly supplemented, such as the 'Brentanian' model in figure 4.10, which also satisfies Weak Company but not Strong Company. Finally, as Gilmore (in press, §1.5) notes, A.42 admits also the model of figure 4.11, which means that Quasi-Supplementation, like Weak and Strong Company, is weak enough to avoid the incompatibility of Weak Supplementation with the conjunction of anti-extensionalism and universalism.

So A.42 is strictly weaker than A.10. And despite some similarities, it also differs from all other weakenings considered so far. Indeed, A.42 differs in ways that clearly speak in its favor. It has all the virtues of Weak Company, but is not as weak: the infinitely descending chains in figure 4.12 are not quasi-supplemented. It has the virtues of Strong Company but is not as strong, and yet it's strong enough to rule out the unpleasant models of figure 4.13: those models are not quasi-supplemented, either. And A.42 is also not as strong as Strict Supplementation, since it admits the model of figure 4.10 as well as a larger variety of non-extensional models. In Gilmore's judgment, all of this makes Quasi-Supplementation the best candidate as a 'core principle' governing mereological decomposition, one that deserves the high ratings typically assigned to Weak Supplementation (including perhaps the claim to analyticity) while avoiding its 'vices' and the limits of its other various competitors.

Nevertheless, there is some reason to think that Quasi-Supplementation, too, has unpleasant consequences. After all, this principle does not require that every proper part be itself disjoint from a second proper part; only that the existence of one proper part entails the existence of two proper parts disjoint from each other. In other words, all it requires is that every composite object has two disjoint proper parts *somewhere* down the line. And while this may be a virtue in some cases, as with the model of figure 4.10, it also means that A.42 is compatible with a whole range of structures that don't seem to map onto the intuitive gloss of part-whole supplementation.

Consider, for example, the model in figure 4.14, left. This model satisfies A.42, since c and d are disjoint parts of every a_i. Yet $a_1 \ldots a_n$ is a linear subset, with no other elements in the model incomparable with any a_i. Similarly with the model on the right, which has the additional property of violating PP–Extensionality. These structures vividly illustrate the odd effects of allowing the two proper parts required by the consequent of A.42 to be other than the one mentioned in the antecedent. There may perhaps be philosophical reasons not to dismiss them at the outset. Since both expand

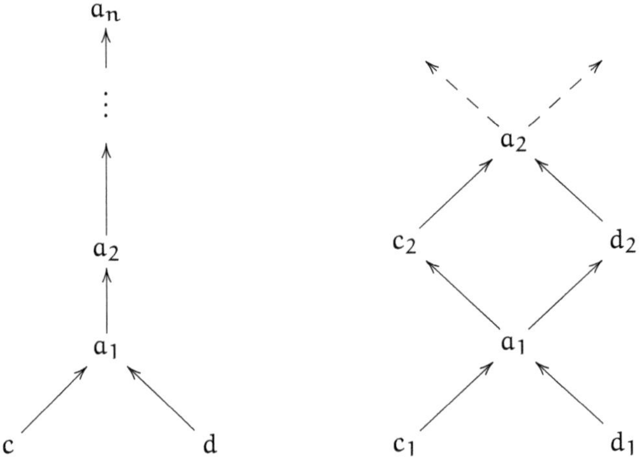

Figure 4.14: Two models of Quasi-Supplementation

the model of figure 4.10, one may, for instance, consider a higher-order extension of Brentano's theory of accidents. The structure on the left would reflect the fact that Socrates (a_1) is part of sitting Socrates (a_2), who in turn is part of thinking sitting Socrates, and so on. On the right we would instead have that Socrates (a_1) is part of sitting Socrates (c_2) and also of thinking Socrates (d_2), both of whom would be part of thinking sitting Socrates (a_3), and so on. However, on this interpretation both models would seem to be missing several elements. On the left there is no element corresponding to thinking Socrates, for instance, and on the right the same issue arises at the higher levels. One may add the missing elements, and the final product may well deliver a good picture of Brentanism. But the odd models in figure 4.14 remain. Alternatively, one might think that structures of this sort are rather akin to a mereology based on set membership, as with Fine's (2007) example of Socrates and singleton Socrates. There is, for instance, a clear difference between {c, d}, {{c, d}}, {{{c, d}}}, and so on, all of which decompose into c and d exactly as in the left model. But then, again, in such a model we would presumably also need elements corresponding to {c}, {{c}}, {{{c}}}, etc., which, if added, would immediately violate A.42.

None of these models, of course, satisfies Weak Supplementation, as they all violate the weaker principles considered above except for Weak Company (which is an obvious consequence of A.42). So the overall picture confirms the complex trade-off between relative strengths and weaknesses mentioned earlier. One way or the other, as soon as we leave the *terra firma* of classical mereology, unexpected parthood structures are bound to show up somewhere; tweaking the supplementation idea to avoid extensionality or other results that one may find philosophically objectionable is no exception. This is by no means an argument to the effect that Weak Supplementation expresses an analytic truth after all. But it suggests that controversies concerning that axiom are not local. If a moral can be drawn, it would rather go in the direction recommended by Donnelly (2011) in the quotation given at the beginning of this chapter, which actually comes from her analysis of supplementation. It is hard to square the demands of A.10 with all views on mereological decomposition. It is equally hard, if not hopeless, to suppose that weaker principles may be found that will preserve the core idea while fitting all possible theories and all desiderata.

4.5 NULL OBJECTS

There is, to be sure, one decomposition thesis regarding which one finds widespread agreement. It's the thesis that decomposition never results in a bottom element that is part of everything. Standardly, the thesis in question is taken to mean that as long as there are at least two things, there exist no such elements—no 'null objects'. This corresponds to the No Zero theorem we met in chapter 2, and in classical mereology it follows from the Remainder axiom A.4 (assuming Reflexivity).

(T.2) $\exists x \exists y \neg x = y \rightarrow \neg \exists x \forall y \, Pxy$ *No Zero*

(Some authors, e.g. Krifka, 1990, p. 491, identify the thesis with just the consequent of T.2. However, this unduly rules out the innocuous one-element model.)

In fact, we saw that precisely here, the absence of a zero element, lies the main difference between classical mereology and the theory of complete Boolean algebras. This was the gist of Tarski's (1935) fundamental result in chapter 2. However, the thesis in question does not require the full strength of A.4. For instance, the non-existence of a null object already follows from the Weak Supplementation principle A.10. For if there were such an object, n, then for every y distinct from n we would have $PPny$, and hence by A.10 there would have to be something that is part of y and disjoint from n, which is impossible if n is to be part of everything. Similarly, T.2 follows from the weaker Quasi-Supplementation principle A.42. For this principle says that $PPny$ implies the existence of two disjoint parts of y, and this is incompatible with n's being part of everything.

More generally, T.2 is usually accepted on independent grounds, for reasons that need not follow from one's favorite supplementation principle. Both Weak and Strong Company, for instance, are compatible with the existence of a null element n (a simple model would in both cases be one in which proper parthood forms a linear dense order, with u at the top and n at the bottom), but someone endorsing these principles might still be intransigent about its non-existence.

Indeed, even someone rejecting the Antisymmetry axiom A.2 may want to assert something along these lines. The formulation in T.2 would not do, for it clashes with certain scenarios that the friend of mutual parts would want to accept. A case in point is the mereological loop we met in section 3.2 (figure 4.15), where, assuming Reflexivity, *every* element is part of everything.

Figure 4.15: Two null objects?

(This model also shows that T.2 doesn't follow from the Strict Supplementation principle A.38, which holds vacuously, highlighting another salient difference between this principle and Weak or Quasi-Supplementation.) There is, however, a simple way to reformulate T.2 so as to capture the intended thesis in the absence of Antisymmetry. A null object is supposed to be a genuine mereological bottom: something that is part of everything *and* has no proper parts of its own. Thus, the idea behind T.2 can be stated more fully as follows.

(T.29) $\exists x \exists y \neg x = y \rightarrow \neg \exists x \forall y (Pxy \wedge \neg PPyx)$ *Strict No Zero*

In antisymmetric contexts the additional conjunct in the consequent is redundant, hence T.29 is equivalent to T.2. Logically, however, T.29 is weaker than T.2, and the model of figure 4.15 shows why: neither element satisfies the additional conjunct and therefore T.29 comes out true. In fact, we can see that this weaker principle is implied also by Strict Supplementation (again, given Reflexivity), since Pny and $\neg PPyn$ would imply PP_2ny whenever $y \neq n$, and thus the same argument given for Weak Supplementation would apply.[77] Precisely for this reason, because T.29 is neutral with respect to the assumption of Antisymmetry, it may therefore be convenient to identify the widespread view that there are no null objects with this weaker, more explicit thesis.

Now, historically the view has its roots in Leśniewski's nominalistic scruples. As we noted in section 2.1.2, Leśniewski felt strongly about the non-existence of a null object. He spoke of its set-theoretic counterpart—the null set, or empty class—as a "mythological" conception (Leśniewski, 1927–1931, p. 202), severely criticizing Fraenkel's positing of "a set that, although a set, is

77 By contrast, T.29 would still be false in a linear dense model with a bottom element and so it does not follow from Weak or Strong Company, just like T.2.

properly speaking not really a set at all" (Fraenkel, 1919, p. 13) and quoting with full endorsement Frege's blunt remark *à propos* Schröder (1890–1895):

> A class ... consists of objects; it is an aggregate, a collective unity, of them; if so, it must vanish when these objects vanish. If we burn down all the trees of a wood, we thereby burn down the wood. Thus there can be no empty class. (Frege, 1895, p. 89)

Actually, Frege was not alone in his skepticism over the empty class. Russell felt the same way, calling it "a fiction" (Russell, 1903, p. 81), and we know that Dedekind, too, had excluded the empty class from his theory, describing it as something that may at best be "appropriate to imagine" for certain investigations (Dedekind, 1888, p. 46). Even the *Axiom der Elementarmengen* of Zermelo (1908, p. 202), which marks the official postulation of the *Nullmenge* in set theory, refers to it as "a (fictitious) set".[78] Still, it is a fact that standard set theory is committed to taking this fiction seriously, whereas mereologists are largely in agreement that there is no room for such a fiction in the field of the part-whole relation. Indeed, within the context of set theory, one can try to make the null set philosophically digestible by identifying it with some arbitrarily chosen individual (*Urelement*) to be treated as an honorary subset of itself and of all sets, as Fraenkel *et al.* (1973, p. 24) suggested.[79] But the null individual? What could do the trick? As Geach (1949, p. 522) noted, it would have to exist "nowhen and nowhere", or perhaps "always and everywhere",[80] and many philosophers find this absurd (Simons, 1987, p. 13), if not altogether senseless (van Inwagen, 2002a, p. 191). In the words of David Lewis:

> It is well-nigh unintelligible how anything could behave as the null individual is said to behave. It is a very queer thing indeed, and we have no good reason to believe in it. (Lewis, 1991, p. 11)

All this being said, not everybody agrees. Some authors have urged that the notion of a null object "is no better or worse than that of the null class"

---

78 Zermelo commented repeatedly on the empty set in his correspondence with Fraenkel, saying that it is "not a genuine set", that he introduced it "only for formal reasons", that its legitimacy was becoming "more and more doubtful" to him, and that "perhaps one can dispense with it" (letters of 31 March and 9 May 1921, cited in Ebbinghaus, 2007a, p. 135).

79 The suggestion is absent from the first edition (Fraenkel and Bar-Hillel, 1958). A similar idea may be found in Lewis (1991, 1993b), who emphasizes that the chosen individual "needn't be a special individual with a whiff of nothingness about it" (1991, p. 13). Any individual would do, even Possum the cat, though Lewis eventually settles on something much bigger, identifying the null set with the fusion of all individuals (= things that are members, but do not themselves have members). For misgivings, see Potter (1993) and Hand (1995).

80 The second phrase comes from an added footnote in the reprint edition (Geach, 1972, p. 201). As it turns out, precisely that seems to be the view of Efird and Stoneham (2005) (with replies in Coggins, 2010, §3.2 and Darby and Watson, 2010).

(Martin, 1965, pp. 723f).[81] Others have argued that "there is no strong reason for rejecting the empty individual as an arbitrary individual, once one accepts improper parts and arbitrary sums, for example" (Mosterin, 1994, p. 521). Even Carnap, the arch-critic of Heidegger's "das Nichts" (Carnap, 1931), thought a null object would be a "natural and convenient choice" for certain purposes, such as providing a default denotation for all defective definite descriptions (Carnap, 1947, p. 37).[82] Other philosophers who found it reasonable to posit a mereologically null entity include Bunt (1985) in the context of his ensemble theory, Meixner (1997) for the mereology of states of affairs, Humberstone (2000) in relation to spatial regions, Landman (2004) in the domain of events, Zalta (2016) in connection with the mereology of concepts, and Fine (2017) in his treatment of states, or situations, as truthmakers.[83] Bunge (1966) even countenances several null objects, one for each kind of entity.[84]

There have also been attempts to offer substantive philosophical interpretations of the notion of a null object. For instance, Giraud (2013) construes it as a Meinongian individual lacking all nuclear properties,[85] Priest (2014a,b) as a Heideggerian nothing that nothings, and Casati and Fujikawa (2019) as the complement of the fusion of all existing and nonexisting objects, while others have gone as far as construing the null object as the omnipresent devil (Oppy, 1997a, fn. 19) or, at the opposite extreme, as the ultimate incarnation of divine omnipresent simplicity (Hudson, 2006b, 2009).

Let us, then, ask: what would happen if we dropped all scruples and rejected (Strict) No Zero? Indeed, what sort of mereology would we get if

81 Martin himself made abundant use of a null object in his mereological systems, from Martin (1943) to Martin (1988). Strangely, in a later text he also says that "in admitting a null object, we follow Leśniewski rather than Husserl" (Martin, 1992, p. 175). Putnam (1987a, pp. 18f) makes the same mistake in contrasting the world of "some Polish logicians" to Carnap's. In fact that's a double blunder, since Carnap does admit a null individual (see note 82).

82 It was actually with reference to Carnap's proposal that Geach made the remark cited above. Note that Carnap is explicit in identifying the null object with "that thing which is part of every thing". Ironically, many would take *that* to be a defective description (Williamson, 2013, p. 60n). Moreover, as Oliver and Smiley (2013a, p. 611) note, the identification implies that the truth of a statement such as 'The present King of France is not part of every thing' requires that the thing which is part of every thing be *not* part of every thing, resuscitating Heidegger's ghost.

83 See also Roeper (1997), Mormann (2000a,b), Forrest (2002), Janicki and Lê (2007), Arntzenius (2012), and Vakarelov (2017), all of whom emphasize that the null object (or region, etc.) is just a convenient algebraic 'fiction'.

84 Bunge emphatically distances himself from the standard conception of the null object as something that is part of everything, offering instead the following characterization: "The null individual of a given kind is that thing which, added to an arbitrary individual of any kind, yields the latter" (p. 777; see also Bunge, 1977, p. 51). Given the biconditional $Pxy \leftrightarrow x + y = y$ (cf. D.19), this would actually reduce to the standard conception (as in Bunge, 2010, p. 270). We do, however, get one null individual for each kind if we read 'any kind' as 'that kind'.

85 This view is already hinted at in Parsons (1980, p. 22). Cf. also Zalta (2016, §9.10), where a null object is defined as an abstract object that encodes no properties.

we openly *posited* the existence of a null object that is part of everything and has no proper parts?

(A.43) $\exists x \forall y (Pxy \wedge \neg PPyx)$ *Strict Zero*

The answer calls for two sorts of consideration.

First, we just saw that in classical mereology the No Zero and Strict No Zero theses, T.2 and T.29, follow from the Reflexivity and Remainder axioms, A.1 and A.4, so we can't simply reject those theses without forgoing one of these axioms. Or rather, strictly speaking, there would be no contradiction in just adding A.43 and keeping everything else. But then a simple *modus tollens* on either T.2 or T.29 would immediately imply that there cannot be two distinct objects. In other words, the following would be a theorem, which means that the only acceptable models of our theory would be the trivial, one-element algebra.

(T.30) $\exists x \forall y \; x = y$ *Oneness*

In fact, T.30 would be a theorem of any theory including as little as Reflexivity and either Weak Supplementation, Strict Supplementation, or Quasi-Supplementation, since we saw that this is enough to derive T.29. Short of giving up such principles,[86] or changing the underlying logic,[87] this means that adding A.43 to any such theory would again result in triviality.

It might be objected that 'triviality' is the wrong word here. After all, there have been and continue to be philosophers who hold radically monistic ontologies—from the Eleatics (Rea, 2001) to Spinoza (Bennett, 1984) all the way to contemporary authors such as Horgan and Potrč (2000, 2008), for whom the entire cosmos is but one huge extended atom, an enormously complex but partless "blobject".[88] For all we know, it may even be that the best ontology for quantum mechanics, if not for Newtonian mechanics, consists in a lonely atom speeding through configuration-space (Albert, 1996). None of this is trivial. However, none of this amounts to fully endorsing T.30, either. For such theories do not, strictly speaking, assert the existence of one single

86 Hudson (2006b) gives up Weak Supplementation for this reason. Similarly, Segal (2014) trades Weak Supplementation for Strong Company (in his terminology: Very Weak Supplementation).

87 As in Weber and Cotnoir (2015), who make use of null objects as "traces" of inconsistent boundaries but avoid T.30 through a paraconsistent recasting of A.0. See also section 6.3.4.

88 The term comes from Horgan (1991, p. 305). The view in question—existence monism—should be distinguished from the priority monism of Schaffer (2007, 2010), which holds instead that the whole cosmos is the only *basic* concrete object, all other objects—its proper parts—existing derivatively. See the exchange between Horgan and Potrč (2012) and Schaffer (2012b) and, relatedly, Bucchioni (2015). For a defense of existence monism, see also Cornell (2013) (responding to Sider, 2007b) and Cornell (2016); for connections with traditional monism, see Potrč (2003) and, for a Kantian variant, Kriegel (2012).

entity, but only the existence of a single material substance along with entities of other kinds, such as properties or space-time regions. In other words, they only endorse a sortally restricted version of T.30, and in some cases only contingently so. In its full generality, T.30 is much stronger and harder to swallow, and most friends of the null object would rather avoid it.

Note that we speak of *the* null object because the entity postulated by A.43 is bound to be unique by D.1 (if not by A.2). We can give it an official name, 'n', and define it explicitly.

(D.36) $\mathrm{n} := \imath z \forall y (Pzy \wedge \neg Pyz)$ *Null Object*

The problem of triviality, then, is that n seems to be ontologically corrosive; its existence appears to rule out the existence of anything else.

On the other hand—and this is the second part of the answer to our question—it should be obvious that the source of the problem lies in the fact that the presence of n makes it impossible for any two things to be disjoint, which is directly in conflict with the existential requirements of Remainder and the Supplementation principles. However, this simply shows that such requirements may have been formulated without taking n into account.

Consider Remainder. The intuitive idea behind this axiom is that whenever an object x is not part of another, y, the latter must leave a remainder—something corresponding to that portion of x that would be left if y were removed. As we noted in section 2.1.2, this notion has a natural set-theoretic analogue in the notion of a relative complement, or set difference, which is defined as follows: the set difference $X \setminus Y$ is the set of all members of X that are not members of Y. Now, if we wanted to express this notion in terms of the subset relation, rather than in terms of membership, we could say that $X \setminus Y$ is the set whose subsets are exactly those subsets of X that are disjoint from Y. And when are two sets disjoint? They are disjoint when they have no members in common, i.e. when they have no subset in common *except for the empty set* $\varnothing$. The 'except' clause is needed precisely to take care of the fact that $\varnothing$ is included in *every* set: given any set Z, there is no member of $\varnothing$ which is not also a member of Z for the simple reason that $\varnothing$ has no members whatsoever. Well, in the presence of the null object n, something similar applies. We know that there is a close relationship between parthood, P, and the set inclusion relation, $\subseteq$. And just as the null set $\varnothing$ is the 'zero element' with respect to $\subseteq$, n is the zero element with respect to P. Thus, what the Remainder axiom A.4 really should say, in the presence of n, is this: that whenever x is not part of y, there is a remainder comprising exactly those parts of x that have no part in common with y *except for the null object* n. The exception was not written into our formulation of A.4 because we were already thinking in terms of classical mereology, which has no room for n.

But if we wish to be more liberal, and certainly if we want to *posit* the existence of n via A.43, we should rephrase A.4 accordingly:

(A.44) $\forall x \forall y(\neg Pxy \rightarrow \exists z \forall w(Pwz \leftrightarrow (Pwx \wedge SDwy)))$ *Solid Remainder*

where SD is the relation of non-trivial, 'solid' disjointness that obtains between any two things that have no other part in common besides n:

(D.37) $SDxy :\equiv \neg \exists z(Pzx \wedge Pzy \wedge \neg z = n)$ *Solid Disjointness*

(Note that we have $SDny$ for all y, since n itself has no proper parts. Thus, when y is n, its solid remainder in x is the whole of x, just as $X \setminus \varnothing = X$.)

It's easy to see that replacing A.4 with A.44 will deliver a non-trivial variant of classical mereology. For example, the eight-element Boolean algebra we met in chapter 2, figure 2.3 (with P interpreted as $\subseteq$), will be a model. In fact, the theory obtained from classical mereology by trading A.4 for A.44 and adding the Strict Zero axiom A.43 is not merely non-trivial; it is an interesting and powerful theory. For just as classical mereology is essentially a complete Boolean algebra with the bottom element removed (modulo the limitations mentioned at the end of section 2.2.3), so the theory defined by the classical ordering and fusion axioms together with A.43 and A.44 is essentially a complete Boolean algebra (with bottom). We shall not prove this result here.[89] But it should be stressed that it is precisely for this reason—and along these lines—that some authors are willing to endorse the null object as a convenient 'fiction'.[90] From a mathematical point of view, the algebraic neatness of the mereological structures that we obtain by adding a bottom element is obviously very attractive.[91] Indeed, since n qualifies as a fusion of the empty set,[92]

(T.31) $\neg \exists x \varphi x \rightarrow F_{\varphi} n$ *Null Fusion*

89 The proof is a simplified variant of the one given in section 2.2, considering that we can just work with the basic order relations $\sqsubseteq$ and $\leqslant$ rather than going through $\sqsubseteq^{-}$ and $\leqslant^{+}$.

90 See again the authors mentioned in note 83, though their axiom systems for classical mereology are somewhat different from ours and require further modifications (see below for A.10). See also Pontow and Schubert (2006) for an explicit proof of the completeness result mentioned in the text relative to the theory obtained from Eberle's axiomatization (section 2.4.3) by adding A.43 and modifying A.15 and A.18 accordingly.

91 Among other things, the fiction makes it possible to treat all mereological functors as defined for all arguments, restoring a perfect duality between $+$ and $\times$. This means the latter functor could now serve as a primitive just like the former, overcoming the difficulties mentioned at the end of section 2.4.4. Leibniz himself seems to have liked the fiction in his algebraic treatment of composition, helping himself with the notion of a *Nihil* and listing equations such as $A - A = $ *Nihil*, $A \oplus$ *Nihil* $= A$, etc. (see Leibniz, 1903, pp. 265ff and 1966, pp. 124ff).

92 Given $\neg \exists x \varphi x$, we immediately have that $\forall x(\varphi x \rightarrow Pxn)$ (vacuously); and since $\forall y Pny$ by D.36, we also have that $\forall y(\forall x(\varphi x \rightarrow Pxy) \rightarrow Pny)$. Thus $F_{\varphi} n$ by D.6.

the theory in question—classical mereology with null object—can be further simplified. In place of A.5 (Unrestricted Fusion) and A.43 (Strict Zero) we can simply take the following axiom schema, asserting the existence of a fusion for any open formula φ whatsoever.

(A.45) $\exists z F_{\varphi} z$ *Absolutely Unrestricted Fusion*

Weaker mereological theories can be modified in a similar fashion. Just notice that some cases require more adjustments than just changing D to SD. For instance, the Weak Supplementation axiom A.10 says that whenever y is a proper part of x, x must have a further proper part, z, disjoint from y. Obviously, in the presence of n we must reinterpret 'disjoint' in terms of SD. But then we must also reinterpret 'proper part', since we certainly want z to be something more than the ubiquitous nought (we *always* have $PPnx$ and $SDny$, even when $y = n$). In other words, z must be a non-trivial, solid proper part of x.

(D.38) $SPPxy :\equiv PPxy \wedge \neg x = n$ *Solid Proper Parthood*

Thus, fully spelled out, the correct way to rephrase A.10 in theories allowing for the null object is as follows.

(A.46) $\forall x \forall y (PPyx \rightarrow \exists z (SPPzx \wedge SDzy))$ *Solid Weak Supplementation*

Similarly for other supplementation principles and, more generally, for any principle whose intended import depends crucially on the distinction between trivial and solid mereological relations.[93]

4.6 ATOMS AND GUNK

One last important family of decomposition principles concerns the question of atomism. Mereologically, an atom (or 'simple') is typically defined as an entity with no proper parts.

(D.39) $Ax :\equiv \neg \exists y PPyx$ *Atom*

In theories that allow for the null element this definition is not quite right, since that element would be the only atom.[94] To allow for multiple atoms we would need to tweak the definition a bit, and the foregoing discussion

93 This includes some composition principles, such as the variants of the Unrestricted Fusion schema due to Leśniewski (A.11), Goodman (A.15), and Leonard and Goodman (via D.18), all of which involve a fusion predicate defined in terms of potentially trivial relations of overlap and disjointness.

94 For some discussion of the consequences, see Latronico (2009) and Valore (2015).

suggests a natural way to do so: we can replace PP in the definiens with its solid counterpart, SPP. Equivalently:[95]

(D.40) $SAx :\equiv \forall y(PPyx \rightarrow y = n)$ *Solid Atom*

However, here we shall confine ourselves to mereologies without the null object, so D.39 will be just fine. By definition of PP, this means that all atoms are pairwise disjoint and overlap only those things of which they are part.

(T.32) $\forall x \forall y((Ax \wedge Ay \wedge \neg x = y) \rightarrow Dxy)$ *Atom Disjointness*
(T.33) $\forall x(Ax \rightarrow \forall y(Oxy \rightarrow Pxy))$ *Atom Overlap*

Are there any such entities? And, if there are, does everything decompose into atoms? Is everything comprised of at least some atoms? Or is everything made up of atomless "gunk"—as Lewis (1991, p. 20) calls it—that divides forever into smaller and smaller parts?

As we mentioned in chapter 1, these are deep and difficult questions that have been the focus of philosophical investigation since antiquity and throughout the medieval and early modern debates on infinite divisibility, up to Kant's antinomies in the *Critique of Pure Reason*.[96] Along with nuclear physics and Russell's (1918–1919) logical atomism, they made their way into contemporary mereology also thanks to the renewed interest in the foundations of geometry (beginning with Whitehead, 1916) and have been treated extensively in the context of both Leśniewski's and Leonard and Goodman's original theories.[97] Today they are still among the most fundamental questions discussed in mereology, though it is generally agreed that they go beyond the analysis of the parthood concept as such. Unlike the disputes on the status of the ordering axioms or the supplementation principles discussed above, these questions fall squarely outside the scope of any putative program in formal ontology; they belong, as Hudson (2007, p. 291) puts it, to that area of inquiry that may be called "mereological metaphysics".

At the same time, it should be emphasized that the notion defined in D.39 is purely mereological, and is therefore silent on a number of important issues associated with the traditional way of dealing with these questions.

95 That is how atoms are defined in the context of Boolean algebras. Originally Tarski (1935, p. 334) gave several other definitions, following Schröder (1890–1895, §47), but they are all equivalent.

96 For a history, see Pyle (1995) and Zilioli (in press). With regard to ancient atomism, see also Sorabji (1983, chs. 21ff), Furley (1987), and Berryman (2016) on the Greek Presocratics and Keith (1921) and Gangopadhyaya (1980) on the Indian schools. On medieval theories, Wood's introduction to Wodeham (1988) gives a good picture of the Latin debate, along with Pabst (1994) and Grellard and Robert (2008), whereas Pines (1936) and Baffioni (1982) address the Islamic tradition. For the modern period, see Holden (2004) and the texts cited in chapter 1, note 3.

97 For the former, the main references are Tarski (1937), Sobociński (1971a,b), Lejewski (1973), and Clay (1975). For the latter, see Yoes (1967), Eberle (1967; 1970, §2.5–2.9), and Schuldenfrei (1969).

For instance, D.39 is silent on whether atoms should be construed as unextended entities that can only occupy spatial or spatio-temporal points (what Markosian, 1998a calls the "pointy view") or, at any rate, regions of spacetime that do not themselves have proper sub-regions (the "simplace view" of Tognazzini, 2006). Mereologically speaking, extended atoms are perfectly conceivable, just as, in fact, mereologically it is conceivable that there be unextended composites.[98] As Goodman put it:

> An atomic element—or atom—of a system is simply an element of the system that contains no lesser elements for the system. Depending on the system, an electron or a molecule or a planet might be taken as an atom. (Goodman, 1956, fn. 6)

Similarly, there is no presumption that mereological atoms should enjoy other properties that may be taken to be constitutive of a more robust notion, e.g. that their spatial extension be maximally continuous (Markosian's "MaxCon view").[99] Reference to such properties may be necessary to answer what Markosian himself calls the "Simple Question" (what are the necessary and jointly sufficient conditions for an object to qualify as a simple?), or what van Inwagen (1990, pp. 48f) called the "Inverse Special Composition Question" (what are the conditions necessary and sufficient for a thing to have proper parts?),[100] but they run afoul of the purely mereological notion of an atom. For all D.39 says, it may also be that such Questions only admit of a brutal answer, as argued by McDaniel (2007b): there may be no correct, finitely statable, non-circular answer except for saying that it is a brute fact that something does, or does not, qualify as a mereological atom.[101]

Now, to return to our questions (lower case), traditionally the main options are identified with the two extreme answers, to the effect that either

98 The notion of an extended atom, which may be traced back to Democritus's conception, is amply discussed in recent literature, beginning with Bigelow (1995, pp. 21ff), MacBride (1998, pp. 220ff), and Olson (1998) and then e.g. Scala (2002), Simons (2004), Parsons (2004b, 2007), Braddon-Mitchell and Miller (2006), Hudson (2006a), McDaniel (2007a), Dumsday (2015), Kleinschmidt (2016), and others. For a guided tour, see Gilmore (2018, §5). The idea of an unextended composite is less common, but it may be found e.g. in Wasserman (2003), McDaniel (2006, 2007b), and Saucedo (2011) and is fully discussed in Pickup (2016).

99 This view is further discussed in McDaniel (2003), Markosian (2004a,b), Steen (2011), and Dumsday (2017). One worry is that it automatically rules out the possibility of gunk, as argued by Hudson (2001, pp. 84ff) and Markosian (2005, §2), though see Fowler (2008) for a reply.

100 The two questions are equivalent, at least given D.39. Van Inwagen's is so called with reference to his "Special Composition Question", which asks for the conditions under which some things jointly compose something. That question will be examined in chapter 5, though it should be noted that his "Inverse Question" is really the inverse of what Markosian (2014, p. 72) calls a "Question About Parthood": under what conditions is one object part of another? For more on these Questions, see Carroll and Markosian (2010, §8.10) and Kovacs (2014).

101 Could it be *indeterminate* whether something is an atom? This view has its defenders (e.g. McKinnon, 2003), though it presupposes that P itself can be indeterminate. We shall come back to this possibility—and the difficulties it raises—in chapter 6, section 6.3.

everything decomposes into atoms, or else there are no atoms at all. In formal treatments, these two theses are in turn identified with the mereological axioms of Atomism and Atomlessness already mentioned in sections 2.3.1 and 3.3.2, respectively, which can now be abbreviated as follows.

(A.6) $\forall x \exists y (Ay \wedge Pyx)$ *Atomism*

(A.31) $\forall x \neg Ax$ *Atomlessness*

Obviously these axioms are mutually incompatible, but taken in isolation they can consistently be added to any mereological theory considered so far (modulo the adjustments mentioned above if we assume the existence of a null object), and this is one more sign that the question of atomism is not, strictly speaking, a question about parthood. Given our favorite mereology, adding A.6 yields a corresponding *atomistic* extension; adding A.31 yields an *atomless* (or *gunky*) extension. Since finitude together with the antisymmetry of parthood imply that mereological decomposition must eventually come to an end, it is clear that the finite models of any theory endorsing A.2 are always atomistic. Accordingly, antisymmetric atomless mereologies admit only models of infinite cardinality. An example of such a model, establishing the consistency of the atomless extension of classical mereology, is provided by the family of all regular open sets of a Euclidean space, with P interpreted as set inclusion (Tarski, 1935).[102] On the other hand, the consistency of an atomistic extension is always guaranteed by the trivial one-element model, though one can also have models of atomistic mereologies with infinite domains. A case in point is provided by the closed intervals on the real line, or the closed sets of a Euclidean space (Eberle, 1970).

This much is clear enough. What else can we say about these conflicting views, and about other views that lie in between?

4.6.1 *Atomism*

Concerning Atomism, one important remark concerns the very thought that A.6 captures the view it is intended to capture. After all, this axiom doesn't quite say that everything *decomposes into* atoms, i.e. is ultimately *composed of* atoms; it merely says that everything *has* atoms, i.e. atomic parts. As such, it rules out atomless structures, but is this enough?

In a way, the answer is in the affirmative. For, assuming Transitivity and Strong Supplementation, A.6 is equivalent to

(T.34) $\forall x F_{Ay \wedge Pyx} x$ *Strong Atomism*

102 Actually this model appears only in the 1956 English version of Tarski (1935); see p. 341, fn. 2. An open set is 'regular' just in case it equals the interior of its own closure.

And this literally says that everything is ultimately composed of atoms: everything is a fusion of its own atomic parts. To see that A.6 implies T.34, recall by D.6 that, in general, $F_{Ay \wedge Pya}a$ is a conjunction of two claims:

(4.5) $\forall y((Ay \wedge Pya) \rightarrow Pya)$

(4.6) $\forall z(\forall y((Ay \wedge Pya) \rightarrow Pyz) \rightarrow Paz)$

The first of these claims is a logical truth, so we only need to show the second. Accordingly, suppose for arbitrary b that $\neg Pab$. By Strong Supplementation we immediately have that there is something, c, such that $Pca \wedge \neg Ocb$, and by A.6 we know c must have some atomic part, d. By Transitivity, Pda, and since $\neg Ocb$, we also have that $\neg(Pdc \wedge Pdb)$ by D.2. Thus, since Pdc, we have that $\neg Pdb$, and hence, since Ad and Pda, that $\exists y((Ay \wedge Pya) \wedge \neg Pyb)$. Therefore $\neg Pab \rightarrow \exists y((Ay \wedge Pya) \wedge \neg Pyb)$, whence 4.6 follows by contraposition and generalization.

Thus, although A.6 does not *say* that everything is ultimately composed of atoms, it implies it—at least so long as P is transitive and strongly supplemented. (Of course, non-standard mereologies in which either postulate is rejected may not warrant the implication, so in such theories T.34 would perhaps be a better way to express the assumption of atomism.) And this is not just because we are reading 'composed' via D.6. The same point applies if composition is understood in terms of the alternative fusion predicates F' and F'' defined in D.13 and D.16. Indeed, in such cases the implication requires only that P be transitive and reflexive (see Varzi, 2017, §2).

In another way, however, A.6 may still be deemed unsatisfactory. For this axiom, like T.34 and its F' and F'' variants, admits of models that seem to run afoul of the atomistic doctrine. A simple example is a chain of decomposition that never 'bottoms out', as in figure 4.16: here it is true that there are atoms, the a_is, and it is true that everything has (proper or improper) atomic parts, validating A.6. Yet it is also true that every composite, c_i,

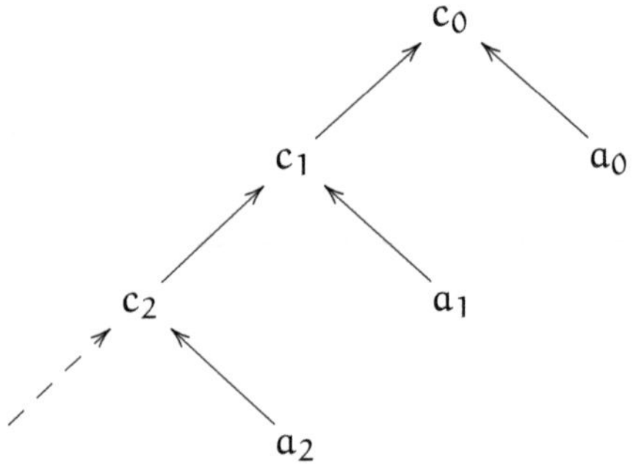

Figure 4.16: An infinitely descending atomistic model

has composite proper parts, the c_js ($j > i$), so the pattern of decomposition that goes down the left branch looks awfully similar to a gunky precipice. (For a concrete example, from Eberle, 1970, p. 75, let each c_i be the set of all non-negative integers $\geqslant i$, with $a_i = \{i\}$, and interpret P as the relation of set inclusion. The same model appears in Cotnoir, 2013c and Shiver, 2015.)

Now, some authors take this sort of case to demonstrate that A.6 is intrinsically inadequate:

> If every composite has a composite proper part, then it is false that everything is ultimately composed of atoms; it is, at least partly, composites all the way down.
> Shiver (2015, p. 609)

This is not correct. The model satisfies A.6 along with T.34 (and the corresponding variants in terms of F' and F''), so it does not violate the idea that everything decomposes into atoms. It simply shows that gunky worlds are not the only worlds with infinite descending proper-parthood chains.[103] However, it is true is that the model defies a parallel idea, namely that everything can actually be *decomposed* into its atomic constituents. The decomposition process goes on forever, and this may be disturbing enough. It might be thought to be disturbing especially if (*pace* Tallant, 2013) atomism is meant to carry the weight of metaphysical grounding: as Jonathan Schaffer would put it, in a model of this sort the atomist's ontology seems to drain away "down a bottomless pit" (Schaffer, 2007, p. 184); being is "infinitely deferred, never achieved" (Schaffer, 2010, p. 62). Are there any ways available to the atomist to avoid this charge?[104] Classical mereology might seem to provide the resources, since the model of figure 4.16 is ruled out by the Remainder axiom A.4. (There is, for instance, no remainder of c_2 in c_0.) But the friend of atomism is not committed to accepting Remainder, even less to endorsing classical mereology holus-bolus, and at any rate there is no guarantee the same diagnosis would apply in all problematic cases. Indeed, on standard models of geometry, extended regions are made up of infinitely-many pointy simples, and this is enough to get infinite descending chains even with classical mereology. Are there any other options?

One option that might come to mind is to require that every model be finite, or that there exist only a finite set of atoms. Yet such requirements, besides being philosophically harsh and contentious even among nominalist

103 As stressed e.g. by Nolan (2006b, pp. 163f) and Brzozowski (2008, pp. 212f). For other atomistic models with this property, see Tsai and Varzi (2016) and the further discussion in Tsai (2015, §3; 2017).

104 That is, any ways other than rejecting the assumption that the grounding relation should always bottom out, as suggested by Cameron (2008a), Rosen (2010), Bliss (2013), and others. (Dixon, 2016, p. 460 and Rabin and Rabern, 2016, p. 366 actually discuss infinitely descending grounding structures that are perfectly isomorphic to that of figure 4.16.) For a compact overview of the relevant literature, see Tahko (2018a, §2).

atomists,[105] cannot be formally implemented in first-order mereology: the former because of the compactness theorem of first-order logic (Gödel, 1930), which makes it impossible for a consistent theory to be satisfiable in all and only the finite domains, and the latter in view of a result by Hodges and Lewis (1968), to the effect that no atomistic extension of classical mereology can be enriched with a formula that is true in every finite intended model but not in any infinite atomic intended model. That is, we cannot postulate that there are finitely many atoms unless we say something more specific about their number (e.g. that there are at most so many, or exactly so many) or we enlarge the language with suitable new predicates.[106] Similar difficulties affect the related thought that everything should decompose into a finite number of atoms, as required e.g. by Suppes (1972, pp. 308f).

The only reasonable option would seem to be a genuine strengthening of Atomism in the spirit of what may be called 'Superatomism' (Cotnoir, 2013c). Given any object x, A.6 guarantees the existence of a maximal parthood chain of x that bottoms out at an atom; Superatomism would require that *every* such chain bottoms out—a property that fails in the model of figure 4.16. Unfortunately, this way of strengthening A.6 runs into problems of its own. For one thing, its formulation requires quantification over sets. In our language, the best we can offer is an axiom schema.

(A.47) $\forall z(F_\varphi z \to \exists x(\varphi x \wedge \forall y(PPyx \to \neg\varphi^x_y)))$ *Superatomism*

But this schema suffers from the usual limitations of first-order languages: the sets in the domain may outnumber the available φs. As with universalism, a proper formulation of Superatomism would really call for stronger resources, e.g. second-order logic. In view of the connection between mereology and Boolean algebras, the models of superatomistic mereology could then be recovered from the general theory of superatomic algebras (Mostowski and Tarski, 1939).[107] Yet there is a further problem. As Hudetz (2014) and Uzquiano (2017) have shown, it turns out that superatomistic classical mereology has no infinite models, and this, as mentioned, is a cost the atomist may not want to incur. Thus, to the extent that it can be formulated at all, superatomism would appear to call for weaker, non-classical mereologies.[108]

105 Even Goodman, proclaiming his atomism and commenting on the "renunciation of infinity" announced in Goodman and Quine (1947, §2), is adamant that "finitism, although a friendly companion of nominalism, is neither identical with nor necessary to it" (Goodman, 1972, p. 154).

106 For more on this topic, see Hellman (1969), Hendry (1982), and Niebergall (2009a, §2, 2016). Note that Hodges and Lewis's result does not follow automatically from the compactness theorem. Compactness implies that there's no sentence that is true in arbitrarily large finite models but false in all infinite ones. An axiom of finitude would instead specify finitude for a limited class of models, viz. the *intended* models of the atomistic theory. See Hellman (1969, p. 416ff).

107 For an overview of these algebras, see Day (1967); for an advanced survey, Roitman (1989).

108 For a fuller picture of these issues, and some additional options, see also Dixon (in press).

So much for the strength and limits of the Atomism axiom A.6. Let us now look briefly at the overall effects of adding this axiom to a given mereological theory, beginning with classical mereology.

First of all, we note that the atomistic extension of A.1–A.5 has the following variant of the extensionality theorem T.1.

(T.35) $\forall x \forall y(\forall z(Az \rightarrow (Pzx \leftrightarrow Pzy)) \rightarrow x = y)$ *Atomistic Extensionality*

For suppose, for arbitrary a and b, that $\neg a = b$. By A.2 we have that either $\neg Pab$ or $\neg Pba$. Take the former case (the two cases are symmetric). By A.4 and A.1 there must be some remainder, c, such that Pca and Dcb, and by A.6 there must be an atom, d, such that Pdc. By D.4 we immediately have that Ddb, and hence $\neg Pdb$ by A.1. But we also have that Pda by A.3. Therefore $\exists z(Az \wedge Pza \wedge \neg Pzb)$. By contraposition and generalization, we obtain T.35.

What this means is that atomistic classical mereology is truly "hyperextensional" in Goodman's (1958) sense: no two of its entities are generated from the same atoms.[109] In particular, if there are only a finite number k of atoms, it follows from the algebraic results of section 2.2.1 that there are exactly $2^k - 1$ entities overall. But there are other interesting consequences of T.35. For instance, it follows immediately that the Unrestricted Fusion axiom schema A.5 can be restated in terms of atoms. More precisely, let us say that something is a φ-atom if and only if it is an atomic part of some φer.

(D.41) $A_\varphi x :\equiv Ax \wedge \exists y(\varphi y \wedge Pxy)$ *φ–Atom*

Then the point is that we can replace A.5 with the following schema, which just asserts the conditional existence of φ-atom fusions.

(A.48) $\exists y \varphi y \rightarrow \exists z F_{A_\varphi x} z$ *Atomistic Fusion*

And the reason is precisely that, in view of T.35, a fusion of the φers *just is* a fusion of φ-atoms, since there is no difference in atomic parts.[110]

---

109 Strictly speaking, Goodman understands 'atom' in terms of PP_2, as in D.42 below. In classical mereology the difference is immaterial, but in weaker theories this might affect the intended import of T.35. For example, the non-antisymmetric model in figure 4.15 would involve two atoms with the same parts, and it isn't clear in what sense this would violate Goodman's nominalistic, scruples. For an interesting case of this sort, see Johansson (2009).

110 To see this, suppose $F_\varphi a$ and $F_{A_\varphi x} b$, and let c be an arbitrary atom. If $A_\varphi c$, then we immediately have that Pcb from the first conjunct of D.6, which says that b is an upper bound of the A_φ's. And since a is likewise an upper bound of the φers, we also have that Pca (by D.41 and Transitivity). On the other hand, suppose $\neg A_\varphi c$. Then Remainder gives us $b - c$, which must be an upper bound of the A_φ's, hence $Pb(b-c)$ by the second conjunct of D.6, and so $\neg Pcb$ (using Transitivity). Similarly, $a - c$ must be an upper bound of the φers (since c is not a φer by D.41 and Reflexivity), and we obtain that $\neg Pca$. Thus, in both cases $Pca \leftrightarrow Pcb$, and since c was arbitrary, this means that a's atomic parts are exactly the same as b's.

The same point could be made with reference to the alternative fusion axiom schemas considered at the end of chapter 2, including Goodman's own (A.15). Indeed, in that particular formulation, the axiom schema could be further simplified as follows

$$\text{(A.49)}\quad \exists x\varphi x \rightarrow \exists z\forall y(Ay \rightarrow (Pyz \leftrightarrow \exists x(\varphi x \wedge Pyx))) \qquad \textit{Atomistic Fusion}''$$

or even as follows

$$\text{(A.50)}\quad \exists x(Ax \wedge \varphi x) \rightarrow \exists y\forall x(Ax \rightarrow (Pxy \leftrightarrow \varphi x)) \qquad \textit{Atom Fusion}''$$

from which Goodman's A.15 can easily be derived by taking φx to be the condition $\exists z(Pxz \wedge \varphi^x_z)$.[111]

Another notable consequence of A.6 is that the Remainder axiom, too, could now be stated more specifically in terms of atomistic remainders.

$$\text{(A.51)}\quad \forall x\forall y(\neg Pxy \rightarrow \exists z\forall w(Aw \rightarrow (Pwz \leftrightarrow (Pwx \wedge \neg Pwy))) \qquad \textit{Atomistic Rem.}$$

For recall that atoms overlap exactly those things of which they are part (T.33). This means that, for any a and b and any atom c, we are sure to have that $Pca \wedge Dcb$ if and only if $Pca \wedge \neg Pcb$. Therefore, if $\neg Pab$, an atom will be part of the remainder postulated by A.4 if and only if it is part of the atomistic remainder postulated by A.51, and so these remainders must be identical. Similarly for various other supplementation principles. For instance, Strong Supplementation (A.18) would become:[112]

$$\text{(A.52)}\quad \forall x\forall y(\neg Pxy \rightarrow \exists z(Az \wedge Pzx \wedge \neg Pzy)) \qquad \textit{Atomistic Strong Supplementation}$$

Finally, it is worth noting that such results have significant implications for the axiomatic characterization of atomistic mereologies. In the case of classical mereology, perhaps the most elegant example is the theory we get

---

111 This is noted in Eberle (1970, p. 69). As for the equivalence between A.15 and A.49, suppose we have that $F''_\varphi a$ and $\forall y(Ay \rightarrow (Pyb \leftrightarrow \exists x(\varphi x \wedge Pyx)))$, and let c be an arbitrary atom. Then we have that $Oca \leftrightarrow \exists x(\varphi x \wedge Ocx)$ (by D.16) and $Pcb \leftrightarrow \exists x(\varphi x \wedge Pcx)$. By T.33, together with Reflexivity, an atom overlaps something if and only if it is part of it, so we can replace O by P in the first of these formulas to obtain $Pca \leftrightarrow \exists x(\varphi x \wedge Pcx)$, and from this and the second formula we obtain that $Pca \leftrightarrow Pcb$. Since c was arbitrary, it follows that a's atomic parts are exactly the same as b's, and so must be identical by T.35.

112 A.18 and A.52 have the same antecedent, so to see that they are mereologically equivalent we just need to check the equivalence of the consequents. That is, for arbitrary a, b we must check that $\exists z(Pza \wedge Dzb)$ if and only if $\exists z(Az \wedge Pza \wedge \neg Pzb)$. From right to left, this follows immediately from T.33 (Atom Overlap) together with D.2 and D.4. Conversely, pick c so that $Pca \wedge Dcb$. By A.6, there must be some atom, d, such that Pdc. Since Pca, we have that Pda by A.3. And since Dcb, we have that $\neg Pdb$ by D.4. Thus, d is a witness for $\exists z(Az \wedge Pza \wedge \neg Pzb)$, as desired. In the literature, A.52 is sometimes known as the Exhaustion axiom (Meixner, 1997, p. 53).

from the Eberle axiomatization of section 2.4.3 by keeping the ordering axioms and replacing the Strong Supplementation axiom A.18 and the Unrestricted Fusion″ axiom schema A.15 with the atomistic variants given above, A.52 and A.49 (or A.50). In this system, the Atomism axiom itself, A.6, is derivable from A.52 using Reflexivity and Antisymmetry.[113] Moreover, A.52 is stronger that A.18, which implies Reflexivity from Transitivity.[114] It follows that we have a complete axiomatization of atomistic classical mereology by taking as axioms just A.2, A.3, A.52, and A.49 (or A.50).[115]

In the case of theories weaker than classical mereology, similar simplifications will apply. For instance, Eberle (1967) offers simplified axiom systems for various theories obtained by dropping the fusion axiom schema altogether or replacing it with weaker closure principles (for binary sums, products, etc.). Generally speaking, all such theories can be studied by analogy with the corresponding quasi-Boolean algebras, just as atomistic classical mereology can be studied by looking at its Boolean counterparts, e.g. the field of all subsets of an initial set of atoms.[116]

4.6.2 *Atomlessness*

Atomless mereologies have a distinguished pedigree. They have been central to research in the foundations of geometry as well as to recent literature on the philosophy of space and time, metaphysical grounding, or the semantics of mass terms.[117] Their formal treatment goes all the way back to Whitehead's relational theory of space (1916, §4) and his later mereology of events (1919, §27), both of which included as an explicit postulate that every object or event has a proper part.[118] Actually, the later theory involved a further,

113 If $\forall x \forall y\, x = y$, then $\forall x Ax$ by D.1 and D.39, so $\forall x \exists y (Ay \wedge Pyx)$ by A.1. If $\neg \forall x \forall y\, x = y$, then by A.2 we have a, b such that $\neg Pab$, and by A.52 we obtain $Pca \wedge \neg Pcb$ for some atom c. Now suppose $\forall y Pny$ for some null object n. Then Pnc, hence $c = n$ by D.1 and D.39, contradicting $\neg Pcb$. Thus $\forall x \exists y \neg Pxy$, and by A.52 we obtain again that $\forall x \exists y (Ay \wedge Pyx)$.

114 This was proven in section 4.2. Actually the direct proof from A.52 to Reflexivity does not even require Transitivity, since $(\neg Paa \to \exists z(Az \wedge Pza \wedge \neg Pza)) \to Paa$ is a logical truth.

115 The version with A.49 is mentioned in Simons (1987, p. 43), though without noting the redundancy of A.1. The version with A.50 (again with A.1) may be found in Eberle (1967). See also Eberle (1970, §2.7), where the same theory is axiomatized with O as primitive. Another elegant axiomatization is the one used by Hodges and Lewis (1968), about which see chapter 6, note 10.

116 Atomic (or 'atomistic') Boolean algebras occupy the second part of Tarski (1935). For a brief survey, see e.g. Givant and Halmos (2009, ch. 14).

117 The first line of research owes much to the pioneering work of Whitehead mentioned below. On the philosophy of space and time more generally, recent indicative references include Forrest (1996a), Arntzenius (2003; 2012, ch. 4), Russell (2008), and Vakarelov (2015). On the implications for the theory of grounding, see Schaffer (2003, 2010), Brzozowski (2016), and the essays in Bliss and Priest (2018). On mass terms, see e.g. Zimmerman (1995) and Olson (2012).

118 See also Whitehead (1929, pt. IV, ch 2), though here the Atomlessness axiom A.31 is replaced by a stronger requirement to the effect that everything has an *interior*, non-tangential proper part

dual condition, to the effect that every event *is* a proper part. So Whitehead's world was not only gunky; it was also, in the terminology introduced by Schaffer (2010, p. 64), "junky". This is reminiscent of some ancient anti-atomists, most notably Anaxagoras, who thought quite generally that the laws governing decomposition and composition are perfectly symmetric.[119]

> Neither of the small is there a least, but always a lesser ... And also in the case of the large there is always a larger. (Anaxagoras, Fr. 3, from Simplicius, *On Aristotle's Physics*, 164.17–18; Simplicius, 2011, p. 72)

We shall come back to junk in chapter 5, section 5.5, where we also consider a parallel view concerning coatomism (the thesis that everything is part of something that is not a proper part). Here we are just concerned with the first half of Whitehead's postulate, or rather its extension to arbitrary entities, corresponding to the Atomlessness axiom A.31. And, again, we shall discuss the axiom in general terms, without attaching any special connotation to the notion of atomless gunk that it delivers (such as, for instance, the requirement that gunky objects can exist only in gunky space-time).[120]

Thus understood, the first thing to note about A.31 is that it is in an important sense stronger than the atomistic axiom A.6. This is a result due essentially to Hendry (1982): if we start from classical mereology and add A.31, the corresponding atomless extension turns out to be *maximally consistent* (and decidable), in the sense that all sentences in the language are either affirmed or denied within the theory. By contrast, adding A.6 results in a theory that is decidable but not maximally consistent; it would become so if, and only if, one added either a further postulate asserting the existence of a specific finite number $k > 0$ of atoms,

(A.53) $\exists_k x\, Ax$ *Size*

(as suggested in de Laguna, 1921, 1922 and Nicod, 1924, ch. I.4). This strengthening of A.31 is crucial for a proper formulation of Whitehead's point-free theory of space and has been a major source of inspiration for the development of later theories, as in Menger (1940), Grzegorczyk (1960), Clarke (1981, 1985), and Roeper (1997), but it is strictly mereotopological and thus goes beyond our present concerns (as does Tarski's 1929 treatment, which involves a different extra-mereological primitive). For details, see Varzi (in press); for a general picture, see the essays in Coppola and Gerla (2013) and the monographs by Gorzka (2003), Gruszczyński (2016), and Hellman and Shapiro (2018). Whitehead's mereotopological approach has received extensive application also in the field of qualitative spatial reasoning, about which see the surveys in Cohn and Hazarika (2001), Vakarelov (2007), and Hahmann and Grüninger (2012).

119 On Anaxagoras's conception in relation to contemporary mereological theories, see Marmodoro (2015; 2017, chs. 2 and 3). A related view was held by Chrysippus and the Stoics, at least with respect to gunk; see Nolan (2006b) and Marmodoro (2017, ch. 6).

120 See e.g. McDaniel (2006) and Giberman (2012) on the idea that gunky objects can reside in a pointy space, or space-time. On the very possibility of atomless gunk, see also Sider (1993) and Zimmerman (1996a) for influential arguments (with early replies in Salsbery, 1996 and Mason, 2000), and Van Cleve (1981) for a defense against Kant's attempt to refute it.

or else the set of all numerative formulas asserting the existence of more than a specific number (and thus, collectively, of infinitely many things):

(A.54) $\exists_{\geqslant k} x \, Ax$ *Minimum Size*

(Here, and more generally, $\exists_k x \varphi x$ is short for $\exists_{\geqslant k} x \varphi x \wedge \neg \exists_{\geqslant k+1} x \varphi x$, and $\exists_{\geqslant k} x \; \varphi x$ in turn is just $\exists x \varphi x$ if $k = 1$, and is $\exists x_1 \ldots \exists x_k (\varphi x_1 \wedge \cdots \wedge \varphi x_k \wedge \neg x_1 = x_2 \wedge \cdots \wedge \neg x_{k-1} = x_k)$ for $k > 1$.)[121] Of course, these results only hold for formulations of classical mereology in a pure first-order language, with no extra-logical symbols besides the binary predicate P; if the language contained individual constants, for instance, then statements such as Pc_1c_2 would be neither provable nor disprovable within the theory. Still, from a model-theoretic viewpoint the results are significant enough, as are several related facts. For example, atomless classical mereology turns out to be $\aleph_0$-categorical, which means that it has exactly one countably infinite model up to isomorphism; the extension of atomistic mereology obtained by adding all instances of A.54, which is also a theory of infinite models, is not.[122]

This being said, and recalling that in classical mereology the strength of Atomlessness shows up e.g. in the Denseness thesis (A.30), there is also a sense in which this axiom is by itself not very strong. Here the worry is not so much that A.31 does not *say* that everything divides forever into smaller and smaller parts, which is how gunk is usually understood. If we wished, we could be more explicit:

(T.36) $\forall x \forall y (Pyx \rightarrow \neg Ay)$ *Gunk*

But obviously, given just Reflexivity, this reduces to A.31. Rather, just as the Atomism axiom A.6 is too weak to rule out unpleasant atomistic infinite models, so too the formulation of the Atomlessness axiom A.31, or T.36, may be found too weak to capture the idea of a gunky world.

For one thing, both A.31 and T.36 presuppose Antisymmetry. Absent A.2, even the finite, two-element loop in figure 4.15 would qualify as gunky, contrary to the intended notion.[123] To rule out such models independently

121 The necessity and sufficiency of A.53 and A.54 follow from the main result of Hodges and Lewis (1968), by which every sentence of atomistic classical mereology is equivalent to a truth-functional compound of instances of A.54 itself. See also Hendry (1980) for refinements.

122 It is precisely by establishing its $\aleph_0$-categoricity that Hendry proves the maximal consistency of atomless classical mereology. This is the Łoś-Vaught test: if an elementary theory has only infinite models and is categorical for some cardinal, it is maximally consistent (Łoś, 1954; Vaught, 1954). The non-categoricity of the infinitist extension of atomistic mereology—and thus of classical mereology itself—is proved in Hellman (1969, pp. 421f). Of course, the finitist extension obtained by adding an instance of A.53 is categorical, given Hodges and Lewis's result.

123 Though infinite loops, like the cosmic 'circular scale' of Rucker's (1981) novel, would presumably be gunky in the intended sense.

of A.2, one should really understand Atomlessness in terms of the stronger notion of proper part defined in D.15, i.e. with reference to the following alternative notion of 'atom':

(D.42) $Ax :\equiv \neg\exists y PP_2 yx$ *Strict Atom*

Likewise, note that unless we assume Weak Supplementation (A.10), or at least Quasi-Supplementation (A.42) or Strong Company (A.40), the infinitely descending patterns in figure 4.12 will qualify as models of A.31 and T.36, though again such patterns do not quite correspond to what philosophers ordinarily have in mind when they talk about atomless gunk. It is indeed an interesting question whether some supplementation principle is presupposed by the ordinary concept of gunk (see Gilmore, in press). To the extent that it is, however, then we may want to be explicit, and this may result in simpler axiomatizations. For example, Weak Supplementation and Atomlessness can be merged into a single principle:

(A.55) $\forall x \forall y (Pxy \to \exists z (PPzy \land (Dzx \lor x = y)))$ *Atomless Weak Supplem.*

(We leave the equivalence as an exercise.) Similarly, Quasi-Supplementation and Atomlessness could be merged into a single axiom asserting explicitly that everything has at least two disjoint proper parts:

(A.56) $\forall x \exists y \exists z (PPyx \land PPzx \land Dyz)$ *Atomless Quasi-Supplementation*

Or one might consider an even stronger axiom, to the effect that everything can be decomposed into two complementary parts (two 'halves')—an atomless strengthening of the Unique Remainder principle T.15:

(A.57) $\forall x \exists y \exists z\, x - y = z$ *Splitting*

In classical mereology these and similar options are all equivalent. Still, generally speaking they are of variable strength, and in weaker mereologies their import and relative differences should be carefully assessed (as in Masolo and Vieu, 1999, §3).

There is, in addition, another, more important sense in which the Atomlessness axiom A.31 may be found too weak. After all, infinite divisibility is loose talk. Given A.31 (also on the strict understanding of 'atom' corresponding to D.42), gunk may have denumerably many, possibly continuum-many parts; but can it have more? Is there an upper bound on the cardinality on the number of pieces of gunk? Should it be allowed that for *every* cardinal number there may be more than that many pieces of gunk? A.31 is silent on these questions. Yet these are certainly aspects of atomless mereology that deserve scrutiny. It might even be thought that the world is not mere gunk but "hypergunk", as Nolan (2004, p. 305) calls it—gunk such that, for any set of its parts, there is a set of its parts of strictly greater cardinality.[124] In other words, hypergunk would be gunk with a proper class of parts. It is not clear what it would take for such a conception to be consistent (Nolan himself conjectured that a set-theoretic model might be constructed using the resources of inaccessible cardinal axioms), and even if it were, there may be philosophical disagreement concerning whether the possibility of hypergunk is merely logical (Hazen, 2004) or genuinely metaphysical (Reeder, in press). Nonetheless the question is indicative of the sort of leeway that A.31 leaves, and that one might want to regiment.[125]

Finally, an interesting question about atomless mereologies, discussed at some length in the late 1960s (Yoes, 1967; Eberle, 1968; Schuldenfrei, 1969) and taken up more recently by Simons (1987, pp. 44f) and Engel and Yoes (1996), is whether they can deliver a suitable analogue of the atomistic extensionality thesis T.35. Is there any predicate that can play the role of 'A' in an atomless mereology? Such a predicate would identify the 'base' (in the topological sense) of the theory and would enable a mereology to vindicate Goodman's hyperextensional intuitions even in the absence of atoms. The question is therefore significant especially from a nominalistic perspective (as Goodman, 1978 acknowledges). But it has ramifications also in connection with other views, for instance, if we wish to preserve the same point-geometric intuition in a point-free theory of space, or if we are interested in some non-atomistic version of Lewis's (1986c) doctrine of Humean supervenience, according to which the entire universe would be no more than "a vast mosaic of local matters of particular fact" (see e.g. Borghini and Lando, 2011, in press).

In special cases there is no difficulty in providing a positive answer. For example, in the partially ordered, strongly supplemented atomless model consisting of the open regular subsets of the real line, the open intervals with rational end points form a base in the relevant sense, indeed a countable

---

124 The idea, if not the term, may already be found in Nolan (1996, pp. 258f). As Nolan (2004, p. 305) notes, hypergunk has some affinities with Peirce's conception of the divisibility of the continuum in his 1898 Cambridge Lectures (Peirce, 1992, pts. III and VIII), at least as reconstructed by Putnam (1995, p. 11).

125 *Pace* Ladyman and Ross (2007, pp. 20 and 33, fn. 35), who find them preposterous, questions concerning the exact structure of gunk have been found relevant to a number of topics. Examples include the Banach-Tarski paradox (Forrest, 2004), the continuity of motion (Hawthorne and Weatherson, 2004) and of qualitative variation (Arntzenius and Hawthorne, 2005), the measure-theoretic structure of the continuum (Arntzenius, 2008; Russell, 2008; Lando and Scott, 2019; Chen, in press), and the relation between divisibility and indefinite extensibility (Russell, 2016). Nolan himself took the conceivability of hypergunk to be relevant to (and problematic for) the metaphysics of modality, particularly with regard to certain familiar assumptions about the size of possible worlds.

base (Simons, 1987, p. 44). It is doubtful, however, whether such answers capture the intended philosophical intuition. And even so, it is an open matter whether a general answer can be given that applies to any sort of domain, short of taking trivial basic predicates such as '$x = x$'. (Hyperextensionality would then reduce to the P–Extensionality thesis T.9.) If not, the only option would appear to be an account where the notion of a base is relativized to entities of a given kind φ. In the terminology of Simons (*ibid.*), we could say that the ψs *form a base for* the φs if and only if the following variants of A.6 and A.52 are satisfied.

(A.58) $\forall x(\varphi x \to \exists y(\psi y \wedge Pyx))$ ψ-*Grounding*

(A.59) $\forall x \forall y((\varphi x \wedge \varphi y) \to (\forall z(\psi z \to (Pzx \leftrightarrow Pzy)) \to x = y))$ ψ-*Extensionality*

An atomistic mereology would then correspond to the limit case where ψ is identified with A for every choice of φ. In an atomless mereology, by contrast, the base would depend in each case on the level of 'granularity' set by the relevant specification of φ. And while it may be impossible to come up with the appropriate specifications in a pure mereological language, a suitably enriched language might provide the resources to model interesting philosophical views. For instance, someone might hold that all physical bodies (the φs) are composed of small physical atoms (the ψs) and insist that physical composition is hyperextensional in the relevant sense: no two bodies can be made up of the same physical atoms. Yet this need not imply that physical atoms are themselves mereologically simple; they could be gunky atoms.

4.6.3 *Hybrid Theories*

Enriching the language would allow us also to model philosophical views that lie somewhere between the two extreme positions represented by Atomism and Atomlessness. Certainly one may hold that all entities of a certain kind φ—say, physical bodies, including the physical atoms that compose them—are fully atomistic in the mereological sense, and yet suspend judgment on the ultimate decompositional structure of other kinds of entity. This would amount to assuming a relativized version of Atomism, corresponding to the instance of A.58 obtained by identifying ψ with A:

(A.60) $\forall x(\varphi x \to \exists y(Ay \wedge Pyx))$ φ–*Atomism*

Similarly, one might e.g. concur with Whitehead that all entities of a certain kind φ—space-time regions—are mereologically gunky while suspending judgment on that being true of other entities as well. Given Reflexivity and

Transitivity, this would amount to a suitably relativized version of Atomlessness, more precisely of the Gunk principle T.36:

(A.61) $\forall x(\varphi x \rightarrow \forall y(Pyx \rightarrow \neg Ay))$ *φ–Gunk*

It is certainly possible also to combine two or more requirements of this sort, endorsing e.g. an ontology of atomistic objects in gunky space-time regions, with both A.60 and A.61 specified accordingly. These and similar principles of relative commitment are easily stated. But is there anything interesting to be said about non-relative, purely mereological intermediate positions?

There are three main options one may consider. The first two are simply the denial of Atomlessness and the denial of Atomism, which amount to asserting the existence of at least *some* atoms and the existence of at least *some* gunk, respectively, without further qualification.

(A.62) $\exists x Ax$ *Weak Atomism*
(A.63) $\exists x \forall y(Pyx \rightarrow \neg Ay)$ *Weak Gunk*

The third option amounts to the conjunction of these two theses, corresponding to the claim that there are both atoms *and* gunky objects.

Mathematically, the first two options are not by themselves particularly interesting. Among other things, it will be clear that within classical mereology A.62 and A.63 are mutually compatible (whence the third option), so neither is going to yield a maximally consistent theory when independently added to A.1–A.5. The third option, in turn, may seem like no more than a "curious hybrid" of the first two (Simons, 1987, p. 41). However, on closer look, this option turns out to have surprisingly interesting properties, philosophically as well as mathematically.

Following Hendry (1982, p. 454) and Pietruszczak (2000b, thm. VI.6.3), note first that a model of the theory obtained by adding both A.62 and A.63 to classical mereology will always have a universal element, u, that divides into two disjoint parts: an atomistic part u_A, which is the fusion of all atomic parts of u, and a gunky part u_G, the fusion of all atomless parts. And while $u = u_A + u_G$, there will, of course, be 'hybrid' parts of u that properly overlap both u_A and u_G and so are part of neither. More generally, any mereology whose axioms include A.62 and A.63 along with unrestricted binary sums will assert not only the existence of some atoms and some gunk, but also the existence of (non-universal) things made of both atoms and gunk.

(T.37) $\exists z(\exists x(Pxz \wedge Ax) \wedge \exists x(Pxz \wedge \forall y(Pyx \rightarrow \neg Ay)))$ *Hybridism*

(Proof: Just take z to be the sum of a witness for x in A.62 and a witness for x, or any proper part thereof, in A.63.) This is more than a mere curiosity.

According to Zimmerman (1996a), for instance, both Suárez and Brentano held a metaphysical conception of extended objects as wholes composed of two radically different kinds of parts, viz. extended parts, which would be infinitely divisible into extended parts within extended parts, and unextended, lower-dimensional (including zero-dimensional) parts, which would be necessarily present at or along the boundaries of extended parts. If so, then we would have two distinguished philosophical examples of theories committed to T.37. A related example, following Brower (2014), would be a hylomorphic conception of substances of the sort Aquinas seems to have held, with forms as indivisible simples, or atomistic anyway, and matter as infinitely divisible gunk.

But Hybridism is even more interesting mathematically, especially if we focus on the hybrid extension of classical mereology. It is clear that this theory is not maximally consistent, for it does not specify the number of atoms in its models. Like atomistic classical mereology, however, it gives rise to two natural sorts of extension, one obtained by postulating the existence of a specific finite number of atoms, as in A.53 (Size), the other by adding all instances of A.54 (Minimum Size), forcing the existence of infinitely many things. Now, Hendry (1982) proved that any extension of the first sort results in a maximally consistent, decidable theory. He also conjectured that the same is true of the second sort of extension, and the conjecture has been confirmed by Niebergall (2007) and, independently, Tsai (2018, pp. 822f). Moreover, it turns out that any other maximally consistent extension of classical mereology, besides the atomistic and atomless extensions already mentioned earlier, must *include* this latter theory. It follows, therefore, that we have a complete picture of the maximally consistent extensions of classical mereology. They are exactly the following:

- the atomless extension, obtained by adding A.31 to A.1–A.5;
- the finitist and infinitist atomistic extensions obtained by adding A.6 along with either an instance of A.53 or all instances of A.54, respectively;
- the hybrid extensions obtained in a similar way by adding A.62 and A.63 along with either an instance of A.53 or all instances of A.54.

Since these are the *only* maximally consistent extensions, this result also gives us a clear picture of the overall scope of classical mereology, at least insofar as we hold to a standard first-order logical setting. Anything that can be done, reasoning exclusively in terms of P, must be done within one of these theories.

5 COMPOSITION

What is combination, and what is that which can combine?
Of what things, and under what conditions is combination a property?
And, further, does combination exist in fact, or is it false to assert its existence?

— Aristotle, *De generatione et corruptione*, 327a32–34 (1984, p. 535)

We turn at last to questions concerning mereological composition, which in classical mereology is governed by the Unrestricted Fusion axiom schema. As we noted, generally speaking, composition and decomposition may be seen as 'two sides of the same coin', and considerations regarding one side are sometimes difficult to disentangle from questions regarding the other side. In chapter 4 we saw how this may affect the choice of adequate decomposition principles, over and above the ordering axioms that one assumes in the background. We need to do the same with regard to composition principles.

The chapter is organized as follows. We begin by reviewing the idea that composition can fully be analyzed in terms of mereological fusion. In our formulation, this notion was given a purely algebraic definition: a fusion is a minimal upper bound relative to the parthood ordering determined by A.1–A.3. However, we saw that other axiom systems present in the literature, including those of Leśniewski's Mereology and of Leonard and Goodman's Calculus of Individuals, rely on different fusion predicates. Given all other axioms and definitions, the relative differences are virtually immaterial, and that is why those systems and our own axiomatization turn out to identify the same theory, classical mereology. Nevertheless, in weaker theories each fusion predicate may behave differently, and it is important to be clear about the differences. That will be our first task. We shall take a closer look at those three main ways of defining fusions and compare them with one another to clearly identify the conditions under which they may diverge, along with some general principles that may be added to guarantee convergence.

With this picture in the background, we then proceed to examining the main philosophical questions that arise in relation with these classical treatments. We start with questions concerning the conditions of *identity* and *existence* of fusions, including what has come to be known as the "Special Composition Question" (van Inwagen, 1987). In particular, we examine in

Mereology. A. J. Cotnoir and Achille C. Varzi, Oxford University Press. © A. J. Cotnoir and Achille C. Varzi 2021. DOI: 10.1093/oso/9780198749004.003.0005

some detail the answer corresponding to the controversial doctrine of mereological *universalism*, which is inherent in the Unrestricted Fusion axiom of classical mereology, along with the thesis known as "Composition as Identity" (Lewis, 1991, §3.6). Next we consider the related question of whether fusions are always *unique*, and how this impacts mereological extensionality. We then examine a number of weaker algebraic principles for fusions satisfied in classical mereology, focusing primarily on *commutativity*, *associativity*, and *idempotence*. Along the way, we also look at the *operationalist* approach to mereology due to Fine (2010), which accepts many different forms of composition (some of which violate each of these principles) as 'building' operations. Finally, similar to the questions raised regarding the existence of a bottom level of decomposition over against atomless gunk, we consider parallel questions regarding the existence of a top level of composition over against 'worldless junk'. These questions pertain to the existence of a mereological 'universe' of which everything is part, and we consider a number of reasons for and against thinking that there is such a thing.

5.1 FUSIONS

We begin in this section by taking a closer look at the three main notions of mereological fusion recalled above (plus some minor variants). The first notion corresponds to our official definition from chapter 2, section 2.1.3. The other two were introduced only briefly in sections 2.4.1 and 2.4.2 and correspond to the classical definition of Leśniewski (1916) and the alternative definition used by Leonard and Goodman (1940), particularly in the later formulation due to Goodman (1951). We shall refer to these three notions as *algebraic* fusions, *Leśniewski* fusions, and *Goodman* fusions, respectively.

5.1.1 *Types of Fusion*

On the algebraic definition, a fusion is just a minimal upper bound with respect to the parthood relation. As such, we saw in section 2.2 that algebraic fusions are common in Boolean algebras and lattice theory, i.e. whenever an order relation $\sqsubseteq$ is available, and are also called 'least upper bounds' or 'suprema'. In mereology, their first use goes back to Kubiński (1968, 1971), though a version of the same definition based on Leśniewski's logical framework may already be found in some unpublished work by Jan Drewnowski from the years 1922–1928 (see Świętorzecka and Łyczak, in press, §§4 and 6) and Leśniewski himself, following an early suggestion by Tarski, considered it as an alternative to his own definition (Leśniewski, 1927–1931, pt. VIII). More recently, algebraic fusions have also been used to express the notion of composition in mereological systems that are not fully classical, such as Bostock's (1979) and van Benthem's (1983), and are frequently found in the linguistics literature that employs mereological models, as in Sharvy (1980, 1983), Link (1983, 1998), Krifka (1990), or Landman (1991, 2000). We will sometimes call them F-type fusions, or simply F-fusions, reflecting the facts of our notation.

(D.6) $F_{\varphi}z :\equiv \forall x(\varphi x \to Pxz) \land \forall y(\forall x(\varphi x \to Pxy) \to Pzy)$ F-*type Fusion*

It is worth stressing that the algebraic reading of such fusions as minimal upper bounds is split between the two conjuncts of the definition: the first conjunct requires that z be 'above' (i.e. include among its parts) every φ, and in that sense the fusion qualifies as an upper bound thereof; the second conjunct requires that z be 'below' (i.e. part of) any upper bound of the φs there might be, and in that sense it counts as minimal. One often speaks of *the* fusion of the φs, because in classical mereology there can only be one thing z satisfying both conditions (see T.3). However, it will be recalled that this property depends on the Antisymmetry axiom A.2. In theories that do not endorse A.2, algebraic fusions need not be unique. Thus it is generally better to speak of algebraic fusions as 'minimal' rather than 'least' upper bounds—a terminology that is now rather standard (following Hovda, 2009).

There is a kindred definition of fusion that also has a rightful claim to be called a 'minimal' upper bound, and is perhaps more closely related to the order-theoretic sense of the term.[1]

(D.43) $F^{*}_{\varphi}z :\equiv \forall x(\varphi x \to Pxz) \land \forall y(\forall x(\varphi x \to Pxy) \to \neg PPyz)$ F^{*}-*type Fusion*

This definition has appeared in the philosophical literature somewhat more rarely.[2] It says a fusion is an upper bound that has no upper bound as a proper part. Although similar to D.6, in non-classical contexts it is not equivalent, as the familiar non-extensional model in figure 5.1 shows. Here the two top elements, a and b, both count as F^{*}-type fusions of c and d, since we have that both $\neg PPab$ and $\neg PPba$, yet neither is an F-type fusion of c and d, for neither Pab nor Pba. By contrast, the following way of defining

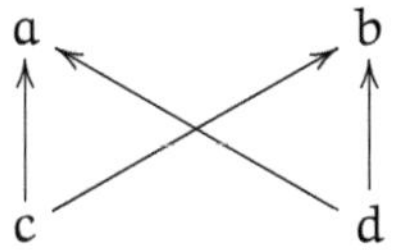

Figure 5.1: F^{*}-type fusions but no F-type fusions

1 See e.g. the definition of 'minimal element' in Davey and Priestly (2002, p. 16).
2 See Varzi (2009) and Cotnoir (2016a).

algebraic fusions, which may be found in some of the works cited above (e.g. Bostock, 1979, p. 117), is equivalent to D.6 even in non-extensional contexts, provided only that P obeys Reflexivity and Transitivity.[3]

(D.44) $F_{\varphi}z :\equiv \forall y(Pzy \leftrightarrow \forall x(\varphi x \to Pxy))$ F-*type Fusion (Alt.)*

Our second main type of fusions, which we term Leśniewski fusions,[4] are used frequently in the philosophical literature, also thanks to the influential works of Tarski (1929, 1935) and, more recently, van Inwagen (1987, 1990) and Lewis (1991).[5] Here is the definition again, from section 2.4.1.

(D.13) $F'_{\varphi}z :\equiv \forall x(\varphi x \to Pxz) \land \forall y(Pyz \to \exists x(\varphi x \land Oyx))$ F′-*type Fusion*

This definition, too, has two conjuncts, the first being the same as in D.6: it says a fusion must be an upper bound of the φs. The second conjunct, however, is different. It doesn't say the upper bound must be *minimal*; it stipulates, rather, that every part of the fusion must *overlap* at least one of the φs.

Finally, our third type of fusion—Goodman fusions—corresponds to the definition we met in section 2.4.2 and is perhaps even more popular, being taken up in four major monographs devoted to mereology: Eberle (1970), Simons (1987), Libardi (1990), and Casati and Varzi (1999).[6]

(D.16) $F''_{\varphi}z :\equiv \forall y(Oyz \leftrightarrow \exists x(\varphi x \land Oyx))$ F″-*type Fusion*

This definition ditches the upper-bound requirement altogether and opts instead for a characterization fully in terms of overlap: something is a fusion of the φs if and only if it is overlapped by exactly those things that overlap at least one of the φs. Since overlap is the opposite of disjointness, the same definition could also be given in terms of D. That was the original choice in Leonard and Goodman (1940) (see again section 2.4.2) and it is worth

3 Note that D.44 is logically equivalent to the conjunction of (a) $\forall y(Pzy \to \forall x(\varphi x \to Pxy))$ and (b) $\forall y(\forall x(\varphi x \to Pxy) \to Pzy)$. Since (b) coincides with the second conjunct of D.6, we only need to check that (a) is interderivable with the first, i.e. $\forall x(\varphi x \to Pxz)$. In one direction, it suffices to instantiate (a) to $Pzz \to \forall x(\varphi x \to Pxz)$ and then drop Pzz by Reflexivity. Conversely, suppose for arbitrary a that Pza. Given any b, we can instantiate $\forall x(\varphi x \to Pxz)$ to obtain $\varphi^x_b \to Pbz$ and Transitivity will give us $Pbz \to Pba$. Thus $\varphi^x_b \to Pba$, which generalizes to $\forall x(\varphi x \to Pxa)$. Hence $Pza \to \forall x(\varphi x \to Pxa)$, which in turn generalizes to (a).

4 These fusions are sometimes called 'sums', following Leśniewski's original usage; see chapter 2, note 14. Here we shall continue to use 'sum' for finitary fusions (in each sense of 'fusion').

5 At least this is true of the spirit of D.13, if not the letter. Recall that Tarski's definition used variables for sets rather than placeholders for formulas, and both van Inwagen and Lewis define fusions using plural quantification. The difference is not immaterial, and we shall come back to it in chapter 6, but it does not affect the main thread of the present chapter.

6 Also Ridder (2002), in the official outline of classical mereology (§1.3), uses this definition. Other surveys of classical mereology that do the same include Cook (2009), Niebergall (2009a, 2011), Calosi (2011), and Link (2014, ch. 13).

noting that Leśniewski himself had considered this definition as one more equivalent alternative to his own (Leśniewski, 1927–1931, pt. x).

(D.18) $F''_{\varphi}z :\equiv \forall y(Dyz \leftrightarrow \forall x(\varphi x \to Dyx))$ *F''-type Fusion (Alt.)*

Note that, given the symmetry of D, this is very similar to the alternative definition of F-type fusion given in D.44, with just D in place of P. However, nowadays the parallel definition in terms of O is much more common, so we shall restrict our attention to D.16.

5.1.2 *Comparisons*

Given these alternate definitions of mereological fusion, we want to compare them more directly and see where they agree and where they differ. In the opening pages of *Parts of Classes*, David Lewis writes:

> The fusion of all cats is that large, scattered chunk of cat-stuff which is composed of all the cats there are, and nothing else. It has all cats as parts. There are other things that have all cats as parts. But the cat-fusion is the least such thing: it is included as a part in any other one ... It has no part that is entirely distinct from each and every cat. Rather, every part of it overlaps some cat. We would equivalently define the cat-fusion as the thing that overlaps all and only those things that overlap some cat. (Lewis, 1991, pp. 1f)

As we mentioned, Lewis will eventually settle on a version of classical mereology based on Leśniewski fusions. But it is telling that here he is appealing to all three notions together, characterizing a cat-fusion first in algebraic terms, then in Leśniewskian terms, and finally in Goodmanian terms. Are these notions really the same? We know that in classical mereology every non-empty condition φ has a fusion of each kind. But do those fusions always match? And how do fusions of one type relate to fusions of the other types in theories weaker than classical mereology?

Let us start with *algebraic* fusions. Generally speaking, it's easy to see that sometimes an algebraic fusion exists even in the absence of a corresponding Leśniewski or Goodman fusion. The model in figure 5.2 is a simple case in point. Here u counts as an F-type fusion of a and b but not as an F'-type fusion, since there is some part of u, namely c, that doesn't overlap a or b.

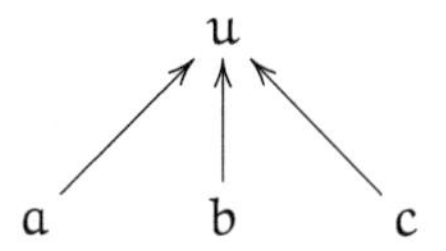

Figure 5.2: F-type fusions but no F'-type or F''-type fusions

Similarly, u is not an F''-type fusion of a and b, since c itself overlaps u but not a or b. Of course this is not a model of classical mereology (it does not satisfy Remainder), but the question applies generally. Are there any conditions one may require to ensure that every algebraic fusion is also a Leśniewski or a Goodman fusion?

Concerning Leśniewski fusions, Hovda (2009, §3.1) observes that the following principle would do.[7]

(T.38) $\forall y \forall z((F_\varphi z \wedge Pyz) \to \exists x(\varphi x \wedge Oyx))$ *Filtration*

Given any condition φ, this principle says that every part of an F-type fusion of the φs must overlap at least one of the φs. It is clear that this principle rules out the model in figure 5.2, precisely because c violates the consequent when φ is the condition '$x = a \vee x = b$'. More generally, we can see that T.38 suffices to guarantee that every algebraic fusion is a Leśniewski fusion for any condition φ. For suppose that $F_\varphi z$. By D.6 we already have the first conjunct of D.13. To get the second conjunct, assume that Pyz for arbitrary y. Then we have the antecedent of T.38 and we immediately obtain the consequent, $\exists x(\varphi x \wedge Oxy)$. Thus $Pyz \to \exists x(\varphi x \wedge Oxy)$, as required. Generalizing, it follows that z satisfies both conjuncts of D.13, i.e. $F'_\varphi z$.

Similarly, Simons (1987, p. 37) notes that the following principle may be added to ensure that algebraic fusions are also Goodman fusions, at least as long as P is transitive.

(T.39) $\forall y \forall z((F_\varphi z \wedge Oyz) \to \exists x(\varphi x \wedge Oyx))$ *Strong Overlap*

To see this, suppose for arbitrary φ and z that $F_\varphi z$. We want to show that $F''_\varphi z$, i.e. $\forall y(Oyz \leftrightarrow \exists x(\varphi x \wedge Oyx))$. In the left-to-right direction, this follows immediately from T.39. For the other direction, assume $\exists x(\varphi x \wedge Oyx)$, i.e. there is some a such that φ^x_a and Oya. By the first conjunct of D.6, a must be part of z, and by D.2, it must have a part of its own, c, in common with y. By Transitivity, c must be part of z, too, and so we obtain that Oyz.

One way to put these results is to say that Filtration and Strong Overlap make up for the 'difference' between algebraic fusions and, respectively, Leśniewski and Goodman fusions. However, it should be stressed that both principles are rather strong as they stand, to the point that neither is provable as a theorem of classical mereology. A simple counterexample is provided in both cases by a one-element model in which the only element in

7 Filtration has some affinities with the Distributivity principle of Landman (1991, p. 315):

$$\forall x \forall y \forall z(Px(y+z) \to (Pxy \vee Pxz \vee \exists v \exists w(Pvy \wedge Pwz \wedge x = v + w)))$$

However, this principle only governs binary algebraic sums. As Hovda (2009, p. 68) notes, it yields Filtration when the domain is finite, but not generally.

the domain fails to satisfy the condition expressed by φ, thereby verifying the antecedent and falsifying the consequent of both T.38 and T.39.[8] Now, models of this sort are perfectly acceptable also from the perspective of a number of non-classical mereological theories, except of course for theories committed to Atomlessness (A.31) or at least Weak Gunk (A.63). It follows, therefore, that adding either T.38 or T.39 would secure the desired result concerning algebraic fusions, but at a cost that many will find unacceptable.[9] More generally, any mereology admitting models in which there is a bottom element that is part of everything and where nothing in the domain satisfies a given condition φ will countenance F-type fusions that are neither F′-type fusions nor F″-type fusions, since the bottom element will vacuously qualify as a minimal upper bound of the φs (satisfying D.6) even though there aren't any φs it can overlap (violating both D.13 and D.16).

Nevertheless, in mereology we are generally interested in non-empty fusions. Even the Unrestricted Fusion axiom schema of classical mereology involves an existential antecedent in each of the three variants corresponding to the main notions of fusion. Thus, generally speaking, we may content ourselves with suitably weakened versions of T.38 and T.39.

(A.64) $\exists x \varphi x \rightarrow \forall y \forall z((F_\varphi z \wedge Pyz) \rightarrow \exists x(\varphi x \wedge Oyx))$ *∃-Filtration*

(A.65) $\exists x \varphi x \rightarrow \forall y \forall z((F_\varphi z \wedge Oyz) \rightarrow \exists x(\varphi x \wedge Oyx))$ *∃-Strong Overlap*

These principles will suffice to guarantee the desired results when φ is non-empty, as the arguments above will still apply. In other words, A.64 and A.65 guarantee that any algebraic fusion of a specifiable *non-empty* collection of things is also a Leśniewski fusion and a Goodman fusion of those things, respectively. In particular, since both principles are theorems of classical mereology,[10] this means that classically every non-empty algebraic fusion is

8 The falsity of the consequent follows directly from the assumption that nothing satisfies φ. To see that the antecedents of T.38 and T.39 are both true, let a be the unique element in the domain. We must check that $F_\varphi a \wedge Paa$ and $F_\varphi a \wedge Oaa$. Assuming the model is reflexive, we immediately have that Paa and Oaa, so we only need to check that $F_\varphi a$. Now, nothing satisfies φ, so $\forall x(\varphi x \rightarrow Pxa)$ is vacuously true. Moreover, a is part of everything and so, *a fortiori*, $\forall y(\forall x(\varphi x \rightarrow Pxy) \rightarrow Pay)$. Thus a satisfies both conjuncts of D.6, as required.

9 Thus, Hovda's claim that in a classical mereology *à la* Leśniewski we can trade the Unrestricted Fusion′ axiom schema A.11 for the Unrestricted Fusion schema A.5 by adding Filtration (as in the "third way" of Hovda, 2009, p. 82) is, strictly speaking, false. However, it turns out that adding the weaker principle of ∃-Filtration introduced below (A.64) will suffice, as shown in Varzi (2019, §2). Similarly for Simons's claim that in a classical mereology *à la* Goodman we can trade the Unrestricted Fusion″ schema A.15 for A.5 by adding Strong Overlap, though adding the weaker principle of ∃-Strong Overlap introduced below (A.65) will do.

10 Here is a proof of A.64 (without using A.5). Assume $\exists x \varphi x$ and $F_\varphi z$. Pick y so that Pyz and suppose for *reductio* that y is disjoint from every φer. Clearly $y \neq z$, since every φer is part of z by D.6 (and thus overlaps z by Reflexivity). By Antisymmetry, this means that $\neg Pzy$ and so, by Remainder, there is a difference $w = z - y$. Now, any φer must be part of w, otherwise

indeed a fusion also according to the other definitions, warranting Lewis's language in the passage quoted above.

(T.40) $\exists x\varphi x \to \forall z(F_\varphi z \to (F'_\varphi z \wedge F''_\varphi z))$ *Classical Fusions*

Let us now consider *Goodman* fusions. If something is a Goodman fusion, does it follow it is an algebraic or a Leśniewski fusion? The short answer, again, is no. A simple counterexample is the diagram in figure 5.3, left, which displays a model in which everything overlaps everything; in particular, something overlaps c if and only if it overlaps either a or b. Counterintuitively, then, this means that c is a Goodman fusion of a and b, though obviously not an algebraic or a Leśniewski fusion. Another case in point is once again the non-extensional model on the right, where a turns out to be an F''-type fusion of a and b even though b is not part of a (and vice versa).

Figure 5.3: F''-type fusions but no F-type or F'-type fusions

This shows clearly that something can go badly wrong with the definition of F''-type fusions in merely partial-ordered models. What principles can be added to fix these problems?

In both models of figure 5.3, the relevant Goodman fusions are not even upper bounds of the things they fuse, whereas algebraic and Leśniewski fusions explicitly state that they must be upper bounds. This thought suggests a simple bridging principle.

(A.66) $\forall z(F''_\varphi z \to \forall x(\varphi x \to Pxz))$ *Upper Bound*

It's easy to see that if something is a Goodman fusion, in the presence of A.66 it is an algebraic fusion as well, at least when P is transitive. For suppose for some arbitrary condition φ that $F''_\varphi z$, i.e. $\forall y(Oyz \leftrightarrow \exists x(\varphi x \wedge Oyx))$. Suppose also, for *reductio*, that $\neg F_\varphi z$. Given A.66, z must be an upper bound of the φs, so the only way it can fail to be their algebraic fusion is for it not to be *minimal*, i.e. there must exist some w such that $\forall x(\varphi x \to Pxw)$ but $\neg Pzw$. Now we have two cases regarding this w: either (i) w itself is a

---

it would overlap $z - w$, which is just y, contradicting our hypothesis. Moreover, since Pwz and z is part of every upper bound of the φs (by D.6), w must be part of those upper bounds, too (by Transitivity). But then w is a minimal upper bound of the φs, i.e. $F_\varphi w$, and so $w = z$ by Uniqueness (T.3). Thus $z - y = z$, contradicting Pyz. The proof of A.65 is similar.

Goodman fusion of the φs, or (ii) it is not. In case (i) we have by D.16 that $\forall y(Oyw \leftrightarrow \exists x(\varphi x \wedge Oyx))$. But then we have $\forall y(Oyz \leftrightarrow Oyw)$, i.e. z and w overlap the same things, which means w is a Goodman fusion of z and w. By A.66, this implies that Pzw: contradiction. On the other hand (ii) suppose $\neg F''_\varphi w$. This means that for some y either (a) Oyw and $\neg\exists x(\varphi x \wedge Oxy)$ or (b) $\neg Oyw$ and $\exists x(\varphi x \wedge Oxy)$. Case (a) conflicts with our assumption for *reductio*, namely $\forall x(\varphi x \rightarrow Pxw)$. Similarly, for case (b) the assumption implies that $\exists x(Pxw \wedge Oxy)$, which implies that Oyw by Transitivity: contradiction. Hence $F_\varphi z$ after all.

In fact, in the presence of A.66 we can show that Goodman fusions are Leśniewski fusions as well, at least as long as P is reflexive. For suppose we have $F''_\varphi z$. Then A.66 immediately gives us $\forall x(\varphi x \rightarrow Pxz)$, which is the first conjunct of D.13. To obtain the second conjunct, assume Pyz, and hence Oyz (by A.1). Then we may appeal to the definition of F''-type fusions, D.16, and the left-to-right direction gives us $\exists x(\varphi x \wedge Oyx)$, as required.

It is worth noting that A.66 has been largely ignored in the literature, except for Gruszczyński (2013). Somewhat interestingly, it has virtually the same strength as the Strong Supplementation axiom A.18. More precisely, recall from chapter 4 that, given Reflexivity and Transitivity, Strong Supplementation is equivalent to

(T.21) $\forall x \forall y(\forall z(Ozx \rightarrow Ozy) \rightarrow Pxy)$ *O–Supervenience*

Then the point is that our Upper Bound principle A.66 is equivalent to T.21, and hence, given just Reflexivity and Transitivity, to Strong Supplementation.[11] To see that it entails T.21, assume for arbitrary a and b that $\forall z(Oza \rightarrow Ozb)$. Then we have $\forall z(Ozb \leftrightarrow (Oza \vee Ozb))$ (by sheer logic), which means that b is an F''-type fusion of a and b. So A.66 gives us Pab, as desired, whence T.21 follows by generalization. For the converse entailment, assume for some b that $F''_\varphi b$. (If there isn't any, A.66 is vacuously true and we are done.) By D.16, this means that every z satisfies the biconditional $Ozb \leftrightarrow \exists x(\varphi x \wedge Ozx)$. We need to show that $\forall x(\varphi x \rightarrow Pxb)$, so suppose a is some thing satisfying φx and let us show that Pab. Now, for any z, either z overlaps a, or it doesn't. If Oza, then a is a witness for $\exists x(\varphi x \wedge Ozx)$, and the right-to-left direction of our biconditional gives us Ozb. So $Oza \rightarrow Ozb$. If $\neg Oza$, then again we have $Oza \rightarrow Ozb$ by material implication. Thus $\forall z(Oza \rightarrow Ozb)$, and so Pab by T.21.

Given the equivalence of Upper Bound and O–Supervenience, it is perhaps not surprising that Goodman used a biconditional version of the latter

11 That Strong Supplementation itself suffices for Goodman fusions to qualify as algebraic and Leśniewski fusions (given also Reflexivity and Transitivity) is shown in Pietruszczak (2000b, thm. IV.3.1 and lm. II.8.2).

principle as definition of P (see D.14 in section 2.4.2). Nonetheless the point is worth stressing. One needs (virtually) the full strength of Strong Supplementation to turn Goodman fusions into algebraic or Leśniewski fusions, and Strong Supplementation is a *de*composition principle. Since adding Goodman's Unrestricted Fusion″ schema A.15 to Strong Supplementation and the ordering axioms yields classical mereology, as in Eberle's axiomatization of section 2.4.3, it follows that in classical mereology every Goodman fusion is indeed a fusion also in the other senses.

(T.41) $\forall z(F''_{\varphi}z \rightarrow (F_{\varphi}z \wedge F'_{\varphi}z))$ *Classical Fusions (bis)*

But really this depends on both sides of the coin—composition and decomposition. And it must be the right sides. Matching A.15 with Weak Supplementation, for instance, would not suffice, as the four-element model in figure 5.3 shows.[12]

Let us finally turn to *Leśniewski* fusions. If something is a Leśniewski fusion of the φs, is it also an algebraic or Goodman fusion? With regard to the latter, this time the answer is in the affirmative, assuming only Transitivity. To see why, suppose for an arbitrary (satisfiable) φ that $F'_{\varphi}z$. We have to check that z satisfies the biconditional in D.16, i.e. $Oyz \leftrightarrow \exists x(\varphi x \wedge Oyx)$ for arbitrary y. For the left-to-right direction, assume Oyz. Let a be a common part. Since Paz, by the second conjunct of D.13 we have for some x that $\varphi x \wedge Oax$, and since Pay, by Transitivity we obtain Oyx. So $\exists x(\varphi x \wedge Oyx)$ as required. For the right-to-left direction, assume for some x that $\varphi x \wedge Oyx$. It follows by the first conjunct of D.13 that Pxz, and because Oyx, Transitivity again gives us Oyz.

So here we finally have one clear entailment that does not require any bridge principles besides a modest ordering axiom: as long as P is transitive, every Leśniewski fusion is a Goodman fusion. By contrast, it's easy to see that a Leśniewski fusion need not be an algebraic fusion even if P obeys all ordering axioms. A case in point is once again the non-extensional butterfly model of figure 5.1 (or figure 5.3, right), where c and d have no algebraic fusion even though both a and b count as their Leśniewski fusions. There are even models in which *everything* has a Leśniewski fusion, thereby satisfying the unrestricted axiom schema A.11, even in the absence of corresponding algebraic fusions, as in figure 5.4. Here c and d have three

12 This is why the popular theory defined by these two axioms together with A.1–A.3 does *not* amount to classical mereology. See again notes 43 and 54 in chapter 2. Cf. also Lorenz (1977) and Forrest (2017), who Goodmanize Tarski's (1929, 1935) system by pairing the Transitivity axiom A.3 with the F″-variant of the Unique Unrestricted Fusion′ schema A.12. Does that amount to an axiomatization of classical mereology? (What about adding Reflexivity, as in Lorenz, 1984, or Antisymmetry, as in Forrest, 2012, or both Reflexivity and Antisymmetry, as in Lorenz, 2013?)

upper bounds, namely a, b, and the top element u. None of these upper bounds is minimal in the sense required by D.6, so again c and d do not have an algebraic fusion in the model. Yet each of a, b, and u qualifies as a Leśniewski fusion of c and d according to D.13, and u itself counts as a Leśniewski (and algebraic) fusion of a and b.

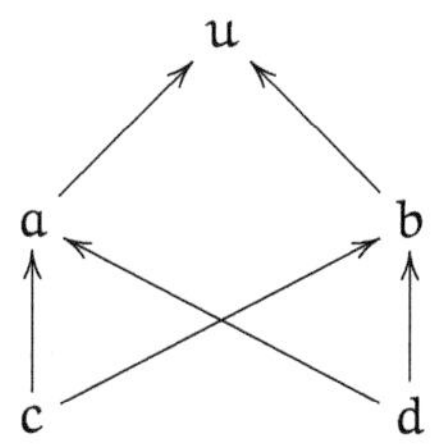

Figure 5.4: F'-type fusions but no F-type fusions

What sort of mereological principles might we add to transform all Leśniewski fusions into algebraic fusions? Here it will be instructive to distinguish two cases, depending on whether or not we want the answer to depend on the general principles of composition that we assume in the background.

If we assume the Unrestricted Fusion′ schema (A.11), or even its finitary variant (A.36), then it turns out that a suitable decomposition principle will again provide the link we need, as with Goodman fusions. This time, however, the Weak Supplementation principle A.10 will suffice. Indeed, it's clear that A.10 immediately rules out the model of figure 5.4, since that model is not weakly supplemented; we have e.g. that $PPau$ even though u has no (proper) parts disjoint from a. But here is a proof that A.10 will always work (from Hovda, 2009, pp. 66f). Suppose for an arbitrary (satisfiable) φ that $F'_\varphi z$. Then by D.13 we already have it that $\forall x(\varphi x \rightarrow Pxz)$, which is the first conjunct of D.6. So we just need to establish the second conjunct, namely $\forall y(\forall x(\varphi x \rightarrow Pxy) \rightarrow Pzy)$. To this end, assume for arbitrary y that $\forall x(\varphi x \rightarrow Pxy)$ and let a be an F'-type fusion of y and z. Suppose for *reductio* that $a \neq y$. Since Pya (by the first conjunct of D.13), we must have $PPya$. So, by Weak Supplementation, there is some b such that $PPba$ and Dby, hence $\neg Oby$ (by D.2 and D.4). Since we must have either Oby or Obz (by D.1 and the second conjunct of D.13), it follows that Obz. But then b and z must have a common part, say c (by D.2). Now recall that $F'_\varphi z$, so Pcz implies that Ocx for some x such that φx (again by the second conjunct of D.13). And because Pxy (by choice of y), it follows that Ocy (by Transitivity). Hence, since Pcb, Oby: contradiction. So we must have $a = y$. And since Pza (by the first conjunct of D.13), we obtain Pzy as required.

Since Unrestricted Fusion′ plus Weak Supplementation, along with Transitivity, yield an axiomatization of classical mereology (see again section 2.4.1), we see once more that classical mereology allows us to match one notion of fusion with the others—in this case, Leśniewski fusions with algebraic and (as shown earlier) Goodman fusions.

(T.42) $\forall z(F'_{\varphi}z \rightarrow (F_{\varphi}z \wedge F''_{\varphi}z))$ *Classical Fusions (ter)*

And again, it is noteworthy that the full matching is guaranteed by a principle that is really meant to govern mereological *de*composition. However, generally speaking, we may be interested in matching Leśniewski fusions with the others, in particular with algebraic fusions, regardless of any substantive axiom governing their existence. This is the second case we mentioned. What sort of principle can be added to make up for the conceptual 'difference' between the two types of fusion?

Gruszczyński and Pietruszczak (2014, p. 132) note that the following monotonicity schema would do, at least so long as P is reflexive.

(A.67) $\forall y \forall z((F'_{\varphi}z \wedge F'_{\psi}y \wedge \forall x(\varphi x \rightarrow \psi x)) \rightarrow Pzy)$ *Monotonicity*

The adequacy of this schema can easily be appreciated by seeing that in reflexive contexts it is equivalent to the following.

(T.43) $\forall y \forall z((F'_{\varphi}z \wedge \forall x(\varphi x \rightarrow Pxy)) \rightarrow Pzy)$ *Minimal Upper Bound*

This says explicitly that every Leśniewski fusion must be minimal, just like A.66 says explicitly that every Goodman fusion must be an upper bound, so its adequacy is straightforward. To see that T.43 implies A.67, suppose for arbitrary y and z that $F'_{\varphi}z$ and $F'_{\psi}y$. By D.13, $F'_{\psi}y$ gives us $\forall x(\psi x \rightarrow Pxy)$. Thus, if we also have $\forall x(\varphi x \rightarrow \psi x)$, we obtain that $\forall x(\varphi x \rightarrow Pxy)$ and hence, by T.43, Pzy. Conversely, to see that A.67 implies T.43, suppose $F'_{\varphi}z$ and also $\forall x(\varphi x \rightarrow Pxy)$. It will suffice to take ψx to be the condition 'Pxy'. For then we immediately have that $\forall x(\varphi x \rightarrow \psi x)$. Moreover, $\forall x(Pxy \rightarrow Pxy)$ is a logical truth and $\forall w(Pwy \rightarrow \exists x(Pxy \wedge Owx))$ follows from the fact that every part of y overlaps itself (by Reflexivity), so we also have that $F'_{\psi}y$ (by D.13). We can therefore invoke A.67 and infer by *modus ponens* that Pzy, as required.

In fact, we can drop the Reflexivity proviso altogether. Monotonicity alone will do, since it entails Reflexivity. The reason is that A.67, in the special case where ψ coincides with φ, logically implies that $\forall z(\neg Pzz \rightarrow \neg F'_{\varphi}z)$, i.e. no z such that $\neg Pzz$ can ever be an F'-fusion. In particular, no such z can be an F'-fusion of its proper parts, $\forall z(\neg Pzz \rightarrow \neg F'_{PPxz}z)$. But as Gruszczyński and Pietruszczak (*ibid.*, p. 129) note, this last formula implies its own contrary,

$\forall z(\neg Pzz \to F'_{PPxz}z)$.[13] The only way this can be the case, short of contradiction, is for both formulas to be vacuously true, i.e. we must have $\forall zPzz$.

So Monotonicity is sufficient enough for every Leśniewski fusion to qualify as an algebraic fusion. It is also necessary, since algebraic fusions are monotonic by definition. A.67 is thus the principle we were looking for. One might still wonder whether, as was the case with A.66 and Strong Supplementation, there is some tight connection between this schematic principle and the Weak Supplementation axiom A.10 after all. The answer to this question is yes and no. Obviously A.10 does not imply A.67, not even under the standard ordering axioms, witness the butterfly model (taking both φx and ψx to be the condition '$x = c \vee x = d$'). In the opposite direction, however, Gruszczyński and Pietruszczak (*ibid.*, §6.5) have shown that the entailment holds so long as P obeys the Antisymmetry axiom A.2.[14] To see this, notice first of all that A.2 and A.67 jointly entail the following thesis.

(T.44) $\forall y \forall z((F'_{\varphi}z \wedge F'_{\varphi}y) \to z = y)$ *Fusion′ Uniqueness*

This is because $\forall x(\varphi x \to \varphi x)$ is a logical truth, so if $F'_{\varphi}z$ and $F'_{\varphi}y$, by A.67 we have both Pzy and Pyz, hence $z = y$ by A.2. Next, given Reflexivity, it's easy to see that T.44 in turn implies Tarski's (1937) singularity axiom, which we met in section 2.4.3.

(A.17) $\forall y \forall z(F'_{x=y}z \to z = y)$ *Singular Fusion′*

The reason is that Reflexivity immediately implies

(T.45) $\forall y\ F'_{x=y}y$ F'*–Reflexivity*

and thus, whenever $F'_{x=y}z$, we also have $F'_{x=y}y$ and T.44 gives us $z = y$. So now, to derive Weak Supplementation, assume for arbitrary a and b that $PPab$ and suppose for *reductio* that $\neg\exists z(Pzb \wedge Dza)$. Then $\forall y(Pyb \to Oya)$ (by D.2 and D.4). Since we also have Pab, by D.13 we obtain that $F'_{x=a}b$.

13 Assume that $\forall z(\neg Pzz \to \neg F'_{PPxz}z)$ and suppose that $\neg Paa$. Obviously we have $\neg F'_{PPxa}a$, but we want to obtain the opposite, $F'_{PPxa}a$. To this end, pick any b and suppose that Pba. Then b must be distinct from a and so we have that $PPba$. Moreover, either Pbb or $\neg Pbb$. If Pbb, then Obb by D.2. If $\neg Pbb$, then our assumption gives us that $\neg F'_{PPxb}b$, which means that $\forall x(PPxb \to Pxb) \wedge \forall y(Pyb \to \exists x(PPxb \wedge Oyx))$ is false (by D.13). Since the first conjunct is a consequence of D.1, we can infer that $\neg\forall y(Pyb \to \exists x(PPxb \wedge Oyx))$ and so there must be some c such that $Pcb \wedge \neg\exists x(PPxb \wedge Ocx)$. From the first conjunct we obtain again that Obb by D.2. Thus, either way we have that $PPba \wedge Obb$, whence $\exists x(PPxa \wedge Obx)$. By conditionalization we obtain $Pba \to \exists x(PPxa \wedge Obx)$, which generalizes to $\forall y(Pya \to \exists x(PPxa \wedge Oyx))$. But by D.1 we also have $\forall x(PPxa \to Pxa)$. Thus a satisfies both conjuncts of D.13 for the condition '$PPxa$', which means that $F'_{PPxa}a$.

14 Interestingly, the other ordering axioms (Reflexivity and Transitivity) turn out instead to entail the equivalence of A.67 with Strong Supplementation. See Pietruszczak (2000b, pp. 97f).

But then $a = b$ by A.17: contradiction. Thus, $PPab \rightarrow \exists z(Pzb \wedge Dza)$. This is the Weak P-Supplementation principle T.25. Given A.1, we know from section 4.3 that it coincides with Weak Supplementation.

To complete the picture, at this point one might well wonder whether the bridge principles for algebraic fusions, namely Filtration (T.38) and Strong Overlap (T.39), or perhaps ∃-Filtration (A.64) and ∃-Strong Overlap (A.65), are closely related to Remainder (A.4), since this was the decomposition axiom we paired with algebraic fusions in our axiomatization of classical mereology. Here the answer is mostly in the negative. We know that A.64 and A.65 are theorems of classical mereology, and since their proof does not require A.5, we can say that both principles follow from the ordering axioms A.1–A.3 along with just Remainder. However, all other entailments fail. The unconditional bridge principles don't follow, since Remainder is vacuously satisfied in any (partially ordered) one-element model even though, as we saw, the model violates T.38 and T.39 when φ is an empty condition. And none of the bridge principles entails Remainder, not even jointly. This is shown, for instance, by the (partially ordered) three-element model we met in figure 5.3, left. That model violates Remainder, since we have e.g. that $\neg Pac$ although there's nothing disjoint from c. But since everything overlaps everything, the model satisfies both Filtration and Strong Overlap—hence, *a fortiori*, their ∃-weakenings—by virtue of their having true consequents.

Let us recapitulate our positive findings. We have seen that in classical mereology the three notions of fusion are virtually equivalent, with just one small exception: in degenerate, one-element models, the unique element of the domain qualifies as a Leśniewski or Goodman fusion of the φs if and only if it is a φ, whereas it counts as an algebraic fusion regardless. These facts correspond to the Classical Fusions principles T.40, T.41, and T.42. For the rest, the relationships among the different types of fusion are as follows.

- F*-type algebraic fusions* (D.6): These fusions qualify as Leśniewski fusions in the presence of Filtration (T.38) and they qualify as Goodman fusions in the presence of Strong Overlap (T.39). For non-empty fusions, it is enough to assume ∃-Filtration (A.64) and ∃-Strong Overlap (A.65), respectively.
- F'*-type Leśniewski fusions* (D.13): These fusions always qualify as algebraic fusions so long as P is monotonic (A.67) and as Goodman fusions so long as P is transitive (A.3).
- F''*-type Goodman fusions* (D.16): In the presence of Upper Bound (A.66), these fusions qualify as algebraic fusions so long as P is transitive (A.3) and as Leśniewski fusions so long as P is reflexive (A.1).

These relationships are summarized schematically in figure 5.5 (where the arrows indicate logical inclusion).

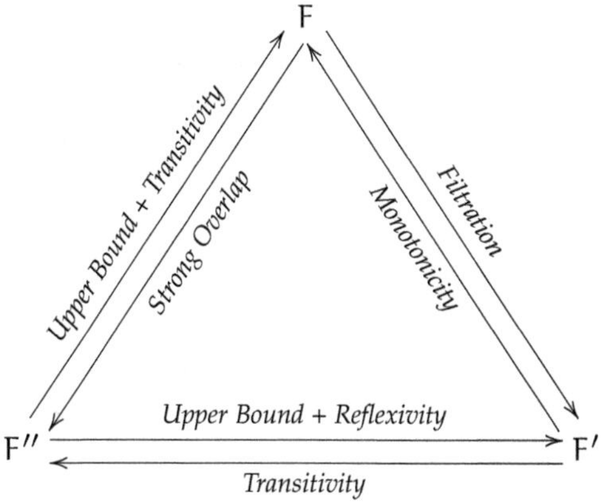

Figure 5.5: Relationships between types of fusion

Note that these entailments do not just mean that if a fusion of some type exists, then a fusion of a different type exists as well if certain conditions are met. In each case we have something stronger, namely, we showed *of a particular* fusion of some type or other that under certain conditions *it itself* is also a fusion of another type. There are, of course, models in which distinct objects exist where one of them serves as a fusion of a certain collection of φs in one sense of 'fusion' and another object serves as a fusion of the very same φs in a different sense. The (partially ordered) model in figure 5.6 is just such a case. In this model, a_2 is an F-type fusion of b_1 and b_3 but not, say, an F''-type fusion; yet there are things that qualify as F''-type fusions of b_1 and b_3, for instance, the bottom element n. Similarly, n itself is an F''-type fusion of a_1 and a_3 but not, say, an F'-fusion; yet there is something that qualifies as an F'-type fusions of a_1 and a_3, namely the top element u. Finally, u itself is an F'-fusion of, say, b_1 and b_2 but not an F-type fusion; yet there is something that serves as an F-type fusion of b_1 and b_2, namely a_2.

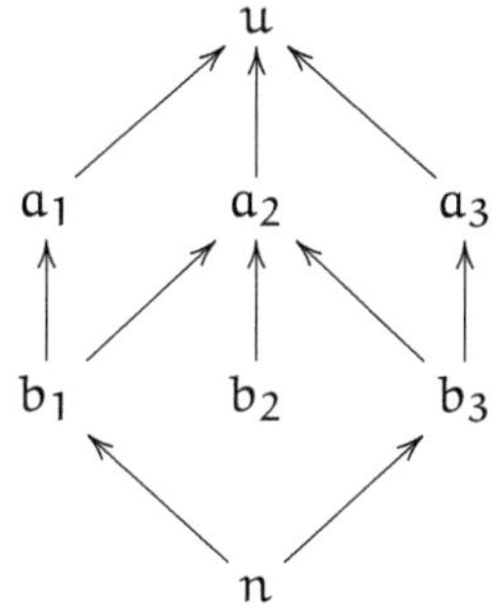

Figure 5.6: Distinct fusions of different types

Whether models of this sort are admissible is partly determined by the constraints we have seen—but only partly. The rest will depend on the other axioms of the specific theory under consideration, beginning with those axioms that deal explicitly with the existence and identity conditions of mereological fusions.

5.2 EXISTENCE AND IDENTITY

Peter van Inwagen (1987, 1990) distinguishes two sorts of questions regarding mereological composition. The first is the *General Composition Question*: what is the nature of mereological composition? The second is the *Special Composition Question*: under what conditions does composition occur?[15] So far we have been focusing on how to *define* composition in terms of fusions, hence on issues related to the general question.[16] We now turn to the special question, addressing different putative conditions under which mereological fusions may be said to *exist*. We also address the question as to the putative conditions under which, if fusions do exist, they are supposed to be *unique*. At the end of the section we return to the general question and examine an answer that is often associated with the classical way of dealing with the existence and uniqueness of fusions: the answer consisting in saying that composition is essentially a many-one relation of *identity*.

5.2.1 *Existence*

The Special Composition Question has been the subject of an intense debate among philosophers. For the most part, the literature has focused on the conditions of composition for material objects, in line with van Inwagen's original concerns.[17] Occasionally the question has been addressed with regard to other sorts of entity, such as events (Bennett, 1988, ch. 10; Savellos, 2000), collective actions (Chant, 2006, 2010; Ludwig, 2014), phenomenal states (Goff, 2011, 2017), or non-individual entities such as universals and

15 An early formulation of this question may be found in Hestevold (1981), though limited to finitary composition: when is it that two objects are mereologically "conjoined"?

16 At least insofar as 'composition' is analyzed in terms of 'part'. Strictly speaking, van Inwagen understands the general question as asking for a non-mereological analysis, and as such the question lies beyond the scope of this book. Van Inwagen himself is skeptical about the possibility of an adequate answer, since the concepts 'part', 'sum', and 'compose' form a tight "mereological circle" (1990, p. 51), but see e.g. Yablo (2016) on the kindred question, what is it for x to be part of y? Cf. also Simons (2016a) on whether mereological propositions need or can have truth-makers of any sort. Relatedly, see Kleinschmidt (2019) for the idea that composition should be treated as a primitive, generalizing the approach outlined in section 2.4.4.

17 This is typical also of critical surveys (e.g. Markosian, 2008) or textbook accounts (e.g. Tallant, 2011, ch. 2; Ney, 2014, ch. 3; Loux and Crisp, 2017, ch. 9; Koons and Pickavance, 2017, ch. 22).

states of affairs (McDaniel, 2009a). In its most general form, however, the question may be asked with respect to any domain of entities whatsoever. When do some things compose something?[18]

Since 'compose' can be understood in different ways, one for each notion of 'fusion', one should of course be careful: strictly speaking, there are several Special Composition Questions.[19] But there is another worry worth mentioning. Regardless of its scope, and regardless of how exactly 'compose' is understood, some philosophers have argued that the Special Composition Question is unanswerable. More precisely, the question would be either illegitimate or trivial. It would be illegitimate insofar as it is ultimately a question about what there is, and questions about what there is admit of no neutral formulation. As Putnam (1987a, pp. 16ff) put it, no ontologically neutral perspective would be available to compare, say, a world in which only two things exist, a and b, and a world in which there exist three things, a, b, and their mereological sum, $a + b$; the word 'exist', says Putnam, does not have a univocal meaning that is "fixed in advance".[20] On the other hand, if the question is asked within the context of a particular mereological theory (what Carnap, 1950 would call an "internal" question), then it would be trivial insofar as the answer must already be contained in the axioms of the theory. This is also why some authors would say the Special Composition Question is "factually empty", giving rise to disputes that are "merely verbal"' (Hirsch, 2002b, 2005; Balaguer, 2018).

These worries can hardly be dismissed.[21] However, there is no pressure to understand the Special Composition Question in terms of a dispute about what there is. Any mereologist, in the course of developing a formal theory, must make some decision concerning the existence conditions of fusions, a decision that will eventually take the form of a composition axiom, and in this sense the question is neither illegitimate nor trivial. It is just another question of the sort we have been discussing all along: What sort of axiom shall we adopt?[22] It may well be that this is already asking too much. Some authors think that whenever some entities compose a bigger one, it is just

18 In this form, the question parallels one that is central in the foundations of set theory: when do some things form a set? For explicit connections, see Linnebo (2010) and Hewitt (2015a).

19 For the record, van Inwagen (1987, 1990) formulated the question in terms of F'-type fusions.

20 This is Putnam's famous incommensurability thesis concerning a world "*à la* Carnap" and a world "*à la* Polish logician". See also Putnam (1987b; 1988, ch. 7; 2004, ch. 2).

21 Witness the extensive literature they generated, including Goggans (1999), Sidelle (2002), Dorr (2005), Koslicki (2005), McGrath (2008) (with reply in Hirsch, 2008), Cameron (2008b), Bennett (2009), Chalmers (2009), Sider (2009), Eklund (2009), Thomasson (2009), Miller (2010, 2014), Horden (2014), Warren (2015), Daly and Liggins (2015), and Belleri (2017). Van Inwagen himself responds to Putnam in van Inwagen (2002a,b, 2009). On Putnam, cf. also Brenner-Golomb and van Brakel (1989), Raatikainen (2001), Horgan and Potrč (2008, §3.5.2), and Zielinska (2016).

22 It is precisely in this sense that questions on the conditions for set existence have been central to the development of axiomatic set theory. See Fraenkel *et al.* (1973, §2.3) for a classic discussion.

a brute fact that they do so (Markosian, 1998b), a particular fact obeying no general principle (Gabriel, 2017), perhaps a matter of contingent fact (Cameron, 2007).[23] If so, then there is no room for an axiomatic treatment. But if we are unhappy with such answers, if we are looking for a *principled* way of drawing the line so as to specify the circumstances under which the facts obtain,[24] then the question is, not only legitimate, but challenging.

On this understanding, a number of different responses to the challenge have been proposed. Following Korman (2015a, ch. 3), we may distinguish three broad classes of answers to the Special Composition Question. First are *permissive* answers, according to which composition always or very frequently occurs, typically including cases going far beyond the ordinary objects of experience. Second are *eliminative* answers, according to which composition never or very rarely occurs, typically excluding cases of ordinary objects of experience. Finally, there are *conservative* answers, according to which composition only sometimes occurs, respecting intuitive judgments about ordinary objects of experience.

Classical mereology, as we know, includes a conditional axiom schema of unrestricted composition, which can take any of the following forms.

(A.5) $\exists x \varphi x \rightarrow \exists z\, F_{\varphi} z$ *Unrestricted Fusion*

(A.11) $\exists x \varphi x \rightarrow \exists z\, F'_{\varphi} z$ *Unrestricted Fusion′*

(A.15) $\exists x \varphi x \rightarrow \exists z\, F''_{\varphi} z$ *Unrestricted Fusion″*

This is the paradigm of a permissive answer to the Special Composition Question, corresponding to the doctrine we have been calling *universalism*: for any condition φ whatsoever, as long as it is satisfiable, there exists something composed of all and only the things that satisfy that condition.[25] In

23 On the last option, see also Nolan (2005, p. 36), Miller (2009a, 2010), and Parsons (2013a).

24 How to construe this desideratum is itself a matter of debate. The strongest formulation is perhaps Terry Horgan's "Principle of the Non-arbitrariness of Composition":

> If one bunch of physical simples compose a genuine physical object, but another bunch of simples do not compose any genuine object, then there must be some reason *why*. (Horgan, 1993, p. 695)

However, here we shall take it that, generally speaking, a principled way of drawing the line need not rest on a full metaphysical *explanation* of the sort Horgan appears to demand (as it need not depend on the assumption of atomism).

25 'Universalism' is van Inwagen's label. More precisely, van Inwagen uses "universalism" for the thesis that any plurality of material objects have an F'-type fusion, and "super-universalism" for the stronger thesis that any plurality of entities whatsoever have an F'-type fusion (1987, p. 35; 1990, p. 74). Here we generally speak of 'universalism' for both theses and with regard to any notion of fusion. For other terminology, see chapter 2, note 15. Of course, strictly speaking, none of the axiom schemas A.5, A.11, and A.15 fully captures the universalist intuition, since those schemas only assert the existence of a fusion for arbitrary *specifiable* pluralities (and there are only countably many such). On this limitation, again, we refer to chapter 6, section 6.1.

fact, universalism has had a long and impressive list of adherents since the original endorsement by Leśniewski (1916) and Leonard and Goodman (1940).[26] However, it is not a prerogative of classical mereology. In section 4.3.2 we saw that it may be difficult to uphold the Unrestricted Fusion axioms in weaker systems, such as weakly supplemented non-extensional mereologies; but, for example, the non-wellfounded mereology of Cotnoir and Bacon (2012), which forgoes Antisymmetry, is closed under each of A.5, A.11, and A.15. Moreover, universalism is not the only permissive view. One might also adopt a principle of mereological *plenitude* (Hawthorne, 2006), according to which any function from possible worlds to filled regions of space-time corresponds to an object (in those worlds, at those regions).[27]

Now, permissivism is of course committed to the existence of all sorts of entities that common sense would have us reject, and for this reason it is often condemned as ontologically extravagant. We already mentioned, for instance, that many philosophers feel uneasy about scattered objects (section 4.1.3); yet it is clear that the Unrestricted Fusion axioms place no limit on the existence of such things, no matter how far-fetched they might seem. Consider again Lewis's cat-fusion. Or consider a sum of two distant stars (Eberle, 1970, p. 41), or a sum composed of a person's left foot and the carburetor of their neighbor's car (Chisholm, 1976, p. 222), or perhaps a fusion of London Bridge, certain sub-atomic particles located far beneath the surface of the moon, and Cal Ripken, Jr. (Markosian, 1998b, p. 228). The permissivist's world is replete with such things.[28] Indeed, permissivism warrants the existence of gerrymandered wholes of all kinds: discontinuous events, such as a sum of Lennon's death and Charles's wedding (Taylor, 1985, p. 25); fusions of arbitrary qualia, such as a color, two sounds, a position, and a moment (Quine, 1951b, p. 559); and so on. Depending on one's ontology, permissivism will also license the existence of fusions of categorially heterogeneous entities, such as a sum of you and the color blue (van Inwagen, 1987, p. 35) or a sum of one of your occurrent thoughts, an attack of measles, and a lump of cheese (Geach, 1991, p. 253).

26 Korman (2015a, p. 14) lists McTaggart (1921, §129) and Goodman and Quine (1947) along with Cartwright (1975), Quine (1981), Thomson (1983), Lewis (1986a, 1991), Van Cleve (1986, 2008), Heller (1990), Jubien (1993), Armstrong (1997), Sider (1997, 2001), Rea (1998a), Fine (1999), Hudson (2000, 2001), Varzi (2003), Bigelow and Pargetter (2006), Braddon-Mitchell and Miller (2006), Baker (2007), Schaffer (2009), and Sattig (2015). Later authors include Russell (2017), Lando (2017, pt. 3), and Fairchild and Hawthorne (2018).

27 Like universalism, plenitudinism is not unpopular among contemporary philosophers. Besides Hawthorne (2006), Korman's list of adherents (in some form or other) includes Fine (1982, 1999), Yablo (1987), Sosa (1987, 1999), Hawley (2001), Bennett (2004), Johnston (2006), Thomasson (2007), Eklund (2008), Inman (2014), and, again, Sider (2001) and Sattig (2015).

28 Keep in mind that their existence is not meant to imply any process of *physical* fusion, as if the parts had somehow to be joined together to get the whole. Ditto for Lewis's disputed "trout-turkeys" (1991, p. 7): they're just an undetached half trout plus an undetached half turkey.

Permissivists have not typically been moved by such examples, however. As Goodman wrote:

> The contention that a genuine whole or individual cannot consist of widely scattered and very unlike parts misses the point as completely as would the contention that a genuine class cannot consist of widely scattered and very unlike members ... A class for Boole need not have social cohesion; and an individual for me need not have personal integration. (Goodman, 1956, p. 16)

Similarly, here is Judith Thomson on arbitrary fusions of events:

> We may have to invent a name for the result of conjoining two [discontinuous] events, there being none naturally available for it (for example, no nominalization), but it plainly cannot be said that where there is no naturally available name, there is no entity. (Thomson, 1977, p. 81)

And here is William Alston on transcategorial fusions:

> Why deny that there is a composite entity consisting of my computer, the Taj Mahal and the number 16? What harm does it do? It isn't taking up any room that isn't already occupied. It isn't in competition for scarce resources. It isn't polluting the atmosphere ... Admittedly, we seldom have occasion to refer to such entities, but if someone does take it upon himself to single them out for attention, what is there to be said against it? (Alston, 1996, p. 171)

Finally, consider the following passage from David Lewis:

> Speaking restrictedly, of course we can have our intuitively motivated restrictions on composition. But not because composition ever fails to take place; rather, because we sometimes ignore some of all the things there really are. We have no name for the mereological sum of the right half of my left shoe plus the Moon plus the sum of all Her Majesty's ear-rings, except for the long and clumsy name I just gave it; we have no predicates under which such entities fall, except for technical terms like 'physical object' (in a special sense known to some philosophers) or blanket terms like 'entity' and maybe 'thing'; we seldom admit it to our domains of restricted quantification. It is very sensible to ignore such a thing in our everyday thought and language. But ignoring it won't make it go away. And really making it go away without making too much else go away as well—that is, holding a theory according to which classes have mereological sums only when we intuitively want them to—turns out not to be feasible. (Lewis, 1986c, p. 213)

Here we have more than a simple defense of permissivism against its *prima facie* extravagance. Lewis is saying that permissivism is actually compatible with common sense and, indeed, inevitable. It is *compatible* insofar as common sense does not really deny the existence of the problematic fusions; it simply "ignores" them. Much as we restrict our quantifiers when we complain that there's no beer, meaning no beer in the refrigerator, so we tend to restrict our quantifiers when we say those fusions don't exist: there really are no such things among the things we care about.[29] And permissivism would be *inevitable* insofar as there appears to be no "feasible" way of drawing a line between those fusions we find acceptable and those we don't. Intuition leaves room for borderline cases of composition, given that it is sometimes a vague matter whether two or more things are sufficiently homogeneous, spatially connected, causally integrated, etc. to pass muster. To restrict composition in accordance with intuition would therefore require a vague restriction.

> But if composition obeys a vague restriction, then it must sometimes be a vague matter whether composition takes place or not. And that is impossible ... There is such a thing as the sum, or there isn't. It cannot be said that, because the *desiderata* for composition are satisfied to a borderline degree, there sort of is and sort of isn't. (Lewis, 1986c, p. 212)

This line of reasoning, which has come to be known as 'the vagueness argument', has its dissenters.[30] But it would at least show that permissivism has some advantages—evading ontic indeterminacy while avoiding having to draw an unprincipled, possibly anthropocentric line to delineate genuine cases of composition—that may be worth the ontological cost.

What ontological cost, exactly? There's the worry that classical mereology and its attendant universalism seem to allow for too many objects. Yet there's also a sense in which they allow for too few. To see why, for simplicity let us assume atomism. Then, regardless of the number of atoms one begins with, the interaction of universalism with the other axioms of classical mereology imposes a fixed relationship between that number, n, and the overall number of things, which is going to be $2^n - 1$. As Simons (1987, p. 17) points out, this means that the cardinality of intended models of classical mereology is restricted. There are models with 1, 3, 7, 15, 31, etc. elements,

29 This form of "compatibilism"—as Korman (2015a, ch. 5) calls it—is explicitly endorsed by later authors (e.g. Jubien, 2001, fn. 2; Sider, 2001, pp. 137f and 2004, p. 680; Richard, 2006, p. 173) and is accepted also by some critics of permissivism (e.g. Rosen and Dorr, 2002, pp. 156f). For reservations and objections, see Hirsch (2002a, pp. 111f) and Korman (2008; 2014, §3.3).

30 The gist of the argument may already be found in Quine (1981, p. 10) and returns in Heller (1990, §2.9) and Lewis (1991, pp. 80f). It is further elaborated in Sider (1997, §3.1; 2001, §4.9.1) and Van Cleve (2008, §3) and defended e.g. by López de Sa (2006) and Kurtsal Steen (2014). Critics include van Inwagen (1990, §19) and many others: Hudson (2000; 2001, §3.7), Koslicki (2003, §3), Merricks (2005) (with reply in Barnes, 2007 and response in Merricks, 2007), Smith (2006), Nolan (2006a), Elder (2008, §2), Tahko (2009), Effingham (2009a, 2011a,b), Noonan (2010), Wake (2011), Carmichael (2011), Korman (2010b; 2015a, §6.7), Brown (2016), Magidor (2018). For overviews, see Korman (2010a), Korman and Carmichael (2016, §3), and Lando (2017, ch. 13). The argument has an analogue for the Inverse Special Composition Question mentioned in section 4.6, which asks under what conditions something *has* proper parts; see e.g. Hawley (2004).

but no models with, say, cardinality 2, 4, 5, 6, etc.[31] The finite models of classical mereological universalism are bound to involve massive violations of what Comesaña (2008) calls "primitive cardinality"—the intuitive thesis that, for any integer n, there could be exactly n things.

A related issue is that atomistic classical mereology does not seem to have large enough models if the universe has a strongly inaccessible size, i.e. a non-denumerable cardinality that cannot be reached 'from below' by taking powers. That is because, as we saw in chapter 2, all models of atomistic classical mereology are isomorphic to a powerset, hence the size of their domain can *always* be reached from below; there simply cannot be strongly inaccessible models. Such is, as Uzquiano (2006a) calls it, the "price of universality". Indeed, the argument does not even require the assumption of Atomism; the atomless models of classical mereology are represented in substructures of powerset models, too. All that is needed is some guarantee that there aren't strongly inaccessibly many atomless fusions.[32]

So much for strictly existential worries. There are, in addition, a wide range of more specific objections that have been raised against permissivism, especially in the form of the Unrestricted Fusion axioms of classical mereology. Among other things, it has been argued that such axioms do not sit well with certain fundamental intuitions about persistence through time (van Inwagen, 1990, p. 75ff),[33] that they rule out certain plausible theories of space (Forrest, 1996b),[34] that they are incompatible with the possibility of plenitudinous colocation (Hawthorne and Uzquiano, 2011),[35] or that they clash with our practices of using singular terms (Koslicki, 2014) or with the demands of metaphysical grounding (Saenz, 2018),[36] if not with the tenets of major theistic metaphysics (Spencer, 2006; Inman and Pruss, 2019). It has also been contended that unrestricted composition is especially problematic when it comes to diachronic fusions of arbitrary 'temporal parts', for such fusions would have unexplained persistence conditions (Thomson, 1983, p. 213; Koslicki, 2003, p. 127), would lack causal powers (Elder, 2004, ch. 3) or have no properties at all (Elder, 2008, §4), might violate principles of mass/energy conservation (Balashov, 2005, p. 527f), etc.[37] Finally, it has

31 One axiom that contributes to this picture is Remainder (A.4), though Weak Supplementation (A.10) suffices. For instance, the model of figure 4.9 (section 4.4) satisfies each of A.5, A.11, and A.15 and has 2 elements, and can be expanded at will to obtain models of any finite cardinality.

32 For more on this, see Uzquiano (2006b, §2.1) and Hewitt (2015b). Cf. also Hudson (2006b).

33 For discussion and responses, see Rea (1998a, 1999), McGrath (1998, 2001), McDaniel (2001, §5), Hudson (2001, §3.6), Giaretta (2001), Eklund (2002, §7), Hübner (2007, § v.3.2), Polcyn (2012).

34 For responses, see Oppy (1997b; 2006, §7.3) and Mormann (1999; 2000a, §6).

35 See also Uzquiano (2015, §3). For a response, see Cotnoir (2016b).

36 For a response, see Kappes (2019).

37 Hudson (2002b) argues that unrestricted diachronic fusions would also warrant superluminal objects, though there is debate on whether this calls for a restriction on composition (Balashov, 2003a,b; Effingham, 2011a) or a modification of the sufficient condition for motion (Torre, 2015).

been suggested that mereological universalism is prone to paradoxes similar to the ones afflicting naive set theory (Bigelow, 1996). Examining all such arguments would take us too far afield. The last worry, however, is especially important, and we shall come back to it in section 5.4.1.

Let us turn now to *eliminative* views of composition. With regard to the Special Question, these views correspond to answers that lie at the opposite extreme from permissive answers: while the latter affirm that composition occurs under (almost) any conditions, eliminativism says it occurs under (almost) no conditions. In its most radical version, this amounts to a form of mereological *nihilism*, rejecting altogether the possibility of plural composition; the only fusions that exist are singular fusions.[38] Again, there are three main ways of saying this in our language.

(A.68) $\exists z F_\varphi z \to \forall x \forall y(\varphi x \wedge \varphi^x_y \to x = y)$ *Nihilist Fusion*

(A.69) $\exists z F'_\varphi z \to \forall x \forall y(\varphi x \wedge \varphi^x_y \to x = y)$ *Nihilist Fusion′*

(A.70) $\exists z F''_\varphi z \to \forall x \forall y(\varphi x \wedge \varphi^x_y \to x = y)$ *Nihilist Fusion″*

Given just Reflexivity (A.1) and Transitivity (A.3), however, these schemas are equivalent, each reducing to what Hoffman and Rosenkrantz (1997) call "monadism", the thesis that nothing has proper parts.[39]

(T.46) $\forall x \forall y(Pxy \to x = y)$ *Monadism*

Indeed, this is how nihilism is often formulated in the literature: everything is mereologically atomic.[40]

Nihilism is obviously a radical view. It leaves no room for interesting mereological theories. In particular, it's clear that there is just one model of classical mereology in which both nihilism and universalism are true: the one-element model. But nihilism is generally met with hostility on independent grounds. Except perhaps for the existence monists mentioned in section 4.5, the one-element model is hardly an option;[41] yet, as soon as we allow other models, nihilism (and compositional eliminativism more generally) would seem to have intolerable ontological costs. For just as universalism commits us to all sorts of entities that common sense would have us reject, the nihilist

---

38 Again, the label 'nihilism' is from van Inwagen (1987, 1990), though his definition takes the existence of a single φ to be necessary as well as sufficient for the existence of a fusion (which automatically yields Reflexivity when 'fusion' is defined algebraically or *à la* Leśniewski).

39 Monadism is also known as "minimalism", in contrast to the "maximalism" of the universalist (Simons, 2006). That it implies each of A.68–A.70 is straightforward. Conversely, suppose that Pab. Then, given A.1, b qualifies as an F-type and F'-type fusion of a and b, and given A.3 it also qualifies as an F''-type fusion. Hence A.68–A.70 will hold only if $a = b$.

40 For example Cook (2009, p. 187), Blatti (2012, p. 157), Sider (2013, p. 237), Calosi (2016a, p. 223), Cornell (2017, p. 77), and Rettler (2018, §1). Cf. also van Inwagen (1993b, p. 684).

41 See Schaffer (2007) for an argument to the effect that nihilism should culminate in monism.

answer to the Special Question seems to require that we *renounce* all sorts of entities common sense would have us accept. As van Inwagen puts it:

> If this answer is correct, then (if current physics is to be believed) the physical world consists entirely of quarks, leptons, and bosons—there is just nothing else in it, for these particles have no parts and they never add up to anything bigger. Where one might have thought there was a hydrogen atom (the Nihilist holds) there are just two up-quarks, a down-quark, an electron, and assorted photons and gluons ... And what goes for hydrogen atoms (the Nihilist holds) goes for cats and stars: any region of space that one might have thought contained a cat or a star in fact contains only elementary particles. (van Inwagen, 1990, p. 72)

This is way more radical than other eliminative views defended in the literature. For instance, Wheeler (1979) and Unger (1979a,b,c, 1980b) resort to a version of the vagueness argument to conclude that there are indeed no such things as cats and stars (or people). But their nihilism—as they call it—does admit the existence of composite objects; it's just that no such composite behaves the way ordinary objects are supposed to behave. By contrast, mereological nihilism does away with composite objects altogether.[42]

Nevertheless, mereological nihilism has its supporters. There are in fact two main lines of defense against the charge of ontological incongruity that is implicit in van Inwagen's remarks. The first and more popular one corresponds to a metaphysical view that may be traced as far back as Greek atomism and Buddhist nominalism, and rests on the idea that the ontology of common sense is really an illusion, an added opinion, a 'fiction'.[43] Yet the fiction is not unrecoverable. In the words of Gideon Rosen and Cian Dorr:

> You may think that there is such a thing as the molecule A + B ... The compositional nihilist denies this. But of course he doesn't deny that A and B are stuck together, that together they exhibit behaviour that neither would exhibit on its own, that together they contrast with their surroundings, and so on. In short, he denies the existence of the molecule but agrees that there are some things arranged 'molecule-wise'. (Rosen and Dorr, 2002, p 157)

And what goes for molecules goes for cats and stars and everything else. All talk apparently about ordinary composite objects ('There is a K here') can

---

42 The difference is already emphasized by van Inwagen (1987, fn. 5; 1990, p. 73), though it is sometimes neglected; see e.g. Markosian (1998b, fn. 2), Hirsch (2005, fn. 2), Elder (2008, fn. 3), Hansen (2011), and Le Bihan (2015, p. 208). For the record, Unger (1990) has since abandoned his nihilism. Both forms of nihilism should in turn be distinguished from mereological antirealism, the view that nothing instantiates any mereological property (Cowling, 2014).

43 Even Democritus, far from holding the standard atomistic view of composition we attributed to him, might have been a nihilist: "The first principles are atoms and void; everything else exists only in opinion" (*apud* Diogenes Laërtius, *Lives*, IX, 44). For an overview of the issues, see Stokes (1971). On Buddhist nihilism, see Tola and Dragonetti (1995) and Siderits (2003, ch. 4) and, for explicit links to contemporary mereology, Westerhoff (2013; 2018, ch. 1) and Priest (2018, ch. 3).

be paraphrased as talk about mereological simples arranged in suitable ways ('There are particles arranged K-wise here'). The paraphrase would eschew any commitment to composite objects; it would, however, "describe the same facts".[44]

The second line of defense is to maintain that nihilism does not quite deny the existence of ordinary objects such as cats and stars; rather, it denies that such objects are *bona fide* mereological composites. For instance, a nihilist may hold that cats and stars are arrangements of simples, much like crowds are arrangements of people (see Liggins, 2008 and, more recently, Contessa, 2014 and Goldwater, 2015).[45]. Or one may simply reject van Inwagen's tacit assumption that the nihilist's simples can only be the tiny particles of "current physics". After all, there are philosophers who maintain that persons, for instance, are mereologically simple substances whose shapes and sizes match those of their respective bodies (see e.g. Lowe, 1996).[46] The mereological nihilist can say something similar about all ordinary objects; simples may come in all sorts of shapes and sizes and that's what ordinary objects would *be*—extended simples (see e.g. Williams, 2006, §5, Saucedo, 2011, §6, Miller and Hariman, 2017). Either way, the nihilist would still endorse a form of extreme eliminativism with respect to mereological composition; yet this eliminativism would not carry over to the ontology of common sense, which could be preserved in full (exactly the opposite of a nihilism *à la* Unger).

Both lines of defense face a number of challenges. First, no matter how exactly one understands it, we saw that mereological nihilism is virtually committed to Atomism via T.46 (Monadism). Thus, to the extent that atomless worlds (or even worlds satisfying Weak Gunk) are metaphysically possible, nihilism would at best be contingently true (Sider, 1993).[47] Second, any account in terms of arrangements of simples gives rise to what Rasmussen (2014, p. 73) and Tallant (2014) call the "Special Arrangement Question": given any composite-object sortal K, under what circumstances are there things arranged K-wise?[48] Relatedly, there is a worry that the paraphrase

44 The phrase is from van Inwagen (1990, p. 113), who first articulated the paraphrase strategy fully endorsed by Rosen and Dorr. Other supporters of this kind of nihilism include Hossack (2000), Grupp (2006), Cameron (2010a,b), Sider (2013), Brenner (2015a, 2017), and Caves (2018).

45 For a critical discussion of this view, see Long (2019).

46 On this view, see Olson (1998).

47 Of course, philosophers who think the Special Question admits only contingent answers (see above, note 23 and text) will be unmoved by this result. On this, see also Dershowitz (in press). As for the argument itself, Dorr (2002, p. 68, fn. 19) asks: is this any better than objecting to nihilism directly on the grounds that composite things are metaphysically possible? For further responses and discussion of Sider's argument, see Williams (2006), Le Bihan (2013), Markosian (2015), and Benovsky (2016). Sider himself has since revisited his view; see Sider (2013, §§9–10).

48 A similar concern is raised by Bennett (2009, p. 66). For other reservations and objections to the paraphrase strategy, see Uzquiano (2004), McGrath (2005), Lowe (2005a, pp. 527ff), Thomasson

might be too strong unless one thinks we can talk as though there were a K *whenever* there are simples arranged K-wise. For instance, Baker (1997) appears to hold that simples arranged K-wise would not compose a K unless they had been arranged with the intention to produce a K. If so, then the nihilist's paraphrases would have to be refined to make room for such intentional elements, and it is not quite clear *whose* intentions those would be.[49] Lastly, with reference to the extended-simple view, one major worry is that more would be needed to vindicate common sense. Ordinary objects need not be qualitatively uniform, so the view seems to require the existence of *heterogeneous* extended simples, i.e. simples that can enjoy qualitative variation across their spatial or temporal axes. That might allow the nihilist to recover all ordinary talk about ordinary objects, including talk of emergent properties (Cotnoir, 2013d); yet the demands are correspondingly more contentious.[50] Indeed, as Wallace (2013) notes, once the nihilist has accepted this much, it should be an easy matter to accept *scattered* heterogeneous extended simples, simples that occupy scattered regions of space-time despite lacking proper parts of their own.[51] And at that point there would seem to be little difference between nihilism and *bona fide* compositional realism.

We come, finally, to the *conservative* views of composition. These views endorse a moderate answer to the Special Composition Question, often attempting to replicate common-sense opinions about what there is, and may be seen as involving a restriction in the consequent of the fusion schemas of classical mereology. The general format is as follows, where ψ_φ is a placeholder for a formula involving explicit quantification over the φs.

(A.71) $\exists x \varphi x \to (\exists z F_\varphi z \leftrightarrow \psi_\varphi)$ — *ψ–Restricted Fusion*

(A.72) $\exists x \varphi x \to (\exists z F'_\varphi z \leftrightarrow \psi_\varphi)$ — *ψ–Restricted Fusion′*

(A.73) $\exists x \varphi x \to (\exists z F''_\varphi z \leftrightarrow \psi_\varphi)$ — *ψ–Restricted Fusion″*

In fact, this is the general format of *any* answer to the Special Composition Question. But whereas universalism and nihilism correspond to the two

(2007, ch. 1), Olson (2007, §8.6), Elder (2007), Korman (2009), Nolan (2010), Unger (2014, ch. 6), Wilkins (2016), Biro (2017), Rosefeldt (2018), and Waechter and Ladyman (2019, §2.2). For recent responses, see Brenner (2015b, in press), Thunder (2017), Noonan (2019), and Kantin (in press). On the very idea that such paraphrases would make nihilism compatible with common sense, see Hawthorne and Michael (1996), Korman (2015b), and Beebee (2017).

49 Simple minds, perhaps? The question arises also in relation to other, more classical brands of nihilism, such as William James's, for whom no composite sum exists except "*for a bystander* who happens to overlook the units and to apprehend the sum as such" (James, 1890, pp. 158f).

50 In favor of heterogeneous simples, see Parsons (2004a), Markosian (2004a), McDaniel (2009b); against, see Spencer (2010) (with reply in Jaeger, 2014 and response in Spencer, 2014) and Cameron (2015, §4.5, fn. 32). Cf. also the discussion in Hudson (2005, §4.4).

51 This is presumably how the existence monist views the world: as a humongous scattered heterogeneous simple (Schaffer, 2007; Cornell, 2016).

limit cases, where ψ_φ is a mere existence condition or a stark uniqueness condition, respectively,[52] conservative answers correspond to the intermediate cases. In other words, they reflect a form of mereological *aliquidism*,[53] according to which only *some* φs have a fusion.

Conservatism is of course vulnerable to the vagueness argument mentioned above, which would rule out any way of restricting composition in accordance with intuition short of positing ontological indeterminacy.[54] Moreover, one might challenge conservatism on the grounds that the factors which guide our common-sense judgments of unity do not have the sort of ontological significance that should guide the construction of a theory of parts and wholes (Van Cleve, 1986).[55] It is indeed an open question whether *there is* a common-sense conception of composition (Korman and Carmichael, 2017). Nonetheless, conservatism has a large number of adherents, resulting in a wide variety of theoretical options.

There are two main sorts of options, depending on whether or not the restriction expressed by the condition ψ_φ is formulated entirely in the language of mereology. Purely mereological restrictions are not easy to find. One early example was put forward by Rescher (1955), to the effect that all collections of objects that can be extensionally defined have a fusion.

(D.45) $\psi_\varphi :\equiv \forall x(\varphi x \rightarrow \forall y(Pyx \leftrightarrow \forall z(Ozy \rightarrow Ozx)))$ *φ–Extensionality*

However Rescher only took this condition to be sufficient for the existence of a fusion—specifically, an F''-type fusion. As a necessary condition, D.45 is actually quite strong, for it rules out non-extensional models altogether. More precisely, reading any of A.71–A.73 via D.45 would immediately entail PP–Extensionality so long as P is reflexive, since A.1 guarantees that every object is a fusion of itself in each sense of 'fusion'.[56]

Another example would consist in requiring the φs to share a common part, collectively or at least pairwise.

(D.46) $\psi_\varphi :\equiv \exists y \forall x(\varphi x \rightarrow Pyx)$ *Common Lower Bound*

(D.47) $\psi_\varphi :\equiv \forall x \forall y((\varphi x \wedge \varphi^x_y) \rightarrow Oxy)$ *Pairwise Overlap*

52 In the latter case, strictly speaking, A.71 reduces to A.68 only insofar as P satisfies Reflexivity.

53 The label is from Koons and Pickavance (2017, p. 505).

54 For responses, see note 30. We shall come back to ontic indeterminacy in section 6.3.

55 But see e.g. Kriegel (2008) and Gabriel (2015) for dissent.

56 If any given object, a, is a fusion of itself (i.e. a fusion of the φs where φ is '$x = a$') in whichever sense, then D.45 together with the relevant instance of A.71–A.73 will give us that $\forall y(Pya \leftrightarrow \forall z(Ozy \rightarrow Oza))$. Now suppose b has the same proper parts as a. Then whatever overlaps b overlaps a, and so we obtain that Pba. But then we must have $b = a$. Otherwise $PPba$ even though $\neg PPbb$ (by D.1 and A.1), contrary to our supposition. Note that the argument is blocked if PP is defined via D.15 (as PP_2) or treated as primitive with P defined via D.26 (as P_2), unless we also assume A.2 (Antisymmetry) or T.8 (Regularity), respectively.

As Simons (1987, p. 33ff) notes, the rationale behind this suggestion is that mereological overlap epitomizes the sort of internal connection that is distinctive of integral, non-scattered wholes.[57] However, again, while most conservatists would agree that such conditions are sufficient for the existence of fusions, hardly anyone would regard them as necessary. For instance, given D.46 or D.47, no plurality of atoms would ever compose anything, as all atoms are pairwise disjoint (T.32).

The most common alternative is thus to restrict fusions to things that have an *upper* bound, whether collectively (as in Bostock, 1979, p. 118 for F-type fusions) or pairwise (as in Donnelly, 2004, p. 152 for F″-type fusions).[58]

(D.48) $\psi_\varphi :\equiv \exists y \forall x(\varphi x \to Pxy)$ *Common Upper Bound*

(D.49) $\psi_\varphi :\equiv \forall x \forall y((\varphi x \land \varphi^x_y) \to Uxy)$ *Pairwise Underlap*

In this case, the necessity of both restrictions is plausible enough. Indeed, with regard to F-type and F′-type fusions, the necessity of D.48 (and, hence, of D.49) follows from the corresponding definitions, D.6 and D.13, and we saw that F″-type fusions are naturally supplemented by the Upper Bound principle A.66 anyway.[59] On the other hand, one should now be careful in reading D.48 and D.49 as expressing sufficient conditions for the existence of fusions. It's not that, upon adopting either condition, each of A.71–A.73 yields a corresponding fusion whenever some objects satisfy the condition. The fact remains that the relevant definition of 'fusion' must be satisfied as well. Thus, some things may still they lack an F′-type or F″-type fusion even if they have a common upper bound, as in the model of figure 5.2 from section 5.1.2. And there are models that are closed under D.48, or under D.49, while missing fusions of each type. The non-classical models in figure 5.7 (left and right, respectively) illustrate this fact.

Figure 5.7: Common upper bounds and pairwise underlap with missing fusions

57 Simons considers a further condition, reflecting the idea that "for a number of individuals to be connected, it is not necessary that each overlap each other, but it is sufficient if each is connected to the other by a chain of overlappings" (*ibid.*, p. 36). This condition would amount to replacing O in D.46 with its transitive closure and would be weaker than D.46 and D.47, though it is not first-order definable (except in atomistic mereologies with a fixed maximum number of atoms).

58 D.48 is considered also in Simons (1987, p. 36) for F-type and F″-type fusions, and both restrictions are considered in Gruszczyński and Pietruszczak (2014, §10) for F′-type fusions.

59 Donnelly's system actually includes the Strong Supplementation axiom A.18 along with Reflexivity and Transitivity, and we know that this suffices for A.66.

Non-mereological (or 'reductive') accounts are far more popular among conservatists. Typically, they also relate more directly to the Special Composition Question and reflect more closely van Inwagen's guidelines, especially with regard to material objects:[60]

> Whether certain objects add up to or compose some larger object does not depend on anything besides the spatial and causal relations they bear to one another. (van Inwagen, 1990, p. 12)

Van Inwagen himself immediately discards some *prima facie* plausible conditions, such as the requirement that the φs be *in contact* or suitably *fastened* together.[61] But several other more-or-less conservative options are available.

According to *organicism*, a given plurality of φs compose something if and only if their activity constitutes a life. This is van Inwagen's own view (1990, ch. 9); it leaves room for composite living things whilst rejecting all other composites. Similarly, Merricks (2000, 2001) leaves room only for composite conscious things, Olson (2007, ch. 9) defends an animalistic principle of composition, and Dowland (2016) has a principle of composition that does away with organisms but vindicates brains.

According to *regionalism*, it is spatial considerations that play a crucial determinative role. Thus, for Markosian (2014) two or more objects compose when there is something occupying the union of the regions they occupy.[62] For Hoffman and Rosenkrantz (1997), composition obtains instead when the objects are *functionally* united or rigidly *bonded*, while Husmann and Näger (2018) combine bonding with organicism. Others lean toward *patternism* (Petersen, 2019) or *dispositionalism* (Gabriel, 2015), which restrict composition to pluralities that exhibit internal organizational coherence or the disposition to cause us to perceive a unity, respectively. Still others have suggested that the common-sense conception is broadly *teleological*, so that only things which jointly serve a purpose would be said to compose (Bowers, 2019).[63]

There are also *science-based* conservative answers. For instance, Elder (2004) defends an account based on biological kinds and Gillett (2007, 2013) an account based on inter-level mechanistic explanations, while Healey (2013), Caulton (2015), and others rely on evidence from physics.[64] On the other hand, Calosi and Tarozzi (2014) argue that fundamental physics really forces

---

60 For a discussion of this constraint, and whether it can be fully met, see Vander Laan (2010) and Spencer (in press).

61 Contact-based accounts have nonetheless been taken seriously in some literature, inspiring much work in the direction of a topological extension of mereology. See e.g. Bochman (1990) and Smith (1996a). On the prospects of mereotopology in this regard, see Varzi (1996).

62 For a detailed analysis of this view, see Gilmore and Leonard (in press).

63 On teleological answers, see also Rose and Schaffer (2017), with discussion in Kovacs (in press).

64 Other physics-based treatments include Morganti (2013, ch. 5), McKenzie and Muller (2017), and Waechter and Ladyman (2019).

no restriction and Sider (2013, §11) and Brenner (2018) that it is even compatible with nihilism.

Broadly speaking, the worry about these reductive accounts is that the various candidate analyses tend to fail to problems of generality. For any purported condition ψ_φ, one can often generate counterexamples where the φs that satisfy ψ_φ do not intuitively compose anything, or where some φs compose something without satisfying ψ_φ. This has led some philosophers to posit *disjunctive* or *series-style* answers, suggesting that different kinds of objects may obey different conditions.[65] As Sanford (1993, p. 224) put it, we may feel "less pressure to tackle a big, impossible question" if we can deal confidentially with specific cases: Do the log and the plank compose a *table*? Do the rocks compose a *fort*? And so on. This divide-and-conquer strategy is endorsed, for instance, in Lowe (2005a), Thomasson (2007, ch. 7), and Koslicki (2008, ch. 7) and may be seen as involving a shift from the Special Composition Question to what Bennett (2017b, p. 11) calls the "Special Special Composition Question": under what conditions do some things compose an entity of kind K? In his original discussion, van Inwagen (1990, §7) raised several objections to such an approach, including that it would violate the transitivity of parthood. Later authors have argued that the objections can be met (see Silva, 2013 and Carmichael, 2015). And Rosenberg (1993, p. 704) reminds us that precisely this—a series-style account—seems to have been Aristotle's view.

> Some things are characterized by the mode of composition of their matter, e.g. the things formed by mixture, such as honey-water; and others by being bound together, e.g. a bundle; and others by being glued together, e.g. a book; and others by being nailed together, e.g. a casket; and others in more than one of these ways; and others by position, e.g. the threshold and the lintel (for these differ by being placed in a certain way); and others by time, e.g. dinner and breakfast; and others by place, e.g. the winds; and others by the affections proper to sensible things, e.g. hardness and softness, density and rarity, dryness and wetness; and some things by some of these qualities, others by them all, and in general some by excess and some by defect. (*Metaphysics*, VIII, 2, 1042b15–32; Aristotle, 1984, p. 1646)

5.2.2 *Uniqueness*

So much for the existence of fusions. What about their uniqueness? Can two or more fusions fuse the same things? Again, we may distinguish two aspects to this question. First is the formal question, for each definition of

65 Cf. also Hirsch (1993), for whom the search for a uniform, general answer presupposes a non-arbitrary concept of existence that must be rejected. Hawley (2006) argues that the General Composition Question, too, may yield interesting answers if (and perhaps only if) one does not assume from the start that there is single composition relation.

fusion, as to which axioms are (minimally) required in order for every fusion to be unique. Second are the philosophical considerations one might raise for or against the thought that fusions are always unique.

As to the formal question, to some extent we already know the answers. Starting with algebraic fusions (D.6), in chapter 2 we saw that their uniqueness is guaranteed by the Antisymmetry axiom A.2. This is because D.6 requires these fusions to be minimal upper bounds, which means that if we have $F_\varphi a$ and $F_\varphi b$ we must have Pab and Pba and thus, by A.2, $a = b$.

(T.3) $\forall z \forall w((F_\varphi z \wedge F_\varphi w) \to z = w)$ *Fusion Uniqueness*

Concerning Leśniewski fusions (D.13), again we already know the answer: their uniqueness is guaranteed by Antisymmetry together with the Monotonicity principle A.67. This was shown in section 5.1.2.

(T.44) $\forall z \forall w((F'_\varphi z \wedge F'_\varphi w) \to z = w)$ *Fusion′ Uniqueness*

The role of Monotonicity should come as little surprise here, since we saw that it serves as a bridging principle from Leśniewski fusions to algebraic fusions. Then Antisymmetry does the job.

As for Goodman fusions (D.16), the picture regarding their uniqueness is as follows. Suppose $F''_\varphi a$ and $F''_\varphi b$. By D.16, this means that something overlaps a if and only if it overlaps one of the φs if and only if it overlaps b, and so we have $\forall z(Oza \leftrightarrow Ozb)$. Using O-Supervenience (T.21) we could then infer that $Pab \wedge Pba$, and Antisymmetry would secure that $a = b$.

(T.47) $\forall z \forall w((F''_\varphi z \wedge F''_\varphi w) \to z = w)$ *Fusion″ Uniqueness*

Again, this should come as little surprise. For we saw that O-Supervenience is equivalent to the Upper Bound principle A.66, in the presence of which every Goodman fusion is an algebraic fusion. Thus, effectively, we see that Goodman fusions are unique if they meet the conditions for being unique algebraic fusions, where Antisymmetry does the job.

It is noteworthy that Antisymmetry plays a central role in securing the uniqueness of each type of fusion. Indeed, not only is A.2 involved in the sufficiency conditions; in each case it is also necessary for uniqueness, at least when P is reflexive or transitive. For suppose we have Pab and Pba with $a \neq b$, contrary to A.2, and let the φs be a and b themselves. Given either A.1 or A.3, it must be that Paa and Pbb. By D.6, it follows that both a and b are F-type fusions of the φs, and so we have a counterexample to T.3. By D.13, it also follows that a and b are F'-type fusions of the φs (since A.1 guarantees that every part of a overlaps a, hence one of the φs, and similarly for b), and so we have a counterexample to T.44 as well. Finally,

A.3 implies that something overlaps a if and only if it overlaps either a or b if and only if it overlaps b, which means a and b also qualify as F''-type fusions of the φs by D.16, yielding a counterexample to T.47.

So Antisymmetry is crucially tied up with each type of fusion uniqueness. This is telling, for in chapter 3 we saw that Antisymmetry is closely related to extensionality, and fusion uniqueness is itself a form of extensionality: no two fusions ever fuse the same things. As a further question, one may therefore wonder whether mereological extensionality *just is* fusion uniqueness, at least in some sense of 'fusion'. Specifically, does any of T.3, T.44, and T.47 amount to the claim that no two composites can have the same proper parts?

$$\text{(T.1)}\quad \forall x(\exists w PPwx \rightarrow \forall y(\forall z(PPzx \leftrightarrow PPzy) \rightarrow x = y)) \qquad \text{PP–}\textit{Extensionality}$$

The answer is in the negative.[66] To begin with F-type fusions, it's easy to see that T.3 and T.1 are logically independent. On the one hand, we know the latter thesis may fail even when the former is true, witness the familiar non-extensional model in figure 5.8, left. In this model, a_1 and a_2 have the same proper parts, namely b_1 and b_2, violating T.1; yet T.3 is satisfied. In particular, b_1 and b_2 have *no* F-type fusions and so the corresponding instance of T.3 holds vacuously. On the other hand, since PP-Extensionality does not force Antisymmetry even in the presence of Reflexivity and Transitivity, T.1 may be true when T.3 is false, as in the model on the right. Here a_1 and a_2 are distinct fusions of the same atoms, b_1 and b_2; yet T.1 holds.[67] In particular, the two fusions have different proper parts, since each is a proper part of the other but not of itself. Of course, we can always find conditions that would rule out these models and secure the desired entailments.

Figure 5.8: Uniqueness of F-type fusions versus PP-Extensionality

66 Contrary to what is sometimes suggested in the literature. For instance, Rosen and Dorr (2002, p. 154), Bennett (2015, p. 251), and Korman and Carmichael (2016, §5) identify PP–extensionality with T.44 while Calosi and Tarozzi (2014, p. 76) identify it with T.47. Such claims are true in classical mereology but not necessarily in weaker theories, as shown below. Cf. also Sattig (2015, p. 3), where T.44 is called "Extensionality", and Saenz (2015, p. 2209), where T.1 is called "Uniqueness".

67 At least when PP is defined standardly via D.1. With PP defined via D.15, i.e. as PP_2, we know from section 4.3.3 that the model violates T.1. Indeed, it's clear that in the latter case T.1 entails T.3 so long as P (and hence PP_2) is transitive. For any two F-type fusions of the same things must be part of each other by the second conjunct of D.6, and so any PP_2-part of one must also be a PP_2-part of the other by A.3.

Specifically, assuming Antisymmetry would secure the entailment from T.1 to T.3 (trivially, since we know it guarantees uniqueness of F-type fusions *tout court*), while the converse entailment would follow immediately if we assumed that every composite object is an F-type fusion of its proper parts.

(T.48) $\forall z(\exists x \mathrm{PP}xz \rightarrow \mathrm{F}_{\mathrm{PP}xz}z)$ *Proper-Parts Fusion*

In classical mereology both conditions hold (the latter as a corollary of Reflexivity and Strong Supplementation),[68] hence T.1 and T.3 may be identified. In weaker theories, however, this need not be.

With F′-type and F″-type fusions, the picture is different. Both types of fusion satisfy the corresponding variant of T.48 so long as P is reflexive and, in the second case, transitive, hence the relevant uniqueness principles T.44 and T.47 entail PP–Extensionality under minimal conditions.[69] The converse entailments, however, may still fail. This is shown again by the non-antisymmetric model of figure 5.8, right, where a_1 and a_2 count as distinct fusions of b_1 and b_2 in every sense of 'fusion'. But T.44 and T.47 may also fail in extensional contexts that do not violate Antisymmetry. A case in point is the model in figure 5.9, left. Here a_1 and a_2 do not share the same proper parts, since each has an immediate part that is not part of the other; yet both qualify as fusions (F′-type and F″-type) of the same three atoms, c_1, c_2, and c_3. There are also models which, while violating T.44 and T.47 as well as T.1, contain elements that satisfy the demands of PP-Extensionality while qualifying as distinct F′-type or F″-type fusions of the same atoms, as with a_1 and a_2 in figure 5.9, right (from Simons, 1987, p, 249).

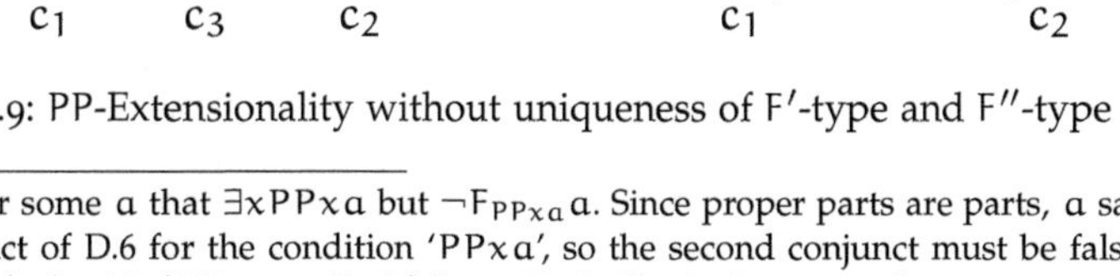

Figure 5.9: PP-Extensionality without uniqueness of F′-type and F″-type fusions

68 Suppose for some a that $\exists x \mathrm{PP}xa$ but $\neg \mathrm{F}_{\mathrm{PP}xa}a$. Since proper parts are parts, a satisfies the first conjunct of D.6 for the condition '$\mathrm{PP}xa$', so the second conjunct must be false: there is some b such that $\forall x(\mathrm{PP}xa \rightarrow \mathrm{P}xb)$ but $\neg \mathrm{P}ab$. By A.18, a must have a part, c, such that $\mathrm{D}cb$. Clearly $c \neq a$, since a overlaps b by A.1: it has proper parts by assumption, and each of them is part of b. Thus $\mathrm{PP}ca$. But then $\mathrm{P}cb$ and, hence, $\neg \mathrm{D}cb$ (again by A.1). Contradiction.

69 Suppose $\exists x \mathrm{PP}xa$. We have that $\forall z(\mathrm{PP}za \rightarrow \mathrm{P}za)$. Given A.1, we also have that a overlaps its proper parts and each such part overlaps itself, hence $\forall y(\mathrm{P}ya \rightarrow \exists x(\mathrm{PP}xa \wedge \mathrm{O}yx))$. Thus a satisfies both conjuncts of D.13 for the condition '$\mathrm{PP}xa$', which means that $\mathrm{F}'_{\mathrm{PP}xa}a$. The proof that $\mathrm{F}''_{\mathrm{PP}xa}a$ (using A.1 and A.3) is left as an exercise.

Again, no such models would be admitted in classical mereology. In particular, it's clear that the two models above are not strongly supplemented and violate both Monotonicity (A.67) and the Upper Bound principle (A.66),[70] consistent with a_1 and a_2 failing to qualify as algebraic fusions. Assuming such principles, along with the Antisymmetry axiom A.2, would remove all oddities and secure the relevant entailments from T.1 to T.44 and T.47. Yet such assumptions do not come for free, and we know their philosophical cost is not negligible.

There is, then, a close connection between uniqueness of fusions and mereological extensionality, but there are also important differences that may show up in the context of non-classical mereologies.[71] Turning now to our second question—the philosophical question as to whether or when, in fact, fusions are unique—one would expect the range of answers to be driven by these considerations. To some extent this is true. Philosophers who distinguish between 'integral wholes' and 'mere fusions', for instance, tend to reject the Proper-Parts Fusion principle T.48 along with its variants in terms of F′-type or F″-type fusions: when it comes to artifacts or natural substances, such as a statue or a cat, the whole would possesses a kind of unity that a mere fusion fails to deliver. Following Aristotle, in such cases

> the whole is not, as it were, a mere heap, but the totality is something besides the parts. (*Metaphysics*, VIII, 2, 1045a9–10; Aristotle, 1984, p. 1650)

Such philosophers (e.g. Lowe, 1989) may therefore be inclined to say that fusions are always unique while rejecting extensionality, at least insofar as they acknowledge the existence of fusions in the first place.[72] By contrast,

70 To be sure, in both models a_1 and a_2 count as upper bounds of the atoms they fuse. Yet A.66 still fails insofar as, say, a_1 is a Goodman fusion of a_2 even though a_2 is not part of a_1.

71 These differences are subtly intertwined with the non-equivalence between T.1 itself and the other extensionality principles discussed in chapter 3. For instance, the model of figure 5.8, left, violates PP-Extensionality along with O-Extensionality (T.10) but not P-Extensionality (T.9), the model on the right satisfies PP-Extensionality but neither P- nor O-Extensionality, and the models of figure 5.9 satisfy both PP- and P-Extensionality but not O-Extensionality. For a systematic comparison, see Pietruszczak (2013, §§ II.5–8).

72 Actually, this is easier said than done. On the standard definition of PP (D.1), any F-type fusion of the proper parts of an integral whole x would have to be part of x by the second conjunct of D.6. Thus, either the fusion is identical to x, or else it is a proper part of x. In the first case we get the Proper-Parts Fusion principle T.48 for free; in the second, extensionality is safe unless we allow the fusion to be a proper part of itself. On the other hand, we just noted that the F′-type and F″-type counterparts of T.48 can be rejected only at the cost of forgoing either Reflexivity or Transitivity, respectively. For these reasons, the approach in question is best understood in terms of a theory of structured wholes of the sort to be discussed in section 5.3. It should also be noted that on some reading of Aristotle, the notion of a "mere heap" does not quite amount to a mere fusion, but to a mere fusion of material parts. Integral wholes would differ from heaps insofar as they include, in addition, a formal part. This is consistent with extensionality along with fusion uniqueness; see e.g. Koslicki (2007, 2008).

philosophers who accept the Proper-Parts Fusion principle and its variants may want to deny the uniqueness of fusions precisely to allow for violations of extensionality (as in the non-wellfounded mereology of Cotnoir and Bacon, 2012, where each of T.3, T.44, and T.47 fails to be a theorem; cf. also Gilmore, 2010b).

On the other hand, it is a fact that, formal discrepancies notwithstanding, many a philosopher tend to see uniqueness and extensionality as two sides of the same coin—the compositional side and the decompositional side. This is widespread practice especially among the friends of these principles. A classic example is Goodman:

> Extensionalism precludes the composition of more than one entity out of exactly the same entities ... For the extensionalist, two entities are identical if they break down into the same members; for the nominalist, two entities are identical if they break down in any way into the same entities. (Goodman, 1956, pp. 19f)

Here Goodman is giving expression to his radical principle of nominalism: no distinction of entities without distinction of content. But there are even more radical positions. There are philosophers for whom the uniqueness of composition and the extensionality of proper parthood are two sides of the same coin insofar as a composite whole is, in an important sense, *identical* to its parts. It is just the parts "taken together" (Baxter, 1988a, p. 193); it is the parts "counted loosely" (Baxter, 1988b, p. 580); it is, effectively, "the same portion of Reality" (Lewis, 1991, p. 81). How is this conception to be understood, exactly?

5.2.3 *Composition as Identity*

This idea that a whole is identical to its parts has a long and complex history. It was already under consideration among the ancients, making repeated appearance in Plato's writings (especially *Parmenides*, *Theaetetus*, and the *Sophist*), and had provenance and influence through the middle ages up.[73] Boethius, for example, endorsed it explicitly, followed by Peter Abelard:

> Every individual thing is identical with its separate parts connected into one thing. For example, a man is identical with his head, chest, abdomen, feet, and other parts conjoined. (*In Ciceronis Topica*, 1, 2.8; Boethius, 1988, p. 39)

> Whoever attributes existence to this house surely concedes the same to this stone and all the other parts taken together; for this house is nothing other than this stone together with the other parts. (*Dialectica*, v, i, 4; Abelard, 1956, p. 550)

73 On Plato, see Harte (2002, ch. 2). On medieval and early modern accounts, see Pasnau (2011, §28.5), Arlig (2012a; 2013, §2), and Normore and Brown (2014).

Even more explicit, perhaps, was Thomas Hobbes:

> The *whole* and *all the parts taken together* are the same thing. And as ... in *division* it is not necessary to pull the parts asunder; so in *composition*, it is to be understood, that for the making up of a whole there is no need of putting the parts together. (*De corpore*, II, vii, 8; Hobbes, 1839, p. 97)

We find similar views in the writings of several later authors, from Leibniz ("The parts taken together differ only in name from the whole"; *Specimen geometriae luciferae*, 274) to Kant ("Allness, or totality, is nothing other than plurality considered as a unity"; *Critique of Pure Reason*, B 111) all the way to Franz Brentano:

> Each particular atom is a thing and ... any three atoms taken together can also be called a thing; but the latter may not now be called a fourth thing, for it consists in nothing more than the original three atoms. (Brentano, 1933, p. 16)

In contemporary literature, this sort of view is known as 'Composition as Identity', or 'CAI' for short, but there is some debate concerning its full import. For one thing, a lot depends on how exactly one construes the relevant 'as'. On a strong reading, CAI says the relationship between the parts and the whole they compose *just is* identity, i.e. numerical identity, although many-one rather than one-one. On a weaker reading, it says the relationship *is like* identity in many important ways.[74] Both versions originate with the works of Baxter and Lewis cited above (the label itself, 'Composition as Identity', comes from Lewis) and have their current defenders,[75] though clearly they amount to different claims and each is in principle amenable to a number of further qualifications.[76]

Moreover, it's clear that a lot depends on the relevant notion of composition, i.e., effectively, mereological fusion. CAI theorists tend to rely on the F′-type definition. If F-type or F″-type fusions are used instead, one must

74 This way of distinguishing between strong and weak CAI is due to Yi (1999). A similar distinction may also found in Sider (2007a). For a general picture, see Cotnoir (2014b).

75 Bøhn (2009c, 2014a) and Wallace (2009, 2011) endorse strong CAI; Varzi (2000a, 2014a), Cotnoir (2013a), Bricker (2016), and French (2016) weak CAI. Concerning Baxter and Lewis themselves, their views are generally identified with strong and weak CAI, respectively, but this is disputable. For instance, Bøhn (2011) contends that Lewis is in many ways committed to strong CAI, while Baxter would seem to reject strong CAI insofar as he accepts numerical identity only within counts, and "within a count it is never the case that many things are one thing" (Baxter, 1988a, p. 193; cf. also 1988b, pp. 579f, and 1999).

76 See the essays in Cotnoir and Baxter (2014). A related view is what Pearce (2017) calls "mereological idealism", which may be traced back to Berkeley's claim that "it is the mind that maketh each thing to be one" (*Siris*, §356). See also McDaniel (2014b) (with discussion in Calosi, in press-b) for the more radical view that a whole is, in some sense, identical to *each* of its parts individually. A similar doctrine may be traced back to Fazang's Huayan teaching of the six characteristics, about which see Jones (2009, 2019).

be careful. Consider the (non-classical) models of figure 5.10. As we saw in section 5.1.2, these models involve F-type and F″-type fusions that do not qualify as F′-type fusions, and indeed both would violate the intuition behind CAI. In the model on the left, u is the F-type fusion of a, b, c, but also of a, b and of b, c, yet clearly these are three distinct groups of atoms. Similarly on the right, where n is an F″-type fusion of a, of b, and of a and b together. Evidently, these models must be ruled out in order for CAI to make intuitive sense. In other words, if composition is construed as algebraic or Goodman fusion, P must at least satisfy ∃-Filtration (A.64) and Upper Bound (A.66), respectively.

Figure 5.10: F-type and F″-type fusions violating CAI

Now, let us assume fusions are well-behaved. One important feature of strong CAI is that it does not simply speak to their necessary uniqueness and its intimate tie with mereological extensionality (two wholes cannot be identical to the same proper parts); to say that composition is identity is to assert a thesis concerning the very nature of composition. On the weak reading of CAI, this thesis would only be partly informative. But on the strong reading it amounts to a full reductive account: for some things to compose a whole is for them to *be* that whole. Thus, strong CAI may actually be seen as providing an answer to the General Composition Question.[77]

Even more important, though, is CAI's bearing on the Special Composition Question, and here the point applies to both readings.[78] We have seen that permissive answers to the Special Question are often condemned as ontologically extravagant. Conservatists object that unrestricted composition would force us to accept the existence of all sorts of unheard-of entities that common sense does not recognize, such as a fusion of all cats, or the sum of a person's foot and a carburetor. But if CAI is accepted, it would go some way toward alleviating these worries. David Lewis writes:

> Given a prior commitment to cats, say, a commitment to cat-fusions is not a *further* commitment. The fusion is nothing over and above the cats that compose it ... Commit yourself to their existence all together or one at a time, it's the same commitment either way. (Lewis, 1991, p. 81)

77 Not an answer van Inwagen (1994) would accept, but see e.g. Spencer (2013) and Bøhn (2014a).

78 CAI is also relevant to the Simple Question and the Inverse Special Composition Question mentioned in section 4.6. See again Spencer (2013) and, respectively, Hawley (2014, §5).

Similarly, David Armstrong writes:

> Mereological wholes are not ontologically additional to all their parts, nor are the parts additional to the whole that they compose. (Armstrong, 1997, p. 12)

This suggests that the friend of CAI can reap the theoretical benefits of permissivism at no ontological cost. If one already accepts the existence of certain things, accepting the existence of their fusion is, as Lewis says, "ontologically innocent" (1991, p. 81). The fusion may be a strange and uninteresting entity, but ontologically speaking the commitment it carries is "redundant" (p. 82). It is, as Armstrong says, an "ontological free lunch" (1997, p. 13).

Part of the plausibility of this suggestion rests on an intuitive *no double-counting* constraint. Consider an example from Donald Baxter:

> Someone with a six-pack of orange juice may reflect on how many items he has when entering a 'six items or less' line in a grocery store. He may think he has one item, or six, but he would be astonished if the cashier said 'Go to the next line please, you have seven items'. (Baxter, 1988b, p. 579)

Astonishment at the cashier would be justified, one would think, because the cashier has counted the same things twice. Of course, in a case like this there are practical reasons to think so. As Baxter says elsewhere (2005, p. 377), "You can't sell the cans to people and continue to own the six-pack yourself". Yet the bar on double counting is not merely a practical affair. It may be seen as a genuine ontological constraint, and Lewis's claim that a whole and the parts are the same "portion of Reality" was intended precisely in this sense.

One way of explaining this constraint is in terms of mereological 'covers'. As with a grocery store receipt, a good inventory of Reality must be complete: everything must show up somewhere. But it must also be judicious: nothing should show up more than once. Thus the inventory should cover all Reality short of overlap: it should include an entity x if and only if x is disjoint from any other entity that is itself included in the inventory—a condition that is violated when a whole is listed along with the parts it fuses.[79]

But there are other ways of explaining the constraint. Armstrong (1997), for instance, puts in in terms of "symmetrical supervenience" between wholes and parts, and similarly Mellor (2008). Others have appealed to internal or grounding relations (Cameron, 2014; Loss, 2016) or to so-called Hume's dictum, to the effect that no contingent thing necessitates the existence of any other (Bøhn, 2014b). Still others have proposed to relativize ontological commitment to "concepts" (Bøhn, 2009c, 2016) or by reference to Frege's

79 This account is detailed in Varzi (2000a). Similar accounts in terms of "tiling", "partitions", and "scales" are given in Schaffer (2010), Cotnoir (2013a), and Schumm *et al.* (2018). For discussion, see Slater (2003), Berto and Carrara (2009), Kitamura (2012), Hawley (2013), and Kim (2019). See also Botti (in press) for an account in terms of variable "metaphysical information".

thesis that we can only count "things of a kind" (Wallace, 2011; Kleinschmidt, 2012).[80] There are also purely formal treatments, as in Sider (2015), where the relation 'x is nothing over and above the φs' is treated as a primitive and suitably axiomatized.[81] Under plausible assumptions, the resulting theory turns out to be intimately related to classical mereology.

With all this, CAI is not without criticism. One general worry is that, precisely because 'redundant', 'double counting', 'nothing over and above', etc. can be understood in so many ways, the view is not properly defined (van Inwagen, 1994).[82] But CAI has been attacked on specific grounds, too, both in regard to its motivations and because of its implications.

A first line of criticism is that CAI would not deliver the ontological innocence it promises. The primary source is Yi (1999), who argues that (i) weak CAI won't do, and (ii) strong CAI is false. Yi's reasons for (i) are aimed specifically against the version of weak CAI he attributes to Lewis, so there is room for replies, but the argument for (ii) is meant to apply generally. Let a be a fusion of distinct b and c. Strong CAI yields that a is identical to b and c. But a is one of a. Thus, substituting, a is one of b and c—absurd. A different objection comes from Turner (2013), who argues that mere existence facts fail to fix many-one identity facts. But perhaps the most common objection is the one put forward by van Inwagen (1994, p. 213; 2002a, p.191) and Koslicki (2008, § II.3.2). Since philosophers may disagree about whether certain things have a fusion, this very fact—they argue—would show that fusions carry a further ontological commitment after all.[83]

---

80 In the *Grundlagen*, Frege repeatedly illustrates his thesis with examples that involve many-one identities. For instance:

> I am able to think of the *Iliad* either as one poem, or as 24 Books, or as some large Number of verses. (Frege, 1884, §22)
>
> *One* pair of boots may be the same visible and tangible phenomenon as *two* boots. Here we have a difference in number to which no physical difference corresponds. (§25)
>
> I can say with equal truth both 'It is a copse' and 'It is five trees' ... Now what changes here from one judgement to the other is neither any individual object, nor the whole, the agglomeration of them, but rather my terminology. (§46)

Baxter himself refers to some of these passages, though he explicitly disavows a corresponding sort-relative explanation of CAI, since it would "fail" when the whole and the parts fall under the same sortal; see Baxter (2005, p. 378). For more discussion of sortal relativism in relation to CAI, see Carrara and Lando (2017) and Lipman (in press).

81 Strictly speaking, in Sider's formulation the second argument of the relation ranges over arbitrary sets. See also Sider (2007a, §3) for an earlier treatment based on plural logic.

82 For recent responses, see Benovsky (2015), Lando (2017, §15.2), and Smid (2017a).

83 For further objections to the innocence of composition, see Oliver (1994), Harte (2002, §1.4), Carrara and Martino (2009, 2011a), Simons (2016b), Mertz (2016, §1.5), Feldbacher-Escamilla (2019), and the argument by Forrest (1996b) mentioned in section 5.2.1 (with replies by Oppy, 1997b and Mormann, 1999). For arguments in its defense, see Smid (2015) and French (2016). See also Bennett (2015) and Hawley (2014, 2018a) for in-depth analyses of Lewis's own conception of 'innocence'.

A second line of attack comes from linguistic considerations. What sort of syntactic sense can be made of CAI's claim that a fusion (singular) is identical to the things it fuses (plural)? This is not just a worry concerning ordinary-language grammar (though see again van Inwagen, 1994, §3).[84] The worry concerns the very possibility of expressing CAI in the regimented language of formal mereology. In fact, CAI theorists tend to resort to formalisms that go beyond the sort of first-order language we have been using, e.g. languages with plural terms and quantifiers.[85] But even so there are concerns. Particularly Sider (2007a, §3), extending Yi's argument above, notes that strong CAI would be at odds with the way we normally talk about pluralities, since it would result in a "collapse" between parthood and plural membership. In our language, this result can be put as follows.[86]

(T.49) $\forall z(F_{\varphi}z \rightarrow \forall x(Pxz \leftrightarrow \varphi x))$ P–*Collapse*

This schema says that something is *part of* a fusion of certain things if and only if it is *one of* those things, and that can't be right. Presumably a fusion of all cats, if it exists, contains many parts that are not cats—e.g. cat tails (by Transitivity) or the fusion itself (by Reflexivity).[87]

A third worry concerns whether CAI really justifies a commitment to compositional permissivism. Some authors argue that it does, since CAI would entail mereological universalism (e.g. Merricks, 2005, p. 630; Sider, 2007a, p. 61). As Cameron (2012) points out, however, generally speaking, CAI only establishes a biconditional: some things compose a whole if and only if they are identical to it.[88] This does not entail that, given some things, they do in fact compose a whole. One way of reading P–Collapse is precisely that the φs have a fusion only if 'φ' satisfies the consequent; there would be no fusion of all the cats, for instance. Of course, the entailment goes through if one assumes that every plurality of things is identical with some thing, as some CAI theorists hold (e.g. Bøhn, 2014a and Bricker, 2016). But then, given CAI, universalism *just is* the assumption in question.[89] Moreover, McDaniel

84 Cf. also Sider (2007a, p. 56) and Cameron (2012, fn. 4). For a response, see Cotnoir (2013a, §1).

85 This is the sort of language used by Lewis (1991), to which we return in section 6.1.2. For related approaches, see Hovda (2014).

86 Assume $F_{\varphi}z$. If Pxz, then z is also a fusion of x and z. Thus, given strong CAI, z is identical to the φs and also to x and z together, so these pluralities are the same. Since x is one of x and z, it follows that it is one of the φs, i.e. φx. Conversely, if φx, then Pxz follows by the first conjunct of D.6. Note that the argument applies also to F'-type fusions (as in Sider's original version). For F''-type fusions, the second inference requires the Upper Bound principle A.66.

87 Here is where an explicit cover-based account of CAI would help. See Cotnoir (2013a).

88 It is more customary to identify CAI with just the 'only if' direction of this biconditional. When properly regimented, however, the other direction follows by Leibniz's law on the mere assumption that everything is composed of itself. See Sider (2007a, fn. 24).

89 For more reservations about the entailment, see Falls (in press) and Lechthaler (in press-b). For more on CAI and the Special Composition Question, see Sider (2015, §§4–5) and Spencer (2017).

(2010a) offers a direct argument against the entailment. He argues that a mereological nihilist who accepts an extensionality constraint on properties is forced to accept CAI. Since nihilists reject universalism, it would follow that CAI does not entail it.[90]

Indeed, given P–Collapse, one could even argue in the opposite direction to show that (strong) CAI entails nihilism, at least so long as parthood is reflexive. For let a be any object and let 'φx' be the condition of being identical with a. We know that Reflexivity implies the singularity principle A.17, to the effect that a is the only (F'-type) fusion of itself. Thus, something is part of the fusion of the φs if and only if it is part of a. But then P–Collapse implies that something is part of a if and only if it is identical with a, which means that a must be mereologically atomic. Generalizing, this yields the Monadism principle T.46 in its full strength, hence mereological nihilism.[91] (Corollary: since the only model satisfying both nihilism and universalism is the one-element model, CAI's route to compositional permissivism, if successful, would lead straight to existence monism.)

More metaphysically minded objections may be found as well. The most central is the objection from Leibniz's law. Consider Lewis:

> Even though the many and the one are the same portion of Reality, and the character of that portion is given once and for all whether we take it as many or take it as one, still we do not really have a generalized principle of indiscernibility of identicals. It does matter how you slice it—not to the character of what's described, of course, but to the form of the description. What's true of the many is not exactly what's true of the one. (Lewis, 1991, p. 87)

The trouble is that the orthodox view of identity *requires* indiscernibility, witness the inclusion of L.7 among our logical axioms. Compare Sider:

> Whatever else one thinks about identity, Leibniz's law must play a central role ... To deny it would arouse suspicion that their use of 'is identical to' does not really express identity. (Sider, 2007a, pp. 56f)

So the friends of CAI seem faced with a dilemma. On the one hand, fully endorsing Leibniz's law is hardly an option, for the reasons stated by Lewis.[92] This is especially troublesome for strong CAI, which is committed to the 'are' of composition being literally another form of the 'is' of identity. On the other hand, weaker versions of CAI are free to forgo the parallel between

90 Bøhn (2014a) replies.

91 One version of this argument, with sets in place of pluralities, may be found in Gruszczyński (2015). Other versions have been given by Calosi (2016a) and Loss (2018) and, implicitly, Sider (2014, §6). See also Yi (2014, §4; in press, §2.3) and Calosi (2016b, §4; 2018, §4) for variants of the argument that do not depend on P–Collapse.

92 Lewis's concerns have a purely semantic parallel in the treatment of coreferentiality and related phenomena; see e.g. Carrara and Lando (2016).

composition and identity precisely on these grounds (as does Lewis), but the cost is high. If composition does not obey the laws of identity, much of CAI's initial appeal would seem undermined.[93] In short, CAI theorists would be caught in the classic problem of the one and the many, exactly as in Plato's writings on the subject.[94]

Another objection is that CAI appears committed to a strong form of mereological essentialism—the thesis that every whole has its parts necessarily. The argument comes from Merricks (1999), though the main gist is already in Abelard: if the parts are identical to the whole, and identity is not a temporary or contingent relation, then *this* whole is necessarily composed of *these* parts.[95] Of course the argument is disturbing only insofar as mereological essentialism is. (Wallace, 2014a, for instance, doesn't think it is.) We will address that issue in chapter 6. But one might wish to avoid the commitment if one can.[96]

Finally, CAI is sometimes questioned on the grounds of its incompatibility with various philosophical desiderata. For instance, McDaniel (2008) argues

93 This line of objection has surfaced repeatedly in the recent literature on CAI, culminating in the detailed critique in Yi (in press). A middle-ground position is that of Baxter (1999, 2014), who does not generally accept the indiscernibility of identicals and thinks there are principled reasons for rejecting it in the case of parts and wholes. See also Turner (2014), where these commitments are thoroughly examined. Further intermediate positions have been offered more recently, based e.g. on reformulating CAI in terms of atomistic composition (Loss, in press-a) or intensional composition (Lechthaler, in press-a) or on restricting the demands of Leibniz's Law to properties that are not slice-sensitive (Bricker, in press). Responses on behalf of strong CAI have been varied, too, ranging from the above-mentioned idea that counting is sort relative (Bøhn, 2014a, in press) to distinguishing different meanings of 'one' (Payton, in press).

94 See again Harte (2002, ch. 2). The objection is also common among later writers in antiquity and the early middle ages, especially Aristotle's commentators. A good example is Philoponus:

> If the whole is single then its parts must be many (i.e. at least two) and if we assert that each of those [parts] exists in actuality this would result in one and the same thing being both many (at least two) and one. This would amount to saying that one and the same thing is simultaneously single and not-single and also plural and not-plural. This would be a genuine internal contradiction, hence impossible. (*A Treatise Concerning the Wholes and the Parts*, I, 81; Philoponus, 2015, p. 195)

Similar considerations may be found in other philosophical traditions. For instance, Tsong-kha-pa's arguments against Abhidharma reductionism exploit the same *reductio*:

> The parts of a chariot are the axle, the wheels, the nails, etc. The chariot is not intrinsically one with those parts. If it were one, there would be fallacies such as the following: just as the parts are plural, so the chariot also would be many; just as the chariot is single, so the parts also would be single. (*Lamrim Chenmo*, III, ii, 22; Tsong-kha-pa, 2000–2004, vol. 3, p. 279)

95 Cf. Abelard's passage quoted above, which continues thus:

> Therefore, as this house exists, so also must this stone and all the other parts taken together ... Whence, if this stone is not, this house is not. (*Dialectica*, V, i, 4; Abelard, 1956, p. 550)

96 See e.g. Borghini (2005) for a response based on counterpart theory and Lechthaler (2017, §6.3.5) for one based on non-rigid plural reference. See also Carrara and Lando (2019, in press-a) for a version of CAI that combines the necessity of identity with the contingency of composition.

that any acceptable version of CAI ought to validate a certain plural duplication principle that appears to be inconsistent with the possibility of strongly emergent properties, while Bailey (2011) argues that CAI is in conflict with widely accepted principles about ontological grounding. Precisely because they rest on substantive philosophical premises, objections such as these do not amount to a refutation of CAI as such. But, again, it is an interesting question whether they can be resisted on their own merits.[97]

5.3 STRUCTURED COMPOSITES

Let us turn now to consider views that explicitly reject the claim that wholes are nothing over and above their parts. These are views according to which composite objects tend to be *structured* in ways that are not adequately captured by classical mereology. Indeed, one of the most frequently voiced criticisms of classical mereology is precisely that it conceives of wholes as completely unstructured when, in fact, the existence and identity conditions of most ordinary objects would seem to depend crucially on the "configuration" or "manner of arrangement" of their proper parts (Koslicki, 2008).

We have already seen a number of putative examples: the statue (which has a specific shape profile) as against the mere lump of clay, a watch as against the mere aggregate of its springs and gears, or even a ham sandwich as opposed to the ham and bread slices out of which it is made. To cite one more example that goes back to Aristotle:

> The substance of any compound thing is not merely that it is made from these things, but that it is made from them in such and such a way, as in the case of a house; for here the materials do not make a house irrespective of the way they are put together. (*Topics*, VI, 13, 150b24–26; Aristotle, 1984, p. 253)

This is the exact opposite of Abelard's view quoted above. Of course Abelard himself shared the intuition. While insisting that a house is nothing other than its parts, he clearly stressed the importance of the way the parts are arranged:

> One cannot say that in order for this house to be, it suffices that the matter exists; otherwise the timber and the stones could be described as this house even before fabrication; rather, a formal arrangement is also necessary. (*Dialectica*, V, i, 4; Abelard, 1956, pp. 550f)

But Abelard didn't think the arrangement is a constituent of the house; it is simply a precondition for the timber and stones to be *described as* a 'house',

97 Bøhn (2012, §3), Sider (2014, §5) respond to McDaniel, with further replies in Calosi (2016b) and Javier-Castellanos (2016). See also Bricker (in press, §6). In response to Bailey, see e.g. Loss (2016) for a version of CAI in which the parts ground the whole to which they are identical.

or rather "this house".[98] Contemporary classical mereologists would offer similar accounts, and here indeed the theory may be showing its debt to the original nominalist motives of Leśniewski and of Leonard and Goodman. The view in question, by contrast, holds precisely that the arrangement of the parts *is* a constituent of the house. It is a structure-making constituent.

We find the same idea in many other contexts. In the natural sciences, for instance, it is common to insist that physical compounds are structure-laden, e.g. that a molecule is not a mere agglomerate of chemical atoms (Harré and Llored, 2013), or that quantum wholes are, at least in some cases, determined by the very process of physical composition (Calosi and Morganti, 2016). Biological organisms are another obvious case in point (Findlay and Thagard, 2012). But the structure of a composite whole need not consist in the spatial or temporal arrangement of its parts: a deck of cards is a good example of something intuitively structured (four suits, thirteen ranks), yet its structure is not merely spatio-temporal, as the cards need not be arranged in any particular way. Nor is the concern limited to material objects; mathematical entities (groups, lattices, categories, etc.) are perhaps paradigm cases of structured abstract objects (Mormann, 2009), as are linguistic constructions, argument forms, or musical works construed as types (Koslicki, 2008, ch. 9; 2017). The example of a syllable as against its vowels and consonants was indeed another favorite of Aristotle's (e.g. *Metaphysics*, VII, 17, 1041b12–16).

Now, just what it is for a whole to be *structured* is, of course, a complex question by itself, and there is a full literature (starting with Tranöy, 1959) devoted to unpacking and taxonomizing the concept. In this section, we briefly consider three main ways in which a whole may be thought to have a structure that defies classical mereology. The operation of composition may be sensitive to *levels*, sensitive to *order*, or sensitive to *repetition*.

5.3.1 *Levels*

To say that composition is sensitive to *levels* is to conceive of composite objects as hierarchically structured. In early treatments, this conception was inspired mainly by Gestalt-theoretic considerations (Rescher and Oppenheim, 1955)[99] or with reference to general system theory (Bertalanffy, 1968;

98 Similar views inspire the writings of other medieval nominalists, e.g. Ockham. For useful discussion, see Cross (1999), Normore (2006), Arlig (2007, 2012a), and Zupko (2018).

99 The thesis that a whole is more than a mere sum of parts was a central tenet of Gestalt psychology (the "Supersummativity" principle) from Ehrenfels (1890) to Köhler (1920), Koffka (1935), and Rausch (1937). It soon reached popularity among phenomenologists working within the framework of Husserl's part-whole theory (Gurwitsch, 1929) and made its way into analytic philosophy through Grelling and Oppenheim (1938, 1939) and Angyal (1939). For relevant overviews and discussion, see Smith and Mulligan (1982, §6) and Simons (1987, §9.7); for a recent formal proposal in this spirit, see Wiegand (2007, 2010).

Bunge, 1979).[100] Today it is more common to draw directly on Aristotle's metaphysics and the hierarchical conception is typically associated with a (broadly) hylomorphic account on which 'forms' play a direct structural role (as in Johnston, 2006, Koslicki, 2008, or Inman, 2018).[101]

A distinct example of a leveled conception of objects is Kit Fine's (1999) theory of embodiments.[102] As we saw in section 3.3.2, according to this theory most material objects submit to a hierarchical division into immediate parts, each of which will have further immediate parts, and so on, much like most sets come with a hierarchical structure of members, members of members, and so on. At each level of the hierarchy, the object or objects at that level will typically have a unique decomposition into their immediate parts. This is because immediate parthood is not transitive, indeed antitransitive (see T.13). And if we take this relation as metaphysically more fundamental than plain parthood, at least in some domains, the outcome is a leveled mereology. In Fine's own words:

> Traditional mereology would have us believe otherwise. Indeed, its very notion of part was conceived by analogy with the notion of subset. But, if I am right, it is the hierarchical conception of sets and their members, rather than the linear conception of set and subset or of aggregate and component, that provides us with the better model for the structure of part-whole in its application to material things. (Fine, 1999, p. 72)

The shift from subsethood to set membership is emblematic of this way of modeling part-whole structures. In set theory, we can build singleton sets, $\{x\}$, and iterate up the hierarchy $\{\{x\}\}$, $\{\{\{x\}\}\}$, etc.[103] This sort of construction is disallowed if the building relation behaves like set inclusion, as in classical mereology, witness the following theorem.

(T.50) $\forall z\, F_{x=z}z$ F–*Reflexivity*

Indeed, T.50 is a theorem in any mereology with the Reflexivity axiom A.1: given the definition of fusion in D.6, $F_{x=z}z$ amounts to the conjunction $\forall x(x = z \rightarrow Pxz) \wedge \forall y(\forall x(x = z \rightarrow Pxy) \rightarrow Pzy)$, which is logically equivalent to $Pzz \wedge \forall y(Pzy \rightarrow Pzy)$, hence to Pzz. And if fusions are unique (T.3), this means we can never generate anything but the object itself when we

100 In his early writings, Bertalanffy actually used "Systemzustand" (systemic state) synonymously with "Gestalt"; see e.g. Bertalanffy (1929, p. 89).

101 See also Koslicki (2018). Other authors include Rea (2011), Toner (2013), Koons (2014), Jaworski (2014, 2019), Evnine (2016), Goswick (2018), and Roudaut (2018). The critical literature on this move is equally extensive; see e.g. Britton (2012), Marmodoro (2013), Oderberg (2014), Robinson (2014), Skrzypek (2017), Renz (2018), and Fiocco (2019).

102 The roots of the theory may already be found in Fine (1982, 1994). For detailed studies, see Jacinto and Cotnoir (2019) and Jansen (2019).

103 On hierarchical mereology as a foundation for set theory, see Caplan *et al.* (2010).

apply the composition operation to it; all we can get out of a given entity z is z itself. Similarly for F'-type fusions (as already noted in section 5.1.2, theorem T.45) and F''-type fusions (where $F''_{x=z}z$ reduces to the logical truth $\forall y(Oyz \leftrightarrow Oyz)$). It is precisely for this reason that, according to Goodman (1956), parthood is a nominalistically acceptable generating relation, in contrast to "platonistic" set membership.[104]

In classical mereology we also have the following principle, which we listed as a natural axiom for systems based on the binary sum operator $+$ (section 2.4.4).

(A.22) $\forall x \forall y \forall z \; x+(y+z)=(x+y)+z$ *Associativity*

In systems based on P, A.22 follows as a theorem from the definition of sum (D.9) and the underlying associativity of logical disjunction.[105] Similarly if summation is defined in terms of the alternative fusion operators F' and F''. The idea is that taking the sum of x and y first, and then summing the result with z, is no different than taking the sum of y and z and then summing it with x. The 'level' of summation at which you include an object as part makes no difference to the final result. Not so if parthood is modeled as (the reflexive closure of) set membership, as the model in figure 5.11 shows.

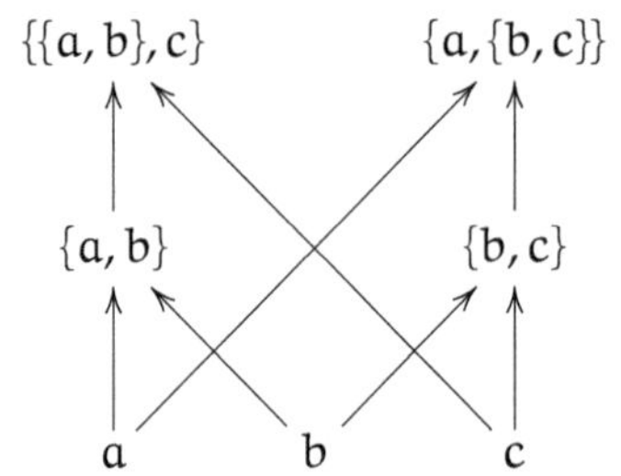

Figure 5.11: A model violating Associativity

Moreover, if we accept the equivalence between Pxy and $x+y=y$ corresponding to Leonard's definition D.19 (matching the algebraic definition of $\sqsubseteq$ in 2.7), we know that A.22 implies the Transitivity axiom A.3, since if $x+y=y$ and $y+z=z$, then $x+z=z$ follows by substitution. Absent A.22, however, Transitivity may fail. For instance, the model in figure 5.11

104 As noted in section 1.2.2, Leśniewski felt exactly the same way, condemning set theory on the grounds that it "demands the differentiation of some object from the collection which contains this one sole object as an element" (Leśniewski, 1916, p. 130). For an extended discussion of "mysterious singletons" from the perspective of classical mereology, see also Lewis (1991, ch. 2). On their significance in set theory, and history thereof, see Oliver and Smiley (2006).

105 For proof, see section 2.2.3.

is compatible with a being part of $\{a, b\}$ and $\{a, b\}$ part of $\{\{a, b\}, c\}$ even though a itself is not part of $\{\{a, b\}, c\}$. (On the other hand, if we take the model to be closed under Transitivity, then we have a concrete case where PP-Extensionality and Uniqueness of F'-type and F''-type fusions may come apart, as noted in section 5.2.2.)

5.3.2 *Order*

Another way wholes may be thought to be structured is for the order in which the parts are summed together to affect the result. Classical mereological summation is not order-sensitive in this way, as reflected in the following thesis.

(A.21) $\forall x \forall y\ x + y = y + x$ *Commutativity*

Like A.22, this thesis was listed as an axiom for the system based on $+$, and in systems based on P it is an immediate consequence of D.9 (owing to the underlying commutativity of logical disjunction). Yet there are cases where it may be suggested that Commutativity fails to hold.

Consider again the putative counterexamples to extensionality mentioned in section 4.2.2: word types made up of the same letter types (Hempel, 1953), tunes composed of the same notes (Rosen and Dorr, 2002), etc. Here the idea is precisely that the order in which the components are summed together makes a difference to the resulting wholes, to the point of being perhaps the *only* difference. For a different sort of example, Bader (2013) suggests that the states of affairs Rab and Rba have the same components—the two objects a and b together with a non-symmetric relation R—as parts, but are nonetheless distinct. One may respond that all these cases would violate A.21 only indirectly; the sum operator $+$ would not even apply, since the relevant fusions would not be unique. But one may also think of concrete cases where uniqueness is not at issue. In a written token of the word 'TIM', for instance, the three letter tokens must be arranged in a precise sequence; in a printed book, the pages must follow one another in a specific order; etc. Cases such as these may be taken to satisfy the demands of extensionality and fusion uniqueness; yet their proper treatment would seem to call for a non-commutative mereology. Indeed, for all his hyperextensionalism, even Goodman would seem to rely on sequential individuals of this sort in his efforts (with Quine) to characterize a nominalistically acceptable language:

> Our nominalistic syntax must contain, besides the six shape-predicates, some means of expressing the *concatenation* of expressions. We shall write '$Cxyz$' to mean that y and z are composed of whole characters of the language ... and that the inscription x consists of y followed by z. (Goodman and Quine, 1947, p. 112)

It should be stressed that classical mereology is not inherently irreconcilable with such cases. For one thing, we could take Goodman and Quine to be suggesting that mereology is only part of the story; to account for ordered inscriptions, one needs to supplement the axioms of mereology with further axioms governing the concatenation predicate C. As Eberle (1970, pp. 85f) points out, such an extended theory would presumably include as a thesis that the concatenate of any two inscriptions is a mereological composite:

(5.1) $\forall x \forall y \forall z (Cxyz \to x = y + z)$ *Summation*

But presumably it would also include a thesis to the effect that concatenation is exclusive, i.e. more precisely

(5.2) $\forall x \forall y \forall z (Cxyz \to \neg \exists w Cwzy)$ *Exclusiveness*

If so, combining 5.1 with Commutativity would be unproblematic. And if such a theory proves adequate to deal with ordered inscriptions, it may perhaps be generalized to account for ordered wholes of any sort. (Eberle himself worked out a theory of "links" that might serve the purpose; see Eberle, 1970, §2.10.4.)

Additionally, one may consider ways of reconciling Commutativity with the existence of ordered wholes even within the purview of a purely mereological theory. The most obvious way would be to insist that such wholes have more parts than 'meet the eye', the hidden parts serving to force the right order on the evident parts. For example, if one allows for hylomorphic composites, as in the neo-Aristotelian mereology of Koslicki (2007, 2008), the hidden parts could be relational 'forms' of the appropriate sort.

These options notwithstanding, the presence of A.21 as an axiom or as a theorem is a clear sign that classical mereological summation is not well suited for dealing with compositional order. Both strategies testify more to the limits of classical mereology than to its strengths, and would involve significant formal and metaphysical compromises. To the extent that these costs are deemed too high, there is scope for developing a genuine non-commutative mereology.[106]

5.3.3 *Repetition*

Even more controversial is perhaps the fact that classical mereological summation is insensitive to repetition. For instance, summing a part with itself

106 Apart from non-extensional or non-antisymmetric mereologies defying uniqueness, where A.21 may fail owing to $x + y$ being undefined for some x and y, no such theory is available to date, save for the brief remarks in Apostel (1982, §3). There is, however, a significant literature on non-commutative (or 'skew') Boolean algebras; see Cornish (1980) and Leech (1990, 1996).

cannot yield a new object. This was the third principle we mentioned in connection with the axiom system based on +.

(A.20) $\forall x\ x + x = x$ *Idempotence*

And indeed, if we accept the equivalence between Pxy and $x + y = y$, then A.20 is simply equivalent to the Reflexivity axiom A.1. More generally, however, one might want to question the equivalence itself, particularly the following direction.

(T.51) $\forall x \forall y (Pxy \rightarrow x + y = y)$ *Subpotence*

On this understanding of parthood and summation (which follows from the definition of + and the underlying idempotence of disjunction), if an object is already included as a part of a whole, then including it 'again' will not change anything.

Effingham and Robson (2007, p. 635) call this feature of classical mereology the "Parts Just Once" principle: a composite whole "cannot have the same object as a proper part many times over". What exactly is meant by parthood "many times over"? Karen Bennett writes:

> Two people are cousins twice over, or 'double cousins', as they are called, just in case they are the children of pairs of siblings. Similarly, the *being three feet from* relation can hold multiple times between the same two entities: consider two antipodal points on a sphere, such that the shortest distance between them along the surface is three feet. Since there are many (infinitely many) three-foot-long arcs between them on the surface, the points are three feet from each other many times over. But ... *parthood*? I have two hands, yes, but each is part of me once and once only. (Bennett, 2013, 83–84)

However, Bennett goes on to argue that we *can* make sense of the idea of an entity's having a part many times over. Her account makes creative use of the functional distinction between a *role* and an *occupant* of that role. This distinction—she argues—allows us to rethink the notion of parthood as involving two separate relations: *being a parthood slot* and *filling a parthood slot*. For something x to be part of y is for x to fill one of y's parthood slots. Thus, on this conception wholes come 'pre-structured', as it were; they are structural shells waiting to be filled in. And since the theory allows for a single entity to fill multiple parthood slots at the same time, the Parts Just Once principle may fail.[107]

---

107 The slot idea is also considered, informally, in Harte (2002, ch. 4) and in Koslicki (2005, pp. 115f and 235ff). For critical discussion of Bennett's mereological treatment, see Fisher (2013) and Cotnoir (2015, §2); for developments and applications, see Garbacz (2017), Masolo and Vieu (2018), and Sattig (in press).

In the case of material bodies, Smith (2009) suggests the phenomenon may also be understood as an object x having a proper part y that is multiply located in distinct subregions of the location of x.[108] If an object can be located in different regions at the same time, then so can its parts and we would have violations of Idempotence and Subpotence. One purported case of this sort is Effingham and Robson's own example of a brick wall composed of a single time-traveling—hence multiply located—brick (Effingham and Robson, 2007, pp. 633f). In section 4.3.1 we mentioned it as a potential counterexample to Weak Supplementation, but obviously such a wall would also violate the Parts Just Once principle.[109]

For those who think that time travel is metaphysically impossible, Gilmore (2007) offers a different example based on the notion of a 'timelike curve'. A timelike curve is the continuous path of a physical object through spacetime. If it lasts long enough and takes the appropriate trajectory, the object may return to its own past and 'coexist' with an earlier version of itself without ever traveling backwards (since locally the path is always oriented forwards). Indeed, Gödel (1949) has shown that the General Theory of Relativity is even compatible with the occurrence of *closed* timeline curves, i.e. curves that intersect themselves. So Gilmore's example is not only metaphysically possible; it is an actual physical possibility:

> Consider ... the career of a hydrogen atom, which we shall call 'Adam'. Adam is spatially bi-located throughout its two-billion-year-long career. For any given moment of external time (or 'global simultaneity slice') t in the relevant universe, Adam is present at t 'twice over' ... Suppose that, at each moment of Adam's proper time, Adam is chemically bonded to itself at a different moment of its proper time, thus forming a molecule of H_2, which we shall call 'Abel' ... These objects trace out the same path over the course of their careers, but ... the distinctness of Adam and Abel can be argued for in a number of ways. Adam, being a mere hydrogen atom, has certain chemical properties that Abel lacks. Abel, being a hydrogen molecule, is more massive than Adam. (Gilmore, 2007, pp. 186f)

In this case, again, we have something (Abel) that is composed of a single multi-located part (Adam). This violates the Subpotence principle T.51 and, hence, Idempotence: Adam is part of itself, but the sum of Adam with itself is not identical with Adam; it is identical with Abel.

Perhaps the most familiar example of multi-location involves universals. As we saw in section 3.1.2, so-called 'immanent' universals are traditionally

108 On the interplay between mereology and location theories, see again Casati and Varzi (1999), Donnelly (2010), Gilmore (2018) and the essays in Kleinschmidt (2014).

109 On the other hand, once repetitions are allowed, one may consider revisiting the Weak Company principle A.39. As Saenz (2014, p. 136) notes, if the underlying intuition is that a whole with a proper part "needs other parts in addition", as Simons (1987, p. 26) actually has it, then the other parts need not be numerically distinct from the first; they can be the same part *again*.

said to be wholly present wherever they are instantiated. Additionally, it is sometimes argued that such universals can be structured by virtue of having other universals as constituents, the *locus classicus* being Armstrong (1986). As Lewis (1986a) notes, these two features violate the Parts Just Once principle:

> Each methane molecule has not one hydrogen atom but four. So if the structural universal *methane* is to be an isomorph of the molecules that are its instances, it must have the universal *hydrogen* as a part not just once, but four times over ... But what can it mean for something to have a part four times over? What are there four of? (Lewis, 1986a, p. 34)

From this, Lewis concludes *pace* Armstrong that structural universals cannot possibly exist, since 'structure' can only be understood mereologically (see also Lewis, 1986b). But one might agree with Forrest (1986) and Hawley (2010) that Lewis's 'mereology or magic' is a false dichotomy. A nonclassical mereology dispensing with Idempotence (along with Weak Supplementation) would provide the resources for a third way.[110]

5.3.4 *Compositional Pluralism*

While discussing a structured conception of wholes, it is important to consider views that accept both structured and unstructured wholes. The view that there is more than one basic mode of composition is known as *compositional pluralism* and has seen a growing number of defenders in recent years. Armstrong (1997) is a classic case in point, accepting both mereological composition for ordinary objects (in fact, as we saw, he thinks mereological composition is a form of identity) and structural composition for states of affairs. Another influential example is Paul (2002), who accepts distinct notions of spatial parts and qualitative parts for her mereological bundle theory.[111] McDaniel (2004, 2009a), a contemporary defender of Armstrongian compositional pluralism, argues that composition for structural wholes satisfies different rules and has a different logical form than composition for mereological wholes.[112] Mumford and Anjum (2011, ch. 4) argue for compositional pluralism by appeal to distinct ways that causal powers

110 See, for example, Bigelow (1986) for an early attempt. Besides Bennett (2013), recent proposals include Mormann (2010, 2012), Sharpe (2012), Bader (2013), Forrest (2013, 2016), Cotnoir (2015), McFarland (2018), and Azzano (in press). (Lewis's misgivings about structural universals are also addressed in Pagés, 2002 and Kalhat, 2008, though without any explicit reference to the repetition problem.) For a general overview, see Fisher (2018).

111 For related views, see Olson (2017) and Longenecker (2018). Variants of Paul's mereological bundle theory of universals (further developed in Paul, 2006, 2012, 2017) may also be found in Shiver (2014), Lafrance (2015), Benocci (2018), and Keinänen and Tahko (2019).

112 Cf. also McDaniel (2010c; 2014a; 2017, §2.3) and the authors mentioned in chapter 1, note 28.

can be composed. And Bennett (2017a) argues that there are several canonical "building relations", though differing in ways that are consistent with the claim that there is "deep and genuine unity" among them.[113] Of course, there are ways of resisting compositional pluralism on behalf of classical mereology (as recommended by Lewis, 1991 and detailed in Lando, 2017). In fact, Hawley (2006) argues that even if there are different principles of composition for different kinds of objects, this needn't commit us to compositional pluralism, in the same way that differing principles of identity need not commit us to pluralism about identity. Nevertheless compositional pluralism is a growing option and has developed into a rich number of formal proposals.

Perhaps the most comprehensive treatment is the neo-Aristotelian framework of Fine (2010). Fine is concerned with arguing for the conjunction of compositional pluralism and *operationalism*, which is the view that the operation of composition, rather than the relation of parthood, should be taken as the sole mereological primitive.[114] In other words, parthood should be defined from composition, not vice versa. A parthood relation is *basic*, in Fine's terms, when it is not definable in terms of other ways of being a part, but may be defined from a particular composition relation.

Now, Fine accepts the composition operation of classical mereology as one candidate among many equally legitimate notions of composition, some of which yield structured composites. Fine begins with a primitive composition operator Σ that can be applied to any number of objects $x_1, x_2, \ldots$ Where $\Sigma(x_1, x_2, \ldots) = y$, each of x_1, x_2, etc. is a *component* of y. The parthood relation is then defined as the transitive closure of componenthood. Thus, x is a part of y, in the sense induced by the given composition operator Σ, whenever there is a way of 'building' y from x (and other things perhaps) by one or more applications of Σ. It's easy to see that, on this definition, parthood is always sure to be a pre-order (weak or strict, depending on the composition operator in question). Antisymmetry—or, in some cases, Asymmetry—would follow from the following principle:[115]

(5.3) $x = \Sigma(\ldots\Sigma(\ldots, x, \ldots)\ldots) \to x = \Sigma(\ldots, x, \ldots)$ *Anticyclicity*

It is worth noting that Fine presupposes that each Σ is functional, i.e. outputs of its application are always unique. On the other hand, a composition

113 See also Hovda (2016, 2017), for whom the existence of multiple varieties of parthood (or part-like relations) does not rule out that they be governed and organized by general principles.

114 Fine provides several arguments for operationalism, though some of them depend on a prior assumption of pluralism. For a different approach to the idea that composition should be taken as primitive, see Kleinschmidt (2019).

115 For suppose $x = \Sigma(\ldots\Sigma(\ldots, x, \ldots)\ldots)$ but $x \neq y = \Sigma(\ldots, x, \ldots)$; then x is a component of y, hence part of it, and y is part of x. This is a violation of Antisymmetry (or Asymmetry).

operator may be partial, i.e. not always defined, and may be sensitive to the order of the arguments to which it applies.

By listing a number of key principles that may or may not hold for Σ, we can generate a number of potential composition operations that behave in accordance with the rules.

(5.4) $\Sigma(x) = x$ *Collapse*

(5.5) $\Sigma(\ldots\Sigma(\ldots x, y \ldots)\ldots\Sigma(\ldots u, v \ldots)\ldots) = \Sigma(\ldots x, y \ldots u, v \ldots)$ *Leveling*

(5.6) $\Sigma(\ldots x, x \ldots y, y \ldots) = \Sigma(\ldots x \ldots y \ldots)$ *Absorption*

(5.7) $\Sigma(\ldots x, y, z \ldots) = \Sigma(\ldots y, z, x \ldots)$ *Permutation*

The first principle, 5.4, is akin to T.50 above (F–Reflexivity). It 'collapses' the distinction between an object and the composite generated from just that object. Some composition operations, such as classical mereological summation, satisfy this principle; others, such as the set-building operation, do not (due to singletons being distinct from their members). The second principle, 5.5, is simply a generalized version of A.22, the Associativity law for $+$: it flattens any hierarchical levels that would otherwise be formed by iterating the composition operation. Sets, again, are a typical example where embedding composites within the composition operator matters; we have e.g. that $\{\{x, y\}, \{z, w\}\} \neq \{x, y, z, w\}$. The Absorption principle, 5.6, asserts that repetition of some components does not matter to the identity of the composite. This is closely related to A.20 (Idempotence) and its generalized cousin T.51 (Subpotence). Both classical mereological sums and sets are insensitive to repetitions of this sort, but so-called multisets, for example, are not; we have e.g. that $[x, y, y] \neq [x, y]$.[116] So the multiset-building operation will not conform to 5.6. Finally, the Permutation principle 5.7 is a more general form of the Commutativity principle for $+$ (A.21) and forces a composition operator to be insensitive to the order of the components. Classical mereological sums, sets, and multisets all satisfy this principle, although strings and sequences, for example, do not; we have e.g. that $\langle x, y, z\rangle \neq \langle y, x, z\rangle$.

These four principles result in a number of different possible composition operators depending on whether or not they are satisfied. Following Fine, we may label them as C, L, A, and P, respectively, and slash through a label to indicate that the relevant principle is not satisfied. Then, for example, the sums of classical mereology satisfy CLAP, sets satisfy $\not{C}\not{L}AP$, and multisets $\not{C}\not{L}\not{A}P$. Strings would be given by $CL\not{A}\not{P}$ while sequences correspond to $\not{C}\not{L}\not{A}\not{P}$.[117] As a result, the framework provides for a general and flexible

116 Multisets are defined precisely as set-like entities that allow for multiple occurrences of its members. See e.g. Blizard (1989).

117 Of the possible variants, $\not{C}LA\not{P}$ and $CLA\not{P}$ violate the Anticyclicity principle 5.3, and so Fine (2010, fn. 12) thinks they should be disallowed.

approach to composition operators that allow for large variety of structured wholes.[118] Fine writes:

> From the present perspective, the operation of summation is one tiny star in a vast mereological firmament, and there is no reason to think of it as possessing better mereological credentials than any of the others. It is indeed distinguished by the fact that it is blind to all aspects of the whole other than the parts from which it was formed. But it is hard to see why sensitivity to structure in the other operations should somehow impede their ability to form wholes. (Fine, 2010, p. 576)

So mereological summation may well be a good, possibly unique way of composing *unstructured* wholes. But the compositional pluralist will maintain that there are other, equally good ways of composing *structured* wholes.

It remains to be seen whether such a variety of composition operations can co-exist. This is a complicated matter. For example, McCarthy (2015) argues that mereological and structural composition operations cannot co-exist if it is assumed that the latter always determine a unique whole, and if they always determine a unique plurality of immediate parts. Whether such assumption should hold, however, is part of the problem.

5.4 THE UNIVERSE

Let us finally turn to some general questions about the overall import of our composition axioms, paralleling our discussion of mereological decomposition. Just as we might wonder whether decomposition eventually results in a bottom 'null' element that is part of everything (section 4.5), so too might one wonder whether composition results in a top element that has everything as a part—a 'universal' object. And just as decomposition gives rise to important options regarding the existence of a bottom level of partless 'atoms' (section 4.6), so may we ask whether similar options arise with regard to composition. We conclude the present chapter by addressing these two questions in turn.

In classical mereology, the first question has a straight answer. Recall our definition of the universe from chapter 2 as the fusion of everything there is.

(D.8) $u := \sigma x \, \exists y \, x = y$ *Universe*

Given the Unrestricted Fusion axiom schema A.5, the existence of u follows immediately from the fact that $\forall x \exists y \, x = y$ is a theorem of the underlying

118 Note that reference to 5.4–5.7 does not allow us to uniquely specify a composition operator. The Weak Supplementation principle A.10, for instance, cannot be proved (or disproved) for the parthood relations associated with CLAP operators, so a CLAP mereology need not be fully classical. See Cotnoir (2015, p. 440) for more on this point.

logic, A.0. Since everything is part of u by the first conjunct in the definition of 'fusion' (D.6), u can therefore serve as the algebraic 'top' of our models. In weaker theories this need not be the case, though the existence of such an element may be assumed as an axiom.

(A.74) $\exists x \forall y \, Pyx$ *Top*

Moreover, classical mereology is antisymmetric, which means that fusions are unique (T.3) and hence the universe is unique too, justifying the use of the sigma-operator in D.8. Without Antisymmetry, there might be several distinct top elements, and so one might wish to distinguish this situation from a stricter assumption concerning the universe.

(A.75) $\exists x \forall y (Pyx \wedge \neg PPxy)$ *Strict Top*

This is the dual of the Strict Zero principle A.43. In antisymmetric contexts, the additional conjunct is redundant, so A.75 is equivalent to A.74.

Now, as we have seen, there is extensive philosophical debate over composition principles, particularly over the classical mereologist's commitment to universalism via A.5. Non-universalists might wish to consider a postulate stating explicitly that there is no top element, or its strict variant, except in the trivial case where there exists only one thing.[119]

(A.76) $\exists x \exists y \neg x = y \rightarrow \neg \exists x \forall y \, Pyx$ *No Top*

(A.77) $\exists x \exists y \neg x = y \rightarrow \neg \exists x \forall y (Pyx \wedge \neg PPxy)$ *Strict No Top*

Formally (and intuitively) these principles are the exact duals of the No Zero principles T.2 and T.29. But whereas the latter follow from the Remainder axiom A.4 (and, indeed, from the much weaker Quasi-Supplementation principle A.42), A.76 and A.77 are inconsistent with A.5. Are there philosophical reasons to endorse either? Conservative answers to the Special Composition Question need not tell us, and indeed it would seem that organicism, regionalism, and such-like views are all compatible with models that comprise (well-behaved) universal elements. Nonetheless, there are further reasons why A.76 or A.77 may be taken seriously.

5.4.1 *A Russell Paradox?*

One potential source of puzzlement over the existence of a universe, and unrestricted fusion principles generally, comes from set theory. Readers

119 In particular, note that the purely mereological restrictions expressed by D.48 (Common Upper Bound) and D.49 (Pairwise Underlap) would be trivially satisfied in any domain that includes a universal element.

familiar with its standard Zermelo-Fraenkel formulation (ZFC)[120] will know that the theory is incompatible with the existence of a universal set on pain of Russell's (1902) paradox.[121] One might wonder, then, why parallel considerations do not also impugn the existence of a universal fusion in mereology.

It is indeed instructive to see why the assumption of a universal set in ZFC would lead to the paradox. Naive set theory has the following principle, which is similar to (the consequent of) our fusion axiom A.5.[122]

(5.8) $\exists z \forall x (x \in z \leftrightarrow \varphi x)$ *Unrestricted Comprehension*

From this, Russell's antinomy follows immediately by letting φ be the formula $\neg x \in x$ and instantiating x to the witness for z, i.e. the set R of all sets that are not members of themselves.

(5.9) $R \in R \leftrightarrow \neg R \in R$

In ZFC, 5.8 is replaced by a weaker axiom schema, which only requires the existence, for any given set y, of a *subset* of y characterized by φ.[123]

(5.10) $\forall y \exists z \forall x (x \in z \leftrightarrow (x \in y \wedge \varphi x))$ *Restricted Comprehension*

This is meant to block the paradox. But suppose there is a universal set U such that $\forall x\, x \in U$. Letting φ be the formula $\neg x \in x$, by 5.10 we have

(5.11) $\exists z \forall x (x \in z \leftrightarrow (x \in U \wedge \neg x \in x))$

The witness for z in 5.11 is the Russell set R. And because every set is in U, we can simplify the right-hand side of the biconditional to obtain

(5.12) $\forall x (x \in R \leftrightarrow \neg x \in x)$

This immediately takes us back to the contradiction in 5.9, so we conclude by *reductio* that there cannot be a universal set U.

120 From Zermelo (1908) and Fraenkel (1922). For a classic introduction to ZFC (with historical details) see Fraenkel *et al.* (1973).

121 Not every set theory faces this problem. Quine's *New Foundations* (1937), for instance, has a universal set but avoids the paradox by restricting the naive Comprehension principle (see below) to 'stratified' formulas. Another variant with a universal set is due to Church (1974). For further details, see Forster (1992) and Holmes (1998); for general discussion, Bremer (2010).

122 Informally from Cantor (1895–1897), where it is stated that any number of objects "of our intuition or our thought" form a set (p. 85). It is the formal analogue of this principle that can be derived from the problematic Basic Law V of Frege (1893).

123 Zermelo's original nomenclature was "Axiom of Separation" (*Axiom der Aussonderung*). In some literature, the schema is also known as "Axiom of Subsets" (Fraenkel and Bar-Hillel, 1958, p. 38) or "Axiom of Specification" (Halmos, 1960, p. 6).

Should a similar line of reasoning convince us that there cannot be a universal object u? As we mentioned, some authors think so. For instance, Bigelow (1996, §5) is suspicious that mereology applied unrestrictedly would face an analogue of Russell's paradox and recommends restricting A.5 along the lines of 5.10. Here is a natural suggestion.[124]

(A.78) $\exists x \varphi x \to (\exists z F_{\varphi} z \leftrightarrow \exists y \forall x(\varphi x \to Pxy))$ *Restricted Composition*

This is essentially the result of adopting Bostock's Common Upper Bound restriction on composition (D.48); it only commits one to *subfusions*, i.e. fusions that are bounded from above by some already existing object, just as Restricted Comprehension only commits one to subsets. Replacing A.5 with A.78 would thus be sufficient to block the derivation of the Top principle A.74, hence the existence of u. However, we know that none of this is strictly necessary. We know *already* that classical mereology doesn't face an analogue of Russell's paradox: for all its permissivism, its axioms are consistent (relative to ZFC), since they have set-theoretic models. This should come as no surprise, since one of Leśniewski's motivations for developing mereology was precisely to provide a theory of collections that wouldn't suffer from Russell's paradox.[125] Yet the question remains: *why* doesn't classical mereology have a corresponding paradox?

There are (at least) two reasons why the paradox doesn't arise: a superficial reason, and a deeper one. The superficial reason is that the axiom schema of Unrestricted Fusion is not *absolutely* unrestricted; it applies exclusively to conditions that are satisfiable—those defining conditions φ that have at least one instance. We would need to find some satisfiable φ parallel to '$\neg x \in x$' in order to generate a paradoxical object, but what could it be? Classical parthood is more analogous to subsethood than it is to membership. Focusing on F-type Unrestricted Fusion, particularly on the equivalent formulation of A.5 based on D.44,

(5.13) $\exists x \varphi x \to \exists z \forall y(Pzy \leftrightarrow \forall x(\varphi x \to Pxy))$

124 Bigelow's own formulation, which he labels "Mereological Separation", is somewhat different and ultimately defective. See Hudson (2001, pp. 95ff) for discussion and amendments.

125 Leśniewski offered three distinct treatments of the paradox. The first (Leśniewski, 1914) appeals to mereological intuitions about collections (see Sinisi, 1976 for commentary). The second treatment is a formal refinement of the first and is included in the original exposition of Mereology (Leśniewski, 1916, §9). The third analysis is unpublished, although it derives from the fully worked out formal system in Leśniewski (1927–1931). An exposition of that analysis was eventually published by Sobociński (1949–1950), which is the *locus classicus* for Leśniewski's views on Russell's paradox. For further studies, see Ridder (2002, §1.1.3), Pietruszczak (2002), Gessler (2005, §II.5; 2007, §1.2), Urbaniak (2008; 2014a, §2.8.4), and Miszczyński (2010, 2011, 2013). The consistency of Leśniewski's Mereology, as based on the logical framework of Ontology, was proved by Clay (1968) and Lejewski (1969). See also Clay (1974a,b).

shows that the main candidate is '$\neg Pxx$'; yet this condition is ruled out by the Reflexivity axiom A.1. So the fusion of all things that aren't part of themselves is not required to exist. Indeed, the main line of argument in Leśniewski (1914) purports to establish exactly this, that 'x is a class not subordinate to itself' is an unsatisfiable predicate. (Note that the full strength of A.1 is crucial here. If, for example, we only had the weaker axiom

(A.79) $\forall x(\exists y Pyx \rightarrow Pxx)$ *Quasi-Reflexivity*

'$\neg Pxx$' might be satisfiable and Unrestricted Fusion would yield a contradiction from $\exists x \neg Pxx$, as shown in Pietruszczak, 1996, pp. 114f.[126])

But there is a deeper reason underlying the lack of a Russell paradox for mereology: it's simply not the case that every part of a fusion must satisfy the defining condition φ.[127] For example, the fusion of all cats isn't itself a cat. In fact, lots of proper parts of that fusion aren't cats either—they are feet, whiskers, feet-whiskers, or whatnots.[128] This is in contradistinction to sets, where we always have that $y \in \{x : \varphi x\}$ if and only if y is a φ.

This difference underlies Leśniewski's distinction between two fundamentally different ways of conceiving of classes: the *collective* conception and the *distributive* conception.[129] Sets are conceived of as distributive classes; mereological wholes on the ordinary (unstructured) conception, by contrast, are collective classes. There are a number of different ways of characterizing the distinction. In the terminology of sections 5.3.1 and 5.3.3, collective classes satisfy Idempotence (A.20) and Associativity (A.22), whereas distributive classes do not. Or more generally, using the framework of Fine (2010) outlined in section 5.3.4, collective classes satisfy both Collapse (5.4) and Leveling (5.5), whereas distributive classes do not.[130] Alternatively, following

126 More precisely, Pietruszczak's proof uses the Unrestricted Fusion′ schema (A.11).

127 That is: so long as we do not independently assume the P-Collapse principle T.49. But then, again, we saw that T.49 entails mereological nihilism so long as P is reflexive.

128 Leśniewski himself offers the following example:

> If every object subordinate to the class (of objects) n were an n, then every object subordinate to the class of quarters of the sphere Q would be a quarter of the sphere Q. As we know … any half P of the sphere Q is subordinate to the class of quarters of the sphere Q; from whence it would follow, therefore, that a half P of the sphere Q is a quarter of the sphere Q, which is obviously false. (Leśniewski, 1914, p. 123, amended according to the translation in Sinisi, 1976, p. 26)

129 In Leśniewski (1927–1931, pt. III), where the distinction arises out of a disagreement with Frege (1895). For a reconstruction, see Sinisi (1969) and Gessler (2007, ch. 3).

130 According to Sinisi (1976, p. 25), Leśniewski's conception of collective classes is encapsulated in the thesis that the class of a class of objects is the same as that class, corresponding to the conjunction of theorems LXXII and XCVII in Leśniewski (1927–1931, pp. 274 and 280). Sobociński (1949–1950, p. 33) adds two more theses: a collective class of φs is always unique; and if there is only one x satisfying φ, then the collective class of φs is just x. For further details and critical discussion, see Urbaniak (2008).

Sobociński (1949–1950, p. 33), we might note that the collective class of all the books found on a given desk at this time is the same as the collective class of all the printed pages presently on that desk, whereas the distributive classes so defined are not identical. In this sense, the collective/distributive opposition matches Leonard and Goodman's way of distinguishing wholes from classes in the passage cited in section 1.2.2, which in turn is reminiscent of Frege's:

> If we are given a whole, it is not yet determined what we are to envisage as its parts. As parts of a regiment I can regard the battalions, the companies or the individual soldiers, and as parts of a sand pile, the grains of sand or the silicon and oxygen atoms. On the other hand, if we are given a class, it is determined what objects are members of it. (Letter to Russell, 7 June 1902, in Frege, 1976, p. 140)

So another way of putting the point is this: distributive classes have a unique decomposition into their elements; collective classes do not.[131] Consequently, a distributive class of the φs is such that all of its elements (members) are φ, whereas a collective class of φs may have elements (parts) that are not φ.[132]

To sum up, then, we have two concurring thoughts. On the one hand, in mereology there there is no difficulty in denying existence to some putative counterparts of Russell's set, such as the fusion of all things that are not part of themselves. So long as P is reflexive, the condition '$\neg$Pxx' is unsatisfiable and, hence, the Unrestricted Fusion axiom A.5 is harmless. On the other hand, consider e.g. the fusion of all things that are not *proper* part of themselves. In this case A.5 will apply non-vacuously and the fusion will exist, since '$\neg$PPxx' is satisfiable. Indeed, everything satisfies '$\neg$PPxx', so the fusion will be a universal object. But because a fusion of the φs need not be a φ, there is no Russell contradiction in saying the universe is not a proper part of itself. On the contrary, $\neg$PPuu is plainly true.

So no analogue of Russell's paradox arises in classical mereology, and we can see why. One might still wonder why we don't run into *other* paradoxical situations that are usually associated with the notion of a universal entity. For instance, a further reason why there cannot be a universal set in ZFC relates to Cantor's (1891) theorem: if there were such a set, it would have to include its own powerset, which is impossible. Why doesn't mereology

131 Once unique decomposition is relaxed, however, trouble can be found. For example, Uzquiano (2006a, p. 145) uses a number of set-theoretic assumptions—together with the claim that the parts of a set are all and only its subsets—to derive a version of unique decomposition for fusions of singletons. He then derives a Russell paradox via the fusion of all singletons which are not parts of their members. The same point may be found in Fine (2005, p. 567).

132 Further delineations of the distinction may be found in Vernant (2000, §2) and Gessler (2005, § II.4) and, with technical details, in Pietruszczak (1996; 2000a, § I.2) and Gruszczyński and Pietruszczak (2010). See also Potter (2004, § 2.1) for an account from a set-theoretic perspective (with no explicit reference to Leśniewski).

suffer from a similar problem? Here the answer follows from a more general consideration regarding the overall strength of mereology as an alternative to set theory. As we mentioned in section 1.2.2, Leśniewski (1927–1931) did prove a mereological analogue of Cantor's theorem. It states (roughly) that if there is more than one φ, and the φs are pairwise disjoint, then there are fewer (*mniej*) φs than collective classes thereof (see p. 314, thm. CXCVIII). This seems to be as close as one can get to Cantor's theorem in mereology (Urbaniak, 2015, §7). But then, again, it is wholly unproblematic. As a collective class of everything there is, the parts of the universe are not pairwise disjoint. So the theorem does not apply and the paradox does not arise.[133]

5.4.2 *Super-Universal Wholes*

A different sort of objection to the existence of the universe stems from considering entities which plausibly have the universe as a constituent, member, or part. Consider the example from Tillman and Fowler (2012, p. 526) mentioned in section 3.2.1: the proposition that u exists. Or consider the truthmaker for that proposition, the state of affairs of u's existing, the complex property of being such that u exists, the ordered pair ⟨u, existing⟩, etc. It would appear that all such cases involve entities that *comprise* the universe amongst other things. How can that be, if the universe itself is supposed to comprise everything? A similar example comes from Uzquiano (2006a, p. 145): under the assumption that singleton formation is unrestricted, we must have that {u} exists. This would be an odd case of a singleton—a singleton that is itself a proper part of its only member.[134]

As noted in chapter 3, one way to deal with cases of this sort is to revisit the partial ordering axioms A.1–A.3. This is Tillman and Fowler's own conclusion: the world may be populated by much stranger things than cats and ordinary fusions, and an adequate mereology of those stranger things may take us beyond classical wisdom—for instance, it may be non-wellfounded. Alternatively, one may of course deny the existence of those things by denying more generally the existence of the relevant sorts of entity: there are *no* singular structured propositions, *no* states of affairs, etc. Or one may accept their existence but deny their constituents are *part* of them, endorsing a compositional pluralism of sorts. Such alternatives, however, have obvious

133 Gabriel Uzquiano (p.c.) has suggested that one might obtain a mereological version of Cantor's theorem that is even closer to the original by weakening the condition 'the φs are pairwise disjoint' to 'different φs form different collective classes'. Even so, the argument in the text still applies, since the parts of the universe do not satisfy this weaker condition, either. For more on Cantor's theorem in Mereology, see Clay (1965); for more on the universe, Łyczak *et al.* (2016).

134 Lewis (1991, p. 18f) is forced to reject unrestricted singleton formation; but Lewis (1986c, p. 211) accepts the existence of trans-world sets and trans-world fusions, which would appear to be super-universal in the relevant sense.

costs, especially for a mereological monist who sees mereology as a formal ontological theory. So one may conclude that the only acceptable alternative to relinquishing the ordering axioms is to relinquish the universe. And this is not just a matter of rejecting the Unrestricted Fusion axiom as such. As already noted, non-universalists avoid *commitment* to u, yet their views may be compatible with u's existence. For instance, it may be a brute fact that only some fusions exist and the universe might be among them (Markosian, 1998b). Rather, the rejection of the universe would have to come in the form of an explicit postulate. In other words, these are cases where one may seriously consider endorsing A.76 (No Top) or A.77 (Strict No Top).

Another issue that some have raised regarding the existence of a mereological universe concerns the status of *transcategorial* fusions, fusions of entities belonging to two or more ontological categories such as material objects, events, properties, numbers, etc. To go back to the examples of section 5.2.1, a foot-carburetor or a death-wedding may be strange enough; but if composition is truly unrestricted (what van Inwagen, 1987, p. 35 calls "super-universalism"), our ontology would also include foot-weddings and death-carburetors, and then also foot-virtues, wedding-numbers, color-propositions, and what not. In the words of Peter Forrest:

> The worst case is the existence of sums of items from [several] different categories, such as: a kettle, the process in the kettle in which water boils, the spatiotemporal region in which the process occurs, the property of being at 100°C, and the relation of contiguity. Even though all those items might be thought of in connection with the activity of boiling water, it seems queer to say there is something which is the sum of them. (Forrest, 1998, p. 318)

We know how the classical mereologist will respond, especially the friend of CAI. But many will be inclined to agree with Forrest and think that such "ontological chimeras"—as both Forrest (2007, p. 238) and Simons (2009b, p. 116) call them—should be banned. It needn't be an absolute ban. As Tillman and Fowler (2012, p. 533) point out, *some* transcategorial fusions are perfectly conceivable and have a respectable metaphysical pedigree: think of structured propositions, states of affairs, certain versions of the 'bundle' theory of objects, or neo-Aristotelian hylomorphic theories of substances as mereological compounds of a 'material' part and a 'formal' part. There are also theories that allow for things comprising 'positive' as well as 'negative' parts, e.g. a donut (Hoffman and Richards, 1984). At the limit, however, the universal entity u would involve parts from *all* ontological kinds, no matter *what* kinds they are, and this is certainly harder to accept.

One specific objection comes from Simons (2003, 2006), who asks what category u would belong to. Never mind that *any* transcategorial fusion may be hard to classify. When it comes to the all-encompassing universe, there would seem to be only four, logically exhaustive options—and no principled way to make a choice.

- The universe is in one of the categories occupied by its proper parts. (But why should a single category get this exclusive privilege?)
- The universe is in a different, *sui generis* category unshared by any of its proper parts. (But, again, why should the universe enjoy such a privilege?)
- The universe is in more than one category, possibly in all categories occupied by its proper parts. (But wouldn't this be an *ad hoc* exception to the idea that categories are mutually exclusive?)
- The universe is in no category at all. (And wouldn't this be an *ad hoc* exception, too?)

There are ways of resisting this objection. For instance, one may hold that no transcategorial fusion can fully belong to a single category (by definition); it belongs *partly* to each category occupied by its fundamental parts (Smid, 2015, p. 3264). If so, then the last option would not be exceptionally *ad hoc*, as the universe would be one such chimera among many. Alternatively, one could pick the first option on the grounds that the privilege need not be unwarranted (Varzi, 2006b, §2). After all, if the universe has parts in all categories, then so do lots of other things: the universe minus Dion's foot, the universe minus the number 16, etc. All such parts are transcategorial in exactly the same way. So assigning the universe to *their* category, whatever that might be, would seem like a reasonable, principled choice. (A complication: if the universe belongs to a category, and if categories themselves are capable of being parts, then the universe must be a member of a category that is itself a proper part of the universe.)

These replies notwithstanding, philosophically the objection raises a genuine challenge for universalism. In section 4.5 we saw that the main philosophical reason why classical mereologists reject the existence of a null object—a mereological zero—stems from its unfathomable nature. Even David Lewis, we noted, discards it on the grounds that it is "a very queer thing" (Lewis, 1991, p. 11). Here we see that the notion of a universal object—a mereological top—gives rise to similar metaphysical worries. What sort of thing is it? The latter worries leaves classical mereologists unmoved. But the asymmetry is striking.

5.5 COATOMS AND JUNK

The mereological asymmetry between top and bottom brings us to our last topic. As we saw in chapter 4, the long history of the debate on infinite divisibility finds expression in a number of interesting theses concerning mereological decomposition, the most important of which are Atomism (A.6) and Atomlessness (A.31). There are directly parallel questions regarding composition. Consider the following definition.

(D.50) $\mathsf{C}x :\equiv \neg\exists y \mathsf{PP}xy$ *Coatom*

A coatom is the dual of a mereological atom, or simple, as defined in D.39. Whereas something is an atom if and only if it has no proper parts (a minimal element with respect to the parthood ordering), something is a coatom if and only if it is not a proper part of anything (a maximal element). All questions we examined in connection with the notion of an atom will therefore have a counterpart in relation to coatoms. And while the latter have received comparatively little attention in the mereological literature,[135] they deserve scrutiny. Dual questions need not receive dual answers, especially if, as in classical mereology, composition and decomposition do not behave symmetrically.

The existence of the universe is relevant here. Given the definitions, it follows immediately that in mereologies with a universal element, u, there are no other coatoms except for u itself. Thus, while classical mereology is neutral with respect to the existence of atoms as opposed to gunk (or hybrid compounds), it trivializes the converse question by asserting the unconditional existence of a unique coatom in all of its models. This is precisely the asymmetry noted above. On the other hand, recall that in the case of atoms, the definition in D.39 could be adapted to mereologies that allowed for a null element n (which would otherwise qualify as the only atom); see D.40. Similarly, in a setting with a universal top element we may tweak D.50 to obtain a more general, non-trivial notion of a coatom.

(D.51) $\mathsf{SC}x :\equiv \forall y(\mathsf{PP}xy \to y = u)$ *Solid Coatom*

This definition states that a coatom can only be a proper part of the universe if it is a proper part of anything at all.[136] And clearly classical mereology is silent on the existence of such elements. Finite models of size $n > 1$ will perforce involve solid coatoms; infinite models—for instance, models satisfying the Denseness axiom A.30—may have none.

One consequence of this definition is that, despite atoms and coatoms being in some sense 'opposite', it is perfectly possible for an entity to belong

135 The very notion of a coatom is virtually absent from the literature. Exceptions include Meixner (1997) and Valore (2016), who call coatoms "complete wholes", or simply "wholes", and Sanson (2016), who calls them "caps".

136 This is how coatoms are usually defined in algebra. Some authors call such elements "anti-atoms" (Goodstein, 1963; Rutherford, 1965), or simply "dual atoms" (Grätzer, 1968). Others speak of "counterpoints" (Curry, 1963), using "point" for a non-zero atom (Birkhoff, 1940).

to both categories simultaneously. For example, consider the three-element model of classical mereology, with exactly two atoms a and b (figure 5.12). According to D.51, a and b are (solid) coatoms as well. In what follows, however, we shall for the most part rely on D.50.

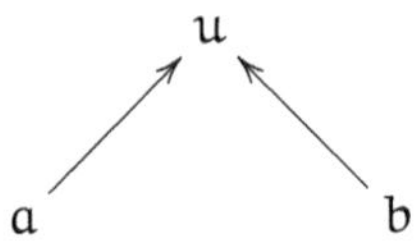

Figure 5.12: Atoms that are (solid) coatoms

Corresponding to the strong claims of Atomism (A.6) and Atomlessness (A.31) we may now consider the following general principles.[137]

(A.80) $\forall x \exists y (Cy \land Pxy)$ *Coatomism*

(A.81) $\forall x \neg Cx$ *Coatomlessness*

Coatomism is dual to Atomism and states that every object is part of some coatom; whether or not there is an all-encompassing universe, all mereological composition ends in maximal wholes. Coatomlessness, in turn, is dual to Atomlessness and states that there are no coatoms at all; everything is a proper part of something. If we wish, we can be more explicit and express Coatomlessness as the thesis that all things compose forever into larger and larger wholes.

(T.52) $\forall x \forall y (Pxy \to \neg Cy)$ *Junk*

This is the dual of T.36, the thesis that everything is made of atomless gunk, and it is in this form that the principle is sometimes discussed in the literature: everything is "junk" (in the already-mentioned terminology of Schaffer, 2010, p. 64).[138] Given Reflexivity, however, T.52 is equivalent to A.81.

Here, again, it should be noted that these principles presuppose that parthood is antisymmetric. Absent the Antisymmetry axiom A.2, the two-element loop of figure 3.2 would qualify as a junky model, though that kind of structure is clearly not what philosophers have in mind when discussing these options. In non-antisymmetric settings, the principles should

137 Our nomenclature reflects the correspondence. In the mereological literature, A.81 is sometimes called "Downwards Seriality" (Lucas, 2000, §9.12), "Ascent" (Varzi, 2014b, §3), "Inverse Gunkness" (Adžić and Arsenijević, 2014, §2), or "Junk" (see below).

138 Some authors, following Parsons (2007, p. 209) and Sorensen (2016, p. 71), call it "knug"—the reverse spelling of 'gunk'. Note that 'junk' is sometimes used with a different meaning, as in Van Cleve (2008, p. 323), where it refers to the rich ontology that comes with universalism.

be formulated using the alternate definition of PP in D.15, i.e. PP_2 (Cotnoir, 2014a). Moreover, just as Atomism does not by itself rule out the possibility of worlds with infinite descending parthood chains, it is important to note that Coatomism does not rule out the dual possibility of worlds that are infinitely ascending. The model obtained by reversing the (non-classical) atomistic structure in figure 4.16 would be an obvious case in point, though it would be badly unsupplemented and would violate No Zero. But it's easy to add the missing elements, as in figure 5.13.

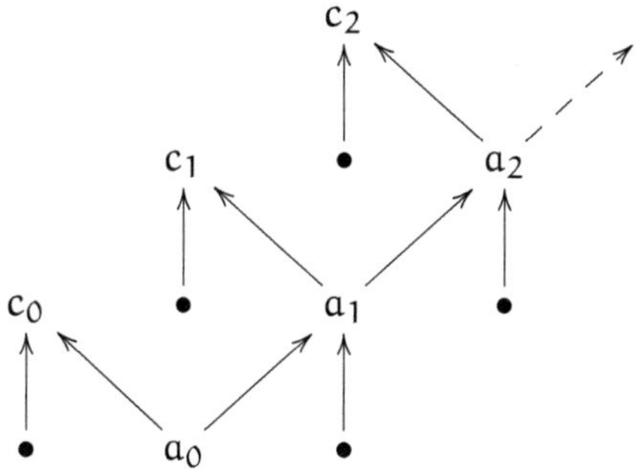

Figure 5.13: An infinitely ascending coatomistic model

Now, whether junk is metaphysically possible is contentious, certainly more contentious than the possibility of gunk (which, as we saw, is central to many contemporary philosophical views). Indeed, there is even controversy over whether junk is conceivable. On the one hand, it will be recalled that Anaxagoras, in the anti-atomistic fragment quoted in section 4.6, claimed that "also in the case of the large there is always a larger". And we mentioned that in his writings on the mereology of events, Whitehead had a postulate that entails both Atomlessness and Coatomlessness (1919, p. 101; 1920, p. 76). Occasionally, the possibility of junky worlds has also been entertained by philosophers attracted to Atomism. A classic example is Leibniz, who (in the guise of Theophilus) held that even though everything is ultimately composed of monads,

> there is never an infinite whole in the world, though there are always wholes greater than others *ad infinitum* (Leibniz, *New Essays*, I, xiii, 21).

More recently, some philosophers have argued that junk is at least conceivable using thought experiments. One might imagine, for example, that a universe just like ours is contained as a particle in some much larger replica universe, which is itself merely a particle in another replica universe, and so on (Bøhn, 2009a, p. 29). Or one might point to the fact that junk admits of well-defined mathematical models. A case in point would be the set of all regular open regions of the Euclidean plane that have a non-zero distance from a given singular point $(0,0)$, with P interpreted as set inclusion (Mormann, 2014, §5). Other auhors have appealed to hypotheses coming from actual physics and from 'multiverse' cosmological theories (Morganti, 2009) or to formal considerations pertaining to the theory of spatio-temporal location (Eagle, 2019, §5). Or one might simply argue for the possibility of junk via the possibility of gunk, resorting to symmetry considerations (Bøhn, 2009b, p. 200).

On the other hand, there are philosophers who regard junk as inconceivable. The leading representative is Jonathan Schaffer:

> The impossibility of junk also follows from the platitude that a possible object must exist *at a possible world*. No world—provided that worlds are understood as possible concrete cosmoi—could contain worldless junk because a world that contained junk would be an entity not a proper part of another entity at that world. A world would top-off the junk. (Schaffer, 2010, p. 65)

The argument here is that, if worlds are understood as concrete entities (as opposed to e.g. sets of propositions), the very thought that a world contains a junky object is incoherent.[139] This is precisely the verdict of classical mereology, on the understanding that a concrete world is just a universal fusion and that to exist *at* a world is to be part *of* that fusion. But there are other ways philosophers have argued for the same conclusion. For instance, Watson (2010) takes up the case against conceivability by objecting directly to Bøhn's (2009a) thought experiments.

It has been argued that the dispute is symptomatic of the troubles that affect any theory involving quantification over absolutely everything (some of which relate to the paradoxes of naive set theory mentioned above).[140] Philosophically, however, the dispute is especially important for the debate on metaphysical grounding. Schaffer himself introduced the notion of junk only to reject it on behalf of *priority monism*, the view that wholes are ontologically prior to their parts. But this is a typical case where one's philosopher's *modus ponens* is another philosopher's *modus tollens*. Tallant (2013), for instance, rejects priority monism precisely because he accepts the possibility of junk. Indeed, he thinks the world might be both junky and gunky, which

139 But see Sanson (2016), who suggests modeling junky possibilities by allowing that parts of possible worlds collectively represent complete possibilities.

140 See Spencer (2012, §2), though his remarks focus on mereologies with plural quantification. On the underlying troubles, see the essays in Rayo and Uzquiano (2006) and the survey in Florio (2014). Relatedly, Jacinto and Cotnoir (2019) argue, on grounds of Cantor's theorem, that Fine's (1999) theory of embodiments discussed earlier should be understood as indefinitely extensible, and provide a class of formal models of Fine's mereology all of which validate Coatomlessness (§7.2, thm. 6).

would threaten the opposite view, *priority pluralism*, as well as any other priority thesis based on mereology.[141] This is close to what Anaxagoras and Whitehead had in mind, a situation known in recent literature as "hunk" (from Bøhn, 2009a, §2).[142]

(A.82) $\forall x \exists y \exists z(\mathsf{PP}yx \wedge \mathsf{PP}xz)$ *Hunk*

Whatever their broader philosophical significance, mereologically these issues translate directly into questions about what sort of theories can best accommodate the views at stake. We know how things stand with regard to classical mereology: A.1–A.5 are compatible with gunk, thanks to the non-existence of a null element n, but not with either junk or hunk, owing to the existence of u. So classical mereology need not be atomistic but is necessarily coatomistic, as already noted by Goodman (1978). This is where the algebraic asymmetry is metaphysically disturbing. Of course one can minimize the worry by understanding 'atom' and 'coatom' in terms of the narrower, 'solid' notions defined in D.40 and D.51, in which case none of the relevant principles would be provable. Some critics, however, have put pressure on this easy 'way out'. Particularly, Bøhn (2009a) argues that the very possibility of worlds that are junky in the broad sense corresponding to D.50 means that mereological universalism cannot be metaphysically necessary. This matches Sider's (1993) gunk argument against the necessity of nihilism,[143] and would leave classical mereologists without a principled reason to resolve the 'vagueness argument' in favor of their extreme answer to the Special Composition Question. One could still respond that the vagueness argument itself, if accepted, would have the effect of ruling out junk altogether, since Coatomlessness demands a conservative answer. It is incompatible with universalism for the reason we have just seen, and it is incompatible with nihilism (as Bøhn, 2009b, p. 194 notes) insofar as it implies that everything is a proper part of something, hence that something is composite. However, this would be a dodgy response. The vagueness argument is targeted against restrictions on composition that aim to track vague intuitions, with the consequence that it would sometimes be indeterminate whether composition takes place or not. But there is nothing vague in the restriction demanded by junky worlds. No common-sense intuition is guiding that restriction. It's rather that composition never comes to an end.

141 For a reply, see Kitamura (2016). For related discussion, see Morganti (2015), Thomson (2016, §2.6), Tallant (2018, §5.4), Inman (2018, §7.1), Tahko (2018b).

142 Giberman (in press) suggests the palindrome "knunk" might be a better term (combining 'knug' and 'gunk'; cf. note 138), though Giberman is concerned with worldly structures in a strict sense (totalities of concreta) rather than in the present, loose sense (mereological models).

143 See section 5.2.1, note 47. For a reply to Bøhn's argument, see again Watson (2010) (with rejoinder in Bøhn, 2010 and further discussion in Mormann, 2014).

Since the source of the difficulty lies in the identification of universalism with the Unrestricted Fusion axiom A.5, a universalist who wishes to accept the possibility of junk or hunk might wish to retreat from A.5 and adopt weaker axioms. One explicit suggestion in this direction comes from Contessa (2012), who offers the following axiom.

(A.83) $\forall x \forall y \exists z\ x + y = z$ *Unrestricted Sum*

This axiom postulates the existence of a (unique) sum for any pair of objects.[144] By repeated applications, it will generate all finite fusions but not, of course, infinite fusions. So endorsing A.83—what Contessa calls "weak universalism"—only commits one to the existence of a universe in finite models.[145] And because junky models are perforce infinite, weak universalism is consistent with Coatomlessness.

It is indeed plausible that only permissivists would endorse A.83: the axiom guarantees the existence of all sorts of disparate and gerrymandered wholes, including 'worst case' instances of ontological chimeras. Nonetheless one might naturally wonder whether weak universalism is really a form of mereological universalism at all. Bøhn (2009a) explicitly calls it a "restricted form of composition". Moreover, the retreat is not without costs. Among other things, Cotnoir (2014a) suggests a tension with the Remainder axiom, A.4, while Giberman (2015) argues that even A.83 rules out certain plausible junky structures, e.g. structures with an infinitely ascending 'spruce' whose elements fuse with something else.[146]

Perhaps a better option is the composition axiom schema put forward by Bostock (1979, p. 118).

(A.84) $(\exists x \varphi x \wedge \exists y \forall x(\varphi x \rightarrow Pxy)) \rightarrow \exists z F_{\varphi} z$ *Bounded Fusion*

This is essentially the Restricted Composition principle A.78 mentioned in section 5.4.1, though in simple conditional form. It says that if the φs have an upper bound, then they must have a least upper bound, i.e. a fusion. Unlike

144 Strictly speaking, uniqueness is not essential to Contessa's proposal, though it is implied by his choice of words ("For any two objects, there is always a third object that is the mereological sum of the other two"; p. 456). Here we follow suit, though without the proviso that the sum and the summands be all distinct. It should also be noted that Contessa does not specify the relevant notion of 'sum'. Here we understand it in terms of F-type fusion, though one might prefer reading 'sum' in terms of F'-type or F''-type fusion, or even as a primitive (as in section 2.4.4).

145 Mereologies closed under finitary fusion are not new to the literature, witness Grzegorczyk (1955, pp. 91f). The first extensive studies go back to Eberle (1967, 1970), albeit restricted to F''-type sums. For F'-type sums, see Pietruszczak (2013, §III.4). Something like A.83 is also hinted at in Bøhn (2012, p. 216), though he takes it to imply that *only* finite fusions exist (fn. 14). A principle asserting the existence of all and only finite fusions is discussed more fully—and ultimately rejected—in Bøhn (2009a, p. 30; 2009b, p. 195).

146 Though see Smith (2019, §4 and fn. 10) for a response to both.

A.83, this axiom commits one to infinitary fusions, so long as the relevant φs are bounded from above. Yet A.84 is still compatible with the existence of junk, since infinite collections may be unbounded. Obviously this is weaker than full-blown mereological universalism (and does not imply A.83). However, the retreat is well behaved. As Bostock notes (p. 121), adding an explicit axiom asserting the existence of a top element (A.74) is all that's needed to bring us back to classical strength.[147]

A universalist might also be tempted by a third, stronger option. Just as classical mereology avoids commitment to a null object and makes room for gunk by restricting A.5 to conditions that are satisfied by *some* objects, one may perhaps avoid commitment to the universe and make room for junk by further requiring the relevant condition not to be satisfied by *all* objects.

(A.85) $(\exists x \varphi x \wedge \exists x \neg \varphi x) \rightarrow \exists z F_\varphi z$ *Almost Unrestricted Fusion*

Unfortunately, this option won't do. A.85 is indeed compatible with No Zero (T.2) as well as with No Top (A.76), as any two-element discrete order will show. However, while No Zero will in fact be true in every other model of A.1–A.4, No Top will fail. For let φ_1 and φ_2 be conditions of the form '$\neg x = a_1$' and '$\neg x = a_2$'. Since identity is reflexive, such conditions cannot be universally satisfied and A.85 will guarantee the existence of the corresponding fusions, z_1 and z_2, in any model with at least two elements. But as soon as we have further elements, the condition '$x = z_1 \vee x = z_2$' will also meet the two constraints in the antecedent of A.85, and so the axiom will give us a corresponding fusion, $z_1 + z_2$. Assuming $\neg a_1 = a_2$, we immediately have that $z_1 + z_2 = u$, violating No Top. A.85 rules out junk.

What about retaining the Unrestricted Fusion schema A.5 in its full generality and revising instead some other aspect of classical mereology? Classically, the existence of a universal fusion is incompatible with junk because PP is a strict partial order: u cannot be a proper part of anything short of being a proper part of itself (by Transitivity), which is impossible (by Irreflexivity or Asymmetry). But we know there's room for non-classical mereologies where the ordering axioms do not fully hold. In particular, a non-wellfounded mereology in which PP, treated as primitive, is neither irreflexive nor asymmetric allows for self-parts and mereological loops. Since such a theory is compatible with Unrestricted Fusion (as in Cotnoir and Bacon,

147 Bostock's mereology was devised for the foundations of arithmetic in the rational numbers, so it is as robust as it can be while admitting gunk and junk. A similar system is presented in Lucas (2000, §9.12). Further properties of systems in which A.5 is weakened to A.84, or rather its F′-type variant, are examined in Pietruszczak (2013, §III.8) and Gruszczyński and Pietruszczak (2014, §10). (These authors also consider the strengthening of A.84 obtained by adopting the Pairwise Underlap condition D.49 we met in section 5.2.1.) Cf. also Linnebo *et al.*'s (2016) mereological treatment of the Aristotelian continuum for an in-depth discussion of related issues.

2012), it follows that it can provide consistent models of universalism with junk. However, it should be stressed that these models—e.g. a model culminating in a top element that is a proper part of itself—do not correspond to what philosophers have in mind when discussing junk. Earlier we said that in non-antisymmetric settings one should understand Coatomism and Coatomlessness in terms of the alternate definition of PP in D.15 (PP_2). With PP treated as primitive, a similar remark applies to non-asymmetric contexts. In particular, A.81 should be strengthened to the following principle (with P defined as in D.12).

(A.86) $\forall x \exists y (\mathsf{PP}xy \land \neg \mathsf{P}yx)$ *Strict Coatomlessness*

And clearly this principle is inconsistent with A.5 regardless of wellfoundedness. If u is the fusion of everything, everything is part of u, hence there can't be any y such that $\mathsf{PP}uy$ *and* $\neg\mathsf{P}yu$.

So much for the tension between (Strict) Coatomlessness and mereological universalism. Let us just add that once A.5 is suitably weakened, Coatomlessness is just one option; one may equally well endorse non-trivial forms of Coatomism, with several maximal wholes that do not further compose. Moreover, each option can be consistently combined with either Atomism (A.6) or Atomlessness (A.31). Clearly any finite structure is a model of Atomism + Coatomism, and it's easy to see that the model we mentioned in connection with the conceivability of junk (the regular open regions of the Euclidean plane at non-zero distance from $\langle 0, 0 \rangle$) is also gunky, hence a model of Atomlessness + Coatomlessness. But mixed theories are also consistent. A simple model of Atomism + Coatomlessness is given by the set of all finite subsets of the positive integers, with P interpreted as the subset relation $\subseteq$; a model of Atomlessness + Coatomism is given by the same set, interpreting P as the converse of $\subseteq$. (Note that while these models violate A.5, they satisfy A.1–A.4 along with the weaker composition principles A.83 and A.84.)

Of course one might opt instead for weaker theories. As with atoms and gunk, one might hold that there are *some* coatoms, or there is *some* junk, whilst remaining neutral on the question of whether everything is part of a coatom or everything is junky.

(A.87) $\exists x \mathsf{C}x$ *Weak Coatomism*

(A.88) $\exists x \forall y (\mathsf{P}xy \to \neg \mathsf{C}y)$ *Weak Junk*

And, of course, there is always the hybrid view expressed by the conjunction of these two theses.

Indeed, as in section 4.6.3, other views are possible. One may hold that composition of entities of a certain kind φ—say, material objects—always results in coatoms, and yet suspend judgment on the ultimate compositional structure of other kinds of entity. That would amount to a relativized version of Coatomism, matching A.60.

(A.89) $\forall x(\varphi x \rightarrow \exists y(Cy \wedge Pxy))$ *φ–Coatomism*

One might think that entities of a given kind φ are junky—e.g. events *à la* Whitehead, or pure sets—while suspending judgment on this being true of other things. That would give us the dual of A.61.

(A.90) $\forall x(\varphi x \rightarrow \forall y(Pxy \rightarrow \neg Cy))$ *φ–Junk*

And similarly for any combination of such theses—for instance:

(A.91) $\forall x(\varphi x \rightarrow \forall y((Pyx \rightarrow \neg Ay) \wedge (Pxy \rightarrow \neg Cy)))$ *φ–Hunk*

As Bøhn (2009a, p. 28) reminds us, Leibniz himself endorsed a view of this sort with regard to the material world (on a pointy conception of atoms and a naive conception of the continuum):

> For, although there are atoms of substance, namely monads, which lack parts, there are no atoms of bulk [*moles*], that is, atoms of the least possible extension, nor are there any ultimate elements, since a continuum cannot be composed out of points. In just the same way, there is nothing greatest in bulk nor infinite in extension, even if there is always something bigger than anything else. ("On Nature itself", in Leibniz, 1989, p. 162)

These and similar principles of relative commitment are easily formulated, and can prove useful to model actual metaphysical views. As with their decompositional counterparts, however, they call for suitably enriched languages that go beyond the scope of pure mereological theorizing.

6

LOGIC

> *Stress is laid on the importance of considering language, which is an instrument of our thinking and is imperfect, as are all human creations.*
>
> — Susan Stebbing, *Logic in Practice* (1934, p. viii)

Throughout the foregoing we have been working within a framework that rests on a fundamental assumption, namely, that mereology is essentially a theory in classical first-order logic, with the parthood relation represented by a binary predicate. In this final chapter we consider various ways of extending or modifying the framework in response to a number of worries, some technical, some philosophical, that arise naturally in connection with that assumption. We begin in section 6.1 by considering extensions of classical mereology aimed at overcoming the expressive limits of standard first-order languages. We focus specifically on second-order extensions and on parallel formulations in languages with plural reference and quantification. We also discuss Lewis's megethology and applications to the philosophy of mathematics. In section 6.2 we consider several ways of modifying the framework to make room for mereological considerations involving time and modality, such as the possibility that an object may have different parts at different times, or that it could have had different parts from the ones it actually has. Lastly, in section 6.3 we survey a number of theories that can be developed in order to deal with the phenomenon of mereological indeterminacy, i.e. the fact that in some cases the very question of whether something is part of something else does not appear to have a definite answer. We do so by considering, first, the idea that the indeterminacy in question is merely linguistic, and therefore does not affect the parthood relation as such, and then several ways of modifying the logical framework to allow for objectively indeterminate, or even overdeterminate, mereological relationships.

6.1 EXPRESSIVE POWER

Classical mereology is a reasonably powerful theory, and it was meant to be so by its nominalistic forerunners, who were thinking of mereology as

Mereology. A. J. Cotnoir and Achille C. Varzi, Oxford University Press. © A. J. Cotnoir and Achille C. Varzi 2021. DOI: 10.1093/oso/9780198749004.003.0006

a good alternative to set theory. Its axioms can be neatly divided into ordering, decomposition, and composition principles; its models correspond to well-studied mathematical structures; its maximally consistent extensions form a well-defined family. As we mentioned, it is also decidable, whereas weaker theories such as Minimal Mereology and Minimal Extensional Mereology (see sections 4.2.2 and 4.3.1) are not.[1] Of course one may think that classical mereology is in fact *too* powerful. The last three chapters were in part devoted precisely to this thought, which led us to consider a number of weaker theories regardless of their mathematical virtues (or defects). But one may as well worry about the opposite question: is classical mereology as powerful as it is meant to be? This is a difficult question to address in the abstract, so one can hardly expect a straightforward answer. Nonetheless, there is a certain consensus that the answer is not quite in the affirmative. For all its *prima facie* strength and mathematical virtues, classical mereology suffers from several limitations, at least insofar as it is formulated as a first-order theory of the sort defined by A.1–A.5 and their extensions.

One important limitation was mentioned already in chapter 2: any such theory lacks the resources to say everything a mereologist would like to say. Most notably, it cannot say that *every* collection of things has a fusion. It can only postulate the existence of a fusion for collections that can be specified by means of formulas in the language. One can do so with the help of an infinitary axiom schema, which is why Unrestricted Fusion has the form it has; but since the language has a countable vocabulary (hence a countable set of formulas), only countably many collections can be identified this way. If the domain is infinite, uncountably many fusions will perforce be left out.

A second limitation is more general, and is intrinsic to every first-order theory. Take as an example the axioms of atomistic classical mereology (A.1–A.5 plus A.6) and add every instance of the Minimum Size schema A.54 to ensure there are infinitely many atoms. Where $\aleph_0$ is the countably infinite size, this theory will only have models with at least $\aleph_0$-many atoms, and should intuitively have a domain of size at least $2^{\aleph_0}$. (Recall from section 2.3.2 that all complete atomistic Boolean algebras have powerset representations; and recall the set-theoretic fact that if a set A has size κ, its powerset $\mathcal{P}(A)$ has size 2^{κ}.) That is, the domain of these models should be uncountable. Yet there are, in fact, countable models of this theory—models whose domain has size $\aleph_0$—as the so-called Löwenheim-Skolem theorems show.[2] In this case, a great many fusions have gone missing.

There are, in addition, actual limits to what one can *do* in mereological theories of this sort. For example, we know from section 4.6.3 that classical

1 For a comprehensive picture of decidability in mereology, see Tsai (2009, 2011, 2013a,b).

2 For a textbook presentation of the theorems, see e.g. Chang and Keisler (1973, §2.1); for an in-depth exposition, Ebbinghaus (2007b).

mereology has a limited number of (types of) maximally consistent extensions, including the atomistic extension we just mentioned, and no such extension appears to have the resources to provide a relative interpretation of even a small amount of what counts as accepted mathematics. Niebergall (2007, 2009b, §1.2) has shown that Peano arithmetic, or even the weaker theory known as Robinson Arithmetic (which does not have the axiom schema of mathematical induction), cannot be relatively interpreted in this sort of mereology. For a serious candidate alternative to set theory, this is obviously a disappointing result.

All of these limitations point to the of lack of expressive power of mereology insofar as it is defined and developed within a standard, first-order logico-linguistic framework. But there are alternatives. In this section we briefly outline the main options.

6.1.1 *Second-Order Mereology*

It is worth recalling that some early theories, such as Tarski's (1929) version of Leśniewski's Mereology and Leonard and Goodman's (1940) original formulation of the Calculus of Individuals, were stronger than the theory defined by A.1–A.5. They involved explicit quantification over sets in their statements of the Unrestricted Fusion postulate A.5 (or, more accurately, its variants A.11 and A.15) and this fact allowed them to overcome some of the limitations mentioned above. Quantifying over sets does not require that one be able to specify them by means of formulas in the language; one can say straight out, with the help of set variables, that *every* non-empty set of things has a fusion, and indeed one can say so by means of a single axiom.[3] The idea of resorting to a first-order axiom schema with an unbound metavariable came only with Goodman (1951) and was initially motivated by the nominalist ban on 'platonistic' modes of quantification.[4] Much literature that followed adopted the same expedient, and we have followed suit. Yet this deviation from the original theories is not immaterial; the resulting axiom system is strictly weaker. Indeed it is irredeemably weaker. It is an established fact that classical mereology, as originally understood, is *not elementarily axiomatizable* (Pietruszczak, 2000b, § III.2).[5]

3 Of course, if that were merely first-order quantification over sets, the theory would be no better off in terms of non-standard models. But the formal language of Leonard and Goodman (1940) is the type-theoretic language of Russell (1903). See Niebergall (2009b, p. 170) for discussion on this point.

4 Even though, strictly speaking, Goodman's nominalism does not necessarily abjure quantifying over sets: "Nominalism does not protect us from starting with ridiculous atoms; it protects us from manufacturing gimcracks out of sound atoms by the popular devices of platonism" (Goodman, 1956, p. 25; cf. Goodman, 1986, p. 160).

5 See also Pietruszczak (2015) and the Addendum to Tsai (2015).

To be sure, the expedient of resorting to an axiom schema—hence, effectively, to an infinity of axioms—is not the only option available for someone working within a standard first-order setting. Contrary to common lore, first-order classical mereology, too, can be finitely axiomatized. An elegant formulation of this result is due to Tsai (2018).[6] With P as a primitive, a finite axiomatization can be obtained from: the partial-order axioms (A.1–A.3), Strong Supplementation (A.18), Strong Complementation′ (A.34), Unrestricted Sum (A.83), and the existence of a universe (A.74), together with the following crucial instance of A.5.[7]

(A.92) $\exists x Ax \rightarrow \exists z F_{Ax} z$ *Fusion of Atoms*

This axiom says simply that whenever there are atoms, there is something they all compose. Only this instance of A.5 is needed. Or rather, since A.34, A.74, and A.83 can also be seen as special cases of A.5,[8] only these four instances are required instead of the infinitely many ones posited by the Unrestricted Axiom schema.[9] (Indeed, in an atomistic mereology the fusion of all atoms adds up to u, whose existence is already guaranteed by A.74, so A.92 would be redundant. Similarly, if there are no atoms at all, then A.92 is vacuously true and hence, again, superfluous. Thus an immediate corollary of Tsai's result is that the extensions of classical mereology obtained by endorsing either Atomism, A.6, or Atomlessness, A.31, can be finitely axiomatized even *without* the special help of A.92; the other seven axioms will suffice.[10])

---

6 A similar result is stated in Niebergall (2009a, p. 343; 2011, p. 288), with unpublished proof in Niebergall (2009c). An even earlier finite axiomatization along these lines, ignored in subsequent literature, was given by Pietruszczak (2000b, § VI.9, orig. §VI.7).

7 Tsai uses the F''-variants of A.83 and A.92. But given his other axioms, we can prove the $\exists$-Strong Overlap principle A.65, which means our F-type axioms entail the F''-variants (see section 5.1.2). Here is a proof. Assume $\exists x \varphi x$ and $F_\varphi z$. Pick y so that Oyz and for *reductio* suppose $\forall x(\varphi x \rightarrow Dyx)$. Since every φer is part of z by D.6 (first conjunct) and P is transitive and reflexive, we must have $\neg Pzy$. By A.34, y has a complement, y', such that $\forall w(Pwy' \leftrightarrow Dwy)$. So every φer is part of y', since by supposition every φer is disjoint from y. But then y' is an upper bound of the φs, and hence Pzy by D.6 (second conjunct). Contradiction. So $\neg\forall x(\varphi x \rightarrow Dyx)$, hence $\exists x(\varphi x \wedge Oyx)$ as required by A.65.

8 This is obvious for A.74 and A.83, given the definitions of u and $+$ in section 2.1.3. As for A.34, Tsai (2018, fn. 1) notes that in classical mereology it is equivalent to $\forall w(\exists x Dxw \rightarrow \exists z \forall y(Oyz \leftrightarrow \exists x(Dxw \wedge Oyx)))$, which is an instance of A.15 and thus, indirectly, of A.5.

9 Tsai also lists Unrestricted Product (A.37), though this further instance is not needed: when $x = u$ (or $y = u$), $x \times y$ reduces to y (to x); otherwise, given Oxy, $x \times y$ is just $(x' + y')'$, whose existence follows from A.34 and A.83. By contrast, note that Strong Supplementation is not redundant despite A.34. This is shown by a partial order with four elements, a, b, c, u, such that Pab, Pbu, and Pcu. (Thanks to Hsing-chien Tsai for clarifying this point.)

10 This reinforces the claims of sections 4.6.1 and 4.6.2 concerning the simplifications afforded by such theories. In fact, one can push such simplifications even further. The atomistic extension of classical mereology of Hodges and Lewis (1968) mentioned in section 4.6.1, based on O as

This is an important result. Not only does it deliver an actual alternative to the expedient of an axiom schema; given the compactness theorem of classical logic, it also follows that *any* first-order axiomatization of classical mereology includes, within itself, a finite axiomatization.[11] The result is appealing also from a strictly nominalist perspective, considering that standard set theory (ZFC) is not finitely axiomatizable short of inconsistency.[12] Nevertheless the picture does not change. Finitely axiomatized or not, the expressive limitations of first-order classical mereology remain. In particular, trading the full strength of Unrestricted Fusion for a few instances is certainly not going to make up the missing fusions. The only hope to transcend these limits is to shift to languages that are genuinely more powerful. In the literature, two main strategies have been considered, and the first is precisely the one we find exemplified in the early formulations of classical mereology due to Tarski (1929) and Leonard and Goodman (1940): a language that permits explicit quantification into predicate position. Let us see in brief how this can be done.

Syntactically, the shift is rather straightforward. For our purposes we will only need our quantifiers to bind *one-place* predicates, using a system sometimes called *monadic second-order logic*. If we label the language of our first-order logic in A.0 as L^1, then let the language with P as a primitive predicate be called $\langle L^1, P \rangle$. We now extend L^1 by adding a countable stock of one-place second-order variables X, Y, Z, ..., giving us the monadic second-order language $\langle L^2, P \rangle$. The grammar of this language is essentially the same as the grammar of $\langle L^1, P \rangle$ given in section 1.5, except that we also have atomic formulas of the form 'Xx' (for 'x is X'). Then we can use our quantifiers to bind both sorts of variables, writing e.g $\exists x \forall Y Yx$ for 'Some x is every Y', $\exists X \forall y (Xy \to Pyz)$ for 'For some X, every y that is X is part of z', etc.

Semantically, we have some options. There are two main ways of interpreting $\langle L^2, P \rangle$: *standard* models, where the domain of second-order quantifiers must comprise the full powerset of the first-order domain, and so-called *general* or *Henkin* models, where second-order quantifiers range over

---

primitive with P defined *à la* Goodman (D.14), consists exclusively of A.6 together with the Overlapping Parts axiom A.13 and the following variants of A.34 and A.83:

$$\forall x(\exists z \forall y(Pyz \leftrightarrow Dyx) \leftrightarrow \neg \forall y Oyx)$$
$$\forall x \forall y \exists z \forall w(Owz \leftrightarrow (Owx \vee Owy))$$

The same axiomatization may be found in Niebergall (2009a, 2011), who also briefly considers the parallel atomless system obtained by replacing A.6 with A.31.

11 The compactness theorem (from Gödel, 1930) guarantees that a first-order theory T implies a formula φ if and only if there is some finite $T' \subseteq T$ that implies φ. If T is a first-order axiomatization of classical mereology, it must imply the conjunction of Tsai's axioms (along with its consequences). Hence there must be some finite $T' \subseteq T$ that suffices for the job.

12 This has been known since Montague (1961). The same is not true of other axiom systems for set theory, such as those of von Neumann (1925) and Bernays (1937) and of Quine (1937).

some non-empty subset of that powerset.[13] These different semantics yield drastically differing metatheoretic results. Full second-order languages with standard semantics violate the Löwenheim-Skolem theorems, they fail to be compact, and no deductive system for them can be complete.[14] By contrast, second-order languages with Henkin semantics satisfy all the usual metatheorems of first-order languages, including the Löwenheim-Skolem theorems, compactness, and completeness.[15] Second-order languages with Henkin semantics have effectively the expressive power of a two-sorted first-order language. But under standard semantics, second-order languages have much more oomph: many important second-order theories (e.g. arithmetic and analysis) are *categorical*, in the sense that all their models are isomorphic.[16] For some mereological theories, the difference between Henkin and standard models is immaterial (for instance, theories stating there are exactly n-many atoms are categorical in both cases; see Niebergall, 2009b, §4.2). But for most systems, the difference matters.[17]

To focus on classical mereology, let us first adapt our existing definitions of fusions (D.6, D.13, D.16) to the new language. This can be done as follows, where 'X' is a monadic second-order variable.

(D$_*$1) $F_X z :\equiv \forall x(Xx \to Pxz) \wedge \forall y(\forall x(Xx \to Pxy) \to Pzy)$ *2nd-Order Fusion*
(D$_*$2) $F'_X z :\equiv \forall x(Xx \to Pxz) \wedge \forall y(Pyz \to \exists x(Xx \wedge Oyx))$ *2nd-Order Fusion′*
(D$_*$3) $F''_X z :\equiv \forall y(Oyz \leftrightarrow \exists x(Xx \wedge Oyx))$ *2nd-Order Fusion″*

The corresponding Unrestricted Fusion axiom schemas (A.5, A.11, A.15) can now be written as single axioms:

(A$_*$1) $\forall X(\exists x Xx \to \exists z F_X z)$ *2nd-Order Unrestricted Fusion*
(A$_*$2) $\forall X(\exists x Xx \to \exists z F'_X z)$ *2nd-Order Unrestricted Fusion′*
(A$_*$3) $\forall X(\exists x Xx \to \exists z F''_X z)$ *2nd-Order Unrestricted Fusion″*

These axioms assert the existence of a fusion of the relevant type for every non-empty set of things over which we are quantifying with our second-order variables.

One would like each of A$_*$1–A$_*$3 to entail all instances of its corresponding first-order axiom schema, where e.g. for each ψ appearing in the latter we assign to X the set of all objects satisfying ψ. In standard models, we are guaranteed that such a set is always available, and so the entailment goes

13 The distinction goes back to Henkin (1950).
14 See Shapiro (1991, §4.2) for precisely stated results and proofs.
15 See Shapiro (1991, §4.3).
16 For proofs, see again Shapiro (1991, §4.2).
17 Much of the presentation that follows is indebted to Niebergall (2009b), which contains a lot more material than can be discussed here. See also Niebergall (2009a, §4).

through. With Henkin models there is no guarantee that the set of all ψs exists. To overcome this problem, we can however force the existence of that set axiomatically: for all $\langle L^2, P\rangle$ formulas ψ with no occurrences of 'X', we add the following to our logical axioms.

(A_*4) $\exists X \forall x(Xx \leftrightarrow \psi x)$ *Comprehension*

A Comprehension schema of this sort (which holds automatically in standard models) is sufficient to guarantee the desired result. For instance, all Henkin models satisfying A_*4 will satisfy (the universal closure of) every instance of the following second-order fusion schema, where ψ is any $\langle L^2, P\rangle$ formula with no occurrences of 'z':[18]

(T_*1) $\exists x\psi x \rightarrow \exists z F''_{\psi} z$ *2nd-Order Unrestricted Fusion'' Schema*

Note that the first-order schema A.15 itself is an instance of T_*1, since $\langle L^1, P\rangle$ is included in $\langle L^2, P\rangle$ (and, again, every instance of T_*1 is satisfied in standard models). Alternatively, we might opt for a weaker version of Comprehension, including only instances of A_*4 where ψ is an $\langle L^2, P\rangle$ formula with no occurrences of 'X' and no bound second-order variables. This weaker form of Comprehension will still suffice for the entailment from A_*3 to every instance of A.15. But the weaker version will not always result in the truth of every instance of T_*1.[19]

Standard second-order systems are of special interest, here, precisely because they give us classical mereologies in the sense of Tarski (1929) and Leonard and Goodman (1940). In particular, they have sufficient expressive power to guarantee a full correspondence between their models and complete Boolean algebras without a 'zero' element, as promised in section 2.2.[20] Thus, the first important limitation of first-order mereology mentioned above is overcome. But there is more. These systems have sufficient expressive power to rule out undesired non-standard models. For example, consider the theory of infinitary atomistic classical mereology discussed in the beginning, i.e. A.1–A.5 plus A.6 plus every instance of A.54. If we use A_*1 instead of A.5, all standard models of the theory will have a domain with the expected cardinality of at least $2^{\aleph_0}$. And moreover, all models of size $2^{\aleph_0}$ are isomorphic. In other words, this theory is $2^{\aleph_0}$-categorical.[21]

18 Niebergall (2009b, p. 183), Lemma 6.
19 See Niebergall (2009b, pp. 181ff) for details.
20 This is how the correspondence was announced in Tarski (1935). For a proof, see again Niebergall (2009b, §3), who actually uses an axiom system comprised of the two variants of A.34 and A.83 mentioned in note 10 together with Overlapping Parts (A.13) and the 2nd-Order Unrestricted Fusion'' axiom A_*3. For other axioms systems, see e.g. the proofs in Pietruszczak (2000b, ch. 3) and Pontow and Schubert (2006, §4).
21 Niebergall (2009b, pp. 190f), Lemma 21.

There remains the fact that such benefits come at the ontological cost associated with second-order quantification. Particularly, a nominalist might share Quine's scruples that second-order logic is "set theory in sheep's clothing" (Quine, 1970, p. 66) and is therefore unacceptable.[22] To be sure, second-order systems have sometimes been used for avowed nominalistic purposes. Apart from the original formulation of the Calculus of Individuals, a primary example is Hartry Field's *Science without Numbers* (1980), which relies on the monadic second-order mereology of space-time points—described as "the complete logic of Goodmanian sums" (p. 38)—as a way of securing quantification over space-time regions. Yet even Field expressed reservations about this strategy in the preface to the second edition of his work (Field, 2016, pp. P22–P24), opting for schematic fusions instead.

6.1.2 *Plural Quantification and Megethology*

The second strategy available to transcend the limits of first-order mereology is more 'nominalist-friendly'. It consists in enriching our first-order language $\langle L^1, P\rangle$ by allowing for *plural* quantification. This is actually close to what Leśniewski's Mereology would look like if we tried to do justice to the peculiarities of its underlying logical system (Ontology), which is neither first-order nor second-order but rather employs quantifiable terms that admit singular as well as plural interpretations (see especially Leśniewski, 1927–1931, part XI: "On 'singular' propositions of the type '$A\varepsilon b$'").[23]

Plural logic as we know it today was developed by George Boolos (1984, 1985a) with an eye toward providing a nominalistically acceptable language with the expressive power of second-order logic and another eye on plural quantification as it occurs in ordinary language.[24] Some ordinary sentences are provably inexpressible in first-order terms, but can easily be handled using plural quantifiers. A famous example is the so-called Geach-Kaplan sentence reported in some writings of Quine's (1973, p. 111; 1974, p. 238) and picked up by Boolos himself (1984, p. 432), 'Some critics admire only one another', meaning 'There are critics each *of whom* admires only other ones *of them*'. Another example, already mentioned in section 3.3, is the transitive closure of a given relation, also called the *ancestral* of the relation, which isn't

22 Though this view has since been challenged in various ways and on various grounds; see e.g. Rayo and Yablo (2001), Wright (2007), and Turner (2015).

23 Cf. chapter 1, note 17. Here Simons (1982c; 1987, §§4.3–4.5; 1992) is especially helpful. See also Simons (1997b) for explicit comparisons with contemporary plural logic as presented below and Simons (1982b) for related views and historical background.

24 For a brief introduction to plural logic, see Linnebo (2017); for a fuller treatment, Oliver and Smiley (2013b). See also McKay (2006) for a more natural-language oriented approach and the essays in Carrara *et al.* (2016) for applications and discussion. At some point, plural logic was also known as "plethynticology" (after Burgess and Rosen, 1997, § II.C.1b).

first-order definable but can be defined using plural quantifiers.[25] Here's a definition of the transitive closure of the 'parent of' relation.

> Napoleon is Peter's ancestor iff, whenever there are some people such that each parent of Peter is one of them, and each parent of one of them is one of them, then Napoleon is one of them. (Lewis, 1991, p. 63, following Boolos, 1985a, pp. 328f)

To formalize plural quantification, we can use plural variables, written by doubling first-order variables as in 'xx', 'yy', 'zz', etc., and bind them with the familiar quantifiers $\exists$ and $\forall$. Notice that the above examples employ the 'is one of' locution to indicate the relationship between a single thing and a plurality. In plural logic, this is treated as a primitive binary predicate, typically written '$\prec$', and corresponds closely to the copula of Leśniewski's Ontology, ε. It takes a singular variable in its first argument place and a plural variable in the second. In principle, other predicates could be allowed to take both singular and plural arguments, especially if one's aim is to model ordinary language (consider: 'The risk *outweighs* the benefits', 'The benefits *outweigh* the risk', etc.). For most purposes, however, one may ignore this option and treat all other predicates, except perhaps the identity predicate $=$, as n-ary functors that combine with singular variables in the usual fashion. Thus, for instance, the Geach-Kaplan sentence can be formalized as

$$(6.1)\quad \exists xx(\forall y(y \prec xx \to Cy) \land \forall y \forall z((y \prec xx \land Ayz) \to (z \prec xx \land \neg y = z)))$$

In words: 'There are some things, the xx, such that each of them is a critic, and such that for all y and z, if y is one of the xx and admires z, then z is one of the xx and is distinct from y'.

Let us, then, extend $\langle L^1, P\rangle$ to a two-sorted language $\langle L^{\prec}, P\rangle$ with both singular and plural variables and $\prec$ as an additional logical constant next to $=$. In a way, this is just a notational variant of $\langle L^2, P\rangle$; we are just trading each second order variable X for a plural variable xx and re-writing each atomic formula Xx as $x \prec xx$.[26] And indeed, a semantics for $\langle L^{\prec}, P\rangle$ can easily be given by taking the plural variables to range over subsets of the domain of quantification assigned to the singular variables, interpreting $\prec$ as the membership relation. On this *set-based* semantics (which admits standard as well as Henkin models), plural logic is essentially a first-order rendering of monadic second-order logic.[27] But $\langle L^{\prec}, P\rangle$ can also be given a bona fide

25 Ancestorhood is easily defined in second-order logic, following Frege (1879, §26). As Rossberg and Cohnitz (2009, fn. 18) note, the unavailability of Frege's definition in a first-order setting turned out to be a recurring concern in early contemporary nominalist programs, from Goodman and Quine (1947, pp. 108f) to Goodman (1951, §IX.5) and Henkin (1962, pp. 188f).

26 See Smirnov (1983) for a parallel analysis of Leśniewski's Ontology.

27 A Quinean might say that, on this semantics, plural logic actually unmasks the "sheep's clothing" of monadic second-order logic.

plurality-based semantics, where the plural variables do not range over sets but, rather, range plurally over things in the domain of the singular variables, with $\prec$ interpreted literally as the relation *is one of*. It is this plurality-based semantics that Boolos advocated, and that a nominalist might find congenial. One can still distinguish between standard and Henkin models, depending on whether the plural variables are taken to range over all pluralities from the domain or just some, and only the latter will have the limitative properties of first-order logic (such as the Löwenheim-Skolem theorems).[28] But a plurality-based semantics will bear no commitment to sets, or to properties; it will not call for any entities beyond the ones already included in the first-order domain.[29]

Axiomatically, one might adopt instances of the following schema, where ψ is any formula in which the plural variable xx has no free occurrences.

(A_*5) $\exists x\psi x \rightarrow \exists xx\forall x(x \prec xx \leftrightarrow \psi x)$ *Plural Comprehension*

This schema guarantees the existence of a plurality for every satisfiable condition ψ: if there is at least one thing that is ψ, there is a plurality comprising all and only those things that are ψ. Since a condition may have a unique satisfier, this means that one-member pluralities are allowed.[30] However, unlike the second-order Comprehension schema A_*4, A_*5 is restricted to satisfiable conditions.[31] For this reason, some have thought that instances of A_*5 are straightforwardly *logically true* (Boolos, 1985b), or at least *ontologically innocent* (Boolos, 1984; Lewis, 1991, 1993b).[32] The non-existence of empty pluralities is sometimes assumed explicitly as a further axiom.

(A_*6) $\forall xx\exists x\, x \prec xx$ *Non-emptiness*

---

28 Plurality-based Henkin semantics are not common, but see e.g. Florio and Linnebo (2016, §2 and Appendices). Note that we follow the popular convention of using 'plurality' as a grammatically singular convenience for *some things* (plural).

29 In this sense, the semantics in question may also be seen as offering a nominalist-friendly interpretation of monadic second-order logic, in contrast with Quine's contention. As Boolos puts it, "we need not think that there are collections of (say) Cheerios in addition to the Cheerios" (Boolos, 1984, p. 449). For more on the relationships between plural logic and monadic first-order logic, see Linnebo (2017, §2) and Uzquiano (2018a, §§3.2–3.4).

30 Thus, if we allowed all predicates to take both singular and plural arguments, trading 'is one of' for 'are some of', on a plurality-based semantics we could do away with singular variables altogether (Rayo, 2002, §11). This would result in a one-sorted language that is even closer to Leśniewski's, though not in line with standard practice.

31 Very few authors allow for empty pluralities, though see e.g. Burgess and Rosen (1997, §II.C.i.b) and Linnebo (2010), where the antecedent of A_*5 is dropped altogether and Plural Comprehension is identified with the consequent.

32 This is matter of controversy. For an overview of the issues, see Linnebo (2017, §5). For actual discussion, see e.g. Yi (2002, 2005–2006), Hossack (2000), Oliver and Smiley (2001, 2013b), and Rayo (2002) versus Resnik (1988), Parsons (1990, §6), Hazen (1993), Shapiro (1993), Rouilhan (2002), Linnebo (2003), and Florio and Linnebo (2016).

Given our plural language with a plurality-based semantics, we can now reformulate mereological theories within it in ways that parallel the second-order treatment in section 6.1.1. The definitions of the various types of fusion become:

$$(D_*4)\quad F_{xx}z :\equiv \forall x(x \prec xx \to Pxz) \land \forall y(\forall x(x \prec xx \to Pxy) \to Pzy) \qquad \textit{Pl. Fusion}$$
$$(D_*5)\quad F'_{xx}z :\equiv \forall x(x \prec xx \to Pxz) \land \forall y(Pyz \to \exists x(x \prec xx \land Oyx)) \qquad \textit{Pl. Fusion}'$$
$$(D_*6)\quad F''_{xx}z :\equiv \forall y(Oyz \leftrightarrow \exists x(x \prec xx \land Oyx)) \qquad \textit{Pl. Fusion}''$$

Correspondingly, the universalist intuition behind the fusion axiom schemas A.5, A.11, and A.15 can again be expressed by means of single axioms, and without the limitations deriving from the need to identify pluralities by means of formulas in the language:[33]

$$(A_*7)\quad \forall xx(\exists x\, x \prec xx \to \exists z F_{xx}z) \qquad \textit{Plural Unrestricted Fusion}$$
$$(A_*8)\quad \forall xx(\exists x\, x \prec xx \to \exists z F'_{xx}z) \qquad \textit{Plural Unrestricted Fusion}'$$
$$(A_*9)\quad \forall xx(\exists x\, x \prec xx \to \exists z F''_{xx}z) \qquad \textit{Plural Unrestricted Fusion}''$$

Of course, in the presence of Non-emptiness the antecedent of these axioms may in each case be dropped. Moreover, Plural Comprehension will guarantee that the relative comparisons of section 5.1.2 apply *mutatis mutandis*. In particular, all three axioms will be provably equivalent from the remaining axioms of classical mereology, A.1–A.4.

Plural Comprehension has other interesting consequences. A notable one is that each fusion axiom will imply a corresponding "covering" thesis (Sider, 2014, p. 212). For instance:

$$(T_*2)\quad \forall x \forall y(Pxy \to \exists xx(F_{xx}y \land x \prec xx)) \qquad \textit{Plural Covering}$$

This thesis says that any part of a given thing y is one of some things whose plural F-fusion is y itself. Similarly for F'-type and F''-type fusions.[34] Such theses cannot be expressed in standard first-order mereology, although it is noteworthy that an analogue of the F'-version of T_*2 features explicitly in Leśniewski's system (1927–1931, thm. CCLXIII). Likewise for other important theses one may consider, including the thesis that the 'are' of mereological composition is just a plural form of the 'is' of identity, i.e. strong CAI (section 5.2.3). As long as the identity predicate is allowed to take both singular

33 It is worth noting that van Inwagen's original formulation of the Special Composition Question used plural quantified variables (written as 'xs', 'ys', etc.); see van Inwagen (1987, p. 22) and the detailed explanation in van Inwagen (1990, pp. 23ff).

34 In each case, the relevant variant of T_*2 can be proved by taking xx to comprise x and y itself (assuming A.1). But typically xx will have other witnesses. For instance, in the presence of A.4, one can take xx to comprise x and its relative complement, $y - x$.

and plural arguments, a literal rendering of that thesis is now readily available. For instance:

$$(\mathrm{A}_*10)\quad \forall xx \forall z(F_{xx}z \rightarrow xx = z) \qquad \textit{Strong Composition as Identity}$$

Indeed, a radical CAI theorist may want to go further and strengthen A_*10 and the like to a biconditional (what Sider, 2007a, p. 59 calls "Superstrong CAI"), or perhaps even to a direct definition in lieu of A_*7–A_*9 (as Bøhn, 2014a, p. 145 recommends).

$$(\mathrm{D}_*7)\quad F'''_{xx}z :\equiv xx = z \qquad \textit{Plural Fusion}'''$$

If so, then our CAI theorist might also wish to strengthen T_*2 in the same spirit, with the result that mereology as a whole would be reduced to the general theory of pluralities.[35]

$$(\mathrm{D}_*8)\quad Pxy :\equiv \exists xx(F'''_{xx}y \wedge x \prec xx) \qquad \textit{Parthood}$$

So, not only does plural mereology overcome the model-theoretic limits of first-order mereology mentioned at the beginning of the chapter; it also provides the resources to express substantive views about parts and wholes that standard first-order mereology is unable to handle, including radically reductive views. And because they can be expressed formally, the import of such views *vis-à-vis* other mereological principles can be assessed more fully. For instance, we can now see that strong CAI does not by itself entail that fusion is unrestricted, i.e. A_*7, since A_*10 does not specify *when* the relevant identities hold (and similarly for the F'-type and F''–type variants of these principles).[36] And we can see why strong CAI is at odds with the usual laws of identity. Given just the following instance of Leibniz's law,

$$(\mathrm{A}_*11)\quad \forall xx \forall yy(xx = yy \rightarrow \forall z(z \prec xx \leftrightarrow z \prec yy)) \qquad \textit{Plural Indiscernibility}$$

A_*10 quickly yields the plural analogue of P-Collapse (T.49), i.e.

$$(\mathrm{T}_*3)\quad \forall xx \forall z(F_{xx}z \rightarrow \forall y(Pyz \leftrightarrow y \prec xx)) \qquad \textit{Plural Collapse}$$

35 This is essentially Bøhn's (2014a) proposal, though he does away with $\prec$ as well by invoking a modified grammatical apparatus that allows D_*8 to be written as $Pxy :\equiv \exists zz F_{xzz}y$. Cf. also Bricker (2016, §4), who endorses both D_*7 and D_*8 and derives the definiens of D_*5 as a theorem (under suitable assumptions). However, Bricker's generalized identity relation does not fully obey Leibniz's law and his view diverges from strong CAI in important respects.

36 See again the debate between Cameron (2012) versus Merricks (2005) and Sider (2007a) cited in section 5.2.3. As noted there, the point applies also if A_*10 is strengthened to a biconditional, or to a definition such as D_*8, though in that case one would obviously get Unrestricted Composition for free if identity were assumed to obey the axiom $\forall xx \exists y\, xx = y$ (what Bricker, 2016, p. 271 calls "E pluribus unum").

and we know this is unacceptable. Munkustrap's tail is part of the fusion of Munkustrap and Jellylorum, but it is not one of *them*.[37] More precisely, T_*3 is unacceptable insofar as plural logic is governed by the Plural Comprehension principle A_*5, which tells us that *there is* a plurality comprised of Munkustrap and Jellylorum. It is unlikely that a strong CAI theorist may be willing to deny this. But, technically, one may consider restricting A_*5 somehow, and this would path the way to the study of novel, non-standard ways of developing mereology within the framework of a plural logic.[38]

Because of all these reasons, plural formulations of mereology have become increasingly popular among philosophers. In relation to classical mereology, perhaps the most influential example is the mereological framework of David Lewis's *Parts of Classes* (1991), whose similarity with Leśniewski's original Mereology he notes explicitly.[39] Lewis's framework is axiomatized using Transitivity (A.3), Plural Unrestricted Fusion′ (A_*8), and a plural version of the uniqueness principle for F'-type fusions (T.44):

$$(A_*12)\quad \forall xx \forall z \forall w((F'_{xx}z \wedge F'_{xx}w) \rightarrow z = w) \qquad \textit{Uniqueness of Plural Fusion}'$$

Under a plural-logic reading of Leśniewski's framework, this is exactly the axiom system of Mereology that we met informally in section 1.2.2 and then again, more formally, in section 2.4.1.[40]

Indeed, Lewis's framework proves especially illuminating when it comes to assessing the strength and benefits of a plural formulation of mereology. For him classical mereology with plural quantification is not just a theory of parts and wholes; it is authentic "megethology". Provided the range of the plural variables encompasses all pluralities from the domain, the additional expressive power turns out to be enough "to define distinctions in the size of things" (Lewis, 1991, p. 88) and "to let us express interesting hypotheses about the size of Reality" (1993b, p. 3). ('Megethology' comes from μέγεθος, 'size'.[41]) For example, Lewis identifies definable axioms which, when added

37 The proof of T_*3 matches the informal argument for T.49 given in section 5.2.3, note 86, using Plural Covering to get $y \prec xx$ from Pyz in the left-to-right direction. It is in the present form (though based on F') that P-Collapse was originally discussed by Sider (2007a).

38 For instance, Sider (2014, p. 215) suggests the following "Weak Comprehension" principle:

$$\exists x \psi x \rightarrow \exists z(F'_{\psi}z \wedge \exists xx \forall x(x \prec xx \leftrightarrow Pxz))$$

while Loss (in press-a) considers the atomistic variant of this principle obtained by replacing 'Pxz' with '$Ax \wedge Pxz$' (so that Strong CAI would equate every composite entity with the plurality of its atomic parts). See also Loss (in press-b) for a general assessment of such moves.

39 See Lewis (1991, ch. 3, fn. 5). Lewis also acknowledges the similarity of his framework with the ensemble theory of Bunt (1985), which, however, uses sets instead of pluralities.

40 Actually, Leśniewski's axioms also included Antisymmetry, though we saw it is redundant.

41 Lewis may have meant it as a neologism, though the term has a few occasional precedents in the history of mathematics (beginning with John Dee's *Mathematicall Praeface*, 1570) and appears in several manuscripts on the theory of magnitudes in Brentano's *Nachlass* (Binder, 2019).

to the classical mereology of countably infinite atoms, have only models of size $2^{\aleph_0}$ and no larger (1991, §3.7). This theory is categorical *tout court*.[42]

But, more importantly, Lewis's theory delivers a full picture of the scope of mereology as a foundational framework for set theory. Lewis's main aim is reductive: he wants to understand standard iterative set theory with minimal resources. And he shows that this can be done using plural classical mereology together with just a primitive singleton-forming operator (governed by axioms that closely resemble the axioms for 'successor' in Peano arithmetic).[43] Using only these resources, Lewis manages to recover all of ZFC, vindicating the intuition that "mysterious singletons" make all the difference between the framework of megethology and standard set theory.[44]

> Take a non-empty class to have exactly its non-empty subclasses as parts, hence its singleton subclasses as atomic parts. Then standard set theory becomes the theory of the member-singleton function—better, the theory of all singleton functions—within the framework of megethology. (Lewis, 1993b, p. 23, Abstract)

One can even eliminate the singleton function if one permits quantification over relations (i.e., effectively, dyadic plural quantification), or similarly if one can define a pairing function on the domain.[45] Burgess *et al.* (1991) showed that pairing is in fact definable in plural mereology on the assumption that the universe is infinite and atomistic (or with infinitely many atoms and not too much gunk).[46] However, it is well known that any formal theory based in a monadic second-order language that admits a pairing function is equivalent to that same theory in *full* second-order logic (Shapiro, 1991, p. 221). Given the close relationship between $\langle L^{\prec}, P\rangle$ and $\langle L^2, P\rangle$, one might therefore question whether the 'innocent' resources presupposed in *Parts of Classes* are nominalistically acceptable after all.

That mereology alone will not suffice for a nominalist grounding of set theory has been shown by Hamkins and Kikuchi (2016) directly with reference to the structure $\langle V, \subseteq\rangle$, where V is the universe of all sets.[47] They also proved, however, that every model of set theory $\langle V, \in\rangle$ would be definable

42 For more on cardinality in Lewis's framework, see Carrara and Martino (2011b). Cf. also Carrara and Martino (2015) on grounding megethology on plural reference *without* mereology.

43 Set theory can be reduced using other mereologies, such as the framework of Fine (2010). See Caplan *et al.* (2010) for a way to carry out the program. For more on Lewis's own theory, see Ridder (2002, ch. 5), Burgess (2015), Richard (2015), and Werner (2015).

44 In fact, Lewis (1991, p. 101) proves a plural (rather than schematic) formulation of the set-theoretic axiom of Restricted Comprehension (5.10), which is for him a theorem. He also assumes a plural choice principle (pp. 72f) in order to prove the axiom of choice for sets (pp. 103f).

45 A pairing function is a binary function f such that $f(x, y) = f(z, w)$ only if $x = z$ and $y = w$. With a pairing-forming operator treated as primitive (instead of the singleton function), one can actually carry out Lewis's program with first-order mereology; see Carrara and Martino (2016).

46 See also Hazen (1997, 2000) on simulating quantification over relations even without atoms.

47 See Hamkins and Kikuchi (2016, thm. 12).

from a corresponding singleton-expanded model $\langle V, \subseteq, s \rangle$ by taking '$x \in y$' to mean '$s(x) \subseteq y$'.[48] So, again, from the viewpoint of the foundations of mathematics, there is reason to conclude that classical mereology enriched with a singleton operator "is basically equivalent to membership-based set theory" (*ibid.*, p. 302).

The emerging picture is thus indicative of the intrinsic limits of mereology as a foundational theory for all of mathematics, but also of its potential when combined with other tools.[49] Goodman and Quine's (1947) early use of mereology to provide a formalist, "purely nominalistic" syntax language;[50] Słupecki's (1958) attempt to extend mereology to ground the theory of types; Hellman's (1996) modal extension of Lewis's framework on behalf of a structuralist program; the recent proposals of Urbaniak (2016), who expands Leśniewski's framework to prove abstraction principles for neologicism, and of Welch and Horsten (2016), who rely on mereology to give a philosophical interpretation of proper classes—in all these cases, the question is not whether mereology alone suffices. The question, in the end, is whether the additional tools are acceptable.

6.2 TIME AND MODALITY

We now turn to the second worry concerning our basic mereological framework—its apparent unfitness to deal with the ductility of much ordinary and philosophical discourse about parts and wholes. This worry may also be put in terms of expressive limits, though in this case the limits are significant especially from a metaphysical standpoint. On the assumption that at least some things can undergo mereological change (as with the case of Dion and Theon from chapter 3),[51] we may wish to say that what counts as part of an object at some time may not be part of it at a different time. Or we may want to say that an object has the parts it has only contingently, i.e. that it could have been composed of different parts than the ones it actually has. Yet such talk would seem to escape the expressive resources of a language whose only non-logical constant is the binary predicate 'x is part of y'.

Even if we wanted to *disavow* mereological ductility, we would need to make room for temporal and modal considerations in order to express our

48 Hamkins and Kikuchi (2016, thm. 13). Cf. Lewis's mereological definition: x is a member of y if and only if y is a class and the singleton of x is part of y (Lewis, 1991, p. 16). The definition in Bunt (1985, p. 61) is similar, though without the restriction on y being a class, resulting in a *sui generis* membership relation that differs from that in set theory.

49 See Hellman (2017) for a general discussion of this point.

50 See also the use of mereology for "protosyntax" in Quine (1951a).

51 The case of mereological diminution illustrated by the Dion/Theon puzzle has of course a parallel in mereological increase; see Chisholm (1976, pp. 157ff) and Olson (2006). For other paradigmatic cases of mereological change, see Hirsch (1982, ch. 1) and Price (1988).

view. For instance, Chisholm (1973, p. 581f) identifies the denial of any temporal and modal change of parts with the following two theses, respectively.

- *Mereological Constancy* If x is ever a part of y, then it is part of y at every time at which y exists.
- *Mereological Essentialism* If x is part of y, then it is part of y in every possible world in which y exists.

Theses of this sort have occasionally been held by philosophers, from Boethius ("If a part of a whole perishes, the whole will no longer exist"; *De divisione*, 879c) to Abelard ("No thing has more or fewer parts at one time than at another"; *Dialectica*, III, ii, 9) to Leibniz ("We cannot say, speaking according to the great truth of things, that the same whole is preserved when a part is lost"; *New Essays*, II, xxvii, 11) all the way to Chisholm himself.[52] Yet it would appear that both theses transcend the exiguous language of our mereological theories, including the logically richer extensions considered above.[53] They transcend it even if, in a way, their truth would *justify* such a language. Similarly for other theses of this sort, including various ways of combining them and perhaps also their holistic counterparts.[54]

- *Hological Constancy* If x is ever a part of y, then it is part of y at every time at which x exists.
- *Hological Essentialism* If x is part of y, then it is part of y in every possible world in which x exists.

How can we do justice to such theses? How can we account for the view of someone who, for example, accepts constancy but rejects essentialism, or accepts one form of constancy/essentialism but not the other?[55] There

52 See Chisholm (1973; 1976, app. B). Later literature on these and related theses includes Wiggins (1979), Van Cleve (1986), Simons (1987, §5.3 and §7.4), Willard (1994), Jubien (2001; 2009, §1.6), Grygianiec (2005, 2006, 2007), Steen (2008), Miller (2008) (with reply in Nicolas, 2009), Wallace (2014a), and Moore (2015). See also Sharvy (1983, §3), Tanksley (2010), and Steen (2016, suppl.) on mereological essentialism for masses and Daniels and Goswick (2017) for events. On the historical precedents, especially Abelard, see Henry (1972, §III.8; 1991a, §2.5; 1991b), Martin (1998, §3; 2019), and Arlig (2005, 2007, 2012a, 2013).

53 In fact, those extensions generate further questions. For instance, if x is one of yy, is it necessarily one of them? See Rumfitt (2005, §7), Williamson (2010, §8), Uzquiano (2011a), Hewitt (2012), and Linnebo (2016). Cf. also Sharvy (1968), Parks (1972), Wiggins (1980, §4.4), Van Cleve (1985), and Forbes (1985, ch. 5) for classic discussions on the essentiality of set membership.

54 On combining Mereological Constancy and Essentialism, see Plantinga (1975) and Chisholm (1975). The holistic variants are not as widely discussed, but see e.g. Ruben (1983), where Ho[lo]logical Essentialism is explicitly stated (and rejected), and Dainton (2010, §8.2). Cf. also Koslicki (2008, pp. 112ff), where the same thesis is called "Reverse Mereological Essentialism", and Koons and Pickavance (2017, §23.4), where it is called "Rigid Parthood".

55 For example, Boethius (*loc. cit.*) endorses mereological constancy but not its holistic counterpart. So does McTaggart (1906, §84) with regard to essentialism. See also Chisholm (1976, p. 146).

are also philosophers who embrace such principles with regard to some entities but not others, as when Chisholm himself distinguishes *entia per se* from *entia per alio* precisely on the ground that the latter, but not the former, obey Mereological Essentialism, or when 'integral wholes' are distinguished from 'mere fusions' on the grounds that the former can undergo various kinds of mereological change while the latter cannot 'by definition'.[56] How can theses of this sort be *expressed* in the language of mereology?

Generally speaking, there are three main strategies one may consider, each of which is to some degree a special case of a more general way of coping with the phenomenon of change at large.[57] First, one could bypass these issues altogether by appealing to an explicit *metaphysical framework* that has room for all the relevant mereological distinctions. In particular, one could say that mereological ductility is strictly speaking an illusion, a false impression stemming from the misguided conception of changeable wholes as three-dimensional, enduring entities; the illusion—and the difficulties it generates—dissolves as soon as we view such wholes as four-dimensional entities that extend in time just as they extend in space (i.e. as things composed of spatio-temporal parts), if not as five-dimensional wholes that extend also across possible worlds (being composed of spatio-temporal-modal parts). Alternatively, one could take at face value the need to revisit the fundamental presupposition that parthood is a *binary relation* and reformulate mereology in terms of relational primitives of greater arity, as in 'x is part of y at time t', or 'x is part of y at time t in world w', etc. Finally, one could deal with these issues by changing, not the language of mereology, but the underlying logical apparatus, specifically by embedding mereology into a framework that is designed precisely for dealing with the logic of temporal and modal discourse—a quantified *modal logic*.

6.2.1 *Temporal and Modal Parts*

The first strategy is perhaps easier to assess if we first focus on mereological change exclusively with regard to time. The idea that ordinary objects are four-dimensional entities composed of spatio-temporal parts, like ordinary processes and events, has indeed a distinguished pedigree in contemporary metaphysics. It finds its roots in the works of Whitehead (1920), Broad (1923), Russell (1927), and Carnap (1928) and made its way into the treatment

56 As in Wiggins (1979, 1980), Lowe (1989, ch, 6), Baker (2000, ch. 7; 2007, ch. 9), Elder (2003; 2004, ch. 3), or Meirav (2003, 2009). See also the discussion in van Inwagen (2006) and Sanford (2011).

57 For systematic overviews of these general strategies, see Haslanger (2003), Wasserman (2004, 2006), Goswick (2013), and Gallois (2016). In principle, each strategy would apply, but here we only focus on those that have been explicitly considered in relation to mereological change. See note 70.

of these issues especially via Quine and, notably, Goodman.[58] Here is a clear statement by Quine:

> The key to [the] difficulty is to be sought not in the idea of identity but in the ideas of thing and time. A physical thing—whether a river or a human body or a stone—is at any one moment a sum of simultaneous momentary states of spatially scattered atoms or other small physical constituents. Now just as the thing at a moment is a sum of these spatially small parts, so we may think of the thing over a period as a sum of the temporally small parts which are its successive momentary states. Combining these conceptions, we see the thing as extended in time and in space alike. (Quine, 1950, p. 210)

And here is Goodman, writing a few years after the development of the Calculus of Individuals:

> We feel no need to hypostatize an underlying core of individuality to explain how a leg and a top, which differ so drastically, can belong to one table. Yet when we consider the table at different moments, we are sometimes told that we must inquire what it is that persists through these temporally different cross sections. The simple answer is that, as with the leg and the top, the unity overlies rather than underlies the diverse elements: these cross sections, though they happen to be temporally rather than spatially less extensive than the whole object in question, nevertheless stand to it in the same relation of element to a larger totality. (Goodman, 1951, pp. 93f)

Of course, strictly speaking there is a difference between the ontological claim that things are composed of temporal parts and the explanatory claim that things persist in virtue of having such parts (i.e. that they "perdure", following Lewis, 1986c, p. 202), but for our purposes we can identify the two.[59] Indeed, strictly speaking four-dimensionalism does not even require an ontology of temporal parts: things could extend over time just as an extended simple may spread out in space, without division into proper parts.[60] Let us set this possibility aside. And let us set aside any questions concerning Atomism versus Atomlessness. Four-dimensionalism is often explained in

58 Later advocates of four-dimensionalism form a long list, from Taylor (1955) and Smart (1955) to Lewis (1971, 1986c), Noonan (1976, 1980), Armstrong (1980), Robinson (1982), Heller (1984, 1990), Le Poidevin (1991), Jubien (1993), and Hudson (2001, 2005). See also Sider (1997, 2001), though his view differs significantly from orthodox four-dimensionalism (cf. below, note 62). To some extent, four-dimensionalism is also a natural view to hold on a standard interpretation of the special theory of relativity—a point already emphasized by Broad (1923, ch. 2) and eventually by Smart (1972) and pressed by Balashov (1999, 2010). For overviews and general discussion, see McGrath (2007b), Sider (2008), and Hawley (2018b).

59 The difference is carefully addressed in Wasserman (2016).

60 This is clarified in Parsons (2000a), with further discussion in Noonan (2009), Miller (2009b), and Hudson (2005, ch. 4). See also Carlson (2017) on the dual view, nihilist perdurantism (temporal parts without spatial parts).

ways that suggest a commitment to mereological simples, as in the passage by Quine quoted above, and surely that was also Goodman's ultimate view. Even today it is not uncommon to characterize the ontology of four-dimensionalism in terms of fusions of *momentary* or *instantaneous* temporal parts.[61] We shall follow suit, for it makes things easier. Generally speaking, however, this is not required and indeed some early proponents, such as Whitehead, were as we know committed to atomlessness. Four-dimensionalism is compatible with temporal gunk as it is with spatial gunk.[62]

With these provisos, it should be clear how this sort of view lends itself to a simple way of accounting for mereological change in the standard language of mereology. Take again the case of Dion, whose foot is amputated at some point in time during his life, say t_0. The intuitive way to describe this scenario, on the assumption that Dion, y, survives the loss of his foot, x, is to make assertions of the following form, where $t < t_0 < t'$.[63]

(6.2) $Pxy \text{ at } t \wedge \neg Pxy \text{ at } t'$

This is of course not a formula in the language of mereology, which is precisely our problem. But from a four-dimensional perspective 6.2 is loose talk. Four-dimensionally, our assertion amounts to this: that while the t-part of x is part of (the t-part of) y, its t'-part is not part of (the t'-part of) y. In other words, 6.2 should be construed as having one of the following forms

(6.3) $Px_ty \wedge \neg Px_{t'}y$

(6.4) $Px_ty_t \wedge \neg Px_{t'}y_{t'}$

where the subscripts identify the relevant momentary parts. And these are perfectly ordinary mereological formulas. Momentary parts are things in the field of P, just like the temporally extended wholes to which they belong.

Now, this is not to say that four-dimensionalists can express every claim about the diachronic behavior of parthood in the basic language of mereology. Clearly, such theses as Mereological or Holological Constancy involve quantification over times, so their explicit formulation would require that we expand our language with a suitable predicate, T, extending over moments of time. Moreover, we would need a further relational predicate, say E, to

61 See e.g. Crisp (2003, p. 216) and Effingham (2009b, p. 301).

62 At least this applies to so-called 'worm four-dimensionalism', which is the theory of temporal *parts* we are interested in; the variant known as 'stage-theoretic four-dimensionalism', which is a theory of temporal *counterparts* (Sider, 1996, 2001; Hawley, 2001), has arguably less leeway in this regard. See Zimmerman (1996b), Stuchlik (2013), and Giberman (2019). See also Leonard (2018) for a parallel worry concerning endurantism.

63 When $t = t_0$, or $t_0 = t'$, intuitions diverge. This is the classic problem of the moment of change (see Mortensen, 2016). Since the problem is not peculiar to mereological change, and does not affect the main point, we can for the moment ignore it, but see section 6.3.4.

connect each thing with the times at which it exists.[64] And we would of course need axioms governing these new predicates, beginning with

$(A_*13)\ \forall x \forall y(Exy \to Ty)$ *Temporary Existence*

In such a language we could actually define momentary parts explicitly, viz. as fusions of simultaneous parts.[65]

$(D_*9)\ x_t := \sigma y(Pyx \wedge \forall z(Eyz \leftrightarrow z = t))$ t–*Part*

And we could easily state (or reject) the two Constancy theses.

$(T_*4)\ \forall x \forall y \forall t(Px_t y \to \forall t'(Eyt' \to Px_{t'} y))$ *Mereological Constancy*
$(T_*5)\ \forall x \forall y \forall t(Px_t y \to \forall t'(Ext' \to Px_{t'} y))$ *Hológical Constancy*

But all this is beyond the point. The point is simply that, generally speaking, we can continue to reason in terms of plain parthood. Mereological 'change' in time is no different from mereological 'change' in space, precisely in the sense explained by Goodman. Just as Dion may be said to change in space insofar as he has qualitatively different spatial parts, so he can be said to change in time insofar as he has qualitatively different temporal parts.

At this point it's easy to see how this strategy could in principle be extended to deal also with modal change. We only have to think of modality as another dimension along which objects can be said to extend and have parts. This is by itself not a popular move. Lewis (1983b), a champion of four-dimensionalism along with realism about possible worlds, does consider it, but eventually rejects it in favor of counterpart theory,[66] and Simons (1987, p. 361), himself not a friend of four-dimensionalism, mentions the idea *en passant* just to dismiss it. To our knowledge, the first author to have embraced *five*-dimensionalism seriously was George Schlesinger:

> We may say that many full-fledged individuals are five-dimensional; they have four physical dimensions, three in space, one in time and a fifth, logical, conceptual or modal dimension. We obtain a complete individual by combining all its cosmic chunks, i.e. by adding together all its four-dimensional parts to be found in each possible world containing them. (Schlesinger, 1985, p. 256)

There are a few other supporters, following Schlesinger or independently inspired, but on the whole it can hardly be said that five-dimensionalism is

64 E would essentially be a (weak) location predicate, axiomatized as in Casati and Varzi (1999, ch. 7), Varzi (2007a, §3), or Parsons (2007). For a thorough overview, see Gilmore (2018).

65 Given A_*13, the definition forces t to be a time, so this is in the spirit of Sider (1997, p. 206; 2001, p. 60). Extended temporal parts can then be defined as fusions of momentary parts.

66 For a comparative analysis, see Varzi (2001a). Quine himself thought the move would be plausible enough, were it not for "independent trouble with possible worlds" (Quine, 1976, p. 861).

a widespread view.[67] Still, it's clear that on this view the intuitive idea that objects might have different parts from the ones they actually have can be modeled exactly as the idea that their parts may vary over time. For instance, to say that Dion, who did not in fact lose his right hand, might nevertheless have lost it would amount to saying that while all of Dion's actual temporal parts include a corresponding temporal part of his hand, some of his temporal parts in other worlds fail to do so. The details are perfectly parallel to the temporal-part account outlined above, on the understanding that in order to be explicit about such claims as Mereological and Holological Essentialism we would need to enrich our language further, adding a suitable predicate, W, to quantify explicitly about worlds (and treating E as a relation of existence at a time in a world).

With all this, a general assessment of this first strategy for dealing with issues of mereological ductility will have to depend on one's overall philosophical attitude. To some extent, the strategy has precisely the advertised advantage of requiring no adjustments to the formal apparatus of mereology as we know it. But, pretty clearly, this advantage comes at the cost of substantive metaphysical commitments that seem to be quite independent of the needs of a formal theory about part-whole relations. Popular as it may be, the four-dimensional conception of objects can hardly be a prerequisite of mereology, and is in fact rejected upfront by a number of philosophers as "abolishing" change altogether (Geach, 1965, p. 323) and "radically at odds with common sense" (Paul, 2002, p. 587), if not as a "metaphysical quagmire" (Hacker, 1982, p. 4), a "crazy metaphysics" (Thomson, 1983, p. 213), etc. Many a philosopher will feel the same about the five-dimensional conception needed to handle modal ductility.

The very idea that the temporal and modal dimensions are on a par with the three dimensions of space is—regardless of the claim that objects are literally spread out in all such dimensions—hardly uncontroversial. With respect to time, some contingent support would seem to come from the special theory of relativity; yet, again, not everyone agrees and some would strongly disagree. Čapek (1976, p. XXVI), for instance, considers the "fallacy of spatialization of time" to be "one of the most persistent features of our intellectual tradition".[68] When it comes to modality, the analogy with space—or, for that matter, with time—is even more contentious.[69]

67 For an early endorsement, see Brennan (1988, ch. 5). The view is reaffirmed in Schlesinger (1994) and, independently, in Hale (1991). Later supporters include Benovsky (2006a,b,c), Yagisawa (2010), Cresswell (2010), Rini and Cresswell (2012, ch. 15), Ueberroth (2013), Wallace (2014a,b, 2019), Graham (2015), Miller and Duncan (2015), Vacek (2017), and De (2018).

68 With specific reference to the early four-dimensionalist literature mentioned in the beginning, detailed and more pointed objections in this spirit may be found already in Meiland (1966). Another influential criticism is Butterfield (1985).

69 For recent discussions, see Meyer (2006) and Torrengo (2011).

6.2.2 *More Arguments for Parthood*

The second strategy for dealing with such issues is radically different. It proceeds from the acknowledgment that parthood is not a binary relation after all. In the words of Judith Thomson:

> It is really the most obvious common sense that a physical object can acquire and lose parts. Parthood surely is a three-place relation, among a pair of objects and a time. (Thomson, 1983, p. 213)

More generally, the idea is that if we want to account for statements of the form 'x is part of y at z', where z is a time, a world, or any other parameter with respect to which things may be said to undergo mereological change, then we have to increase the arity of the primitive parthood relation. We have to take such locutions at face value, rather than try and reduce them to parthood claims *simpliciter*.[70]

In recent literature this approach is rather popular. There is, in fact, no comprehensive treatment. Beginning with Thomson's own "Cross-temporal Calculus of Individuals" (Thomson, 1983, §6), proposals have for the most part been formulated to deal with specific issues within the framework of specific philosophical views, with no aim at completeness, even less formal neutrality.[71] Nonetheless, one can go some way toward a general picture.

To illustrate, suppose we have a language with a three-place predicate P of relative parthood as a primitive along with the additional predicates needed to be explicit about the special role of the third parameter. Focusing on the temporal case, the easiest way to do so without changing the underlying logic would be to proceed along the lines described in section 6.2.1, adding just a time predicate T (for 'is a time') and a binary existence predicate E (for 'exists at'). These new predicates would have to be axiomatized somehow, possibly with the help of a further relational predicate to specify the ordered structure of time, but we can skip all details and assume only what is strictly necessary, namely the Temporary Existence axiom, A_*13, along with a parallel axiom concerning the intended reading of P.

(A_*14) $\forall x \forall y \forall z(\mathsf{P}xyz \to \mathsf{T}z)$ *Temporary Parthood*

70 Actually there are ways of taking statements of the form 'x is part of y at z' at face value without changing the arity of the parthood relation. For instance, one could read them as involving an adverbial modifier (as in 'x is part of y at-z-ly'), or a sentential operator (as in 'at z: x is part of y'). Such accounts would reflect more general ways of dealing with the problem of change at large, but have not been explicitly pursued in the context of mereology.

71 Examples may be found in Simons (1987, §5.2), Sider (1997, 2001, §3.2), Brogaard (1999), Hudson (2001), Bittner *et al.* (2004) (followed by Bittner and Donnelly, 2007; Donnelly and Bittner, 2009; Donnelly, 2009, 2010), Masolo (2009), Giaretta and Spolaore (2011), and Hovda (2013, §1.2). See also Nenchev and Vakarelov (2009) and Nenchev (2011) for a related approach.

Together, these two axioms would suffice to force the last argument of E and P to be a time, a fact that we may highlight by displaying it as a subscript (writing e.g. '$E_t x$' for 'Ext' and '$P_t xy$' for '$Pxyt$'). For convenience, let us also assume that times are not themselves structured by P:

(A$_*$15) $\forall x \forall y \forall z (Pxyz \to \neg Ty)$ *Time Apartness*

This simplifies things considerably, though a fuller account would of course call for some treatment of time's internal structure (e.g. atomistic vs. gunky).

With this picture in place, the bulk of the apparatus would be rather straightforward. To begin with, the auxiliary mereological relations introduced in chapter 2 could easily be adjusted. For instance:

(D$_*$10) $PP_t xy :\equiv P_t xy \wedge \neg x = y$ *t–Proper Parthood*
(D$_*$11) $O_t xy :\equiv \exists z (P_t zx \wedge P_t zy)$ *t–Overlap*
(D$_*$12) $D_t xy :\equiv \neg \exists z (P_t zx \wedge P_t zy)$ *t–Disjointness*

The relativized version of other mereological notions could be obtained from the corresponding absolute notions in a similar fashion, by replacing in each case the binary predicates in the definiens with the corresponding three-place counterparts. In particular, the fusion predicate F could be relativized as follows, where '$\varphi_t x$' abbreviates '$E_t x \wedge \varphi x$'.[72]

(D$_*$13) $F_{t\varphi} z :\equiv \forall x (\varphi_t x \to P_t xz) \wedge \forall y (\forall x (\varphi_t x \to P_t xy) \to P_t zy)$ *t–Fusion*

In addition, one could also consider notions that in a standard setting tend to be underplayed. An interesting case in point is the following.[73]

(D$_*$14) $C_t xy :\equiv P_t xy \wedge P_t yx$ *t–Coincidence*

This predicate corresponds to the relation of mereological coincidence that, on some views, two or more things may satisfy at some stages of their lives. For example, in chapters 3 and 4 we saw that the mutual-part solution to the Dion/Theon puzzle consists precisely in this: when Dion loses his foot, he comes to coincide with his proper part Theon. A classically-minded mereologist would of course reject this account. But even so, the predicate in question may be helpful to state the rejection, as in

(A$_*$16) $\forall x \forall y \forall t (C_t xy \to x = y)$ *Identity of Coincidents*

72 Thomson (1983, p. 216) has an analogous relativization of Goodman-style fusion, as do Simons (1987, p. 185), Bittner *et al.* (2004, p. 39), and, with minor variations, Bittner and Donnelly (2007, p. 290). Cf. also Needham (2010, p. 162; 2017, p. 61). The other authors cited in note 71 start from Leśniewski-style fusions, as does van Inwagen (2006), but the relativization is similar.
73 We already have 'C' for 'coatom'. Since coincidence is ternary, no confusion should arise.

In fact, this thesis might be too strong even for a classically-minded mereologist. Four-dimensionalists, for instance, would deny it, since on their view temporary coincidence is just overlap *simpliciter*: different things may share a common temporal part (as the case of Dion and Theon would show).[74] A four-dimensionalist would rather say that things are identical if they *always* coincide, that is, if they are part of each other throughout their career and, therefore, truly indiscernible from a mereological standpoint.[75]

$(A_*17)\ \forall x \forall y(\forall t((E_t x \vee E_t y) \rightarrow C_t xy) \rightarrow x = y)$ *Sameness*

Many other useful relations could be defined and investigated along these lines.[76] For our purposes, however, the interesting questions concern the axiomatic framework. How should the ordering, decomposition, and composition axioms of standard mereology be adapted to a language of this sort, where all vocabulary is relativized to times? Concerning ordering, A.1–A.3 admit of immediate counterparts.

$(A_*18)\ \forall x \forall t(E_t x \rightarrow P_t xx)$ *Conditional Reflexivity*

$(A_*19)\ \forall x \forall y \forall t((P_t xy \wedge P_t yx) \rightarrow x = y)$ *Antisymmetry*

$(A_*20)\ \forall x \forall y \forall z \forall t((P_t xy \wedge P_t yz) \rightarrow P_t xz)$ *Transitivity*

The Reflexivity axiom A_*18 could be strengthened by dropping the antecedent, but this would mean that things can have (relational) properties even when they do not exist, which is controversial.[77] Indeed, most philosophers would rule out that possibility explicitly, requiring that things can have properties *only* when they exist (what Fine, 1981 calls the "Falsehood Principle"). In the present context, this would amount to assuming the following axiom.

$(A_*21)\ \forall x \forall y \forall t(P_t xy \rightarrow (E_t x \wedge E_t y))$ *Existence*

Given A_*21, A_*18 would immediately turn into a biconditional, and one could therefore treat E as a defined predicate.[78]

$(D_*15)\ E_t x :\equiv P_t xx$ t–*Existence*

74 This is the account hinted at in chapter 4, note 48.

75 Strictly speaking, this thesis should be formulated so as to avoid that all times be identified just because do not themselves exist *at* times; the details will depend on the axioms on T.

76 A good source is still Simons (1987, §5.2).

77 Simons himself, despite viewing the classical ordering axioms as analytic, refrains from assuming an unconditional version of A_*18 (Simons, 1987, p. 179), just as he doesn't embrace A.1 for mereologies based on free logic rather than classical logic (1987, p. 58; 1991a, p. 293).

78 As in the mereologies of Bitter and Donnelly cited in note 72. See also Thomson (1998, fn. 3). Thomson (1983, p. 215) has a similar definition, though based on the irreflexivity of D_t.

The Antisymmetry axiom A_*19 is, of course, just the Identity of Coincidents principle A_*16 in primitive notation. As we said, this is in the spirit of classical mereology, but some philosophers might find it too strong. For such philosophers, Thomson (1983, p. 216) offers as an alternative the Sameness principle A_*17, which may be accepted by three- and four-dimensionalists alike. But perhaps even A_*17 is too strong. One might insist that things of different sorts, such as a statue and its matter, would be distinct even in circumstances of permanent coincidence, e.g. because their life spans *might* have differed.[79] Fine (2000) even argues that there can be necessarily permanent coincidents of the *same* sort. If so, then A_*17 would be just as unacceptable as A_*19. All one should say is that coincidence behaves *like* identity and this would already be guaranteed by the other axioms.[80]

(T$_*$6) $\forall x \forall t(E_t x \to C_t xx)$ *C–Reflexivity*

(T$_*$7) $\forall x \forall y \forall t(C_t xy \to C_t yx)$ *C–Symmetry*

(T$_*$8) $\forall x \forall y \forall z \forall t((C_t xy \land C_t yz) \to C_t xz)$ *C–Transitivity*

(T$_*$9) $\forall x \forall y \forall t(C_t xy \to \forall z(P_t zx \leftrightarrow P_t zy))$ *C–Indiscernibility*

As for Transitivity, note that A_*20 requires the time variable to be the same throughout. If the times at which x is part of y and y part of z were different, there would be no guarantee that x is part of z at either time, or for that matter at any time: occasional parthood is not transitive. By contrast, the following thesis would be a simple logical consequence of A_*20.

(T$_*$10) $\forall x \forall y \forall z(\exists t(P_t xy \land P_t yz) \to \exists t P_t xz)$ *Occasional Transitivity*

Except for the worries concerning Antisymmetry, the three ordering axioms A_*18–A_*20 are rather common in the literature.[81] They also have the consequences we might expect with regard to other notions, such as PP_t, which is easily seen to be a strict ordering. When it comes to decomposition and composition principles, however, things are not so simple.

To begin with the former, consider first the classical Remainder axiom, A.4. Its straightforward relativization would be as follows.

(6.5) $\forall x \forall y \forall t(\neg P_t xy \to \exists z \forall w(P_t wz \leftrightarrow (P_t wx \land D_t wy)))$

Yet there are at least two senses in which this formulation would fail to capture the intended import of A.4 in a time-relative context. For one thing,

79 This objection is rather common even among philosophers who do not share the mutual-part approach. See e.g. Koslicki (2008, pp. 26f). For an extensive discussion, see Miller (2006b).

80 Specifically: T_*6 and T_*7 follow from A_*18 whereas T_*8 and T_*9 from A_*20.

81 Time travel scenarios of the sort discussed in chapter 3 would of course raise problems. See also Gilmore (2009, §3.2.3) for more general worries about the Transitivity axiom A_*20.

the consequent is too weak. It should require, not only that a remainder exists in the atemporal sense corresponding to the existential quantifier, but also that it exists at t in the sense corresponding to E. In other words, it should include an explicit clause to the effect that $E_t z$. Otherwise z could have witnesses that do not qualify at all as *remainders* (e.g. because they vacuously satisfy the relevant biconditional by virtue of satisfying $\forall w D_t zw$). On the other hand, as soon as we restrict the consequent of 6.5 to things existing at t, the antecedent becomes too strong. As it stands, it concerns any pair of things satisfying the condition $\neg P_t xy$, even when x does not exist at t. But why should this necessitate a remainder *at* t? Why should it be that, among the things that exist today, one ought to serve as a remainder of Dion minus his foot? Clearly the antecedent must also be restricted. So, putting things together, we obtain that a better relativization of A.4 should look like this:

$$(A_*22)\quad \forall x \forall y \forall t((E_t x \wedge \neg P_t xy) \rightarrow \exists z(E_t z \wedge \forall w(P_t wz \leftrightarrow (P_t wx \wedge D_t wy)))) \quad \mathit{Rm}$$

Similar remarks apply to weaker decomposition principles one might consider. For example, in Sider (2001, p. 58) we find a relativized version of Strong Supplementation and Simons (1987, p. 179) has a version of Weak Supplementation.[82]

$$(A_*23)\quad \forall x \forall y \forall t((E_t x \wedge \neg P_t xy) \rightarrow \exists z(P_t zx \wedge D_t zy)) \quad \textit{Strong Supplementation}$$
$$(A_*24)\quad \forall x \forall y \forall t(PP_t yx \rightarrow \exists z(PP_t zx \wedge D_t zy)) \quad \textit{Weak Supplementation}$$

These principles are offered in the context of mereological theories that assume the Existence axiom A_*21. Absent this axiom A_*23 and A_*24 would still be meaningful, but in each case one might want to strengthen the consequent by requiring that $E_t z$. If so, then the antecedent of A_*24 should be adjusted accordingly.

Let us stress that these decomposition principles would preserve the essential features that make their atemporal counterparts controversial in the first place, so the temporal relativization would not by itself be a way to overcome those worries. For instance, in the absence of Antisymmetry, the three-place variant of Weak Supplementation would still fail whenever x and y coincide at t. Nevertheless, the temporal relativization might prove helpful to disentangle different ways in which such principles can be asserted

82 More precisely, Simons's version of A_*24 is a relativization of Strict Supplementation (A.38), since he defines $PP_t xy$ as $P_t xy \wedge \neg P_t yx$. Moreover, strictly speaking Sider's version of A_*23 includes '$E_t y$' as a further conjunct in the antecedent. In the form given here, the axiom may be found e.g. in Donnelly and Bittner (2009, p. 176) and Donnelly (2010, p. 224), who assume A_*21, and in Olson (2006, p. 743), who identifies it with Sider's and discusses A_*24 as well (as do e.g. McGrath, 2007a, fn. 10 and, treating PP_t as a primitive, Effingham, 2010a, p. 334).

or rejected, and it could be argued that precisely here lies the advantage of relativizing parthood. For a concrete example, consider the doctrine of *mereological potentialism* (Smith, 1987, §7). On this doctrine, the only things that 'really' exist are full-fledged, bounded substances, and things such as Dion's undetached foot, or Theon before the amputation, are mere 'potential' entities that actual division would not simply unveil but literally bring into existence.[83] With 'existence' understood in terms if E, this doesn't rule out the possibility of reasoning about the mereological structure of Dion before the amputation (*contra* A_*21). In particular, one might say that before the amputation Theon is a proper part of Dion, and that this part is at that time supplemented by the foot, vindicating both A_*24 and A_*23. Yet the stronger versions of these principles, obtained by adding '$E_t z$' in the consequent, would be rejected.

Turning finally to the laws of composition, we may again start from the straightforward relativization of a classical axiom schema, say A.5.

(A_*25) $\forall t(\exists x \varphi_t x \rightarrow \exists z(E_t z \wedge F_{t\varphi} z))$ *Unrestricted Fusion*

This schema would suggest itself as the natural counterpart of A.5. And in a way it is: modulo the expressive limitations discussed in section 6.1 above, A_*25 encapsulates the spirit of mereological universalism. It states that every specifiable plurality of things existing at any given time t has a t-fusion. However, there are other principles a universalist might want to endorse, and not only insofar as A_*25 could be stated in terms of different fusion operators. As Thomson (1983, pp. 216f) and Simons (1987, pp. 183ff) noted, and Sider (2001, §4.9.2) further clarified, there is the additional fact that t-fusions would not exhaust the sense in which composition may occur in a time-relative setting.

Following Sider, we can put it in terms of the Special Composition Question. In section 5.2 we saw that universalism is the answer to that question within classical mereology. However, when parthood is indexed to times, the question itself admits of different formulations. One is the *Synchronic Composition Question*: given various things existing at a given time, under what conditions is there something that at that time is composed of those things? To this question, A_*25 provides the answer we would expect from a classically-minded mereologist: under *any* conditions. But we may also ask

83 For a fuller account, see Smith (1994, §3.4). The doctrine has its roots in Aristotle (*Metaphysics*, VII, 16, 1040b10–16; *Physics*, VII, 5, 250a24–25), though its clearest formulations emerge in the early modern debate on matter's divisibility. See Pfeiffer (2018) along with Holden (2004, ch. 2) and Pasnau (2011, ch. 26). For contemporary variants, see Johansson (2006b, 2008) and the counterpart-theoretic treatment in Casati and Varzi (1999, ch. 6). Some accounts of extended simples may also be seen in this light: for Markosian (1998a, p. 223), such simples have no "metaphysical parts", despite there being a "conceptual part" for each sub-region of the space they occupy.

a *Diachronic Composition Question*: given various times and various things existing at each, under what conditions is there something that at those times is composed of those things? This is not a question about fusions at-a-time; it is a question about cross-temporal fusions. And in this regard A_*25 is completely silent. It states that there is, say, something composed of Theon and Dion's foot at t, and also something composed of Caesar and Cleopatra's nose at t′; but it doesn't tell us whether there's something that at t is composed of Theon and Dion's foot and at t′ of Caesar and Cleopatra's nose. A devoted universalist might want to countenance such things as well.[84] Surely a four-dimensionalist universalist *à la* Goodman would want to do so.[85] But even a plenitudinous three-dimensionalist might want to countenance arbitrary diachronic fusions, claiming that for any times and any things existing at those times there is something that at those times is composed exactly of those things.[86]

To cover such stronger theses, the relevant notion of diachronic fusion must be distinguished from the synchronic notion defined in D_*13. It can be defined as follows, where ξ is any formula in which t occurs free (intuitively, a formula that defines a class or interval of times).

$$(D_*16)\ F_{\xi,\varphi}z :\equiv \forall t((\xi t \wedge \exists x\varphi_t x) \rightarrow F_{t\varphi}z) \qquad \textit{ξ-Fusion}$$

Then the universalist answer to the Diachronic Composition Question would amount to the following axiom schema, obviously stronger than A_*25.

$$(A_*26)\ \exists t(\xi t \wedge \exists x\varphi_t x) \rightarrow \exists z F_{\xi,\varphi}z \qquad \textit{Unrestricted Diachronic Fusion}$$

(Note that this schema is doubly schematic: it yields a distinct individual axiom for every choice of ξ and each condition φ.)

Indeed, A_*26 is not even as strong as it might sound. For as Sider again points out, there is a crucial difference between saying that certain things

84 Recall that already Leibniz spoke of the aggregate comprising "all the Roman emperors" (see chapter 1, note 7), though strictly speaking he would describe such an aggregate as a "mere phenomenon" that exists only insofar as the emperors are *considered* together—a conception sometimes classified as phenomenalism (Adams, 1983) if not as idealism (Adams, 1994, pt. III).

85 For a general appraisal of the link between perdurantism and universalism, see Miller (2006c).

86 One reason why a three-dimensionalist may be led to this view (*pace* Steen, 2017) is that it offers a response to certain arguments from vagueness that would otherwise undermine the endurantist conception of persistence. For the arguments, see Heller (1990, pp. 49ff), Le Poidevin (2000), and Sider (2001, §4.9); for the response, Koslicki (2003, p. 121f), Markosian (2004c), Lowe (2005b), Miller (2005, 2006a), Anthony (2010), Kurtsal Steen (2010), Magidor (2015) and, in a way, Hawthorne (2006) and Inman (2014). For comparisons, see Hudson (2001, §3.7), Balashov (2005), and Varzi (2005, 2007b). Note that there would still be a difference between the two sorts of universalism, since a four-dimensionalist would take such diachronic fusions to be perduring entities having the relevant time-bound fusions as *parts* (simpliciter), whereas a three-dimensionalist would take them to be enduring entities that at each time *are* those fusions.

existing at certain times have a diachronic fusion and saying that they have a *minimal* diachronic fusion, i.e. a fusion that exists exactly at those times.

(D_*17) $MF_{\xi\varphi}z :\equiv F_{\xi\varphi}z \wedge \forall t(E_t z \leftrightarrow (\xi t \wedge \exists x \varphi_t x))$ *Minimal ξ-Fusion*

For instance, if ξ identifies two separate times at which Dion exists, t and t', and each φ_i identifies the corresponding class of body cells in Dion's body, then presumably Dion is a ξ-fusion of the φs, witnessing for z in A_*26. He is not, however, a minimal ξ-fusion, for he exists through other times. Is there also such a thing, a temporally discontinuous ξ-fusion existing only at t and t'? A_*26 does not say. More generally, A_*26 is silent about Sider's *Hard Diachronic Composition Question*: given various times and various things existing at each, under what conditions is there a minimal fusion of those things at those times? So, if a universalist answer to *this* question is wanted, A_*26 must be strengthened accordingly.

(A_*27) $\exists t(\xi t \wedge \exists x \varphi_t x) \rightarrow \exists z MF_{\xi\varphi}z$ *Unrestricted Minimal Diachronic Fusion*

This should suffice to complete the picture, at least insofar as classical mereology is concerned. Needless to say, there is room for weaker theories, just as one could consider stronger theories obtained by adding axioms dealing with the question of atomism or with the theses of mereological constancy, which in this language can easily be stated.

(T_*11) $\forall x \forall y \forall t(P_t xy \rightarrow \forall t'(E_{t'}y \rightarrow P_{t'}xy))$ *Mereological Constancy*
(T_*12) $\forall x \forall y \forall t(P_t xy \rightarrow \forall t'(E_{t'}x \rightarrow P_{t'}xy))$ *Holological Constancy*

Let us simply conclude by stressing that while we have focused on the temporal case, the same approach could be followed to develop theories where parthood is relativized to other dimensions, beginning with the cosmic dimension needed to account for cases of modal change. Formally the move from 'x is part of y at time t' to 'x is part of y in world *w*' is immaterial. One might also want to treat parthood as a four-place relation, 'x is part of y at time t in world *w*' (as in Plantinga, 1975), in which case the space of viable theories would increases accordingly. Given the possibility of time travel, and multi-location more generally, a (non-modal) four-place relation 'x is part of y at time t at place p' may also be considered (Hudson, 2001, §2.1), and some authors have considered a four-place parthood relation that is relativized twice with respect to the same dimension, once for the part and once for the whole, as in 'x, at moment t of its proper time, is part of y, at moment t' of its proper time' (Gilmore, 2007), or 'x at region r is part of y at region r'' (Gilmore, 2009; Kleinschmidt, 2011). The details may vary, even significantly; but the nature of the enterprise would be essentially the same.

6.2.3 *Modal Mereology*

Concerning the third strategy for dealing with temporal and modal considerations, we can be brief. As we mentioned, in this case the idea is simply to embed mereology in a language that is independently suited for this purpose—a language equipped with temporal or modal operators governed by appropriate logical principles that would apply generally, not only to the special case of part-whole reasoning. For instance, in temporal logic we typically have a sentential operator for 'it is always the case that'. In modal logic we have an operator for 'it is necessarily the case that'. Writing '$\Box$' for either operator, and representing singular existence by the defined predicate $\mathsf{E}x :\equiv \exists z\, z = x$, the corresponding Constancy and Essentialism theses would have a straightforward formulation.[87]

(T_*13) $\forall x \forall y(Pxy \to \Box(Ey \to Pxy))$ *Mereological Constancy/Essentialism*

(T_*14) $\forall x \forall y(Pxy \to \Box(Ex \to Pxy))$ *Holological Constancy/Essentialism*

Similarly for any other thesis we might wish to consider beyond the axioms and theorems of the pure mereological theory that we take as our starting point. For example, the Sameness principle A_*17, to the effect that thoroughly coinciding things are identical, would become

(A_*28) $\forall x \forall y(\Box((Ex \lor Ey) \to (Pxy \land Pyx)) \to x = y)$ *Sameness*

The behavior of P would be governed by our mereological axioms. But because 'P' is not a logical constant, the flexibility in its interpretation across the admissible models of the extended language would ensure all sorts of temporal or modal ductility unless we explicitly stipulate otherwise (e.g. by assuming T_*13 and T_*14 themselves as further axioms).[88]

This strategy has at least three advantages and one limitation, plus a technical complication. One obvious advantage is that it would not require any revisions of the basic mereological framework. We can continue to think of parthood as a binary, absolute relation, and we can do so without the metaphysical costs involved in the first strategy considered in section 6.2.1. A

87 For a general overview of temporal (or tense) logic, see Goranko and Galton (2015). On modal logic, see Hughes and Cresswell (1996). On combining time and modality, see Thomason (2002). It should be noted that in recent literature 'modal logic' is often used as an umbrella term covering both sorts of logic along with many others, each of which is obtained by imposing specific conditions on abstract operators, such as $\Box$, to fix the intended interpretation.

88 Uzquiano (2014) gives perhaps the clearest illustration of this strategy with regard to modality. With regard to time, see Hovda (2013). Early work in either areas include Simons (1987, ch. 7), Kazmi (1990), and Needham (2012). Note that this approach in principle is compatible with the strategies discussed in the previous sections. For instance, Simons has a modal mereology of this sort based on a three-place parthood relation indexed to times.

second advantage is that this way of proceeding would not require that we explicitly quantify over times or worlds in the object language—a crucial feature of the second strategy that some may find objectionable on ontological grounds. Although there are systematic ways of translating from a language with temporal or modal operators to a language that quantifies over times and worlds, the former kind of language provides for greater neutrality, leaving the task of explaining the exact import of those operators to the semantic metatheory. Moreover, the translation need not be first-order; in some cases, a modal principle can only be translated with the help of second-order quantification over classes of worlds/times, giving rise to the general nominalist concerns discussed earlier.[89] Finally, a third important advantage of this approach is that it would allow one to distinguish clearly between principles that one accepts or rejects because of specific mereological intuitions and principles one accepts or rejects because of one's general views regarding temporal and modal logic.

The last point is especially delicate, and is connected to the second, so here is a simple illustration. Adapting from Uzquiano (2014, pp. 39ff), suppose we start from classical mereology and we share the modal intuition that whatever is the case is necessarily possible, corresponding to the so-called Brouwerian principle $\varphi \to \Box\neg\Box\neg\varphi$. Within the framework of a modal logic governed by this principle, it can generally be shown that familiar arguments for the necessity of non-identity do not extend to the parthood relation. That is, we can generally prove

$$(T_*15)\quad \forall x \forall y(\neg x = y \to \Box\neg x = y) \qquad \textit{Necessity of Non-Identity}$$

but we cannot prove

$$(T_*16)\quad \forall x \forall y(\neg PPxy \to \Box\neg PPxy) \qquad \textit{Necessity of Non-Parthood}$$

What this means is that in this setting classical mereology would warrant two seemingly conflicting thoughts. On the one hand, because T_*15 is provable, Dion cannot become identical with Theon upon losing his foot. On the other hand, because T_*16 is not provable, he can become a proper part of the fusion of Theon's parts, e.g. if both of Dion's feet were safely amputated and the fusion continued to exist (scattered). But, of course, classically Theon just

89 To illustrate, the modal thesis that whatever is necessarily/always the case is in fact the case, $\Box\varphi \to \varphi$, may be translated as a first-order quantification to the effect that every world/time counts as 'accessible' from itself (where accessibility is just an ordinary binary relation); but, for instance, the thesis that whatever is necessarily possible is possibly necessary, or its temporal counterpart, i.e. $\Box\neg\Box\neg\varphi \to \neg\Box\neg\Box\varphi$, cannot be expressed by a first-order formula, not even by a family of first-order formulas, and calls for higher-order quantification. For details and further examples, see e.g. Hughes and Cresswell (1996, chs. 10, 12); for an advanced overview, van Benthem (2001).

is the fusion of his own parts. So classically we have that Dion can in principle become a *proper* but not an *improper* part of Theon. Now, perhaps this is just what the classical mereologist would want to say. But for someone who found it hard to accept this outcome, and to choose between competing answers concerning who survives when, the situation should be carefully assessed. Is the source of the conflict to be found in the assumption that parthood is antisymmetric, which rules out the possibility of mutual proper parts, or is it due to the modal principle that whatever is the case is necessarily possible? Should the conflict be resolved by adding mereological axioms that would prove T_*16, or by blocking the proof of T_*15? In a way, these are questions that could also be raised in the context of a relativized mereology of the sort described in section 6.2.2. The above-mentioned inter-translatability between the two approaches rests on the fact that the principles of modal logic can be made to correspond with specific conditions on a domain of quantification that includes possible worlds, hence our questions translate to questions about whether the conflict should be resolved in terms of mereological axioms or in terms of such conditions. However, we saw that generally speaking there is no guarantee that the latter be *first-order* characterizable.[90] So when it comes to disentangling these issues, if not to *see* them in the first place, the two approaches are not on a par and the present one can easily claim an advantage.

There is, however, also a disadvantage, or rather a limitation. For precisely because we would not explicitly talk about times and worlds, we cannot, on this approach, represent statements making specific mereological claims, i.e. claims asserting that something is or is not part of something at a specific time or in a specific world. We can, for example, deny certain instances of the essentialist claims in T_*13 and T_*14, or in T_*16, but we cannot say at which times or in which worlds those instances fail. In temporal logic we may also rely on suitable operators to distinguish what is now the case from what is the case in the past or in the future, and this would allow us to track important distinctions. For instance, using $\mathbb{P}$ for 'it was (at some time) the case that', we can differentiate between cases of mereological diminution and cases of mereological increase by means of such formulas as

(6.6) $\mathbb{P}Pxy \wedge \neg Pxy$

(6.7) $\mathbb{P}\neg Pxy \wedge Pxy$

But we cannot be more specific. This is not by itself a limit insofar as we are interested in mereology as a general theory, a theory of the general laws

90 As it happens, the specific case at issue is of the first sort; the modal principle $\varphi \rightarrow \Box\neg\Box\neg\varphi$ can be expressed as the requirement that if a world w is accessible from a world w', then w' is accessible from w. The point is that this kind of translation is not always available.

that govern the parthood relation. Indeed the axioms and theorems of a mereology relativized to times, or worlds, would also be stated as quantified formulas, not as formulas concerning what happens to be the case at specific times or specific worlds. In this sense, the present approach is on a par with the approach outlined in section 6.2.2. But when it comes to *applying* mereology, i.e. to discussing specific cases of mereological change, the difference will show up.

Finally, here is the technical complication we alluded to. It comes from the fact that temporal and modal operators do not interact well with classical logic. Specifically, it turns out that all normal systems of temporal or modal logics based on classical logic have the following theorem:

(T_*17) $\forall x \Box \exists y\, x = y$ *Eternity/Necessity of Existence*

This says that every existing thing exists eternally, or necessarily, which is obviously unacceptable if we want to make allowance for temporary or contingent existence. For this reason it is common practice to develop temporal and modal logics within the framework of a quantification theory that is weaker than classical logic, specifically, a so-called 'free' logic. This is essentially the logic we get if we restrict our axiom schemas L.4–L.7 to bound variables (hence, to existing things), which is enough to block the proof of T_*17.[91] Now, the shift from classical logic to free logic is not by itself a problem. But it has an impact that goes beyond the logic of the temporal and modal operators; it forces us to reconsider mereology itself, which was axiomatized within the framework of classical logic (via axiom A.0). So it's not enough to embed a mereological theory into the broader framework of temporal or modal logic; before proceeding with the embedding, we have to 'free' the theory, and that is no straightforward job. More precisely, we already stated all our axioms as involving no free variables, so we know that they are meant to hold exclusively of existing things. (In this sense, the task is not as difficult as that of developing a free mereology in the sense of Simons, 1987, §2.5, 1991a, where free variables are allowed.[92]) But what follows from the axioms, which is determined by the underlying logical theory, would need to be carefully assessed.

91 The point goes back to Kripke (1963). Free logics have been developed independently of modal logic and are so called, following Lambert (1960), insofar as they are meant to be 'free' from the existence assumptions of classical logic. For an overview, see Nolt (2018).

92 The systems of Eberle (1970) have the same feature, as does the system of Link (2014, §13.3). Cf. also Tennant (2013), who provides a sequent-calculus version of classical mereology based on free logic. As we mentioned in chapter 2, note 67, there is a sense in which Leśniewski's own formulation of Mereology is 'free' in this sense, since his quantifiers do not have ontological import. For more on this important aspect of Leśniewski's system, see Lejewski (1954b) and Prior (1965) along with the detailed studies of Küng and Canty (1970), Sagal (1973), Kielkopf (1977), Küng (1977), Simons (1981, 1985b, 1995), and Rickey (1985).

6.3 INDETERMINACY

We turn, finally, to the third worry mentioned in the beginning. All the theories examined so far presuppose that parthood is a perfectly determinate relation: given any two entities x and y, there is always a fact of the matter as to whether or not x is part of y. However, in some cases this seems problematic. Perhaps there is no room for indeterminacy in the idealized mereology of space and time as such; but when it comes e.g. to the mereology of ordinary spatio-temporal particulars, the picture may well be different. Think of objects such as clouds, forests, heaps of sand. What exactly are their constitutive parts? What are the mereological boundaries of a desert, a river, a mountain? Some stuff is positively part of Mount Everest and some is positively not part of it, but there is borderline stuff whose mereological relationship to Everest seems dubious. Even living organisms may, on closer look, give rise to indeterminacy issues. Surely Dion's body comprises his head and does not comprise this book. But what about the cherry Dion is currently chewing? It used to be disjoint from him and soon it will be part of him, yet meanwhile its mereological status is unclear. Is it part of Dion? Will it be part of him only after he swallowed it? After he started digesting it? After he digested it completely? And what goes for living organisms goes for everything. What are the mereological boundaries of a neighborhood, a crowd, a rock band? What about events such as walks, concerts, wars? What about the extensions of such concepts as baldness, wisdom, personhood?

These worries are of no little import, and it may be thought that some mereological principles would have to be revisited accordingly. For example, the PP-Extensionality theorem of classical mereology, T.1, says that composite things with the same proper parts are identical, but in the presence of indeterminacy this may call for qualifications. The model in figure 6.1, left, depicts a and b as non-identical by virtue of their having distinct determinate parts; yet one might prefer to describe a situation of this sort as one in which the identity between a and b is itself indeterminate, owing to the indeterminate status of the two outer atoms c_1 and c_3. Conversely, in the model on the right a and b have the same determinate proper parts, yet again one might prefer to suspend judgment concerning their identity, owing to the indeterminate status of the middle atom c_2.

Figure 6.1: Objects with indeterminate parts (dotted lines).

6.3.1 *De Dicto and De Re*

As it turns out, a lot here depends on how exactly one construes the relevant notion of indeterminacy. Suppose we say:

(6.8) It is indeterminate whether Rock is part of Everest

where Rock is a well-defined piece of rock somewhere in the relevant periphery. There are two ways of understanding this claim, depending on whether the phrase 'it is indeterminate whether' is assigned wide scope, as in 6.9, or narrow scope, as in 6.10.

(6.9) It is indeterminate whether Everest is such that Rock is part of it.
(6.10) Everest is such that it is indeterminate whether Rock is part of it.

These two understandings are not equivalent, and their impact on the presuppositions of our mereological apparatus is correspondingly different.

On the first reading, the indeterminacy in 6.8 is merely *de dicto*: we are saying that the statement

(6.11) Everest is such that Rock is part of it

fails to have a determinate truth-value. This need *not* imply that we have a case of indeterminate parthood. Following Lewis (1986c, 1993a), Heller (1990), and others,[93] one could argue that the indeterminacy of 6.11 is due entirely to the vagueness of 'Everest': our linguistic practices do not, on closer look, specify exactly which portion of reality correspond to that name. In particular, they do not specify whether the name denotes something whose proper parts include Rock and, as a consequence, the truth conditions of 6.11 are not fully determined. But this is not to say that the stuff out there is mereologically indeterminate. Each one of a variety of slightly distinct chunks of reality has an equal claim to being the referent of the vaguely introduced name 'Everest', and each such thing has a perfectly precise mereological structure; it's just that some of them include Rock among their parts while others do not and so we can't tell. Alternatively, one could hold that the indeterminacy of 6.11 is due, not to the vagueness of the name 'Everest', but to a certain vagueness affecting the English predicate 'part of', as urged by Donnelly (2014). There is no one parthood relation; rather, several slightly different relations are equally eligible as extension of our predicate, and while some such relations link Rock to Everest, others do not. This would also provide a key to such models as in figure 6.1. A solid line would

93 Beginning with Mehlberg (1958, §29). Similar accounts may be found in Hughes (1986), McGee (1997), McGee and McLaughlin (2000), Varzi (2001b), and Bittner and Smith (2003), *inter alia*.

indicate that all parthood relations agree on the relevant link; a dotted line would register a disagreement. But this would only show the models are defective insofar as they are representing several relations at once; the relations themselves can be perfectly standard. Either way—whether we blame it on 'Everest' or on 'part of'—a *de dicto* reading of 6.8 will locate the indeterminacy in the way we speak, not in the way the world is (or isn't). And what goes for 6.8 goes for any claim of that form. Linguistic vagueness is a widespread phenomenon and we need some way to deal with it: an adequate semantic theory, or perhaps a pragmatic or even an epistemic theory.[94] But none of this would have any ontological import. Our parthood ascriptions may be indeterminate. But the principles of mereology, understood as principles governing the parthood *relation*, or all the relations that qualify as admissible extensions of the parthood predicate, would be unaffected.[95]

Things are different on the second way of reading 6.8 (and the like). On this reading, corresponding to 6.10, the relevant indeterminacy is truly *de re*: we are saying *of* the mighty mountain we call 'Everest' that it is indeterminate whether its parts include a certain rock. So this reading does clash with the standard assumptions of mereology. The indeterminacy of 6.11 would not lie in the name we use to pick out the mountain, or in the predicate 'part of', but in the part-whole structure of the mountain itself. Similarly, the dotted lines in figure 6.1 would not reflect a defect in the models but a genuine, objective lack of determinateness in the situations they depict. This sort of reading may be questioned: already Russell (1923) argued that the idea of worldly indeterminacy betrays a "fallacy of verbalism", and some have gone as far as saying that it is simply not "intelligible" (Dummett, 1975, p. 314), if not ruled out "*a priori*" (Jackson, 2001, p. 657). Nonetheless, several philosophers feel otherwise and the thought that there may be vague objects for which the parthood relation is not fully determined has received increasing attention in the literature, from Johnsen (1989), Tye (1990), and van Inwagen (1990, ch. 17) to Morreau (2002), Smith (2005), and many others.[96] Even the opponents may come to admit that an *a priori* ban is unwarranted—a strong but debatable "metaphysical prejudice", as Burgess (1990, p. 263) calls it.[97] The worry is therefore legitimate: how would such a thought impact on the mereological axioms and theses considered so far?

94 See e.g. Hudson (2001, ch. 3) for an explicit endorsement of Williamson's (1994) epistemic account in relation to the present issues. For a survey of the main options, see Keefe (2000).

95 Some principles may, however, give rise to new concerns and clashes of intuition. See e.g. Donnelly (2014, pp. 56ff) on the Unrestricted Fusion axiom (with consequences for the 'vagueness argument' for mereological universalism mentioned in section 5.2.1).

96 For example, McKinnon (2003), Akiba (2000, 2004), Hyde (2008, §5.3), Williams (2008a), Barnes and Williams (2009, 2011), Rosen and Smith (2004), Carmichael (2011), Korman (2015a, §9.5), and, to some extent, Sattig (2013; 2014; 2015, ch. 7).

97 Dummett himself came to see his earlier remark as a prejudice in Dummett (1981, p. 440).

There is no straightforward way to address this question. Broadly speaking, the thought is that an atomic formula in our language, 'Pxy', may sometimes be indeterminate, but this is consistent with two views: (i) there may simply be no fact of the matter as to whether the formula holds, i.e. 'Pxy' may be *neither true nor false* of the objects in question, or (ii) part-whole relationships are not absolute and 'Pxy' may be *true to some degree*. Both views may be articulated in a variety of ways.

6.3.2 *Ontic Indeterminacy*

On the first sort of view, it could again be argued that no modification of our basic mereological machinery is strictly necessary, provided we take 'Pxy' to be true just when x is determinately part of y and false (with '$\neg Pxy$' true) just when x is determinately not part of y, and similarly for '$x = y$' if indeterminacies of identity are also allowed. Thus, the Reflexivity axiom A.1 should be read as asserting that everything is determinately part of itself, the Irreflexivity axiom A.7 that everything is determinately not a proper part of itself, the Antisymmetry axiom A.2 that things that are determinately part of each other are determinately identical, and so on. A number of questions arise, however, regarding how to deal explicitly with cases of indeterminacy.

For example, do objects with indeterminate parts have indeterminate identity? Many philosophers have taken the answer to be obviously in the affirmative (as in Evans, 1978) or have argued specifically to that effect (Weatherson, 2003), or have defended the affirmative answer against the idea that it amounts to a *reductio* (Barnes and Williams, 2009). Others, such as Sainsbury (1989), Burgess (1990), Edgington (2000), or Tye (2000), and more recently Paganini (2017), hold the opposite view: mereologically indeterminate objects would be in many ways elusive, but they would have precise identity conditions like any other object. Still others maintain that the answer depends on the strength of the underlying mereology. For instance, Parsons (2000b, §5.6.1) argues that on an extensional mereology with unrestricted binary sums, the *de re* indeterminacy of 6.11 would be inherited by

(6.12) Everest is identical with the sum of Everest and Rock.

so long as one accepts the following additional principle:

(6.13) If it is indeterminate whether x is part of y, then there is no part of the sum of x and y that is determinately not part of y.

A related question is: does countenancing things with indeterminate parts entail that composition is indeterminate, i.e. that there is sometimes no matter of fact whether some things have a mereological fusion? A popular view, much influenced by van Inwagen (1990, ch. 18), says it does. Others, such as Morreau (2002, §2), argue instead that the entailment is unwarranted: perhaps the *de re* indeterminacy of 6.11 is inherited by some instances of

(6.14) Everest is composed of x and Rock.

(for example, x could stand for something that is just like Everest except that Rock is determinately not part of it); yet this would not amount to saying that composition is indeterminate, for the following might be true all the same—and it surely is for the friend of mereological universalism.

(6.15) There is something composed of x and Rock.

Similarly, it is common to think that compositional indeterminacy entails existential indeterminacy (as in the vagueness argument for universalism; see section 5.2.1) but the link may not be straightforward. For instance, Donnelly (2009) argues that the entailment may require the following thesis.[98]

(6.16) If it is indeterminate whether the φs compose something, then the φs (indeterminately) compose an indeterminately existing thing.

Note that part of the issue here depends on how exactly one understands indeterminate composition. The antecedent of 6.16 is meant *de re*, but even *de re* indeterminacy can be ambiguous. The following need not be equivalent:

(6.17) The φs are such that it is indeterminate whether they compose x.
(6.18) x is such that it is indeterminate whether the φs compose it.

Finally, there is of course the general question of how one should handle logically complex statements concerning, at least in part, mereologically indeterminate objects. And here there are several options. A natural choice is to rely on a three-valued semantics of some sort, the 'third' value being, strictly speaking, not a truth *value* but rather a truth-value *gap*. In this spirit, both Johnsen (1989) and Tye (1990) endorse the truth conditions of Kleene (1938) while Hyde (2008), for instance, those of Łukasiewicz (1920). However, other choices are available, including non-truth-functional accounts.

For example, Morreau (2002) recommends a form of supervaluationism. This sort of account was originally put forward by Fine (1975) as a way to deal with *de dicto* indeterminacy, the idea being that a statement involving vague expressions should count as true (false) if and only it is true (false) under every semantic 'sharpening' of those expressions.[99] Still, a friend of

98 On this point, see also Hawley (2002, 2004), Merricks (2005), and Carmichael (2011).

99 Supervaluationism was first developed by van Fraassen (1966, 1969) to provide a semantics of free logic. For an overview of its applications to vagueness, see Keefe (2008).

de re indeterminacy may exploit the same idea and speak instead of *ontological* sharpenings—what Sainsbury (1989) calls "approximants" and Cohn and Gotts (1996) "crispings" of vague objects, or what Parsons (2000b) calls "resolutions" and Akiba (2000) "precisifications" of the world as a whole.[100] As a result, one would be able to explain why, for example, 6.19 appears to be true and 6.20 false for every value of x and y (assuming determinate parts satisfy the Transitivity axiom A.3), whereas both conditionals may turn out to be equally indeterminate on Kleene's semantics and equally true on Łukasiewicz's (e.g. when x is Rock and y a determinate part of Everest).

(6.19) If x is part of y and y is part of Everest, then x is part of Everest.
(6.20) If x is part of y and y is part of Everest, then x is not part of Everest.

Alternatively, one could rely on a logical framework that is explicitly designed to handle the locution 'it is indeterminate whether'—not as a way to report a semantic condition in the metalanguage but as a genuine sentential operator in the object language. This would amount to seeing mereological indeterminacy as a special case of a general phenomenon that once again lies beyond the expressive power of a standard first-order language, much as mereological change may be seen as a special case of a general phenomenon that calls for a language with temporal or modal operators (section 6.2.3). By itself, the apparatus would be neutral regarding whether there *are* cases of mereological indeterminacy. But as with temporal and modal logics, the interaction of the new operator with the other formula-building operators, especially the quantifiers, would at least allow one to express *de re* indeterminacy and to study its logical behavior. Indeed, Evans's (1978) argument against vague objects was given in a language of this sort, with '$\nabla\varphi$' expressing 'It is indeterminate whether φ', and much discussion that followed focused precisely on the modal logic of ∇ that the argument presupposed.[101] The friend of ontic indeterminacy may want to handle things differently.

We shall not go into the details of this approach. Let us simply note one advantage that it might claim over the other options, which concerns the possibility of *higher-order* indeterminacy. Perhaps it is indeterminate whether Rock is part of Everest. But perhaps it is indeterminate whether things are truly so; it might be indeterminate whether it is indeterminate whether Rock is part of Everest—and so on. Higher-order *de re* indeterminacy of this sort can hardly be accommodated within the framework of a three-valued semantics, which simply replaces one sharp boundary (here: between positive

100 Related proposals may be found in the writings of several other authors; see e.g. Stell (2004), Williams (2008b), Bynoe (2008), Barnes (2010), Bennett (2010), Barnes and Williams (2011), and Abasnezhad and Hosseini (2014). See also the discussion in Abasnezhad and Jenkins (2018).

101 The literature is extensive, but see e.g. Rasmussen (1986) and Heck (1998). Evans himself took ∇ to be governed by the modal logic known as S5 (Hughes and Cresswell, 1996, ch. 3).

and negative cases of parthood) with *two* boundaries (between positive and indeterminate cases, and between indeterminate and negative cases). That is, it can hardly be accommodated short of pushing the problem to the meta-language, and then perhaps to the meta-metalanguage, and so on. But a modal language would allow one to handle higher-order indeterminacy quite naturally. Just as we can study the effect of iterating the operator $\Box$ in a temporal or modal logic, so one could study the logical behavior of formulas in which the indeterminacy operator ∇, or perhaps a determinacy operator $\triangle$, is iterated two or more times.[102]

6.3.3 *Fuzzy Mereology*

The second way of dealing with *de re* indeterminacy is significantly different. It proceeds from the intuition that the phrase 'it is indeterminate whether' is loose talk. As van Inwagen (1990, p. 221) puts it, generally speaking it is not just a matter of *whether* a given object a is part of an object b; the question is *to what degree* a is part of b. For example, given two borderline rocks, it may be that one is (much) closer to Everest's peak than the other, and to capture this intuition it is not enough to say that neither rock is determinately part of Everest; one should say that the first rock is part of Everest to a (much) greater degree than the second. To think that the parthood relation is an all-or-nothing affair is, on this view, to miss out on a fundamental feature of the mereological structure of the world.

It should be noted that this intuition can in principle be accommodated also within a *de dicto* conception of indeterminacy. For instance, the super-valuational account mentioned above can be generalized by introducing a measure on the class of relevant semantic sharpenings: rather than checking whether a statement is true (false) under *every* sharpening of its vague expressions, one would check *how many* sharpenings make it true (false).[103] However, it is mainly in relation to *de re* indeterminacy that the intuition has been taken seriously. And typically the approach has not been to 'ontologize' a generalized form of supervaluationism. The popular way of developing a degree-theoretic account of mereological indeterminacy has been to 'fuzzify'

102 There are two ways of understanding a determinacy operator $\triangle$. One way corresponds to the locution 'It is determinate whether', which makes $\triangle$ dual to ∇. This is the reading suggested by Evans (1978), though his claim that the resulting logic would be as strong as S5 can't be right: the T principle $\triangle\varphi \rightarrow \varphi$ would obviously fail when φ is false (Gibbins, 1982). Indeed, the resulting modal logic would not even be normal, since it would also violate the K principle $\triangle(\varphi \rightarrow \psi) \rightarrow (\triangle\varphi \rightarrow \triangle\psi)$, e.g. when φ is a logical falsehood (Pellettier, 1984). The second reading of $\triangle$ corresponds to 'It is determinate that'. This is not dual to ∇ and is best treated as primitive, with '$\nabla\varphi$' defined as '$\neg\triangle\varphi \wedge \neg\triangle\neg\varphi$'. See e.g. Keefe (2000, §§ 1.5–1.6) for general discussion. For a recent illustration of this approach, see Bacon (2018, ch. 16).

103 See e.g. Lewis (1970, appendix) and Kamp (1975) for generalizations along these lines.

the parthood relation in ways that closely parallel the fuzzification of membership in Zadeh's (1965) set theory, leading to such proposals as Polkowski and Skowron's (1994) "rough mereology", Gerla and Miranda's (2004) theory of "graded inclusion", Smith's (2005) "concrete mereology", and Parsons's (2011) or Sadegh-Zadeh's (2012) "fuzzy mereologies". There is some leeway concerning matters of detail.[104] But generally speaking the approach is uniform across the literature, and can be described as follows.

Think of the parthood relation in terms of its characteristic function. Classically, this function is fully bivalent: it takes a certain designated value, say 1, for those ordered pairs that stand in the relation and a different value, say 0, for all other pairs. Thus, any mereological model $\langle D, \leqslant \rangle$ may equally be thought of as a structure $\langle D, \pi \rangle$, where π is the characteristic function of $\leqslant$, and the relevant satisfaction condition for atomic formulas

(6.21) 'Pxy' is satisfied by a, b if and only if $a \leqslant b$

may be revisited accordingly:

(6.22) 'Pxy' is true of a, b if and only if $\pi(a, b) = 1$, and 'Pxy' is false of a, b if and only if $\pi(a, b) = 0$.

From this perspective, it's clear that the possibility of *de re* mereological indeterminacy amounts to dropping the assumption of bivalence. And while the approach of section 6.3.2 may be seen as dropping the assumption one way, by allowing π to have *no* value for some arguments (making the second clause in 6.22 non-redundant), the degree-theoretic approach drops the assumption the other way, by allowing π to have *other* values—typically, any value δ in the closed real interval $[0, 1]$. As a result, the satisfaction conditions for the atomic formulas will still be fully defined. But instead of delivering the classical rule in 6.22, π will deliver a many-valued rule:

(6.23) 'Pxy' is true of a, b to degree δ if and only if $\pi(a, b) = \delta$.

Now, what this means, effectively, is that mereology would come with a non-classical semantics, so one way to implement this approach is simply to act on the underlying logical machinery: rather than assuming classical logic (our A.0), one can start from a many-valued or fuzzy logic of sorts and revisit the axioms of mereology on such grounds.[105] At the same time, in practice one never proceeds this way. As soon as one thinks parthood comes

104 Rough mereology actually grew out of a variant of Zadeh's fuzzy set theory known as rough set theory (Pawłak, 1982). However, its proponents do not hesitate to describe it as "a counterpart of fuzzy set theory within mereology" (Polkowski, 2001, p. VIII).
105 For an introductory survey of fuzzy logics and related systems, see Cintula *et al.* (2017).

in degrees, intuitions concerning a number of mereological principles will depend crucially on intuitions concerning the minimum degrees to which the relevant atomic formulas must be true, and this can hardly be handled by the logical apparatus.[106] The standard way to proceed is to work explicitly at the semantic level, characterizing the parthood relation directly in terms of conditions on π rather than by means of axioms on 'P'. What conditions should be assumed? How would they affect the axioms of classical mereology and its competitors?

As it turns out, with regard to some basic principles the answer to these questions is rather straightforward, but going further gives rise to several complications and calls for difficult decisions. Consider, for instance, the partial ordering axioms A.1–A.3. Classically, these correspond to the following general conditions on π.

(6.24) $\pi(a, a) = 1$ *π-Reflexivity*

(6.25) If $\pi(a, b) = 1$ and $\pi(b, a) = 1$, then $a = b$ *π-Antisymmetry*

(6.26) If $\pi(b, c) = 1$, then $\pi(a, b) \leq \pi(a, c)$ *π-Transitivity*

When the range of π is extended from $\{0, 1\}$ to $[0, 1]$, the same conditions would seem to work equally well. After all, just as Everest's fuzziness does not prevent it from being definitely self-identical, it should not prevent it from being definitely part of itself. If Everest and Chomolungma are definitely part of each other, then their fuzziness should not interfere with their being one and the same mountain. And if Everest is definitely part of the Himalayas, then Rock should be part of the Himalayas at least to the degree that it is part of Everest. Perhaps one may consider a stronger form of π-Antisymmetry, as in Smith (2005, p. 397).[107]

(6.27) If $\pi(a, b) > 0$ and $\pi(b, a) > 0$, then $a = b$ *Strong π-Antisymmetry*

Or one could consider a more general form of π-Transitivity, as in Sadegh-Zadeh (2012, p. 399).

(6.28) If $\pi(a, b) > 0$ and $\pi(b, c) > 0$, then $\pi(a, c) > 0$ *General π-Transitivity*

106 Indeed, this might be a reason to think that the move to a non-bivalent characteristic function is the wrong way to go; one should rather move to a part-whole-degree relation, writing e.g. '$P_\delta xy$' for 'x is part of y to degree δ', and figure out the relevant axioms in the usual way. Such a course would be analogous to the sort of relativization we saw in section 6.2.2 in regard to time and modality, and would have an obvious advantage: it would take care of the idea that parthood comes in degrees without requiring any departure from classical semantics and, hence, from classical logic. Again, this is not a common way to proceed, though the axiomatic treatment of 'rough inclusion' in Polkowski and Skowron (1996) comes close to it.

107 Strictly speaking, Smith works with a notion of (concrete) part that involves a double world-time index, but here we may ignore such details.

But such adjustments wouldn't raise major conceptual difficulties.[108] Things get harder, though, as soon as we move beyond the ordering axioms.

Take, for instance, the Weak Supplementation principle A.10. One natural way of expressing it in terms of π would be as follows.

(6.29) If $\pi(a, b) = 1$ and $a \neq b$, then $\pi(c, b) = 1$ for some c such that, for all d, either $\pi(d, c) = 0$ or $\pi(d, a) = 0$.

There are, however, fifteen other possibilities, corresponding to the variants of 6.29 obtained by re-writing one or both occurrences of '$= 1$' as '> 0' and one or both occurrences of '$= 0$' as '< 1'. In the presence of bivalence, all such variants would amount to the same. Yet they would differ if π is allowed to take non-integral values, and the question of which version best reflects the supplementation intuition would have no obvious answer. (See e.g. the discussion in Smith, 2005, p. 397.) And this is just the beginning: it's clear that similar issues arise with regard to virtually every principle examined in the previous chapters, concerning decomposition as well as composition. (See e.g. the reformulations of Unrestricted Fusion in Polkowski and Skowron, 1994, p. 86, Parsons, 2011, p. 6, and Tsai, 2012, p, 472.)

On the other hand, when it comes to some major worries that are typically raised in connection with *de re* indeterminacy, the present framework would be less open to controversy than the approach of section 6.3.2. For example, the question of whether mereological indeterminacy implies indeterminate identity would generally be answered in the negative, especially if one adheres to the spirit of extensionality. For then it is natural to say that composite objects are identical if and only if they have exactly the same proper parts to the same degree—and that is not a vague matter.[109] Likewise, the question of whether mereological indeterminacy implies indeterminate existence would generally be answered in the affirmative. van Inwagen (1990, p. 228) takes this to be an obvious consequence of the approach, but Smith (2005, pp. 399ff) goes further and provides a detailed analysis of how one can calculate the degree to which a given non-empty collection of things has a fusion, i.e. the "degree of existence" of the fusion. (Roughly, the idea is to begin with the fusion as it would exist if every element of the collection were determinately part of it, and then calculate the actual degree of existence of the fusion as a function of the degree to which each element of the collection is actually part of it).

108 As opposed to intuition battles, e.g. concerning 6.25 vs. 6.27, or 6.26 vs. 6.28 vs. Smith's variant:

$$\min(\pi(a, b), \pi(b, c)) \leq \pi(a, c)$$

Suppose Rock is part of Everest to some positive degree, and Everest is part of Tibet to some positive degree. Rock is definitely in Nepal. To what degree is it part of Tibet?

109 The same is true of fuzzy sets *vis-à-vis* fuzzy membership; see Zadeh (1965, p. 340).

The one question that remains open is whether all this really amounts to an account of mereological *indeterminacy*. After all, fuzzifying the characteristic function π amounts to requiring that there always be an exact degree to which anything counts as a part of anything: Rock_1 will be part of Everest to degree .0.4, Rock_2 to degree 0.45, Rock_3 perhaps to degree 0.45978. It seems somewhat "ironic" (Sanford, 1976, p. 201) that mereological indeterminacy should result in such refined and infinitely precise discriminations. Indeed, that is a common complaint, extending a concern we already raised regarding the non-bivalent theories of section 6.3.2:

> The shared disadvantage concerns higher-order vagueness: many-valued theories implausibly assume a sharp cut-off point between definite (1 or 0) and indefinite cases. The three-valued theory, by having only one intermediate case, does not take account of the fact that some cases, while indeterminate, are nearer to the truth than others. The fuzzy theory takes this into account but makes the even more absurd assumption that ... there are exactly determined objects of every degree of candidacy. (Simons, 1999, p. 92)

It could be argued that *de dicto* theories will suffer from parallel worries, especially on a supervaluational construal: 'sharpening' is not a sharp concept. But in that case one could respond that the irony concerns the modeling of our linguistic practices, and concede that the metalanguage is itself vague. Here it would concern the modeling of the world itself.

6.3.4 *Overdeterminacy and Paraconsistency*

Someone who takes seriously the possibility of *de re* mereological indeterminacy may want to go further and consider the opposite possibility as well, namely, that parthood relationships may in some cases suffer from genuine *over*determinacy.

Consider again the puzzle illustrated by Peirce's example of the boundary separating a black drop of ink from its white surrounding, which we briefly mentioned in section 4.1.2: is the boundary black or white? Or consider Aristotle's formulation of the puzzle in the temporal continuum: at the instant a moving object comes to rest, is it in motion or at rest? (*Physics*, VI, 3, 234a–b) This is the classic problem of change (Mortensen, 2016), and mereologically it can be seen as arising whenever we examine the relationship between a thing and its (relative) complement in the presence of continuity. Where one ends, the other begins, but which of the two gets to 'own' the cut-off boundary? The case of Dion and his foot is another example. In section 6.2.1 we said that if the amputation takes place at t_0, we may describe the situation by saying that the foot is part of Dion at $t < t_0$ but not at $t' > t_0$. But what about the limit cases, where $t = t_0$, or $t_0 = t'$? One may of course view such riddles as a *reductio* of the very notion of a boundary. That was Peirce's moral: "The logical conclusion ... is that the points of the boundary do not exist" (Peirce, 1893, p. 98). Indeed, that is why someone may be led to endorse Atomlessness (A.31), or at least to posit spatio-temporal Gunk (A.61), as in Whitehead's mereology of events and his point-free theory of space.[110] But for those who are willing to accept boundary points as *bona fide* entities, the puzzles must be taken at face value. One might concede that the boundary between a thing and its complement belongs to neither, or that we are dealing with another case of mereological indeterminacy. That would take us back to the options of the previous sections. But one may as well take the opposite stance and view this as a genuine case of mereological overdeterminacy: the boundary belongs to both.[111]

Formally, this option is of course at odds with the laws of classical logic, particularly the laws governing the Boolean behavior of negation. The (relative) complement of any given thing x is by definition something all of whose parts are disjoint from x (D.5, D.11), so a mutual sharing of boundary parts is automatically ruled out in any mereology based on A.0 or, indeed, any mereology logically committed to the law of non-contradiction. Hegel was forthright about this point:

> Something, as an immediate existence, is the limit with respect to another something; but it has this limit *in it* and is something through the mediation of that limit, which is just as much its non-being. The limit is the mediation in virtue of which something and other each *both is and is not*. (Hegel, 1812-1816, p. 99)

Some may therefore take such considerations to motivate a *dialetheic* metaphysics, according to which the world itself might involve true contradictions.[112] And this, in turn, would require that classical logic be abandoned and replaced by a paraconsistent logic, which is to say a logic that rejects the classical *ex falso quodlibet* inference $\varphi \wedge \neg\varphi \vdash \psi$.[113] After all, a dialetheist who accepts some contradictions will not want to accept every sentence whatsoever; their view needn't be trivial.

There are several ways of achieving this. Generally speaking, the key idea would be to use a paraconsistent logic in which classical Boolean negation

110 For more on this line of reasoning, we refer again to Varzi (1997, 2015) and the literature cited in chapter 4, note 117.

111 There are other options. For instance, Brentano (1976) held that whenever x is in contact with y there are *two* boundaries—one belonging to x and one to y—that coincide spatially without x and y overlapping mereologically. This view has received formal treatment in some recent literature (from Chisholm, 1984, 1993 and Smith, 1995, 1997 to Baumann *et al.*, 2014, 2016 and Cotnoir, 2019b), but it requires an explicit step into topology and location theory, so we shall not consider it here.

112 For a brief overview of dialetheism, see Priest *et al.* (2018).

113 On paraconsistent logics, see Priest (2002); on the relationship between dialetheism and paraconsistency, Priest (2009).

is weakened to a so-called De Morgan negation: it satisfies double-negation elimination, the De Morgan laws for conjunction and disjunction, and the law of excluded middle, but allows some forms of inconsistency. (A simple example would be Priest's 1979 quantified "Logic of Paradox", LPQ.[114]) A key feature of such a logic, besides the failure of *ex falso quodlibet*, is the invalidity of disjunctive syllogism, i.e. the inference $\varphi \vee \psi, \neg\varphi \vdash \psi$.

Now, weakening the underlying logic this way and retaining the axioms for classical mereology results in some decidedly non-classical behavior. In a paraconsistent context, the *parts* of a given object y (the xs for which Pxy) are independent of its *non-parts* (the xs for which $\neg Pxy$). That is, it is paraconsistently acceptable that a part might also be a non-part of the same object. Call such things *inconsistent parts*.

To see how this works, consider the model in figure 6.2. We may think of this as a model for Peirce's black drop, a, and its white complement, $-a$, with a common inconsistent boundary b. The left diagram shows the parts of each element, which are connected to their wholes by arrows, or by chains of arrows, since we may continue to assume that parthood is transitive. So we have Pba, $Pb(-a)$, Pbu, etc. The second diagram uses dotted arrows to show each element's non-parts. So we have $\neg Pba$, $\neg Pb(-a)$, $\neg Pab$, etc. As non-parthood is not transitive, one cannot chain together dotted arrows (e.g. we have $\neg Pab$ and $\neg Pbu$ but not $\neg Pau$). Our boundary, b, is a bottom element that is both a part and a non-part, and hence an inconsistent part, of every other object.

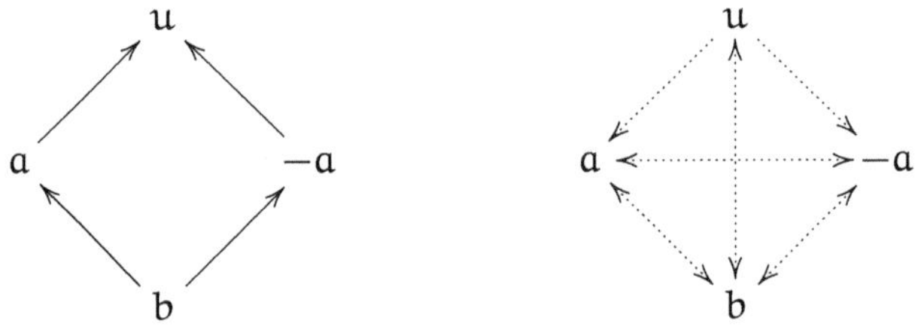

Figure 6.2: Parts and non-parts (dotted lines)

The first thing to note about such a model is that the Remainder axiom A.4 yields only De Morgan—not Boolean—complements: an object and its

114 LPQ is based on the truth conditions of Kleene's (1938) three-valued semantics mentioned earlier, but with the third value construed as a truth-value *glut* rather than a truth-value gap, i.e. as meaning 'both true and false', or 'paradoxical'. Thus, representing the three values in decreasing order as 1 (only true), $\frac{1}{2}$ (true and false), and 0 (only false), a conjunction has the minimum value of its conjuncts, a disjunction has the maximum value of its disjuncts, etc., and negation behaves classically with respect to 1 and 0 but stays fixed with respect to $\frac{1}{2}$. Importantly, in LPQ both 1 and $\frac{1}{2}$ are designated values.

complement can overlap, as is the case with a and $-a$. This is precisely what we wanted. However, the underlying tolerance for inconsistencies also gives us that a and $-a$ are disjoint, since all of a's parts are non-parts of $-a$. Thus we have $\mathrm{O}a(-a)$ as well as $\mathrm{D}a(-a)$, showing that overlap may hold simultaneously with disjointness.[115]

Another violation of classical behavior concerns Weak Supplementation (A.10), which the model does not satisfy: we have $\mathrm{PP}ba$ even though a has no proper part disjoint from b (assuming nothing is a non-part of itself). In fact the model violates weaker forms of supplementation too, including Quasi-Supplementation (A.42) and both Weak and Strong Company (A.39 and A.40). This is highly non-standard. However, on the paraconsistent picture the failure of such principles makes sense, since b is a part of a but also a non-part of a. There need be no residue of a without b, since b is already 'removed', so to speak.

Relatedly, both a and $-a$ have proper parts; indeed they have the same proper parts, namely b and nothing else. Yet clearly, $a \neq -a$. So we have a failure of PP–Extensionality (T.1). Once again, though, this is understandable. In a paraconsistent setting, having the same proper parts does not amount to mereological indiscernibility, hence it can't be sufficient for identity; things additionally need to have the same *non-parts*. In figure 6.2, a's non-parts are b, u, and $-a$ whereas $-a$'s non-parts are b, u, and a. So the elements a and $-a$ are mereologically discernible after all, hence distinct. Similarly, the model violates O–extensionality (A.14), since everything overlaps everything else, but this is not surprising: mereological indiscernibility is more demanding than mere overlap-indiscernibility.

Finally, it is worth noting that paraconsistent mereologies may in principle allow for the existence of several universal objects, each of which has everything as a part but different things as non-parts. A simple example is the model in figure 6.3, where the two top elements, u_1 and u_2, stand in different non-parthood relations with respect to a and b. Similarly, there

Figure 6.3: Universal objects with distinct non-parts

115 Here we are working informally with Priest's LPQ. To check that $-a$ is genuinely the complement of a, given D.11, it suffices to verify that $-a$ is the fusion of everything disjoint from a. Note that $\exists z(\mathrm{P}za \wedge \mathrm{P}z(-a))$ is false (and true), since b is a non-part of both. Thus $\neg\exists z(\mathrm{P}za \wedge \mathrm{P}z(-a))$ is true (and false). Indeed, only $-a$ and b count as disjoint from a, and the minimal upper bound of those elements is $-a$.

can be several distinct null objects, each of which is part of everything but is a non-part of different things.

All of this is rather informal, but can be made precise. As an example, a fully developed paraconsistent mereology for application to puzzles about boundaries is given by Weber and Cotnoir (2015). The underlying logic of their system is the weak relevant logic DKQ of Routley (1979), which has also been used in the context of paraconsistent set theory,[116] and the mereological axioms comprise a paraconsistent recasting of a classical mereology due to Hovda (2009, §4), which includes the ordering axioms (A.1–A.3), Strong Complementation* (A.35), and Unrestricted Fusion (A.5) along with both No Zero (T.2) and O–Inclusion (T.22) treated as axioms. In order to give a full account of a paraconsistent theory of boundaries, the authors also show how to extend this theory to include topological operators—a paraconsistent 'mereotopology'.

But boundary puzzles are not the only domain of application for paraconsistent mereology. Another application concerns the 'problem of nothingness' in the context of contemporary Meinongianism. According to Meinong (1904), every intentional state is directed toward an object.[117] On the assumption that one can take intentional attitudes toward nothingness, it would thus appear that nothingness is both an object and the utter absence of any object.[118] Priest (2014a) develops a paraconsistent mereology based on LPQ to handle precisely this problem, where the quantifiers are 'free' of existential commitment. Nothingness, on Priest's view, is the fusion of the empty set—the null object. So Priest's mereology, which takes PP as a primitive and defines P using D.12, contains as axioms just Asymmetry (A.8), Transitivity (A.9), O–Extensionality (A.14), and the F''-type variant of the Absolutely Unrestricted Fusion schema (A.45).

A similar system may be found in Priest (2014b, ch. 6), except that Asymmetry is explicitly dropped. This is motivated by Priest's metaphysics of unity, particularly his "gluon" theory.[119] However the move is not straightforward. On the one hand, in the presence of D.12, the transitivity of PP together with O–Extensionality entail the antisymmetry of P (A.2),[120] which in LPQ is equivalent to $\forall x \forall y((\neg x = y \wedge (\neg PPxy \vee \neg PPyx)) \vee x = y)$. This formula is not quite the Asymmetry axiom A.8, but it means that for any x and y that are distinct (and not also identical) we have $PPxy \rightarrow PPyx$. On

116 See e.g. Brady (2006) and Weber (2010).

117 This is generally known as the 'Intentionality Thesis', which Meinong inherited from Brentano (1874, § II.i.5); see Jacquette (2015, esp. ch. 9).

118 A similar problem faces interpreters of the late Heidegger; see Casati and Fujikawa (2015) and Casati (2016).

119 Gluons are things that 'glue' several parts together into a unity. The notion was first introduced in Priest (1995, ch. 12).

120 This is noted in Cotnoir (2018), along with a way of fixing the problem.

the other hand, it is not entirely clear why gluon theory should rule out Asymmetry. Priest's argument proceeds by showing for some gluon g that $PPgg$. But that same line of reasoning can be used to show that $\neg PPgg$, so paraconsistently we don't really have a violation of Irreflexivity and, hence, of Asymmetry.[121]

Another option would be to construe nothingness as the complement of the universe. Casati (2016, ch. 4) and Casati and Fujikawa (2019) extend Weber and Cotnoir's framework for exactly this purpose, adding the following axiom.

(A_*29) $\exists x \exists y(\neg Pxy \wedge F_{z=z}y)$ *Non-totalness*

From A_*29, paraconsistent complementation immediately yields the existence of a unique complement of u (more precisely, a complement* in the sense of D.34) that is part of everything but also disjoint from the universe—an inconsistent null object.[122] This mereological account, they argue, has advantages over Priest's.

6.4 NON-CLASSICAL LOGICS AND NON-CLASSICAL MEREOLOGIES

Such theories must of course be assessed on their own merits, as with any other theory considered in this book. From a general perspective, however, they also give us an opportunity to conclude with an important remark that goes beyond the specific cases. It concerns the broader question of the interplay between mereology and logic.

We started in chapter 2 with classical mereology as an axiomatic theory based on classical first-order logic (A.0), and in the following three chapters we considered a number of alternative, non-classical theories that can be obtained by revisiting our initial stock of axioms (A.1–A.5). Earlier in this chapter we saw that there are in fact several reasons one may want to go beyond this setting and provide such theories, classical or non-classical, with stronger and more expressive logical foundations, such as second-order or plural logic, or modal logic. But we also saw a number of reasons that may lead one to revisit the underlying logic in more radical ways, shifting to

121 Here is Priest's argument (2014b, p. 89). Take some y with proper parts and a gluon, g, that has every property of any part of y (a "prime gluon"). There must be some part x of y such that $PPgx$ (for instance, let x be a sum of g and some other part z of y). It follows that $PPgg$. But then, by the same pattern: since $\neg PPxg$, it follows that $\neg PPgg$.

122 One might wonder how a null object can be permitted in a mereology with the No Zero principle T.2. Note that a classically null object n would be such that Pnx for all x and $\neg Pnx$ for no x. In figure 6.2, b isn't classically nil, since it is among a's non-parts. Since we have more than one object around, T.2 gives $\neg\exists x \forall y Pxy$, which is just equivalent to $\forall x \exists y \neg Pxy$ (even in a paraconsistent setting). But a is a witness for y when x is instantiated by b.

genuine alternative frameworks such as three-valued, fuzzy, or even paraconsistent logics. In each of these cases, the outcome is once again a non-classical mereology. Yet this 'non-classicality' is significantly different from the more familiar cases examined earlier. Many-valued or paraconsistent mereologies do not originate from misgivings about the axioms of classical *mereology*; they stem from more general concerns about the underlying principles of classical *logic*. They are non-classical for reasons that have little or nothing to do with one's intuitions about parthood *per se*.

This phenomenon is not uncommon in other areas. Particularly, set theory has received many alternative formulations, some of which depart from classical ZFC precisely by virtue of relying on different logical foundations. We already mentioned, for instance, that the relevant logic DKQ employed by Weber and Cotnoir (2015) has also been used for the purpose of developing paraconsistent set theories, and the same is true of other systems of paraconsistent logic.[123] Similarly, there are of course variants of ZFC that are based on fuzzy logic.[124] In view of the tight connection between mereology and set theory, it is not surprising that mereologists have pursued similar programs. But there are other options. In set theory, another important alternative to classical ZFC is represented by constructive theories based on intuitionistic logic.[125] One may therefore consider recasting mereology, too, in intuitionistic terms. The literature does not offer much, but see e.g. Ciraulo (2013), whose mereological theory corresponds to an intuitionistic overlap algebra rather than a (complete) Boolean algebra, and Maffezioli and Varzi (in press), who develop a mereology that is acceptable from the standpoint of constructive reasoning and satisfies the extensionality principles of classical mereology.[126]

There are also independent reasons why a mereologist might want to leave the *terra firma* of classical logic. Consider, for instance, the fact that many mereological notions, such as product, difference, complement, etc. are defined with the help of the iota operator, ɿ. Classically this operator is governed by Russell's (1905) theory of descriptions, which treats ɿ-terms as incomplete symbols to be eliminated in terms of existence and uniqueness claims. As a result, basic statements involving such terms turn out to be false whenever the relevant existence and uniqueness conditions are not satisfied. For instance, a formula of the form '$x = y \times z$' will be false whenever

123 See e.g. Priest (2006, ch. 18) and Carnielli and Coniglio (2016, ch. 8).

124 See e.g. Hájek and Haniková (2003) for a recast of axiomatic ZFC in fuzzy logic.

125 See Crosilla (2019) for a first survey.

126 There is also a literature on so-called "Heyting mereologies" (Forrest, 2002, 2012; Mormann, 2012, 2013; Russell, 2016). Despite the name (Arend Heyting was the father of intuitionistic logic), such theories are based on classical logic. Since they lack Weak Supplementation, they are therefore non-classical *mereologies* in the familiar sense. (Essentially, they deliver a parthood relation whose structure is not a Boolean but a Heyting algebra; see Johnstone, 1982.)

Dyz, '$x = y - z$' will be false whenever PPyz, and '$x = -u$' will always be false. This is how Leonard and Goodman (1940) handle such notions in their Calculus of Individuals, and we decided to do the same (see section 1.5). Yet Russell's theory has had its fair share of opposition. Some may prefer treating definite descriptions as *bona fide* singular terms that may or may not be uniquely satisfied. In that case adjustments would be required, and again we have two main options. A friend of classical logic will go for a (mildly) non-classical *mereology*, e.g. a mereology with a null object serving as the default denotation for all defective definite descriptions (following Carnap, 1947, p. 37). The second option is to allow for genuinely non-denoting descriptions and trade classical logic for a suitable free logic with ι-terms, as in Simons (1987, §2.5 and 1991a). Then the outcome would be a mereology that is (mildly) non-classical because so is the underlying *logic*.[127]

These are just some examples. Nonetheless, they are indicative of the large space of possibilities that mereologists face when they engage in the task of developing rigorous formal theories to give expressions to their views on parthood relationships—and of the subtle but important ambivalence involved in the notion of a 'non-classical' account. In this book we focused mainly on one way to understand that notion, as with the majority of the mereological literature. The other way is also important and opens up a wide spectrum of venues that, so far, have been barely broached.

127 Free description theories go back to the early days of free logic. For an overview of the philosophical motivations, see Lambert (1987); for technical surveys, see Bencivenga (1986, §12) and Lehmann (2002, §4). It is worth noting that set theory, too, may be revisited in a similar fashion; see Bencivenga (1976).

BIBLIOGRAPHY

This bibliography lists all contemporary literature referenced in the text or in the footnotes. Works by ancient, medieval, or early modern philosophers are included only if cited in some specific edition; otherwise we followed a reference format that should enable most editions to be used. When a foreign title is available also in English translation, all page numbers given in the text and footnotes refer to the latter. Similarly for entries that mention later editions.

Abasnezhad, A. and Hosseini, D., 2014. Vagueness in the world: A supervaluationist approach. In Akiba, K. and Abasnezhad, A., eds., *Vague Objects and Vague Identity: New Essays on Ontic Vagueness*, pp. 239–255. Springer, Dordrecht.

Abasnezhad, A. and Jenkins, C. S. I., 2018. Metaphysical vagueness without vague objects. *Thought*, 7: 278–283.

Abelard, P., 1956. *Dialectica*, ed. by L. M. De Rijk. Van Gorcum, Assen.

Aczel, P., 1988. *Non-Well-Founded Sets*. CSLI Publications, Stanford (CA).

Adams, R. M., 1983. Phenomenalism and corporeal substance in Leibniz. *Midwest Studies in Philosophy*, 8: 217–257.

Adams, R. M., 1994. *Leibniz: Determinist, Theist, Idealist*. Oxford University Press, Oxford.

Adžić, M. and Arsenijević, M., 2014. Gunkology and pointilism: Two mutually supervening models of the region-based and the point-based theory of the infinite two-dimensional continuum. In Macchia, G., Orilia, F., and Fano, V., eds., *Space and Time: A Priori and a Posteriori Studies*, pp. 137–170. De Gruyter, Berlin.

Akiba, K., 2000. Vagueness as a modality. *The Philosophical Quarterly*, 50: 359–370.

Akiba, K., 2004. Vagueness in the world. *Noûs*, 38: 407–429.

Albert, D. Z., 1996. Elementary quantum metaphysics. In Cushing, J. T., Fine,

A. I., and Goldstein, S., eds., *Bohmian Mechanics and Quantum Theory: An Appraisal*, pp. 277–284. Kluwer, Dordrecht.

Albertazzi, L. and Libardi, M., eds., 1994. *Mereologies*. Special issue of *Axiomathes*, volume 5/1.

Allen, R., 2000. Identity and becoming. *The Southern Journal of Philosophy*, 38: 527–548.

Allen, R., 2005. The mereology of events. *Sorites*, 16: 23–37.

Alston, W. P., 1996. *A Realist Conception of Truth*. Cornell University Press, Ithaca (NY).

Amerini, F., Binini, I., and Mugnai, M., eds., 2019. *Mereology in Medieval Logic and Metaphysics: Proceedings of the 21st European Symposium of Medieval Logic and Semantics*. Edizioni della Normale, Pisa.

Angyal, A., 1939. The structure of wholes. *Philosophy of Science*, 6: 25–37.

Anthony, M., 2010. Improper parts, restricted existence, and use: Three arguments against Ted Sider's four-dimensionalism. *Res Cogitans*, 1: 1–13.

Apostel, L., 1982. Some remarks on ontology. In Agassi, J. and Cohen, R. S., eds., *Scientific Philosophy Today: Essays in Honor of Mario Bunge*, pp. 1–44. Reidel, Dordrecht.

Aquinas, T., 1961. *Commentary on the Metaphysics of Aristotle*, Eng. trans. by J. P. Rowan. Regnery, Chicago (IL).

Aquinas, T., 2006. *Summa Theologiae*, ed. by T. Gilby with Eng. trans. by T. McDermott *et al*. Cambridge University Press, Cambridge.

Arci, A., 2012. *Parti diafane: Introduzione alla mereologia di Aristotele*. Lampi di stampa, Cologno Monzese.

Aristotle, 1984. *Complete Works: The Revised Oxford Translation*, ed. by J. Barnes. Princeton University Press, Princeton (NJ).

Arlig, A. W., 2005. A study in early medieval mereology: Boethius, Abelard, and Pseudo-Joscelin. Ph.D. thesis, Ohio State University, Columbus (OH).

Arlig, A. W., 2007. Abelard's assault on everyday objects. *American Catholic Philosophical Quarterly*, 81: 209–227.

Arlig, A. W., 2011a. Mereology. In Lagerlund, H., ed., *Encyclopedia of Medieval Philosophy*, pp. 763–771. Springer, Dordrecht.

Arlig, A. W., 2011b. Is there a medieval mereology? In Cameron, M. and Marenbon, J., eds., *Methods and Methodologies: Aristotelian Logic East and West, 500–1500*, pp. 161–189. Brill, Leiden.

Arlig, A. W., 2012a. Parts, wholes and identity. In Marenbon, J., ed., *The Oxford Handbook of Medieval Philosophy*, pp. 445–467. Oxford University Press, New York.

Arlig, A. W., 2012b. Peter Abelard on material constitution. *Archiv für Geschichte der Philosophie*, 94: 119–146.

Arlig, A. W., 2013. Some twelfth-century reflections on mereological essentialism. *Oxford Studies in Medieval Philosophy*, 1: 83–112.

Arlig, A. W., 2019. Medieval mereology. In Zalta, E. N., ed., *The Stanford Encyclopedia of Philosophy*. http://plato.stanford.edu/archives/fall2019/entries/mereology-medieval.

Armstrong, D. M., 1978. *A Theory of Universals*, volume 2: *Universals and Scientific Realism*. Cambridge University Press, Cambridge.

Armstrong, D. M., 1980. Identity through time. In van Inwagen, P., ed., *Time and Cause: Essays Presented to Richard Taylor*, pp. 67–78. Reidel, Dordrecht.

Armstrong, D. M., 1986. In defense of structural universals. *Australasian Journal of Philosophy*, 64: 85–88.

Armstrong, D. M., 1991. Classes are states of affairs. *Mind*, 100: 189–200.

Armstrong, D. M., 1997. *A World of States of Affairs*. Cambridge University Press, Cambridge.

Arntzenius, F., 2003. Is quantum mechanics pointless? *Philosophy of Science*, 70: 1447–1457.

Arntzenius, F., 2008. Gunk, topology and measure. *Oxford Studies in Metaphysics*, 4: 225–247.

Arntzenius, F., 2012. *Space, Time, and Stuff*. Oxford University Press, Oxford.

Arntzenius, F. and Hawthorne, J., 2005. Gunk and continuous variation. *The Monist*, 88: 441–465.

Azzano, L., in press. Structural properties, mereology, and modal magic. In Carrara and Lando (in press-b).

Bacon, A., 2018. *Vagueness and Thought*. Oxford University Press, Oxford.

Bader, R. M., 2013. Multiple-domain supervenience for non-classical mereologies. In Hoeltje, M., Schnieder, B., and Steinberg, A., eds., *Varieties of Dependence: Ontological Dependence, Grounding, Supervenience, Response-Dependence*, pp. 347–368. Philosophia, Munich.

Baffioni, C., 1982. *Atomismo e antiatomismo nel pensiero islamico*. Istituto Universitario Orientale, Naples.

Bailey, A. M., 2011. The incompatibility of composition as identity, priority pluralism, and irreflexive grounding. *Analytic Philosophy*, 52: 171–174.

Baker, L. R., 1997. Why constitution is not identity. *The Journal of Philosophy*, 94: 599–621.

Baker, L. R., 2000. *Persons and Bodies: A Constitution View*. Cambridge University Press, Cambridge.

Baker, L. R., 2007. *The Metaphysics of Everyday Life*. Cambridge University Press, Cambridge.

Balaguer, M., 2018. Why the debate about composition is factually empty (or why there's no fact of the matter whether anything exists). *Synthese*, 195: 3975–4008.

Balashov, Y., 1999. Relativistic objects. *Noûs*, 33: 644–662.

Balashov, Y., 2003a. Temporal parts and superluminal motion. *Philosophical Papers*, 32: 1–13.

Balashov, Y., 2003b. Restricted diachronic composition, immanent causality, and objecthood: A reply to Hudson. *Philosophical Papers*, 32: 23–30.
Balashov, Y., 2005. On vagueness, 4D and diachronic universalism. *Australasian Journal of Philosophy*, 83: 523–531.
Balashov, Y., 2010. *Persistence and Spacetime*. Oxford University Press, Oxford.
Barnes, E., 2007. Vagueness and arbitrariness: Merricks on composition. *Mind*, 116: 105–113.
Barnes, E., 2010. Ontic vagueness: A guide for the perplexed. *Noûs*, 44: 601–627.
Barnes, E., 2018. Symmetric dependence. In Bliss and Priest (2018), pp. 50–69.
Barnes, E. and Williams, J. R. G., 2009. Vague parts and vague identity. *Pacific Philosophical Quarterly*, 90: 176–187.
Barnes, E. and Williams, J. R. G., 2011. A theory of metaphysical indeterminacy. *Oxford Studies in Metaphysics*, 6: 103–148.
Barnes, J., 1988. Bits and pieces. In Barnes, J. and Mignucci, M., eds., *Matter and Metaphysics: Fourth Symposium Hellenisticum*, pp. 225–294. Bibliopolis, Naples.
Barnett, D., 2004. Some stuffs are not sums of stuff. *The Philosophical Review*, 113: 89–100.
Barwise, K. J. and Etchemendy, J. W., 1987. *The Liar: An Essay on Truth and Circularity*. Oxford University Press, New York.
Barwise, K. J. and Moss, L., 1996. *Vicious Circles: On the Mathematics of Non-Well-Founded Phenomena*. CSLI Publications, Stanford (CA).
Batchelor, R., 2013. Complexes and their constituents. *Theoria*, 79: 326–352.
Baumann, R., Loebe, F., and Herre, H., 2014. Axiomatic theories of the ontology of time in GFO. *Applied Ontology*, 9: 171–215.
Baumann, R., Loebe, F., and Herre, H., 2016. Towards an ontology of space for GFO. In Ferrario, R. and Kuhn, W., eds., *Formal Ontology in Information Systems: Proceedings of the 9th International Conference*, pp. 53–66. IOS Press, Amsterdam.
Baumgartner, W., 2013. Franz Brentano's mereology. In Fisette, D. and Fréchette, G., eds., *Themes from Brentano*, pp. 227–245. Rodopi, Amsterdam.
Baumgartner, W. and Simons, P. M., 1993. Brentanos Mereologie. *Brentano Studien*, 4: 53–77. Eng. trans. by P. M. Simons: Brentano's mereology, in Albertazzi and Libardi (1994), pp. 55–76.
Baxter, D. L. M., 1988a. Many-one identity. *Philosophical Papers*, 17: 193–216.
Baxter, D. L. M., 1988b. Identity in the loose and popular sense. *Mind*, 97: 576–582.
Baxter, D. L. M., 1988c. Hume on infinite divisibility. *History of Philosophy Quarterly*, 5: 133–140.
Baxter, D. L. M., 1999. The discernibility of identicals. *Journal of Philosophical Research*, 24: 37–55.

Baxter, D. L. M., 2005. Altruism, grief, and identity. *Philosophy and Phenomenological Research*, 70: 371–383.

Baxter, D. L. M., 2014. Identity, discernibility, and composition. In Cotnoir and Baxter (2014), pp. 244–253.

Beall, J. C. and Restall, G., 2006. *Logical Pluralism*. Clarendon Press, Oxford.

Beebee, H., 2017. Do ordinary objects exist? Yes. In Barnes, E., ed., *Current Controversies in Metaphysics*, pp. 149–163. Routledge, London.

Beeson, M. J., 1979. Continuity in intuitionistic set theories. In Boffa, M., van Dalen, D., and McAloon, K., eds., *Logic Colloquium 78*, pp. 1–52. North-Holland, Amsterdam.

Beeson, M. J., 1985. *Foundations of Constructive Mathematics: Metamathematical Studies*. Springer, Berlin.

Bell, D., 2001. Some Kantian thoughts on propositional unity. *Proceedings of the Aristotelian Society, Supplementary Volume*, 75: 1–16.

Belleri, D., 2017. A pluralistic way out of epistemic deflationism about ontological disputes. In Coliva, A. and Pedersen, N. J. L. L., eds., *Epistemic Pluralism*, pp. 317–344. Palgrave Macmillan, London.

Bencivenga, E., 1976. Set theory and free logic. *Journal of Philosophical Logic*, 5: 1–15.

Bencivenga, E., 1986. Free logics. In Gabbay, D. M. and Guenthner, F., eds., *Handbook of Philosophical Logic*, volume 3, pp. 373–426. Reidel, Dordrecht.

Bennett, B., 2010. Spatial vagueness. In Jeansoulin, R., Papini, O., Prade, H., and Schockaert, S., eds., *Methods for Handling Imperfect Spatial Information*, pp. 15–47. Springer, Berlin.

Bennett, J., 1984. *A Study of Spinoza's Ethics*. Hackett, Indianapolis (IN).

Bennett, J., 1988. *Events and Their Names*. Hackett, Indianapolis (IN).

Bennett, K., 2004. Spatio-temporal coincidence and the grounding problem. *Philosophical Studies*, 118: 339–371.

Bennett, K., 2009. Composition, colocation, and metaontology. In Chalmers, D., Manley, D., and Wasserman, R., eds., *Metametaphysics: New Essays on the Foundations of Ontology*, pp. 38–76. Clarendon Press, Oxford.

Bennett, K., 2011. Koslicki on formal proper parts. *Analysis*, 71: 286–290.

Bennett, K., 2013. Having a part twice over. *Australasian Journal of Philosophy*, 91: 83–103.

Bennett, K., 2015. 'Perfectly understood, unproblematic, and certain': Lewis on mereology. In Loewer, B. and Schaffer, J., eds., *A Companion to David Lewis*, pp. 250–261. Wiley-Blackwell, Oxford.

Bennett, K., 2017a. *Making Things Up*. Oxford University Press, Oxford.

Bennett, K., 2017b. Part and whole, again. *Philosophical Issues*, 27: 7–25.

Benocci, M., 2018. The repeatability argument and the non-extensional bundle theory. *Australasian Journal of Philosophy*, 96: 432–446.

Benovsky, J., 2006a. A modal bundle theory. *Metaphysica*, 7: 21–33.

Benovsky, J., 2006b. Four-dimensionalism and modal perdurants. In Valore, P., ed., *Topics on General and Formal Ontology*, pp. 137–159. Polimetrica, Milan.

Benovsky, J., 2006c. *Persistence Through Time and Across Possible Worlds*. Ontos, Frankfurt.

Benovsky, J., 2015. 'Nothing over and above' or 'Nothing'? On eliminativism, reductionism, and composition. *Polish Journal of Philosophy*, 9: 7–17.

Benovsky, J., 2016. Eliminativism and gunk. *Teorema*, 35: 59–66.

Bernays, P., 1937. A system of axiomatic set theory—Part I. *The Journal of Symbolic Logic*, 2: 65–77.

Berryman, S., 2016. Ancient atomism. In Zalta, E. N., ed., *The Stanford Encyclopedia of Philosophy*. http://plato.stanford.edu/archives/win2016/entries/atomism-ancient.

Bertalanffy, L. von., 1929. Vorschlag zweier sehr allgemeiner biologischer Gesetze. Studien über theoretische Biologie III. *Biologisches Zentralblatt*, 49: 83–111.

Bertalanffy, L. von., 1968. *General System Theory: Foundations, Development, Applications*. Braziller, New York.

Berto, F. and Carrara, M., 2009. To exist and to count: A note on the minimalist view. *Dialectica*, 63: 343–356.

Betti, A., 2004. Leśniewski's early liar, Tarski and natural language. *Annals of Pure and Applied Logic*, 147: 267–287.

Betti, A., 2008. Polish axiomatics and its truth: On Tarski's Leśniewskian background and the Ajdukiewicz connection. In Patterson, D., ed., *New Essays on Tarski and Philosophy*, pp. 44–71. Oxford University Press, Oxford.

Betti, A., 2014. Leśniewski, Tarski and the axioms of mereology. In Mulligan, K., Kijania-Placek, K., and Placek, T., eds., *The History and Philosophy of Polish Logic: Essays in Honour of Jan Woleński*, pp. 242–258. Palgrave Macmillan, London.

Betti, A. and Loeb, I., 2012. On Tarski's foundations of the geometry of solids. *The Bulletin of Symbolic Logic*, 18: 230–260.

Bigelow, J., 1986. Towards structural universals. *Australasian Journal of Philosophy*, 64: 94–96.

Bigelow, J., 1995. *The Reality of Numbers: A Physicalist's Philosophy of Mathematics*. Oxford University Press, Oxford.

Bigelow, J., 1996. God and the new math. *Philosophical Studies*, 84: 127–154.

Bigelow, J., 2010. Quine, mereology, and inference to the best explanation. *Logique et Analyse*, 53: 465–482.

Bigelow, J. and Pargetter, R., 2006. Real work for aggregates. *Dialectica*, 60: 485–503.

Binder, T., 2019. *Franz Brentano und sein philosophischer Nachlass*. De Gruyter, Berlin.

Birkhoff, G., 1940. *Lattice Theory*. American Mathematical Society, New York. 3rd edition: 1967.

Biro, J., 2017. Saving the ship. *European Journal of Analytic Philosophy*, 13/2: 43–54.

Bittner, T. and Donnelly, M., 2007. A temporal mereology for distinguishing between integral objects and portions of stuff. In Holte, R. C. and Howe, A., eds., *Proceedings of the 22nd AAAI Conference on Artificial Intelligence*, pp. 287–292. AAAI Press, Vancouver.

Bittner, T., Donnelly, M., and Smith, B., 2004. Individuals, universals, collections: On the foundational relations of ontology. In Varzi, A. C. and Vieu, L., eds., *Formal Ontology in Information Systems: Proceedings of the 3rd International Conference*, pp. 37–48. IOS Press, Amsterdam.

Bittner, T. and Smith, B., 2003. Vague reference and approximating judgments. *Spatial Cognition and Computation*, 3: 137–156.

Blatti, S., 2012. Material constitution. In Manson, N. A. and Barnard, R. W., eds., *The Continuum Companion to Metaphysics*, pp. 149–169. Continuum, London.

Blecksmith, R. and Null, G. T., 1990. Matrix representation of Husserl's part-whole-foundation theory. *Notre Dame Journal of Formal Logic*, 32: 87–111.

Bliss, R., 2013. Viciousness and the structure of reality. *Philosophical Studies*, 166: 399–418.

Bliss, R. and Priest, G., eds., 2018. *Reality and Its Structure: Essays in Fundamentality*. Oxford University Press, Oxford.

Blizard, W. D., 1989. Multiset theory. *Notre Dame Journal of Formal Logic*, 30: 36–66.

Bochman, A., 1990. Mereology as a theory of part-whole. *Logique et Analyse*, 33: 75–101.

Boethius, 1988. *In Ciceronis Topica*, Eng. trans. by E. Stump. Cornell University Press, Ithaca (NY).

Boethius, 1998. *De divisione liber*, ed. and Eng. trans. by J. Magee. Brill, Leiden.

Boffa, M., 1968. Les ensembles extraordinaires. *Bulletin de la Société Mathématique de Belgique*, 20: 3–15.

Bogaard, P. A., 1979. Heaps or wholes: Aristotle's explanation of compound bodies. *Isis*, 70: 11–29.

Bøhn, E. D., 2009a. An argument against the necessity of unrestricted composition. *Analysis*, 69: 27–31.

Bøhn, E. D., 2009b. Must there be a top level? *The Philosophical Quarterly*, 59: 193–201.

Bøhn, E. D., 2009c. Composition as identity: A study in ontology and philosophical logic. Ph.D. thesis, University of Massachusetts, Amherst (MA).

Bøhn, E. D., 2010. The necessity of universalism versus the possibility of junky worlds: A rejoinder. *Analysis*, 70: 296–298.

Bøhn, E. D., 2011. Commentary on Lewis (1991). In Carrara *et al.* (2011), pp. 151–158.
Bøhn, E. D., 2012. Monism, emergence, and plural logic. *Erkenntnis*, 76: 211–223.
Bøhn, E. D., 2014a. Unrestricted composition as identity. In Cotnoir and Baxter (2014), pp. 143–165.
Bøhn, E. D., 2014b. From Hume's dictum via submergence to composition as identity or mereological nihilism. *Pacific Philosophical Quarterly*, 95: 336–355.
Bøhn, E. D., 2016. Composition as identity and plural Cantor's theorem. In Varzi and Gruszczyński (2016), pp. 411–428.
Bøhn, E. D., in press. Composition as identity: Pushing forward. In Carrara and Lando (in press-b).
Bolzano, B., 1837. *Wissenschaftslehre*. Seidel, Sulzbach. 2nd edition, ed. by W. Schultz: Meiner, Leipzig, 1929–1931; Eng. trans. by R. George and P. Rusnock: *Theory of Science*, Oxford University Press, Oxford, 2014.
BonJour, L., 1998. *In Defense of Pure Reason: A Rationalist Account of A Priori Justification*. Cambridge University Press, Cambridge.
Boole, G., 1847. *The Mathematical Analysis of Logic*. Macmillan, Cambridge.
Boolos, G., 1971. The iterative conception of set. *The Journal of Philosophy*, 68: 215–231.
Boolos, G., 1984. To be is to be a value of a variable (or to be some values of some variables). *The Journal of Philosophy*, 81: 430–449.
Boolos, G., 1985a. Nominalist platonism. *The Philosophical Review*, 94: 327–344.
Boolos, G., 1985b. Reading the *Begriffsschrift*. *Mind*, 94: 331–344.
Borges, J. L., 1945. El Aleph. *Sur*, 131: 52–66. Eng. trans. by A. Hurley: The Aleph, in Borges's *Collected Fictions*, pp. 274–286, Penguin, London, 1998.
Borghini, A., 2005. Counterpart theory vindicated: A reply to Merricks. *Dialectica*, 59: 67–73.
Borghini, A. and Lando, G., 2011. Natural properties, supervenience, and mereology. In Carrara *et al.* (2011), pp. 79–104.
Borghini, A. and Lando, G., in press. Mereological monism and Humean supervenience. *Synthese*.
Bosley, R. N. and Tweedale, M. M., eds., 2006. *Basic Issues in Medieval Philosophy*. Broadview Press, Peterborough (ON).
Bostock, D., 1979. *Logic and Arithmetic*, volume 2: *Rational and Irrational Numbers*. Clarendon Press, Oxford.
Botti, M., in press. Composition as analysis: The meta-ontological origins (and future) of composition as identity. In Carrara and Lando (in press-b).
Bowers, J., 2019. A teleological answer to the special composition question. *Dialectica*, 73: 231–246.

Bowin, J. F., 2003. Chrysippus' puzzle about identity. *Oxford Studies in Ancient Philosophy*, 24: 239–251.

Braddon-Mitchell, D. and Miller, K. L., 2006. The physics of extended simples. *Analysis*, 66: 222–226.

Brady, R., 2006. *Universal Logic*. CSLI Publications, Stanford (CA).

Breitkopf, A., 1978. Axiomatisierung einiger Begriffe aus Nelson Goodmans. *Erkenntnis*, 12: 229–247.

Bremer, M., 2010. *Universality in Set Theories: A Study in Formal Ontology*. Ontos, Frankfurt.

Brennan, A. A., 1988. *Conditions of Identity: A Study of Identity and Survival*. Clarendon Press, Oxford.

Brenner, A., 2015a. Mereological nihilism and theoretical unification. *Analytic Philosophy*, 56: 318–337.

Brenner, A., 2015b. Mereological nihilism and the special arrangement question. *Synthese*, 192: 1295–1314.

Brenner, A., 2017. Mereological nihilism and personal ontology. *The Philosophical Quarterly*, 67: 464–485.

Brenner, A., 2018. Science and the special composition question. *Synthese*, 195: 657–678.

Brenner, A., in press. Mereology and ideology. *Synthese*.

Brenner-Golomb, N. and van Brakel, J., 1989. Putnam on Davidson on conceptual schemes. *Dialectica*, 43: 263–269.

Brentano, F., 1874. *Psychologie vom empirischen Standpunkte*. Duncker und Humblot, Leipzig. 2nd edition, ed. by O. Kraus: Meiner, Leipzig, 1924; Eng. trans. by A. C. Rancurello, D. B. Terrell, and L. L. McAlister: *Psychology from an Empirical Standpoint*, Routledge & Kegan Paul, London, 1973.

Brentano, F., 1933. *Kategorienlehre*, ed. by A. Kastil. Meiner, Leipzig. Eng. trans. by R. M. Chisholm and N. Guterman: *The Theory of Categories*, Nijhoff, The Hague, 1981.

Brentano, F., 1976. *Philosophische Untersuchungen zu Raum, Zeit und Kontinuum*, ed. by S. Körner and R. M. Chisholm. Meiner, Hamburg. Eng. trans. by B. Smith: *Philosophical Investigations on Space, Time and the Continuum*, Croom Helm, London, 1988.

Bricker, P., 2016. Composition as a *kind* of identity. *Inquiry*, 59: 264–294.

Bricker, P., in press. Composition as identity, Leibniz's law, and slice-sensitive emergent properties. In Carrara and Lando (in press-b).

Britton, T., 2012. The limits of hylomorphism. *Metaphysica*, 13: 145–153.

Broad, C. D., 1923. *Scientific Thought*. Harcourt, New York.

Brogaard, B., 1999. Temporal mereology. Ph.D. thesis, State University of New York, Buffalo (NY).

Brower, J. E., 2014. *Aquinas's Ontology of the Material World: Change, Hylomorphism, and Material Objects*. Oxford University Press, Oxford.

Brown, C., 2005. *Aquinas and the Ship of Theseus: Solving Puzzles about Material Objects*. Continuum, London.

Brown, C., 2007. Souls, ships, and substances: A response to Toner. *American Catholic Philosophical Quarterly*, 81: 655–668.

Brown, C. H., 1976. General principles of human anatomical partonomy and speculations on the growth of partonomic nomenclature. *American Ethnologist*, 3: 400–424.

Brown, C. H., Kolar, J., Torrey, B. J., Trương-Quang, T., and Volkman, P., 1976. Some general principles of biological and non-biological folk classification. *American Ethnologist*, 3: 73–85.

Brown, J. D. K., 2016. Natural objects. *Journal of the American Philosophical Association*, 2: 254–271.

Brzozowski, J., 2008. On locating composite objects. *Oxford Studies in Metaphysics*, 4: 193–222.

Brzozowski, J., 2016. Monism and gunk. In Jago, M., ed., *Reality Making*, pp. 57–74. Oxford University Press, Oxford.

Bucchioni, G., 2015. Tout intégral et théories de la composition. *Revue Philosophique de Louvain*, 113: 679–705.

Bunge, M., 1966. On null individuals. *The Journal of Philosophy*, 63: 776–778.

Bunge, M., 1977. *Treatise on Basic Philosophy*, volume 3: *Ontology I: The Furniture of the World*. Reidel, Dordrecht.

Bunge, M., 1979. *Treatise on Basic Philosophy*, volume 4: *Ontology II: A World of Systems*. Reidel, Dordrecht.

Bunge, M., 2010. *Matter and Mind: A Philosophical Inquiry*. Springer, Berlin.

Bunt, H. C., 1985. *Mass Terms and Model-Theoretic Semantics*. Cambridge University Press, Cambridge.

Burge, T., 1977. A theory of aggregates. *Noûs*, 11: 97–117.

Burgess, J. A., 1990. Vague objects and indefinite identity. *Philosophical Studies*, 59: 263–287.

Burgess, J. P., 2004. *E pluribus unum*: Plural logic and set theory. *Philosophia Mathematica*, 12: 193–221.

Burgess, J. P., 2015. Lewis on mereology and set theory. In Loewer, B. and Schaffer, J., eds., *A Companion to David Lewis*, pp. 459–469. Wiley-Blackwell, Oxford.

Burgess, J. P., Hazen, A. P., and Lewis, D. K., 1991. Appendix on pairing. In Lewis (1991), pp. 121–149.

Burgess, J. P. and Rosen, G., 1997. *A Subject with No Object: Strategies for Nominalistic Interpretation of Mathematics*. Clarendon Press, Oxford.

Burke, M. B., 1992. Copper statues and pieces of copper: A challenge to the standard account. *Analysis*, 52: 12–17.

Burke, M. B., 1994. Dion and Theon: An essentialist solution to an ancient puzzle. *The Journal of Philosophy*, 91: 129–139.

Burke, M. B., 1996. Tibbles the cat: A modern sophisma. *Philosophical Studies*, 84: 63–74.

Burkhardt, H. and Degen, W., 1990. Mereology in Leibniz's logic and philosophy. *Topoi*, 9: 3–13.

Burkhardt, H. and Dufour, C., 1991. Part/whole I: History. In Burkhardt, H. and Smith, B., eds., *Handbook of Metaphysics and Ontology*, pp. 663–673. Philosophia, Munich.

Burkhardt, H., Seibt, J., Imaguire, G., and Gerogiorgakis, S., eds., 2017. *Handbook of Mereology*. Philosophia, Munich.

Butterfield, J., 1985. Spatial and temporal parts. *The Philosophical Quarterly*, 35: 32–44.

Bynoe, W., 2008. Existential and mereological vagueness. Ph.D. thesis, King's College, London.

Bynoe, W., 2011. Against the compositional view of facts. *Australasian Journal of Philosophy*, 89: 91–100.

Calosi, C., 2011. Mereologia. *Aphex*, 3: 23–77.

Calosi, C., 2014. Universalismo ed estensionalismo. (Ovvero: la posizione di Varzi non è Rea). *Isonomia/Epistemologica*, 4: 95–103.

Calosi, C., 2016a. Composition is identity and mereological nihilism. *The Philosophical Quarterly*, 66: 219–235.

Calosi, C., 2016b. Composition, identity, and emergence. In Varzi and Gruszczyński (2016), pp. 429–443.

Calosi, C., 2018. Failure or boredom: The pendulum of composition as identity. *American Philosophical Quarterly*, 55: 281–292.

Calosi, C., in press-a. An elegant universe. *Synthese*.

Calosi, C., in press-b. Is parthood identity? In Carrara and Lando (in press-b).

Calosi, C. and Graziani, P., eds., 2014. *Mereology and the Sciences: Parts and Wholes in the Contemporary Scientific Context*. Springer, Cham.

Calosi, C. and Morganti, M., 2016. Humean supervenience, composition as identity and quantum wholes. *Erkenntnis*, 81: 1173–1194.

Calosi, C. and Tarozzi, G., 2014. Parthood and composition in quantum mechanics. In Calosi and Graziani (2014), pp. 53–84.

Cameron, R. P., 2007. The contingency of composition. *Philosophical Studies*, 136: 99–121.

Cameron, R. P., 2008a. Turtles all the way down: Regress, priority, and fundamentality. *The Philosophical Quarterly*, 58: 1–14.

Cameron, R. P., 2008b. Truthmakers and ontological commitment: Or how to deal with complex objects and mathematical ontology without getting into trouble. *Philosophical Studies*, 140: 1–18.

Cameron, R. P., 2010a. Quantification, naturalness, and ontology. In Hazlett, A., ed., *New Waves in Metaphysics*, pp. 8–26. Palgrave Macmillan, London.

Cameron, R. P., 2010b. How to have a radically minimal ontology. *Philosophical Studies*, 151: 249–64.

Cameron, R. P., 2012. Composition as identity doesn't settle the special composition question. *Philosophy and Phenomenological Research*, 84: 531–554.

Cameron, R. P., 2014. Parts generate the whole, but are not identical to it. In Cotnoir and Baxter (2014), pp. 90–107.

Cameron, R. P., 2015. *The Moving Spotlight: An Essay on Time and Ontology*. Oxford University Press, Oxford.

Cantor, G., 1878. Ein Beitrag zur Mannigfaltigkeitslehre. *Journal für die reine und angewandte Mathematik*, 84: 242–258.

Cantor, G., 1891. Über eine elementare Frage der Mannigfaltigkeitslehre. *Jahresbericht der Deutschen Mathematiker-Vereinigung*, 1: 75–78. Eng. trans. by W. B. Ewald: On an elementary question in the theory of manifolds, in Ewald, W. B., ed., *From Kant to Hilbert: A Source Book in the Foundations of Mathematics*, volume 2, pp. 920–922, Clarendon Press, Oxford, 1996.

Cantor, G., 1895–1897. Beiträge zur Begründung der transfiniten Mengenlehre. *Mathematische Annalen*, 46: 481–512; 49: 207–246. Eng. trans. by P. Jourdain: *Contributions to the Founding of the Theory of Transfinite Numbers*, Open Court, Chicago (IL), 1915.

Čapek, M., 1976. Introduction. In Čapek, M., ed., *The Concepts of Space and Time: Their Structure and Their Development*, pp. XVII–XLII. Reidel, Dordrecht.

Caplan, B., Tillman, C., and Reeder, P., 2010. Parts of singletons. *The Journal of Philosophy*, 107: 501–533.

Carlson, B. M., 2017. Nihilist perdurantism: A new ontology of material objects. Ph.D. thesis, University of Kentucky, Lexington (KY).

Carmichael, C., 2011. Vague composition without vague existence. *Noûs*, 45: 315–327.

Carmichael, C., 2015. Toward a commonsense answer to the special composition question. *Australasian Journal of Philosophy*, 93: 475–490.

Carmichael, C., in press. How to solve the puzzle of Dion and Theon without losing your head. *Mind*.

Carnap, R., 1928. *Der logische Aufbau der Welt*. Weltkreis-Verlag, Berlin. Eng. trans. by R. A. George: *The Logical Structure of the World [and] Pseudoproblems in Philosophy*, University of California Press, Berkeley (CA), 1967.

Carnap, R., 1931. Überwindung der Metaphysik durch logische Analyse der Sprache. *Erkenntnis*, 2: 219–241. Eng. trans. by A. Pap: The elimination of metaphysics through logical analysis of language, in Ayer, A. J., ed., *Logical Positivism*, pp. 60–81, Free Press, Glencoe (IL), 1952.

Carnap, R., 1934. *Logische Syntax der Sprache*. Springer, Vienna. Eng. trans. by A. Smeaton: *The Logical Syntax of Language*, Kegan Paul, London, 1937.

Carnap, R., 1947. *Meaning and Necessity: A Study in Semantics and Modal Logic*. University of Chicago Press, Chicago (IL).

Carnap, R., 1950. Empiricism, semantics, and ontology. *Revue Internationale de Philosophie*, 4: 20–40.

Carnap, R., 1954. *Einführung in die symbolische Logik, mit besonderer Berücksichtigung ihrer Anwendungen*. Springer, Vienna. Eng. trans. by W. G. Meyer and J. Wilkinson: *Introduction to Symbolic Logic and Its Applications*, Dover, New York, 1958.

Carnielli, W. and Coniglio, M. E., 2016. *Paraconsistent Logic: Consistency, Contradiction and Negation*. Springer, Cham.

Carrara, M., Arapinis, A., and Moltmann, F., eds., 2016. *Unity and Plurality: Logic, Philosophy, and Linguistics*. Oxford University Press, Oxford.

Carrara, M., Ciuni, R., and Lando, G., eds., 2011. *Composition, Counterfactuals, Causation*. Special issue of *Humana.Mente*, volume 19.

Carrara, M. and Lando, G., 2016. Composition, indiscernibility, coreferentiality. *Erkenntnis*, 81: 119–142.

Carrara, M. and Lando, G., 2017. Composition and relative counting. *Dialectica*, 71: 489–529.

Carrara, M. and Lando, G., 2019. La composizione come identità da un punto di vista modale. *Rivista Italiana di Filosofia del Linguaggio*, 13/3: 26–39.

Carrara, M. and Lando, G., in press-a. Contingent composition as identity. In Carrara and Lando (in press-b).

Carrara, M. and Lando, G., eds., in press-b. *Mereology and Identity*. Special issue of *Synthese*.

Carrara, M. and Martino, E., 2009. On the ontological commitment of mereology. *The Review of Symbolic Logic*, 2: 164–174.

Carrara, M. and Martino, E., 2011a. Four theses on the alleged innocence of mereology. In Carrara *et al.* (2011), pp. 57–77.

Carrara, M. and Martino, E., 2011b. On the infinite in mereology with plural quantification. *The Review of Symbolic Logic*, 4: 54–62.

Carrara, M. and Martino, E., 2015. Grounding megethology on plural reference. *Studia Logica*, 103: 697–711.

Carrara, M. and Martino, E., 2016. The mereological foundation of megethology. *Journal of Philosophical Logic*, 45: 227–235.

Carroll, J. W. and Markosian, N., 2010. *An Introduction to Metaphysics*. Cambridge University Press, Cambridge.

Carter, W. R., 1983. In defense of undetached parts. *Pacific Philosophical Quarterly*, 64: 126–143.

Carter, W. R., 1997. Dion's left foot (and the price of Burkean economy). *Philosophy and Phenomenological Research*, 75: 371–379.

Cartwright, H. M., 1984. Parts and partitives: Notes on what things are made of. *Synthese*, 58: 251–277.

Cartwright, R., 1975. Scattered objects. In Lehrer, K., ed., *Analysis and Metaphysics: Essays in Honor of R. M. Chisholm*, pp. 153–171. Reidel, Dordrecht.

Casari, E., 2000. On Husserl's theory of wholes and parts. *History and Philosophy of Logic*, 21: 1–43.

Casari, E., 2007. On the relationship between parts and wholes in Husserl's phenomenology. In Boi, L., Kerszberg, P., and Patras, F., eds., *Rediscovering Phenomenology: Phenomenological Essays on Mathematical Beings, Physical Reality, Perception and Consciousness*, pp. 67–102. Springer, Dordrecht.

Casati, F., 2016. Being: A dialetheic interpretation of the late Heidegger. Ph.D. thesis, University of St Andrews, St Andrews.

Casati, F. and Fujikawa, N., 2015. Better than zilch? *Logic and Logical Philosophy*, 24: 255–264.

Casati, F. and Fujikawa, N., 2019. Nothingness, Meinongianism and inconsistent mereology. *Synthese*, 196: 3739–3772.

Casati, R. and Varzi, A. C., 1999. *Parts and Places: The Structures of Spatial Representation*. MIT Press, Cambridge (MA).

Caulton, A., 2015. Is mereology empirical? Composition for fermions. In Bigaj, T. and Wüthrich, C., eds., *Metaphysics in Contemporary Physics*, pp. 293–322. Rodopi Brill, Amsterdam.

Cavendish, M., 2001. *Observations upon Experimental Philosophy*, ed. by E. O'Neill. Cambridge University Press, Cambridge.

Caves, R. L. J., 2018. Emergence for nihilists. *Pacific Philosophical Quarterly*, 99: 2–28.

Chalmers, D., 2009. Ontological anti-realism. In Chalmers, D., Manley, D., and Wasserman, R., eds., *Metametaphysics: New Essays on the Foundations of Ontology*, pp. 77–130. Clarendon Press, Oxford.

Champollion, L., 2017. *Parts of a Whole: Distributivity as a Bridge between Aspect and Measurement*. Oxford University Press, Oxford.

Champollion, L. and Krifka, M., 2016. Mereology. In Dekker, P. and Aloni, M., eds., *The Cambridge Handbook of Formal Semantics*, pp. 369–388. Cambridge University Press, Cambridge.

Chang, C. C. and Keisler, H. J., 1973. *Model Theory*. North-Holland, Amsterdam. 3rd edition: 1990.

Chant, S. R., 2006. The special composition question in action. *Pacific Philosophical Quarterly*, 87: 422–441.

Chant, S. R., 2010. Two composition questions in action. In Hazlett, A., ed., *New Waves in Metaphysics*, pp. 27–53. Palgrave Macmillan, London.

Chen, L., in press. Infinitesimal gunk. *Journal of Philosophical Logic*.

Chisholm, R. M., 1973. Parts as essential to their wholes. *The Review of Metaphysics*, 26: 581–603.

Chisholm, R. M., 1975. Mereological essentialism: Some further considerations. *The Review of Metaphysics*, 28: 477–484.

Chisholm, R. M., 1976. *Person and Object: A Metaphysical Study*. Open Court, La Salle (IL).

Chisholm, R. M., 1978. Brentano's conception of substance and accident. *Grazer Philosophische Studien*, 5: 197–210.

Chisholm, R. M., 1984. Boundaries as dependent particulars. *Grazer Philosophische Studien*, 10: 87–95.

Chisholm, R. M., 1987. Scattered objects. In Thomson, J. J., ed., *On Being and Saying: Essays for Richard Cartwright*, pp. 167–173. MIT Press, Cambridge (MA).

Chisholm, R. M., 1993. Spatial continuity and the theory of part and whole: A Brentano study. *Brentano Studien*, 4: 11–24.

Church, A., 1974. Set theory with a universal set. In Henkin, L., Addison, J., Chang, C. C., Craig, W., Scott, D., and Vaught, R. L., eds., *Proceedings of the Tarski Symposium*, pp. 297–308. American Mathematical Society, Providence (RI).

Cintula, P., Fermüller, C. G., and Noguera, C., 2017. Fuzzy logic. In Zalta, E. N., ed., *The Stanford Encyclopedia of Philosophy*. http://plato.stanford.edu/archives/fall2017/entries/logic-fuzzy.

Ciraulo, F., 2013. Intuitionistic overlap structures. *Logic and Logical Philosophy*, 22: 201–212.

Clarke, B. L., 1981. A calculus of individuals based on 'connection'. *Notre Dame Journal of Formal Logic*, 22: 204–219.

Clarke, B. L., 1985. Individuals and points. *Notre Dame Journal of Formal Logic*, 26: 61–75.

Clay, R. E., 1961. Contributions to mereology. Ph.D. thesis, University of Notre Dame, Notre Dame (IN).

Clay, R. E., 1965. The relation of weakly discrete to set and equinumerosity in mereology. *Notre Dame Journal of Formal Logic*, 6: 325–340.

Clay, R. E., 1966. On the definition of mereological class. *Notre Dame Journal of Formal Logic*, 7: 359–360.

Clay, R. E., 1968. The consistency of Leśniewski's mereology relative to the real number system. *The Journal of Symbolic Logic*, 33: 251–257.

Clay, R. E., 1974a. Relation of Leśniewski's mereology to Boolean algebra. *The Journal of Symbolic Logic*, 39: 638–648.

Clay, R. E., 1974b. Some mereological models. *Notre Dame Journal of Formal Logic*, 15: 141–146.

Clay, R. E., 1975. Single axioms for atomistic and atomless mereology. *Notre Dame Journal of Formal Logic*, 16: 345–351.

Clay, R. E., 1980. Introduction to Leśniewski's logical systems. *Annali dell'Istituto di Discipline filosofiche dell'Università di Bologna*, 2: 5–31.

Cobreros, P., Egré, P., Ripley, D., and van Rooij, R., 2012. Tolerant, classical, strict. *Journal of Philosophical Logic*, 41: 347–385.

Coggins, G., 2010. *Could There Have Been Nothing? Against Metaphysical Nihilism*. Palgrave Macmillan, London.

Cohn, A. G. and Gotts, N. M., 1996. Representing spatial vagueness: A mereological approach. In Aiello, L. C., Doyle, J., and Shapiro, S. C., eds., *Principles of Knowledge Representation and Reasoning: Proceedings of the 5th International Conference*, pp. 230–241. Morgan Kaufmann, San Francisco (CA).

Cohn, A. G. and Hazarika, S. M., 2001. Qualitative spatial representation and reasoning: An overview. *Fundamenta Informaticae*, 46: 1–29.

Cohn, A. G. and Varzi, A. C., 2003. Mereotopological connection. *Journal of Philosophical Logic*, 32: 357–390.

Cohnitz, D. and Rossberg, M., 2006. *Nelson Goodman*. Acumen, Chesham.

Cohnitz, D. and Rossberg, M., 2019. Nelson Goodman – Supplement: The Calculus of Individuals in its different versions. In Zalta, E. N., ed., *The Stanford Encyclopedia of Philosophy*. http://plato.stanford.edu/archives/sum2019/entries/goodman/supplement.html.

Comesaña, J., 2008. Could there be exactly two things? *Synthese*, 162: 31–35.

Contessa, G., 2012. The junk argument: Safe disposal guidelines for mereological universalists. *Analysis*, 72: 455–457.

Contessa, G., 2014. One's a crowd: Mereological nihilism without ordinary-object eliminativism. *Analytic Philosophy*, 55: 199–221.

Cook, R. T., 2000. Monads and mathematics: The logic of Leibniz's mereology. *Studia Leibnitiana*, 32: 1–19.

Cook, R. T., 2009. *A Dictionary of Philosophical Logic*. Edinburgh University Press, Edinburgh.

Copp, D., 1984. What collectives are: Agency, individualism and legal theory. *Dialogue*, 23: 249–269.

Coppola, C. and Gerla, G., eds., 2013. *Mereology and Point-Free Geometry*. Special issue of *Logic and Logical Philosophy*, volume 22/2–3.

Cornell, D. M., 2013. Monism and statespace: A reply to Sider. *Analysis*, 73: 230–236.

Cornell, D. M., 2016. Taking monism seriously. *Philosophical Studies*, 173: 2397–2415.

Cornell, D. M., 2017. Mereological nihilism and the problem of emergence. *American Philosophical Quarterly*, 54: 77–87.

Cornish, W. H., 1980. Boolean skew algebras. *Acta Mathematica Academiae Scientiarum Hungaricae*, 36: 281–291.

Correia, F., 2004. Husserl on foundation. *Dialectica*, 58: 349–367.

Correia, F. and Schnieder, B., 2012a. Grounding: An opinionated introduction. In Correia and Schnieder (2012b), pp. 1–36.

Correia, F. and Schnieder, B., eds., 2012b. *Metaphysical Grounding: Understanding the Structure of Reality*. Cambridge University Press, Cambridge.

Costa, E., in press. Whole-parts relations in early modern philosophy. In Jalobeanu, D. and Wolfe, C. T., eds., *Encyclopedia of Early Modern Philosophy and the Sciences*. Springer, Cham.

Cotnoir, A. J., 2010. Anti-symmetry and non-extensional mereology. *The Philosophical Quarterly*, 60: 396–405.
Cotnoir, A. J., 2013a. Composition as general identity. *Oxford Studies in Metaphysics*, 8: 295–322.
Cotnoir, A. J., 2013b. Strange parts: The metaphysics of non-classical mereologies. *Philosophy Compass*, 8: 834–845.
Cotnoir, A. J., 2013c. Beyond atomism. *Thought*, 2: 67–72.
Cotnoir, A. J., 2013d. Parts as counterparts. *Thought*, 2: 228–241.
Cotnoir, A. J., 2014a. Universalism and junk. *Australasian Journal of Philosophy*, 92: 649–664.
Cotnoir, A. J., 2014b. Composition as identity: Framing the debate. In Cotnoir and Baxter (2014), pp. 3–23.
Cotnoir, A. J., 2015. Abelian mereology. In Varzi and Gruszczyński (2015), pp. 429–447.
Cotnoir, A. J., 2016a. Does universalism entail extensionalism? *Noûs*, 50: 121–132.
Cotnoir, A. J., 2016b. How many angels can be in the same place at the same time? A defense of mereological universalism. *Mind*, 125: 959–965.
Cotnoir, A. J., 2017. Mutual indwelling. *Faith and Philosophy*, 34: 123–151.
Cotnoir, A. J., 2018. A note on Priest's mereology. *Australasian Journal of Logic*, 15: 642–645.
Cotnoir, A. J., 2019a. Logical nihilism. In Kellen, N., Pedersen, N. J. L. L., and Wyatt, J., eds., *Pluralisms in Truth and Logic*, pp. 301–329. Palgrave Macmillan, London.
Cotnoir, A. J., 2019b. Unity, identity, and topology: How to make donuts and cut things in half. In Başkent, C. and Ferguson, T. M., eds., *Graham Priest on Dialetheism and Paraconsistency*, pp. 217–229. Springer, Cham.
Cotnoir, A. J., in press. Is weak supplementation analytic? In Carrara and Lando (in press-b).
Cotnoir, A. J. and Bacon, A., 2012. Non-wellfounded mereology. *The Review of Symbolic Logic*, 5: 187–204.
Cotnoir, A. J. and Baxter, D. L. M., eds., 2014. *Composition as Identity*. Oxford University Press, Oxford.
Cotnoir, A. J. and Varzi, A. C., 2019. Natural axioms for classical mereology. *The Review of Symbolic Logic*, 12: 201–208.
Cowling, S., 2014. No simples, no gunk, no nothing. *Pacific Philosophical Quarterly*, 95: 246–260.
Crane, J. K., 2012. Biological-mereological coincidence. *Philosophical Studies*, 161: 309–325.
Cresswell, M. J., 2010. Predicate wormism: A Quinean account of *de re* modality. *Logique et Analyse*, 53: 449–464.
Crisp, T. M., 2003. Presentism. In Loux, M. J. and Zimmerman, D. W., eds.,

The Oxford Handbook of Metaphysics, pp. 211–245. Oxford University Press, Oxford.

Crosilla, L., 2019. Set theory: Constructive and intuitionistic ZF. In Zalta, E. N., ed., *The Stanford Encyclopedia of Philosophy*. http://plato.stanford.edu/archives/spr2019/entries/set-theory-constructive.

Cross, R., 1999. Ockham on part and whole. *Vivarium*, 37: 143–167.

Crosson, F. J., 1962. Formal logic and formal ontology in Husserl's phenomenology. *Notre Dame Journal Formal Logic*, 3: 259–269.

Cruse, D. A., 1979. On the transitivity of the part-whole relation. *Journal of Linguistics*, 15: 29–38.

Curry, H. B., 1963. *Foundations of Mathematical Logic*. McGraw-Hill, New York.

Dainton, B., 2010. *Stream of Consciousness: Unity and Continuity in Conscious Experience*. Routledge, London.

Daly, C. and Liggins, D., 2015. Agnosticism about ontology. In Daly, C., ed., *The Palgrave Handbook of Philosophical Methods*, pp. 158–175. Palgrave Macmillan, London.

Daniels, P. R., 2014. Occupy wall: A mereological puzzle and the burdens of endurantism. *Australasian Journal of Philosophy*, 92: 91–101.

Daniels, P. R. and Goswick, D. L., 2017. Do events have their parts essentially? *Acta Analytica*, 32: 313–320.

Dapoigny, R. and Barlatier, P., 2013. A typed approach for contextualizing the part-whole relation. In Brézillon, P., Blackburn, P., and Dapoigny, R., eds., *Modeling and Using Context: Proceedings of the 8th International and Interdisciplinary Conference*, pp. 1–14. Springer, Berlin.

Dappiano, L., 1993. Le parti e l'intero nella concezione di Aristotele: La hologia come progetto di metafisica descrittiva, I. *Axiomathes*, 4: 75–103.

Darby, G. and Watson, D., 2010. Lewis's principle of recombination: Reply to Efird and Stoneham. *Dialectica*, 64: 435–445.

Davey, B. A. and Priestly, H. A., 2002. *Introduction to Lattices and Order*, 2nd edition. Cambridge University Press, Cambridge.

Day, G. W., 1967. Superatomic Boolean algebras. *Pacific Journal of Mathematics*, 23: 479–489.

De, M., 2018. On the Humphrey objection to modal realism. *Grazer Philosophische Studien*, 95: 159–179.

de Laguna, T., 1921. Extensive abstraction: A suggestion. *The Philosophical Review*, 30: 216–218.

de Laguna, T., 1922. Point, line, and surface, as sets of solids. *The Journal of Philosophy*, 19: 449–461.

Dedekind, R., 1888. *Was sind und was sollen die Zahlen?* Vieweg, Braunschweig. 2nd edition: 1893; Eng. trans. by W. W. Beman: The nature and meaning of numbers, in Dedekind's *Essays on the Theory of Numbers*, pp. 29–115, Open Court, Chicago (IL), 1901.

Denkel, A., 1995. Theon's tale: Does a Cambridge change result in a substantial change? *Analysis*, 55: 166–170.

Dershowitz, N. S., in press. Nihilism, but not necessarily. *Erkenntnis*.

Dixon, T. S., 2016. What is the well-foundedness of grounding? *Mind*, 125: 439–468.

Dixon, T. S., in press. Between atomism and superatomism. *Journal of Philosophical Logic*.

Doepke, F., 1982. Spatially coinciding objects. *Ratio*, 4: 45–60.

Doepke, F., 1996. *The Kinds of Things: A Theory of Personal Identity Based on Transcendental Arguments*. Open Court, Chicago (IL).

Donnelly, M., 2004. A formal theory for reasoning about parthood, connection, and location. *Artificial Intelligence*, 160: 145–172.

Donnelly, M., 2009. Mereological vagueness and existential vagueness. *Synthese*, 168: 53–79.

Donnelly, M., 2010. Parthood and multi-location. *Oxford Studies in Metaphysics*, 5: 203–243.

Donnelly, M., 2011. Using mereological principles to support metaphysics. *The Philosophical Quarterly*, 61: 225–246.

Donnelly, M., 2014. A linguistic account of mereological vagueness. In Akiba, K. and Abasnezhad, A., eds., *Vague Objects and Vague Identity: New Essays on Ontic Vagueness*, pp. 43–65. Springer, Dordrecht.

Donnelly, M. and Bittner, T., 2009. Summation relations and portions of stuff. *Philosophical Studies*, 143: 167–185.

Donnelly, M. and Smith, B., 2003. Layers: A new approach to locating objects in space. In Kuhn, W., Worboys, M. F., and Timpf, S., eds., *Spatial Information Theory: Proceedings of COSIT 2003*, pp. 50–65. Springer, Berlin.

Dorr, C., 2002. The simplicity of everything. Ph.D. thesis, Princeton University, Princeton (NJ).

Dorr, C., 2005. What we disagree about when we disagree about ontology. In Kalderon, M. E., ed., *Fictionalism in Metaphysics*, pp. 234–286. Clarendon Press, Oxford.

Dowland, S. C., 2016. Embodied mind sparsism. *Philosophical Studies*, 173: 1853–1872.

Drewnowski, J. F., 1934. Zarys programu filozoficznego. *Przegląd Filozoficzny*, 37: 3–38, 150–181, 262–292.

Dummett, M. A. E., 1975. Wang's paradox. *Synthese*, 30: 301–324.

Dummett, M. A. E., 1981. *The Interpretation of Frege's Philosophy*. Duckworth, London.

Dumsday, T., 2015. Atoms vs. extended simples: Towards a dispositionalist reconciliation. *Philosophia*, 43: 1023–1033.

Dumsday, T., 2017. MaxCon extended simples and the dispositionalist ontology of laws. *Synthese*, 194: 1627–1641.

Dunglison, R., 1857. *Medical Lexicon: A Dictionary of Medical Science*, 15th edition. Blanchard & Lea, Philadelphia (PA).

Eagle, A., 2010a. Location and perdurance. *Oxford Studies in Metaphysics*, 5: 53–94.

Eagle, A., 2010b. Duration in relativistic spacetime. *Oxford Studies in Metaphysics*, 5: 113–118.

Eagle, A., 2016. Multiple location defended. *Philosophical Studies*, 173: 2215–2231.

Eagle, A., 2019. Weak location. *Dialectica*, 73: 149–181.

Ebbinghaus, H.-D., 2007a. *Ernst Zermelo: An Approach to His Life and Work*. Springer, Berlin.

Ebbinghaus, H.-D., 2007b. Löwenheim-Skolem theorems. In Jacquette, D., ed., *Handbook of the Philosophy of Science*, volume 5: *Philosophy of Logic*, pp. 587–614. Elsevier, Amsterdam.

Eberl, J. T., 2009. Do human persons persist between death and resurrection? In Timpe, K., ed., *Metaphysics and God: Essays in Honor of Eleonore Stump*, pp. 188–205. Routledge, London.

Eberle, R. A., 1967. Some complete calculi of individuals. *Notre Dame Journal of Formal Logic*, 8: 267–278.

Eberle, R. A., 1968. Yoes on non-atomic systems of individuals. *Noûs*, 2: 399–403.

Eberle, R. A., 1970. *Nominalistic Systems*. Reidel, Dordrecht.

Eddon, M., 2009. Why four-dimensionalism explains coincidence. *Australasian Journal of Philosophy*, 88: 721–728.

Edgington, D., 2000. Indeterminacy *de re*. *Philosophical Topics*, 28: 27–44.

Effingham, N., 2009a. Universalism, vagueness and supersubstantivalism. *Australasian Journal of Philosophy*, 87: 35–42.

Effingham, N., 2009b. Composition, persistence and identity. In Le Poidevin, R., Simons, P. M., McGonigal, A., and Cameron, R. P., eds., *The Routledge Companion to Metaphysics*, pp. 296–309. Routledge, London.

Effingham, N., 2010a. Mereological explanation and time travel. *Australasian Journal of Philosophy*, 88: 333–345.

Effingham, N., 2010b. The metaphysics of groups. *Philosophical Studies*, 149: 251–267.

Effingham, N., 2011a. Undermining motivations for universalism. *Noûs*, 45: 696–713.

Effingham, N., 2011b. Sider, Hawley, Sider and the vagueness argument. *Philosophical Studies*, 154: 241–250.

Effingham, N. and Robson, J., 2007. A mereological challenge to endurantism. *Australasian Journal of Philosophy*, 85: 633–640.

Efird, D. and Stoneham, T., 2005. Genuine modal realism and the empty world. *European Journal of Analytic Philosophy*, 1: 21–37.

Ehrenfels, C. von., 1890. Über 'Gestaltqualitäten'. *Vierteljahrsschrift für wissenschaftliche Philosophie*, 14: 249–292. Eng. trans. by B. Smith: On 'Gestalt' qualities, in Smith, B., ed., *Foundations of Gestalt Theory*, pp. 82–117, Philosophia, Munich, 1988.

Eklund, M., 2002. Peter van Inwagen on material beings. *Ratio*, 15: 245–256.

Eklund, M., 2008. The picture of reality as an amorphous lump. In Sider, T., Hawthorne, J., and Zimmerman, D. W., eds., *Contemporary Debates in Metaphysics*, pp. 382–396. Blackwell, Oxford.

Eklund, M., 2009. Carnap and ontological pluralism. In Chalmers, D., Manley, D., and Wasserman, R., eds., *Metametaphysics: New Essays on the Foundations of Ontology*, pp. 130–156. Clarendon Press, Oxford.

Elder, C. L., 2003. Destruction, alteration, simples, and world-stuff. *The Philosophical Quarterly*, 53: 24–38.

Elder, C. L., 2004. *Real Natures and Familiar Objects*. MIT Press, Cambridge (MA).

Elder, C. L., 2007. On the phenomenon of 'dog-wise arrangement'. *Philosophy and Phenomenological Research*, 74: 132–155.

Elder, C. L., 2008. Against universal mereological composition. *Dialectica*, 62: 433–454.

Engehausen, A., Pribbenow, S., and Töter, U., 1997. Taxonomie und partonomien. In Kluwe, R. H., ed., *Strukturen und Prozesse intelligenter Systeme*, pp. 157–178. Deutscher Universitäts Verlag, Wiesbaden.

Engel, R. and Yoes, M. G., 1996. Exponentiating entities by necessity. *Australasian Journal of Philosophy*, 74: 293–304.

Engelhard, K., 2005. *Das Einfache und die Materie: Untersuchungen zu Kants Antinomie der Teilung*. De Gruyter, Berlin.

Epstein, B., 2015. *The Ant Trap: Rebuilding the Foundations of the Social Sciences*. Oxford University Press, Oxford.

Evans, G., 1978. Can there be vague objects? *Analysis*, 38: 208.

Evnine, S., 2011. Constitution and composition: Three approaches to their relation. *ProtoSociology*, 27: 212–235.

Evnine, S., 2016. *Making Objects and Events: A Hylomorphic Theory of Artifacts, Actions, and Organisms*. Oxford University Press, Oxford.

Fairchild, M. and Hawthorne, J., 2018. Against conservatism in metaphysics. *Royal Institute of Philosophy Supplements*, 82: 45–75.

Falls, E., in press. Composition as identity, universalism, and generic quantifiers. *Erkenntnis*.

Favaretti Camposampiero, M., 2019a. Mereology and mathematics: Christian Wolff's foundational programme. *British Journal for the History of Philosophy*, 27: 1151–1172.

Favaretti Camposampiero, M., 2019b. Il nesso delle parti: Mereologia e scienza secondo Christian Wolff. In D'Anna, G., Massimilla, E., Piro, F., Sanna,

M., and Toto, F., eds., *Morfologie del rapporto parti-tutto: Totalità e complessità nelle filosofie dell'età moderna*, pp. 239–255. Mimesis, Milan.
Feferman, A. B. and Feferman, S., 2004. *Alfred Tarski: Life and Logic*. Cambridge University Press, Cambridge.
Feldbacher-Escamilla, C. J., 2019. Is mereology ontologically innocent? Well, it depends . . . *Philosophia*, 47: 395–424.
Field, H., 1980. *Science without numbers: A Defense of Nominalism*. Oxford University Press, Oxford.
Field, H., 2016. *Science without Numbers: A Defense of Nominalism*, 2nd edition. Oxford University Press, Oxford.
Findlay, S. D. and Thagard, P., 2012. How parts make up wholes. *Frontiers in Physiology*, 3: 1–10.
Fine, K., 1975. Vagueness, truth and logic. *Synthese*, 30: 265–300.
Fine, K., 1981. Model theory for modal logic, Part III: Existence and predication. *Journal of Philosophical Logic*, 10: 293–307.
Fine, K., 1982. Acts, events, and things. In Leinfellner, W., Kraemer, E., and Schank, J., eds., *Language and Ontology: Proceedings of the 6th International Wittgenstein Symposium*, pp. 97–105. Hölder-Pichler-Tempsky, Vienna.
Fine, K., 1994. Compounds and aggregates. *Noûs*, 28: 137–158.
Fine, K., 1995. Part-whole. In Smith, B., ed., *The Cambridge Companion to Husserl*, pp. 463–468. Cambridge University Press, Cambridge.
Fine, K., 1999. Things and their parts. *Midwest Studies in Philosophy*, 23: 61–74.
Fine, K., 2000. A counter-example to Locke's thesis. In Varzi (2000b), pp. 357–361.
Fine, K., 2003. The non-identity of a material thing and its matter. *Mind*, 112: 195–234.
Fine, K., 2005. Class and membership. *The Journal of Philosophy*, 102: 547–572.
Fine, K., 2007. Response to Kathrin Koslicki. *Dialectica*, 61: 161–166.
Fine, K., 2010. Towards a theory of part. *The Journal of Philosophy*, 107: 559–589.
Fine, K., 2012. Guide to ground. In Correia and Schnieder (2012b), pp. 37–80.
Fine, K., 2017. A theory of truthmaker content I: Conjunction, disjunction and negation. *Journal of Philosophical Logic*, 46: 625–674.
Fiocco, M. O., 2019. Each thing is fundamental: Against hylomorphism and hierarchical structure. *American Philosophical Quarterly*, 56: 289–301.
Fiorini, S. R., Gärdenfors, P., and Abel, M., 2014. Representing part–whole relations in conceptual spaces. *Cognitive Processing*, 15: 127–142.
Fisher, A. R. J., 2013. Bennett on parts twice over. *Philosophia*, 41: 757–761.
Fisher, A. R. J., 2018. Structural universals. *Philosophy Compass*, 13/10: 13 pp.
Fitzgerald, M. J., 2009. Time as a part of physical objects: The modern 'Descartes-minus argument' and an analogous argument from fourteenth-century logic (Heytesbury and Albert of Saxony). *Vivarium*, 47: 54–73.

Florio, S., 2014. Unrestricted quantification. *Philosophy Compass*, 9: 441–454.
Florio, S. and Linnebo, Ø., 2016. On the innocence and determinacy of plural quantification. *Noûs*, 50: 565–583.
Floyd, J., 2011. Prefatory note to the Frege-Wittgenstein correspondence. In De Pellegrin, E., ed., *Interactive Wittgenstein: Essays in Memory of Georg Henrik von Wright*, pp. 1–14. Springer, Dordrecht.
Forbes, G., 1985. *The Metaphysics of Modality*. Clarendon Press, Oxford.
Forrest, P., 1986. Neither magic nor mereology: A reply to Lewis. *Australasian Journal of Philosophy*, 64: 89–91.
Forrest, P., 1996a. From ontology to topology in the theory of regions. *The Monist*, 79: 34–50.
Forrest, P., 1996b. How innocent is mereology? *Analysis*, 56: 127–131.
Forrest, P., 1998. Mereology. In Craig, E., ed., *Routledge Encyclopedia of Philosophy*, volume 6, pp. 317–320. Routledge, London.
Forrest, P., 2002. Nonclassical mereology and its application to sets. *Notre Dame Journal of Formal Logic*, 43: 79–94.
Forrest, P., 2004. Grit or gunk: Implications of the Banach-Tarski paradox. In Hudson (2004), pp. 351–370.
Forrest, P., 2007. Mereological summation and the question of unique fusion. *Analysis*, 67: 237–242.
Forrest, P., 2010. Mereotopology without mereology. *Journal of Philosophical Logic*, 39: 229–254.
Forrest, P., 2012. *The Necessary Structure of the All-pervading Aether: Discrete or Continuous? Simple or Symmetric?* Ontos, Frankfurt.
Forrest, P., 2013. Exemplification and parthood. *Axiomathes*, 23: 323–341.
Forrest, P., 2016. The mereology of structural universals. In Varzi and Gruszczyński (2016), pp. 259–283.
Forrest, P., 2017. Theoretical mereology. In Burkhardt *et al.* (2017), pp. 554–562.
Forster, T. M., 1992. *Set Theory with a Universal Set*. Oxford University Press, Oxford.
Forti, M. and Honsell, F., 1983. Set theory with free construction principles. *Annali della Scuola Normale Superiore di Pisa, Classe di Scienze*, 10: 493–522.
Fowler, G., 2008. A gunk-friendly MaxCon. *Australasian Journal of Philosophy*, 86: 611–627.
Fraenkel, A. A., 1919. *Einleitung in die Mengenlehre*. Springer, Berlin.
Fraenkel, A. A., 1922. Zu den Grundlagen der Cantor-Zermeloschen Mengenlehre. *Mathematische Annalen*, 86: 230–237.
Fraenkel, A. A., 1927. Die Gleichheitsbeziehung in der Mengenlehre. *Journal für die reine und angewandte Mathematik*, 157: 79–81.
Fraenkel, A. A. and Bar-Hillel, Y., 1958. *Foundations of Set Theory*. North-Holland, Amsterdam.

Fraenkel, A. A., Bar-Hillel, Y., and Levy, A., 1973. *Foundations of Set Theory*, 2nd revised edition. North-Holland, Amsterdam.

Frege, G., 1879. *Begriffsschrift, eine der arithmetischen nachgebildete Formelsprache des reinen Denkens*. Nebert, Halle. Eng. trans. by S. Bauer-Mengelberg: *Begriffsschrift*, a formal language, modeled upon that of arithmetic, for pure thought, in van Heijenoort (1967), pp. 1–82.

Frege, G., 1884. *Die Grundlagen der Arithmetik: Eine logisch-mathematische Untersuchung über den Begriff der Zahl*. Koebner, Breslau. Eng. trans. by J. L. Austin: *The Foundations of Arithmetic: A Logico-mathematical Enquiry into the Concept of Number*, Blackwell, Oxford, 1950; 2nd edition: 1974.

Frege, G., 1893. *Grundgesetze der Arithmetik, begriffsschriftlich abgeleitet*, volume 1. Pohle, Jena. Eng. trans. (including volume 2) by P. Ebert and M. Rossberg with C. Wright: *Basic Laws of Arithmetic, Derived Using Concept-Script*, Oxford University Press, Oxford, 2013.

Frege, G., 1895. Kritische Beleuchtung einiger Punkte in E. Schröders *Vorlesungen über die Algebra der Logik*. *Archiv für systematische Philosophie*, 1: 433–456. Eng. trans. by P. T. Geach: A critical elucidation of some points in E. Schroeder's *Vorlesungen ueber die Algebra der Logik*, in Geach, P., and Black, M., eds., *Translations from the Philosophical Writings of Gottlob Frege*, pp. 86–106, Blackwell, Oxford, 1952.

Frege, G., 1969. *Nachgelassene Schriften*, ed. by H. Hermes, F. Kambartel, and F. Kaulbach. Meiner, Hamburg. Eng. trans. by P. Long and R. White: *Posthumous Writings*, Blackwell, Oxford, 1979.

Frege, G., 1976. *Wissenschaftlicher Briefwechsel*, ed. by G. Gabriel *et al*. Meiner, Hamburg. Abridged Eng. trans. by H. Kaal: *Philosophical and Mathematical Correspondence*, University of Chicago Press, Chicago (IL), 1980.

Frege, G., 1989. Briefe an Ludwig Wittgenstein aus den Jahren 1914–1920, ed. by A. Janik and C. P. Berger. *Grazer Philosophische Studien*, 33–34: 5–33. Revised edition and Eng. trans. by B. Dreben and J. Floyd: Frege-Wittgenstein correspondence, in De Pellegrin, E., ed., *Interactive Wittgenstein: Essays in Memory of Georg Henrik von Wright*, pp. 15–73, Springer, Dordrecht, 2011.

French, R., 2016. An argument for the ontological innocence of mereology. *Erkenntnis*, 81: 683–704.

French, S. and Krause, D., 2006. *Identity in Physics: A Historical, Philosophical, and Formal Analysis*. Clarendon Press, Oxford.

Fried, E., 2013. Prolegomena to any future mereology of the body. *Theoretical Medicine and Bioethics*, 34: 359–384.

Friedman, H., 1973. The consistency of classical set theory relative to a set theory with intuitionistic logic. *The Journal of Symbolic Logic*, 38: 315–319.

Furley, D. J., 1987. *The Greek Cosmologists*, volume 1: *The Formation of the Atomic Theory and Its Earliest Critics*. Cambridge University Press, Cambridge.

Gabriel, J., 2015. From unity to wholeness. *Metaphysica*, 16: 1–24.
Gabriel, J., 2017. Particularism about composition. *Ratio*, 30: 15–30.
Galen, C., 1821. *Opera Omnia*, volume 1: *Adhortatio ad artes addiscendas [et al.]*, ed. by C. G. Kühn. Knobloch, Leipzig.
Gallois, A., 1998. *Occasions of Identity: A Study in the Metaphysics of Persistence, Change, and Sameness*. Clarendon Press, Oxford.
Gallois, A., 2016. Identity over time. In Zalta, E. N., ed., *The Stanford Encyclopedia of Philosophy*. http://plato.stanford.edu/archives/win2016/entries/identity-time.
Galluzzo, G., 2015. Aquinas on parts, wholes, and Aristotelian anti-reductionism. *Documenti e studi sulla tradizione filosofica medievale*, 26: 241–276.
Galluzzo, G., 2018. Are matter and form parts? Aristotle's and neo-Aristotelian hylomorphism. *Discipline Filosofiche*, 28: 65–87.
Gangopadhyaya, M., 1980. *Indian Atomism: History and Sources*. Bagchi, Kolkata.
Garbacz, P., 2007. A first order theory of functional parthood. *Journal of Philosophical Logic*, 36: 309–337.
Garbacz, P., 2017. Slot mereology revised. *Australasian Journal of Philosophy*, 95: 171–177.
Garrett, B. J., 1985. Noonan, 'best candidate' theories, and the ship of Theseus. *Analysis*, 45: 212–215.
Geach, P. T., 1949. On rigour in semantics. *Mind*, 58: 518–522.
Geach, P. T., 1958. Entailment. *Proceedings of the Aristotelian Society, Supplementary Volume*, 32: 157–172.
Geach, P. T., 1965. Some problems about time. *Proceedings of the British Academy*, 51: 320–336.
Geach, P. T., 1972. *Logic Matters*. Blackwell, Oxford.
Geach, P. T., 1980. *Reference and Generality: An Examination of Some Medieval and Modern Theories*, 3rd edition. Cornell University Press, Ithaca (NY).
Geach, P. T., 1991. Replies. In Lewis, H. A., ed., *Peter Geach: Philosophical Encounters*, pp. 247–306. Kluwer, Dordrecht.
Gerla, G. and Miranda, A., 2004. Graded inclusion and point-free geometry. *International Journal of Pure and Applied Mathematics*, 11: 63–81.
Gerstl, P. and Pribbenow, S., 1995. Midwinters, end games, and body parts: A classification of part-whole relations. *International Journal of Human-Computer Studies*, 43: 865–889.
Gessler, N., 2005. *Introduction à l'œuvre de S. Leśniewski, Fascicule III: La méréologie*. Centre de recherches sémiologiques, Neuchâtel.
Gessler, N., 2007. *Introduction à l'œuvre de S. Leśniewski, Fascicule V: Leśniewski, lecteur de Frege*. Centre de recherches sémiologiques, Neuchâtel.
Ghiselin, M. T., 1997. *Metaphysics and the Origin of Species*. SUNY Press, Albany (NY).

Ghiselin, M. T., 2007. Is the Pope a Catholic? *Biology and Philosophy*, 22: 283–291.

Giaretta, P., 2001. Individuation and mereological universalism. In Miéville (2001), pp. 55–74.

Giaretta, P. and Spolaore, G., 2011. A mereology for the change of parts. In Trobok, M., Miščević, N., and Žarnić, B., eds., *Between Logic and Reality: Modeling Inference, Action and Understanding*, pp. 243–259. Springer, Berlin.

Gibbins, P. F., 1982. The strange modal logic of indeterminacy. *Logique et Analyse*, 25: 443–446.

Giberman, D., 2012. T-gunk and exact occupation. *American Philosophical Quarterly*, 49: 165–174.

Giberman, D., 2015. Junky non-worlds. *Erkenntnis*, 80: 437–443.

Giberman, D., 2019. On stage with gunk. *Australasian Journal of Philosophy*, 97: 228–238.

Giberman, D., in press. What it takes to be hunky. *Thought*.

Gilbert, M., 1989. *On Social Facts*. Princeton University Press, Princeton (NJ).

Gillett, C., 2007. Understanding the new reductionism: The metaphysics of science and compositional reduction. *The Journal of Philosophy*, 104: 193–216.

Gillett, C., 2013. Constitution, and multiple constitution, in the sciences: Using the neuron to construct a starting framework. *Minds and Machines*, 23: 309–337.

Gilmore, C., 2007. Time travel, coinciding objects, and persistence. *Oxford Studies in Metaphysics*, 3: 177–198.

Gilmore, C., 2009. Why parthood might be a four-place relation, and how it behaves if it is. In Honnefelder, L., Runggaldier, E., and Schick, B., eds., *Unity and Time in Metaphysics*, pp. 83–133. De Gruyter, Berlin.

Gilmore, C., 2010a. Coinciding objects and duration properties: Reply to Eagle. *Oxford Studies in Metaphysics*, 5: 95–111.

Gilmore, C., 2010b. Sider, the inheritance of intrinsicality, and theories of composition. *Philosophical Studies*, 151: 177–197.

Gilmore, C., 2014. Parts of propositions. In Kleinschmidt (2014), pp. 156–208.

Gilmore, C., 2018. Location and mereology. In Zalta, E. N., ed., *The Stanford Encyclopedia of Philosophy*. http://plato.stanford.edu/archives/fall2018/entries/location-mereology.

Gilmore, C., in press. Quasi-supplementation, plenitudinous coincidentalism, and gunk. In Garcia, R. K., ed., *Substance: New Essays*. Philosophia, Munich.

Gilmore, C. and Leonard, M., in press. Composition and the logic of location: An argument for regionalism. *Mind*.

Gilmore, P. C., 1974. The consistency of partial set theory without extensionality. In Jech, T. J., ed., *Axiomatic Set Theory: Proceedings of the Symposium in Pure Mathematics*, pp. 147–153. American Mathematical Society, Providence (RI).

Ginsberg, E., 1929. Zur Husserlschen Lehre von den Ganzen und Teilen. *Archiv für systematische Philosophie und Soziologie*, 32: 108–120.

Giraud, T., 2013. An abstract mereology for Meinongian objects. *Humana. Mente*, 25: 177–210.

Givant, S. and Halmos, P. R., 2009. *Introduction to Boolean Algebras*. Springer, New York.

Gödel, K., 1930. Die Vollständigkeit der Axiome des logischen Funktionenkalküls. *Monatshefte für Mathematik und Physik*, 37: 349–360. Eng. trans. by S. Bauer-Mengelberg: The completeness of the axioms of the functional calculus of logic, in van Heijenoort (1967), pp. 582–591.

Gödel, K., 1944. Russell's mathematical logic. In Schilpp, P. A., ed., *The Philosophy of Bertrand Russell*, pp. 123–153. Northwestern University Press, Evanston (IL).

Gödel, K., 1949. An example of a new type of cosmological solution of Einstein's field equations of gravitation. *Review of Modern Physics*, 21: 447–450.

Goff, P., 2011. There is no combination problem. In Blamauer, M., ed., *The Mental as Fundamental: New Perspectives on Panpsychism*, pp. 131–140. Ontos, Frankfurt.

Goff, P., 2017. The phenomenal bonding solution to the combination problem. In Brüntrup, G. and Jaskolla, L., eds., *Panpsychism: Contemporary Perspectives*, pp. 283–302. Oxford University Press, Oxford.

Goggans, P., 1999. How not to have an ontology of physical objects. *Philosophical Studies*, 94: 295–308.

Goldman, A. I., 1970. *A Theory of Human Action*. Prentice-Hall, Englewood (NJ).

Goldwater, J. P. B., 2015. No composition, no problem: Ordinary objects as arrangements. *Philosophia*, 43: 367–379.

Goodman, N., 1941. *A Study of Qualities: An Essay in Elementary Constructional Theory*. Ph.D. thesis, Harvard University, Cambridge (MA). Published by Garland, New York, 1990.

Goodman, N., 1951. *The Structure of Appearance*. Harvard University Press, Cambridge (MA). 3rd edition: Reidel, Dordrecht, 1977.

Goodman, N., 1956. A world of individuals. In Bochenski, J. M., Church, A., and Goodman, N., *The Problem of Universals: A Symposium*, pp. 13–31. University of Notre Dame Press, Notre Dame (IN).

Goodman, N., 1958. On relations that generate. *Philosophical Studies*, 9: 65–66.

Goodman, N., 1972. *Problems and Projects*. Bobbs-Merrill, Indianapolis (IN).

Goodman, N., 1978. Reply to Breitkopf. *Erkenntnis*, 12: 289–290.

Goodman, N., 1986. Nominalisms. In Hahn, L. E. and Schilpp, P. A., eds., *The Philosophy of W. V. Quine*, pp. 159–161. Open Court, Chicago (IL).

Goodman, N. and Quine, W. V. O., 1947. Steps toward a constructive nominalism. *The Journal of Symbolic Logic*, 12: 105–122.

Goodstein, R. L., 1963. *Boolean Algebra*. Pergamon, Oxford.

Goranko, V. and Galton, A. P., 2015. Temporal logic. In Zalta, E. N., ed., *The Stanford Encyclopedia of Philosophy*. http://plato.stanford.edu/archives/win2015/entries/logic-temporal.

Górska, E., 1999. *On Parts and Wholes: A Cognitive Study of English Schematic Part Terms*. Zakład Graficzny Uniwersytetu Warszawskiego, Warsaw.

Górska, E., 2002a. On partonomy and taxonomy. *Studia Anglica Posnaniensia*, 39: 103–111.

Górska, E., 2002b. The level of specificity of part terms and their function and usage. In Lewandowska-Tomaszczyk, B. and Turewicz, K., eds., *Cognitive Linguistics Today*, pp. 501–515. Lang, Frankfurt.

Gorzka, C., 2003. *Mereologia a topologia i geometria bezpunktowa*. Wydawnictwo Naukowe Uniwersytetu Mikołaja Kopernika, Toruń.

Goswick, D. L., 2013. Change and identity over time. In Dyke, H. and Bardon, A., eds., *A Companion to the Philosophy of Time*, pp. 365–386. Wiley-Blackwell, Oxford.

Goswick, D. L., 2018. The hard question for hylomorphism. *Metaphysics*, 1: 52–62.

Graham, A., 2015. From four- to five-dimensionalism. *Ratio*, 28: 14–28.

Grandy, R. E., 1975. Stuff and things. *Synthese*, 31: 479–485.

Grätzer, G. A., 1968. *Universal Algebra*. Van Nostrand, Princeton (NJ).

Grellard, C. and Robert, A., eds., 2008. *Atomism in Late Medieval Philosophy and Theology*. Brill, Leiden.

Grelling, K. and Oppenheim, P., 1938. Der Gestaltbegriff im Lichte der neuen Logik. *Erkenntnis*, 7: 211–225. Eng. trans. by P. M. Simons: The concept of Gestalt in the light of modem logic, in Smith, B., ed., *Foundations of Gestalt Theory*, pp. 191–205, Philosophia, Munich, 1988.

Grelling, K. and Oppenheim, P., 1939. Logical analysis of 'Gestalt' as 'functional whole'. Preprint distributed at the *Fifth International Congress for the Unity of Science*, Harvard University, Cambridge (MA), April 17–19; published in Smith, B., ed., *Foundations of Gestalt Theory*, pp. 210–216, Philosophia, Munich, 1988.

Grossmann, R., 1973. *Ontological Reduction*. Indiana University Press, Bloomington (IN).

Grupp, J., 2006. Mereological nihilism: Quantum atomism and the impossibility of material constitution. *Axiomathes*, 16: 245–386.

Gruszczyński, R., 2013. Mereological fusion as an upper bound. *Bulletin of the Section of Logic*, 42: 135–149.

Gruszczyński, R., 2015. On mereological counterparts of some principle for sets. *Logique et Analyse*, 58: 535–546.

Gruszczyński, R., 2016. *Niestandardowe teorie przestrzeni*. Wydawnictwo Naukowe Uniwersytetu Mikołaja Kopernika, Toruń.

Gruszczyński, R. and Pietruszczak, A., 2010. How to define a mereological (collective) set. *Logic and Logical Philosophy*, 19: 309–328.

Gruszczyński, R. and Pietruszczak, A., 2014. The relations of *supremum* and *mereological sum* in partially ordered sets. In Calosi and Graziani (2014), pp. 123–140.

Gruszczyński, R. and Varzi, A. C., 2015. Mereology then and now. In Varzi and Gruszczyński (2015), pp. 409–427.

Grygianiec, M., 2005. W obronie mereologicznego esencjalizmu. *Filozofia Nauki*, 13: 57–69.

Grygianiec, M., 2006. Identyczność osobowa w czasie: Konsekwencje esencjalizmu. *Filozofia Nauki*, 14: 49–56.

Grygianiec, M., 2007. Zasady mereologicznego esencjalizmu. *Filozofia Nauki*, 15: 27–40.

Grzegorczyk, A., 1955. The systems of Leśniewski in relation to contemporary logical research. *Studia Logica*, 3: 77–97.

Grzegorczyk, A., 1960. Axiomatizability of geometry without points. *Synthese*, 12: 228–235.

Guarino, N., Pribbenow, S., and Vieu, L., eds., 1996. *Modeling Parts and Wholes*. Special issue of *Data & Knowledge Engineering*, volume 20/3.

Guillon, J.-B., in press. Coincidence as parthood. In Carrara and Lando (in press-b).

Guizzardi, G., 2009. The problem of transitivity of part-whole relations in conceptual modeling revisited. In van Eck, P., Gordijn, J., and Wieringa, R., eds., *Advanced Information Systems Engineering: Proceedings of the 21st International Conference*, pp. 94–109. Springer, Berlin.

Gurwitsch, A., 1929. Phänomenologie der Thematik und des reinen Ich. Studien über Beziehungen von Gestalttheorie und Phänomenologie. *Psychologische Forschung*, 12: 279–381. Eng. trans. by F. Kersten: Phenomenology of thematics and of the pure ego: Studies of the relation between Gestalt theory and phenomenology, in Gurwitsch's *Studies in Phenomenology and Psychology*, pp. 175–285, Northwestern University Press, Evanston (IL), 1966.

Haber, M. H., 2015. The biological and the mereological: Metaphysical implications of the individuality thesis. In Pradeu, T. and Guay, A., eds., *Individuals Across the Sciences*, pp. 295–316. Oxford University Press, Oxford.

Hacker, P. M. S., 1982. Events and objects in space and time. *Mind*, 91: 1–19.

Hahmann, T. and Grüninger, M., 2012. Region-based theories of space: Mereotopology and beyond. In Hazarika, S. M., ed., *Qualitative Spatio-Temporal Representation and Reasoning: Trends and Future Directions*, pp. 1–62. IGI Publishing, Hershey (PA).

Hájek, P. and Haniková, Z., 2003. A development of set theory in fuzzy logic.

In Fitting, M. and Orłowska, E., eds., *Beyond Two: Theory and Applications of Multiple-Valued Logic*, pp. 273–285. Physica-Verlag, Heidelberg.

Hale, S., 1991. Modal realism without counterparts. *Southwest Philosophy Review*, 7: 77–86.

Halmos, P. R., 1960. *Naive Set Theory*. Van Nostrand, Princeton (NJ).

Hamkins, J. D. and Kikuchi, M., 2016. Set-theoretic mereology. In Varzi and Gruszczyński (2016), pp. 285–308.

Hand, M., 1995. What the null set could not be. *Australasian Journal of Philosophy*, 73: 429–431.

Hansen, K., 2011. Argument Petera Ungera za nihilizmem mereologicznym. *Filozofia Nauki*, 19: 85–97.

Harré, R. and Llored, J.-P., 2013. Molecules and mereology. *Foundations of Chemistry*, 15: 127–144.

Harte, V., 2002. *Plato on Parts and Wholes: The Metaphysics of Structure*. Clarendon Press, Oxford.

Hartz, G. A., 2006. *Leibniz's Final System: Monads, Matter, and Animals*. Routledge, London.

Haslanger, S., 1994. Parts, compounds, and substantial unity. In Scaltsas, T., Charles, D., and Gill, M. L., eds., *Unity, Identity, and Explanation in Aristotle's Metaphysics*, pp. 129–170. Clarendon Press, Oxford.

Haslanger, S., 2003. Persistence through time. In Loux, M. J. and Zimmerman, D. W., eds., *The Oxford Handbook of Metaphysics*, pp. 315–354. Oxford University Press, Oxford.

Hawley, K., 2001. *How Things Persist*. Clarendon Press, Oxford.

Hawley, K., 2002. Vagueness and existence. *Proceedings of the Aristotelian Society*, 102: 125–140.

Hawley, K., 2004. Borderline simple or extremely simple. In Hudson (2004), pp. 385–404.

Hawley, K., 2006. Principles of composition and criteria of identity. *Australasian Journal of Philosophy*, 84: 481–493.

Hawley, K., 2008. Persistence and determination. *Royal Institute of Philosophy Supplements*, 62: 197–212.

Hawley, K., 2010. Mereology, modality and magic. *Australasian Journal of Philosophy*, 88: 117–133.

Hawley, K., 2013. Cut the pie any way you like? Cotnoir on general identity. *Oxford Studies in Metaphysics*, 8: 323–330.

Hawley, K., 2014. Ontological innocence. In Cotnoir and Baxter (2014), pp. 70–89.

Hawley, K., 2017. Social mereology. *Journal of the American Philosophical Association*, 3: 395–411.

Hawley, K., 2018a. Almost identical, almost innocent. *Royal Institute of Philosophy Supplements*, 82: 249–263.

Hawley, K., 2018b. Temporal parts. In Zalta, E. N., ed., *The Stanford Encyclopedia of Philosophy*. http://plato.stanford.edu/archives/spr2018/entries/temporal-parts.

Hawthorne, J., 2006. *Metaphysical Essays*. Clarendon Press, Oxford.

Hawthorne, J. and Michael, M., 1996. Compatibilist semantics in metaphysics: A case study. *Australasian Journal of Philosophy*, 74: 117–134.

Hawthorne, J. and Uzquiano, G., 2011. How many angels can dance on the point of a needle? Transcendental theology meets modal metaphysics. *Mind*, 120: 53–81.

Hawthorne, J. and Weatherson, B., 2004. Chopping up gunk. In Hudson (2004), pp. 339–350.

Hazen, A. P., 1993. Against pluralism. *Australasian Journal of Philosophy*, 71: 132–144.

Hazen, A. P., 1997. Relations in Lewis's framework without atoms. *Analysis*, 57: 243–248.

Hazen, A. P., 2000. Relations in Lewis's framework without atoms: A correction. *Analysis*, 60: 351–353.

Hazen, A. P., 2004. Hypergunk. In Hudson (2004), pp. 322–338.

Healey, R., 2013. Physical composition. *Studies in History and Philosophy of Modern Physics*, 44: 48–62.

Heck, R. G. Jr., 1998. That there might be vague objects (so far as concerns logic). *The Monist*, 81: 274–296.

Hegel, G. W. F., 1812-1816. *Wissenschaft der Logik*. Schrag, Nuremberg. 2nd edition, ed. by L. von Henning: Duncker und Humblot, Berlin, 1833; Eng. trans. by G. di Giovanni: *The Science of Logic*, Cambridge University Press, Cambridge, 2010.

Heller, M., 1984. Temporal parts of four dimensional objects. *Philosophical Studies*, 46: 323–334.

Heller, M., 1990. *The Ontology of Physical Objects: Four-Dimensional Hunks of Matter*. Cambridge University Press, Cambridge.

Heller, M., 2000. Temporal overlap is not coincidence. In Varzi (2000b), pp. 362–380.

Hellman, G., 1969. Finitude, infinitude, and isomorphism of interpretations in some nominalistic calculi. *Noûs*, 3: 413–425.

Hellman, G., 1996. Structuralism without structures. *Philosophia Mathematica*, 4: 100–123.

Hellman, G., 2017. Mereology in philosophy of mathematics. In Burkhardt *et al.* (2017), pp. 412–424.

Hellman, G. and Shapiro, S., 2018. *Varieties of Continua: From Regions to Points and Back*. Oxford University Press, Oxford.

Hempel, C. G., 1953. Reflections on Nelson Goodman's *The Structure of Appearance*. *The Philosophical Review*, 62: 108–116.

Hendry, H. E., 1980. Two remarks on the atomistic calculus of individuals. *Noûs*, 14: 235–237.

Hendry, H. E., 1982. Complete extensions of the calculus of individuals. *Noûs*, 16: 453–460.

Henkin, L., 1950. Completeness in the theory of types. *The Journal of Symbolic Logic*, 15: 81–91.

Henkin, L., 1962. Nominalistic analysis of mathematical language. In Nagel, E., Suppes, P., and Tarski, A., eds., *Logic, Methodology and Philosophy of Science: Proceedings of the 1960 International Congress*, pp. 187–193. Stanford University Press, Stanford (CA).

Henry, D. P., 1972. *Medieval Logic and Metaphysics: A Modern Introduction*. Hutchinson, London.

Henry, D. P., 1989. Mereology and metaphysics: From Boethius of Dacia to Leśniewski. In Szaniawski, K., ed., *The Vienna Circle and the Lvov-Warsaw School*, pp. 203–224. Kluwer, Dordrecht.

Henry, D. P., 1991a. *Medieval Mereology*. Grüner, Amsterdam.

Henry, D. P., 1991b. Abelard and medieval mereology. In Lewis, H. A., ed., *Peter Geach: Philosophical Encounters*, pp. 49–64. Kluwer, Dordrecht.

Herre, H., 2010. The ontology of mereological systems: A logical approach. In Poli, R. and Seibt, J., eds., *Theory and Applications of Ontology: Philosophical Perspectives*, pp. 57–82. Springer, Dordrecht.

Hershenov, D. B., 2008. A hylomorphic account of thought experiments concerning personal identity. *American Catholic Philosophical Quarterly*, 82: 481–502.

Hershenov, D. B. and Koch-Hershenov, R., 2006. Personal identity and purgatory. *Religious Studies*, 42: 439–451.

Hestevold, H. S., 1981. Conjoining. *Philosophy and Phenomenological Research*, 41: 371–385.

Hewitt, S. T., 2012. Modalising plurals. *Journal of Philosophical Logic*, 41: 853–875.

Hewitt, S. T., 2015a. When do some things form a set? *Philosophia Mathematica*, 23: 311–337.

Hewitt, S. T., 2015b. A cardinal worry for permissive metaontology. *Metaphysica*, 16: 159–165.

Hirsch, E., 1982. *The Concept of Identity*. Oxford University Press, Oxford.

Hirsch, E., 1993. *Dividing Reality*. Oxford University Press, Oxford.

Hirsch, E., 2002a. Against revisionary ontology. *Philosophical Topics*, 30: 103–127.

Hirsch, E., 2002b. Quantifier variance and realism. *Philosophical Issues*, 12: 51–73.

Hirsch, E., 2005. Physical-object ontology, verbal disputes, and common sense. *Philosophy and Phenomenological Research*, 70: 67–97.

Hirsch, E., 2008. Language, ontology, and structure. *Noûs*, 42: 509–529.
Hobbes, T., 1839. *The English Works*, volume 1: *Elements of Philosophy, the First Section, Concerning Body*, ed. by W. Molesworth. Bohn, London.
Hodges, W. and Lewis, D. K., 1968. Finitude and infinitude in the atomic calculus of individuals. *Noûs*, 2: 405–410 (with Errata in 3: 109, 1969).
Hoffman, D. D. and Richards, W. A., 1984. Parts of recognition. *Cognition*, 18: 65–96.
Hoffman, J. and Rosenkrantz, G. S., 1994. *Substance among Other Categories*. Cambridge University Press, Cambridge.
Hoffman, J. and Rosenkrantz, G. S., 1997. *Substance: Its Nature and Existence*. Routledge, London.
Holden, T., 2002. Infinite divisibility and actual parts in Hume's *Treatise*. *Hume Studies*, 28: 3–25.
Holden, T., 2004. *The Architecture of Matter: Galileo to Kant*. Clarendon Press, Oxford.
Holmes, M. R., 1998. *Elementary Set Theory with a Universal Set*. Academia-Bruylant, Louvain-la-Neuve.
Horden, J., 2014. Ontology in plain English. *The Philosophical Quarterly*, 64: 225–242.
Horgan, T., 1991. Metaphysical realism and psychologistic semantics. *Erkenntnis*, 34: 297–322.
Horgan, T., 1993. On what there isn't. *Philosophy and Phenomenological Research*, 53: 693–700.
Horgan, T. and Potrč, M., 2000. Blobjectivism and indirect correspondence. *Facta Philosophica*, 2: 249–270.
Horgan, T. and Potrč, M., 2008. *Austere Realism: Contextual Semantics Meets Minimal Ontology*. MIT Press, Cambridge (MA).
Horgan, T. and Potrč, M., 2012. Existence monism trumps priority monism. In Goff, P., ed., *Spinoza on Monism*, pp. 51–76. Palgrave, London.
Hossack, K., 2000. Plurals and complexes. *The British Journal for the Philosophy of Science*, 51: 411–443.
Hovda, P., 2009. What is classical mereology? *Journal of Philosophical Logic*, 38: 55–82.
Hovda, P., 2013. Tensed mereology. *Journal of Philosophical Logic*, 42: 241–283.
Hovda, P., 2014. Logical considerations on composition as identity. In Cotnoir and Baxter (2014), pp. 192–210.
Hovda, P., 2016. Parthood-like relations: Closure principles and connections to some axioms of classical mereology. *Philosophical Perspectives*, 30: 183–197.
Hovda, P., 2017. Varieties of parthood. In Yang, S. C.-M., Lee, K. Y., and Ono, H., eds., *Philosophical Logic, Current Trends in Asia: Proceedings of AWPL-TPLC 2016*, pp. 259–286. Springer, Singapore.

Hübner, J., 2007. *Komplexe Substanzen*. De Gruyter, Berlin.

Hudetz, L., 2014. Mereological atomism and infinite divisibility. Talk given at the *Eighth European Congress of Analytic Philosophy*, University of Bucharest, Bucharest, August 29.

Hudson, H., 2000. Universalism, four-dimensionalism, and vagueness. *Philosophy and Phenomenological Research*, 60: 547–560.

Hudson, H., 2001. *A Materialist Metaphysics of the Human Person*. Cornell University Press, Ithaca (NY).

Hudson, H., 2002a. The liberal view of receptacles. *Australasian Journal of Philosophy*, 80: 432–439.

Hudson, H., 2002b. Moving faster than light. *Analysis*, 62: 203–205.

Hudson, H., ed., 2004. *Simples*. Special issue of *The Monist*, volume 87/3.

Hudson, H., 2005. *The Metaphysics of Hyperspace*. Clarendon Press, Oxford.

Hudson, H., 2006a. Simple statues. *Philo*, 9: 32–38.

Hudson, H., 2006b. Confining composition. In Mann and Varzi (2006), pp. 631–651.

Hudson, H., 2007. Simples and gunk. *Philosophy Compass*, 2: 291–302.

Hudson, H., 2009. Omnipresence. In Flint, T. P. and Rea, M., eds., *The Oxford Handbook of Philosophical Theology*, pp. 199–216. Oxford University Press, Oxford.

Hughes, C., 1986. Is a thing just the sum of its parts? *Proceedings of the Aristotelian Society*, 86: 213–233.

Hughes, G. E. and Cresswell, M. J., 1996. *A New Introduction to Modal Logic*. Routledge, London.

Humberstone, L., 2000. Parts and partitions. *Theoria*, 66: 41–82.

Husmann, J. and Näger, P. M., 2018. Physical composition by bonding. In Jansen, L. and Näger, P. M., eds., *Peter van Inwagen: Materialism, Free Will and God*, pp. 65–96. Springer, Cham.

Husserl, E., 1894. Psychologische Studien zur elementaren Logik. *Philosophische Monatshefte*, 30: 159–191. Eng. trans. by D. Willard: Psychological studies in the elements of logic, *The Personalist*, 58: 297–320, 1977.

Husserl, E., 1900–1901. *Logische Untersuchungen*. Niemeyer, Halle. 2nd edition: 1913 (volumes 1 and 2/I) and 1921 (volume 2/II); Eng. trans. by J. N. Findlay: *Logical Investigations*, Routledge & Kegan Paul, London, 1970.

Husserl, E., 1913. Ideen zu einer reinen Phänomenologie und phänomenologischen Philosophie. Erstes Buch: Allgemeine Einführung in die reine Phänomenologie. *Jahrbuch für Philosophie und phänomenologische Forschung*, 1: 1–323. Eng. trans. by W. R. B. Gibson: *Ideas: General Introduction to Pure Phenomenology*, Allen & Unwin, London, 1931.

Husserl, E., 1929. *Formale und transzendentale Logik: Versuch einer Kritik der logischen Vernunft*. Niemeyer, Halle. Eng. trans. by D. Cairns: *Formal and Transcendental Logic*, Nijhoff, The Hague, 1969.

Husserl, E., 1939. *Erfahrung und Urteil: Untersuchungen zur Genealogie der Logik*, ed. by L. Landgrebe. Academia, Prague. Eng. trans. by J. S. Churchill and K. Ameriks: *Experience and Judgment: Investigations in a Genealogy of Logic*, Northwestern University Press, Evanston (IL), 1973.

Hutchinson, G. E., 1978. *An Introduction to Population Ecology*. Yale University Press, New Haven (CT).

Hyde, D., 2008. *Vagueness, Logic and Ontology*. Ashgate, Aldershot.

Inman, R. D., 2014. Neo-Aristotelian plenitude. *Philosophical Studies*, 168: 583–597.

Inman, R. D., 2018. *Substance and the Fundamentality of the Familiar: A Neo-Aristotelian Mereology*. Routledge, London.

Inman, R. D. and Pruss, A. R., 2019. On Christian theism and unrestricted composition. *American Philosophical Quarterly*, 56: 345–360.

Iris, M. A., Litowitz, B. E., and Evens, M. W., 1988. Problems of the part-whole relation. In Evens, M. W., ed., *Relational Models of the Lexicon*, pp. 261–288. Cambridge University Press, Cambridge.

Jacinto, B. and Cotnoir, A. J., 2019. Models for hylomorphism. *Journal of Philosophical Logic*, 48: 909–955.

Jackson, F., 2001. Responses. *Philosophy and Phenomenological Research*, 62: 653–664.

Jacquette, D., 1996. Hume on infinite divisibility and sensible extensionless indivisibles. *Journal of the History of Philosophy*, 34: 61–78.

Jacquette, D., 2015. *Alexius Meinong, the Shepherd of Non-Being*. Springer, Cham.

Jaeger, A. J., 2014. A tale of two parts. *Res Philosophica*, 91: 477–484.

James, W., 1890. *The Principles of Psychology*. Holt & Co., New York.

Janicki, R. and Lê, D. T. M., 2007. Towards a pragmatic mereology. *Fundamenta Informaticae*, 75: 295–314.

Jansen, C. M., 2019. De-Fining material things. *Dialectica*, 73: 459–477.

Javier-Castellanos, A. A., 2016. Duplication and collapse. *Thought*, 5: 196–202.

Jaworski, W., 2014. Hylomorphism and the metaphysics of structure. *Res Philosophica*, 91: 179–201.

Jaworski, W., 2019. Hylomorphism and part-whole realism. *Ancient Philosophy Today: Dialogoi*, 1: 108–127.

Jech, T. J., 1978. *Set Theory*. Academic Press, New York.

Jenkins, C. S. I., 2011. Is metaphysical grounding irreflexive? *The Monist*, 94: 267–276.

Johansson, I., 2004. On the transitivity of parthood relations. In Hochberg, H. and Mulligan, K., eds., *Relations and Predicates*, pp. 161–181. Ontos, Frankfurt.

Johansson, I., 2006a. Formal mereology and ordinary language. Reply to Varzi. *Applied Ontology*, 1: 157–161.

Johansson, I., 2006b. Identity puzzles and supervenient identities. *Metaphysica*, 7: 7–33.

Johansson, I., 2008. Formalizing common sense: An operator-based approach to the Tibbles-Tib problem. *Synthese*, 163: 217–225.

Johansson, I., 2015. Applied mereology. *Metascience*, 24: 239–245.

Johansson, I. and Lynøe, N., 2008. *Medicine and Philosophy: A Twenty-First Century Introduction*. Ontos, Frankfurt.

Johansson, J., 2009. Constituted simples? *Philosophia*, 37: 87–89.

Johnsen, B., 1989. Is vague identity incoherent? *Analysis*, 49: 103–112.

Johnston, M., 1992. Constitution is not identity. *Mind*, 101: 89–105.

Johnston, M., 2002. Parts and principles: False axioms in mereology. *Philosophical Topics*, 30: 129–166.

Johnston, M., 2005. Constitution. In Jackson, F. and Smith, M., eds., *The Oxford Handbook of Contemporary Philosophy*, pp. 636–675. Oxford University Press, Oxford.

Johnston, M., 2006. Hylomorphism. In Mann and Varzi (2006), pp. 652–698.

Johnstone, P. T., 1982. *Stone Spaces*. Cambridge University Press, Cambridge.

Jones, N. J., 2009. Fazang's total power mereology: An interpretive analytic reconstruction. *Asian Philosophy*, 19: 199–211.

Jones, N. J., 2010. Mereological heuristics for Huayan Buddhism. *Philosophy East and West*, 60: 355–368.

Jones, N. J., 2019. The architecture of Fazang's six characteristics. *British Journal for the History of Philosophy*, 27: 468–491.

Jubien, M., 1993. *Ontology, Modality, and the Fallacy of Reference*. Cambridge University Press, Cambridge.

Jubien, M., 2001. Thinking about things. *Philosophical Perspectives*, 15: 1–15.

Jubien, M., 2009. *Possibility*. Clarendon Press, Oxford.

Kalhat, J., 2008. Structural universals and the principle of uniqueness of composition. *Grazer Philosophische Studien*, 76: 57–77.

Kamp, J. A. W., 1975. Two theories about adjectives. In Keenan, E., ed., *Formal Semantics of Natural Language*, pp. 123–155. Cambridge University Press, Cambridge.

Kantin, H., in press. Why compositional nihilism dissolves puzzles. *Synthese*.

Kappes, Y., 2019. On the grounds of sums: Reply to Saenz. *Australasian Journal of Philosophy*, 97: 824–829.

Kaulbach, F., Oeing-Hanhoff, L., and Beck, H., 1974. Ganzes/Teil. In Ritter, J., ed., *Historisches Wörterbuch der Philosophie*, volume 3, pp. 3–20. Schwabe, Basel.

Kazmi, A. A., 1990. Parthood and persistence. *Canadian Journal of Philosophy* (Supplement), 20: 227–250.

Kearns, J. T., 1967. The contribution of Leśniewski. *Notre Dame Journal of Formal Logic*, 8: 61–93.

Kearns, S., 2011. Can a thing be part of itself? *American Philosophical Quarterly*, 48: 87–93.

Keefe, R., 2000. *Theories of Vagueness*. Cambridge University Press, Cambridge.

Keefe, R., 2008. Vagueness: Supervaluationism. *Philosophy Compass*, 3: 315–324.

Keet, C. M. and Artale, A., 2008. Representing and reasoning over a taxonomy of part-whole relations. *Applied Ontology*, 3: 91–110.

Keinänen, M. and Tahko, T. E., 2019. Bundle theory with kinds. *The Philosophical Quarterly*, 69: 838–857.

Keith, A. B., 1921. *Indian Logic and Atomism: An Exposition of the Nyāya and Vaiçeṣika Systems*. Clarendon Press, Oxford.

Keller, L., 2013. The metaphysics of propositional constituency. *Canadian Journal of Philosophy*, 43: 655–678.

Ketland, J. and Schindler, T., 2016. Arithmetic with fusions. *Logique et Analyse*, 59: 207–226.

Khushf, G., 2013. Beware of mereologists bearing gifts: Prolegomena to a medical metaphysics. *Theoretical Medicine and Bioethics*, 34: 385–408.

Kielkopf, C. F., 1977. Quantifiers in Ontology. *Studia Logica*, 36: 301–307.

Kim, J., 2019. Baxter and Cotnoir on composition as identity. *Chul Hak Sa Sang*, 73: 105–125.

King, J., 2007. *The Nature and Structure of Content*. Oxford University Press, Oxford.

Kitamura, N., 2012. Another sense of the ontological innocence of mereology: From a neo-Aristotelian point of view. *Philosophy* (Japan), 129: 73–86.

Kitamura, N., 2016. Defending priority views from the gunk/junk argument. *Philosophia*, 44: 155–165.

Kleene, S. C., 1938. On notation for ordinal numbers. *The Journal of Symbolic Logic*, 3: 150–155.

Kleinschmidt, S., 2007. Some things about stuff. *Philosophical Studies*, 135: 407–423.

Kleinschmidt, S., 2011. Multilocation and mereology. *Philosophical Perspectives*, 25: 253–276.

Kleinschmidt, S., 2012. Many-one identity and the Trinity. *Oxford Studies in Philosophy of Religion*, 4: 84–96.

Kleinschmidt, S., ed., 2014. *Mereology and Location*. Oxford University Press, Oxford.

Kleinschmidt, S., 2016. Placement permissivism and logics of location. *The Journal of Philosophy*, 113: 117–136.

Kleinschmidt, S., 2017. Extensionality of proper part containment. *The Philosophical Quarterly*, 67: 835–844.

Kleinschmidt, S., 2019. Fusion first. *Noûs*, 53: 689–707.

Klima, G. and Hall, A., eds., 2018. *Hylomorphism and Mereology: Proceedings of the Society for Medieval Logic and Metaphysics*. Cambridge Scholars Publishing, Newcastle upon Tyne.

Koestler, A., 1967. *The Ghost in the Machine*. Hutchinson, London.

Koestler, A., 1969. Beyond atomism and holism – The concept of the holon. In Koestler, A. and Smythies, J. R., eds., *Beyond Reductionism: New Perspectives in the Life Sciences*, pp. 192–216. Hutchinson, London.

Koestler, A., 1978. *Janus: A Summing Up*. Hutchinson, London.

Koffka, K., 1935. *Principles of Gestalt Psychology*. Kegan Paul, Trench, & Trübner, London.

Köhler, W., 1920. *Die physischen Gestalten in Ruhe und im stationären Zustand: Eine naturphilosophische Untersuchung*. Vieweg, Braunschweig. Condensed Eng. trans. by W. D. Ellis: Physical Gestalten, in Ellis, W. D., ed., *A Source Book of Gestalt Psychology*, pp. 17–55, Routledge, London, 1938.

Koons, R. C., 2014. Staunch vs. faint-hearted hylomorphism: Toward an Aristotelian account of composition. *Res Philosophica*, 91: 151–177.

Koons, R. C. and Pickavance, T. H., 2017. *The Atlas of Reality: A Comprehensive Guide to Metaphysics*. Wiley-Blackwell, Oxford.

Korman, D. Z., 2008. Unrestricted composition and restricted quantification. *Philosophical Studies*, 140: 319–334.

Korman, D. Z., 2009. Eliminativism and the challenge from folk belief. *Noûs*, 43: 242–264.

Korman, D. Z., 2010a. The argument from vagueness. *Philosophy Compass*, 5: 891–901.

Korman, D. Z., 2010b. Strange kinds, familiar kinds, and the charge of arbitrariness. *Oxford Studies in Metaphysics*, 5: 119–144.

Korman, D. Z., 2014. Debunking perceptual beliefs about ordinary objects. *Philosopher's Imprint*, 14/13: 1–21.

Korman, D. Z., 2015a. *Objects: Nothing out of the Ordinary*. Oxford University Press, Oxford.

Korman, D. Z., 2015b. Fundamental quantification and the language of the ontology room. *Noûs*, 49: 298–321.

Korman, D. Z. and Carmichael, C., 2016. Composition. In *Oxford Handbooks Online*. Oxford University Press, Oxford.

Korman, D. Z. and Carmichael, C., 2017. What do the folk think about composition, and does it matter? In Rose, D., ed., *Experimental Metaphysics*, pp. 187–206. Bloomsbury, London.

Koslicki, K., 1999. The semantics of mass-predicates. *Noûs*, 33: 46–91.

Koslicki, K., 2003. The crooked path from vagueness to four-dimensionalism. *Philosophical Studies*, 114: 107–134.

Koslicki, K., 2005. On the substantive nature of disagreements in ontology. *Philosophy and Phenomenological Research*, 71: 85–105.

Koslicki, K., 2006. Aristotle's mereology and the status of form. In Mann and Varzi (2006), pp. 715–736.

Koslicki, K., 2007. Towards a neo-Aristotelian mereology. *Dialectica*, 61: 127–159.

Koslicki, K., 2008. *The Structure of Objects*. Oxford University Press, Oxford.

Koslicki, K., 2014. Mereological sums and singular terms. In Kleinschmidt (2014), pp. 209–235.

Koslicki, K., 2017. Structure. In Burkhardt *et al.* (2017), pp. 512–519.

Koslicki, K., 2018. *Form, Matter, Substance*. Oxford University Press, Oxford.

Kosslyn, S. M., Heldmeyer, K. H., and Glass, A. L., 1980. Where does one part end and another begin? A developmental study. In Becker, J., Wilkening, F., and Trabasso, T., eds., *Information Integration by Children*, pp. 147–168. Erlbaum, Hillsdale (NJ).

Kotarbiński, T., 1929. *Elementy teorii poznania, logiki formalnej i metodologii nauk*. Ossolineum, Lvov. Eng. trans. by O. Wojtasiewicz: *Gnosiology: The Scientific Approach to the Theory of Knowledge*, Pergamon, Oxford, 1966.

Kovacs, D. M., 2014. What do we want to know when we ask the Simple Question? *The Philosophical Quarterly*, 64: 254–266.

Kovacs, D. M., in press. Intuitions about objects: From teleology to elimination. *Mind*.

Krecz, C. A., 1986. Parts and pieces. *Philosophy and Phenomenological Research*, 46: 381–400.

Kretzmann, N., 1982. Syncategoremata, exponibilia, sophismata. In Kretzmann, N., Kenny, A., and Pinborg, J., eds., *The Cambridge History of Later Medieval Philosophy*, pp. 211–245. Cambridge University Press, Cambridge.

Kriegel, U., 2008. Composition as a secondary quality. *Pacific Philosophical Quarterly*, 89: 359–383.

Kriegel, U., 2012. Kantian monism. *Philosophical Papers*, 41: 23–56.

Kriegel, U., 2015. Thought and thing: Brentano's reism as truthmaker nominalism. *Philosophy and Phenomenological Research*, 91: 153–180.

Kriegel, U., 2018a. *Brentano's Philosophical System: Mind, Being, Value*. Oxford University Press, Oxford.

Kriegel, U., 2018b. Brentano's dual-framing theory of consciousness. *Philosophy and Phenomenological Research*, 97: 79–98.

Krifka, M., 1990. Four thousand ships passed through the lock: Object-induced measure functions on events. *Linguistics and Philosophy*, 13: 487–520.

Krifka, M., 1998. The origins of telicity. In Rothstein, S., ed., *Events and Grammar*, pp. 197–235. Kluwer, Dordrecht.

Kripke, S. A., 1963. Semantical considerations on modal and intuitionistic logic. *Acta Philosophica Fennica*, 16: 83–94.

Kubiński, T., 1968. Uwagi o modelach systemu mereologii Leśniewskiego. *Ruch Filozoficzny*, 26: 336–338.

Kubiński, T., 1971. A report on investigations concerning mereology. *Acta Universitatis Wratislaviensis*, 139: 48–69.

Küng, G., 1977. The meaning of the quantifiers in the logic of Leśniewski. *Studia Logica*, 36: 309–322.

Küng, G. and Canty, J. T., 1970. Substitutional quantification and Leśniewskian quantifiers. *Theoria*, 36: 165–182.

Kurtsal Steen, İ., 2010. Three-dimensionalist's semantic solution to diachronic vagueness. *Philosophical Studies*, 150: 79–96.

Kurtsal Steen, İ., 2014. Almost-ontology: Why epistemicism cannot help us avoid unrestricted composition or diachronic plenitude. *Pacific Philosophical Quarterly*, 95: 130–139.

Ladyman, J. and Ross, D., 2007. *Every Thing Must Go: Metaphysics Naturalized*. Oxford University Press, Oxford.

Lafrance, J.-D., 2015. A bundle of universals theory of material objects. *The Philosophical Quarterly*, 65: 202–219.

Lambert, K., 1960. The definition of E(xistence)! in free logic. In *International Congress for Logic, Methodology and Philosophy of Science: Abstracts of Contributed Papers*, p. 40. Stanford University (mimeo), Stanford (CA).

Lambert, K., 1987. On the philosophical foundations of free description theory. *History and Philosophy of Logic*, 8: 57–66.

Lambrix, P., 2000. *Part-Whole Reasoning in an Object-Centered Framework*. Springer, Berlin.

Landman, F., 1991. *Structures for Semantics*. Kluwer, Dordrecht.

Landman, F., 2000. *Events and Plurality: The Jerusalem Lectures*. Kluwer, Dordrecht.

Landman, F., 2004. *Indefinites and the Type of Sets*. Blackwell, Oxford.

Lando, G., 2007. Tractarian ontology: Mereology or set theory? *Forum Philosophicum*, 12: 24–39.

Lando, G., 2017. *Mereology: A Philosophical Introduction*. Bloomsbury, London.

Lando, T. and Scott, D., 2019. A calculus of regions respecting both measure and topology. *Journal of Philosophical Logic*, 48: 825–850.

Latronico, V., 2009. Al nominalista non manca proprio nulla? La dispensabilità dell'insieme vuoto in mereologia. *Rivista di storia della filosofia*, 64: 63–73.

Laycock, H., 2011. Any sum of parts which are water is water. In Carrara *et al.* (2011), pp. 41–55.

Le Bihan, B., 2013. Why a gunk world is compatible with nihilism about objects. *Studia Philosophica Estonica*, 6: 1–14.

Le Bihan, B., 2015. No physical particles for a dispositional monist? *Philosophical Papers*, 44: 207–232.

Le Blanc, A., 1983. A study of the axiomatic foundations of mereology. M.A. thesis, University of Manchester, Manchester.

Le Blanc, A., 1985a. Axioms for mereology. *Notre Dame Journal of Formal Logic*, 26: 429–436.

Le Blanc, A., 1985b. New axioms for mereology. *Notre Dame Journal of Formal Logic*, 26: 437–443.

Le Poidevin, R., 1991. *Change, Cause and Contradiction: A Defence of the Tenseless Theory of Time*. Macmillan, London.

Le Poidevin, R., 2000. Continuants and continuity. In Varzi (2000b), pp. 381–398.

Lechthaler, M., 2017. Composition and identities. Ph.D. thesis, University of Otago, Dunedin.

Lechthaler, M., in press-a. Intensional composition as identity. *Grazer Philosophische Studien*.

Lechthaler, M., in press-b. No universalism without gunk? Composition as identity and the universality of identity. In Carrara and Lando (in press-b).

Leech, J., 1990. Skew Boolean algebras. *Algebra Universalis*, 27: 497–506.

Leech, J., 1996. Recent developments in the theory of skew lattices. *Semigroup Forum*, 52: 7–24.

Lehmann, S., 2002. More free logic. In Gabbay, D. M. and Guenthner, F., eds., *Handbook of Philosophical Logic*, 2nd edition, volume 5, pp. 197–259. Kluwer, Dordrecht.

Leibniz, G. W., 1890. *Die philosophischen Schriften*, volume 7: *Scientia Generalis, Characteristica [et al.]*, ed. by C. I. Gerhardt. Weidmannsche Buchhandlung, Berlin.

Leibniz, G. W., 1903. *Opuscules et fragments inédits*, ed. by L. Couturat. Alcan, Paris.

Leibniz, G. W., 1966. *Logical Papers: A Selection*, ed. and Eng. trans. by G. H. R. Parkinson. Clarendon Press, Oxford.

Leibniz, G. W., 1989. *Philosophical Essays*, ed. and Eng. trans. by R. Ariew and D. Garber. Hackett, Indianapolis (IN).

Leibniz, G. W., 2002. *The Labyrinth of the Continuum: Writings on the Continuum Problem, 1672–1686*, ed. and Eng. trans. by R. T. W. Arthur. Yale University Press, New Haven (CT).

Lejewski, C., 1954a. A contribution to Leśniewski's Mereology. *Rocznik Polskiego Towarzystwa Naukowego na Obczyźnie*, 5: 43–50.

Lejewski, C., 1954b. Logic and existence. *The British Journal for the Philosophy of Science*, 5: 104–119.

Lejewski, C., 1955. A new axiom for Mereology. *Rocznik Polskiego Towarzystwa Naukowego na Obczyźnie*, 6: 65–70.

Lejewski, C., 1957. Review of Rescher (1955). *The Journal of Symbolic Logic*, 22: 213–214.

Lejewski, C., 1963. A note on a problem concerning the axiomatic foundations of Mereology. *Notre Dame Journal of Formal Logic*, 4: 135–139.

Lejewski, C., 1967. A single axiom for the mereological notion of proper part. *Notre Dame Journal of Formal Logic*, 8: 279–285.

Lejewski, C., 1969. Consistency of Leśniewski's Mereology. *The Journal of Symbolic Logic*, 34: 321–328.

Lejewski, C., 1973. A contribution to the study of extended mereologies. *Notre Dame Journal of Formal Logic*, 14: 55–67.

Lejewski, C., 1978. A note concerning the notion of mereological class. *Notre Dame Journal of Formal Logic*, 19: 251–263.

Lejewski, C., 1980. A note concerning the notion of mereological class. Postscript. *Notre Dame Journal of Formal Logic*, 21: 679–682.

Lejewski, C., 1983. A note on Leśniewski's axiom system for the mereological notion of ingredient or element. In Sinisi (1983), pp. 63–71.

Lenzen, W., 2000. Guilielmi Pacidii Non plus ultra, oder: Eine Rekonstruktion des Leibnizschen Plus-Minus-Kalküls. *Logical Analysis and History of Philosophy*, 3: 71–118.

Lenzen, W., 2004. Leibniz's logic. In Gabbay, D. M. and Woods, J., eds., *Handbook of the History of Logic*, volume 3, pp. 1–83. North-Holland, Amsterdam.

Leonard, H. S., 1930. Singular terms. Ph.D. thesis, Harvard University, Cambridge (MA).

Leonard, H. S., 1967. Comments on 'The calculus of individuals and its uses'. Published posthumously in Burkhardt *et al.* (2017), pp. 127–128.

Leonard, H. S. and Goodman, N., 1937. A calculus of individuals (Abstract). *The Journal of Symbolic Logic*, 2: 63–64.

Leonard, H. S. and Goodman, N., 1940. The calculus of individuals and its uses. *The Journal of Symbolic Logic*, 5: 45–55.

Leonard, M., 2016. What is mereological harmony? *Synthese*, 193: 1949–1965.

Leonard, M., 2018. Enduring through gunk. *Erkenntnis*, 83: 753–771.

Leśniewski, S., 1914. Czy klasa klas, nie podporządkowanych sobie, jest podporządkowana sobie? *Przegląd Filozoficzny*, 17: 63–75. Eng. trans. by S. J. Surma and J. Wójcik: Is the class of classes not subordinated to themselves, subordinated to itself?, in Leśniewski (1992), pp. 115–128.

Leśniewski, S., 1916. *Podstawy ogólnej teoryi mnogości. I.* Prace Polskiego Koła Naukowego w Moskwie, Sekcya matematyczno-przyrodnicza, Moskow. Eng. trans. by D. I. Barnett: Foundations of the general theory of sets. I, in Leśniewski (1992), pp. 129–173.

Leśniewski, S., 1927–1931. O podstawach matematyki. *Przegląd Filozoficzny*, 30: 164–206; 31: 261–291; 32: 60–101; 33: 77–105; 34: 142–170. Eng. trans. by V. Sinisi: On the foundations of mathematics, in Sinisi (1983), pp. 7–52; Eng. trans. by D. I. Barnett (referenced): On the foundations of mathematics, in Leśniewski (1992), pp. 174–382.

Leśniewski, S., 1931. Über Definitionen in der sogenannten Theorie der Deduktion. *Comptes rendus des séances de la Société des Sciences et des Lettres de Varsovie*, Classe III, 24: 289–309. Eng. trans. by E. C. Luschei: On definitions in the so-called theory of deduction, in McCall (1967), pp. 170–187; also in Leśniewski (1992), pp. 629–648.

Leśniewski, S., 1938. Einleitende Bemerkungen zur Fortsetzung meiner Mitteilung u.d.T. 'Grundzüge eines neuen System der Grundlagen der Mathematik'. *Collectanea Logica*, 1: 1–60. Eng. trans. by W. Teichmann and S. McCall: Introductory remarks to the continuation of my article 'Grundzüge eines neuen System der Grundlagen der Mathematik', in McCall (1967), pp. 116–169; also in Leśniewski (1992), pp. 649–710.

Leśniewski, S., 1992. *Collected Works*, ed. by S. J. Surma, J. T. Srzednicki, D. I. Barnett, and F. V. Rickey. Kluwer, Dordrecht.

Lewis, D. K., 1970. General semantics. *Synthese*, 22: 18–67.

Lewis, D. K., 1971. Counterparts of persons and their bodies. *The Journal of Philosophy*, 68: 203–211.

Lewis, D. K., 1983a. New work for a theory of universals. *Australasian Journal of Philosophy*, 61: 343–377.

Lewis, D. K., 1983b. Postscripts to 'Counterpart theory and modal logic'. In *Philosophical Papers*, volume 1, pp. 39–46. Oxford University Press, Oxford.

Lewis, D. K., 1986a. Against structural universals. *Australasian Journal of Philosophy*, 64: 25–46.

Lewis, D. K., 1986b. Comment on Armstrong and Forrest. *Australasian Journal of Philosophy*, 64: 92–93.

Lewis, D. K., 1986c. *On the Plurality of Worlds*. Blackwell, Oxford.

Lewis, D. K., 1991. *Parts of Classes*. Blackwell, Oxford.

Lewis, D. K., 1993a. Many, but almost one. In Bacon, J., Campbell, K., and Reinhardt, L., eds., *Ontology, Causality and Mind: Essays in Honour of D. M. Armstrong*, pp. 23–42. Cambridge University Press, Cambridge.

Lewis, D. K., 1993b. Mathematics is megethology. *Philosophia Mathematica*, 1: 3–23.

Leys, J., 2007. The Droste effect image transformation. *Computers & Graphics*, 31: 516–523.

Libardi, M., 1990. *Teorie delle parti e dell'intero: Mereologie estensionali*. Quaderni del Centro Studi per la Filosofia Mitteleuropea, Trento.

Libardi, M., 1994. Applications and limits of mereology: From the theory of parts to the theory of wholes. In Albertazzi and Libardi (1994), pp. 13–54.

Liggins, D., 2008. Nihilism without self-contradiction. *Royal Institute of Philosophy Supplements*, 62: 177–196.

Link, G., 1983. The logical analysis of plurals and mass terms: A lattice-theoretical approach. In Bäuerle, R., Schwarze, C., and von Stechow, A., eds., *Meaning, Use and Interpretation of Language*, pp. 302–323. De Gruyter, Berlin.

Link, G., 1998. *Algebraic Semantics in Language and Philosophy*. CSLI Publications, Stanford (CA).

Link, G., 2014. *Collegium Logicum: Logische Grundlagen der Philosophie und der Wissenschaften*, volume 2. Mentis, Münster.

Linnebo, Ø., 2003. Plural quantification exposed. *Noûs*, 37: 71–92.

Linnebo, Ø., 2010. Pluralities and sets. *The Journal of Philosophy*, 107: 144–164.

Linnebo, Ø., 2016. Plurals and modals. *Canadian Journal of Philosophy*, 46: 654–676.

Linnebo, Ø., 2017. Plural quantification. In Zalta, E. N., ed., *The Stanford Encyclopedia of Philosophy*. http://plato.stanford.edu/archives/sum2017/entries/plural-quant.

Linnebo, Ø., Shapiro, S., and Hellman, G., 2016. Aristotelian continua. *Philosophia Mathematica*, 24: 214–246.

Lipman, M. A., in press. On relativist approaches to many-one identity. In Carrara and Lando (in press-b).

Loeb, I., 2014. From mereology to Boolean algebra: The role of regular open sets in Alfred Tarski's work. In Mulligan, K., Kijania-Placek, K., and Placek, T., eds., *The History and Philosophy of Polish Logic: Essays in Honour of Jan Woleński*, pp. 259–277. Palgrave Macmillan, London.

Lombard, P., 2007. *The Sentences, Book 1: The Mystery of the Trinity*, Eng. trans. by G. Silano. Pontifical Institute of Medieval Studies, Toronto.

Long, A. A. and Sedley, D. N., eds., 1987. *The Hellenistic Philosophers*, volume 1: *Translations*. Cambridge University Press, Cambridge.

Long, J., 2019. One's an illusion: Organisms, reference, and non-eliminative nihilism. *Philosophia*, 47: 459–475.

Longenecker, M. T.-S., 2018. Non-concrete parts of material objects. *Synthese*, 195: 5091–5111.

López de Sa, D., 2006. Is 'everything' precise? *Dialectica*, 60: 397–409.

Lorenz, K., 1977. On the relation between the partition of a whole into parts and the attribution of properties to an object. *Studia Logica*, 36: 351–362.

Lorenz, K., 1984. Mereologie. In Mittelstraß, J., ed., *Enzyklopädie Philosophie und Wissenschaftstheorie*, volume 2, pp. 849–850. Bibliographisches Institut, Mannheim.

Lorenz, K., 2013. Mereologie. In Mittelstraß, J., ed., *Enzyklopädie Philosophie und Wissenschaftstheorie*, 2nd edition, volume 5, pp. 341–343. Metzler, Stuttgart.

Łoś, J., 1954. On the categoricity in power of elementary deductive systems and some related problems. *Colloquium Mathematicae*, 3: 58–62.

Loss, R., 2016. Parts ground the whole and are identical to it. *Australasian Journal of Philosophy*, 94: 489–498.

Loss, R., 2018. A sudden collapse to nihilism. *The Philosophical Quarterly*, 68: 370–375.

Loss, R., in press-a. On atomic composition as identity. In Carrara and Lando (in press-b).
Loss, R., in press-b. Composition, identity and plural ontology. *Synthese*.
Loux, M. J. and Crisp, T. M., 2017. *Metaphysics: A Contemporary Introduction*, 4th edition. Routledge, London.
Lowe, E. J., 1989. *Kinds of Being: A Study of Individuation, Identity, and the Logic of Sortal Terms*. Blackwell, Oxford.
Lowe, E. J., 1996. *Subjects of Experience*. Cambridge University Press, Cambridge.
Lowe, E. J., 2001. Identity, composition, and the simplicity of the self. In Corcoran, K., ed., *Soul, Body and Survival: Essays on the Metaphysics of Human Persons*, pp. 139–158. Cornell University Press, Ithaca (NY).
Lowe, E. J., 2005a. How are ordinary objects possible? *The Monist*, 88: 510–533.
Lowe, E. J., 2005b. Vagueness and endurance. *Analysis*, 65: 104–112.
Lowe, E. J., 2013. Mereological extensionality, supplementation, and material constitution. *The Monist*, 96: 131–148.
Lowe, V., 1953. Professor Goodman's concept of an individual. *The Philosophical Review*, 62: 117–126.
Lucas, J. R., 2000. *The Conceptual Roots of Mathematics*. Routledge, London.
Ludwig, K., 2014. The ontology of collective action. In Chant, S. R., Hindriks, F., and Preyer, G., eds., *From Individual to Collective Intentionality: New Essays*, pp. 112–133. Oxford University Press, Oxford.
Łukasiewicz, J., 1920. O logice trójwartościowej. *Ruch Filozoficzny*, 5: 170–171. Eng. trans. by H. Hiż: On three-valued logic, in McCall (1967), pp. 16–18.
Luschei, E. C., 1962. *The Logical Systems of Leśniewski*. North-Holland, Amsterdam.
Łyczak, M., Porwolik, M., and Świętorzecka, K., 2016. The universe in Leśniewski's Mereology: Some comments on Sobociński's reflections. *Axioms*, 5/3: 13 pp.
Lyons, J., 1977. *Semantics*. Cambridge University Press, Cambridge.
MacBride, F., 1998. Where are particulars and universals? *Dialectica*, 52: 203–227.
Maddy, P., 1988. Believing the axioms, I. *The Journal of Symbolic Logic*, 53: 481–511.
Maffezioli, P., 2016a. Analytic rules for mereology. *Studia Logica*, 104: 79–114.
Maffezioli, P., 2016b. Sequents for non-wellfounded mereology. In Varzi and Gruszczyński (2016), pp. 351–369.
Maffezioli, P. and Varzi, A. C., in press. Intuitionistic mereology. In Carrara and Lando (in press-b).
Magidor, O., 2011. Arguments by Leibniz's law in metaphysics. *Philosophy Compass*, 6: 180–195.
Magidor, O., 2015. Why neither diachronic universalism nor the argument

from vagueness establishes perdurantism. *Canadian Journal of Philosophy*, 45: 113–126.
Magidor, O., 2018. Epistemicism, distribution, and the argument from vagueness. *Noûs*, 52: 144–170.
Mandelbrot, B. B., 1983. *The Fractal Geometry of Nature*. Macmillan, London.
Mann, W. and Varzi, A. C., eds., 2006. *Parts and Wholes*. Special issue of *The Journal of Philosophy*, volume 103/12.
Markman, E. M., 1981. Two different principles of conceptual organization. In Lamb, M. E. and Brown, A. L., eds., *Advances in Developmental Psychology*, pp. 199–236. Erlbaum, Hillsdale (NJ).
Markosian, N., 1998a. Simples. *Australasian Journal of Philosophy*, 76: 213–26.
Markosian, N., 1998b. Brutal composition. *Philosophical Studies*, 92: 211–249.
Markosian, N., 2004a. Simples, stuff, and simple people. In Hudson (2004), pp. 405–428.
Markosian, N., 2004b. SoC it to me? Reply to McDaniel on MaxCon simples. *Australasian Journal of Philosophy*, 82: 332–340.
Markosian, N., 2004c. Two arguments from Sider's *Four-Dimensionalism*. *Philosophy and Phenomenological Research*, 68: 665–673.
Markosian, N., 2005. Against ontological fundamentalism. *Facta Philosophica*, 7: 69–84.
Markosian, N., 2008. Restricted composition. In Sider, T., Hawthorne, J., and Zimmerman, D. W., eds., *Contemporary Debates in Metaphysics*, pp. 341–363. Blackwell, Oxford.
Markosian, N., 2014. A spatial approach to mereology. In Kleinschmidt (2014), pp. 69–90.
Markosian, N., 2015. The right stuff. *Australasian Journal of Philosophy*, 93: 665–687.
Marmodoro, A., 2013. Aristotle's hylomorphism without reconditioning. *Philosophical Inquiry*, 37: 5–22.
Marmodoro, A., 2015. Anaxagoras's qualitative gunk. *British Journal for the History of Philosophy*, 23: 402–422.
Marmodoro, A., 2017. *Everything in Everything: Anaxagoras's Metaphysics*. Oxford University Press, Oxford.
Marschall, B., 2019. Conceptualizing Kant's mereology. *Ergo*, 6: 374–404.
Martin, C. J., 1998. The logic of growth: Twelfth-century Nominalists and the development of theories of the Incarnation. *Medieval Philosophy and Theology*, 7: 1–15.
Martin, C. J., 2019. Only God can make a tree. Abaelard on wholes and parts and some evidence of his later thinking about them. *Oxford Studies in Medieval Philosophy*, 7: 44–66.
Martin, R. M., 1943. A homogeneous system for formal logic. *The Journal of Symbolic Logic*, 8: 1–23.

Martin, R. M., 1965. Of time and the null individual. *The Journal of Philosophy*, 62: 723–736.

Martin, R. M., 1988. *Metaphysical Foundations: Mereology and Metalogic*. Philosophia, Munich.

Martin, R. M., 1992. *Logical Semiotics and Mereology*. Benjamins, Amsterdam.

Mascaró, J., ed., 1965. *The Upanishads*. Penguin, London.

Masolo, C., 2009. Parthood simpliciter vs. temporary parthood. In Lakemeyer, G., Morgenstern, L., and Williams, M.-A., eds., *Proceedings of the 9th International Symposium on Logical Formalizations of Commonsense Reasoning*, pp. 97–102. UTSePress, Sydney.

Masolo, C. and Vieu, L., 1999. Atomicity vs. infinite divisibility of space. In Freksa, C. and Mark, D., eds., *Spatial Information Theory: Proceedings of COSIT 1999*, pp. 235–250. Springer, Berlin.

Masolo, C. and Vieu, L., 2018. Graph-based approaches to structural universals and complex states of affairs. In Borgo, S., Hitzler, P., and Kutz, O., eds., *Formal Ontology in Information Systems: Proceedings of the 10th International Conference*, pp. 69–82. IOS Press, Amsterdam.

Mason, F. C., 2000. How not to prove the existence of 'atomless gunk'. *Ratio*, 13: 175–185.

Maudlin, T., 1998. Part and whole in quantum mechanics. In Castellani, E., ed., *Interpreting Bodies: Classical and Quantum Objects in Modern Physics*, pp. 46–60. Princeton University Press, Princeton (NJ).

McCall, S., ed., 1967. *Polish Logic 1920–1939*. Clarendon Press, Oxford.

McCarthy, T. G., 2015. A note on unrestricted composition. *Thought*, 4: 202–211.

McDaniel, K., 2001. Tropes and ordinary physical objects. *Philosophical Studies*, 104: 269–290.

McDaniel, K., 2003. Against MaxCon simples. *Australasian Journal of Philosophy*, 81: 265–275.

McDaniel, K., 2004. Modal realism with overlap. *Australasian Journal of Philosophy*, 82: 137–152.

McDaniel, K., 2006. Gunky objects in a simple world. *Philo*, 9: 39–46.

McDaniel, K., 2007a. Extended simples. *Philosophical Studies*, 133: 131–141.

McDaniel, K., 2007b. Brutal simples. *Oxford Studies in Metaphysics*, 3: 233–265.

McDaniel, K., 2008. Against composition as identity. *Analysis*, 68: 128–133.

McDaniel, K., 2009a. Structure-making. *Australasian Journal of Philosophy*, 87: 251–274.

McDaniel, K., 2009b. Extended simples and qualitative heterogeneity. *The Philosophical Quarterly*, 59: 325–331.

McDaniel, K., 2010a. Composition as identity does not entail universalism. *Erkenntnis*, 73: 97–100.

McDaniel, K., 2010b. Parts and wholes. *Philosophy Compass*, 5: 412–425.

McDaniel, K., 2010c. A return to the analogy of being. *Philosophy and Phenomenological Research*, 81: 688–717.
McDaniel, K., 2014a. Compositional pluralism and composition as identity. In Cotnoir and Baxter (2014), pp. 130–142.
McDaniel, K., 2014b. Parthood is identity. In Kleinschmidt (2014), pp. 13–32.
McDaniel, K., 2017. *The Fragmentation of Being*. Oxford University Press, Oxford.
McFarland, A., 2018. Causal powers and isomeric chemical kinds. *Synthese*, 195: 1441–1457.
McGee, V., 1997. Kilimanjaro. *Canadian Journal of Philosophy* (Supplement), 27: 141–163.
McGee, V. and McLaughlin, B., 2000. The lessons of the many. *Philosophical Topics*, 28: 129–151.
McGrath, M., 1998. Van Inwagen's critique of universalism. *Analysis*, 58: 116–121.
McGrath, M., 2001. Rea on universalism. *Analysis*, 61: 69–76.
McGrath, M., 2005. No objects, no problem? *Australasian Journal of Philosophy*, 83: 457–486.
McGrath, M., 2007a. Four-dimensionalism and the puzzles of coincidence. *Oxford Studies in Metaphysics*, 3: 143–176.
McGrath, M., 2007b. Temporal parts. *Philosophy Compass*, 2: 730–746.
McGrath, M., 2008. Conciliatory metaontology and the vindication of common sense. *Noûs*, 42: 482–508.
McGuinness, B. F., 1988. *Wittgenstein: A Life. Young Ludwig, 1889–1921*. University of California Press, Berkeley (CA).
McKay, T. J., 2006. *Plural Predication*. Clarendon Press, Oxford.
McKenzie, K. and Muller, F. A., 2017. Bound states and the special composition question. In Massimi, M., Romeijn, J.-W., and Schurz, G., eds., *EPSA15 Selected Papers: The 5th Conference of the European Philosophy of Science Association*, pp. 233–241. Springer, Cham.
McKinnon, N., 2003. Vague simples. *Pacific Philosophical Quarterly*, 84: 394–397.
McTaggart, J. M. E., 1906. *Some Dogmas of Religion*. Arnold, London.
McTaggart, J. M. E., 1921. *The Nature of Existence*, volume 1. Cambridge University Press, Cambridge.
McTaggart, J. M. E., 1927. *The Nature of Existence*, volume 2. Cambridge University Press, Cambridge.
Mehlberg, H., 1958. *The Reach of Science*. Toronto University Press, Toronto.
Meiland, J. W., 1966. Temporal parts and spatio-temporal analogies. *American Philosophical Quarterly*, 3: 64–70.
Meinong, A., 1904. Über Gegenstandstheorie. In Meinong, A., ed., *Untersuchungen zur Gegenstandstheorie und Psychologie*, pp. 1–51. Barth, Leipzig.

Eng. trans. by I. Levi, D. B. Terrell, and R. M. Chisholm: The theory of objects, in R. M. Chisholm, ed., *Realism and the Background of Phenomenology*, pp. 76–117, Free Press, Glencoe (IL), 1960.

Meirav, A., 2000. Non-unique composition. *Synthese*, 124: 323–342.

Meirav, A., 2003. *Wholes, Sums and Unities*. Kluwer, Dordrecht.

Meirav, A., 2009. The principle of summation. *Erkenntnis*, 71: 175–190.

Meixner, U., 1997. *Axiomatic Formal Ontology*. Kluwer, Dordrecht.

Mellor, D. H., 1982. The reduction of society. *Philosophy*, 57: 51–75.

Mellor, D. H., 2006. Wholes and parts: The limits of composition. *South African Journal of Philosophy*, 25: 138–145.

Mellor, D. H., 2008. Micro-composition. *Royal Institute of Philosophy Supplements*, 62: 65–80.

Mendelson, E., 1964. *Introduction to Mathematical Logic*. Van Nostrand, Princeton (NJ).

Menger, K., 1940. Topology without points. *Rice Institute Pamphlets*, 27: 80–107.

Merricks, T., 1999. Composition as identity, mereological essentialism, and counterpart theory. *Australasian Journal of Philosophy*, 77: 192–195.

Merricks, T., 2000. No statues. *Australasian Journal of Philosophy*, 78: 47–52.

Merricks, T., 2001. *Objects and Persons*. Clarendon Press, Oxford.

Merricks, T., 2005. Composition and vagueness. *Mind*, 114: 615–637.

Merricks, T., 2007. Remarks on vagueness and arbitrariness. *Mind*, 116: 115–119.

Merricks, T., 2015. *Propositions*. Clarendon Press, Oxford.

Mertz, D. W., 2016. *On the Elements of Ontology: Attribute Instances and Structure*. De Gruyter, Berlin.

Meyer, U., 2006. Worlds and times. *Notre Dame Journal of Formal Logic*, 47: 25–37.

Miéville, D., 1984. *Un développement des systèmes logiques de Stanisław Leśniewski: Protothétique – Ontologie – Méréologie*. Lang, Berlin.

Miéville, D., ed., 2001. *Méréologie et modalités: Aspects critiques et développements*. Special issue of *Travaux de Logique*, volume 14.

Miller, G. A. and Johnson-Laird, P. N., 1976. *Language and Perception*. Belknap Press, Cambridge (MA).

Miller, K. L., 2005. Blocking the path from vagueness to four dimensionalism. *Ratio*, 18: 317–331.

Miller, K. L., 2006a. Non-mereological universalism. *European Journal of Philosophy*, 14: 404–422.

Miller, K. L., 2006b. *Issues in Theoretical Diversity: Persistence, Composition, and Time*. Kluwer, Dordrecht.

Miller, K. L., 2006c. Sparse parts. *Sorites*, 17: 31–48.

Miller, K. L., 2008. Essential stuff. *Ratio*, 21: 55–63.

Miller, K. L., 2009a. Defending contingentism in metaphysics. *Dialectica*, 63: 23–49.

Miller, K. L., 2009b. Ought a four-dimensionalist to believe in temporal parts? *Canadian Journal of Philosophy*, 39: 619–646.

Miller, K. L., 2010. The existential quantifier, composition and contingency. *Erkenntnis*, 73: 211–235.

Miller, K. L., 2014. Defending substantivism about disputes in the metaphysics of composition. *The Journal of Philosophy*, 111: 529–556.

Miller, K. L. and Duncan, M., 2015. Modal persistence and modal travel. *Ratio*, 28: 241–255.

Miller, K. L. and Hariman, J., 2017. What is an ersatz part? *Grazer Philosophische Studien*, 94: 524–551.

Miszczyński, R., 2010. Stanisława Leśniewskiego pierwsze rozwiązanie antynomii Russella. *Prace Naukowe Akademii im. Jana Długosza w Częstochowie. Seria: Filozofia*, 7: 5–17.

Miszczyński, R., 2011. Stanisława Leśniewskiego drugie rozwiązanie antynomii Russella. *Prace Naukowe Akademii im. Jana Długosza w Częstochowie. Seria: Filozofia*, 8: 163–172.

Miszczyński, R., 2013. Stanisława Leśniewskiego trzecia analiza antynomii Russella. *Prace Naukowe Akademii im. Jana Długosza w Częstochowie. Seria: Filozofia*, 10: 163–181.

Moltmann, F., 1997. *Parts and Wholes in Semantics*. Oxford University Press, New York.

Moltmann, F., 1998. Part structures, integrity, and the mass-count distinction. *Synthese*, 116: 75–111.

Molto, D., 2018. The mereology of Latin Trinitarianism. *Religious Studies*, 54: 395–418.

Monaghan, P., 2016. The largest proper parts of a mereological whole: A refutation of classical extensional mereology. *Metaphysica*, 17: 19–26.

Montague, R. M., 1961. Semantic closure and non-finite axiomatizability I. In Buss, S. R., ed., *Infinitistic Methods: Proceedings of the Symposium on Foundations of Mathematics*, pp. 45–69. Pergamon, Oxford.

Moore, D., 2015. Mereological essentialism and mereological inessentialism. *Croatian Journal of Philosophy*, 15: 67–85.

Moran, A., 2018. The paradox of decrease and dependent parts. *Ratio*, 31: 273–284.

Morganti, M., 2009. Ontological priority, fundamentality and monism. *Dialectica*, 63: 271–288.

Morganti, M., 2013. *Combining Science and Metaphysics: Contemporary Physics, Conceptual Revision and Common Sense*. Palgrave Macmillan, London.

Morganti, M., 2015. Dependence, justification and explanation: Must reality be well-founded? *Erkenntnis*, 80: 555–572.

Mormann, T., 1999. Neither mereology nor Whiteheadian account of space yet convicted. *Analysis*, 59: 174–182.

Mormann, T., 2000a. Topological representations of mereological systems. In Faye, J., Scheffler, U., and Urchs, M., eds., *Things, Facts and Events*, pp. 463–486. Rodopi, Amsterdam.

Mormann, T., 2000b. Mereologie. Einige mathematische Explorationen. In Peres, C. and Greimann, D., eds., *Wahrheit, Sein, Struktur: Auseinandersetzungen mit Metaphysik*, pp. 249–271. Rodopi, Amsterdam.

Mormann, T., 2009. Updating classical mereology. In Glymour, C., Westerstahl, D., and Wang, W., eds., *Logic, Methodology and Philosophy of Science: Proceedings of the 13th International Congress*, pp. 326–343. King's College Publications, London.

Mormann, T., 2010. Structural universals as structural parts: Towards a general theory of parthood and composition. *Axiomathes*, 20: 229–253.

Mormann, T., 2012. On the mereological structure of complex states of affairs. *Synthese*, 187: 403–418.

Mormann, T., 2013. Heyting mereology as a framework for spatial reasoning. *Axiomathes*, 23: 137–164.

Mormann, T., 2014. Set theory, topology, and the possibility of junky worlds. *Notre Dame Journal of Formal Logic*, 55: 79–90.

Morreau, M., 2002. What vague objects are like. *The Journal of Philosophy*, 99: 333–361.

Mortensen, C., 2016. Change and inconsistency. In Zalta, E. N., ed., *The Stanford Encyclopedia of Philosophy*. http://plato.stanford.edu/archives/win2016/entries/change.

Morzycki, M., 2016. *Modification*. Cambridge University Press, Cambridge.

Mosterin, J., 1994. Mereology, set theory, biological ontology. In Prawitz, D. and Westerståhl, D., eds., *Logic and Philosophy of Science in Uppsala: Papers from the 9th International Congress of Logic, Methodology and Philosophy of Science*, pp. 511–524. Kluwer, Dordrecht.

Mostowski, A. and Tarski, A., 1939. Boolesche Ringe mit geordneter Basis. *Fundamenta mathematicae*, 32: 69–86. Eng. trans. by M. Mączyński: Boolean rings with an ordered basis, in A. Mostowski, *Foundational Studies: Selected Works*, ed. by K. Kuratowski *et al.*, volume 2, pp. 75–91, North-Holland, Amsterdam, 1979.

Moyer, M., 2006. Statues and lumps: A strange coincidence? *Synthese*, 148: 401–423.

Moyer, M., 2009. Does four-dimensionalism explain coincidence? *Australasian Journal of Philosophy*, 87: 479–488.

Mugnai, M., 2019. Leibniz's mereology in the essays on logical calculus of 1686–1690. In De Risi, V., ed., *Leibniz and the Structure of Sciences*, pp. 47–69. Springer, Cham.

Mumford, S. and Anjum, R. L., 2011. *Getting Causes from Powers*. Oxford University Press, Oxford.

Myro, G., 1986. Identity and time. In Grandy, R. E. and Warner, R., eds., *Philosophical Grounds of Rationality: Intentions, Categories, Ends*, pp. 383–409. Clarendon Press, Oxford.

Nagel, E., 1952. Wholes, sums, and organic unities. *Philosophical Studies*, 3: 17–32.

Nardi, D. and Brachman, R. J., 2003. An introduction to description logics. In Baader, F., Calvanese, D., McGuinness, D. L., Nardi, D., and Patel-Schneider, P. F., eds., *The Description Logic Handbook: Theory, Implementation and Applications*, pp. 1–40. Cambridge University Press, Cambridge.

Needham, P., 2010. Transient things and permanent stuff. *Australasian Journal of Philosophy*, 88: 147–166.

Needham, P., 2012. Modality, mereology and substance. In Woody, A. I., Hendry, R. F., and Needham, P., eds., *Handbook of the Philosophy of Science*, volume 6: *Philosophy of Chemistry*, pp. 231–254. Elsevier, Amsterdam.

Needham, P., 2017. *Macroscopic Metaphysics: Middle-Sized Objects and Longish Processes*. Springer, Cham.

Nenchev, V., 2011. Logics for stable and unstable mereological relations. *Central European Journal of Mathematics*, 9: 1354–1379.

Nenchev, V. and Vakarelov, D., 2009. An axiomatization of dynamic ontology of stable and unstable mereological relations. In Drossos, C., Peppas, P., and Tsinakis, C., eds., *Proceedings of the 7th Panhellenic Logic Symposium*, pp. 137–141. Patras University Press, Patras.

Ney, A., 2014. *Metaphysics: An Introduction*. Routledge, London.

Nicod, J., 1924. *La géométrie dans le monde sensible*. Alcan, Paris. Eng. trans. by P. P. Wiener: Geometry in the Sensible World, in Nicod's *Foundations of Geometry and Induction*, pp. 3–192, Routledge & Kegan Paul, London, 1930.

Nicolas, D., 2009. Mereological essentialism, composition, and stuff: A reply to Kristie Miller. *Erkenntnis*, 71: 425–429.

Niebergall, K.-G., 2007. Zur logischen Stärke von Individuenkalkülen. In Bohse, H. and Walter, S., eds., *Ausgewählte Sektionsbeiträge der GAP.6: Sechster Internationaler Kongress der Gesellschaft für Analytische Philosophie*, pp. 85–103. Mentis, Paderborn.

Niebergall, K.-G., 2009a. Calculi of individuals and some extensions: An overview. In Hieke, A. and Leitgeb, H., eds., *Reduction, Abstraction, Analysis: Proceedings of the 31st International Wittgenstein Symposium*, pp. 335–354. Ontos, Frankfurt.

Niebergall, K.-G., 2009b. On 2nd order calculi of individuals. *Theoria*, 65: 169–202.

Niebergall, K.-G., 2009c. Zur Metatheorie mereologischer Theorien. Unpublished ms.

Niebergall, K.-G., 2011. Mereology. In Horsten, L. and Pettigrew, R., eds., *The Continuum Companion to Philosophical Logic*, pp. 271–298. Continuum, London.

Niebergall, K.-G., 2016. Mereology and infinity. In Varzi and Gruszczyński (2016), pp. 309–350.

Nolan, D. P., 1996. Recombination unbound. *Philosophical Studies*, 84: 239–262.

Nolan, D. P., 2004. Classes, worlds, and hypergunk. In Hudson (2004), pp. 303–321.

Nolan, D. P., 2005. *David Lewis*. Acumen, Chesham.

Nolan, D. P., 2006a. Vagueness, multiplicity and parts. *Noûs*, 40: 716–737.

Nolan, D. P., 2006b. Stoic gunk. *Phronesis*, 51: 162–183.

Nolan, D. P., 2010. Metaphysical language, ordinary language and Peter van Inwagen's *Material Beings*. *Humana.mente*, 13: 237–246.

Nolan, D. P., 2018. Cosmic loops. In Bliss and Priest (2018), pp. 91–106.

Nolt, J., 2018. Free logic. In Zalta, E. N., ed., *The Stanford Encyclopedia of Philosophy*. http://plato.stanford.edu/archives/fall2018/entries/logic-free.

Noonan, H. W., 1976. The four-dimensional world. *Analysis*, 37: 32–39.

Noonan, H. W., 1980. *Objects and Identity: An Examination of the Relative Identity Thesis and Its Consequences*. Nijhoff, The Hague.

Noonan, H. W., 1999. Tibbles the cat: Reply to Burke. *Philosophical Studies*, 95: 215–218.

Noonan, H. W., 2009. Perdurance, location and classical mereology. *Analysis*, 69: 448–452.

Noonan, H. W., 2010. A flaw in Sider's vagueness argument for unrestricted mereological composition. *Analysis*, 70: 669–672.

Noonan, H. W., 2019. The challenge to nihilism. *Analytic Philosophy*, 60: 55–66.

Normore, C. G., 2006. Ockham's metaphysics of parts. In Mann and Varzi (2006), pp. 737–754.

Normore, C. G. and Brown, D. J., 2014. On bits and pieces in the history of philosophy. In Cotnoir and Baxter (2014), pp. 24–43.

Null, G. T., 1983. A first-order axiom system for non-universal part-whole and foundational relations. In Embree, L., ed., *Phenomenological Essays in Memory of Aron Gurwitsch*, pp. 463–484. University Press of America, Lanham (MD).

Null, G. T., 1995. Art and part: Mereology and the ontology of art. In Crowell, S. G., ed., *The Prism of the Self: Philosophical Essays in Honor of Maurice Natanson*, pp. 255–275. Kluwer, Dordrecht.

Null, G. T., 1997. Conditional identity and irregular parts. In Evans, J. C. and Stufflebeam, R. S., eds., *To Work at the Foundations: Essays in Memory of Aron Gurwitsch*, pp. 65–128. Kluwer, Dordrecht.

Null, G. T., 2007. The ontology of intentionality I: The dependence ontological account of order. *Husserl Studies*, 23: 33–69.

Obojska, L., 2012. Algebraiczne aspekty mereologii nieekstensjonalnej. *Roczniki Filozoficzne*, 60: 105–124.

Obojska, L., 2013a. *U źródeł zbiorów kolektywnych: O mereologii nieantysymetrycznej*. Wydawnictwo Uniwersytetu Przyrodniczo-Humanistycznego, Siedlce.

Obojska, L., 2013b. Some remarks on supplementation principles in the absence of antisymmetry. *The Review of Symbolic Logic*, 6: 343–347.

Odell, J. J., 1994. Six different kinds of composition. *Journal of Object-Oriented Programming*, 5: 10–15.

Oderberg, D. S., 2005. Hylemorphic dualism. *Social Philosophy and Policy*, 22: 70–99.

Oderberg, D. S., 2012. Survivalism, corruptionism, and mereology. *European Journal for the Philosophy of Religion*, 4: 1–26.

Oderberg, D. S., 2014. Is form structure? In Novotný, D. D. and Novák, L., eds., *Neo-Aristotelian Perspectives in Metaphysics*, pp. 164–180. Routledge, London.

Ojeda, A. E., 2009. The partitive structure of linguistic space and time. In Reinheimer Rîpeanu, S., ed., *Studia linguistica in honorem Mariæ Manoliu*, pp. 241–260. Editura Universităţii din Bucureşti, Bucharest.

Oliver, A., 1993. Classes and Goodman's nominalism. *Proceedings of the Aristotelian Society*, 93: 179–191.

Oliver, A., 1994. Are subclasses parts of classes? *Analysis*, 54: 215–223.

Oliver, A. and Smiley, T., 2001. Strategies for a logic of plurals. *The Philosophical Quarterly*, 51: 289–306.

Oliver, A. and Smiley, T., 2006. What are sets and what are they for? *Philosophical Perspectives*, 20: 123–155.

Oliver, A. and Smiley, T., 2013a. Zilch. *Analysis*, 73: 601–613.

Oliver, A. and Smiley, T., 2013b. *Plural Logic*. Oxford University Press, Oxford.

Olson, E. T., 1995. Why I have no hands. *Theoria*, 61: 182–197.

Olson, E. T., 1997. Dion's foot. *The Journal of Philosophy*, 94: 260–265.

Olson, E. T., 1998. Human atoms. *Australasian Journal of Philosophy*, 76: 396–406.

Olson, E. T., 2006. The paradox of increase. *The Monist*, 89: 390–417.

Olson, E. T., 2007. *What Are We? A Study in Personal Ontology*. Oxford University Press, New York.

Olson, E. T., 2012. Identity, quantification, and number. In Tahko, T. E., ed., *Contemporary Aristotelian Metaphysics*, pp. 66–82. Cambridge University Press, Cambridge.

Olson, E. T., 2017. Properties as parts of ordinary objects. In Keller, J. A., ed.,

Being, Freedom, and Method: Themes from the Philosophy of Peter van Inwagen, pp. 62–79. Oxford University Press, Oxford.

Oppenheim, P. and Putnam, H., 1958. Unity of science as a working hypothesis. *Minnesota Studies in the Philosophy of Science*, 2: 3–36.

Oppy, G., 1997a. Pantheism, quantification and mereology. *The Monist*, 80: 320–337.

Oppy, G., 1997b. Countable fusion not yet proven guilty: It may be the Whiteheadian account of space whatdunnit. *Analysis*, 57: 249–253.

Oppy, G., 2006. *Philosophical Perspectives on Infinity*. Cambridge University Press, Cambridge.

Pabst, B., 1994. *Atomentheorien des lateinischen Mittelalters*. Wissenschaftliche Buchgesellschaft, Darmstadt.

Padmanabhan, R. and Rudeanu, S., 2008. *Axioms for Lattices and Boolean Algebras*. World Scientific, Singapore.

Padoa, A., 1901. Essai d'une théorie algébrique des nombres entiers, précédé d'une introduction logique à une théorie déductive quelconque. In *Bibliothèque du Congrès International de Philosophie*, volume 3: *Logique et Histoire des Sciences*, pp. 309–365. Colin, Paris. Partial Eng. trans. by J. van Heijenoort: Logical introduction to any deductive theory, in van Heijenoort (1967), pp. 118–123.

Paganini, E., 2017. Vague objects within classical logic and standard mereology, and without indeterminate identity. *Journal of Philosophical Logic*, 46: 457–465.

Pagés, J., 2002. Structural relations and formal relations. *Synthese*, 131: 215–221.

Palmer, S. E., 1977. Hierarchical structure in perceptual representation. *Cognitive Psychology*, 9: 441–474.

Parks, Z., 1972. Classes and change. *Journal of Philosophical Logic*, 1: 162–169.

Parsons, C., 1990. The structuralist view of mathematical objects. *Synthese*, 84: 303–346.

Parsons, J., 2000a. Must a four-dimensionalist believe in temporal parts? In Varzi (2000b), pp. 399–418.

Parsons, J., 2004a. Distributional properties. In Jackson, F. and Priest, G., eds., *Lewisian Themes: The Philosophy of David K. Lewis*, pp. 173–180. Clarendon Press, Oxford.

Parsons, J., 2004b. Dion, Theon, and DAUP. *Pacific Philosophical Quarterly*, 85: 85–91.

Parsons, J., 2007. Theories of location. *Oxford Studies in Metaphysics*, 3: 201–232.

Parsons, J., 2011. Fuzzy mereology. Unpublished ms.

Parsons, J., 2013a. Conceptual conservatism and contingent composition. *Inquiry*, 56: 327–339.

Parsons, J., 2013b. An extensionalist's guide to non-extensional mereology. Unpublished ms.

Parsons, J., 2013c. The Earth and the Aleph. Unpublished ms.

Parsons, J., 2014. The many primitives of mereology. In Kleinschmidt (2014), pp. 3–12.

Parsons, T., 1980. *Nonexistent Objects*. Yale University Press, New Haven (CT).

Parsons, T., 2000b. *Indeterminate Identity: Metaphysics and Semantics*. Clarendon Press, Oxford.

Pasnau, R., 2011. *Metaphysical Themes, 1274–1671*. Clarendon Press, Oxford.

Paul, L. A., 2002. Logical parts. *Noûs*, 36: 578–596.

Paul, L. A., 2006. Coincidence as overlap. *Noûs*, 40: 623–659.

Paul, L. A., 2010. The puzzles of material constitution. *Philosophy Compass*, 5: 579–590.

Paul, L. A., 2012. Building the world from its fundamental constituents. *Philosophical Studies*, 158: 221–256.

Paul, L. A., 2017. A one category ontology. In Keller, J. A., ed., *Being, Freedom, and Method: Themes from the Philosophy of Peter van Inwagen*, pp. 32–61. Oxford University Press, Oxford.

Pawłak, Z., 1982. Rough sets. *International Journal of Computer and Information Sciences*, 11: 341–356.

Payton, J. D., in press. How to identify wholes with their parts. In Carrara and Lando (in press-b).

Pearce, K. L., 2017. Mereological idealism. In Goldschmidt, T. and Pearce, K. L., eds., *Idealism: New Essays in Metaphysics*, pp. 200–216. Oxford University Press, Oxford.

Peirce, C. S., 1893. The logic of quantity. Published posthumously in Hartshorne, C. and Weiss, P., eds., *Collected Papers of Charles Sanders Peirce*, volume 4, pp. 59–131, Harvard University Press, Cambridge (MA), 1933.

Peirce, C. S., 1992. *Reasoning and the Logic of Things: The Cambridge Conferences Lectures of 1898*, ed. by K. L. Ketner. Harvard University Press, Cambridge (MA).

Pellettier, F. J., 1984. The not-so-strange modal logic of indeterminacy. *Logique et Analyse*, 27: 415–422.

Peterman, A., 2019. Margaret Cavendish on motion and mereology. *Journal of the History of Philosophy*, 57: 471–499.

Petersen, S., 2019. Composition as pattern. *Philosophical Studies*, 176: 1119–1139.

Pfeifer, K., 1980. *Actions and Other Events: The Unifier-Multiplier Controversy*. Lang, New York.

Pfeiffer, C., 2018. Aristotle and the thesis of mereological potentialism. *Philosophical Inquiry*, 42: 28–66.

Philoponus, 2015. *On Aristotle, Categories 1–5; A Treatise Concerning the Whole and the Parts*, Eng. trans. by R. Sirkel, M. Tweedale, J. Harris, and D. King. Bloomsbury, London.

Pickup, M., 2016. Unextended complexes. *Thought*, 5: 257–264.

Pietruszczak, A., 1996. Mereological sets of distributive classes. *Logic and Logical Philosophy*, 4: 105–122.

Pietruszczak, A., 2000a. Kawałki mereologii. In Perzanowski, J. and Pietruszczak, A., eds., *Logika & filozofia logiczna*, pp. 357–374. Wydawnictwo Naukowe Uniwersytetu Mikołaja Kopernika, Toruń. Eng. trans. by R. Gruszczyński: Pieces of mereology, *Logic and Logical Philosophy*, 14: 211–234, 2015.

Pietruszczak, A., 2000b. *Metamereologia*. Wydawnictwo Naukowe Uniwersytetu Mikołaja Kopernika, Toruń. Revised edition and Eng. trans. by M. Carmody: *Metamereology*, Nicolaus Copernicus University Scientific Publishing House, Toruń, 2018.

Pietruszczak, A., 2002. Paradoks Russella a początki mereologii. *Ruch Filozoficzny*, 59: 123–129.

Pietruszczak, A., 2012. Ogólna koncepcja bycia częścią całości. Mereologia a nieprzechodnia relacja bycia częścią. In Golińska-Pilarek, J. and Wójtowicz, A., eds., *Identyczność znaku czy znak identyczności?*, pp. 205–228. Wydawnictwa Uniwersytetu Warszawskiego, Warsaw.

Pietruszczak, A., 2013. *Podstawy teorii części*. Wydawnictwo Naukowe Uniwersytetu Mikołaja Kopernika, Toruń.

Pietruszczak, A., 2014. A general concept of being a part of a whole. *Notre Dame Journal of Formal Logic*, 55: 359–381.

Pietruszczak, A., 2015. Classical mereology is not elementarily axiomatizable. In Varzi and Gruszczyński (2015), pp. 485–498.

Pineda, D., 2006. A mereological characterization of physicalism. *International Studies in the Philosophy of Science*, 20: 243–266.

Pines, S., 1936. *Beiträge zur islamischen Atomenlehre*. Heine, Berlin. Revised edition and Eng. trans. by T. Langermann and M. Schwarz: *Studies in Islamic Atomism*, Magnes Press, Jerusalem, 1997.

Plantinga, A. C., 1975. On mereological essentialism. *The Review of Metaphysics*, 28: 468–476.

Plato, 1997. *Complete Works*, ed. by J. M. Cooper. Hackett, Indianapolis (IN).

Polcyn, K., 2012. Objects, their parts, and essences. *Filozofia Nauki*, 20: 5–11.

Poli, R., 1993. Husserl's conception of formal ontology. *History and Philosophy of Logic*, 14: 1–14.

Polkowski, L. T., 2001. *Approximate Reasoning by Parts: An Introduction to Rough Mereology*. Springer, Berlin.

Polkowski, L. T. and Skowron, A., 1994. Rough mereology. In Ras, Z. W. and Zemankova, M., eds., *Proceedings of the 8th International Symposium on Methodologies for Intelligent Systems*, pp. 85–94. Springer, Berlin.

Polkowski, L. T. and Skowron, A., 1996. Rough mereology: A new paradigm for approximate reasoning. *International Journal of Approximate Reasoning*, 15: 333–365.

Pontow, C., 2004. A note on the axiomatics of theories in parthood. *Data & Knowledge Engineering*, 50: 195–213.

Pontow, C. and Schubert, R., 2006. A mathematical analysis of theories of parthood. *Data & Knowledge Engineering*, 59: 107–138.

Potrč, M., 2003. Blobjectivist monism. In Bächli, A. and Petrus, K., eds., *Monism*, pp. 125–155. Ontos, Frankfurt.

Potter, M., 1993. Critical notice of Lewis (1991). *The Philosophical Quarterly*, 43: 362–366.

Potter, M., 2004. *Set Theory and Its Philosophy: A Critical Introduction*. Oxford University Press, Oxford.

Pribbenow, S., 1999. Parts and wholes and their relations. In Rickheit, G. and Habel, C., eds., *Mental Models in Discourse Processing and Reasoning*, pp. 359–382. North-Holland, Amsterdam.

Pribbenow, S., 2002. Meronymic relationships: From classical mereology to complex part-whole relations. In Green, R., Bean, C. A., and Myaeng, S. H., eds., *The Semantics of Relationships: An Interdisciplinary Perspective*, pp. 35–50. Springer, Dordrecht.

Price, M. S., 1988. On a paradox of mereological change. *Philosophical Studies*, 54: 109–124.

Priest, G., 1979. The logic of paradox. *Journal of Philosophical Logic*, 8: 219–241.

Priest, G., 1995. *Beyond the Limits of Thought*. Cambridge University Press, Cambridge.

Priest, G., 1997. Sylvan's box: A short story and ten morals. *Notre Dame Journal of Formal Logic*, 38: 573–582.

Priest, G., 2002. Paraconsistent logic. In Gabbay, D. M. and Guenthner, F., eds., *Handbook of Philosophical Logic*, 2nd edition, volume 6, pp. 287–393. Kluwer, Dordrecht.

Priest, G., 2003. A site for sorites. In Beall, J. C., ed., *Liars and Heaps: New Essays on Paradox*, pp. 9–24. Oxford University Press, Oxford.

Priest, G., 2006. *In Contradiction: A Study of the Transconsistent*, 2nd edition. Oxford University Press, Oxford.

Priest, G., 2009. Paraconsistency and dialetheism. In Gabbay, D. M. and Woods, J., eds., *Handbook of the History of Logic*, volume 8, pp. 129–204. North-Holland, Amsterdam.

Priest, G., 2014a. Much ado about nothing. *Australasian Journal of Logic*, 11: 146–158.

Priest, G., 2014b. *One, Being an Investigation into the Unity of Reality and of Its Parts, Including the Singular Object Which Is Nothingness*. Oxford University Press, Oxford.

Priest, G., 2015. The net of Indra. In Tanaka, K., Deguchi, Y., Garfield, J. L., and Priest, G., eds., *The Moon Points Back*, pp. 113–127. Oxford University Press, New York.

Priest, G., 2018. *The Fifth Corner of Four: An Essay on Buddhist Metaphysics and the Catuṣkoṭi*. Oxford University Press, Oxford.

Priest, G., Berto, F., and Weber, Z., 2018. Dialetheism. In Zalta, E. N., ed., *The Stanford Encyclopedia of Philosophy*. http://plato.stanford.edu/archives/fall2018/entries/dialetheism.

Prior, A. N., 1965. Existence in Leśniewski and Russell. In Crossley, J. N. and Dummett, M. A. E., eds., *Formal Systems and Recursive Functions: Proceedings of the 8th Logic Colloquium*, pp. 149–155. North-Holland, Amsterdam.

Prior, A. N., 1966. Time, existence and identity. *Proceedings of the Aristotelian Society*, 66: 183–192.

Proclus, 1933. *The Elements of Theology*, Eng. trans. by E. R. Dodds. Clarendon Press, Oxford.

Proclus, 1987. *Commentary on Plato's Parmenides*, Eng. trans. by G. R. Morrow and J. M.Dillon. Princeton University Press, Princeton (NJ).

Proietti, C. and Smid, J., in press. Mereology and time travel. *Philosophical Studies*.

Putnam, H., 1987a. *The Many Faces of Realism*. Open Court, Chicago (IL).

Putnam, H., 1987b. Truth and convention: On Davidson's refutation of conceptual relativism. *Dialectica*, 41: 69–77.

Putnam, H., 1988. *Representation and Reality*. MIT Press, Cambridge (MA).

Putnam, H., 1995. Peirce's continuum. In Ketner, K. L., ed., *Peirce and Contemporary Thought: Philosophical Inquiries*, pp. 1–23. Fordham University Press, New York.

Putnam, H., 2004. *Ethics without Ontology*. Harvard University Press, Cambridge (MA).

Pyle, A., 1995. *Atomism and Its Critics: From Democritus to Newton*. Thoemmes, Bristol.

Quine, W. V. O., 1936. Set-theoretic foundations for logic. *The Journal of Symbolic Logic*, 1: 45–57.

Quine, W. V. O., 1937. New foundations for mathematical logic. *The American Mathematical Monthly*, 44: 70–80.

Quine, W. V. O., 1948. On what there is. *The Review of Metaphysics*, 2: 21–38.

Quine, W. V. O., 1950. *Methods of Logic*. Holt, Rinehart & Winston, New York.

Quine, W. V. O., 1951a. *Mathematical Logic*. Harvard University Press, Cambridge (MA).

Quine, W. V. O., 1951b. Review of Goodman (1951). *The Journal of Philosophy*, 48: 556–563.

Quine, W. V. O., 1963. *Set Theory and Its Logic*. Belknap Press, Cambridge (MA).

Quine, W. V. O., 1970. *Philosophy of Logic*. Prentice-Hall, Englewood (NJ). 2nd edition: Harvard University Press, Cambridge (MA), 1986.

Quine, W. V. O., 1973. *The Roots of Reference*. Open Court, La Salle (IL).

Quine, W. V. O., 1974. *Methods of Logic*, 3rd edition (3rd printing, with relevant corrections). Routledge & Kegan Paul, London.

Quine, W. V. O., 1976. Worlds away. *The Journal of Philosophy*, 73: 859–863.

Quine, W. V. O., 1981. Things and their place in theories. In *Theories and Things*, pp. 1–23. Harvard University Press, Cambridge (MA).

Quine, W. V. O., 1985. *The Time of My Life: An Autobiography*. MIT Press, Cambridge (MA).

Quine, W. V. O. and Goodman, N., 1940. Elimination of extra-logical postulates. *The Journal of Symbolic Logic*, 5: 104–109.

Quinton, A., 1976. Social objects. *Proceedings of the Aristotelian Society*, 76: 1–27.

Raatikainen, P., 2001. Putnam, languages and worlds. *Dialectica*, 55: 167–174.

Rabin, G. O. and Rabern, B., 2016. Well founding grounding grounding. *Journal of Philosophical Logic*, 45: 349–379.

Rasmussen, J., 2014. *Defending the Correspondence Theory of Truth*. Cambridge University Press, Cambridge.

Rasmussen, S. A., 1986. Vague identity. *Mind*, 95: 81–91.

Rausch, E., 1937. Über Summativität und Nicht-Summativität. *Psychologische Forschung*, 21: 209–289.

Raven, M. J., 2013. Is ground a strict partial order? *American Philosophical Quarterly*, 50: 191–199.

Rayo, A., 2002. Word and objects. *Noûs*, 36: 436–464.

Rayo, A. and Uzquiano, G., eds., 2006. *Absolute Generality*. Clarendon Press, Oxford.

Rayo, A. and Yablo, S., 2001. Nominalism through de-nominalization. *Noûs*, 35: 74–92.

Rea, M. C., 1995. The problem of material constitution. *The Philosophical Review*, 104: 525–552.

Rea, M. C., 1998a. In defense of mereological universalism. *Philosophy and Phenomenological Research*, 58: 347–360.

Rea, M. C., 1998b. Sameness without identity: An Aristotelian solution to the problem of material constitution. *Ratio*, 11: 316–328.

Rea, M. C., 1999. McGrath on universalism. *Analysis*, 59: 200–203.

Rea, M. C., 2001. How to be an Eleatic monist. *Philosophical Perspectives*, 15: 129–151.

Rea, M. C., 2010. Universalism and extensionalism: A reply to Varzi. *Analysis*, 70: 1–7.

Rea, M. C., 2011. Hylomorphism reconditioned. *Philosophical Perspectives*, 25: 341–358.

Reeder, P., in press. Quick and easy recipes for hypergunk. *Australasian Journal of Philosophy*.

Renz, G., 2018. Form as structure: It's not so simple. *Ratio*, 31: 20–36.

Rescher, N., 1955. Axioms for the part relation. *Philosophical Studies*, 6: 8–11.

Rescher, N. and Oppenheim, P., 1955. Logical analysis of Gestalt concepts. *The British Journal for the Philosophy of Science*, 6: 89–106.

Resnik, M. D., 1988. Second-order logic still wild. *The Journal of Philosophy*, 85: 75–87.

Rettler, B., 2018. Mereological nihilism and puzzles about material objects. *Pacific Philosophical Quarterly*, 99: 842–868.

Richard, M., 2006. Context, vagueness, and ontology. In Greenough, P. and Lynch, M., eds., *Truth and Realism*, pp. 162–174. Clarendon Press, Oxford.

Richard, S., 2011. Whitehead's mereotopology and the project of formal ontology. *Logique et Analyse*, 54: 249–285.

Richard, S., 2015. Lewis et la fondation méréologique des mathématiques. *Klesis*, 31: 65–100.

Rickey, V. F., 1977. A survey of Leśniewski's logic. *Studia Logica*, 36: 407–426.

Rickey, V. F., 1985. Interpretations of Leśniewski's Ontology. *Dialectica*, 39: 181–192.

Ridder, L., 2001. Whiteheads Theorie der Ausdehnung. *Logical Analysis and History of Philosophy*, 4: 143–172.

Ridder, L., 2002. *Mereologie: Ein Beitrag zur Ontologie und Erkenntnistheorie*. Klostermann, Frankfurt.

Rini, A. A. and Cresswell, M. J., 2012. *The World-Time Parallel: Tense and Modality in Logic and Metaphysics*. Cambridge University Press, Cambridge.

Ripley, D., 2012. Conservatively extending classical logic with transparent truth. *The Review of Symbolic Logic*, 5: 354–378.

Ritchie, K., 2013. What are groups? *Philosophical Studies*, 166: 257–272.

Robin, C., 1851. *Tableaux d'anatomie comprenant l'exposé de toutes les parties à étudier dans l'organisme de l'homme et dans celui des animaux*. Baillière, Paris.

Robinson, D., 1982. Re-identifying matter. *The Philosophical Review*, 91: 317–341.

Robinson, H., 2014. Modern hylomorphism and the reality and causal power of structure: A skeptical investigation. *Res Philosophica*, 91: 203–214.

Roeper, P., 1997. Region-based topology. *Journal of Philosophical Logic*, 26: 251–309.

Roitman, J., 1989. Superatomic Boolean algebras. In Monk, J. D. and Bonnet, R., eds., *Handbook of Boolean Algebras*, volume 3, pp. 719–740. North-Holland, Amsterdam.

Rose, D. and Schaffer, J., 2017. Folk mereology is teleological. In Rose, D., ed., *Experimental Metaphysics*, pp. 135–186. Bloomsbury, London. Abridged version in *Noûs*, 51: 238–270.

Rosefeldt, T., 2018. Should metaphysics care about linguistics? *Journal for General Philosophy of Science*, 49: 161–178.

Rosen, G., 1995. Armstrong on classes as states of affairs. *Australasian Journal of Philosophy*, 73: 613–625.

Rosen, G., 2010. Metaphysical dependence: Grounding and reduction. In Hale, B. and Hoffmann, A., eds., *Modality: Metaphysics, Logic, and Epistemology*, pp. 109–135. Oxford University Press, Oxford.

Rosen, G. and Dorr, C., 2002. Composition as a fiction. In Gale, R. M., ed., *The Blackwell Guide to Metaphysics*, pp. 151–74. Blackwell, Oxford.

Rosen, G. and Smith, N. J. J., 2004. Worldly indeterminacy: A rough guide. *Australasian Journal of Philosophy*, 82: 185–198.

Rosenberg, J. F., 1993. Comments on Peter van Inwagen's *Material Beings*. *Philosophy and Phenomenological Research*, 53: 701–708.

Rosiak, M., 1995. Ontologia ufundowania: Ogólna teoria części i całości w 'Badaniach logicznych' Edmunda Husserla. *Filozofia Nauki*, 3: 25–63.

Rosiak, M., 1996. Formalizacja ontologii ufundowania. *Filozofia Nauki*, 4: 41–80.

Rosiak, M., 1998a. Twardowski and Husserl on wholes and parts. In Kijania-Placek, K. and Woleński, J., eds., *The Lvov-Warsaw School and Contemporary Philosophy*, pp. 85–100. Kluwer, Dordrecht.

Rosiak, M., 1998b. Husserlowska koncepcja ontologii formalnej, logiki formalnej i ich wzajemnych relacji. *Kwartalnik Filozoficzny*, 26: 67–78.

Rossberg, M., 2009. Leonard, Goodman, and the development of the *Calculus of Individuals*. In Ernst, G., Steinbrenner, J., and Scholz, O. R., eds., *From Logic to Art: Themes from Nelson Goodman*, pp. 51–69. Ontos, Frankfurt.

Rossberg, M. and Cohnitz, D., 2009. Logical consequence for nominalists. *Theoria*, 65: 147–168.

Rotkale, L., 2018. The form is not a proper part in Aristotle's *Metaphysics* Z.17, 1041b11–33. *Metaphysics*, 1: 75–87.

Roudaut, S., 2018. A dynamic version of hylomorphism. *Axiomathes*, 28: 13–36.

Rouilhan, P. de., 2002. On what there are. *Proceedings of the Aristotelian Society*, 102: 183–200.

Routley, R., 1979. Dialectical logic, semantics and metamathematics. *Erkenntnis*, 14: 301–331.

Ruben, D.-H., 1983. Social wholes and parts. *Mind*, 92: 219–238.

Ruben, D.-H., 1985. *The Metaphysics of the Social World*. Routledge, London.

Ruben, D.-H., 1999. Actions and their parts. In Rockmore, T., ed., *Proceedings of the 20th World Congress of Philosophy*, volume 2: *Metaphysics*, pp. 73–80. Philosophy Documentation Center, Bowling Green (OH).

Rucker, R., 1981. *Spacetime Donuts*. Ace Books, New York.

Rumfitt, I., 2005. Plural terms: Another variety of reference. In Bermudez,

J. L., ed., *Thought, Reference, and Experience: Themes from the Philosophy of Gareth Evans*, pp. 84–123. Clarendon Press, Oxford.
Russell, B., 1902. Letter to Frege, Eng. trans. by B. Woodward. In van Heijenoort (1967), pp. 124–125.
Russell, B., 1903. *The Principles of Mathematics*. Allen & Unwin, London.
Russell, B., 1905. On denoting. *Mind*, 14: 479–493.
Russell, B., 1918–1919. The philosophy of logical atomism. *The Monist*, 28: 495–527; 29: 33–63, 190–222, 345–380.
Russell, B., 1923. Vagueness. *The Australasian Journal of Psychology and Philosophy*, 1: 84–92.
Russell, B., 1927. *The Analysis of Matter*. Allen & Unwin, London.
Russell, G., 2018. Logical nihilism: Could there be no logic? *Philosophical Issues*, 28: 308–324.
Russell, J. S., 2008. The structure of gunk: Adventures in the ontology of space. *Oxford Studies in Metaphysics*, 4: 248–274.
Russell, J. S., 2016. Indefinite divisibility. *Inquiry*, 59: 239–263.
Russell, J. S., 2017. Composition as abstraction. *The Journal of Philosophy*, 114: 453–470.
Rutherford, D., 1965. *Introduction to Lattice Theory*. Oliver & Boyd, Edinburgh.
Rychter, P., 2011. How coincidence bears on persistence. *Philosophia*, 39: 759–770.
Sadegh-Zadeh, K., 2012. Fuzzy formal ontology. In Seising, R. and Sanz, V., eds., *Soft Computing in Humanities and Social Sciences*, pp. 383–400. Springer, Berlin.
Saenz, N. B., 2014. Wholly, grounding, truth. Ph.D. thesis, University of Colorado, Boulder (CO).
Saenz, N. B., 2015. A grounding solution to the grounding problem. *Philosophical Studies*, 172: 2193–2214.
Saenz, N. B., 2018. Sums and grounding. *Australasian Journal of Philosophy*, 96: 102–117.
Sagal, P. S., 1973. On how best to make sense of Leśniewski's Ontology. *Notre Dame Journal of Formal Logic*, 14: 259–262.
Sainsbury, R. M., 1989. What is a vague object? *Analysis*, 49: 99–103.
Salice, A., 2017. Brentano, Franz. In Burkhardt *et al.* (2017), pp. 119–125.
Salmon, N., 1986. *Frege's Puzzle*. MIT Press, Cambridge (MA).
Salsbery, K. J., 1996. Van Inwagen and gunk: A response to Sider. *Sorites*, 7: 21–27.
Sanford, D. H., 1976. Competing semantics of vagueness: Many values versus super-truth. *Synthese*, 33: 195–219.
Sanford, D. H., 1993. The problem of the many, many composition questions, and naive mereology. *Noûs*, 27: 219–228.
Sanford, D. H., 2003. Fusion confusion. *Analysis*, 63: 1–4.

Sanford, D. H., 2011. Can a sum change its parts? *Analysis*, 71: 235–239.

Sanford, D. H., 2017. Naïve mereology. In Burkhardt *et al.* (2017), pp. 369–371.

Sanson, D., 2016. Worlds enough for junk. *Res Philosophica*, 93: 45–62.

Sattig, T., 2008. Identity in 4D. *Philosophical Studies*, 140: 179–195.

Sattig, T., 2013. Vague objects and the problem of the many. *Metaphysica*, 14: 211–223.

Sattig, T., 2014. Mereological indeterminacy: Metaphysical but not fundamental. In Akiba, K. and Abasnezhad, A., eds., *Vague Objects and Vague Identity: New Essays on Ontic Vagueness*, pp. 25–42. Springer, Dordrecht.

Sattig, T., 2015. *The Double Lives of Objects: An Essay in the Metaphysics of the Ordinary World*. Oxford University Press, Oxford.

Sattig, T., in press. Part, slot, ground: Foundations for neo-Aristotelian mereology. *Synthese*.

Saucedo, R., 2011. Parthood and location. *Oxford Studies in Metaphysics*, 6: 225–284.

Savellos, E. E., 2000. When are events parts? *Philosophical Papers*, 29: 223–247.

Scala, M., 2002. Homogeneous simples. *Philosophy and Phenomenological Research*, 64: 393–397.

Scanlon, J., 1975. Formal logic and formal ontology. *Research in Phenomenology*, 5: 95–107.

Schaff, P. and Wace, H., eds., 1899. *Nicene and Post-Nicene Fathers*, volume 9: *Hilary of Poitiers, John of Damascus*. Scribner, New York.

Schaffer, J., 2003. Is there a fundamental level? *Noûs*, 37: 498–517.

Schaffer, J., 2007. From nihilism to monism. *Australasian Journal of Philosophy*, 85: 175–191.

Schaffer, J., 2009. On what grounds what. In Chalmers, D., Manley, D., and Wasserman, R., eds., *Metametaphysics: New Essays on the Foundations of Ontology*, pp. 347–383. Clarendon Press, Oxford.

Schaffer, J., 2010. Monism: The priority of the whole. *The Philosophical Review*, 119: 31–76.

Schaffer, J., 2012a. Grounding, transitivity, and contrastivity. In Correia and Schnieder (2012b), pp. 122–138.

Schaffer, J., 2012b. Why the world has parts: Reply to Horgan and Potrč. In Goff, P., ed., *Spinoza on Monism*, pp. 77–91. Palgrave Macmillan, London.

Schalley, A. C., 2017. Common sense reasoning about parts and wholes. In Burkhardt *et al.* (2017), pp. 152–160.

Schlesinger, G. N., 1985. Spatial, temporal, and cosmic parts. *Southern Journal of Philosophy*, 23: 255–271.

Schlesinger, G. N., 1994. *Timely Topics*. St. Martin's Press, New York.

Schmidt, F., 1971. Ganzes und Teil bei Leibniz. *Archiv für Geschichte der Philosophie*, 53: 267–278.

Schmitt, F. F., 2003a. Socializing metaphysics: An introduction. In Schmitt, F. F., ed., *Socializing Metaphysics: The Nature of Social Reality*, pp. 1–37. Rowman & Littlefield, Lanham (MD).

Schmitt, R., 2003b. Frege's letters to Wittgenstein about the *Tractatus*. *Bertrand Russell Society Quarterly*, 120: 13–31.

Schröder, E., 1890–1895. *Vorlesungen über die Algebra der Logik (Exakte Logik)*. Teubner, Leipzig.

Schrödinger, E., 1952. *Science and Humanism: Physics in Our Time*. Cambridge University Press, Cambridge.

Schuldenfrei, R., 1969. Eberle on nominalism in non-atomic systems. *Noûs*, 3: 427–430.

Schumm, A., Rohloff, W., and Piccinini, G., 2018. Composition as trans-scalar identity. Unpublished ms.

Scott, D., 1960. A different kind of model for set theory. Talk given at the *1st International Congresses in Logic, Methodology and Philosophy of Science*, Stanford (CA), August 24 – September 2.

Sedley, D., 1982. The Stoic criterion of identity. *Phronesis*, 27: 255–275.

Segal, A., 2014. Causal essentialism and mereological monism. *Philosophical Studies*, 169: 227–255.

Seibt, J., 2009. Forms of emergent interaction in general process theory. *Synthese*, 166: 479–512.

Seibt, J., 2015. Non-transitive parthood, leveled mereology, and the representation of emergent parts of processes. *Grazer Philosophische Studien*, 91: 165–190.

Seibt, J., 2017. Transitivity. In Burkhardt *et al.* (2017), pp. 570–579.

Shapiro, S., 1991. *Foundations without Foundationalism: A Case for Second-Order Logic*. Clarendon Press, Oxford.

Shapiro, S., 1993. Modality and ontology. *Mind*, 102: 455–481.

Sharpe, K. W., 2012. Structural properties and parthood. *Southwest Philosophy Review*, 28: 111–120.

Sharvy, R., 1968. Why a class can't change its members. *Noûs*, 2: 303–314.

Sharvy, R., 1980. A more general theory of definite descriptions. *The Philosophical Review*, 89: 607–624.

Sharvy, R., 1983. Mixtures. *Philosophy and Phenomenological Research*, 44: 227–239.

Sheehy, P., 2006a. Sharing space: The synchronic identity of social groups. *Philosophy of the Social Sciences*, 36: 131–148.

Sheehy, P., 2006b. *The Reality of Social Groups*. Ashgate, Aldershot.

Shields, C., 2019. Hylomorphic offices. *Ancient Philosophy Today: Dialogoi*, 1: 215–236.

Shiver, A., 2014. Mereological bundle theory and the identity of indiscernibles. *Synthese*, 191: 901–913.

Shiver, A., 2015. How do you say 'Everything is ultimately composed of atoms'? *Philosophical Studies*, 172: 607–614.

Sidelle, A., 2002. Is there a true metaphysics of material objects? *Noûs*, 36: 118–145.

Sider, T., 1993. Van Inwagen and the possibility of gunk. *Analysis*, 53: 285–289.

Sider, T., 1996. All the world's a stage. *Australasian Journal of Philosophy*, 74: 433–53.

Sider, T., 1997. Four-dimensionalism. *The Philosophical Review*, 106: 197–231.

Sider, T., 2001. *Four-Dimensionalism: An Ontology of Persistence and Time*. Clarendon Press, Oxford.

Sider, T., 2004. Replies to Gallois, Hirsch and Markosian. *Philosophy and Phenomenological Research*, 58: 674–687.

Sider, T., 2007a. Parthood. *The Philosophical Review*, 116: 51–91.

Sider, T., 2007b. Against monism. *Analysis*, 67: 1–7.

Sider, T., 2008. Temporal parts. In Sider, T., Hawthorne, J., and Zimmerman, D. W., eds., *Contemporary Debates in Metaphysics*, pp. 241–262. Blackwell, Oxford.

Sider, T., 2009. Ontological realism. In Chalmers, D., Manley, D., and Wasserman, R., eds., *Metametaphysics: New Essays on the Foundations of Ontology*, pp. 384–423. Clarendon Press, Oxford.

Sider, T., 2013. Against parthood. *Oxford Studies in Metaphysics*, 8: 237–293.

Sider, T., 2014. Consequences of collapse. In Cotnoir and Baxter (2014), pp. 211–221.

Sider, T., 2015. Nothing over and above. *Grazer Philosophische Studien*, 91: 191–216.

Siderits, M., 2003. *Personal Identity and Buddhist Philosophy: Empty Persons*. Ashgate, Aldershot.

Silva, P., 2013. Ordinary objects and series-style answers to the special composition question. *Pacific Philosophical Quarterly*, 94: 69–88.

Simons, P. M., 1980. Individuals, groups and manifolds. In Haller, R. and Grassl, W., eds., *Language, Logic and Philosophy: Proceedings of the 4th International Wittgenstein Symposium*, pp. 483–486. Hölder-Pichler-Tempsky, Vienna.

Simons, P. M., 1981. A note on Leśniewski and free logic. *Logique et Analyse*, 95-96: 415–420.

Simons, P. M., 1982a. The formalization of Husserl's theory of wholes and parts. In Smith (1982), pp. 113–159.

Simons, P. M., 1982b. Plural reference and set theory. In Smith (1982), pp. 199–260.

Simons, P. M., 1982c. On understanding Leśniewski. *History and Philosophy of Logic*, 3: 165–191.

Simons, P. M., 1985a. The old problem of complex and fact. *Teoria*, 5: 205–226.
Simons, P. M., 1985b. Leśniewski's logic and its relation to classical and free logics. In Dorn, G. and Weingartner, P., eds., *Foundations of Logic and Linguistics: Problems and Their Solutions*, pp. 369–402. Plenum Press, New York.
Simons, P. M., 1986. Tractatus mereologico-philosophicus? A Brentanian look at Wittgenstein, and a moral. *Grazer Philosophische Studien*, 28: 165–186.
Simons, P. M., 1987. *Parts: A Study in Ontology*. Clarendon Press, Oxford.
Simons, P. M., 1991a. Free part-whole theory. In Lambert, K., ed., *Philosophical Applications of Free Logic*, pp. 285–306. Oxford University Press, New York.
Simons, P. M., 1991b. Whitehead und die Mereologie. In Hampe, M. and Maassen, H., eds., *Die Gifford Lectures und ihre Deutung: Materialien zu Whiteheads 'Prozess und Realität'*, volume 2, pp. 369–388. Suhrkamp, Frankfurt. Revised Eng. trans.: Whitehead and mereology, in Durand, G. and Weber, M., eds., *Les principes de la connaissance naturelle d'Alfred North Whitehead*, pp. 215–233, Ontos, Frankfurt, 2007.
Simons, P. M., 1992. Leśniewskian term logic. *Lingua e Stile*, 27: 23–46.
Simons, P. M., 1993. Nominalism in Poland. In Coniglione, F., Poli, R., and Woleński, J., eds., *Polish Scientific Philosophy: The Lvov-Warsaw School*, pp. 207–231. Rodopi, Amsterdam.
Simons, P. M., 1995. Leśniewski and ontological commitment. In Miéville, D. and Vernant, D., eds., *Stanisław Leśniewski aujourd'hui*, pp. 103–119. Groupe de recherches sur la philosophie et le langage, Grenoble.
Simons, P. M., 1997a. Bolzano on collections. *Grazer Philosophische Studien*, 53: 87–108.
Simons, P. M., 1997b. Higher-order quantification and ontological commitment. *Dialectica*, 51: 255–271.
Simons, P. M., 1999. Does the sun exist? The problem of vague objects. In Rockmore, T., ed., *Proceedings of the 20th World Congress of Philosophy*, volume 2: *Metaphysics*, pp. 89–97. Philosophy Documentation Center, Bowling Green (OH).
Simons, P. M., 2003. The universe. *Ratio*, 16: 236–250.
Simons, P. M., 2004. Extended simples: A third way between atoms and gunk. In Hudson (2004), pp. 371–384.
Simons, P. M., 2006. Real wholes, real parts: Mereology without algebra. In Mann and Varzi (2006), pp. 597–613.
Simons, P. M., 2009a. Leśniewski's logic. In Gabbay, D. M. and Woods, J., eds., *Handbook of the History of Logic*, volume 5, pp. 305–320. North-Holland, Amsterdam.
Simons, P. M., 2009b. Why there are no states of affairs. In Reicher, M. E., ed., *States of Affairs*, pp. 111–128. Ontos, Frankfurt.
Simons, P. M., 2013a. Varieties of parthood: Ontology learns from engineering.

In Michelfelder, D. P., McCarthy, N., and Goldberg, D. E., eds., *Philosophy and Engineering: Reflections on Practice, Principles and Process*, pp. 151–163. Springer, Dordrecht.
Simons, P. M., 2013b. Mereology: Parts and wholes. In Kaldis, B., ed., *Encyclopedia of Philosophy and the Social Sciences*, pp. 592–596. SAGE Publications, Los Angeles (CA).
Simons, P. M., 2015. Stanisław Leśniewski. In Zalta, E. N., ed., *The Stanford Encyclopedia of Philosophy*. http://plato.stanford.edu/archives/win2015/entries/lesniewski.
Simons, P. M., 2016a. Mereology and truth-making. In Varzi and Gruszczyński (2016), pp. 245–258.
Simons, P. M., 2016b. The ontology and logic of higher-order multitudes. In Carrara *et al.* (2016), pp. 55–69.
Simons, P. M., 2017a. Mereologie. In Schrenk, M., ed., *Handbuch Metaphysik*, pp. 267–271. Metzler, Stuttgart.
Simons, P. M., 2017b. Whitehead, Alfred North. In Burkhardt *et al.* (2017), pp. 593–598.
Simons, P. M., 2018. Leśniewski and mereology. In Garrido, Á. and Wybraniec-Skardowska, U., eds., *The Lvov-Warsaw School: Past and Present*, pp. 337–359. Birkhäuser, Basel.
Simons, P. M. and Dement, C. W., 1996. Aspects of the mereology of artifacts. In Poli, R. and Simons, P. M., eds., *Formal Ontology*, pp. 255–276. Kluwer, Dordrecht.
Simplicius, 1992. *On Aristotle, Physics 4.1–5 and 10–14*, Eng. trans. by J. O. Urmson. Duckworth, London.
Simplicius, 2011. *On Aristotle, Physics 1.3–4*, Eng. trans. by P. Huby and C. C. W. Taylor. Duckworth, London.
Sinisi, V. F., 1966. Leśniewski's analysis of Whitehead's theory of events. *Notre Dame Journal of Formal Logic*, 7: 323–327.
Sinisi, V. F., 1969. Leśniewski's and Frege on collective classes. *Notre Dame Journal of Formal Logic*, 10: 239–246.
Sinisi, V. F., 1976. Leśniewski's analysis of Russell's antinomy. *Notre Dame Journal of Formal Logic*, 17: 19–34.
Sinisi, V. F., ed., 1983. *Leśniewski's Philosophy of Mathematics*. Special issue of *Topoi*, volume 2/1.
Skrzypek, J., 2017. Three concerns for structural hylomorphism. *Analytic Philosophy*, 58: 360–408.
Slater, M. H., 2003. Minimalism and coincidence: Comments on Varzi. *Dialectica*, 57: 323–329.
Słupecki, J., 1958. Towards a generalized mereology of Leśniewski. *Studia Logica*, 8: 131–154.
Smart, J. J. C., 1955. Spatialising time. *Mind*, 64: 239–241.

Smart, J. J. C., 1972. Space-time and individuals. In Rudner, R. S. and Scheffler, I., eds., *Logic and Art: Essays in Honor of Nelson Goodman*, pp. 3–20. Bobbs-Merrill, Indianapolis (IN).

Smid, J., 2015. The ontological parsimony of mereology. *Philosophical Studies*, 172: 3253–3271.

Smid, J., 2017a. What does 'nothing over and above its parts' actually mean? *Philosophy Compass*, 12/1: 13 pp.

Smid, J., 2017b. 'Identity' as a mereological term. *Synthese*, 194: 2367–2385.

Smirnov, V. A., 1983. Embedding the elementary ontology of Stanisław Leśniewski into the monadic second-order calculus of predicates. *Studia Logica*, 42: 197–207.

Smith, B., ed., 1982. *Parts and Moments: Studies in Logic and Formal Ontology*. Philosophia, Munich.

Smith, B., 1987. The substance of Brentano's ontology. *Topoi*, 6: 39–49.

Smith, B., 1989. Logic and formal ontology. In Mohanty, J. N. and McKenna, W., eds., *Husserl's Phenomenology: A Textbook*, pp. 29–67. University Press of America, Lanham (MD).

Smith, B., 1990. On the phases of reism. In Woleński, J., ed., *Kotarbiński: Logic, Semantics and Ontology*, pp. 137–184. Kluwer, Dordrecht.

Smith, B., 1994. *Austrian Philosophy: The Legacy of Franz Brentano*. Open Court, Chicago (IL).

Smith, B., 1995. Zur Kognition räumlicher Grenzen: Eine mereotopologische Untersuchung. *Kognitionswissenschaft*, 4: 177–184.

Smith, B., 1996a. Mereotopology: A theory of parts and boundaries. In Guarino *et al.* (1996), pp. 287–303.

Smith, B., 1996b. In defense of extreme (fallibilistic) apriorism. *Journal of Libertarian Studies*, 12: 179–192.

Smith, B., 1997. Boundaries: An essay in mereotopology. In Hahn, L. E., ed., *The Philosophy of Roderick Chisholm*, pp. 534–561. Open Court, Chicago (IL).

Smith, B., 1999. Agglomerations. In Freksa, C. and Mark, D., eds., *Spatial Information Theory: Proceedings of COSIT 1999*, pp. 267–282. Springer, Berlin.

Smith, B. and Mulligan, K., 1982. Pieces of a theory. In Smith (1982), pp. 15–109.

Smith, D., 2006. The vagueness argument for mereological universalism. *Pacific Philosophical Quarterly*, 87: 357–368.

Smith, D., 2009. Mereology without weak supplementation. *Australasian Journal of Philosophy*, 87: 505–511.

Smith, D. C., 2019. Gunky objects, junky worlds, and weak mereological universalism. *Erkenntnis*, 84: 41–55.

Smith, D. W., 2003. 'Pure' logic, ontology, and phenomenology. *Revue Internationale de Philosophie*, 2: 21–44.

Smith, N. J. J., 2005. A plea for things that are not quite all there: Or, is there a problem about vague composition and vague existence? *The Journal of Philosophy*, 102: 381–421.

Soames, S., 1987. Direct reference, propositional attitudes, and semantic content. *Philosophical Topics*, 15: 47–87.

Sobociński, B., 1949–1950. L'analyse de l'antinomie russellienne par Leśniewski. *Methodos*, 1: 94–107, 220–228, 308–316; 2: 237–257. Eng. trans. by R. E. Clay: Leśniewski's analysis of Russell's paradox, in Srzednicki and Rickey (1984), pp. 11–44.

Sobociński, B., 1954. Studies in Leśniewski's Mereology. *Rocznik Polskiego Towarzystwa Naukowego na Obczyźnie*, 5: 34–43.

Sobociński, B., 1971a. Atomistic mereology. *Notre Dame Journal of Formal Logic*, 12: 89–103, 203–213.

Sobociński, B., 1971b. A note on an axiom-system of atomistic mereology. *Notre Dame Journal of Formal Logic*, 12: 249–251.

Sokolowski, R., 1968. The logic of parts and wholes in Husserl's *Investigations*. *Philosophy and Phenomenological Research*, 28: 537–553.

Sorabji, R., 1983. *Time, Creation and the Continuum: Theories in Antiquity and the Early Middle Ages*. Cornell University Press, Ithaca (NY).

Sorabji, R., 2005. *The Philosophy of the Commentators, 200–600 AD: A Sourcebook*, volume 3: *Logic and Metaphysics*. Cornell University Press, Ithaca (NY).

Sorabji, R., 2006. *Self: Ancient and Modern Insights about Individuality, Life, and Death*. University of Chicago Press, Chicago (IL).

Sorensen, R. A., 2016. *A Cabinet of Philosophical Curiosities*. Oxford University Press, New York.

Sosa, E., 1987. Subjects among other things. *Philosophical Perspectives*, 1: 155–187.

Sosa, E., 1999. Existential relativity. *Midwest Studies in Philosophy*, 23: 132–43.

Spencer, J. T., 2006. Two mereological arguments against the possibility of an omniscient being. *Philo*, 9: 62–72.

Spencer, J. T., 2010. A tale of two simples. *Philosophical Studies*, 148: 167–181.

Spencer, J. T., 2012. All things must pass away. *Oxford Studies in Metaphysics*, 7: 67–92.

Spencer, J. T., 2013. Strong composition as identity and simplicity. *Erkenntnis*, 78: 1177–1184.

Spencer, J. T., 2014. Two thoughts on 'A tale of two parts'. *Res Philosophica*, 91: 485–490.

Spencer, J. T., 2017. Counting on strong composition as identity to settle the special composition question. *Erkenntnis*, 82: 857–872.

Spencer, J. T., in press. On the explanatory demands of the special composition question. In Carrara and Lando (in press-b).

Srzednicki, J. T. J. and Rickey, V. F., eds., 1984. *Leśniewski's Systems: Ontology and Mereology*. Kluwer, Dordrecht.

Srzednicki, J. T. J. and Stachniak, Z., eds., 1984. *Leśniewski's Systems: Protothetic*. Kluwer, Dordrecht.

Srzednicki, J. T. J. and Stachniak, Z., eds., 1988. *S. Leśniewski's Lecture Notes in Logic*. Kluwer, Dordrecht.

Stalnaker, R., 1984. *Inquiry*. MIT Press, Cambridge (MA).

Stebbing, L. S., 1934. *Logic in Practice*. Methuen, London.

Steen, M., 2008. Chisholm's changing conception of ordinary objects. *Grazer Philosophische Studien*, 76: 1–56.

Steen, M., 2011. More problems for MaxCon: Contingent particularity and stuff-thing coincidence. *Acta Analytica*, 26: 135–154.

Steen, M., 2016. The metaphysics of mass expressions. In Zalta, E. N., ed., *The Stanford Encyclopedia of Philosophy*. http://plato.stanford.edu/archives/win2016/entries/metaphysics-massexpress.

Steen, M., 2017. Temporally restricted composition. *Croatian Journal of Philosophy*, 17: 431–440.

Stell, J. G., 2004. Part and complement: Fundamental concepts in spatial relations. *Annals of Mathematics and Artificial Intelligence*, 41: 1–17.

Stokes, M. C., 1971. *One and Many in Presocratic Philosophy*. Center for Hellenic Studies, Washington (DC).

Stone, J., 2002. Why sortal essentialism cannot solve Chrysippus's puzzle. *Analysis*, 62: 216–223.

Stone, M., 1936. The theory of representations of Boolean algebras. *Transactions of the American Mathematical Society*, 40: 37–111.

Strohmaier, D., 2018. Group membership and parthood. *Journal of Social Ontology*, 4: 121–135.

Stuchlik, J. M., 2013. Not all worlds are stages. *Philosophical Studies*, 116: 309–321.

Stump, E., 1995. Non-Cartesian substance dualism and materialism without reductionism. *Faith and Philosophy*, 12: 505–531.

Stump, E., 2006. Resurrection, reassembly, and reconstitution: Aquinas on the soul. In Niederbacher, B. and Runggaldier, E., eds., *Die menschliche Seele: Brauchen wir den Dualismus?*, pp. 151–172. Ontos, Frankfurt.

Stump, E., 2012. Resurrection and the separated soul. In Davies, B. and Stump, E., eds., *The Oxford Handbook of Aquinas*, pp. 458–466. Oxford University Press, New York.

Suppes, P., 1972. Some open problems in the philosophy of space and time. *Synthese*, 24: 298–316.

Svoboda, D., 2012. Thomas Aquinas on whole and part. *The Thomist*, 76: 273–304.

Świętorzecka, K. and Łyczak, M., in press. Mereology with super-supplementation axioms: A reconstruction of the unpublished manuscript of Jan F. Drewnowski. *Logic and Logical Philosophy*.

Swoyer, C., 1994. Leibniz's calculus of real addition. *Studia Leibnitiana*, 26: 1–30.

Tahko, T. E., 2009. Against the vagueness argument. *Philosophia*, 37: 335–340.

Tahko, T. E., 2018a. Fundamentality. In Zalta, E. N., ed., *The Stanford Encyclopedia of Philosophy*. http://plato.stanford.edu/archives/fall2018/entries/fundamentality.

Tahko, T. E., 2018b. Fundamentality and ontological minimality. In Bliss and Priest (2018), pp. 237–253.

Tallant, J., 2011. *Metaphysics: An Introduction*. Continuum, London.

Tallant, J., 2013. Problems of parthood for proponents of priority. *Analysis*, 73: 429–438.

Tallant, J., 2014. Against mereological nihilism. *Synthese*, 191: 1511–1527.

Tallant, J., 2018. *Truth and the World: An Explanationist Theory*. Routledge, London.

Tanksley, C., 2010. The mereological constancy of masses. *The Philosophical Quarterly*, 60: 343–354.

Tarski, A., 1923. O wyrazie pierwotnym logistyki. *Przegląd Filozoficzny*, 2: 68–89. Eng. trans. by J. H. Woodger: On the primitive term of logistic, in Tarski (1956), pp. 1–14.

Tarski, A., 1929. Les fondements de la géométrie des corps. *Księga Pamiątkowa Pierwszkego Polskiego Zjazdu Matematycznego*, suppl. to *Annales de la Société Polonaise de Mathématique*, 7: 29–33. Eng. trans. by J. H. Woodger (with additions): Foundations of the geometry of solids, in Tarski (1956), pp. 24–29.

Tarski, A., 1935. Zur Grundlegung der Booleschen Algebra. I. *Fundamenta Mathematicae*, 24: 177–198. Eng. trans. by J. H. Woodger (with additions): On the foundations of Boolean algebra, in Tarski (1956), pp. 320–341.

Tarski, A., 1937. Appendix E. In Woodger, J. H., *The Axiomatic Method in Biology*, pp. 161–172. Cambridge University Press, Cambridge.

Tarski, A., 1956. *Logic, Semantics, Metamathematics: Papers from 1923 to 1938*. Clarendon Press, Oxford.

Taylor, B., 1985. *Modes of Occurrence: Verbs, Adverbs and Events*. Basil Blackwell, Oxford.

Taylor, R., 1955. Spatial and temporal analogues and the concept of identity. *The Journal of Philosophy*, 52: 599–612.

Tennant, N., 2013. Parts, classes and *Parts of Classes*: An anti-realist reading of Lewisian mereology. *Synthese*, 190: 709–742.

Tennant, N., 2019. On Tarski's axiomatization of mereology. *Studia Logica*, 107: 1089–1102.

Thomason, R. H., 2002. Combinations of tense and modality. In Gabbay, D. M. and Guenthner, F., eds., *Handbook of Philosophical Logic*, 2nd edition, volume 7, pp. 205–234. Kluwer, Dordrecht.

Thomasson, A. L., 2007. *Ordinary Objects*. Oxford University Press, Oxford.

Thomasson, A. L., 2009. Answerable and unanswerable questions. In Chalmers, D., Manley, D., and Wasserman, R., eds., *Metametaphysics: New Essays on the Foundations of Ontology*, pp. 444–471. Clarendon Press, Oxford.

Thomson, J. J., 1977. *Acts and Other Events*. Cornell University Press, Ithaca (NY).

Thomson, J. J., 1983. Parthood and identity across time. *The Journal of Philosophy*, 80: 201–220.

Thomson, J. J., 1998. The statue and the clay. *Noûs*, 32: 149–173.

Thomson, N., 2016. Metaphysical interdependence. In Jago, M., ed., *Reality Making*, pp. 38–56. Oxford University Press, Oxford.

Thunder, S. D., 2017. Mereological nihilism: Keeping it simple. *Thought*, 6: 278–287.

Tillman, C. and Fowler, G., 2012. Propositions and parthood: The universe and antisymmetry. *Australasian Journal of Philosophy*, 90: 525–539.

Tognazzini, N. A., 2006. Simples and the possibility of discrete space. *Australasian Journal of Philosophy*, 84: 117–128.

Tola, F. and Dragonetti, C., 1995. *On Voidness: A Study on Buddhist Nihilism*. Motilal Banarsidass, Delhi.

Toner, P., 2009. Personhood and death in St. Thomas Aquinas. *History of Philosophy Quarterly*, 26: 121–138.

Toner, P., 2010. St. Thomas Aquinas on death and the separated soul. *Pacific Philosophical Quarterly*, 91: 587–599.

Toner, P., 2013. On Aristotelianism and structures as parts. *Ratio*, 26: 148–161.

Torre, S., 2015. Restricted diachronic composition and special relativity. *The British Journal for the Philosophy of Science*, 66: 235–255.

Torrengo, G., 2011. The modal dimension. In Carrara *et al.* (2011), pp. 105–120.

Tranöy, K. E., 1959. *Wholes and Structures: An Attempt at a Philosophical Analysis*. Munksgaard, Copenhagen.

Tsai, H.-C., 2009. Decidability of mereological theories. *Logic and Logical Philosophy*, 18: 45–63.

Tsai, H.-C., 2011. More on the decidability of mereological theories. *Logic and Logical Philosophy*, 20: 251–265.

Tsai, H.-C., 2012. First-order axiomatization of rough mereology. In Lin, T. Y., Hu, X., Wu, Z., Chen, A. L. P., Broder, A. Z., Ho, H., and Wang, S., eds., *Proceedings of the 2012 IEEE International Conference on Granular Computing*, pp. 471–474. IEEE Computer Society, Washington (DC).

Tsai, H.-C., 2013a. Decidability of general extensional mereology. *Studia Logica*, 101: 619–636.

Tsai, H.-C., 2013b. A comprehensive picture of the decidability of mereological theories. *Studia Logica*, 101: 987–1012.

Tsai, H.-C., 2015. Notes on models of first-order mereological theories. In Varzi and Gruszczyński (2015), pp. 469–482 (with an 'Addendum', p. 483).

Tsai, H.-C., 2017. Infinite 'atomic' mereological structures. In Yang, S. C.-M., Lee, K. Y., and Ono, H., eds., *Philosophical Logic, Current Trends in Asia: Proceedings of AWPL-TPLC 2016*, pp. 287–296. Springer, Singapore.

Tsai, H.-C., 2018. General extensional mereology is finitely axiomatizable. *Studia Logica*, 106: 809–826.

Tsai, H.-C. and Varzi, A. C., 2016. Atoms, gunk, and the limits of 'composition'. *Erkenntnis*, 81: 231–235.

Tsong-kha-pa, 2000–2004. *The Great Treatise on the Stages of the Path to Enlightenment*, ed. by J. W. C. Cutler with Eng. trans. by the Lamrim Chenmo Translation Committee. Snow Lion, Ithaca (NY).

Turner, J., 2013. Existence and many-one identity. *The Philosophical Quarterly*, 63: 313–329.

Turner, J., 2014. Donald Baxter's composition as identity. In Cotnoir and Baxter (2014), pp. 225–243.

Turner, J., 2015. What's so bad about second-order logic? In Torza, A., ed., *Quantifiers, Quantifiers, and Quantifiers: Themes in Logic, Metaphysics, and Language*, pp. 463–487. Springer, Cham.

Tversky, B., 1986. Components and categorization. In Craig, C. G., ed., *Noun Classes and Categorization: Proceedings of a Symposium on Categorization and Noun Classification*, pp. 63–75. Benjamins, Amsterdam.

Tversky, B., 1989. Parts, partonomies, and taxonomies. *Developmental Psychology*, 25: 983–995.

Tversky, B., 1990. Where partonomies and taxonomies meet. In Tsohatzidis, S. L., ed., *Meanings and Prototypes: Studies in Linguistic Categorization*, pp. 334–344. Routledge, London.

Tversky, B., 2005. On exploring parts and wholes. In Gero, J. S. and Maher, M. L., eds., *Computational and Cognitive Models of Creative Design: Preprints of the 6th International Conference*, pp. 3–16. University of Sydney, Sydney.

Tversky, B. and Hemenway, K., 1984. Objects, parts, and categories. *Journal of Experimental Psychology: General*, 113: 169–193.

Twardowski, K., 1894. *Zur Lehre vom Inhalt und Gegenstand der Vorstellungen: Eine psychologische Untersuchung*. Hölder, Vienna. Eng. trans. by R. Grossmann: *On the Content and Object of Presentations: A Psychological Investigation*, Nijhoff, The Hague, 1977.

Tye, M., 1990. Vague objects. *Mind*, 99: 535–557.

Tye, M., 2000. Vagueness and reality. *Philosophical Topics*, 28: 195–209.

Tzouvaras, A., 1993. Significant parts and identity of artifacts. *Notre Dame Journal of Formal Logic*, 34: 445–452.

Tzouvaras, A., 1995. Worlds of homogeneous artifacts. *Notre Dame Journal of Formal Logic*, 36: 454–474.

Ueberroth, J. A., 2013. Possible parthood and modal-mereological composition. *Res Cogitans*, 4: 2–11.

Ujvári, M., 2004. Cambridge change and sortal essentialism. *Metaphysica*, 5: 25–34.

Unger, P. K., 1979a. There are no ordinary things. *Synthese*, 41: 117–154.

Unger, P. K., 1979b. I do not exist. In Macdonald, G. F., ed., *Perception and Identity: Essays Presented to A. J. Ayer with His Replies to Them*, pp. 235–251. Macmillan, New York.

Unger, P. K., 1979c. Why there are no people. *Midwest Studies in Philosophy*, 4: 177–222.

Unger, P. K., 1980a. The problem of the many. *Midwest Studies in Philosophy*, 5: 411–468.

Unger, P. K., 1980b. Skepticism and nihilism. *Noûs*, 14: 517–545.

Unger, P. K., 1990. *Identity, Consciousness, and Value*. Oxford University Press, New York.

Unger, P. K., 2014. *Empty Ideas: A Critique of Analytic Philosophy*. Oxford University Press, New York.

Urbaniak, R., 2008. Leśniewski and Russell's paradox: Some problems. *History and Philosophy of Logic*, 29: 115–146.

Urbaniak, R., 2014a. *Leśniewski's Systems of Logic and Foundations of Mathematics*. Springer, Cham.

Urbaniak, R., 2014b. Słupecki's generalized mereology and its flaws. *History and Philosophy of Logic*, 35: 289–300.

Urbaniak, R., 2015. Stanisław Leśniewski: Rethinking the philosophy of mathematics. *European Review*, 23: 125–138.

Urbaniak, R., 2016. Potential infinity, abstraction principles and arithmetic (Leśniewski style). *Axioms*, 5/2: 20 pp.

Uzquiano, G., 2004. Plurals and simples. In Hudson (2004), pp. 429–451.

Uzquiano, G., 2006a. The price of universality. *Philosophical Studies*, 129: 137–169.

Uzquiano, G., 2006b. Unrestricted unrestricted quantification: The cardinal problem of absolute generality. In Rayo and Uzquiano (2006), pp. 305–332.

Uzquiano, G., 2011a. Plural quantification and modality. *Proceedings of the Aristotelian Society*, 111: 219–250.

Uzquiano, G., 2011b. Mereological harmony. *Oxford Studies in Metaphysics*, 6: 199–224.

Uzquiano, G., 2014. Mereology and modality. In Kleinschmidt (2014), pp. 33–56.

Uzquiano, G., 2015. Recombination and paradox. *Philosopher's Imprint*, 15/19: 1–20.

Uzquiano, G., 2017. Atomism and composition. *Thought*, 6: 232–240.

Uzquiano, G., 2018a. Quantifiers and quantification. In Zalta, E. N., ed., *The*

Stanford Encyclopedia of Philosophy. http://plato.stanford.edu/archives/win2018/entries/quantification.

Uzquiano, G., 2018b. Groups: Toward a theory of plural embodiment. *The Journal of Philosophy*, 115: 423–452.

Vacek, M., 2017. Extended modal dimensionalism. *Acta Analytica*, 32: 13–28.

Vakarelov, D., 2007. Region-based theory of space: Algebras of regions, representation theory, and logics. In Gabbay, D. M., Goncharov, S. G., and Zakharyaschev, M., eds., *Mathematical Problems from Applied Logic: Logics for the XXIst Century*, volume 2, pp. 267–348. Springer, Berlin.

Vakarelov, D., 2015. A Whiteheadian-type theory of space and time. In Petrov, V. and Scarfe, A. C., eds., *Dynamic Being: Essays in Process-Relational Ontology*, pp. 262–305. Cambridge Scholars Publishing, Newcastle upon Tyne.

Vakarelov, D., 2017. Actual existence predicate in mereology and mereotopology. In Polkowski, L., Yao, Y., Artiemjew, P., Ciucci, D., Liu, D., Ślęzak, D., and Zielosko, B., eds., *Rough Sets: International Joint Conference, Proceedings of IJCRS 2017*, part 2, pp. 138–157. Springer, Cham.

Valore, P., 2015. Nothing is part of everything. In Fraisopi, F., ed., *Ontologie: Storia e prospettive della domanda sull'ente*, pp. 407–420. Mimesis, Milan.

Valore, P., 2016. *Fundamentals of Ontological Commitment*. De Gruyter, Berlin.

van Benthem, J., 1983. *The Logic of Time: A Model-Theoretic Investigation into the Varieties of Temporal Ontology and Temporal Discourse*. Kluwer, Dordrecht.

van Benthem, J., 2001. Correspondence theory. In Gabbay, D. M. and Guenthner, F., eds., *Handbook of Philosophical Logic*, 2nd edition, volume 3, pp. 325–408. Kluwer, Dordrecht.

Van Cleve, J., 1981. Reflections on Kant's second antimony. *Synthese*, 47: 481–494.

Van Cleve, J., 1985. Why a set contains its members essentially. *Noûs*, 19: 585–602.

Van Cleve, J., 1986. Mereological essentialism, mereological conjunctivism, and identity through time. *Midwest Studies in Philosophy*, 11: 141–156.

Van Cleve, J., 2008. The moon and sixpence: A defense of mereological universalism. In Sider, T., Hawthorne, J., and Zimmerman, D. W., eds., *Contemporary Debates in Metaphysics*, pp. 321–340. Blackwell, Oxford.

van Fraassen, B., 1966. Singular terms, truth-value gaps, and free logic. *The Journal of Philosophy*, 63: 481–495.

van Fraassen, B., 1969. Presuppositions, supervaluations, and free logic. In Lambert, K., ed., *The Logical Way of Doing Things*, pp. 67–92. Yale University Press, New Haven (CT).

van Heijenoort, J., ed., 1967. *From Frege to Gödel: A Source Book in Mathematical Logic, 1879–1931*. Harvard University Press, Cambridge (MA).

van Inwagen, P., 1981. The doctrine of arbitrary undetached parts. *Pacific Philosophical Quarterly*, 62: 123–137.

van Inwagen, P., 1987. When are objects parts? *Philosophical Perspectives*, 1: 21–47.

van Inwagen, P., 1990. *Material Beings*. Cornell University Press, Ithaca (NY).

van Inwagen, P., 1993a. Naive mereology, admissible valuations, and other matters. *Noûs*, 27: 229–234.

van Inwagen, P., 1993b. Précis of *Material Beings*. *Philosophy and Phenomenological Research*, 53: 683–686.

van Inwagen, P., 1994. Composition as identity. *Philosophical Perspectives*, 8: 207–220.

van Inwagen, P., 2002a. The number of things. *Philosophical Issues*, 12: 176–196.

van Inwagen, P., 2002b. 'Carnap' and 'the Polish logician'. *Acta Analytica*, 17: 7–17.

van Inwagen, P., 2006. Can mereological sums change their parts? In Mann and Varzi (2006), pp. 614–630.

van Inwagen, P., 2007. Impotence and collateral damage: One charge in van Fraassen's indictment of analytical metaphysics. *Philosophical Topics*, 35: 67–82.

van Inwagen, P., 2009. The new antimetaphysicians. *Proceedings and Addresses of the American Philosophical Association*, 83: 45–61.

Vander Laan, D. A., 2010. A relevance constraint on composition. *Australasian Journal of Philosophy*, 88: 135–145.

Varzi, A. C., 1996. Parts, wholes, and part-whole relations: The prospects of mereotopology. In Guarino *et al.* (1996), pp. 259–286.

Varzi, A. C., 1997. Boundaries, continuity, and contact. *Noûs*, 31: 26–58.

Varzi, A. C., 2000a. Mereological commitments. *Dialectica*, 54: 283–305.

Varzi, A. C., ed., 2000b. *Temporal Parts*. Special issue of *The Monist*, volume 83/3.

Varzi, A. C., 2001a. Parts, counterparts, and modal occurrents. In Miéville (2001), pp. 151–171.

Varzi, A. C., 2001b. Vagueness in geography. *Philosophy and Geography*, 4: 49–65.

Varzi, A. C., 2003. Perdurantism, universalism, and quantifiers. *Australasian Journal of Philosophy*, 81: 208–215.

Varzi, A. C., 2005. Change, temporal parts, and the argument from vagueness. *Dialectica*, 59: 485–498.

Varzi, A. C., 2006a. A note on the transitivity of parthood. *Applied Ontology*, 1: 141–146.

Varzi, A. C., 2006b. The universe among other things. *Ratio*, 19: 107–120.

Varzi, A. C., 2007a. Spatial reasoning and ontology: Parts, wholes, and locations. In Aiello, M., Pratt-Hartmann, I., and van Benthem, J., eds., *Handbook of Spatial Logics*, pp. 945–1038. Springer, Dordrecht.

Varzi, A. C., 2007b. Promiscuous endurantism and diachronic vagueness. *American Philosophical Quarterly*, 44: 181–189.

Varzi, A. C., 2008. The extensionality of parthood and composition. *The Philosophical Quarterly*, 58: 108–133.

Varzi, A. C., 2009. Universalism entails extensionalism. *Analysis*, 69: 599–604.

Varzi, A. C., 2010. On the boundary between material and formal ontology. In Smith, B., Mizoguchi, R., and Nakagawa, S., eds., *Interdisciplinary Ontology: Proceedings of the 3rd Meeting*, pp. 3–8. Keio University Press, Tokyo.

Varzi, A. C., 2013. Undetached parts and disconnected wholes. In Svennerlind, C., Almäng, J., and Ingthorsson, R., eds., *Johanssonian Investigations: Essays in Honour of Ingvar Johansson on His Seventieth Birthday*, pp. 696–708. Ontos, Frankfurt.

Varzi, A. C., 2014a. Counting and countenancing. In Cotnoir and Baxter (2014), pp. 47–69.

Varzi, A. C., 2014b. Formal theories of parthood. In Calosi and Graziani (2014), pp. 359–370.

Varzi, A. C., 2015. Boundary. In Zalta, E. N., ed., *The Stanford Encyclopedia of Philosophy*. http://plato.stanford.edu/archives/win2015/entries/boundary.

Varzi, A. C., 2016. Mereology. In Zalta, E. N., ed., *The Stanford Encyclopedia of Philosophy*. http://plato.stanford.edu/archives/spr2016/entries/mereology.

Varzi, A. C., 2017. On being ultimately composed of atoms. *Philosophical Studies*, 174: 2891–2900.

Varzi, A. C., 2019. On three axiom systems for classical mereology. *Logic and Logical Philosophy*, 28: 203–207.

Varzi, A. C., in press. Points as higher-order constructs: Whitehead's method of Extensive Abstraction. In Shapiro, S. and Hellman, G., eds., *The History of Continua: Philosophical and Mathematical Perspectives*. Oxford University Press, Oxford.

Varzi, A. C. and Gruszczyński, R., eds., 2015. *Mereology and Beyond, Part I*. Special issue of *Logic and Logical Philosophy*, volume 24/4.

Varzi, A. C. and Gruszczyński, R., eds., 2016. *Mereology and Beyond, Part II*. Special issue of *Logic and Logical Philosophy*, volume 25/3.

Vaught, R. L., 1954. Applications of the Löwenheim-Skolem-Tarski theorem to problems of completeness and decidability. *Indagationes Mathematicae*, 16: 467–472.

Vermaas, P. and Garbacz, P., 2009. Functional decomposition and mereology in engineering. In Meijers, A., ed., *Handbook of the Philosophy of Science*, volume 9: *Philosophy of Technology and Engineering Sciences*, pp. 235–271. Elsevier, Amsterdam.

Vernant, D., 2000. Sur les fondements de la mathématique de Stanislaw

Leśniewski. In Beets, F. and Gillet, É., eds., *Logique en perspective: Mélanges offerts à Paul Gochet*, pp. 313–363. Ousia, Bruxelles.

Vieu, L., 2006. On the transitivity of functional parthood. *Applied Ontology*, 1: 147–155.

Vieu, L. and Aurnague, M., 2007. Part-of relations, functionality and dependence. In Aurnague, M., Hickmann, M., and Vieu, L., eds., *The Categorization of Spatial Entities in Language and Cognition*, pp. 307–336. Benjamins, Amsterdam.

von Neumann, J., 1925. Eine Axiomatisierung der Mengenlehre. *Journal für die reine und angewandte Mathematik*, 154: 219–240. Eng. trans. by S. Bauer-Mengelberg and D. Føllesdal: An axiomatization of set theory, in van Heijenoort (1967), pp. 393–413.

Waechter, J. and Ladyman, J., 2019. In defence of ordinary objects and a naturalistic answer to the special composition question. In Cumpa, J. and Brewer, B., eds., *The Nature of Ordinary Objects*, pp. 82–128. Cambridge University Press, Cambridge.

Wake, A. V., 2011. Spacetime and mereology. *Erkenntnis*, 74: 17–35.

Wallace, M., 2009. Composition as identity. Ph.D. thesis, University of North Carolina, Chapel Hill (NC).

Wallace, M., 2011. Composition as identity. *Philosophy Compass*, 6: 804–827.

Wallace, M., 2013. Counterparts and compositional nihilism: A reply to A. J. Cotnoir. *Thought*, 2: 242–247.

Wallace, M., 2014a. Composition as identity, mereological essentialism, and modal parts. In Cotnoir and Baxter (2014), pp. 111–129.

Wallace, M., 2014b. The argument from vagueness for modal parts. *Dialectica*, 68: 355–373.

Wallace, M., 2019. The lump sum: A theory of modal parts. *Philosophical Papers*, 48: 403–435.

Wallace, M., in press. The polysemy of 'part'. In Carrara and Lando (in press-b).

Walters, L., 2019. Are the statue and the clay mutual parts? *Noûs*, 53: 23–50.

Wang, H., 1974. *From Mathematics to Philosophy*. Humanities Press, New York.

Wang, H., 1996. *A Logical Journey: From Gödel to Philosophy*. MIT Press, Cambridge (MA).

Warren, J., 2015. Quantifier variance and the collapse argument. *The Philosophical Quarterly*, 65: 241–253.

Wasserman, R., 2002. The standard objection to the standard account. *Philosophical Studies*, 111: 197–216.

Wasserman, R., 2003. Review of Hudson (2001). *Philo*, 6: 307–313.

Wasserman, R., 2004. Framing the debate over persistence. *Metaphysica*, 5: 67–80.

Wasserman, R., 2006. The problem of change. *Philosophy Compass*, 1: 48–57.

Wasserman, R., 2016. Theories of persistence. *Philosophical Studies*, 173: 243–250.

Wasserman, R., 2018a. Material constitution. In Zalta, E. N., ed., *The Stanford Encyclopedia of Philosophy*. http://plato.stanford.edu/archives/fall2018/entries/material-constitution.

Wasserman, R., 2018b. *Paradoxes of Time Travel*. Oxford University Press, Oxford.

Watson, D., 2010. An argument against an argument against the necessity of universal mereological composition. *Analysis*, 70: 78–82.

Watt, R., 2019. Three myths about Kant's second antinomy. *Archiv für Geschichte der Philosophie*, 101: 258–279.

Weatherson, B., 2003. Many many problems. *The Philosophical Quarterly*, 53: 481–501.

Weber, Z., 2010. Transfinite numbers in paraconsistent set theory. *The Review of Symbolic*, 3: 71–92.

Weber, Z. and Cotnoir, A. J., 2015. Inconsistent boundaries. *Synthese*, 192: 1267–1294.

Weingartner, P., 1981. Similarities and differences between the $\in$ of set theory and part-whole-relations. In Weinke, K., ed., *Logik, Ethik und Sprache: Festschrift für Rudolf Freundlich*, pp. 266–287. Oldenbourg, Vienna.

Weir, A., 2015. A robust non-transitive logic. *Topoi*, 34: 99–107.

Welch, P. and Horsten, L., 2016. Reflecting on absolute infinity. *The Journal of Philosophy*, 113: 89–111.

Welsh, P. J., 1978. Primitivity in Mereology. *Notre Dame Journal of Formal Logic*, 19: 25–62, 355–385.

Werner, P., 2015. *David Lewis und seine mereologische Interpretation der Zermelo-Fraenkelschen Mengenlehre: Eine Rekonstruktion*. De Gruyter, Berlin.

Westerhoff, J., 2004. A taxonomy of composition operations. *Logique et Analyse*, 47: 375–393.

Westerhoff, J., 2013. Metaphysical issues in Indian Buddhist thought. In Emmanuel, S. M., ed., *A Companion to Buddhist Philosophy*, pp. 129–150. Wiley-Blackwell, Oxford.

Westerhoff, J., 2018. *The Golden Age of Indian Buddhist Philosophy*. Oxford University Press, Oxford.

Wheeler, S. C., 1979. On that which is not. *Synthese*, 41: 155–173.

Whitehead, A. N., 1916. La théorie relationniste de l'espace. *Revue de Metaphysique et de Morale*, 23: 423–454. Eng. trans. by P. J. Hurley: The relational theory of space, *Philosophy Research Archives*, 5: 712–741, 1979.

Whitehead, A. N., 1919. *An Enquiry Concerning the Principles of Natural Knowledge*. Cambridge University Press, Cambridge.

Whitehead, A. N., 1920. *The Concept of Nature*. Cambridge University Press, Cambridge.

Whitehead, A. N., 1929. *Process and Reality: An Essay in Cosmology*. Cambridge University Press, Cambridge.

Wiegand, O. K., 2007. A formalism supplementing cognitive semantics based on mereology. *Spatial Cognition and Computation*, 7: 33–59.

Wiegand, O. K., 2010. On referring to Gestalts. In Hartimo, M., ed., *Phenomenology and Mathematics*, pp. 183–211. Springer, Dordrecht.

Wiggins, D., 1968. On being at the same place at the same time. *The Philosophical Review*, 77: 90–95.

Wiggins, D., 1979. Mereological essentialism: Asymmetrical essential dependence and the nature of continuants. *Grazer Philosophische Studien*, 7: 297–315.

Wiggins, D., 1980. *Sameness and Substance*. Blackwell, Oxford.

Wilkins, S. M., 2016. Why paraphrase nihilism fails. *Synthese*, 193: 2619–2632.

Willard, D., 1994. Mereological essentialism restricted. In Albertazzi and Libardi (1994), pp. 123–144.

Williams, J. R. G., 2006. Illusions of gunk. *Philosophical Perspectives*, 20: 493–513.

Williams, J. R. G., 2008a. Ontic vagueness and metaphysical indeterminacy. *Philosophy Compass*, 3: 763–788.

Williams, J. R. G., 2008b. Multiple actualities and ontically vague identity. *The Philosophical Quarterly*, 58: 134–154.

Williamson, T., 1990. Review of Simons (1987). *Grazer Philosophische Studien*, 38: 201–210.

Williamson, T., 1994. *Vagueness*. Routledge, London.

Williamson, T., 2010. Necessitism, contingentism, and plural quantification. *Mind*, 119: 657–674.

Williamson, T., 2013. *Modal Logic as Metaphysics*. Oxford University Press, Oxford.

Williamson, T., 2017. Semantic paradoxes and abductive methodology. In Armour-Garb, B., ed., *Reflections on the Liar*, pp. 325–346. Oxford University Press, Oxford.

Wilson, J. M., 2014. No work for a theory of grounding. *Inquiry*, 57: 535–579.

Winston, M. E., Chaffin, R., and Herrmann, D. J., 1987. A taxonomy of part-whole relations. *Cognitive Science*, 11: 417–444.

Wittgenstein, L., 1921. Logisch-philosophische Abhandlung. *Annalen der Naturphilosophie*, 14: 185–262. Eng. trans. by C. K. Ogden: *Tractatus Logico-Philosophicus*, Kegan Paul, London, 1922.

Wittgenstein, L., 1964. *Philosophische Bemerkungen*, ed. by R. Rhees. Blackwell, Oxford. Eng. trans. by R. Hargreaves and R. White: *Philosophical Remarks*, Blackwell, Oxford, 1974.

Wittgenstein, L., 1974. *Letters to Russell, Keynes and Moore*, ed. by G. H. von Wright and B. F. McGuinness. Cornell University Press, Ithaca (NY).

Wodeham, A. de., 1988. *Tractatus de Indivisibilibus*, ed. and Eng. trans. by R. Wood. Kluwer, Dordrecht.

Wright, C., 2007. On quantifying into predicate position: Steps towards a new(tralist) position. In Leng, M., Paseau, A., and Potter, M., eds., *Mathematical Knowledge*, pp. 150–174. Oxford University Press, Oxford.

Yablo, S., 1987. Identity, essence, and indiscernibility. *The Journal of Philosophy*, 84: 293–314.

Yablo, S., 2014. *Aboutness*. Princeton University Press, Princeton (NJ).

Yablo, S., 2016. Parts and differences. *Philosophical Studies*, 173: 141–157.

Yagisawa, T., 2010. *Worlds and Individuals, Possible and Otherwise*. Oxford University Press, Oxford.

Yi, B.-U., 1999. Is mereology ontologically innocent? *Philosophical Studies*, 93: 141–160.

Yi, B.-U., 2002. *Understanding the Many*. Routledge, London.

Yi, B.-U., 2005–2006. The logic and meaning of plurals. *Journal of Philosophical Logic*, 34: 459–506; 35: 239–288.

Yi, B.-U., 2014. Is there a plural object? In Cotnoir and Baxter (2014), pp. 169–191.

Yi, B.-U., in press. Is composition identity? In Carrara and Lando (in press-b).

Yoes, M. G., 1967. Nominalism and non-atomic systems. *Noûs*, 1: 193–200.

Zadeh, L. A., 1965. Fuzzy sets. *Information and Control*, 8: 338–353.

Zalta, E. N., 2016. Principia logico-metaphysica. Unpublished ms.

Zardini, E., 2008. A model of tolerance. *Studia Logica*, 90: 337–368.

Zermelo, E., 1908. Untersuchungen über die Grundlagen der Mengenlehre, I. *Mathematische Annalen*, 65: 261–281. Eng. trans. by S. Bauer-Mengelberg: Investigations in the foundations of set theory I, in van Heijenoort (1967), pp. 199–215.

Zhuangzi, 2013. *The Complete Works*, Eng. trans. by B. Watson. Columbia University Press, New York.

Zielinska, A. C., 2016. Putnam: Relativité conceptuelle et méréologie. *Archives de Philosophie*, 79: 675–692.

Zilioli, U., ed., in press. *Atomism in Philosophy: A History from Antiquity to the Present*. Bloomsbury, London.

Zimmerman, D. W., 1995. Theories of masses and problems of constitution. *The Philosophical Review*, 104: 53–110.

Zimmerman, D. W., 1996a. Could extended objects be made out of simple parts? An argument for atomless gunk. *Philosophy and Phenomenological Research*, 56: 1–29.

Zimmerman, D. W., 1996b. Persistence and presentism. *Philosophical Papers*, 25: 115–126.

Zupko, J., 2018. 'Nothing in nature is naturally a statue': William of Ockham on artifacts. *Metaphysics*, 1: 88–95.

INDEX

This index is divided into four sections. The *Names* section covers all references to the authors (other than ourselves) cited in the main text or in the footnotes. The *Subjects* section lists the main occurrences of key terms and concepts, with some cross-references to track synonyms and related content. The *Featured Formulas* section lists all technical nomenclature regarding formal definitions, axioms, and numbered theses. Finally, the *Symbols* section lists the first occurrences of all technical notation.

NAMES

Names of joint authors are listed as independent entries even when cited tacitly under '*et al.*' (but fully displayed in the *Bibliography*). Editors and translators are not listed unless cited explicitly. Also not included are occurrences of names in standardized phrases, such as 'Venn diagram' or 'Leibniz's law'.

SUBJECTS

This section lists (with some cross-references) the main occurrences of key terms and concepts. For a complete inventory of the nomenclature accompanying our official definitions, axioms, and numbered theses, see the next section, *Featured Formulas*.

FEATURED FORMULAS

This section provides a complete listing, in alphabetical order, of the official nomenclature accompanying all numbered formulas (definitions, axioms, notable theses), with reference to the pages where they are first introduced. For ease of reference, the formulas themselves, ordered by label number, are reproduced at the end of the volume.

SYMBOLS

Page numbers refer to the first occurrence of each symbol.

LIST OF FEATURED FORMULAS

LOGICAL AXIOMS

(L.1)	$\varphi \to (\psi \to \varphi)$	
(L.2)	$(\varphi \to (\psi \to \xi)) \to ((\varphi \to \psi) \to (\varphi \to \xi))$	
(L.3)	$(\neg\varphi \to \neg\psi) \to ((\neg\varphi \to \psi) \to \varphi)$	
(L.4)	$\forall x\varphi \to \varphi^x_y$	provided y is free for x in φ
(L.5)	$\forall x(\varphi \to \psi) \to (\varphi \to \forall x\psi)$	provided x is not free in φ
(L.6)	$x = x$	
(L.7)	$x = y \to (\varphi \to \varphi(^x_y))$	provided y is free for x in φ

DEFINITIONS

(D.1)	$PPxy :\equiv Pxy \wedge \neg x = y$	*Proper Parthood* (PP_1)
(D.2)	$Oxy :\equiv \exists z(Pzx \wedge Pzy)$	*Overlap*
(D.3)	$Uxy :\equiv \exists z(Pxz \wedge Pyz)$	*Underlap*
(D.4)	$Dxy :\equiv \neg\exists z(Pzx \wedge Pzy)$	*Disjointness*
(D.5)	$x - y := \iota z \forall w(Pwz \leftrightarrow (Pwx \wedge Dwy))$	*Difference*
(D.6)	$F_\varphi z :\equiv \forall x(\varphi x \to Pxz) \wedge \forall y(\forall x(\varphi x \to Pxy) \to Pzy)$	*Fusion*
(D.7)	$\sigma x\, \varphi x := \iota z F_\varphi z$	*Unique Fusion*
(D.8)	$u := \sigma x\, \exists y\, x = y$	*Universe*
(D.9)	$a + b := \sigma x(x = a \vee x = b)$	*Sum*
(D.10)	$a \times b := \sigma x(Pxa \wedge Pxb)$	*Product*
(D.11)	$-a := \sigma x\, Dxa$	*Complement*
(D.12)	$Pxy :\equiv PPxy \vee x = y$	*Parthood* (P_1)
(D.13)	$F'_\varphi z :\equiv \forall x(\varphi x \to Pxz) \wedge \forall y(Pyz \to \exists x(\varphi x \wedge Oyx))$	*Fusion′*
(D.14)	$Pxy :\equiv \forall z(Ozx \to Ozy)$	*Parthood*
(D.15)	$PPxy :\equiv Pxy \wedge \neg Pyx$	*Proper Parthood* (PP_2)

(D.16) $F''_{\varphi}z :\equiv \forall y(Oyz \leftrightarrow \exists x(\varphi x \wedge Oyx))$	*Fusion''*
(D.17) $Pxy :\equiv \forall z(Dzy \rightarrow Dzx)$	*Parthood (D–Variant)*
(D.18) $F''_{\varphi}z :\equiv \forall y(Dyz \leftrightarrow \forall x(\varphi x \rightarrow Dyx))$	*Fusion'' (D–Variant)*
(D.19) $Pxy :\equiv x + y = y$	*Parthood*
(D.20) $a + b := \iota z Szab$	*Sum*
(D.21) $Pxy :\equiv x \times y = x$	*Parthood*
(D.22) $N_{\varphi}z :\equiv \forall y(\varphi y \rightarrow Pzy) \wedge \forall x(\forall y(\varphi y \rightarrow Pxy) \rightarrow Pxz)$	*Nucleus*
(D.23) $POxy :\equiv Oxy \wedge \neg Pxy \wedge \neg Pyx$	*Proper Overlap*
(D.24) $IOxy :\equiv Pxy \vee Pyx$	*Improper Overlap*
(D.25) $Ixy :\equiv \forall z(PPzx \rightarrow PPzy)$	*Inclosure*
(D.26) $Pxy :\equiv (\exists z PPzx \rightarrow Ixy) \wedge (\neg\exists z PPzx \rightarrow (PPxy \vee x = y))$	*Parthood* (P_2)
(D.27) $x = y :\equiv Pxy \wedge Pyx$	*Identity*
(D.28) $P_{\varphi}xy :\equiv Pxy \wedge \varphi x$	*φ–Parthood 1*
(D.29) $P_{\varphi}xy :\equiv Pxy \wedge \varphi xy$	*φ–Parthood 2*
(D.30) $IPxy :\equiv PPxy \wedge \neg\exists z(PPxz \wedge PPzy)$	*Immediate Parthood*
(D.31) $PP_{\xi}xy :\equiv PPxy \wedge \xi x$	*Proper ξ–Parthood*
(D.32) $IP_{\xi}xy :\equiv PP_{\xi}xy \wedge \neg\exists z(PPxz \wedge PP_{\xi}zy)$	*Immediate ξ–Parthood*
(D.33) $a' := \iota z \forall x(Pxz \leftrightarrow Dxa)$	*Complement'*
(D.34) $a^* := \iota z(Dza \wedge \forall x((Dxa \rightarrow Pxz) \wedge (Dxz \rightarrow Pxa)))$	*Complement**
(D.35) $S'zxy :\equiv Pxz \wedge Pyz \wedge \forall w(Pwz \rightarrow (Owx \vee Owy))$	*Binary Sum'*
(D.36) $n := \iota z \forall y(Pzy \wedge \neg PPyz)$	*Null Object*
(D.37) $SDxy :\equiv \neg\exists z(Pzx \wedge Pzy \wedge \neg z = n)$	*Solid Disjointness*
(D.38) $SPPxy :\equiv PPxy \wedge \neg x = n$	*Solid Proper Parthood*
(D.39) $Ax :\equiv \neg\exists y PPyx$	*Atom*
(D.40) $SAx :\equiv \forall y(PPyx \rightarrow y = n)$	*Solid Atom*
(D.41) $A_{\varphi}x :\equiv Ax \wedge \exists y(\varphi y \wedge Pxy)$	*φ–Atom*
(D.42) $Ax :\equiv \neg\exists y PP_2 yx$	*Strict Atom*
(D.43) $F^*_{\varphi}z :\equiv \forall x(\varphi x \rightarrow Pxz) \wedge \forall y(\forall x(\varphi x \rightarrow Pxy) \rightarrow \neg PPyz)$	F^**-type Fusion*
(D.44) $F_{\varphi}z :\equiv \forall y(Pzy \leftrightarrow \forall x(\varphi x \rightarrow Pxy))$	F*-type Fusion (Alt.)*
(D.45) $\psi_{\varphi} :\equiv \forall x(\varphi x \rightarrow \forall y(Pyx \leftrightarrow \forall z(Ozy \rightarrow Ozx)))$	*φ–Extensionality*
(D.46) $\psi_{\varphi} :\equiv \exists y \forall x(\varphi x \rightarrow Pyx)$	*Common Lower Bound*
(D.47) $\psi_{\varphi} :\equiv \forall x \forall y((\varphi x \wedge \varphi^x_y) \rightarrow Oxy)$	*Pairwise Overlap*
(D.48) $\psi_{\varphi} :\equiv \exists y \forall x(\varphi x \rightarrow Pxy)$	*Common Upper Bound*
(D.49) $\psi_{\varphi} :\equiv \forall x \forall y((\varphi x \wedge \varphi^x_y) \rightarrow Uxy)$	*Pairwise Underlap*
(D.50) $Cx :\equiv \neg\exists y PPxy$	*Coatom*
(D.51) $SCx :\equiv \forall y(PPxy \rightarrow y = u)$	*Solid Coatom*

(D_*1)	$F_X z :\equiv \forall x(Xx \rightarrow Pxz) \wedge \forall y(\forall x(Xx \rightarrow Pxy) \rightarrow Pzy)$	*2nd-Order Fusion*
(D_*2)	$F'_X z :\equiv \forall x(Xx \rightarrow Pxz) \wedge \forall y(Pyz \rightarrow \exists x(Xx \wedge Oyx))$	*2nd-Order Fusion′*
(D_*3)	$F''_X z :\equiv \forall y(Oyz \leftrightarrow \exists x(Xx \wedge Oyx))$	*2nd-Order Fusion″*
(D_*4)	$F_{xx} z :\equiv \forall x(x \prec xx \rightarrow Pxz) \wedge \forall y(\forall x(x \prec xx \rightarrow Pxy) \rightarrow Pzy)$	*Pl. Fusion*
(D_*5)	$F'_{xx} z :\equiv \forall x(x \prec xx \rightarrow Pxz) \wedge \forall y(Pyz \rightarrow \exists x(x \prec xx \wedge Oyx))$	*Pl. Fusion′*
(D_*6)	$F''_{xx} z :\equiv \forall y(Oyz \leftrightarrow \exists x(x \prec xx \wedge Oyx))$	*Pl. Fusion″*
(D_*7)	$F'''_{xx} z :\equiv xx = z$	*Plural Fusion‴*
(D_*8)	$Pxy :\equiv \exists xx(F'''_{xx} y \wedge x \prec xx)$	*Parthood*
(D_*9)	$x_t := \sigma y(Pyx \wedge \forall z(Eyz \leftrightarrow z = t))$	*t–Part*
(D_*10)	$PP_t xy :\equiv P_t xy \wedge \neg x = y$	*t–Proper Parthood*
(D_*11)	$O_t xy :\equiv \exists z(P_t zx \wedge P_t zy)$	*t–Overlap*
(D_*12)	$D_t xy :\equiv \neg\exists z(P_t zx \wedge P_t zy)$	*t–Disjointness*
(D_*13)	$F_{t\varphi} z :\equiv \forall x(\varphi_t x \rightarrow P_t xz) \wedge \forall y(\forall x(\varphi_t x \rightarrow P_t xy) \rightarrow P_t zy)$	*t–Fusion*
(D_*14)	$C_t xy :\equiv P_t xy \wedge P_t yx$	*t–Coincidence*
(D_*15)	$E_t x :\equiv P_t xx$	*t–Existence*
(D_*16)	$F_{\xi\varphi} z :\equiv \forall t((\xi t \wedge \exists x \varphi_t x) \rightarrow F_{t\varphi} z)$	*ξ-Fusion*
(D_*17)	$MF_{\xi\varphi} z :\equiv F_{\xi\varphi} z \wedge \forall t(E_t z \leftrightarrow (\xi t \wedge \exists x \varphi_t x))$	*Minimal ξ-Fusion*

AXIOMS

(A.1)	$\forall x Pxx$	*Reflexivity*
(A.2)	$\forall x \forall y((Pxy \wedge Pyx) \rightarrow x = y)$	*Antisymmetry*
(A.3)	$\forall x \forall y \forall z((Pxy \wedge Pyz) \rightarrow Pxz)$	*Transitivity*
(A.4)	$\forall x \forall y(\neg Pxy \rightarrow \exists z \forall w(Pwz \leftrightarrow (Pwx \wedge Dwy)))$	*Remainder*
(A.5)	$\exists x \varphi x \rightarrow \exists z F_\varphi z$	*Unrestricted Fusion*
(A.6)	$\forall x \exists y(Pyx \wedge \neg\exists z PPzy)$	*Atomism*
(A.7)	$\forall x \neg PPxx$	*Irreflexivity*
(A.8)	$\forall x \forall y(PPxy \rightarrow \neg PPyx)$	*Asymmetry*
(A.9)	$\forall x \forall y \forall z((PPxy \wedge PPyz) \rightarrow PPxz)$	*Transitivity*
(A.10)	$\forall x \forall y(PPyx \rightarrow \exists z(PPzx \wedge Dzy))$	*Weak Supplementation*
(A.11)	$\exists x \varphi x \rightarrow \exists z F'_\varphi z$	*Unrestricted Fusion′*
(A.12)	$\exists x \varphi x \rightarrow \exists z \forall y(F'_\varphi y \leftrightarrow y = z)$	*Unique Unrestricted Fusion′*
(A.13)	$\forall x \forall y(Oxy \leftrightarrow \exists z(Pzx \wedge Pzy))$	*Overlapping Parts*
(A.14)	$\forall x \forall y(\forall z(Ozx \leftrightarrow Ozy) \rightarrow x = y)$	*O–Extensionality*
(A.15)	$\exists x \varphi x \rightarrow \exists z F''_\varphi z$	*Unrestricted Fusion″*
(A.16)	$\forall x \forall y(Oxy \leftrightarrow \neg Dxy)$	*Exclusion*
(A.17)	$\forall y \forall z(F'_{x=y} z \rightarrow z = y)$	*Singular Fusion′*

(A.18) $\forall x \forall y(\neg Pxy \to \exists z(Pzx \wedge Dzy))$ *Strong Supplementation*
(A.19) $\forall x \forall y \forall z \forall w((Szxy \wedge Swxy) \to z = w)$ *Sum Uniqueness*
(A.20) $\forall x\, x + x = x$ *Idempotence*
(A.21) $\forall x \forall y\, x + y = y + x$ *Commutativity*
(A.22) $\forall x \forall y \forall z\, x + (y + z) = (x + y) + z$ *Associativity*
(A.23) $\forall x\, x \times x = x$ *Idempotence*
(A.24) $\forall x \forall y \forall w\, (w = x \times y \to w = y \times x)$ *Commutativity*
(A.25) $\forall x \forall y \forall z \forall w\, (w = x \times (y \times z) \to w = (x \times y) \times z)$ *Associativity*
(A.26) $\exists x \varphi x \to \exists z N_{\forall y(\varphi y \to Pyx)} z$ *Unrestricted Upper Nucleus*
(A.27) $\forall x \forall y((Pxy \wedge Pyx) \to (\varphi \to \varphi(^x_y)))$ *Indiscernibility*
(A.28) $\forall x \forall y((P^n xy \wedge Pyx) \to x = y)$ *Anticyclicity*
(A.29) $\forall x \forall y(PP^n xy \to \neg PPyx)$ *Acyclicity*
(A.30) $\forall x \forall y(PPxy \to \exists z(PPxz \wedge PPzy))$ *Denseness*
(A.31) $\forall x \exists y PPyx$ *Atomlessness*
(A.32) $\forall x \forall y \forall z((P^m xy \wedge P^n yz \wedge Pxz) \to Pxy)$ *Left Transitivity*
(A.33) $\forall x \forall y \forall z((P^m xy \wedge P^n yz \wedge Pxz) \to Pyz)$ *Right Transitivity*
(A.34) $\forall x(\neg \forall y Pyx \to \exists z\, z = x')$ *Strong Complementation′*
(A.35) $\forall x(\neg \forall y Pyx \to \exists z\, z = x^*)$ *Strong Complementation**
(A.36) $\forall x \forall y \exists z S' zxy$ *Unrestricted Sum′*
(A.37) $\forall x \forall y(Oxy \to \exists z\, z = x \times y)$ *Unrestricted Product*
(A.38) $\forall x \forall y(PP_2 yx \to \exists z(PP_2 zx \wedge Dzy))$ *Strict Supplementation*
(A.39) $\forall x \forall y(PPyx \to \exists z(PPzx \wedge \neg z = y))$ *Weak Company*
(A.40) $\forall x \forall y(PPyx \to \exists z(PPzx \wedge \neg Pzy))$ *Strong Company*
(A.41) $\forall x \forall y(PPyx \to \exists z(PPzx \wedge \neg Pzy \wedge \neg Pyz))$ *Super-Strong Company*
(A.42) $\forall x \forall y(PPyx \to \exists w \exists z(PPwx \wedge PPzx \wedge Dwz))$ *Quasi-Supplementation*
(A.43) $\exists x \forall y(Pxy \wedge \neg PPyx)$ *Strict Zero*
(A.44) $\forall x \forall y(\neg Pxy \to \exists z \forall w(Pwz \leftrightarrow (Pwx \wedge SDwy)))$ *Solid Remainder*
(A.45) $\exists z F_\varphi z$ *Absolutely Unrestricted Fusion*
(A.46) $\forall x \forall y(PPyx \to \exists z(SPPzx \wedge SDzy))$ *Solid Weak Supplementation*
(A.47) $\forall z(F_\varphi z \to \exists x(\varphi x \wedge \forall y(PPyx \to \neg \varphi^x_y)))$ *Superatomism*
(A.48) $\exists y \varphi y \to \exists z F_{A_\varphi x} z$ *Atomistic Fusion*
(A.49) $\exists x \varphi x \to \exists z \forall y(Ay \to (Pyz \leftrightarrow \exists x(\varphi x \wedge Pyx)))$ *Atomistic Fusion″*
(A.50) $\exists x(Ax \wedge \varphi x) \to \exists y \forall x(Ax \to (Pxy \leftrightarrow \varphi x))$ *Atom Fusion″*
(A.51) $\forall x \forall y(\neg Pxy \to \exists z \forall w(Aw \to (Pwz \leftrightarrow (Pwx \wedge \neg Pwy)))$ *Atomistic Rem.*
(A.52) $\forall x \forall y(\neg Pxy \to \exists z(Az \wedge Pzx \wedge \neg Pzy))$ *Atomistic Strong Supplem.*
(A.53) $\exists_k x\, Ax$ *Size*

(A.54)	$\exists_{\geqslant k}x\, Ax$	*Minimum Size*
(A.55)	$\forall x \forall y(Pxy \to \exists z(PPzy \wedge (Dzx \vee x = y)))$	*Atomless Weak Supplem.*
(A.56)	$\forall x \exists y \exists z(PPyx \wedge PPzx \wedge Dyz)$	*Atomless Quasi-Supplem.*
(A.57)	$\forall x \exists y \exists z\, x - y = z$	*Splitting*
(A.58)	$\forall x(\varphi x \to \exists y(\psi y \wedge Pyx))$	*ψ-Grounding*
(A.59)	$\forall x \forall y((\varphi x \wedge \varphi y) \to (\forall z(\psi z \to (Pzx \leftrightarrow Pzy)) \to x = y))$	*ψ-Extensionality*
(A.60)	$\forall x(\varphi x \to \exists y(Ay \wedge Pyx))$	*φ–Atomism*
(A.61)	$\forall x(\varphi x \to \forall y(Pyx \to \neg Ay))$	*φ–Gunk*
(A.62)	$\exists x Ax$	*Weak Atomism*
(A.63)	$\exists x \forall y(Pyx \to \neg Ay)$	*Weak Gunk*
(A.64)	$\exists x \varphi x \to \forall y \forall z((F_\varphi z \wedge Pyz) \to \exists x(\varphi x \wedge Oyx))$	*∃-Filtration*
(A.65)	$\exists x \varphi x \to \forall y \forall z((F_\varphi z \wedge Oyz) \to \exists x(\varphi x \wedge Oyx))$	*∃-Strong Overlap*
(A.66)	$\forall z(F''_\varphi z \to \forall x(\varphi x \to Pxz))$	*Upper Bound*
(A.67)	$\forall y \forall z((F'_\varphi z \wedge F'_\psi y \wedge \forall x(\varphi x \to \psi x)) \to Pzy)$	*Monotonicity*
(A.68)	$\exists z F_\varphi z \to \forall x \forall y(\varphi x \wedge \varphi^x_y \to x = y)$	*Nihilist Fusion*
(A.69)	$\exists z F'_\varphi z \to \forall x \forall y(\varphi x \wedge \varphi^x_y \to x = y)$	*Nihilist Fusion′*
(A.70)	$\exists z F''_\varphi z \to \forall x \forall y(\varphi x \wedge \varphi^x_y \to x = y)$	*Nihilist Fusion″*
(A.71)	$\exists x \varphi x \to (\exists z F_\varphi z \leftrightarrow \psi_\varphi)$	*ψ–Restricted Fusion*
(A.72)	$\exists x \varphi x \to (\exists z F'_\varphi z \leftrightarrow \psi_\varphi)$	*ψ–Restricted Fusion′*
(A.73)	$\exists x \varphi x \to (\exists z F''_\varphi z \leftrightarrow \psi_\varphi)$	*ψ–Restricted Fusion″*
(A.74)	$\exists x \forall y Pyx$	*Top*
(A.75)	$\exists x \forall y(Pyx \wedge \neg PPxy)$	*Strict Top*
(A.76)	$\exists x \exists y \neg x = y \to \neg \exists x \forall y\, Pyx$	*No Top*
(A.77)	$\exists x \exists y \neg x = y \to \neg \exists x \forall y(Pyx \wedge \neg PPxy)$	*Strict No Top*
(A.78)	$\exists x \varphi x \to (\exists z F_\varphi z \leftrightarrow \exists y \forall x(\varphi x \to Pxy))$	*Restricted Composition*
(A.79)	$\forall x(\exists y Pyx \to Pxx)$	*Quasi-Reflexivity*
(A.80)	$\forall x \exists y(Cy \wedge Pxy)$	*Coatomism*
(A.81)	$\forall x \neg Cx$	*Coatomlessness*
(A.82)	$\forall x \exists y \exists z(PPyx \wedge PPxz)$	*Hunk*
(A.83)	$\forall x \forall y \exists z\, x + y = z$	*Unrestricted Sum*
(A.84)	$(\exists x \varphi x \wedge \exists y \forall x(\varphi x \to Pxy)) \to \exists z F_\varphi z$	*Bounded Fusion*
(A.85)	$(\exists x \varphi x \wedge \exists x \neg \varphi x) \to \exists z F_\varphi z$	*Almost Unrestricted Fusion*
(A.86)	$\forall x \exists y(PPxy \wedge \neg Pyx)$	*Strict Coatomlessness*
(A.87)	$\exists x Cx$	*Weak Coatomism*
(A.88)	$\exists x \forall y(Pxy \to \neg Cy)$	*Weak Junk*
(A.89)	$\forall x(\varphi x \to \exists y(Cy \wedge Pxy))$	*φ–Coatomism*

(A.90)	$\forall x(\varphi x \to \forall y(Pxy \to \neg Cy))$	*φ–Junk*
(A.91)	$\forall x(\varphi x \to \forall y((Pyx \to \neg Ay) \wedge (Pxy \to \neg Cy)))$	*φ–Hunk*
(A.92)	$\exists x Ax \to \exists z F''_A z$	*Fusion of Atoms*
(A$_*$1)	$\forall X(\exists x Xx \to \exists z F_X z)$	*2nd-Order Unrestricted Fusion*
(A$_*$2)	$\forall X(\exists x Xx \to \exists z F'_X z)$	*2nd-Order Unrestricted Fusion′*
(A$_*$3)	$\forall X(\exists x Xx \to \exists z F''_X z)$	*2nd-Order Unrestricted Fusion″*
(A$_*$4)	$\exists X \forall x(Xx \leftrightarrow \varphi x)$	*Comprehension*
(A$_*$5)	$\exists x \psi x \to \exists xx \forall x(x \prec xx \leftrightarrow \psi x)$	*Plural Comprehension*
(A$_*$6)	$\forall xx \exists x\, x \prec xx$	*Non-emptiness*
(A$_*$7)	$\forall xx(\exists x\, x \prec xx \to \exists z F_{xx} z)$	*Plural Unrestricted Fusion*
(A$_*$8)	$\forall xx(\exists x\, x \prec xx \to \exists z F'_{xx} z)$	*Plural Unrestricted Fusion′*
(A$_*$9)	$\forall xx(\exists x\, x \prec xx \to \exists z F''_{xx} z)$	*Plural Unrestricted Fusion″*
(A$_*$10)	$\forall xx \forall z(F_{xx} z \to xx = z)$	*Strong Composition as Identity*
(A$_*$11)	$\forall xx \forall yy(xx = yy \to \forall z(z \prec xx \leftrightarrow z \prec yy))$	*Plural Indiscernibility*
(A$_*$12)	$\forall xx \forall z \forall w((F_{xx} z \wedge F_{xx} w) \to z = w)$	*Uniqueness of Plural Fusion′*
(A$_*$13)	$\forall x \forall y(Exy \to Ty)$	*Temporary Existence*
(A$_*$14)	$\forall x \forall y \forall z(Pxyz \to Tz)$	*Temporary Parthood*
(A$_*$15)	$\forall x \forall y \forall z(Pxyz \to \neg Ty)$	*Time Apartness*
(A$_*$16)	$\forall x \forall y \forall t(C_t xy \to x = y)$	*Identity of Coincidents*
(A$_*$17)	$\forall x \forall y(\forall t((E_t x \vee E_t y) \to C_t xy) \to x = y)$	*Sameness*
(A$_*$18)	$\forall x \forall t(E_t x \to P_t xx)$	*Conditional Reflexivity*
(A$_*$19)	$\forall x \forall y \forall t((P_t xy \wedge P_t yx) \to x = y)$	*Antisymmetry*
(A$_*$20)	$\forall x \forall y \forall z \forall t((P_t xy \wedge P_t yz) \to P_t xz)$	*Transitivity*
(A$_*$21)	$\forall x \forall y \forall t(P_t xy \to (E_t x \wedge E_t y))$	*Existence*
(A$_*$22)	$\forall x \forall y \forall t((E_t x \wedge \neg P_t xy) \to \exists z(E_t z \wedge \forall w(P_t wz \leftrightarrow (P_t wx \wedge D_t wy))))$	*Rm*
(A$_*$23)	$\forall x \forall y \forall t((E_t x \wedge \neg P_t xy) \to \exists z(P_t zx \wedge D_t zy))$	*Strong Supplementation*
(A$_*$24)	$\forall x \forall y \forall t(PP_t yx \to \exists z(PP_t zx \wedge D_t zy))$	*Weak Supplementation*
(A$_*$25)	$\forall t(\exists x \varphi_t x \to \exists z(E_t z \wedge F_{t\varphi} z))$	*Unrestricted Fusion*
(A$_*$26)	$\exists t(\xi t \wedge \exists x \varphi_t x) \to \exists z F_{\xi\varphi} z$	*Unrestricted Diachronic Fusion*
(A$_*$27)	$\exists t(\xi t \wedge \exists x \varphi_t x) \to \exists z MF_{\xi\varphi} z$	*Unrestricted Minimal Diachronic Fusion*
(A$_*$28)	$\forall x \forall y(\Box((Ex \vee Ey) \to (Pxy \wedge Pyx)) \to x = y)$	*Sameness*
(A$_*$29)	$\exists x \exists y(\neg Pxy \wedge F_{z=z} y)$	*Non-totalness*

NOTABLE THESES

(T.1)	$\forall x(\exists w PPwx \to \forall y(\forall z(PPzx \leftrightarrow PPzy) \to x = y))$	PP–*Extensionality*
(T.2)	$\exists x \exists y \neg x = y \to \neg \exists x \forall y\, Pxy$	*No Zero*

(T.3)	$\forall z\forall w((F_\varphi z \wedge F_\varphi w) \to z = w)$	*Fusion Uniqueness*
(T.4)	$\forall x\forall y(Pxy \leftrightarrow \exists z(x + z = y))$	*Addition*
(T.5)	$\forall z(N_\varphi z \leftrightarrow F_{\forall y(\varphi y \to Pxy)}z)$	*Upward Duality*
(T.6)	$\forall z(F_\varphi z \leftrightarrow N_{\forall y(\varphi y \to Pyx)}z)$	*Downward Duality*
(T.7)	$\forall x\forall y(PP_2xy \to PP_1xy)$	*PP–Strength*
(T.8)	$\forall x\forall y(Pxy \to (PPxy \vee x = y))$	*Regularity*
(T.9)	$\forall x\forall y(\forall z(Pzx \leftrightarrow Pzy) \to x = y)$	*P–Extensionality*
(T.10)	$\forall x\forall y(\forall z(Ozx \leftrightarrow Ozy) \to x = y)$	*O–Extensionality*
(T.11)	$\forall x\forall y(\forall z(Dzx \leftrightarrow Dzy) \to x = y)$	*D–Extensionality*
(T.12)	$\forall x\forall y\forall z((P_\varphi xy \wedge P_\varphi yz) \to P_\varphi xz)$	*φ–Transitivity*
(T.13)	$\forall x\forall y\forall z((IPxy \wedge IPyz) \to \neg IPxz)$	*Antitransitivity*
(T.14)	$\forall x\forall y(PPxy \leftrightarrow (IPxy \vee \exists z(PPxz \wedge IPzy)))$	*Finite Parts*
(T.15)	$\forall x\forall y(\neg Pxy \to \exists z\, z = x - y)$	*Unique Remainder*
(T.16)	$\forall x\forall y(PPyx \to \exists z\, z = x - y)$	*Weak Remainder*
(T.17)	$\forall x\forall y(\exists z(Pzx \wedge Dzy) \to \exists z\, z = x - y)$	*Maximal Remainder*
(T.18)	$\forall x\forall y(PPyx \to \exists z(Dzy \wedge y + z = x))$	*Additive Remainder*
(T.19)	$\exists z\, z = u \to \forall x(\neg x = u \to u - x = -x)$	*Boolean Complementation*
(T.20)	$\forall x(\neg\forall y Pyx \to \exists z\, z = -x)$	*Absolute Complementation*
(T.21)	$\forall x\forall y(\forall z(Ozx \to Ozy) \to Pxy)$	O–*Supervenience*
(T.22)	$\forall x\forall y(Pxy \to \forall z(Ozx \to Ozy))$	O–*Inclusion*
(T.23)	$\forall x\forall y(\forall z(Dzy \to Dzx) \to Pxy)$	D–*Supervenience*
(T.24)	$\forall x(\exists w PPwx \to \forall y(\forall z(PPzx \to PPzy) \to Pxy))$	*Proper Parts*
(T.25)	$\forall x\forall y(PPyx \to \exists z(Pzx \wedge Dzy))$	*Weak* P–*Supplementation*
(T.26)	$\forall x\forall y(POxy \to \exists z(PPzx \wedge Dzy))$	*Over-Supplementation*
(T.27)	$\forall x\forall y(PP_2yx \to \exists z(Pzx \wedge Dzy))$	*Strict* P–*Supplementation*
(T.28)	$\forall x\forall y(PPyx \to \exists w\exists z(Pwx \wedge Pzx \wedge Dwz))$	*Quasi*-P–*Supplementation*
(T.29)	$\exists x\exists y \neg x = y \to \neg\exists x\forall y(Pxy \wedge \neg PPyx)$	*No Strict Zero*
(T.30)	$\exists x\forall y\; x = y$	*Oneness*
(T.31)	$\neg\exists x\varphi x \to F_\varphi n$	*Null Fusion*
(T.32)	$\forall x\forall y((Ax \wedge Ay \wedge \neg x = y) \to Dxy)$	*Atom Disjointness*
(T.33)	$\forall x(Ax \to \forall y(Oxy \to Pxy))$	*Atom Overlap*
(T.34)	$\forall x F_{Ay \wedge Pyx}x$	*Strong Atomism*
(T.35)	$\forall x\forall y(\forall z(Az \to (Pzx \leftrightarrow Pzy)) \to x = y)$	*Atomistic Extensionality*
(T.36)	$\forall x\forall y(Pyx \to \neg Ay)$	*Gunk*
(T.37)	$\exists z(\exists x(Pxz \wedge Ax) \wedge \exists x(Pxz \wedge \forall y(Pyx \to \neg Ay)))$	*Hybridism*
(T.38)	$\forall y\forall z((F_\varphi z \wedge Pyz) \to \exists x(\varphi x \wedge Oyx))$	*Filtration*

(T.39) $\forall y \forall z((F_{\varphi} z \wedge Oyz) \to \exists x(\varphi x \wedge Oyx))$	*Strong Overlap*
(T.40) $\exists x \varphi x \to \forall z(F_{\varphi} z \to (F'_{\varphi} z \wedge F''_{\varphi} z))$	*Classical Fusions*
(T.41) $\forall z(F''_{\varphi} z \to (F_{\varphi} z \wedge F'_{\varphi} z))$	*Classical Fusions (bis)*
(T.42) $\forall z(F'_{\varphi} z \to (F_{\varphi} z \wedge F''_{\varphi} z))$	*Classical Fusions (ter)*
(T.43) $\forall y \forall z((F'_{\varphi} z \wedge \forall x(\varphi x \to Pxy)) \to Pzy)$	*Minimal Upper Bound*
(T.44) $\forall y \forall z((F'_{\varphi} z \wedge F'_{\varphi} y) \to z = y)$	*Fusion′ Uniqueness*
(T.45) $\forall y\, F'_{x=y} y$	F'–*Reflexivity*
(T.46) $\forall x \forall y(Pxy \to x = y)$	*Monadism*
(T.47) $\forall z \forall w((F''_{\varphi} z \wedge F''_{\varphi} w) \to z = w)$	*Fusion″ Uniqueness*
(T.48) $\forall z(\exists x PPxz \to F_{PPxz} z)$	*Proper-Parts Fusion*
(T.49) $\forall z(F_{\varphi} z \to \forall x(Pxz \leftrightarrow \varphi x))$	P–*Collapse*
(T.50) $\forall z\, F_{x=z} z$	F–*Reflexivity*
(T.51) $\forall x \forall y(Pxy \to x + y = y)$	*Subpotence*
(T.52) $\forall x \forall y(Pxy \to \neg Cy)$	*Junk*
(T$_*$1) $\exists x \psi x \to \exists z F''_{\psi} z$	*2nd-Order Unrestricted Fusion″ Schema*
(T$_*$2) $\forall x \forall y(Pxy \to \exists xx(F_{xx} y \wedge x \prec xx))$	*Plural Covering*
(T$_*$3) $\forall xx \forall z(F_{xx} z \to \forall y(Pyz \leftrightarrow y \prec xx))$	*Plural Collapse*
(T$_*$4) $\forall x \forall y \forall t(Px_t y \to \forall t'(Eyt' \to Px_{t'} y))$	*Mereological Constancy*
(T$_*$5) $\forall x \forall y \forall t(Px_t y \to \forall t'(Ext' \to Px_{t'} y))$	*Holological Constancy*
(T$_*$6) $\forall x \forall t(E_t x \to C_t xx)$	C–*Reflexivity*
(T$_*$7) $\forall x \forall y \forall t(C_t xy \to C_t yx)$	C–*Symmetry*
(T$_*$8) $\forall x \forall y \forall z \forall t((C_t xy \wedge C_t yz) \to C_t xz)$	C–*Transitivity*
(T$_*$9) $\forall x \forall y \forall t(C_t xy \to \forall z(P_t zx \leftrightarrow P_t zy))$	C–*Indiscernibility*
(T$_*$10) $\forall x \forall y \forall z(\exists t(P_t xy \wedge P_t yz) \to \exists t P_t xz)$	*Occasional Transitivity*
(T$_*$11) $\forall x \forall y \forall t(P_t xy \to \forall t'(E_{t'} y \to P_{t'} xy))$	*Mereological Constancy*
(T$_*$12) $\forall x \forall y \forall t(P_t xy \to \forall t'(E_{t'} x \to P_{t'} xy))$	*Holological Constancy*
(T$_*$13) $\forall x \forall y(Pxy \to \Box(Ey \to Pxy))$	*Mereological Constancy/Essentialism*
(T$_*$14) $\forall x \forall y(Pxy \to \Box(Ex \to Pxy))$	*Holological Constancy/Essentialism*
(T$_*$15) $\forall x \forall y(\neg x = y \to \Box \neg x = y)$	*Necessity of Non-Identity*
(T$_*$16) $\forall x \forall y(\neg PPxy \to \Box \neg PPxy)$	*Necessity of Non-Parthood*
(T$_*$17) $\forall x \Box \exists y\, x = y$	*Eternity/Necessity of Existence*

OTHER PRINCIPLES

(3.1) $\forall x \forall y(\forall z(z \in x \leftrightarrow z \in y) \to x = y)$	$\in$–*Extensionality*
(3.2) $\forall x \forall y((x \subseteq y \wedge y \subseteq x) \to x = y)$	$\subseteq$–*Antisymmetry*
(5.3) $x = \Sigma(\ldots \Sigma(\ldots, x, \ldots) \ldots) \to x = \Sigma(\ldots, x, \ldots)$	*Anticyclicity*

(5.4)	$\Sigma(x) = x$	*Collapse*
(5.5)	$\Sigma(\ldots\Sigma(\ldots x, y\ldots)\ldots\Sigma(\ldots u, v\ldots)\ldots) = \Sigma(\ldots x, y\ldots u, v\ldots)$	*Leveling*
(5.6)	$\Sigma(\ldots x, x\ldots y, y\ldots) = \Sigma(\ldots x\ldots y\ldots)$	*Absorption*
(5.7)	$\Sigma(\ldots x, y, z\ldots) = \Sigma(\ldots y, z, x\ldots)$	*Permutation*
(5.8)	$\exists z \forall x(x \in z \leftrightarrow \varphi x)$	*Unrestricted Comprehension*
(5.10)	$\forall y \exists z \forall x(x \in z \leftrightarrow (x \in y \wedge \varphi x))$	*Restricted Comprehension*